P9-DIY-050

Critical Issues in Education

Dialogues and Dialectics

Critical Issues in Education

Dialogues and Dialectics

SEVENTH EDITION

Jack L. Nelson
Rutgers University

Stuart B. Palonsky
University of Missouri

Mary Rose McCarthy
Pace University

FOREWORD BY

Nel Noddings
Stanford University; Teachers College, Columbia University

 Higher Education

Boston   Burr Ridge, IL   Dubuque, IA   New York   San Francisco   St. Louis
Bangkok   Bogotá   Caracas   Kuala Lumpur   Lisbon   London   Madrid   Mexico City
Milan   Montreal   New Delhi   Santiago   Seoul   Singapore   Sydney   Taipei   Toronto

The *McGraw·Hill* Companies

 Higher Education

A DIVISION OF THE MCGRAW-HILL COMPANIES

Published by McGraw-Hill, an imprint of The McGraw-Hill Companies, Inc., 1221 Avenue of the Americas, New York, NY 10020. Copyright © 2010, 2007, 2004, 2000, 1996, 1993 by The McGraw-Hill Companies, Inc. All rights reserved. No part of this publication may be reproduced or distributed in any form or by any means, or stored in a database or retrieval system, without the prior written consent of The McGraw-Hill Companies, Inc., including, but not limited to, in any network or other electronic storage or transmission, or broadcast for distance learning.

This book is printed on acid-free paper.

1 2 3 4 5 6 7 8 9 0 FGR/FGR 0 9

ISBN: 978-0-07-337864-0
MHID: 0-07-337864-X

Editor in Chief: *Michael Ryan*
Publisher: *David S. Patterson*
Executive Editor: *Allison McNamara*
Executive Marketing Manager: *James Headley*
Editorial Coordinator: *Sarah Kiefer*
Production Editors: *Melissa Williams/Les Chappell, Macmillan Publishing Solutions*
Manuscript Editor: *Jillian West*
Cover Designer: *Ashley Bedell*
Cover Photo: © *Dan Trist/Punchstock*
Media Project Manager: *Thomas Brierly*
Production Supervisor: *Louis Swaim*
Composition: This text was set in 10/12 Times Roman by Macmillan Publishing Solutions
Printing: Printed on 45# New Era Matte by Quebecor World, Inc.

Library of Congress Cataloging-in-Publication Data

Nelson, Jack L.
   Critical issues in education : dialogues and dialectics / Jack L. Nelson, Stuart B. Palonsky, Mary Rose McCarthy ; foreword by Nel Noddings.—7th ed.
      p. cm.
   ISBN 0-07-337864-X
   1. Education—United States. 2. Teaching—United States. 3. Educational evaluation—United States. 4. Critical thinking—United States. I. Palonsky, Stuart B. II. McCarthy, Mary Rose, Ph. D. III. Title.
   LA217.2.N45 2010
   370.973—dc22

                                                                                    2009002181

About the Authors

JACK L. NELSON, Rutgers University professor of education emeritus, earned a doctorate from the University of Southern California; an M.A. from California State University, Los Angeles; and a B.A. from the University of Denver. Prior to his thirty years or Rutgers, he taught at State University of New York, Buffalo; San Jose State University; and California State University, Los Angeles. He has been a visiting scholar at the University of California, Berkeley; Stanford University; Colgate University; City University of New York; University of Colorado; and University of Washington. He served several years as a visiting scholar in England at Cambridge University; in Scotland at Jordanhill College; and in Australia at the University of Sydney, Curtin University, and Edith Cowan University. His public school teaching experience includes elementary and secondary levels. *Critical Issues in Education* is his seventeenth book, and he has published over 175 articles, chapters, and reviews. His awards include citations from the American Association of University Professors and the National Council for the Social Studies, and he is listed in *Contemporary Authors* and *Who's Who in America*.

STUART B. PALONSKY is professor of education and director of The Honors College at the University of Missouri. A former public high school teacher in New York and New Jersey, Palonsky taught reading and English to speakers of other languages while serving in the U.S. Army. He graduated from the State University of New York at Oneonta and Michigan State University. His publications include the book *900 Shows a Year: A Look at Teaching from the Teacher's Side of the Desk,* an ethnographic account of high school teaching from a teacher's perspective. In addition, Palonsky has published numerous articles and reviews in education and social science journals and has presented research papers on education issues at national and state conferences. For ten years, Palonsky and Nelson were colleagues at Rutgers University. Nelson was the more prolific scholar; Palonsky, the better tennis player.

MARY ROSE McCARTHY received her PhD from State University of New York at Buffalo in the social foundation of education with a concentration in the history of education. While at Buffalo, she was a presidential fellow and a member of the Buffalo Research Institute on Teacher Education. She is an associate professor in the School of Education at Pace University and currently serves as associate dean.

McCarthy has been a secondary school teacher and administrator, the director of a work cooperative for guests at a Catholic Worker House of Hospitality, and a family life educator for parents whose children were at risk of being placed in foster care. She has written and presented at conferences on women's education, the history of teacher education, teaching high school students with disabilities, classroom management in inclusive settings, and racial desegregation of schools. Her ongoing commitment to work for positive social change is reflected in her current research on educational reform, progressive teacher education, and vestiges of segregation in the education of students with disabilities.

Brief Contents

Part Two
WHAT SHOULD BE TAUGHT?
KNOWLEDGE AND LITERACY

Part Three
HOW SHOULD SCHOOLS BE ORGANIZED
AND OPERATED?
SCHOOL ENVIRONMENT

Contents

Part Two
WHAT SHOULD BE TAUGHT?
KNOWLEDGE AND LITERACY

Part Three
HOW SHOULD SCHOOLS BE ORGANIZED
AND OPERATED?
SCHOOL ENVIRONMENT

Foreword

We live an age of ideology and uncritically held loyalties. Such an attitude is acceptable in, say, sports where we cheer for our favorite team through thick and thin. But it is an unhealthy way to approach politics, education, or religion. And even as consumers, we would do well to step back and take a critical view of the products we buy regularly. Are we really getting the most for our money, or have we been unduly influenced by advertising?

In this very welcome seventh edition of *Critical Issues in Education*, the authors tackle issues such as school finance, gender equity, multiculturalism, school reform, and a host of other controversial topics in education. They believe, as I do, that people learn to be critical thinkers by grappling with critical issues in public debate (Noddings, 2006). It is not enough to learn the formal rules of logic and argument; these must be put to use on genuine problems. Indeed, struggling with critical issues under the guidance of a good teacher may be the best way to learn the formal rules. That comment suggests a critical issue to think about in pedagogy: Should students be required to learn the basic rules, details of information, and algorithms before attempting to solve problems, or should they learn the rules in the process of problem solving? Should our answer differ, depending on the subject matter or age of students? Does it inevitably depend on the knowledge and skills of the teacher?

In addition to revised and updated chapters on such perennial controversial topics as school finance, gender and minority-group equity, choice, and religion, I am especially pleased to see chapters like "Corporations, Commerce, and Schools," "Discipline and Justice," "Values and Character Education," and a new chapter for this edition on "New Immigrants and Schools." These topics are loaded with critical issues.

Most citizens react with appreciation when business organizations take an interest in our public schools. But when is that interest educationally appropriate? How much influence should the Business Roundtable and other corporate organizations have on public education? Perhaps criticisms and recommendations from these groups are too often accepted uncritically (Emery and Ohanian, 2004). We need to ask: Is the criticism well founded? Who profits from the recommendation? Where, if at all, do the aims of education and of business overlap?

Discipline is a topic of major interest to every teacher. We need to discuss methods and tactics critically. Educators are—or should be—accountable for means as well as ends. If, for example, a teacher maintains an orderly classroom, does it matter how she does it? Put so starkly, most of us would respond that of course it matters. What methods are ethically justified? What tactics contribute to the growth of democratic character?

These matters require critical thought. When we encounter discipline problems, there is a temptation to seize any tactic that promises a solution. We sometimes forget to ask: Why are we having this problem? Too often, a faculty leaps to the conclusion that there is "something wrong with these kids"—and sometimes that conclusion is right, but often it is not.

When I was a high school mathematics teacher (more than thirty years ago), kids did not swear in class (and never at the teacher), listened in class (or pretended to), and usually did their homework. Were kids better then? Do students now need character education—perhaps uniforms, ceremonies, and consistent patterns of reward and punishment? Maybe. But consider. At that time, there were no security guards in most schools, no locked exits, no metal detectors. A little earlier—when I was myself a high school student—we had a full hour for lunch and could go where we wished; we had the same teachers for four years in many of our subjects; we knew instantly, in our small school, when a stranger was on campus. Perhaps it is *conditions* and not kids that have changed. If that is the case, how should we proceed to analyze our discipline problem?

I am not suggesting that character education should be rejected out of hand. There is much of value in it. But exactly *what* should we borrow from it? Why should we engage in it? What outcomes can we reasonably expect? And how should we try to reach them? George Orwell said of his own school days (crammed with character education of a highly questionable sort): "I was in a world where it was *not possible* for me to be good. . . . Life was more terrible, and I was more wicked, than I had imagined" (1946/1981, p. 5). Educators must make it both desirable and possible for students to be good. How might the conditions of schooling be changed to support this goal?

The new chapter on immigration and education is a welcome addition. Immigration has, once again, become a hot button issue in politics and social life. We are conflicted about how to handle legal and illegal immigration with justice and fairness while protecting our borders and continuing our tradition as a nation of immigrants. A more recent wrinkle on this topic involves schools. The number and variety of immigrants, their differing educational needs, the resources needed to accommodate those needs, and the public support necessary are among the many areas where critical thinking is required.

The discussion of critical issues is difficult—an enterprise littered with opportunities to attack persons instead of arguments. We human beings have not yet learned how to conduct these discussions effectively. In private social life, we generally avoid topics that might trigger passionate disagreement. It is not considered polite to talk critically about religion or politics. In schools, too, we usually avoid controversial issues, and this avoidance is supported by the careful vetting (censoring?) of school textbooks.

Rejecting the "war model" of debate, we have to learn how to participate intelligently and respectfully in critical discussions. *Critical Issues in Education* makes a significant contribution to the achievement of this goal.

Finally, it is worth repeating something I said in my foreword to an earlier edition: As you read this book, be ready to think and speak up, but be gentle with your opponents.

Nel Noddings
Stanford University; Teachers College, Columbia University

References

EMERY, K., AND OHANIAN, S. (2004). *Why Is Corporate America Bashing Our Public Schools?* Portsmouth, NH: Heinemann.

ORWELL, G. (1946/1981). *A Collection of Essays.* San Diego: Harcourt Brace.

NODDINGS, N. (2006). *Critical Lessons: What Our Schools Might Teach but Do Not.* Cambridge: Cambridge University Press.

Preface

Greetings, and welcome to the seventh edition of *Critical Issues in Education,* a collection of original, competing essays on pervasive controveries about schooling. We have updated and revised all chapters, and we encourage your exploration and critical engagement.

School is controversial. True, it is not as obviously controversial as politics, religion, or sex—but education ranks up high. Just ask relatives and friends what they think of America's schools, and be prepared for some strong opinions. Actually, school issues include the hot topics of politics, religion, and sex—politicians use education as an election device, religion and schools is a continuing debate, and sex-related school topics bring out intense views. There are many other controversies surrounding schooling, from financing to standardized testing, and many opinions about each.

School and Controversies

Persistent school issues reflect basic human disagreements in areas like politics, economics, and social values. The issues and ideologies deserve critical examination of competing views. Newspapers and magazines report educational information like student test scores, school finance decisions, and various school activities. But mass media often ignore or gloss over basic social or ideological conflicts that lie below the surface of the news. And news media can sterilize issues by presenting only one view. Few media provide alternative views of an issue. This implies there is only one correct view on a topic and it obscures important distinctions surrounding school controversies.

For over three hundred years, people on this continent have agreed on the importance of education, but have disagreed over how it should be controlled, financed, organized, conducted, and evaluated. Two centuries ago, a very young United States was debating whether or not to establish free and compulsory education, arguing over who should be educated, who should pay, and what should be taught. We have mass public education now, but some of these same arguments continue about schools.

Some say American schools are in deep trouble and getting worse, with poor teachers and weak programs of study. Others view their schools as remarkably good, with excellent teachers and high-quality programs. New views emerge as debates over education stimulate us to rethink our positions. The terrain of education is rugged and rocky, with few clear paths and many conflicting road signs. It is controversial.

Organization of the Book

An introductory chapter presents background and a process for examining debates in education and reform efforts.

The three following sections are each devoted to a major question about schooling and provide a thematic context:

Part One: Whose Interests Should Schools Serve? Theme: Justice and Equity

Part Two: What Should Be Taught? Theme: Knowledge and Literacy

Part Three: How Should Schools Be Organized and Operated? Theme: School Environment

Each part contains chapters on specific critical issues, and each chapter contains two essays expressing divergent positions on that issue. Obviously, these do not exhaust all the possible positions; they do provide at least two views on the issue. References are provided in each chapter to encourage further exploration. At the end of each chapter are a few questions to consider and discuss.

The three coauthors each took primary responsibility for writing different parts of this volume. For Jack Nelson, this includes Introductions to Part One and Part Two and Chapters 1, 7, 8, 11, 13, 17, and 18. For Stuart Palonsky, it includes Introduction to Part Three and Chapters 5, 12, 14, 16, and 19. And for Mary Rose McCarthy, it includes Chapters 2, 3, 4, 6, 10, and 15. Stu and Jack jointly prepared Chapter 9, with assistance from Valerie Pang.

Acknowledgments

We thank Nel Noddings of Stanford University and Teachers College, Columbia University, for her stimulating Foreword.

We thank colleagues and reviewers who made many suggestions for this revision. We received particularly valuable suggestions from a variety of faculty members and students who have used this book in one or more of its six previous editions. Thanks to them for their important contributions.

We owe great intellectual debts to a long list of scholars, writers, teachers, and others who examine education and society, and who express divergent ideas in the extensive literature available. This includes a variety of educational and social theorists and critics, as well as a corps of school practitioners who live the life of schools. We also are indebted to students, colleagues, and others who provided specific criticism and assistance as we worked through the various topics. In particular, we express appreciation to

Allison McNamara, our primary editor at McGraw-Hill, and the McGraw-Hill education editor.

We owe special thanks to Gwen, Nancy, and Ken for their support, enthusiasm, and criticism when needed.

Many colleagues have reviewed the manuscript of this edition, given us good criticism as the work progressed, or provided provocative ideas to challenge us along the way. We thank them for their help and suggestions. Among these are John B. Aston, Southwest Texas State University; Vic Balaker, Carlsbad–Vinaka Debates; Pat Benne, Wittenberg University; David Blacker, University of Delaware; Deron R. Boyles, Georgia State University; Wade A. Carpenter, Berry College; Mark Caruana, attorney, Carlsbad, California; David Cauble, Western Nebraska Community College; Cathryn A. Chappell, University of Akron; John Cline, Carlsbad–Vinaka Debates; Linda T. Coats, Mississippi State University; Eleanor Cohen, editorial and technological consultant, Vista, California; Jorge Correa, Mount Berry College; Diane Crews, Binghamton University; Frances P. Crocker, Lenoir Rhyne College; Warren Crown, Rutgers University; James Daly, Seton Hall University; Emily de la Cruz, Portland State University; Russell Dennis, Bucknell University; Xu Di, University of West Florida; Annette Digby, University of Arkansas; Kathleen A. Dolgos, Kutztown University; Beverly Durham, school reform advocate, Fishers, Indiana; Gloria Earl, Indiana Wesleyan University; Herbert Edwards, attorney, Harbor Springs, Michigan; Paul Edwards, attorney, Colorado Springs, Colorado; Tracy Faulconer, Pacific University; William and Sheila Fernekes, Hunterdon, New Jersey, Central High School; Mark Garrison, D'Youville College; William Gaudelli III, Teachers College, Columbia University; Karen Graves, Denison University; Harry D. Hall, Indiana Wesleyan University; Julia O. Harper, Azusa Pacific University; Warren R. Heydenberk, Lehigh University; Robert Higgins, curator emeritus, Smithsonian Institution and University of North Carolina, Asheville; Sharon Hobbs, Montana State University; Michael Imber, University of Kansas; Mary Ann Isberg, artist-in-residence, Denver, Colorado; Chris Johnson, University of Arizona; Tony W. Johnson, West Chester University; Jean Ketter, Grinnell College; Ramon Khalona, engineer and technological consultant, Carlsbad, California; Kevin Laws, University of Sydney, Australia; Joslen Letscher, University of Detroit–Mercy; Becky Lewis, University of Buffalo; Charles Love, University of South Carolina–Upstate; Stephen Earl Lucas, The University of Illinois at Urbana-Champaign; Chogallah Maroufi, California State University at Los Angeles; Gary E. Martin, Northern Arizona University; Cornelia McCarthy, Columbia University; Joseph McCarthy, Suffolk University; Barbara Bredefeld Meyer, Illinois State University; David Michels, Carlsbad–Vinaka Debates; Wally Moroz, Edith Cowan University, Perth, Australia; Maxine G. Morris, Missouri Southern State University; John D. Napier, University of Georgia; Nel Noddings, Stanford University; Julie R. Palmour, Piedmont College; Valerie Pang, San Diego State University; Nancy Patterson, Bowling Green State University; Maike Philipsen, Virginia Commonwealth University; Kel Phillipson, technical director, Red Box Digital, London, England; Yasmeen Qadri, University of Central Florida; Adah Ward Randolph, Ohio University; Christopher Roellke, Vassar College; Bonnie

Rose, Riverside City Schools, California; Betty Sauer, Palo Alto Schools; Dawn Shinew, Washington State University, Barbara R. Sjostrom, Rowan University; Leslie Soodak, Pace University; William Stanley, Monmouth University; Susan Talburt, Georgia State University; Ronald K. Templeton, The Citadel; Doris Terr, City Schools of New York; Atilano Valencia, California State University, Fresno; John Vernon, engineering craftsman, Del Mar, California; Mark Vollmer, Director of ABA Learning, Australia; Burt Weltman, William Paterson College; and David and Janelle Wiedemann, political analysis consultants, Centennial, Colorado.

We dedicate this effort to Megan, Kel, Jordan, Warwick, Jonathan, Barbara, Mark, Steven, Kim, Robert, Mary Catherine, Skyler, Olwyn and others of the generations of students and teachers who are at the center of critical education debates in this twenty-first century.

Jack L. Nelson

Stuart B. Palonsky

Mary Rose McCarthy

CHAPTER 1

Introduction: Critical Issues and Critical Thinking

About This Book: Schools are controversial because they are so important. This book presents debates about eighteen pervasive educational issues, in Chapters 2 through 19, organized under three thematic sections:

Part One: Whose Interests Should Schools Serve?

Theme: Justice and Equity

Part Two: What Should Be Taught?

Theme: Knowledge and Literacy

Part Three: How Should Schools Be Organized and Operated?

Theme: School Environment

Controversy requires at least two distinct views; each chapter contains two essays presenting divergent positions on that topic. These position essays are all original, written only for this book, and they include data, research, and arguments that support that view of the issue. Critical thinking is a valuable process for examining and evaluating critical issues and the controversies they inspire (Clabaugh, 2008).

About this Chapter: Chapter 1 covers controversies and critical-thinking processes that use dialogue and dialectic reasoning in examining educational issues. These issues arise in historic, philosophic, and social contexts, so we include some of that background as well as current scholarly research on schooling in terms of politics, economics, policy questions, ideology, and social practice. We note patterns of criticism about schools and proposed reforms, and we conclude with a brief examination of efforts to reform schools and the controversial results.

INTRODUCTION

Education as Controversy: Examples

If you like arguments, you will love the study of education. Few topics elicit more disagreement or have as much at stake for our future. Even if you don't like arguments, your life and our society are influenced by the debates and the resulting decisions. Arguments over education seldom challenge its value. There is broad support for education. We disagree over the purposes, nature, form, and process of education, but not on its fundamental virtues. That still provides plenty of opportunities for bitter fights.

Current controversies about schools and schooling include the No Child Left Behind (NCLB) Act of 2002. A bipartisan bill, it followed, but considerably expanded, several decades of elementary and secondary federal school funding laws. NCLB calls for standards for students and teachers, increased testing, school accountability, decreasing the achievement gap for minorities, and significant penalties for schools that do not perform over time.

The NCLB Act generates partisan and bipartisan attacks and rebuttals from many quarters. Critics note that it is grossly underfunded, excessively punitive, educationally unsound, and inadequate in application. The Department of Education argues in reply that there has been increased educational funding, improved flexibility for states, and better scores for math at the fourth-grade level (Spellings, 2006, 2008). Critics disagree, citing how much it costs states without reimbursement, how it limits the curriculum and thinking while destroying those subjects not on the tests, how basic flaws in the law were not fixed, and how there is virtually no significant improvement in educational quality (Meier and Wood, 2004; McKenzie, 2006, 2007; Sunderman, 2006; AFT, 2005; NEA, 2006; Science News, 2008; Nichols and Berlin, 2008).

Critics from different political sides contend that the law:

- is wrong-headed and short-sighted (to mix metaphors);
- is narrow and restrictive on curriculum, limiting real education;
- is too inclusive and broad in scope and punishment;
- improperly imposes federal controls on a state function;
- misevaluates educational progress by overreliance on testing;
- forces teachers and students into conformity;
- imposes a class orientation, disadvantaging lower income families;
- restricts critical thinking;
- illustrates political interference of the worst kind.

Results of NCLB are mixed: Very limited test score increases in select areas can easily be explained as accidental, but no remarkable improvements. Government research found Reading First, a NCLB required program funded at $1 billion per year, to be ineffective (Institute of Education Sciences, 2008). This program was also plagued with criticisms of conflict of interest and cronyism in contracts and mandates imposed by the U.S. Department of Education (Dillon, 2008). Many now contend the NCLB Act is a giant failure or, worse, a stealthy way to undercut support for public education (Meier and Wood, 2004; McKenzie, 2006, 2008; Neill, 2008; Spring, 2008).

On the traditionalist side, Diane Ravitch (2007) says NCLB is fatally flawed. Progressive Jonathan Kozol (2005) criticizes NCLB because of its top-down standardization and conformity provisions and its stealthy return to racial apartheid in schooling.

Another current example of significant arguments over schools involves evolution and creationism (Johnson, 2006; Rudoren, 2006). This has been a school and social issue since Darwin. The Scopes trial illustrated this over 80 years ago and the effort to place "intelligent design" in the science curriculum carries the controversy forward into the twenty-first century. Intelligent design (ID), a variation of the creationist position, challenges Darwinian theories on natural selection and evolution. The Intelligent Design Network website states their position that "certain features of the universe and of living things are best explained by an intelligent cause rather than an undirected process such as natural selection" (www.intelligentdesignnetwork.org, 2005). Evolutionists find there is no credible scientific evidence that is better than evolutionary theory so far and that religious beliefs should not overwhelm science.

The ID position is expressed in recent publications (Dembski, 2004; Behe, Dembski, and Meyer, 2000; Strobel, 2004; House, 2008). The opposition appears in other sources (Perakh, 2003; Forrest and Gross, 2004; Young and Edis, 2004; Scott, 2004).

Jacoby (2008) states:

> . . . Americans are alone in the developed world in their view of evolution by means of natural selection as "controversial" rather than as settled mainstream science. The continuing strength of religious fundamentalism in America (again, unique in the developed world) is generally cited as the sole reason for the bizarre persistence of anti-evolutionism. . . . The real and more complex explanation may lie not in America's brand of faith but in the public's ignorance about science in general as well as evolution in particular. (p. xvii)

Obviously, what we teach in schools is a reflection of what we consider true, accurate, consistent, and reasoned. This is especially true in science education. The evolution/creationism argument is fundamental to that point and is highly related to schooling questions about church/state relations, the nature of knowledge, curriculum decision making, and academic freedom for teachers and students, among others.

Disputes over NCLB and evolution/creationism illustrate strident school debates involving deeply held views from politics to religion. If school was inconsequential, it would not be worthy of intense, long-lived disputes. Education is not a trivial pursuit, a minor activity that can be avoided with impunity. It is necessary for the survival and development of each person and society. Strong opinions define many controversial topics, but schooling is unusual because few controversial topics have so many personally experienced experts. School is one social institution that virtually all people have experienced for long periods, and most have an opinion about it. So we argue about education and the formal agency we use for education—the schools.

Education and Schooling

Education, of course, is far more than just what goes on in school. But schools are usually at the center of public arguments about education because schools are the social organizations that take on the formalized task of educating. In colonial America, most people received their education outside of schools (Bailyn, 1960). Some of today's reluctant students might prefer that alternative to their life in school, but that is not an option available to many. For these students, school may even be an impediment to education—it interferes with their learning about life. They become educated, despite school.

For the vast majority, however, much of the most important learning, and certainly most of the formal learning, occurs in school. Book learning and computer learning are hallmarks of schools, and society expects schools to remain that central learning location for academic knowledge. In addition to academics, there is some expectation that school also will be a place of intellectual development. Intellectual learning differs from academic learning in its development of skeptical and questioning attitudes and its focus on ideas rather than on information (Gella, 1976; Gouldner, 1979; Barber, 1998; Schneider, 2004; Jacoby, 2008). Academic learning includes formal study of typical subjects: English, science, history, arts, math, social sciences, languages, and so on. Intellectual learning includes raising questions, critical thinking, creative interpretation, and being unlimited by subject-field discipline boundaries in the examination of ideas. Some people become concerned when schools heavily engage in intellectual learning; open examination of ideas and skepticism can lead to controversial topics—a threat to some people.

In addition to academic and intellectual responsibilities of schools, there are also social expectations for schools to take on responsibility for the ethical, physical, and emotional development of children, as well as for their safety, health, and civility. Academic, intellectual, practical, moral, and behavioral responsibilities have long been multiple foci of schools. In addition, schools have accepted some responsibility for addressing such social problems as drugs, sexual mores, and crime. For several decades, we have had proposals for making schools even more the centers of their communities, open all year, seven days a week, early morning to late night, and taking on more social responsibilities (Dryfoos, 2002; Strike, 2004).

The significance of responsibilities schools have is suggested in the strength and intensity of the great debates over schools. Schooling, as a major player in the process of education, is particularly important to society's vitality and the viability of each person. In today's world, those who can't read, write, or calculate adequately bear a heavy burden in daily existence. Those lacking fundamental knowledge and skills suffer social, economic, political, and personal difficulty. The society that does not pay enough attention to schooling also suffers; it is on a downhill slope (Fuentes, 2005).

Nolan (1996) notes:

> Of all the issues that are likely to generate controversy, no issue hits closer to home than the education and care of children. A cursory glance at many of the most heated issues in the culture wars reveals just how pivotal education is.

Multiculturalism, sex education, condom distribution, guns in school, textbook selection, creationism, values clarification—controversies over these issues demonstrate how educational institutions have become a primary focus of the culture wars . . . the battle over the schools then is nothing less than a struggle for the future of America. (p. 37)

Some of the continuing questions about education, schools, and society:

- How should we evaluate schools, teachers, curricula, and society's support of schools?
- How should we address problems of inequality, racism, sexism, and violence in schools?
- Who should be going to school, for how long, to study what, and for what purposes?
- How should schools be financed, and how well?
- What is the best approach to religion, values, character, and academic subjects for schools?
- How should schools be organized and operated?
- Why do we seem clueless about the best education, when there are plenty of clues and firm opinions about it?

Cycles of criticism and reform in education are not new (Cuban, 2003). We have had educational reform advocates for so long that it is impossible to identify their beginnings. Perhaps the first educational reformer, a member of some prehistoric group, rose up to protest that children were not learning the basic skills, as he had. Another member may have proposed a radical new plan to improve children's hunting-and-gathering skills. Some of the bashed skulls lying about prehistoric sites are probably the results of arguments over education.

Critical Thinking, Dialogue, and Dialectics

Questions about schooling stimulate a variety of potential and often competing answers, but there is no single set of clear and uncontested resolutions. Life would be easier, although less interesting, if we had single and simple answers to all our problems. But critical social issues are usually too complex to be adequately resolved by easy or absolute solutions. In fact, simple answers often create new problems, or merely cause the problems they were supposed to solve to rise again.

Quick, easy, and absolute resolutions are readily available in contemporary society—radio talk shows, newspaper editorials and responses, websites and chatrooms, and coffee shops are among the places where we can find clear and forceful answers to most of our problems, including educational issues. These answers may well be simple, clear, and forceful—but often will be contradictory, competing, or inconsistent. Significant debates over complicated human issues such as sex, politics, and religion are engaging partly because they usually are not subject to quick and easy resolution.

A proper skepticism and critical thinking are the friends of wisdom. Critical thinking, the main process and goal of education, involves at least:

- recognition that an important issue deserves considered judgment,
- thoughtful formulation of good questions,
- a search for possible answers and evaluating pertinent evidence,
- consideration of alternative views, and
- drawing of tentative conclusions that are acceptable until another question or a better answer arises.

Critical thinking is far more difficult, and significantly more important, than just finding answers (Emerson, Boes, and Mosteller, 2002; Kinchloe and Weil, 2004). The search for knowledge goes well beyond puzzle pages with answers printed upside down at the bottom or reporting back to a teacher what an encyclopedia says. Dialogue and dialectics can help.

Dialogue and the Case for Dialectic Reasoning

Arguments easily can dissolve into shouting matches, "Says who?" and "Me, that's who!" levels of dialogue, or even fistfights. Whether arguments are trivial or significant, they can be heated and unthinking. It is easy to recognize the merits of our own position, and we are not always eager to admit the virtues of others. Arguments about important topics, however, should not devolve into shouting or personal attack. Knowledge and social improvement depend on rational and civil argument; "Disagreement is a key element of communal deliberations" (Makau and Marty, 2001, p. 7). Active democracy requires it (Gutman and Thompson, 1996, 2004; Hess, 2002; Zurn, 2007). Good arguments can be thoughtful and reasoned, a dialogue between two different points of view—or dialectic reasoning with opposing views.

Reasoned dialogue calls for listening, understanding evidence, and assessing the quality of sources and persuasiveness of the arguments (Audi, 2001; McCabe, 2000). Dialectic reasoning, the examination of opposing ideas to develop a creative and superior idea, is a level beyond dialogue (Sim, 1999; Farrar, 2000; Sciabarra, 2000). Both are practices of critical thinking.

Dialogue and dialectic are dynamic, interactive, and optimistic. They are optimistic since they take the stance that things can and should be improved. Arguments are not the only way to reason. Intuition, for example, is perfectly suitable, as is reading and contemplation.

Dialogue calls for two persons or two ideas—we can have dialogue with ourselves, but we need at least two ideas. Monologues, to others or ourselves, can be valuable for gaining ideas; most textbooks operate as monologues, presenting one view. But dialogue is more dynamic and more challenging. Not all dialogue, however, is civil and productive. It can operate at the lowest level, used to browbeat others into agreement, as in a kind of Socratic attack—Noddings (1995b) notes: "Socrates himself taught by engaging others in dialogue . . . he dominates the dialogue and leads the listeners . . . forcing his listeners gently and not so gently to see the errors in their thinking" (pp. 6, 7). But reasoned

FIGURE 1.1 Dialectic Reasoning: A Simplified Diagram

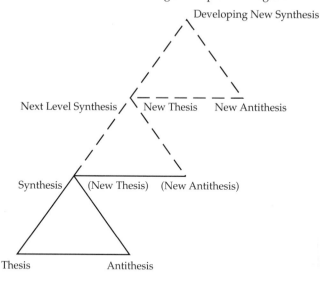

dialogue involves active consideration of a different view and interest in inter-action in discussion (Mercer, 2008; NCDD, 2008). We advocate informed skep-ticism, using reasoned dialogue in examining educational issues—but we go further, encouraging development of a dialectic approach for some issues in the search for improvement in education.

Dialogue does not expect much beyond civil discussion used to gain under-standing. Dialectic reasoning uses disputes and divergent opinions to arrive at a better idea. The dialectic occurs when you pit one argument (thesis) against another (antithesis) in an effort to develop a synthesis superior to either (see Figure 1.1). It is an inquiry into important issues that identifies the main points, important evidence, and logical arguments used by each of at least two diver-gent views on an issue. This requires critical examination of the evidence and arguments on each side of a dispute, granting each side some credibility. A dia-lectic approach is dynamic. A synthesis from one level of dialectic reasoning can become a new thesis at a more sophisticated level, and the process of inquiry continues to spiral (Adler, 1927; Cooper, 1967; Rychlak, 1976; Noddings, 1995b; Blumenfeld-Jones, 2004). True inquiry is life-long.

The purpose for dialectic reasoning between competing ideas is not to defeat one and accept the other, but to search for an improved idea. Dialectic reasoning is not merely the search to certify one side as a winner nor to find a political compro-mise, especially a compromise that pleases neither side very well. It is a search for a higher level of idea that accommodates or incorporates the most important points in the thesis and antithesis. Sciabarra (2000) describes the dialectic process as:

> Dialectical method is neither dualistic nor monistic. A thinker who employs a dialectic method embraces neither a pole nor the middle of a duality of extremes. Rather, the dialectical method anchors the thinker to both camps.

> The dialectic thinker refuses to recognize these camps as mutually exclusive or apparent opposites. . . . He or she strives to uncover the common roots of apparent opposites . . . [and] presents an integrated alternative. . . . (p. 16)

For a simple example on a complicated topic: As Marcuse (1960) notes, many early philosophers considered individual freedom and social freedom as opposites. One could enjoy individual freedom only by trampling on social freedoms, and a society could exert its freedom only by limiting the freedom of individuals. One was a thesis, the other its antithesis; apparently opposite views. A synthesis develops as both freedoms are considered necessary to modern civilization and to individuals, using the view that individual freedoms are best maintained in a free society. Without society, humans have no freedom in practice; there is no freedom in mere survival. Without individual freedoms, society cannot be free in practice; the range of individual freedom depends on agreement with other individuals in a social contract requiring essential equality, a system of laws, and rational thinking.

Philosophers have used the idea of dialectics in many different ways; it has justified opposite radical conclusions like absolute social control, as in forms of Marxism, or absolute individualism and against society, as in some of the libertarian ideas of Ayn Rand (Sciabarra, 1999). But Aristotle, the moderate philosopher who initiated Western political philosophy, could be considered the father of dialectic reasoning. He saw dialectic and rhetoric as mutually supportive arts, with dialectic the logical means for developing arguments and rhetoric the means of persuasion, speaking or writing, that uses the results of dialectic reasoning. Aristotle favored the dialectic because it required examining serious questions from many different positions.

The dialectic approach is fundamentally optimistic: It assumes there are better ideas for improving society and that examining diverse ideas is a productive way to develop them. Many issues can't resolve well into a synthesis at any given time, but that does not denigrate the dialectic approach as a good way to comprehend and critically examine opposing positions. Dialectic reasoning may require more energy than you think necessary for some of the educational issues in this book, and dialogue will be perfectly satisfactory. The dialectic process, though, is a valuable tool for considering knotty social problems. It offers a means for depersonalizing various strongly held opinions to strive for a common good in improving schools (Van Emeren and GootenHorst, 2003; Caranfa, 2004). As with most educative practices, it is not the finding of predetermined right answers, but the process of thinking that is most important. A right answer is good for solving a single problem, but a good process is useful for many problems.

Dialogues and dialectics don't necessarily lead to truth; they can merely repeat errors and bias. Thus, we advocate a healthy, informed skepticism in examining these disputes. In the ancient Greek tradition, exercising skepticism meant to examine or to consider—to raise questions about reasons, evidence, and arguments (Sim, 1999; Wright, 2001). Skepticism is not simply doubt, despair, or cynicism; it is intelligent inquiry. Without skepticism, we easily can fall into "complacent self-deception and dogmatism"; with it, we can "effectively advance the frontiers of inquiry and knowledge," applying this knowledge to "practical life, ethics, and politics" (Kurtz, 1992, p. 9). Dialogues and dialectics on educational issues, with prudent skepticism, are thoughtful forms of inquiry (McLaren and Houston, 2004; Van Luchene, 2004).

DEMOCRATIC VITALITY
AND EDUCATIONAL CRITICISM

Critics of schools are easy to find. People are not bashful about noting school problems, but disagree over what is wrong, who is responsible, and what should be done to change schools. Of all social institutions in a democracy, the school should be the most ready for examination; education rests upon critical assessment and reassessment. That does not mean that all criticism is justified, or even useful. Some of it is simplistic, mean-spirited, or wrong-headedly arrogant. But much of it is thoughtful and cogent. Although some unjustified criticism can be detrimental to education in a democracy, open debate can permit the best ideas to percolate, to be developed and revised, and to be evaluated (DeWiel, 2000).

Over the long haul, schooling has improved and civilization has been served by the debates over education. More people get more education of a better quality across the world now than in previous generations. Despite periodic lapses and declines, the global movement toward increased and improved schooling for more students continues. The debates force us to reconsider ideas about schooling and increase our sophistication about schools and society.

Democratic vitality and educational criticism are good companions. Democracy, as Thomas Jefferson so wisely noted, requires an enlightened public and free dissent. Education is the primary means to enlightenment and to thoughtful dissent. It follows that schools would be among those fundamental social institutions under continuing public criticism in a society striving to improve its democracy.

- Alexis de Tocqueville (1848/1969) introduced his classic study of democracy in the very young United States by stating:

  The first duty imposed on those who now direct society is to educate democracy; to put, if possible, new life into its beliefs. . . . (p. 12)

- Bertrand Russell (1928) noted that education is basic to democracy:

  . . . it is in itself desirable to be able to read and write . . . an ignorant population is a disgrace to a civilized country, and . . . democracy is impossible without education. (p. 128)

- And John Dewey (1916) put schools at the center of democracy:

  The devotion of democracy to education is a familiar fact. . . . a democratic society repudiates the principle of external authority, it must find a substitute in voluntary disposition and interest; these can only be created by education. (p. 87)

Democratic vitality and educational criticism both require open expression of diverse ideas, yet both are based on an optimistic sense of unity of purpose. Diverse ideas and criticism provide necessary tests of our ideas. Criticism easily can appear to be negative, pessimistic, or cynical, but these are not its only forms. Informed skepticism, the purpose for this book, offers a more optimistic view without becoming like Pollyanna. Diverse ideas are sought because we think, optimistically, that education can be improved. Unity of purpose suggests there is a bedrock of agreement on basic values, the criteria against which to judge diverse ideas. Without diverse ideas, there is no vitality and opportunity for progress; without unity of purpose, diverse ideas can be chaotic and irrational.

Global Democratization and Purposes of Education

In these first two decades of the twenty-first century, school remains the most common approach to education around the world. Schools for children of the elite classes have existed since ancient times, but mass education in schools is a relatively recent global phenomenon. Though it is essentially a twentieth-century development, mass schooling has become dominant worldwide as democracy has become the dominant global trend in governments. But democratization is not always positive and progressive. Shapiro and Macedo (2000) pose the kind of problems that confront societies and their schools in developing democratic life:

> The principles and practices of democracy continue to spread even more widely, and it is hard to imagine that there is a corner of the globe into which they will not penetrate. But the euphoria of democratic revolutions is typically short-lived, and its attainment seems typically to be followed by disgruntlement and even cynicism about the actual operation of democratic institutions. . . . Of course, it is far easier to perceive the need for reform than to prescribe specific proposals. (p. 1)

Garforth (1980) points out that "Undoubtedly, democracy at its best is a great educative force, but . . . it is not immune from dishonesty, corruption, and the betrayal of truth" (p. 20). Democratization brings the need for mass schooling and critical literacy (Torres, 2002). Dictatorship seems to work better with less education for the general public; but miseducation of the public in a democracy is dysfunctional. A strong democracy requires a critical citizenry, a public capable of engaging in critical thinking. Critical citizens depend upon critical education (Norris, 1999; Winthrop, 2000; Giroux, 2004). This is a significant concern for the United States, where democracy and mass education are well developed and supported; it is even more significant for nations where these traditions are weaker.

Global Dimensions of Education

Public and private schools are the social institutions organized to provide formal education in modern nations, involving nearly all the student-age populations. Wealthier nations provide and require schooling for the largest proportion of children for the longest period, but less wealthy nations have rapidly increased

FIGURE 1.2 World Population, School Enrollments, Teachers,
and Expenditures, 1980–2010

	1980	1990	2000	2010 est.
Population	4.4 billion	5.3 billion	6.2 billion	6.8 billion
Enrollment	856 million	1.1 billion	1.2 billion	1.4 billion
Teachers	38 million	47 million	60 million	80 million
School Expenditures in U.S. Dollars	$516 billion	$986 billion	$1.8 trillion	$3 trillion

primary school education and are moving to expand secondary and higher education opportunities for more students. In 1950, only 16 percent of the world's students of high school age were in secondary schools, and 3 percent of age-related students were in colleges. By 2000, over 34 percent of high-school-age students around the world were in secondary schools and 8 percent of the age-related students were in college. Figure 1.2 shows the global effort to educate (UNESCO, 2005; U.S. Census Bureau, 2008).

The schools of the world now employ over 70 million teachers, who comprise the world's largest professional occupation. Finding adequate resources to support these teachers and operate schools is a major global issue. The United Nations has undertaken a significant role in improving education and treatment of children. International treaties and conventions on education indicate the importance of schooling worldwide. Still, schools in the poorest nations face serious shortages of basic requirements, from adequate buildings to textbooks. Some schools in all parts of the world are in poor physical condition and are getting worse, but poorer nations suffer more in lack of school facilities and support. This will further increase separation between rich and poor nations since schooling is future-oriented (*UNESCO World Education Report, 2000*).

The world's population is almost 7 billion, doubling since 1960. Developing nations have about 80 percent of the people, up from 70 percent in 1960. The growth rate has slowed, to about 1.2 percent annually, which, along with better education and health, means the population is aging. The median age in developing nations is now about 24 years old, up from about 19 years a quarter-century ago. The median age in more developed nations is 37, up from 29 years in 1975. Illiteracy not addressed when many of these people were younger is an increasing problem, along with the extensive current global effort to provide literacy to youth. That suggests global needs for educational programs for older citizens in addition to the well-known needs for schooling for the under-18-year-olds.

Educational spending, however, differs significantly between wealthier and poorer nations. In 1980, developed nations spent $408 billion on schools, about 5 percent of their Gross Domestic Product (GDP); less developed nations spent $98 billion, about 4 percent of their GDP, and the least developed spent

FIGURE 1.3 School Expenditure, as Percentage of Gross Domestic Product, Selected Nations, 21st Century

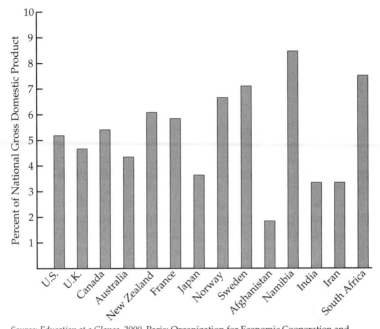

Source: *Education at a Glance, 2000.* Paris: Organization for Economic Cooperation and Development; *World Statistics Pocketbook 2001, Statistical Extracts, 2008.* New York: United Nations Department of Economic and Social Affairs; UNESCO. (2003). *Financing Education.*

$3.8 billion, or not quite 3 percent of GDP. In 2000 the more developed nations spent $1,000 billion, still 5 percent of GDP, and the least developed spent $7 billion, now just 2 percent of GDP (*UNESCO World Education Report, 2000;* UNESCO, 2003). The gap widens (see Figure 1.3).

Global democratization, population growth and distribution in the world, globalization of trade and industry, economic disparities among nations, and increasing age medians are reasons for an increasing interest in education as a primary means for national development and international interchange. Burns et al. (2003) note:

> Education is one of the most powerful instruments known for reducing poverty and inequality and for laying the basis for sustained economic growth. It is fundamental for the construction of democratic societies and dynamic, globally competitive economies. (p. 26)

The *United Nations Economic and Social Council Report on the World Social Condition, 2000* states:

> Education opens doors and facilitates social and economic mobility. . . . Education has assumed a central role in the life of societies, and their general progress has become intimately bound up with the vitality and reach of the educational enterprise. . . . At the global level, it has become the biggest industry, absorbing 5% of the world GDP and generating or helping to generate much more. (p. 16)

Table 1.1 Enrollment and Expenditures in Public and Private Schools, United States 1900–2010 (Projected; in thousands)

	Elementary and Secondary School Enrollees				Expenditures (in millions)	
	Public	%	Private	%	Public	Private
1900	15,500	92	1,350	8	$ 215	n/a
1910	17,800	92	1,550	8	426	n/a
1920	21,500	93	1,690	7	1,036	n/a
1930	25,600	91	2,650	9	2,317	n/a
1940	25,400	91	2,611	9	2,344	n/a
1950	25,111	88	3,380	12	5,838	$ 411
1960	35,150	86	6,300	14	16,700	1,100
1970	45,850	89	5,360	11	43,183	2,500
1980	40,850	88	5,300	12	103,162	7,200
1990	41,200	89	5,230	11	248,900	19,500
2000	47,000	89	5,950	11	389,000	28,400
2010	50,300	89	6,170	11	683,000	54,000

Source: Digest of Education Statistics, 2007. Washington, DC: U.S. Department of Education.
Data for private education are estimated. Private schools include religion-affiliated institutions, some of which include teachers and other staff who are not paid salaries.

In the United States, schooling also involves large numbers—of people, dollars, and locations. The number of U.S. school districts approaches 15,000, and the number of teachers is almost 3.5 million, with school expenditures about $500 billion annually. Table 1.1 summarizes U.S. school enrollments for public and private schools and public school expenditures. Schooling involves significant numbers of people and costs, but school has many payoffs. Unemployment rates are highest for people with less than a high school education, and lowest for those with at least a bachelor's degree; the median income of people 18 years and older increases consistent with education level attained (see Figure 1.4).

Schools are a focus of criticism and reform efforts because schools are among the most public of institutions, are one of the most common experiences people have, and are immensely important to the lifeblood and future of societies. Virtually every person spends long periods of life in schools; teachers may spend a lifetime. Schools carry significant social trust for transmitting cultural heritage, developing economic and political competence, and providing inspiration and knowledge to improve the future society. The nature and form of that heritage, competence, and knowledge form constant battlegrounds for different views of what schools ought to be and ought to be doing.

The public has lofty expectations for education, giving schools the responsibility for much of their children's welfare, values, skills, and knowledge. Schools are also experted to correct such social ills as crime, teenage pregnancy, and adolescent rudeness and to provide self-fulfillment education, ranging from employment skills to personal happiness. Schools, then, are seen as a source of both problems and solutions.

FIGURE 1.4 Relation of Education to Income; Workers 18 Years and Older,
Period 1975–2010

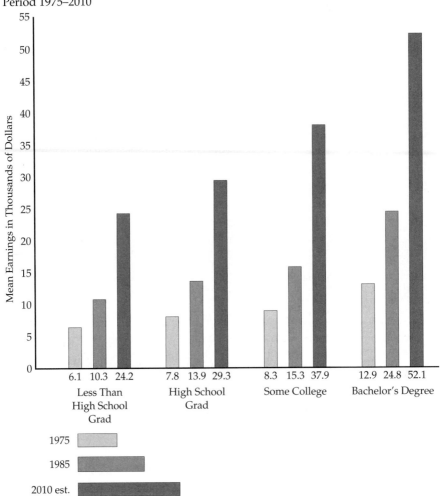

Source: Gauguin, D. A., and DeBrandt, K. A. (2001). *Education Statistics of the United States.* 3rd Ed. Lanham,
MD: Bernan; U.S. Census Bureau. (2008). *Statistical Abstract of the United States,* 2004–2005. Washington, DC:
U.S. Government Printing Office. Digest of Education Statistics 2008, www.nces.ed.gov

THE POLITICAL CONTEXT OF SCHOOLING

Education has emerged again as one of the most highly charged areas in political contests. Candidates offer clean, neat, and simple answers to long-term
school problems with often inconsistent messages about schools:

- Cut class size, but also cut school expenses.
- Repair buildings, but also lower taxes.
- Allow more local control, but impose more national standards and
  support.

- Educate against violence and drug abuse, but also teach only the basics.
- Improve sex education, but do not teach values in school.
- Make teachers more accountable, but give teachers more freedom and responsibility.
- Increase distance learning by computers, but also increase daily school time and the school year.
- Increase school competition for grades and awards, but make schools more collaborative, inclusive, and supportive.

School debates can be schizophrenic. Theodore Sizer said, "Everybody is for high test scores till their kids get low test scores" (Bronner, 1998). It is easy to claim that our own education was vastly superior to what students now get in school, and to advocate a return to the good old days. But how many would actually want their children to return to the reality and limitations of yesterday's schools?

The political nature of educational debates is illustrated by actions surrounding the Sandia Report on schools just a decade ago. The government suppressed for two years a major government-sponsored study showing U.S. schools were better than the first Bush administration wanted to divulge. The Sandia Report showed U.S. schools were far better than government and influential media were reporting.

"Much of the 'crisis' commentary today claims total system-wide failure in education. Our research shows that this is simply not true" (Carson, Huelskamp, and Woodall, 1992, p. 99).

Schools are both political agencies and handy targets from every side of party politics. Schools consume more local budget money than any other social agency, and are among the top consumers of state funds. Schools are a major responsibility under state legislation and local control, subjecting them to political pressures both from those in office and those vying to be.

A TRADITION OF SCHOOL CRITICISM AND REFORM

From the intensity and vigor of public debate over schooling, a debate in Western society at least since the time of Socrates, one would expect either dramatic changes in schools or their abolition in favor of an alternative structure. One of the two accusations leveled against Socrates in the indictment that brought him to trial, and brought on his suicide, was "corruption of the young." Socrates may have paid the ultimate price for being an educational reformer in a political setting that was not ready for his reforms. At least one critic has argued to abolish schools (Illich, 1971), and some have proposed revolutionary changes in schooling (Sinclair, 1924; Rafferty, 1968; Apple, 1990). Most changes have been moderate, however, and no radical attempts have succeeded.

Some school purposes are commonly accepted, such as distributing knowledge and providing opportunity, but controversies arise over what knowledge we should distribute, which children should get which opportunities, and who should be making these decisions. For more than 3,000 years, human societies have recognized the value of education—and argued about what the goal of schooling should be and how to achieve it (Ulich, 1954).

Shifts in criticism and efforts at reform are common in U.S. educational history (Cremin, 1961; Welter, 1962; Karier, 1967; Tyack, 1967; Katz, 1971; Ravitch, 2000; Cuban, 2003; Ross and Gibson, 2006), but schools actually change only modestly. Traditional and progressive agendas differ; schools respond by moving very gradually in one direction with a few widely publicized examples of reform, and then to await the next movement. Kaestle (1985) notes, "[The] real school system is more like a huge tanker going down the middle of a channel, rocking a bit from side to side as it attends to one slight current and then to another" (p. 423).

School Reform in Early Twentieth-Century America

The United States has a long tradition of innovation in education, stemming from its pioneer role in providing mass education at public expense. There are some major failures in this history, most notably the lack of equal educational opportunities for African Americans, Native Americans, women, immigrants, and those of lower income. We have, however, expanded education as a means for developing democracy and offering some social mobility. We may not realize these ambitions, and our real intentions may be less altruistic (Katz, 1968). But idealization of democratic reform through education is in the traditional American rhetoric.

American schools, from the nineteenth century, were expected to blend immigrants into the American mainstream through compulsory education on such subjects as English, American history, and civics. A history of racism, sexism, and ethnic prejudice was commonly ignored in American social life and schools, while we labored under the myth that everyone shared a happy society made up of people who should all talk, think, and form values the same way. Schools were a primary social agency to meld students from divergent cultural backgrounds into the American ideal, which, not unsurprisingly, exhibited European, white, male characteristics and values. English language and belief in the superiority of Western literature, history, politics, and economics dominated the schools. Schools were key institutions in "Americanizing" generations of immigrants.

In the early twentieth century, urbanization and industrialization created the need for different forms of school services. Large numbers of children from the working classes were in schools in urban areas, and the traditional classical curriculum, teaching methods, and leisure-class approach stumbled. Extensive development of vocational and technical courses was the most dominant change in schooling before World War I, as school activities broadened to include medical exams, health instruction, free lunch programs, schools open during vacation periods for working parents, and other community services. These reforms fit the evolving sense of social progressivism (Jacoby, 2008). The progressive education movement, from about 1920 to World War II, incorporated severe criticisms of traditional schooling ideas and such practices as corporal punishment, rigid discipline, rote memorization and drill, stress on the classics, and high failure rates.

Progressives advocated engaging in practical experiences and projects, community activities, study of controversial topics, practicing democracy in the schools, and study of social problems. Schools became more open to students of all classes, and the curriculum moved from more esoteric studies to courses with social applications, such as home economics, business and vocational education, current events, health, sociology, sex education, and consumer math. Sporadic criticisms of progressive thought cropped up throughout that time, but a reform movement from traditionalists gained public interest near the end of the Depression and again following World War II. Graham, summarizing the shift, states:

> Sometime between 1919 and 1955 the phrase "progressive education" shifted from a term of praise to one of opprobrium. To the American public of 1919, progressive education meant all that was good in education; thirty-five years later nearly all the ills in American education were blamed on it. (1967, p. 145)

Gurney Chambers (1948) notes that after the 1929 stock market crash, education came under attack: "Teachers were rebuked for their complacency and inertia, and progressive schools, surprisingly enough, were blamed for the increasing crime and divorce rates and political corruption" (pp. 142–143).

Jacoby (2008), writing about the history of anti-intellectualism in America states: "Ironically, the denigration of professional educators did not really take hold until the middle of the twentieth century. . . . in the eighteenth and nineteenth centuries. . . . the hiring of a schoolmaster was one of the two fundamental markers of civilization in frontier communities (the other being the presence of a minister)" (p. xvi).

Cycles of Educational Reform after World War II

Attacks on schools increased in intensity and frequency during the late 1940s and 1950s. The great school debates of this time involved many issues that extend into the twenty-first century. Church-state issues, including school prayer and use of public funds for religious education and other school services, gained significance. Racial issues, with the landmark Supreme Court decision in *Brown v. Board of Education of Topeka* (1954) and forced busing, became another focus of school controversy. Rapidly increasing tax burdens, to pay for new schools and teachers required by the baby boom, aroused protests from many school critics. Rising expectations for education were driven by the thousands of "non-college-prep" veterans who went to college on the GI Bill. Curricular issues, including disputes over the most effective way to teach reading and over test scores showing students did not know enough history or math or science or English, filled the popular press.

Politically, the McCarthy period "Red Scare" produced rampant public fear of a creeping communistic influence in American life and created suspicions that schools were breeding grounds for "communal" and progressive thought. These, and other factors, led to renewed criticism of schools. For many, there was simply a lingering sense that schools were not doing their job. Two books illustrate the criticisms of this period: Albert Lynd's *Quackery in the Public Schools* (1950, p. 53) and Arthur Bestor's *Educational Wastelands* (1953). Each attacked progressive education, and the "educationists" who advocated it, for turning schools from traditional discipline and subject knowledge toward the "felt needs" of children. As historian Clarence Karier notes, ". . . the educationist who spoke out for 'progressive education' and 'life adjustment education' appeared increasingly out of place in the postwar, cold war period" (1985, p. 238).

Major foundations examined America's schools. The Ford Foundation made education a focal point. Grants were made to the Educational Testing Service to improve measures of student performance. The Carnegie Foundation asked James Bryant Conant, former president of Harvard and U.S. Ambassador to West Germany, to conduct a series of studies of public education. There was much public criticism of the academic failures of American schools. The Soviet launch of *Sputnik* in 1957, ahead of the United States, gave a new focus for educational reform. *Sputnik* was a highly visible catalyst for conservative critics, illustrating a lack of American competitiveness they attributed to progressive reforms in schools during the pre–World War II period. Critics blamed the "permissive" atmosphere in schools for this deficiency.

Excellence and Its Discontents: Post **Sputnik**

Post-*Sputnik* reform included a reinstitution of rigor, discipline, traditional subject teaching, and standards. They added up to the theme, to be repeated in the 1980s, of "Excellence." There are remarkable similarities in the language and rationales used in the earlier reform movement and those used in the 1980s efforts to return schools to traditional work. International competition, advancing technology, and the needs of business are rationales cited in the literature of both periods.

Excellence, ill-defined and excessively used, is a cue word that shows up in many reports and statements from both periods. Gardner's *The Pursuit of Excellence: Education and the Future of America* (1958), is one illustration. Another term common to both periods is *mediocrity*, a threat suggested in the title of Mortimer Smith's book, *The Diminished Mind: A Study of Planned Mediocrity in Our Public Schools* (1954).

The Conant Report, *The American High School Today* (1958), was a moderate book that proposed a standard secondary school curriculum, tracking by ability group, special courses for gifted students, improvements in English composition, better counseling, and other recommendations. Federal funds for reform were increased in the late 1950s and early 1960s. The National Defense Education Act (NDEA) responded to pleas that schools were key to providing "national defense," and that *Sputnik* showed the United States was militarily vulnerable. Funds to improve teaching in science and math, foreign languages, social studies, and English encouraged university scholars in each field to determine better ways to convey the subject matter; many projects attempted to make the curriculum "teacherproof" (as in foolproof) to prevent classroom teachers from teaching it incorrectly. Teacher education came in for its share of criticism, with blasts at teachers' colleges, the progressive techniques they advocated, and quality of students going into teaching. This all sounds hauntingly familiar to those who read current educational criticism.

As the trend toward conservative educational ideas gained support and school practice turned back to standards and "rigor," criticism from the left began to emerge. This liberal criticism was a response to the rote memorization, excessive testing, lock-step schooling, and increased school dropout and failure rates that began to characterize schools. Paul Goodman, George Dennison, Edgar Z. Friedenberg, A. S. Neill in England, Nat Hentoff, John Holt, Herbert Kohl, and Jonathan Kozol attacked schools for their sterility, bureaucracy, boredom, lack of creativity, rigidity, powerlessness of students and teachers, and inadequacy in educating disadvantaged youth. Holt (1964) stated:

> Most children in school fail. . . . They fail because they are afraid, bored, and confused . . . bored because the things they are given and told to do in school are so trivial, so dull, and make such limited and narrow demands on the wide spectrum of their intelligence, capabilities, and talents. . . . Schools should be a place where children learn what they want to know, instead of what we think they ought to know. (pp. xiii, xiv, 174)

This 1960s liberal reform rebelled against conservative authoritarianism and the dehumanization of schools. Reforms included open education, nongraded schools, more student freedom, more electives, less reliance on standardized tests, abolition of dress codes and rigid rules, and more teacher-student equality. The Vietnam War and demonstrations spurred the politics that stimulated much of the late 1960s educational reform literature.

Multicultural education was not on the educational agenda in early America because mass schooling was supposed to produce a melting pot where various cultural strands were blended into the "new American." The civil rights movement in the 1950s and 1960s showed the melting pot thesis about American society was a myth. This led to other approaches to diversity and unity. One was separatism, where each major subcultural group would go its own way with separate social and school structures. Another was an effort to reconstitute a form of the melting pot by enforcing integration in such institutions as housing, restaurants, and schools. Integration often led to resegregation by white flight and establishment of private all-white academies. Multicultural education, which aimed to recognize positive contributions of a variety of national, racial, ethnic, gender, and other groups to American life, developed as a way to recognize both diversity and unity.

The multicultural effort intended to correct a century of schooling that featured white male American or European heroes from the middle and upper social classes. African American, Latino, and women authors now showed up on lists of standard readings in English classes. The societal contributions of Native Americans, blacks, Chicanos, and females were added to history and civics books. Equal physical education opportunities for boys and girls, compensatory education for the disadvantaged, and programs featuring minority and women role models were developed.

Traditionalism Revisited: The 1980s and Beyond

In the early 1980s, reports of falling SAT and ACT scores, drug abuse, vandalism, and chaos in schools increased public receptivity to traditionalist reform. Nervousness about international competition, resurgence of business and technology as dominant features of society, and questions about shifting morality and values provided a political setting that blamed schools for inadequacies. The presidentially appointed National Commission on Excellence in Education (1983) published a highly political document, *A Nation at Risk*, which claimed there was a "rising tide of mediocrity" in schools. Ensuing public debate produced a flurry of legislation to develop "excellence" by increasing the competitive nature of schooling and testable standards.

Student protests of the 1960s died and a negative reaction set in. "Yuppies" (young upwardly mobile professionals) emerged as role models for student style in the 1980s, embracing careerism and corporate fashion. There was an increasing perception of disarray in the American family, and a return to religion for many. Open confrontation with communism subsided as the Iron Curtain collapsed in the late 1980s. Anticommunism, a major influence on conservative educational reform since the 1920s, was replaced by the War on Drugs and character education. Schools were blamed for social ills and challenges to traditional values, and they were expected to respond to these strains by suddenly becoming academically excellent and moralistic—"Just say NO!"

Foundations and individual critics again undertook the study of schools. These include generally conservative reports from the Twentieth Century Fund (1983), College Entrance Examination Board (1983), and National Science Foundation (1983), as well as Mortimer Adler's *The Paideia Proposal* (1982). The more liberal works included John Goodlad's *A Place Called School* (1983) and Theodore Sizer's *Horace's Compromise* (1984). Ernest Boyer's moderate *High School* (1983) for the Carnegie Foundation also was popular.

States pumped up school financing until the 1990s recession, and state officials, having enacted myriad new regulations governing school matters, began claiming some credit for educational change (*Results in Education 1990; The Education Reform Decade*, 1990; Webster and McMillin, 1991). In the main, jaw-boning by the federal government and increased regulatory activity in the states produced little in the way of dramatic change, but many adjustments were undertaken. Most underlying social problems—for example, poverty, family disruption, discrimination, and economic imbalance—worsened during the 1980s, and schools suffer the continuing effects. In the 1990s, the focus of educational criticism and reform shifted from state regulation and test score worries to more diverse views of the national influence on local schools, school choice, curriculum control, at-risk students, restructuring schools for school-based management, teacher empowerment, parental involvement, and shared decision making. These ideas are potentially conflicting, some leading to increased centralization while others lead to increased decentralization.

Into the twenty-first century, the idea of replacing the traditional canons of literature and social thought with modern multicultural material engendered other battles framed within the "Culture Wars." Finn (1990a) and Ravitch (1990), former high officials of the U.S. Department of Education argue for teaching traditional content emphasizing unified American views rather than diverse views from segments of society. The Organization of American Historians, however, supports the teaching of non-Western culture and diversity in schools (Winkler, 1991). Camille Paglia, arguing against feminist positions, says her work "accepts the canonical Western tradition and rejects the modernist idea that culture has collapsed into meaningless fragments" (1990, p. xii). This battle also emerged when Stanford University's faculty debated whether to substitute modern literature for traditional in its basic course, when New York State social studies curriculum revision for multicultural content aroused a firestorm, and when English-only resolutions were adopted by state legislatures.

Other arguments over multicultural education linked it with politically correct speech in schools (*National Review,* 1990; *The Progressive,* 1991; D'Souza, 1991; Winkler, 1991; Banks, 1995). "Politically correct" (PC) speech, defined as speech that does not denigrate any minority group, gender, or sexual preference, attracts protest because it is equivalent to censorship, stifling free expression. Protecting civil rights to free speech appeared to be at odds with protecting the civility of schools and protecting the "multiculturally diverse" from enduring negative comments. The argument against PC speech is that the free marketplace of ideas requires free speech, not courteous speech, and the best response to epithets and slurs is reasoned argument and public disapproval. Although few are open advocates of politically correct regulations in schools, many would like to find a way to limit racist and sexist comments and graffiti. School is an obvious battleground for this issue.

Another continuing issue is the use and abuse of technology in schools (Oppenheimer, 2003). Through the search for knowledge, we develop faster and more comprehensive systems of communication, travel, and research—which then require faster and more comprehensive systems of education to comprehend and extend that knowledge. Doheny-Farina (1996), discussing the coming of virtual society and virtual schools, cites the argument that "Distance education will become the norm, the least expensive way to deliver the educational product, while face-to-face teaching will be only for the well-to-do"(p. 108). He concludes, however, that "most of those [distance learning] materials will be in the form of prescribed packages, which over time will tend to centralize expertise . . ." and that "the virtualization of school removes it from the fabric of the local community" (pp. 110, 116, 117). Educational theorist Michael Apple (1994; Bromley and Apple, 2002) claims that distance learning de-skills teachers, making them switch-turners and simple conduits for other people's ideas and procedures. That will destroy the central characteristic of democratic education: the freedom to learn and to teach.

In the United States, we are reform-minded about all aspects of society and, as in our views on schools, we hold widely disparate views on what societal changes we need to make. Historian David Tyack (1991), discussing the intertwining of school reform with social reform, says, "For over a century and a half, Americans have translated their cultural anxieties and hopes into demands for educational reform" (p. 1).

Evaluation of Reforms

There is general agreement that results of reform efforts have been mixed. No clear evidence indicates that the reforms have significantly changed education. Analyses of the 1980s school reform show great diversity (Giroux, 1989; Finn, 1990b; Darling-Hammond, 1991; *U.S. News and World Report*, 1990; Fiske, 1991; Safire, 1991; Moynihan, 1991; *New York Times*, 1992). Ideological chasms appear among the analysts as they try to explain why the reforms did not seem to work and what should be done now. Stories about drugs, shootings, and gang violence around schools compete with news articles stating that American students can't read, are ignorant in math and science, and fail tests of common knowledge in history and geography (Holt, 1989; *Newsweek*, 1989; *Business Week*, 1990; Hawley, 1990; Novak, 1990).

Critics (Bastian et al., 1985; Presseisen, 1985; Giroux, 1988b) charge that the 1980s school reform movement was dominated by mainstream conservative thought. This conservative agenda includes standardization, more testing, a return to basics, implanting patriotic values, increased regulation, more homework for students, less student freedom, renewed emphasis on dress codes and socially acceptable behavior for students and teachers, stricter discipline, and teacher accountability.

From a liberal/progressive view, schools are defective because they are too standardized, excessively competitive, and too factory-like. Students are measured and sorted in an assembly-line atmosphere where social class, gender, and race determine which students get which treatments. Teachers are deprofessionalized and treated as servile workers. Critical thinking is punished; one kind of curriculum or classroom instruction fits all. Creativity and joy are excluded from the school lexicon because education is supposed to be hard, dreary, boring work (McLaren, 1989; Purpel, 1989; Fisher, 1991; Nathan, 1991; Sacks, 1999; Wraga, 2001; Schoenfeld, 2002). Making schools active, pleasant, student-oriented, critical, and sensitive to social problems is the reform they advocate.

Educational researchers David Berliner and Bruce Biddle (1995) present test scores, international school finance data, and various other indicators of achievement and support, and they conclude school critics are mistaken or uninformed. They discount critics' assertions that student achievement and teacher quality have declined and schools are failing society. Berliner and Biddle summarize their analysis with the response that "these assertions are errant nonsense" (p. 13), and they conclude that "American education has recently been subjected to an unwarranted, vigorous, and damaging attack—a Manufactured

Crisis . . . the major claims of the attack turn out to have been myths; the Manufactured Crisis was revealed as a Big Lie" (p. 343).

Conservative school reform was, however, the main influence on schooling in the United States at the end of the twentieth century. Proposals and action for school change include academically tougher schools, vouchers, charter schools, rigorous standards and more testing, more discipline, privatized management, and training in moral behavior.

Liberal and radical ideas for schools did not disappear (Fullen, 2000; Bracey, 2002b; Giroux, 2004). Teacher empowerment, academic freedom, student rights, limiting testing, providing student choice, and active social criticism and participation are ideas percolating in school reform to come. Reconstructionist ideas placing schools at the center of social change have not been entirely forgotten in the current surge of literature on schools and reform. William Stanley (1992, 2001) rethinks social reconstructionism and examines key ideas from the critical pedagogy movement to offer educational possibilities for the twenty-first century. His focus on practical reasoning provides critical examination of social issues and stimulates positive social action.

Continuing Debates over Schooling

Humans have long argued about what knowledge children should learn, how they should behave, and who should teach them. Basic subjects like reading and mathematics instruction are often at the eye of the hurricane because of their importance in the ongoing lives of students and their future prospects. Reading has long been the focus of debates over phonics and whole-language instruction, though often it is a more ideological and political issue than merely finding the best way to teach (Coles, 2001; *Kappan,* 2001). Arguments over the best approaches to mathematical literacy have included "civil rights" questions (Moses and Cobb, 2001), as well as competing ideologies in curricular reform, which Schoenfeld (2002) claims "gave rise to the math wars and catalyzed the existence of what is in essence a neo-conservative back-to-basics movement. This way lies madness" (p. 22). Nearly all subject fields have experienced the same problems in finding stability in seas of change dependent on ideological and political contexts. They present a bewildering array of educational ideas, from left-wing, right-wing, moderate, and radical positions.

The Changing Focus of Debates

In this early twenty-first century, public debate over education changed from a primary focus on crisis, hand-wringing, and derisive blame to arguments over which political candidate offers more financial support, smaller classes, and better facilities and teachers to schools. The 1980s competition to bash schools and teachers has been partially replaced by a public affirmation that the future of schools and of society are intertwined. Serious disagreements, of course, continue on most school topics and we still get teacher-bashing on occasion. The general tenor of the debates, however, has shifted from castigation and condemnation to diverse proposals for funding, accountability, standards, and specific corrective action. Finance problems may derail most reforms. There are still sharply negative criticisms of the current state of schooling, but more moderate voices are more common in the schooling debates of 2010–2020.

The 1983 claim that schools were floating on a "rising tide of mediocrity," had put the nation at risk, and were responsible for declining American values and economic competitiveness was followed by different analyses of the same kinds of data indicating schools were not as bad as this and subsequent 1980s and 1990s documents and media portrayed to the public (Bracey, 1992, 1994, 1995, 1997, 1998, 2002a; Berliner, 1993; Berliner and Biddle, 1995). The politics of bashing schools and teachers, however, benefits politicians seeking an issue. The politics of school critique and governmental or privatization intervention for reform are attention-getting, and politicians find schools an excellent target. This means more attention paid to school failures than to school successes.

Public Ratings of Schools

One of the most surprising things about the extremely negative school criticism between 1980 and now is that public rating of public schools has remained consistently high. Even with negative publicity about schools, survey evidence shows that public rating of *local* public schools actually has been positive, and often increasingly so, for over a quarter-century. The annual Phi Delta Kappa/ Gallup Poll has surveyed the public since 1974. In 1992, the poll showed the largest one-year increase in the grades people give their local public schools in almost two decades, from 40 percent grading their schools A or B in 1992 to 47 percent rating them that high in 1993 (Elam et al., 1993). In 1998, the annual poll showed 46 percent of all respondents gave their local schools an A or B, and 52 percent of public school parents gave their children's schools an A or B grade (Rose and Gallup, 1998). For the first time in the 33 years the Gallup Poll has sampled the American public on schools, the Gallup Poll of 2001 found that a majority (51 percent) of the public gives public schools an A or B rating, and 62 percent of parents with children in public schools rate them A or B (Rose and Gallup, 2001, 2007). Those closest to the schools seem to rate them much better than media reports would suggest. The public has mixed opinions on the federal NCLB Act, but most were negative (Rose and Gallup, 2005, 2007).

Ironically, people rate their own local schools significantly higher than they rate schools across the nation (only 20 percent in 1998 and 23 percent in 2001 give the nation's schools an A or B). For the school their oldest children attended, the rating is very high (about 65 percent rating them A or B). Gallup interpreted these data to suggest that the more the public knows about actual practices in schools, the better they rate them. The data also indicate that negative publicity from political and media treatment of schooling influences the way people grade schools they know the least.

Decreasing negative criticism of schools might suggest school reforms in the past fifteen years have been successful, but that would be a misreading. No clear evidence exists about the reforms and their consequences; outcomes are still in dispute. Although many claims surround specific reforms, few comprehensive studies show that any school is significantly better or worse now as a result of reforms. Since recent evidence shows schools were never as bad as government and media reported, one could make the case that some reforms actually hindered school progress by improperly blaming and alienating teachers and by forcing more testing and governmental intervention in school requirements and operations. The current concept of school accountability leads to more testing and probably more hand-wringing as test scores do not satisfy the critics. The No Child Left Behind legislation of 2001 exacerbates this.

The political setting of the standards movement, and ideological underpinnings of the schooling culture wars, is illustrated by the furor raised over proposed standards in American history. The federal government provided substantial funds to a center at UCLA, where historians were to establish standards that identified what students in each grade should know about American history. The initial product offered much more contemporary and multicultural information, highlighting contributions of many people from minority groups. Critics attacked the standards as insufficiently patriotic and the Senate voted against them; historians capitulated and changed the standards to reflect the conservative view. Ideology and politics are firmly entrenched in the battles over schooling. It is easy to inflame emotions in this setting. Still, public schools get good ratings from their closest observers, and schools in the United States are rated by the public higher than many other institutions of American society.

Even though local schools are well received, schooling remains one of the most controversial topics in society. Schools benefit from good criticism, but the suppressed evidence should suggest we maintain a level of skepticism about some negative media reports and political statements about schools.

Although polls continue to show general public support of local schools, most of us can identify one or more areas needing correction. Impatient or burned-out teachers, cloddish administrators, frazzled counselors, and outdated textbooks and curricula are examples. Most of us know the virtues as well as warts and blemishes of schools from our direct personal experience. Some critics propose quick and simplistic reforms to improve schools. Fortunately, most people understand that change in schooling is more complex, and that potential consequences of change need more thought.

Reformers see schools as either the cause of some problem or part of the cure. We are led to believe that schools can solve major social problems such as racism, sexism, automobile accidents, AIDS, teenage pregnancy, and drugs. Reform has not been especially productive in student achievement, curing social ills, intellectual development, or student and public happiness about schools. Yet the arguments over reform have helped air ideological and political baggage that weighs on the reforms. Perhaps there is a better word than *reform* to use in discussing school improvement. Reform school was the institution where young social deviants and juvenile criminals were sent; "reform schools" seems a strange phrasing in that context.

Unity and Diversity: A Dialectic

Among the conditions of human civilization is the tension between unifying and diverse ideas. We share a vision of the good life with others, yet recognize human improvement depends on new ideas that may conflict with that vision. Unity provides a focus, but also complacency; diversity provides stimulation, but also dissension. Both comfort and discontent thus reside in unity and diversity. This tension occurs in life, and is most evident in important matters such as schooling. It is also at the center of the culture wars; do we advocate unity or diversity? One is a thesis, the other antithesis.

Diversity and unity commonly are seen as contradictory. Some diverse ideas are too radical, too preposterous, or too challenging to deeply held beliefs for some people. Fundamental religions expect unity and do not accept diversity; criticism of religious dogma is considered heretical and sacrilegious. For those religions, just as for some people who believe they have the only truth, unity of belief is sacrosanct.

On the other hand, some question unity. One argument is that unity of purpose or values is a myth perpetuated by those in power to stay in power. Hard work, frugality, and acceptance of authority are seen as fictional values that are part of an effort by the powerful class to hide their oppressive actions, maintain the social order, and enslave docile workers.

Thus, diversity and unity can be seen as adversarial positions, bound in opposition. Those on the side of unity believe diverse ideas can be censored, ignored, or disdained; those arguing for diversity consider unity to be a facade hiding the basic conflicts in society.

It also is possible to understand diversity and unity as collateral positions, supporting and energizing. This tension between diversity and unity, multiple views and common principles, informs this book about schools. Among current critical issues in education, debates about purposes and practices of schooling, are such matters as school choice, finance, racism, sexism, child welfare, privatization, curriculum, business orientations, academic freedom, unionism, and testing. These issues reflect deeper social and political tensions between unity and diversity, including tensions between liberty and equality, rights and responsibilities, consensus and conflict, and individual and social development. Diverse ideas combined in a unified purpose is an ideal, not easily and perhaps not ever attained. It is a possible synthesis, drawing on two opposing strands as in dialectic reasoning. But what would it look like in practice? How would we define the kind of diversity and unity expressed?

This book presents two differing views on each topic in each chapter. The views expressed aren't always exactly opposing, but they represent publicly expressed ideas about how schooling could be improved. Contrasting these views in terms of evidence presented and logic of each argument can stimulate a realistic dialogue, offering an opportunity to examine issues as they occur in human discourse. Divergent essays sometimes will use the same data or same published works to make opposite cases, but they usually will offer evidence from widely separate literatures. The search for improvement in society and in schooling is a unifying purpose; dialogues require diversity.

School is not only the subject of disputes, it is also the logical place for the thoughtful study of disputes. Schools should be settings where reasoned thought and open inquiry are practiced. They are a suitable location for examining disputes about important issues—those characterized by diverse opinions. Critical issues, those of the greatest significance, often stimulate the most intense disputes.

The next decades of the twenty-first century may be placid or turbulent for schools, a period of recuperation from the latest round of reforms or a new set of attacks. Even in placidity, however, educational issues are sure to arise, cause alarm, and inflame passions. Some of the issues raised will spawn elements of new school reforms and some will lead to school improvement; nearly all will be disputed.

Welcome to this exchange of ideas.

References

ADLER, M. (1927). *Dialectic.* New York: Harcourt Brace.

———. (1982). *The Paideia Proposal.* New York: Macmillan.

AFT. (2005). "NCLB—Let's Get it Right." May 19. American Federation of Teachers. www.AFT.com.

APPLE, M. (1990). *Ideology and Curriculum.* 2nd Ed. London: Routledge.

———. (1994). "Computers and the Deskilling of Teachers." *CPSR Newsletter* 12(2):3.

APPLE, M., and Weis, L., eds. (1983). *Ideology and Practice in Schooling.* Philadelphia: Temple University Press.

AUDI, R. (2001). *The Architecture of Reason.* Oxford: Oxford University Press.

BAILYN, B. (1960). *Education in the Forming of American Society.* Chapel Hill: University of North Carolina Press.

BANKS, J. A. (1995). "The Historical Reconstruction of Knowledge About Race: Implications for Transformative Teaching." *Educational Researcher* 24:15–25.

BARBER, B. (1998). *Intellectual Pursuits.* Lanham, MD: Rowman and Littlefield.

BASTIAN, A., et al. (1985). *Choosing Equality: The Case for Democratic Schooling.* San Francisco: New World Foundation.

BEHE, M., DEMBSKI, W., AND MEYER, S. (2000). *Science and Evidence for Design in the Universe.* San Francisco: Ignatius Press.

BERLINER, D. (1993). "Mythology and the American System of Education." *Kappan* 74:632–640.

BERLINER, D., AND BIDDLE, B. J. (1995). *The Manufactured Crisis: Myths, Fraud, and the Attack on America's Public Schools.* Reading, MA: Addison-Wesley.

BESAG, F., AND NELSON, J. (1984). *The Foundations of Education: Stasis and Change.* New York: Random House.

BESTOR, A. (1953). *Educational Wastelands.* Urbana, IL: University of Illinois Press. (2nd Ed., 1985).

BLUMENFELD-JONES, D. (2004). "The Hope of a Critical Ethics." *Educational Theory* 54(3): 263–279.

BOGGS, C. (1993). *Intellectuals and the Crisis of Modernity.* Albany, NY: SUNY Press.

BOYER, E. (1983). *High School.* New York: Harper and Row.

BRACEY, G. (1992). "The Second Bracey Report on the Condition of Public Education." *Kappan* 74:104–108.

———. (1994). "The Fourth Bracey Report on the Condition of Public Education." *Kappan* 76:115–127.

———. (1995). "Stedman's Myths Miss the Mark." *Educational Leadership* 52:75–78.

———. (1997). *The Truth About America's Schools: The Bracey Reports, 1991–1997.* Bloomington, IN: Phi Delta Kappa.

———. (1998). "The Eighth Bracey Report on the Condition of Public Education." *Kappan* 80(2):112–131.

———. (2002a) "The Twelfth Bracey Report on the Condition of Public Education." *Kappan* 84(2):135–150.

———. (2002b). *The War Against America's Public Schools.* Boston: Allyn and Bacon/Longmans.

BRAMELD, T. (1956). *Toward a Reconstructed Philosophy of Education.* New York: Holt, Rinehart and Winston.

BROMLEY, H., AND APPLE, M., eds. (2002). *Education/Technology/Power.* Albany, NY: SUNY Press.

BRONNER, E., "Candidates Latch onto Education Issue," *San Diego Union-Tribune,* Sept. 20, 1998.

Brown v. Board of Education of Topeka, Shawnee County, Kansas, et al. (1954). 74 Sup. Ct. 686.

BURNS, B., ET AL. (2003). *Achieving Universal Primary Education by 2015.* Washington, DC: The World Bank.

Business Week. (1990). "Using Flash Cards and Grit to Defeat a Secret Shame." July 16, pp. 22, 23.

CARANFA, A. (2004). "Silence as the Foundation of Learning." *Educational Theory* 54(2):211–230.

CARSON, C. C., HUELSKAMP, R. M., AND WOODALL, T. D. (1992). "Perspectives on Education in America." Final Draft, April. Albuquerque, NM: Sandia National Laboratories.

CHAMBERS, G. (1948). "Educational Essentialism Thirty Years After," in *Secondary Education: Origins and Directions,* ed. R. Hahn and D. Bidna. New York: Macmillan, 1970.

CLABAUGH, G. K. (2008). "Thinking Critically About Critical Thinking." *Educational Horizons.* 86 (3), 129–133. Spring.

COLES, G. (2003). *Reading the Naked Truth.* Portsmouth, NH: Heinemann.

COLLEGE ENTRANCE EXAMINATION Board. (1983). *Academic Preparation for College.* New York: College Board.

CONANT, J. B. (1958). *The American High School Today.* New York: McGraw-Hill.

COOPER, D., ed. (1967). *To Free a Generation: The Dialectics of Liberalism.* New York: Collier.

COUNTS, G. S. (1932). *Dare the Schools Build a New Social Order?* New York: John Day.

CREMIN, L. (1961). *The Transformation of the School.* New York: Random House.

———. (1965). *The Genius of American Education.* New York: Random House.

CUBAN. L. (2003). "The Great Reappraisal of Public Education." *American Journal of Education* 110 (November):3–31.

DAHL, G. (1999). *Radical Conservatism and the Future of Politics.* London: Sage.

DARLING-HAMMOND, L. (1991). "Achieving Our Goals: Superficial or Structural Reforms?" *Kappan* 72:286–295.

DE RUGIERRO, G. (1959). *The History of European Liberalism.* R. G. Collingwood, translator. Boston: Beacon Press.

DE TOCQUEVILLE, A. (1848/1969). *Democracy In America.* J. P. Mayer, ed. Garden City, NY: Doubleday.

DEMBSKI, W. (2004). *The Design Revolution.* Downer's Grove, IL: InterVarsity Press.

DENNISON, G. (1969). *The Lives of Children.* New York: Random House.

DEWEIL, B. (2000). *Democracy: A History of Ideas.* Vancouver: UBC Press.

DEWEY, J. (1916). *Democracy and Education.* New York: Macmillan.

DIGEST OF EDUCATIONAL STATISTICS. (2008). www.nces.edu.gov

DILLON, S., "Connecticut to Sue U.S. Over Cost of Testing Law," *New York Times,* April 16, 2005. www.nytimes.com.

———. (2008). "An Initiative on Reading is Rated Ineffective." *New York Times.* www .nytimes.com, May 2.

DOHENY-FARINA, S. (1996). *The Wired Neighborhood.* New Haven, CT: Yale University Press.

DRYFOOS, J. (2002). "Full-Service Community Schools." *Kappan* 83:393–399.

D'SOUZA, D. (1991). *Illiberal Education: The Politics of Race and Sex on Campus.* New York: Free Press.

The Education Reform Decade. (1990). Policy Information Report. Princeton: Educational Testing Service.

ELAM, S., ET AL. (1993). "25th Annual PDK/Gallup Poll." *Kappan* 75 (September).

EMERSON, J. D., BOES, L., AND MOSTELLER, F. (2002). "Critical Thinking in College Students," in *Educational Media and Technology Yearbook,* ed. M. A. Fitzgerald et al. Englewood, CO: Libraries Unlimited.

FARRAR, R. C. (2000). *Sartrean Dialectics.* Lanham, MD: Lexington Books.

FINN, C. (1990a). "Why Can't Our Colleges Convey Our Diverse Culture's Unifying Themes?" *The Chronicle of Higher Education* 36, 40, 41.

———. (1990b). "The Biggest Reform of All." *Kappan* 71:584–593.

FISHER, E. (1991). "What Really Counts in Schools?" *Educational Leadership* 48:10–15.

FISKE, E. B. (1991). *Smart Schools, Smart Kids.* New York: Simon and Schuster.

FORREST, B. C., and Gross, P. R. (2004). *Creationism's Trojan Horse: The Wedge of Intelligent Design.* New York: Oxford University Press.

FRIEDENBERG, E. Z. (1965). *Coming of Age in America.* New York: Random House.

FREIRE, P. (1973). *Education for Critical Consciousness.* New York: Continuum.

FUENTES, C. (2005). *This I Believe.* New York: Random House.

FULLEN, M. (2000). "Three Stories of Education Reform." *Kappan* 83:581–584.

GARDNER, J. (1958). *The Pursuit of Excellence: Education and the Future of America.* New York: Rockefeller Brothers Fund.

GARFORTH, F. W. (1980). *Educative Democracy: John Stuart Mill on Education in Society.* Oxford: Oxford University Press.

GELLA, A. (1976). *The Intelligentsia and the Intellectuals.* London: Sage.

GIROUX, H. (1988a). *Teachers as Intellectuals: Toward a Critical Pedagogy of Learning.* Granby, MA: Bergin and Garvey.

———. (1988b). *Schooling and the Struggle for Public Life.* Granby, MA: Bergin and Garvey.

———. (1989). "Rethinking Educational Reform in the Age of George Bush." *Kappan* 70: 728–730.

———. (2004). "Critical Pedagogy and the Postmodern/Modern Divide." *Teacher Education Quarterly* 37(1):31–47.

GOLDFARB, J.C. (1998). *Civility and Subversion: The Intellectual in Democratic Society.* Cambridge: Cambridge University Press.

GOODLAD, J. I. (1983). *A Place Called School: Prospects for the Future.* New York: McGraw-Hill.

GOODMAN, P. (1964). *Compulsory Miseducation.* New York: Horizon Press.

GOULDNER, A. (1979). *The Future of Intellectuals and the Rise of the New Class.* New York: Seabury Press.

GRAHAM, P. A. (1967). *Progressive Education: From Arcady to Academe.* New York: Teachers College Press.

GREENE, M. (1995). "Art and Imagination: Reclaiming the Sense of Possibility." *Kappan* 76:378–382.

GUTMAN, A., AND THOMPSON, D. (1996). *Democracy and Disagreement.* Cambridge, MA: Harvard University Press.

———. (2004) *Why Deliberative Democracy?* Princeton NJ: Princeton University Press.

HAHN, R., AND BIDNA, D., eds. (1970). *Secondary Education: Origins and Directions.* New York: Macmillan.

HAWLEY, R. A. (1990). "The Bumpy Road to Drug-Free Schools." *Kappan* 72:310–314.

HENTOFF, N. (1977). *Does Anybody Give a Damn?* New York: Alfred Knopf.

———, "God's Place in the Public Schools," *San Diego Union-Tribune,* Aug. 18, 1998.

HESS, D. G. (2002). "Discussing Controversial Public Issues in Secondary Social Studies Classrooms." *Theory and Research in Social Education* 30(1):10–41.

HOLT, J. (1964). *How Children Fail.* New York: Pitman.

HOLT, R. (1989). "Can We Make Our Schools Safe?" *NEA Today* 8:4–6.

HOUSE, H. W. (2008). *Intelligent Design 101.* Grand Rapids, MI: Kregel Publications.

HUELSKAMP, R. (1993). "Perspectives on Education in America." *Kappan* 74:717–720.

ILLICH, I. (1971). *Deschooling Society.* New York: Harper and Row.

International Education Indicators. (1997). National Center for Educational Statistics. Washington, DC: U.S. Department of Education.

JACOBY, R. (1987). *The Lost Intellectuals.* New York: Basic Books.

JACOBY, S. (2008). *The Age of American Unreason.* New York: Pantheon

JENSEN, C. (1994). *Censored: The News That Didn't Make the News—And Why.* New York: Four Walls Eight Windows Press.

JOHNSON, H. L. AND SALZ, A., eds., (2008). *What is Authentic Educational Reform?* New York: Lawrence Erlbaum Associates.

JOHNSON, K., "Anti-Darwinism Bill Fails in Utah," *New York Times,* Feb. 28, 2006. www.nytimes.com.

KAESTLE, C. F. (1985). "Education Reform and the Swinging Pendulum." *Kappan* 66: 410–415.

Kappan. "No Quick and Dirty." (2001). Editor's Page. 83:278.

KARIER, C. (1967). *Man, Society, and Education.* Chicago: Scott, Foresman.

———. (1985). "Retrospective One," in A. Bestor, *Educational Wastelands.* 2nd Ed. Urbana, IL: University of Illinois Press.

KATZ, M. (1968). *The Irony of Early School Reform.* Cambridge, MA: Harvard University Press.

———. (1971). *Class, Bureaucracy, and Schools: The Illusion of Educational Change in America.* New York: Praeger.

KERLINGER, F. (1984). *Liberalism and Conservatism.* Hillsdale, NJ: Erlbaum.

KINCHELOE, J. L. AND WEIL, D. eds., (2004) *Critical Thinking and Learning.* Westport, CT: Greenwood Press.

KOHL, H. (1967). *36 Children.* New York: New American Library.

KOHLBERG, L. (1981). *The Meaning and Measurement of Moral Development.* Worcester, MA: Clark University Press.

KOZOL, J. (1967). *Death at an Early Age.* Boston: Houghton Mifflin.

———. (2005). *The Shame of the Nation: The Restoration of Apartheid Schooling in America.* New York: Crown Publishers.

KURTZ, P. (1992). *The New Skepticism.* Buffalo, NY: Prometheus Books.

LLOYD, T. (1988). *In Defense of Liberalism.* Oxford: Basil Blackwell.

LYND, A. (1950). *Quackery in the Public Schools.* Boston: Little, Brown.

MAKAU, J. M., AND MARTY, D. L. (2001). *Cooperative Argumentation: A Model for a Deliberative Community.* Prospect Heights, IL: Waveland Press.

MARCUSE, H. (1960). *Reason and Revolution.* Boston: Beacon Press.

MARSHALL, C. (1997). *Feminist Critical Policy Analysis I: A Perspective from Primary and Secondary Schooling.* London: Falmer Press.

MARTIN, J. R. (1994). *Changing the Educational Landscape: Philosophy, Women, and Curriculum.* New York: Routledge.

McCABE, M. M. (2000). *Plato and His Predecessors.* Cambridge: Cambridge University Press.

McCOLL, A. (2005). "Tough Call: Is No Child Left Behind Constitutional?" *Kappan* 86(8): 604–610.

McKENZIE, J. (2006). "The Harsh Bigotry of Bad Policy." *No Child Left* 4(3): www.nochildleft.com.

———. (2007). "The Last Word." *No Child Left 5* (5). May.

———. (2008). "After NCLB: Back to the Basics of Inquiry and Comprehension." *From Now On.* 17 (5) 1. May.

McLAREN, P. (1989). *Life in Schools.* New York: Longman.

McLAREN, P., AND HOUSTON, D. (2004). "Revolutionary Ecologies." *Educational Studies* 36(1):27–45.

MEIER, D., AND WOOD, G., eds. (2004). *Many Children Left Behind.* Bellingham, WA: FNO Press.

MERCER, N. (2008). "The Seeds of Time: Why Classroom Dialogue Needs a Temporal Analysis." *Journal of the Learning Sciences* 17(1). 33–59.

MOSES, R., AND COBB. C. E. (2001). *Radical Equations: Math Literacy and Civil Rights.* Boston: Beacon Press.

MOYNIHAN, D. P. (1991). "Educational Goals and Political Plans." *The Public Interest* Winter: 32–49.

NATHAN, J. (1991). "Toward Educational Change and Economic Justice: An Interview with Herbert Kohl." *Kappan* 72:678–681.

NATIONAL COMMISSION ON EXCELLENCE IN EDUCATION. (1983). *A Nation at Risk.* Washington, DC: U.S. Government Printing Office.

National Review. (1990). "Academic Watch." 42, 18.

NATIONAL SCIENCE FOUNDATION. (1983). *Educating Americans for the 21st Century.* Washington, DC: Author.

NCDD (2008). National Coalition for Dialogue and Deliberation Online Newsletter. www.thataway.org

NEA. (2006). "Independent Commission on NCLB." News Release. Feb. www.NEA.org.

NEILL, A. S. (1966). *Summerhill: A Radical Approach to Child Rearing.* New York: Hart.

NEILL, M. (2008). "Beyond NCLB." *Rethinking Schools.* 22(3), 14–17 Spring.

NICHOLS, S. L. AND BERLINER, D. C. (2008). "Testing the Joy Out of Learning," *Educational Leadership.* 65(6). 14–18.

NELSON, J. L., CARLSON, K., AND LINTON, T. L. (1972). *Radical Ideas and the Schools.* New York: Holt, Rinehart and Winston.

Newsweek. (1989). "Kids: Deadly Force." 111:18–20.

New York Times, "Education Life." Special supplement. Jan. 5, 1992.

New York Times, "Stand Firm for Educational Fairness," April 22, 2005.

NODDINGS, N. (1984a). *Awakening the Inner Eye: Intuition and Education.* New York: Teachers College Press.

———. (1984b). *Caring: A Feminine Approach to Ethics and Moral Education.* Berkeley: University of California Press.

———. (1995a). "A Morally Defensible Mission for Schools in the 21st Century." *Kappan* 76:365–368.

————. (1995b). *Philosophy of Education*. Boulder, CO: Westview Press.

NOLAN, J. L. (1996). *The American Culture Wars*. Charlottesville: University of Virginia Press.

NORRIS, P., ed. (1999). *Critical Citizens*. New York: Oxford University Press.

NOVAK, M. (1990). "Scaring Our Children." *Forbes* 144:167.

OPPENHEIMER, T. (2003). *The Flickering Mind*. New York: Random House.

PAGLIA, C. (1990). *Sexual Personae*. New Haven, CT: Yale Press.

PERAKH. M. (2003). *Unintelligent Design*. Buffalo, NY: Prometheus Books.

PIAGET, J. (1950). *The Psychology of Intelligence*. London: Routledge and Kegan Paul.

PIERCE, R. K. (1993). *What Are We Trying to Teach Them, Anyway?* San Francisco: Center for Self-Governance.

PRESSEISEN, B. (1985). *Unlearned Lessons*. Philadelphia: Falmer Press.

The Progressive. (1991). "The PC Monster." 55, 9.

Projections of Education Statistics to 2008. (1996). National Center for Educational Statistics. Washington, DC: U.S. Department of Education.

PUBLIC AGENDA. (2008). Education Overview. www.publicagenda.org

PURPEL, D. (1989). *The Moral and Spiritual Crisis in Education: A Curriculum for Justice and Compassion in Education*. Granby, MA: Bergin and Garvey.

RAFFERTY, M. (1968). *Max Rafferty on Education*. New York: Devon Adair.

RASPBERRY, W, "Public Schools Bad for Education," *San Diego News-Tribune*, Aug. 18, 1998.

RAVITCH, D. (1990). "Multiculturalism: E Pluribus Plures." *American Scholar* 59:337–354.

————. (2007), *New York Times*, Get Congress Out of the Classroom October 3. www .nytimes.com.

RAVITCH, D., AND VITERITTI, J. (1997). *New Schools for a New Century*. New Haven, CT: Yale University Press.

Results in Education: 1990. (1990). The Governors' 1991 Report on Education. Washington, DC: National Governors' Association.

ROSE, L. C., AND GALLUP, A. M. (1998). "The 30th Phi Delta Kappa/Gallup Poll of the Public's Attitudes Toward the Public Schools." *Kappan* 80(1):41–56.

————. (2001). "The 33rd Annual Phi Delta Kappa/Gallup Poll." *Kappan* 83:41–47.

————. (2005). "The 37th Annual Phi Delta Kappa/Gallup Poll." *Kappan* 87(1):41–57.

————. (2007). "The 39th Annual Phi Delta Kappa/Gallup Poll." *Kappan*. 89(1). 41–47. September.

ROSS, E. W. AND GIBSON, R. eds., (2006) *Neoliberalism and Educational Reform*. Cresskill, NJ: Hampton Press.

RUDROREN, J., "Ohio Board Undoes Stand on Evolution," *New York Times*, Feb. 15, 2006. www.nytimes.com.

RUSSELL, B. (1928). *Sceptical Essays*. London: George Allen and Unwin.

RYCHLAK, J. F., ed. (1976). *Dialectic*. Basil, Switzerland: Karger.

SACKS, P. (1999). *Standardized Minds*. Cambridge, MA: Perseus Books.

SAFIRE, W, "Abandon the Pony Express," *New York Times*, April 25, 1991.

SCHNEIDER, C. G. (2004). "Practicing Liberal Education." *Liberal Education* 9(2):8–10.

SCHOENFELD, A. H. (2002). "Making Mathematics Work for All Children." *Educational Researcher* 31:13–25.

SCIABARRA, C. M. (1999). *Ayn Rand: The Russian Radical*. University Park: Pennsylvania State University Press.

————. (2000). *Total Freedom: Toward Dialectical Libertarianism*. University Park: Pennsylvania State University Press.

SCIENCE NEWS (2008). "Negative Implications of No Child Left Behind." www .sciencedaily.com Feb. 16.

SCOTT, E. (2004). *Evolution Versus Creationism*. Westport, CT: Greenwood Press.

SHAPIRO, I., AND MACEDO, S. (2000). *Designing Democratic Institutions, Nomos 42*. New York: New York University Press.

SIM, M. (1999). *From Puzzles to Principles*. Lanham, MD: Lexington Books.

SINCLAIR, U. (1924). *The Goslings*. Pasadena, CA: Sinclair.

SIZER, T. (1984). *Horace's Compromise: The Dilemma of the American High School*. Boston: Houghton Mifflin.

SMITH, M. (1954). *The Diminished Mind: A Study of Planned Mediocrity in Our Public Schools*. New York: Regnery.

SOWELL, T. (1993). *Inside American Education: The Decline, the Deception, the Dogmas*. New York: Free Press.

SPELLINGS, M. (2006). News Release. U.S. Department of Education. March 20. www .ed.gov.

———. (2008) News Release, US Department of Education. www.ed.gov. April 22.

SPRING, JOEL. (2008). "No Child Left Behind as Political Fraud." *In Johnson and Salz, What is Authentic Educational Reform?* New York: Lawrence Erlbaum Associates.

STANLEY, W. B. (1981). "Toward a Reconstruction of Social Education." *Theory and Research in Social Education* 9:67–89.

———. (1992). *Education for Utopia: Social Reconstructionism and Critical Pedagogy in the Postmodern Era*. Albany, NY: SUNY Press.

———, ed. (2001). *Social Studies Research for the 21st Century*. Greenwich, CT: Information Age Publishers.

STRIKE, K. A. (2004). "Community, the Missing Element of School Reform." *American Journal of Education* 110 (May):215–232.

STROBEL, L. (2004). *The Case for a Creator*. Grand Rapids, MI: ZonderVan.

SUNDERMAN, G. L. (2006). "The Unraveling of No Child Left Behind." Report. Civil Rights Project of Harvard University. Feb. www.civilrightsproject.harvard.edu.

TORRES, C. A. (2002). "Globalization, Education, and Citizenship." *American Educational Research Journal* 39(2):363–378.

Twentieth-Century Fund. (1983). *Making the Grade*. New York: Author.

TYACK, D. (1967). *Turning Points in American Educational History*. Waltham, MA: Blaisdell.

———. (1991). "Public School Reform: Policy Talk and Institutional Practice." *American Journal of Education* 100:1–19.

U. S. CENSUS BUREAU. (2008). International Data Base. www.census.gov March 27.

U.S. News and World Report. (1990). "The Keys to School Reform." Feb. 26, 108, 50–53.

ULICH, R. (1954). *Three Thousand Years of Educational Wisdom*. 2nd Ed. Cambridge, MA: Harvard University Press.

UNESCO COUNCIL. (2000). *Report on the World Social Condition, 2000*. New York: United Nations.

UNESCO EFA GLOBAL MONITORING REPORT. (2005). *Education for All*. Paris: UNESCO Publishing.

UNESCO. (2003). *Financing Education*. Paris: UNESCO.

UNESCO World Education Report, 2000. (2000). "The Right to Education: Towards Education for All Throughout Life." Paris: UNESCO Publishing.

VAN EMEREN, F. H., AND GOOTENHORST, R. (2003). "A Pragma-Dialectic Procedure for a Critical Discussion." *Argumentation* 17(4):365–386.

VAN LUCHENE, S. R. (2004). "Rekindling the Dialogue: Education According to Plato and Dewey." *Academe* 90(3):54–7.

WEBSTER, W. E., AND MCMILLIN, J. D. (1991). "A Report on Calls for Secondary School Reform in the United States." NASSP Bulletin 75:77–83.

WEIS, L., AND FINE. M., eds. (2000). *Construction Sites: Excavating Race, Class, and Gender Among Urban Youth.* New York: Teachers College Press.

WELTER, R. (1962). *Popular Education and Democratic Thought in America.* New York: Columbia University Press.

WILLIAMS, R. H. (1997). *Cultural Wars in American Politics.* New York: Aldine de Gruyter.

WINKLER, K. (1991). "Organization of American Historians Backs Teaching of Non-Western Culture and Diversity in Schools." *The Chronicle of Higher Education* 37:5–8.

WINTHROP, N. (2000). *Democratic Theory as Public Philosophy.* Sydney, Australia: Ashgate.

WRAGA, W. (2001). "Left Out: The Villainization of Progressive Education in the United States." Review of Left Back. *Educational Researcher* 30:7.

WRIGHT, L. (2001). *Critical Thinking.* New York: Oxford University Press.

YOUNG, M., AND EDIS, T. (2004). *Why Intelligent Design Fails.* New Brunswick, NJ: Rutgers University Press.

ZURN, C.F. (2007) *Deliberative Democracy and the Institutions of Judicial Review.* Cambridge, UK: Cambridge University Press.

Whose Interests Should Schools Serve?

Justice and Equity

About Part One: The chapters of Part One cover competing ideological interests in regard to schools. Chapters 2 through 9 include divergent views on family choice and school vouchers, equity in school financing, gender equity, standards and school accountability, church/state interests in schooling, privatization of public schools, consumer and corporate interests, and immigration.

Each topic involves basic questions about justice and equity in American society. Definitions and evaluations of justice and equity are commonly filtered through political terms like liberalism and conservatism as well as through personal and ethical principles. We label some practices and policies as "conservative" and others as "liberal," with a few as "radical." And we want to justify our views by using personal or ethical connotations of "good," "right," "proper," "just," and "equitable" to support them. These political and personal filters may not be accurate labels or precise indicators of ideologies or personal positions,

but they are widely used. Schooling battles often fall within the themes of justice and equity.

PART ONE: COMPETING INTERESTS

Schools serve many masters: students, parents, teachers, administrators, government, commerce, media, special interest groups, and varying educational philosophies and laws. These are usually competitive interests with divergent agendas, the realm of politics, economics, social conscience, and ideology (Mauro, 2008). Politics is concerned with the distribution of power among interests, economics with the distribution of wealth, social conscience and ideology with rationales that people use to justify practices and policies.

Justice and equity are basic to a consideration of which interests should be emphasized in schooling. But we have differing views of what

35

constitutes a just or equitable system (Kitching, 2001; Little, 2002; Mitzman, 2003; Kolm, 2005; Barry, 2005; Fuentes, 2005). Evaluating the quality of equity and justice in society and schools involves interests as a major concern (Rawls, 1971, 1999, 2001, 2005; Bowles, Gintis, and Gross, 2005).

We all have interests, and we are members of groups that have interests. We want good things for ourselves, our families, our friends, our associations, and our society. We may also want negative consequences for our enemies, our competitors, and others who oppose our interests. We like to hear that our nation's writers, scientists, athletes, actors, students, or workers have won awards in international competitions. We are dismayed by reports that our children's test scores are lower than scores in other neighborhoods or nations. We compete with a family down the street or some obnoxious cousin, and we want our interests to be successful. There are, of course, times when our personal interests and family or group interests are in opposition, as in family arguments over who should get the family car, what kind of career to pursue, or whether to support a war.

Enlightened self-interest is a pleasant way of describing why we do things that benefit ourselves without hurting others. Novelist and philosopher Ayn Rand (1943, 1957, 1997) is a strong advocate of self-interest, though she incorporates an enlightened provision that individuals should respect others' rights. She considers selfishness a virtue and argues against altruism and its idea that others are more important than oneself. Rand's views provide excellent examples of rugged individualism and "titanic self-assertion" (Gladstein, 1999, p. 1). Anthony Downs (1957, 1997) provides similar support for enlightened self-interest in the marketplace. Enlightened self-interest, where no damage is intended for others and there is a sense of social responsibility, can still create serious conflicts as individual or group interests compete for scarce resources. Who gets to decide whose self-interests are enlightened, and on what criteria?

Unenlightened self-interest, where selfishness without social conscience is the pattern, is just greed. Recent examples at Enron, WorldCom, some financial institutions, and other corporations illustrate this point. Major executives made millions of dollars in salary, perks, and stock options while workers were underpaid, misinformed, and lost retirement and medical benefits—even when the executives knew how badly the company was doing. Graft, corruption, and fraud occur in politics, in schools, in corporate life, and even in religious institutions.

Certainly, individual interests need not be so ruthless and irresponsible. Altruism can be seen as one form of socially beneficial self-interest. "Do unto others as you would have them do unto you" is the Golden Rule, a principle that is shared by virtually every culture in the world. Self-interest provides a rationale for the Golden Rule; we want to have a good life and that depends on others also having a good life. Teachers often recognize that their self-interest is served by having happy and successful students. There are, of course, many selfless people who devote their lives to helping others; Mother Teresa and Martin Luther King come to mind. They have interests, but are not absorbed with their own welfare.

Beyond individual interests are group interests, and these can be very competitive. Special interests have become a term of derision in politics—we label the opposition candidate in an election campaign as being in the clutches of special interest groups. Yet we all belong to various special interest groups, by our own or our family's occupations, geographic area, hobbies, charities, travel, religion, shopping, educational pursuits, and nearly all other endeavors.

Obviously, these interests do not always coincide. We would like lower taxes, but appreciate public benefits such as roads, police, clean parks, and schools. We prefer a healthy environment, but like products that come from chemicals, plastics, and other pollution-producing manufacturers. We join or support groups that advocate those ideas we share, even if at times we act in a manner that is not internally consistent.

Then there are our societal and national interests. Our stated policy, whether under a Democratic or Republican administration, is to defend national interests in international affairs—trade, borders, war, terrorism, and so on. Not remarkably, each nation places national interest as foremost, though clearly the definition and delineation of national interest differs. National interest has been one of the fuels of war, genocide, militarism, border vigilantism, isolation, denial of human rights, trade

restriction, and international posturing (Herbert, 2005; Bandy and Smith, 2005; Pavola and Lowe, 2005). It also has been a fuel for peace, international understanding, freedom, trade agreements, charity, economic development, and the protection of human rights (Nelson and Green, 1980; Hahnel, 2005). Our use of language shows interests at work: the "Axis of Evil" identifies nations and groups our government considers threatening, "Manifest Destiny" was invoked to cover the invasion of Native American territory in the West, the "war on terrorism" is used as grounds for changing accepted patterns of civil rights and civil liberties.

Societal interests involve such matters as general safety and welfare, the environment, health, education, security, transportation, communication, freedom, and order. These topics concern people across such political boundaries as cities, states, and nations. Residents of cities, suburbs, and rural areas are interested in safe highways and airports, good hospitals and schools—these are public interests, whether the social institutions are privately or publicly operated. The public also has a stake in how these quality-of-life areas are handled; many are government controlled and operated, some are government regulated but privately operated, and some are privately controlled and operated, with little governmental oversight.

Schooling is one of the most important of those broad public concerns in the United States. Laws govern nearly all forms of schooling to include required attendance, financing, staff credentials, curriculum, and operational requirements. Most school-age students in the United States attend public schools, controlled and operated by government. But about 15 percent of all students are enrolled in some form of private schooling, including independent schools, religiously affiliated schools, trade schools, and home schooling. In addition, there are efforts to provide vouchers for funding to parents who want to take their children from public schools to private schools, efforts to establish charter schools in the public districts for relief from some governmental regulation, and efforts to privatize public school operation by contracting with corporations.

Ideas of justice and equity provide rationales for mediating, adjudicating, mitigating, criticizing, and evaluating the various conflicts among interests; but justice and equity are not without debate themselves.

Justice and Equity: Sounds Good to Me

Justice sounds simple enough, and is certainly above dispute as a fundamental element in a well-ordered society—or family, organization, school, or relationship with others. We want to live in a society, family, school, or relationship that is just. We rail against situations we consider unjust. The difficulty, of course, is that justice depends on many factors: a set of socially agreed on values and principles, legal and moral traditions, the political and economic situation, technical and practical definitions of terms used, the time period and geographic

location, social and individual conditions, and the eye of the beholder. Justice, then, is dependent on such things as where you happen to be, when, who you are, how you are represented, and what you think of it.

This is not to suggest that justice is just a fuzzy idea that can never be defined, is constantly changing, and is too nebulous to have much impact on your life. Indeed, justice is the forming idea for nearly all political theory, law, ethics, and human relations. It has a history of very specific definitions in particular situations, yet is still under constant redefinition by a variety of people from parents to legislators. Burning witches at the stake was considered justice at one time; using the rod to physically punish misbehaving students was an accepted schoolmarm's role in the school justice system of the past. The ultimate punishment, death, is considered too uncivilized to be justice in some nations; others use it routinely.

The existing concept of justice has an impact on your life in virtually all settings, and can easily be the most important of influences. Consider being accused of a serious crime; consider being the victim. Think of the times you got a grade you think you did not deserve; think of the teacher's view of the same grade. Put yourself into the shoes of someone who suffers from a severe physical or mental disorder, or lives in a dictatorship, or is audited by the IRS. Each of these has a justice component. Everyday complaints about restaurant food or a department store purchase pose questions of justice, albeit more trivial. Waiters and store clerks usually employ a sense of justice in dealing with or ignoring complaining customers. Justice is both an ideal and a practical matter of significance for individuals and society, but it is a concept fraught with difficulties in definition and interpretation.

Justice incorporates ideas of impartiality and fairness, two concepts as difficult to discern as justice. Was Solomon impartial? Could his decision be fair to all? How do we know that any judge is impartial and fair? Was the Supreme Court impartial and fair in deciding the election between George W. Bush and Al Gore in 2000? Was the Supreme Court impartial and fair in their differing historic decisions on slavery, women's suffrage, segregated schools, abortion? Were those stock market analysts impartial when they recommended buying more Enron stock or sub-prime mortgage bundles as they collapsed? Was your teacher fair and impartial when you got the grade you think you did not deserve? Is school a good place to learn about justice, fairness, and impartiality—and do schools provide good models for how justice, fairness, and impartiality should work?

Stuart Hampshire (2000), arguing that the basis of justice lies in human conflicts, states ". . . fairness in procedures for resolving conflicts is the fundamental kind of fairness" (p. 4). Conflicts are a continuing and engaging human condition. Dialogue and dialectics can assist in examining conflicting views, but our sense of justice requires a belief in fair procedures for dealing with them (Fishkin, 1992). The procedural fairness Hampshire advocates may result in unequal conditions.

Divorcing parents who fight over child custody are unlikely to achieve equal condition. Selecting the Teachers of the Year in a school district may incorporate a fair procedure with impartial judging, but results are unequal. But when we think the procedures were generally fair, unequal results can be better tolerated.

The concept of fairness is essential to our ideas of justice—and fair procedures are a basic condition for justice in a legitimate democracy. Legitimacy, in a democracy, is the granting of authority to government by the people—a form of social contract. This is the idea of the consent of the governed, a concept disputed by some political theorists, but it continues to be widely held (Rawls, 1999, 2005). We accept decisions, even if we don't like them, when we feel the procedure is fair. If there is widespread concern that basic procedures are unfair, we have social unrest and the seeds of revolution.

Equity and Equality

Equity is a concept directly related to justice, and includes the idea of equal treatment under natural law or rights, without bias or favoritism. Equity and equality are concepts that can differ significantly. Equality can be measured by condition—each person has exactly the same. Or it can be equality of treatment—each one is treated the same based on some principle such as, "All men are created equal." But often we think that some seem to be more equal than others; we can suspect gender inequality at work in the preceding quote on the equality of men. These are issues of equity and justice. Is it possible to distribute things in a truly equal manner? Political scientist David Spitz (1982) notes that "Equality drives us into an insoluble moral dilemma, and therefore into practices that contradict what we preach. . . . To impose equality of results . . . is to limit equality of opportunity. We cannot have both equalities simultaneously" (p. 105).

Equity does not require equality, but it does expect a process deemed fair. Most of our notions of equality in the United States are procedural—equal treatment under the law, which is similar to the idea of procedural fairness. These ideas provide for opportunity, but do not specify equal results or conditions. The idea of equity provides a concept for judging the procedure of equal treatment. Under equity, exactly equal conditions or results are not required; there is no mandate that good things are distributed to all in an equal manner. Instead, there is an expectation for justice—any unequal distribution must be justified by some significant social or ethical principle (Rawls, 1971, 1999, 2001).

For example, we could justify providing special funds and separate programs for gifted and talented students in school because those students are meritorious and have the potential to give back more to the school and, later, to society. But not everyone would agree this is a democratic or equitable justification or that these students deserve special treatment or make more community contributions. Using Rawlsian theory on distributive justice, McKenzie (1984) studied school programs for gifted and talented students and concluded such programs were undemocratic, unfair

in selection and special treatment, and did not provide for having those specially treated students give something back to the school and society. Tracking students into separate curriculums for college preparation, vocational training, general studies, and special education brings up similar issues of justice and equity. Are inclusion or mainstreaming programs more equitable and just?

In the last quarter of the twentieth century, we decided justice is served when we provide special access to public buildings for people who require a wheelchair. That is based on a principle of equity turned into law that equal access requires special treatment for one group. Equity, then, can include inequality if the basic premise is that of justice. Affirmative action programs are predicated on this idea, making up for previous unjust discrimination. Improved funding for programs such as special education, Head Start, and school lunches for poor families is an equity topic. Special school treatment of the children of minority or immigrant families, whether by ethnic group, nationality, or income, represents another example.

Programs to redress previous inequalities and discrimination based on gender, race, class, or sexual orientation also are equity issues. Inequalities in public financing among local school districts are the subject of several different state supreme court decisions based on equal treatment. Children, their parents, taxpayers, constitutional lawyers, citizens in neighboring school districts, and most of the rest of society have interests in such equity issues. Should new national standards in various subject fields be imposed on all children in every school? Should some public schools be operated by private corporations? Should private schools have access to public money? Should religion be part of public education and should it be supported by public funds? Each of these examples, of course, has been and continues to be hotly contested social and educational policy and practice. As in political discourse, these issues have ideological dimensions.

Interests, Politics and Ideologies

Our interests are incorporated in and modified by ideas—liberal, conservative, radical, reactionary. Although these labels may not identify each of us or our views on various topics, they represent broad, divergent views and they can be used to examine social and educational issues. Ideologies enable people to explain and justify the society they would prefer (Jacoby, 2005). An ideology includes assumptions about the nature and purpose of society and related nature of individuals (Shils, 1968); it provides criteria against which one can judge human life and society (Lane, 1962); and it provides a means for self-identification (Erikson, 1960). Ideologies are broadly coherent structures of attitudes, values, and beliefs that influence individual perceptions and social policy (Piper, 1997).

Political ideologies are widely known, from radical right to radical left with conservatives and liberals somewhere near the center (Freeden, 1998; see also *Journal of Political Ideologies*). The right and left political conflict is often starkly presented.

Ideological debates can be fiery and passionate, if not always reasonable, realistic, or precise.

LIBERALISM, LIBERALS, CONSERVATIVES, AND RADICALS: CONFUSION

Continuing disputes about justice and equity as they apply to individual and social rights are among the grand debates in democratic history and philosophy (Valentyne, 2003; Barry, 2005; Hahnel, 2005; Rawls, 2005). These disputes revolve around disparate opinions about the relative rights of individuals and of society, and how equity among those rights should be determined. Although it is a bit confusing to use a similar term to mean different things, the current models of *conservatives* and *liberals* follow a Western tradition of liberalism.

Liberalism, a belief in freedom and equality, is the dominant political philosophy among Western democracies (de Ruggiero, 1927, 1959; Noddings, 1995; Klosko, 2000; Richardson, 2001; Kolm, 2005). Shapiro (1958), who traces the history of liberalism through major political literature, states: "What has characterized liberalism at all times is its unshaken belief in the necessity of freedom to achieve every desirable aim. . . . Equality is another fundamental liberal principle . . ." (pp. 10, 11). This dual belief separates the philosophy of modern Western nations from some other political ideas, such as divine right of kings, aristocracy by birth and social class, or theocratic rule. In the United States and other Western democracies, we don't argue seriously for a return to colonial-period theocratic governments, European feudal dictatorships, or politically powerful monarchies. We do argue about the relative weight that should be given to individual freedoms and social constraints (Dahl, 1999; Kramer and Kimball, 1999; Riesman, 1999; Geuss 2001; Henderson, 2001; Newey, 2001; Fuentes, 2005). Berlin (1969), points out that

> "Liberty is not the only goal . . . if others are deprived of it . . . then I do not want it for myself. . . . To avoid glaring inequality or widespread misery I am ready to sacrifice some, or all, of my freedom; I may do so willingly and freely: but it is freedom that I am giving up for the sake of justice or equality. . . ." (p. 125)

In the main, both conservatives and liberals in the United States support the basic ideas of democratic freedoms and equality—tenets of traditional liberalism (Dewey, 1930; Lippman, 1934; Russell, 1955; Spitz, 1982; Bellah et al., 1985; Gutman, 1999; Spragens, 1999; Gill, 2001; Tomasi, 2001; Rawls, 2005). The major differences between conservatives and liberals revolve around what are the best definitions or criteria for freedom and equality, what is the best balance between them, how that balance can best be achieved, and how each is served in a specific situation.

In addition to possible confusion with the use of the term *liberalism*, another of the intriguing and often confusing trends in contemporary politics and educational politics is the shifting of ideas between conservatives and liberals as they attempt to influence the

public's interests and plot potentially successful political positions. Political parties move toward the center to capture votes to get their candidates elected, resulting in some blurring of the conservative and liberal markers we are accustomed to using. Basic ideological differences may remain for the Republican and Democratic parties, but individual candidates don't easily fit on all issues in public life. Each party has a conservative and a liberal wing, and there is a large group of people inside and out of the parties who prefer to be considered independent.

New Democrats, like Bill Clinton, work to cut the deficit, stimulate the economy and increase corporate wealth, cut welfare, and actively support imposing national standards on schools. These had been Republican and conservative views. New Republicans, like George W. Bush, increase public spending and the deficit, support the U.S. Department of Education, and give illegal immigrants opportunities—previously Democratic and liberal views. Specific political party positions and the views of individual candidates may not correlate well with divergent underlying political ideologies, from conservative to liberal. But within each party there is often a contest among candidates to be identifed as more conservative, if Republican, or more liberal, if Democrat, as a way of attracting core party voters. This suggests the basic ideological orientation of each of the parties, but conservative and liberal labels don't stick on individuals as well as some might like.

We continue, despite the confusions, to use conservative and liberal labels to identify ideas and issues, and to mark various people. Newt Gingrich (2008), former congressional leader, argues that "liberals" are the cause of much that he opposes. David Brock (2002), a widely read conservative author, confesses to a career of overstatement and falsification of information in his active denigration of "liberal" causes and sanctifying of "conservative" ones. The labels still have meaning, despite the confusions and shifting, in politics and education.

Contemporary political disputes between "conservatives" and "liberals" occur over questions of balance and process, and they spill over into our debates on lawmaking, court proceedings, and schooling. Current conservatives, in general, want to limit governmental interference in individual freedom; current liberals generally want to ensure individual rights by governmental regulation. Conservatives argue for unregulated rights of individuals to own guns; liberals for governmental regulation of gun ownership. There are many areas of muddiness in this separation, giving pause to gross labeling.

One of these areas is abortion, where liberals tend to support women's right to choose and conservatives tend to want government to restrict abortions. Another is free speech, where liberals tend to support more individual freedom and conservatives tend to want limits imposed on opposing views of sexuality, patriotism, politics, and economics. A third example includes some school topics, where liberals tend to support more individual freedom for students and teachers to examine controversial topics, to protest, and to

criticize, and conservatives tend to support government-imposed standards, school and teacher accountability, socially acceptable student behavior, and restrictions on what topics can be studied.

Definitions of conservative and liberal may be slippery, but these terms are commonly applied and widely understood to refer to two distinct groups of ideas and people in any time period. Liberal ideas in one period may be considered conservative in another, and vice versa. Neoconservative and neoliberal views are a rethinking of conservative or liberal ideas (Steinfels, 1979; Rothenberg, 1984; DeMuth and Kristol, 1995; Piper, 1997; Dahl, 1999; Newey, 2001; Richardson, 2001). For example, Simhony and Weinstein (2001) claim that new liberalism goes beyond the stale liberalism/communitarian debates of the 1980s, and aims to reconcile the split between "individuality and sociability," with liberals shifting away from social or government programs as the primary answer to most social and individual problems.

More deeply discordant ideological roots, including a variety of radical positions on what a society and its schools should be, run beyond the mainstream liberal and conservative dialogue. Radical critiques influence the general debate by providing extreme positions, allowing liberals and conservatives to take more popular positions in the center. Radical ideas tend to have limited credibility in mainstream discussions, but liberals and conservatives draw from those ideas in proposing reforms (Dahl, 1999). Critical positions often appear first in the radical literature, then filter into the liberal and conservative rhetoric (Nelson, Carlson, and Linton, 1972; Dahl, 1999; Simhony and Weinstein, 2001).

Mainstream views sound more reasonable as bases for reform, but radical ideas contain the seeds for longer-term and more significant change. In the age when kings and queens were presumed to rule by divine right, democracy was a radical view. In a dictatorship, individual freedom is radical.

One of the major struggles in determining justice in a democracy lies in finding a suitable balance between the interests of individuals and communities. This struggle has many titles, but often is described as an ideological battle between individualism and communitarianism. These ideologies compete in their emphases, and in their more extreme versions offer a dialectic.

INDIVIDUAL AND SOCIAL RIGHTS

More radical factions separate much farther than the mainstream conservative and liberal dialogue on issues of individualism and communitarianism. The radical right wing, known as reactionaries or libertarians, advocates individual freedoms with the least restraint possible.

Nozick (1974) phrases it:

> "Individuals have rights, and there are things no person or group may do to them (without violating their rights). So strong

and far-reaching are these rights that they raise the question of what, if anything, the state and its officials may do. How much room do individual rights leave for the state? . . . Our main conclusions about the state are that a minimal state, limited to the narrow functions of protection against force, theft, fraud, enforcement of contracts, and so on, is justified; that any more extensive state will violate person's rights not to be forced to do certain things, and is unjustified. (p. ix)

In addition to an antistate position, libertarians convey a strong procapitalism view, relatively unfettered entrepreneurship and private enterprise. Excessive governmental control is assumed to kill individual initiative. Government, to libertarians, is an unfortunate development that has grown too large and too encompassing—stifling individual freedoms. Herbert Spencer (1981) writes, "The great political superstition of the past was the divine right of kings. The great political superstition of the present is the divine right of parliaments" (p. 123).

Libertarians want to dismantle the government, abolishing regulation, taxation, and public financing. They would eliminate social security, medicare, welfare, public education, and the right of government to take property under eminent domain; libertarians aim at "nothing short of the privatization of social existence" (Newman, 1984, p. 162). As Thomas Sowell (1999) says: "The welfare state, however, has made many of the respectable, self-supporting poor look like chumps, as the government has lavished innumerable programs on those who violate all rules and refuse to take responsibility for themselves" (p. 89). Not all libertarians share the view that all government is harmful; some recognize a need for some governmental role in mediating disputes, regulating commerce in basic human needs, and protecting society.

On the other side are communitarians of various stripes. Their major critique involves greed and social corruption of unregulated capitalism and the selfishness and self-centeredness that accompanies individualism. They believe community, our social glue, is in serious jeopardy from excessive individualism. Some of these critiques take great pains to separate individualism—a belief in oneself above others—from individuality—an expression of the value of recognizing each person's worth. John Dewey's (1933) treatise on that separation is significant. He develops in other writings on democracy and schooling his concept that individual differences and individual learning are consistent with his concept of education as a social process (Dewey, 1916, 1930). Dewey also writes of a broader set of conflicts:

> There can be no conflict between the individual and the social. For both of these terms refer to pure abstractions. What do exist are conflicts between some individuals and some arrangements in social life; between groups and classes of individuals; between nations and races; between old traditions embedded in institutions and new ways of thinking and acting which spring from those few individuals who attack what is socially accepted. (Dewey, in Ratner, 1939, p. 435)

Communitarians don't always ignore or denigrate the value of individuals; they advocate a balance between individual liberty and social needs for common purposes—balancing rights and order. Amitai Etzioni (1996) notes a major shift from "traditional" social order by edict, authoritarian rule, and rigid control to increasing individual rights.

He argues:

> . . . after the forces of modernity rolled back the forces of traditionalism, these [modernity] forces did not come to a halt; instead, in the last generation (roughly from 1960 on), they pushed ahead relentlessly, eroding the much weakened foundations of social virtue and order while seeking to expand liberty ever more. As a result, we shall see that some societies have lost their equilibrium, and are heavily burdened with the antisocial consequences of excessive liberty (not a concept libertarians or liberals often use). (p. xvii)

More radical communitarians argue for egalitarian answers to the excesses of individualism. They see a breakdown of social values, family structures, social responsibilities, shared interests, and collective purposes that constitute a decent society.

Among their concerns is the greedy continuation of "me" generation mentality and expansion of "yuppiness," antigovernment attacks that can undermine public confidence and lead to debilitating and discriminatory competitiveness, destruction of environmental protections and other regulatory needs, increased private territoriality, and suspicion of others. Unbridled individualism poses, they contend, clear and negative repercussions in charitable works, public welfare, public services, and public education—those major contributions to our civilization. Excessive individualism also appears in efforts to deregulate utilities and corporations, privatize public services, and maintain a social hierarchy based on birth, wealth, and historical status. Individualism is not usually advocated by members of the social class at the bottom. A premise of individualists is that those who have had should continue to have. Egalitarian answers, in opposition, include expansion and guarantees of equal opportunities, forms of affirmative action, progressive taxation and redistribution of wealth, and such programs as national health care, Head Start, and safety net welfare. These intend to correct or mitigate inequalities among groups.

Failures in corporate and accounting self-regulation prompts an upsurge of interest in increasing public regulation and accountability. As in the antitrust period in the early twentieth century, this has ignited public concern about patterns of deregulation, privatization, and rampant individualism that identified the 1990s.

Ideological Roots of School Disputes

Competing ideas with differing expectations for schools include freedom and equality, public and private, individual and society, the masses and the elites, unity and diversity, and the religious and the secular.

Dualisms are false in that they don't exist in complete isolation from each other and don't usually require a pristine choice. We can't have mind without body, and body without mind may be possible, but we have no certain knowledge of that. So we can't choose either body or mind. But we are faced continuously with situations where we must exercise choice among competing interests. Those choices often are between two political ideologies, two opposing sets of interests, or two parts of a dialectic—each side of which entails some potentially good and bad consequences. Dualisms are useful as mental constructions to assist in making that choice or finding a new synthesis; they can assist in reasoned dialogue about competing interests and ideologies. Schooling is one very public activity where such dualisms occur with frequency.

Schools are directly engaged in developing the individuals and society of the future and people care a great deal about what kind of individuals and society will develop. As Apple (1990) states, "the conflicts over what should be taught are sharp and deep. It is not only an educational issue, but one that is inherently ideological and political" (p. vii). Traditionalists share a general view that schools ought to follow time-honored ideas, practices, and authorities from a previous golden age of education. Progressivists share a different view that schools must be flexible, child-centered, and future-oriented.

Each ideology provides different views of schooling, from advocating abolition of public schools to using public schools for social criticism and the overthrow of oppression. Divergent

FIGURE 1 A Spectrum of Political and Educational Views

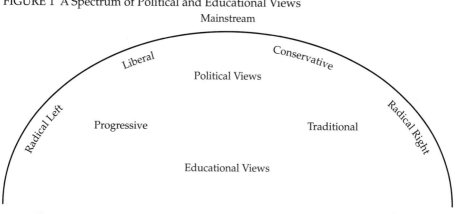

views of schooling and politics can be understood in terms of an ideological continuum: from elitist positions on the extreme right to egalitarian positions on the extreme left, with mainstream conservative and liberal positions in the center (see Figure 1).

Radical right-wing ideas about schooling are not uniform; they come from different special interest groups. Some promote teaching fundamentalist religious dogma. Some seek to censor teaching materials dealing with sex, socialism, atheism, or anything they think is anti-American. And some want to undercut publicly supported schools in favor of elite schooling for a select group of students. Right-wing groups have attacked secular humanism, feminism, abortion rights, sex education, global education, and values education in schools.

Radical educational ideologies from the right include the views of:

libertarians: "get government off our backs and out of our schools,"

abolitionists: "abolish public schooling," and

extreme elitists: "schooling for the best only; the rest into the work pool."

The radical left wing also offers a critical view of schools. Some see education as the way for the masses to uncover the evils of capitalism and the corporate state. Some propose education as the means for revolution, opening all the institutions of society to criticism. Left-wing groups have attacked business-sponsored teaching materials, religious dogma in public schools, tracking, discrimination, social control, and education for patriotic obedience.

Radical left-wing views include those of:

liberationists: "liberate students from oppressive forces in school and society,"

reconstructionists: "use schools to criticize and remake society," and

extreme egalitarians: "abolish all privilege or distinction."

Conservative, liberal, and radical views of society and education provide different rationales for criticism of schools and different proposals for reform. They are general frameworks that underlie individual and group discontent with schools. Radical views are important because they present stark and clearly defined differences between egalitarian and elitistic ideologies. However, mainstream conservative and liberal ideas govern most reform movements because of their general popularity and immense influence over media and government. Liberals, conservatives, and radicals differ in their views of which mainstream position has the schools in its grip (Aronowitz and Giroux, 1993).

The importance of education in society is reflected in controversies surrounding divergent ideological positions and the interests they represent.

Ideologies exist to explain or justify purposes and practices or to challenge them. In education these fundamental goals and general practices have varied during different times and in different locations. Primitive education was dedicated to survival and continuing rituals and life patterns established by elders. Ancient schooling was largely devoted to inculcation of religious learnings. In Athens, philosophic and contemplative schooling supplanted religious, while Spartan education was heavily committed to the military life. Roman schooling was more practical than philosophic and intended for developing strong loyalty and citizenship. Spiritual ideas predominated in schools of the Middle Ages, a preparation for the afterlife. The Renaissance brought different goals for schools—enlightenment, development of human capacities, and individual creativity. For most of

this time, formal schooling was for the elites, usually for families of religious, social, and political leaders. The main schooling arguments concerned how society's leaders should be prepared; strict learning of traditional roles, rituals, and concepts of knowledge—or contemplation of the good—or enlightenment and more flexible learnings.

Mass education arose as democracy developed, fostered especially in schooling in the United States from the mid-nineteenth century, and now spread throughout the industrialized world. Schooling for all developed some different educational goals, under differing ideologies: basic literacy and numeracy, social control, civic responsibility, loyalty and patriotism, vocational and home training, character and values development, health and safety knowlege, human relationships, self-reliance and realization, and solving problems. Schooling also shifted toward more secular, scientific, and technological goals. Consistent with the evolution in democratic political concepts, ideas about schooling shifted from a focus on basic literacy and social control to broader intellectual development and increasing interest in individuality.

Newer developments in educational ideas challenged established purposes and practices in schools, and posed interesting questions on the relation of individuals to their societies, and important issues of justice and equity.

What dimensions of justice and equity should be expected in schools and classrooms? How should schools address justice and equity regarding individual choice, racism, gender, class, wealth, and religion? What interests are at stake? Competing answers to these questions show disparate interests. Chapters 2 through 9 involve schooling issues that raise questions of justice, fairness, and impartiality.

We would like to include in this volume all viewpoints on each educational issue, but that is an obvious impossibility. We have, therefore, limited each chapter to two distinct positions about the topic covered to stress the dialogue or dialectic quality of the issue. These positions draw from liberal-progressive ideas, from conservative-traditional, and from radical critiques from the left or right. Additional references to conservative, liberal, and radical literature are included, and we encourage exploration of these highly divergent views.

References

APPLE, M. (1990). *Ideology and Curriculum.* 2nd Ed. London: Routledge.

ARONOWITZ, S., AND GIROUX, H. (1983). *Education Under Siege.* South Hadley, MA: Bergin and Garvey. (2nd Ed., 1993).

BANDY, J., AND SMITH, J. (2005). *Coalitions Across Borders.* Lanham, MD: Rowman and Littlefield.

BARRY, B. (2005). *Why Social Justice Matters.* Cambridge, UK: Polity.

BELLAH, R. N., ET AL. (1985). *Habits of the Heart: Individualism and Commitment in American Life.* Berkeley: University of California Press.

BERLIN, I. (1969). *Four Essays on Liberty.* Oxford: Oxford University Press.

BOWLES, S., GINTIS, H., AND GROSS, M. O. (2005). *Unequal Chances.* Princeton, NJ: Princeton University Press.

BRAUN, A., AND SCHEINBERG, S. (1997). *The Extreme Right.* Boulder, CO: Westview Press.

BROCK, D. (2002). *Blinded by the Right: The Conscience of an Ex-Conservative.* New York: Crown Publishers.

CHRISTENSON, R. M., ET AL. (1971). *Ideologies and Modern Politics.* New York: Dodd, Mead.

DAHL, G. (1999). *Radical Conservatism and the Future of Politics.* London: Sage.

DEMUTH, C., AND KRISTOL, W. (1995). *The Neoconservative Imagination.* Washington, DC: AEI Press.

DE RUGGERIO, G. (1927). *The History of European Liberalism.* R. G. Collingwood, translator. Boston: Beacon Press. (2nd Ed., 1959).

DEWEY, J. (1916). *Democracy and Education.* New York: Macmillan.

———. (1930). *Individualism Old and New.* New York: Minton, Balch, and Co.

———. (1933). *How We Think.* Boston: D. C. Heath.

DOWNS, A. (1957). *An Economic Theory of Democracy.* New York: Harper/Addison Wesley. (2nd Ed., 1997).

ERIKSON, E. H. (1960). *Childhood and Society.* New York: W. W. Norton.

ETZIONI, A. (1996). *The New Golden Rule.* New York: Basic Books.

FISHKIN, J. S. (1992). *The Dialogue of Justice.* New Haven, CT: Yale University Press.

FREEDEN, M. (1998). *Ideologies and Political Theory.* Oxford: Oxford University Press.

FUENTES, C. (2005). *This I Believe.* New York: Random House.

GEUSS, R. (2001). *History and Illusion in Politics.* Cambridge: Cambridge University Press.

GILL, E. R. (2001). *Becoming Free: Autonomy and Diversity in the Liberal Polity.* Lawrence, KS: University of Kansas Press.

GINGRICH, N. (2008). *Real Change.* Washington, DC: Regnery.

GLADSTEIN, M. R. (1999). *The New Ayn Rand Companion.* Westport, CT: Greenwood.

GOLDBERG, B. (2002). *Bias: A CBS Insider Exposes How the Media Distort the News.* Washington, DC: Regnery Publishers.

GUTMAN, A. (1999). *Democratic Education.* Princeton, NJ: Princeton University Press.

HAHNEL, R. (2005). *Economic Justice and Democracy.* New York: Routledge.

HAMPSHIRE, S. (2000). *Justice Is Conflict.* Princeton, NJ: Princeton University Press.

HENDERSON, D. (2001). *Anti-Liberalism 2000.* London: Institute of Economic Affairs.

HERBERT, B. (2005). *Promises Betrayed.* New York: New York Times Books.

JACOBY, R. (2005). *Picture Imperfect: Utopian Thought for an Anti-Utopian Age.* New York: Columbia University Press.

Journal of Political Ideologies. London: Routledge.

KITCHING, G. (2001) *Seeking Social Justice Through Globalization.* University Park, PA: Pennsylvania State University Press.

KLOSKO, G. (2000). *Democratic Procedures and Liberal Consensus.* New York: Oxford University Press.

KOLM, S-C. (2005). *Macrojustice: The Political Economy of Fairness.* Cambridge: Cambridge University Press.

KRAMER, H., AND KIMBALL, R. (1999). *The Betrayal of Liberalism.* Chicago: Ivan R. Dee.

LANE, R. E. (1962). *Political Ideology.* New York: The Free Press of Glencoe.

LIPPMAN, W. (1934). *The Method of Freedom.* New York: Macmillan.

LITTLE, I. M. D. (2002). *Ethics, Economics, and Politics.* Oxford: Oxford University Press.

MAURO, R. M. (2008). "Political Science Education and the Conceptual Analysis of Ideology." *Journal of Political Ideologies.* 13(1) 55–72. Feb.

MCKENZIE, J. (1984). *A Study of the Relative Democratic Nature of Gifted Education Programs in New Jersey.* Unpublished dissertation, Rutgers University.

MITZMAN, A. (2003). *Prometheus Revisited: The Quest for Global Justice in the Twenty-First Century.* Amherst, MA: University of Massachusetts Press.

NELSON, J., CARLSON, K., AND LINTON, T. (1972). *Radical Ideas and the Schools.* New York: Holt, Rinehart and Winston.

NELSON, J., AND GREEN, V. (1980). *International Human Rights.* Stanfordville, NY: Coleman Publishers.

NEWEY, G. (2001). *After Politics.* New York: Palgrave.

NEWMAN, S. L. (1984). *Liberalism at Wit's End.* Ithaca, NY: Cornell University Press.

NODDINGS, N. (1995). *Philosophy of Education.* Boulder, CO: Westview Press.

NOZICK, R. (1974). *Anarchy, State, and Utopia.* New York: Basic Books.

PAVOLA, J., AND LOWE, I, eds. (2005). *Environmental Values in a Globalizing World.* New York: Routledge.

PIPER, J. R. (1997). *Ideologies and Institutions.* New York: Rowman and Littlefield.

RAND, A. (1943). *The Fountainhead.* New York: New American Library. (2nd Ed., 1957).

———. (1997). *The Journals of Ayn Rand.* D. Harriman, ed. New York: Dutton.

RATNER, J. (1939). *Intelligence in the Modern World: John Dewey's Philosophy.* New York: Random House.

RAWLS, J. (1971). *A Theory of Justice.* Cambridge, MA: Harvard University Press. (2nd Ed., 1999).

———. (1999). *The Law of Peoples.* Cambridge, MA: Harvard University Press.

———. (2001). *Justice as Fairness.* E. Kelly, ed. Cambridge, MA: Harvard University Press.

———. (2005). *Political Liberalism.* Expanded Edition. New York: Columbia University Press.

REISMAN, D. (1999). *Conservative Capitalism.* New York: St. Martins Press.

RICHARDSON, J. L. (2001). *Contending Liberalisms in World Politics.* Boulder, CO: Lynne Rienner Publications.

ROTHENBERG, R. (1984). *The Neoliberals.* New York: Simon and Schuster.

RUSSELL, B. (1955). *Authority and the Individual.* London: Allen and Unwin.

SHAPIRO, J. S. (1958). *Liberalism: Its Meaning and History.* New York: D. Van Nostrand.

SHILS, E. (1968). "The Concept of Ideology." In D. Sills, ed., *The International Encyclopedia of the Social Sciences.* New York: Macmillan.

SIMHONY, A., AND WEINSTEIN, D. (2001). *The New Liberalism.* Cambridge: Cambridge University Press.

SPENCER, H. (1981). *The Man Versus the State.* Indianapolis, IN: Liberty Classics.

SPITZ, D. (1982). *The Real World of Liberalism.* Chicago: University of Chicago Press.

SPRAGENS, T. A. (1999). *Civic Liberalism.* Lanham, MD: Rowman and Littlefield.

SOWELL, T. (1999). *The Quest for Cosmic Justice.* New York: Free Press.

STEINFELS, P. (1979). *The Neoconservatives.* New York: Simon and Schuster.

TOMASI, J. (2001). *Liberalism Beyond Justice.* Princeton: Princeton University Press.

VALENTYNE, P. ed., (2003) *Equality and Justice.* Volumes 1–6, New York: Routledge.

CHAPTER 2

School Choice: Family or Public Funding

Is family choice of schools in the public interest?

POSITION 1: FOR FAMILY CHOICE IN EDUCATION

School choice means better educational opportunity, because it uses the dynamics of consumer opportunity and provider competition to drive service quality...It re-asserts the rights of the parent and the best interests of child over the convenience of the system, infuses accountability and quality into the system, and provides educational opportunity where none existed before.

—The Center for Educational Reform, 2008

Why Educational Choice Is Needed

If your children attended a school in which most students scored below the state average on standardized tests, what could you do? What if they were enrolled in a school with few certified teachers, overcrowded classrooms, few computers, little lab equipment, and not enough books or other supplies? Could you find a way to get them the education they need? If you were unhappy with your child's school because the curriculum was not rigorous enough or because it violated your beliefs and values, how could you remedy the situation? Depending on a family's income, those choices become even more limited.

Dissatisfied families can work to correct problems in their children's public schools. Doing so, however, often involves a long, cumbersome process of political action—meeting with teachers and principals, attending school board meetings, working on committees, and being an active presence in a school. Time and energy commitments usually are more than most parents can make, and risk of failure and frustration is high. Even when these efforts are successful, the resulting changes may come too late for the students whose parents initially tried to make them. Students are in a particular grade for only one year.

Schools often cannot modify programs or policies that quickly. Although work-ing for long-term change is an option, it is a choice that doesn't meet the most immediate needs of parents and children.

Families with enough money can decide to send their children to expensive, nonsectarian private schools. Their budget can absorb the cost of this decision even as the parents continue paying taxes to support public schools. Addition-ally, because there are only a limited number of such schools, attending them may mean students must live away from their families for long periods. This disruption of family life for the sake of a child's education is not often an attractive option for parents or young people, even when the family can afford it. Instead of increasing parental influence in children's lives, this choice weakens it. Private schools remain options only for the wealthiest families since the tuition costs run into the tens of thousands of dollars per child (Broughman and Swaim, 2006; National Associa-tion of Indendent Schools, 2008; U.S. Department of Education, 2007, 2008c).

Parents with more limited financial resources can choose to send their chil-dren to less expensive and more accessible private schools affiliated with religious organizations (McDonald, 2008). In fact, of the almost 28,000 private schools in the United States, close to 80 percent have connections to a religious group (Brough-man and Swaim, 2006). However, this choice is still of limited help. Many families are not comfortable with the differences between their religious beliefs and those of the organization sponsoring the school. In times of economic distress, tuition may become too much of a burden for the family budget to bear.

Indeed, if a family has no surplus funds in its budget, the option of any kind of private school is not available. Most poor children attend urban public schools. Academic achievement lags far behind their counterparts in suburban public schools (KewalRamani, A., Gilbertson, L., Fox, M., and Provasnik, S., 2007). Many parents who live in inner cities and are members of ethnic or racial minority groups are deeply concerned about the quality of their children's education (Black Alliance for Educational Options, 2008). However, without viable family choice programs for all—rich and poor—they cannot translate their concerns into actions. The 2001 No Child Left Behind Act attempts to provide more choice by allowing parents to transfer their children from failing schools to other public schools whose students have higher academic achievement levels. Except for Alabama, North Carolina, and Virginia, all states have enacted some type of "open enrollment" policy. Often, however, these policies mandate transfers only within districts. In some urban areas there are simply not enough successful schools to absorb fully the numbers of students from failing schools that wish to transfer. Most states also allow but do not mandate transfers from a low-performing to a higher-performing district. There is little incentive for districts to accept students from other areas. For the most part, students who wish to transfer out of district do not even receive transportation to their new school (U.S. Department of Education, 2008a).

Because Americans wanted to maintain a high level of local control over schools, districts were established based on geography—meaning cities, towns, villages or any part of those municipalities can become school districts. That way local branches of government, most often school boards, can be elected by and held responsible to residents of the areas the schools serve. In practice, however, these forms of governance have become less responsive to dissatisfied parents. Many critics believe public school bureaucracy has, over time, become elaborate and self-protective (Lips, 2007).

For example, once a district is established, students are assigned to schools based on where they live within and among those districts. The dividing lines are firmly maintained. Moving from school to school within a district often is difficult; moving from district to district (unless the family changes its residence) is almost impossible. Assigning students to schools based on their residence minimizes parents' choice about the school their children can attend. Families' financial situations, not their commitments to their children, determine the amount of educational choice they have. If a family can afford to live where a school matches their hopes and ambitions, then all is well. If a family lives where that match does not exist, and they cannot afford to move to a better district, their relative poverty deprives them of the freedom to choose their children's school.

Others besides parents are concerned about education and have expertise to contribute in deciding what kind of schools and programs will best serve children and our society. Educators have access to research about academic programs that ensure success for children having difficulties with traditional ways of teaching and learning. Health professionals have suggestions about issues affecting children's physical and emotional well-being and how those concerns can be addressed in schools. Businesspeople can offer advice and support to schools in preparing young people for their future in an ever-more demanding job market. However, despite the good will and knowledge these people bring to questions about education, none of them is as concerned about the welfare of an individual child as his or her loving and committed parents. While parental authority with regard to children is not unlimited in this country, we Americans believe that generally it should be the most significant factor in determining most aspects of a child's life. Of those concerned about a child's education, parents have the most long-term relationship with children, giving them insights into what is right for their child that not even the most famous educational expert could ever hope to have. Ultimately, parents should be the final decision makers about *their* child's education. As Americans we should work to ensure that all parents have this right, not just those who have achieved a certain level of economic success.

We are, however, coming to recognize that state-sponsored schools have put a stranglehold on parental choice. We need to allow the educational system to operate within a free and competitive market. "No amount of money or number of programs will create anything more than marginal improvements, because public schools are organized to serve teachers and administrators rather than students and families...only markets will force the unpleasant restructuring necessary to unleash potential" (Manzi, 2008, p. 43).

Family choice is an issue that is not going to go away. The stakes for individuals are too high. The question before us as a country is not if we should create viable family choice programs, but how we should do so. Although the latest Gallup poll shows concern among Americans about such programs,

41 percent said they would favor a proposal in their state to allow parents to send their school-age children to any public, private, or church-related school they chose, with the government paying all or part of the tuition in nonpublic schools. Fifty-seven percent of those with children in public school said they would use vouchers, if available, to send their children to private schools (Rose and Gallup, 2007). Well-crafted choice programs could ease concerns some have expressed about accountability of private schools receiving taxpayer dollars.

Creating Options for Parents and Children

Charter Schools and Open Enrollment

We could create choice programs in several ways. First, we could do so in a limited fashion by encouraging options within public school systems. Government funds still would be used exclusively for those schools, but under such a system parents would have more options if they were dissatisfied with a particular school. We could introduce a more radical change by directing taxpayer dollars from providers of education, public schools, to consumers of educational services, parents and children. Those consumers would be allowed to make choices about where to spend that money.

The first option has been tried with limited success. Some districts have been giving families choices about their children's schooling since the civil rights movement of the 1960s and '70s. Magnet schools that offer specialized curriculum designed to draw students from all across a district were tools in the desegregation plans of many urban districts. Some of those schools continue to operate. Voluntary transfer programs, sometimes called "open-enrollment," also have been in place on a limited basis. Since 1988 eighteen states have enacted legislation allowing transfer both within and among school districts. Another eleven states have regulations allowing transfer only within the same district. Nearly 4 million students participate in open-enrollment programs (U.S. Department of Education, 2008b).

Public school districts have created schools of choice for reasons other than racial integration. Since the 1970s, qualified teachers have been given state permission (called a charter) to create new, more independent schools in which educational innovations could be explored. Now thirty-nine states and the District of Columbia have laws allowing the establishment of schools that are partially autonomous from the districts in which they are located. Members of these school communities believe freedom from state and local regulations enables them to better meet students' needs. In addition, they see charter schools as places where an "alternative vision of schooling" can be lived out—where such educational values as diversity, inquiry, and community can more fully be realized than in traditional public schools (U.S. Charter Schools, 2008).

In the early 1990s researchers concluded that despite positive benefits children who participate in charter schools received, little evidence directly connected these programs with improvement in school performance or student achievement (National Center for Education Statistics, 2004). More recent studies, though, conclude that even this limited form of competition causes improvements in student performance (Betts, 2006; Hoxbie, 2007; Witte, 2008) and encourages school districts to improve their services (Betts, 2006; Forster, 2008).

Vouchers

The second option, providing taxpayer dollars directly to families, puts decisions about children's education back where it belongs, in the hands of their parents. "Vouchers" are one mechanism for transferring taxpayer dollars to families. In such a program, families with children receive a check from the government to be used to pay for the educational program of their choice. According to Milton Friedman, the economist who first proposed vouchers fifty years ago, to work best, each family would receive an amount of money equal to the public school per pupil expenditure. They could then shop around for the school—private or public—that best matches their needs (Hendrie, 2004). Additional subsidies would be available for children with handicapping conditions. Most of the money would come from state and local taxes; additional funds for children with special needs would come from the federal government. There would be no restrictions against parents adding their own money to what they receive from the government to pay for schools that cost more than the voucher amount. Similarly, there would be no regulations preventing using these funds at the school of a parent's choice. Private nonsectarian schools, those with religious affiliations, and government-sponsored schools all would be valid choices. Some proponents of voucher plans suggest that to increase the competitive nature of this system, there should be no added subsidies from the government to any of the options. The amount of funding a school received from taxpayers would be determined by enrollment, which itself would be driven by customer satisfaction (Enrow, 2008).

In the early 1990s experiments with vouchers began with privately funded programs. There are at least eight such programs across the country. Two of the largest are Children First America and the Children's Scholarship Fund. Children First America had helped to create tuition scholarship programs for children in over 70 cities. The Children's Scholarship Fund sponsors nearly 29,000 children across the country. However, these programs cannot meet the need. For example, over 1.25 million applications for funding were received by Children's Scholarship Fund. Leaders of these funds have concluded that philanthropy alone cannot meet American families' desires to choose their children's schools. Tax dollars for vouchers are needed (Children's Scholarship Fund, 2008; Washington Scholarship Fund, 2007).

However, only six states—Florida, Utah, Maine, Ohio, Vermont, Wisconsin, and the District of Columbia have voucher programs. These are very limited— for example, Maine and Vermont's plans only apply to students in districts without public schools, and neither state allows parents to choose religious schools for their children (Kafer, 2005). In Florida, Arizona, Georgia, Ohio, and Utah, students with disabilities are eligible for vouchers to pay their tuition at private schools (Enrow, 2008). Milwaukee and Cleveland have the largest publicly funded voucher programs. Approximately 11,000 students from low-income families receive vouchers to attend private schools in those cities. The schools meet state health and safety standards/regulations, and agree to use random selection processes in admitting voucher students. Families of children who have been able to use vouchers in Milwaukee, Cleveland, and Washington, D.C., to attend the schools of their choice report greater satisfaction with the educational setting than do familes of students attending public schools (Wolf, 2007; Read, 2008; Witte, 2008). There is every reason to believe that, by creating more publicly funded choice programs, we could extend these benefits to many more families. In fact, we should replace the current way of funding education in America with voucher programs in every state in the country. That would give every parent a real choice about their children's education.

Benefits of Voucher Programs

Voucher programs would address concerns about injustices in the American educational system. With adequately funded programs, all parents, regardless of income, would be able to provide their children with an education that meets their needs and interests. What are now privileges of the wealthy would become entitlements of all. For example, many parents feel public schools policies, practices, and teaching violate their religious principles.

Some parents believe schools do not, in fact, take neutral positions but actually teach values that contradict their own (Shaw, 2005; Strom, 2005). Members of some traditions also find school policies to be problematic as their children attempt to practice their religion. Young Muslims often cannot find space within their schools in which they can meet their obligation to pray; they cannot leave school on Fridays, their holy day, to attend services at their mosques (Farquhar, 2008; Zine, 2007). Both Muslims and Jews sometimes find it difficult to obtain food that meets their dietary laws in public school cafeterias. In addition, religious holidays and ritual fasting days often are not acknowledged in public schools. The coeducational nature of public schools also violates the religious beliefs of some students and their families whose traditions teach that boys and girls should be educated separately (Farquhar, 2008; Zine, 2007). Voucher programs would allow parents to remove their children from public schools they find offensive and place them in schools whose curricula or policies did not violate their religious or moral values. They would be able to choose schools that contributed to their children's growth in the family's religious or spiritual tradition. Doing so would no longer be a privilege of the wealthy few.

Voucher programs also could help us address the long-standing problem of segregation in American schools. Even though a family might not have enough money to move out of a neighborhood, parents could use vouchers to choose schools for their children outside of the area in which they live. Families would be able to send their children to schools that did not replicate the racial segregation of their neighborhoods. Vouchers would give private schools the opportunity to accept children whose families are unable to pay tuition and to whom schools could not afford to provide scholarships. In doing so, school populations could become more racially diverse. There is evidence that private schools, especially religiously affiliated private schools, are already less segregated than public schools (Forster, 2006; Greene and Winters, 2006).

In a system where schools compete for students, the institutions' survival would be dependent on consumers' decisions about where to spend their vouchers. Therefore, schools would have more motivation to ensure high levels of customer satisfaction than they do under the current system. Obviously, student achievement would directly affect parents' evaluation of a school. Voucher programs would create an educational system in which more children were likely to succeed. The new funding would help existing private schools and create new ones dedicated to increasing student achievement. The competition would force government schools to improve their students' learning outcomes as well (Hendrie, 2004). Research indicates that public schools have improved in areas where private school voucher programs have been established (Greene and Winters, 2003; Wolf, 2008). This set of benefits is one of the reasons so many parents whose children attend schools with high failure rates are so supportive of voucher programs (Wolf, 2008).

Voucher systems and the resultant competitive educational market also would increase the number of schools designed to meet students' special interests and needs. For example, schools for the performing arts and those emphasizing science and technology would be more available. The increased variety of schools could be expected to stimulate students' motivation since there would be a better match between their interests and a school's offerings. Students who don't fit easily or comfortably in currently designed schools would have a better chance of finding an appropriate place under a voucher system encouraging the creation of innovative programs.

These benefits for parents and students would minimize the amount of social conflict over schools. Because parents could choose their child's educational program and change to another if they were unhappy, their satisfaction with schools could be expected to rise. Research on this seems quite clear. Parents who can choose their children's schools are more satisfied with them than parents who have no choice (Wolf, 2008). Even though many schools would be privately owned, they would give parents and students a more significant voice in school governance than in public schools where they compete with representatives of special interest groups (Center for Educational Reform, 2008; Wolf et al., 2007).

Voucher programs will not only help parents and students. Teachers also will benefit under these plans. School survival will depend on parent satisfaction with student achievement, and since such achievement depends on competent instruction, good teachers will be highly in demand. As a result, teachers' salaries will increase as schools compete to attract these skilled professionals. In addition, as the number and variety of schools increase, teachers will be more able to find schools whose values, missions, and methods match their own. Consequently, teacher satisfaction will rise under voucher programs as well. Voucher programs will also help taxpayers. The cost of attending the private, religious schools in which most vouchers will be used is much less than the monies expended by public schools—often because school district bureaucracies overspend or waste funds (Michos and Aud, 2006).

Concerns about Choice Plans Using Vouchers

Critics of choice plans rightly point out several areas of concern. If voucher plans are implemented, we must be sure they are constitutional, fair, and consistent with American values. All these conditions can be met if voucher plans are carefully designed.

The issue of constitutionality most often is raised when critics question using taxpayer dollars to educate children in schools affiliated with religious groups. This concern is rooted in their understanding of the doctrine of the separation of church and state. The First Amendment states, "Congress shall make no law respecting an establishment of religion." The Supreme Court most often has interpreted that to mean that only the federal government has no authority over religion. For most of our history, state and local government were left to act as they wanted about the matter. However, in the 1940s the court began to look more closely at the issue and created some standards limiting states' and municipalities' relationships to religious institutions. In the process, the Court reached some decisions establishing a greater distance between church and state than previously had existed.

However, the Court also has held that many government policies benefiting religious groups *are* constitutional. For example, tax exemption for churches and religious schools, tax deductions for contributions to religious charities, tax credits for tuition paid to religious schools, transportation for children in those schools, and police or fire protection of religious institutions have all been declared legal. Even more closely related to the question of school choice, the G.I. Bill, Pell Grants, federally subsidized student loans, and state tuition assistance programs for college students have not been declared unconstitutional even though some money from those programs has gone to schools directly affiliated with religious groups.

What the Supreme Court seems to have established is a policy of "neutrality" with regard to such funding. If a program provides benefits to individuals according to neutral guidelines, then it can be declared constitutional, even if the individuals choose to use those benefits for a service provided by a religious group. The government is not itself supporting a religious institution; individuals are doing so through private decisions (*Widmer et al. v. Vincent et al.*, 1981; *Mueller v. Allen*, 1983; *Witters v. Washington Department of Services for the Blind*, 1986; *Zobrest v. Catalina Foothills School District*, 1993; *Agostini v. Felton*, 1997). The court has ruled that the issue is not *what* is funded through taxpayer money, but *how* that funding reaches the religious institution. If an individual makes an independent and private decision to spend tax dollars to which he or she is entitled on a service provided by a religious institution, then the wall between church and state has not been breached (Lewin, 1999; Lindsey, 2000; Rosen, 2000). Using this reasoning, in *Zelman v. Doris Simmons-Harris* (2002) the justices ruled the Cleveland voucher program was legal. In doing so the Court established that it is constitutional for a state to provide families with public money to use at private schools, even those affiliated with religious organizations. This principle has been well-established in federal Pell grants awarded to students attending college who may use the funds to attend any college or university, whether or not it has a religious affiliation.

The admissions policies of private schools to which parents could direct taxpayer dollars is another area of concern to voucher program critics. They are rightly concerned about whether a market system will allow schools to discriminate in their admissions policies. They suggest that religious schools, for example, will be able to admit only those applicants whose parents are members of the religious organization with which the schools are affiliated. They further argue that private schools will be able to refuse students with handicapping conditions that create special educational needs.

While it is certainly justified to worry about unfair admissions policies, current law already protects young people from arbitrary discrimination. In fact, in 2000, these laws were used to correct just such problems in the admissions policies of several high schools participating in the Milwaukee voucher program (Garn, 2008).

However, the Supreme Court also has ruled that private organizations, even those that benefit from indirect taxpayer support, can refuse to admit members whose inclusion would significantly breach the organization's First Amendment right to express its beliefs (*Roberts v. United States Jaycees*, 1984; *Hurley v. Irish American Gay, Lesbian, Bisexual Group of Boston*, 1995; *Boy Scouts of America v. Dale*, 2000). The court has not yet established if this ruling applies to church-affiliated schools.

A third concern raised about vouchers to fund parental choice in education is that people or organizations whose beliefs violate American ideals will be able to maintain schools teaching those beliefs using taxpayer dollars. For example, critics suggest that groups such as the Ku Klux Klan might use voucher funding to establish schools in which they could teach white supremacy (Center for Educational Reform, 2005). These suggestions raise legitimate concerns about regulation. However, those raising these objections seem to forget that laws already exist to prevent anyone in the United States from advocating illegal activities. Teachers or administrators in private schools are not exempt from these statutes. In addition, just because government no longer would be the exclusive operator of schools under voucher programs, it does not necessarily follow that government could not regulate educational institutions receiving taxpayer dollars indirectly. Many countries in Europe fund private and religious schools with public dollars. They establish "inspectorates" to verify those institutions are indeed providing children with an education and nothing illegal takes place in them. Americans could modify those systems to fit our needs without returning to a governmental monopoly in education (Betts, 2006).

Funding schools associated with religious or political minority groups raises some legitimate questions. However, critics seem to forget that tolerance for diverse opinions is at the heart of America's democratic tradition. By suggesting we not fund schools in which opinions or beliefs of a particular group are taught, critics may unwittingly be participating in a form of censorship that in other settings they would find unacceptable. Lack of government funding may prevent these schools from operating and, therefore, prevent them from expressing their beliefs and opinions as they are entitled to do under the First Amendment. The fact that it would be a new task for government to regulate such schools does not mean it would be impossible (Betts, 2006).

Concerns about whether prejudice and bigotry will be taught in voucher-funded schools are legitimate. However, to those most likely to be the target of the hatred, these worries appear to be less important than their children's current forced attendance at public schools that fail to educate but are their only option under the system we have now. Many urban and minority parents believe that, although it is possible if not probable that there will be problems with a voucher-funded educational system, those difficulties will not be worse than the ones they face now (Black Alliance for Educational Options, 2008). They are right. As a society we need the benefits voucher programs will bring. We must accept the challenge of designing them in ways that are faithful to American law and values.

The goal of those who established the American public school system was to provide education for all American children in a way that all those who benefited from their training would share its financial cost. However, achieving that dream never required that government operate schools, only that we should fund them through our taxes. Vouchers provide a way to fund schools without subjecting them to unresponsive bureaucratic control. We no longer can afford not to make the change. All families deserve to be able to choose education that works for their children. Our unwillingness to put the power of good education at their disposal fails to give poor and marginalized children the tools they need to change their situations. Voucher programs will give parents of these and all children real options. They no longer will be recipients of choices made by others with less investment in their children's lives. We need to make family choice a reality—publicly funded vouchers will do just that.

POSITION 2: AGAINST VOUCHERS

Vouchers, in my own belief, represent the single worst, most dangerous idea to enter education discourse in my lifetime.

—Kozol, 2007

There are many ways to provide parents and students with choices about schools and education that are not *as* problematic as voucher programs. Proponents of such programs seem to ignore or demean all other possibilities, painting their alternative as the only one with any real hope of reforming American education. However, in their enthusiasm for their position they underestimate the difficulties inherent in publicly funding payments to private schools.

We should oppose voucher programs allowing parents to use public funds in private schools for several reasons. They will undermine an educational system that, for all its flaws, still enables parents, students, teachers, administrators, and other citizens to learn "what a democratic life means and how it might be led" (Dewey, 1916, p. 7). In violation of the Constitution, they break down the barrier between church and state. They pose legal problems by diverting public funds to private coffers. They will have unacceptable financial consequences for schools and taxpayers, impede continuing development of American values such as diversity and tolerance, and lead to more divisiveness based on unequal economic or social condition. Finally, voucher plans simply will not deliver the improvements in academic achievement their supporters promise.

Differing Forms of Choice

Families already do have choices about the educational system. The Elementary and Secondary Act of 2001, known as No Child Left Behind (NCLB), provides funding for a variety of options for parents, including charter schools, voluntary public school choice, and magnet schools. In addition, if a school fails to meet state standards for two years in a row, the district must provide parents with the opportunity to send their children to a higher-performing school (U.S. Department of Education, 2008).

What the law doesn't provide—yet—are governmental funds to subsidize private decisions about schooling. Parents' and children's concerns are not the only ones to be considered when we decide what kind of education to provide with public funds. Since all taxpayers contribute the funds used for education, they have a right to make choices about schools as well. That is, there are social purposes for schooling that must be considered as significant as the individual purposes of parents for their children.

Americans accepted the notion of the "common school" in the mid-nineteenth century to provide future generations with knowledge, skills, and values they would need to improve society and create positive social interactions within their communities. Through public education, young people would learn how to behave as responsible, productive citizens of a democratic society, learn the importance of voting, and develop the habits of responsible and honest workers. They also would learn tolerance and respect for diverse peoples and different points of view that make up this country (Good and Braden, 2000).

We were willing to hand over hard-earned money to the government for schools because we believed such schools would return "profits" to every member of society, not just to children attending them and their families. The United States has a remarkable record in educating nearly all children through the high school level through public funding of public schools.

Citizens of the United States also decided that choices about education should be made collectively through the electoral and representative processes characteristic of American life. So we established schools managed through elected school boards or other forms of local government. If people disagreed with decisions by elected officials, they could elect others. This process would maintain the right of taxpayers to make choices about schools they supported financially. Voucher plans effectively take away this right.

Voucher proponents want to sidestep this democratic decision-making process and dislike the compromises it demands in such areas as curriculum or policy. Because they *are* compromises, they require everyone to "give in and give up" on some issues. Perhaps dissatisfied parents and other voucher supporters believe they have had to give up too much while others have given too little. Even if they're right, however, that is how the democratic process works. Minority positions, those that cannot mount sufficient public pressure, do not carry the day in our political system. However, democratic institutions also safeguard the rights of minority groups, especially their right to participate, to make the strongest possible case for their position and perhaps, eventually, to sway the majority (Apple and Beane, 1995).

Voucher plans, however, do not really represent an attempt of a minority to gain more influence within the democratic decision-making process regarding education. Instead, they allow parents to bypass it altogether when it comes to school governance and accountability (Paris, 1995). Using taxpayer money, parents will be able to choose to send their children to private schools that avoid the difficulties of working within "democratic procedures that accept as legitimate views from disparate actors with conflicting agendas and incompatible styles" (Henig, 1994, p. 23).

Religion, Tolerance, and Democratic Ideals

Among the choices parents can make with their vouchers will be schools affiliated with religious institutions. Proponents of voucher programs argue such use of taxpayer money is constitutional; it does not follow that it is good public policy. Determining the constitutionality of a policy means only it "could" be implemented, not that it "should" be.

Voucher plans making it easier for students to attend schools that separate people by their religious beliefs can contribute to isolation from, and misunderstanding of, those whose beliefs are different from their own. In an age where we need citizens who are more, not less, capable of accepting religious differences, sectarian schools do not prepare young people adequately enough to deserve public funding. As we have seen, in a democracy it is within the right of the citizens to determine what return it wants on the investment of its tax dollars. In this case, then, it is not a violation of families' rights if society decides only to fund schools that will be most likely to provide students with experiences of, and contact with, people who are unlike themselves and their families. A collective decision to teach students the democratic values of pluralism and tolerance through school experiences of those realities does not lessen parents' rights to choose to teach their children the family's religious values. It is simply a decision of how best to use tax dollars to achieve society's goals.

There is reason from other reports to believe such tolerance is not a universal product of private schools with religious affiliations (Slater, 2005). Studies of textbooks used in some conservative religious schools seems to indicate they could encourage negative, judgmental attitudes toward people not sharing the school community's religious beliefs (Mogra, 2007; Paterson, 2000). Such curricula may encourage students to label other people and to dismiss their arguments on the basis of those stereotypes rather than on their merits. Using government funds to develop such attitudes in students is questionable in light of our historical decision to use public funds for education to create a citizenry committed to democratic ideals of tolerance and compromise. It is not that alternative ideals should not be presented in schools funded by communities whose beliefs they represent. However, they should not be taught at taxpayer expense.

Financial Consequences of Voucher Plans

Whether we consider fully or partially funded voucher plans, they all have negative financial consequences.

Fully funded voucher programs, the kind envisioned by many who want market forces to control education, would mean that parents or guardians of every school-age child in America would receive a check from the government. The basic amount of the check, under most proposals, would be the same for every student. Those with special needs would receive additional funds. Under some plans, the amount a parent received would be equal to the amount currently spent in local public school districts. Under most plans, the amount would be much less, although some proposals include the possibility that government-sponsored schools could continue and those, perhaps, would be funded at their current levels (Hendrie, 2004).

Fully funded voucher schemes have consequences for taxpayers and for teachers. If these plans are implemented, the total amount spent by government on education will increase dramatically. In the United States, more than 5 million students are in private schools that charge an average tuition of over $6,600 (U.S. Department of Education, 2008b). Parents of these students do not currently receive any government funds for these tuition expenses. If they did and we continued to provide the amount of aid to education that we do now, even if we did it in the form of vouchers, the extra cost would be over $22 billion per year. Legislators and their constituents would have to support the increases in taxes required to provide such additional money.

If we decided to maintain educational spending at its current level and not increase taxes, then the $22 billion for students in private schools would be subtracted from the amount of money available for students who attend public schools now. So even if those students received vouchers, their checks would not equal the amount their school districts currently receive for their education.

Some proponents of voucher programs would argue that the decrease in available money would not be a problem because the amount of money available through vouchers still would pay the tuition at a private school. They point out that those private schools currently educate students at an average cost half the price of a public school education. Presence of vouchers would cause an increase in the number of such cost-efficient private schools and force government-sponsored schools to scale back their expenses to stay competitive. This argument, however, is problematic. It ignores the fact that private schools have lower expenditures primarily because of the dramatically lower salaries they pay teachers, especially in the religiously affiliated schools. Sectarian schools are the ones whose tuitions most often fall in the "average" range of $5,050. More elite, nonsectarian schools have much higher average tuition— $13,420 (U.S. Department of Education, 2008b). Teachers in religious schools may have faith commitments that motivate them to work for low wages. That is not necessarily the case for others in the profession.

Supporters of vouchers often argue that the competitive nature of the educational system under their plans will create a "seller's" market for teachers. That is, because good teachers will be in demand, they will be able to ask for and receive higher salaries. However, the structures of the plans they support do not seem to guarantee any such consequence. In fact, under most plans, unless parents could supplement their vouchers with additional tuition, private schools could not raise teachers' salaries and public schools would have to lower them or significantly increase student-to-teacher ratios.

Partially funded voucher plans also have financial implications. These plans usually are proposed as alternatives for students in urban schools where the level of academic achievement is below state standards. The families of students in these "underperforming" schools would be given government funds to seek alternative education for their children. In most proposals, these funds would not equal the amount it costs to educate a child in the public schools. The Milwaukee and Cleveland plans are models of this type of program. They were designed to provide educational opportunity for students of low-income families living in those cities. In both cases, the vouchers provided only partial funding—only a part of the amount spent on students who remained in public schools.

In Milwaukee, students receive vouchers worth the cost of their schooling in a private school, with the maximum award being $6,500. Fifty-five percent is paid by the state. The other 45 percent is deducted from aid that would have gone to the Milwaukee public schools. In Milwaukee public schools, the per pupil cost is $11,885. When a student in Milwaukee is awarded a voucher, the state no longer contributes its share of the per pupil cost for that student to the Milwaukee public schools—even if the child would have attended private school without the voucher. That is, Milwaukee public schools lose state aid for students who would never have even attended them. The state also deducts some of the voucher cost from additional aid the district would have received. As a result, Milwaukee property taxpayers faced a significant increase rise in property taxes to make up for the lost state funds. However, overall, in Wisconsin, voucher proponents can accurately say that the program saved taxpayers $24.6 million in 2007. What that figure fails to provide, however, is a detailed explanation of which taxpayers benefit from the voucher system. Wisconsin state taxpayers saved $29.3 million as a result of the plan; property taxpayers who do not live in Milwaukee saved $42.3 million. There was a $40 million negative impact on property taxpayers—that is, homeowners—in the city itself to fund vouchers for children to attend private, mostly religiously affiliated schools (Costrell, 2008). Even with the revenue from increased local property taxes, the Milwaukee Public School District has had to make significant cuts to programs and reductions in staff (Borsuk, 2007; 2007a).

Supporters of the plans are adamant that they cause school districts no real harm because students for whom the aid was intended left the district. Therefore, they argue, the schools incur no expenses for those children. They ignore the fact, however, that public schools' fixed costs remain the same. Buildings still need heat and electricity. School buses still require fuel and maintenance. Decreased funding due to increased spending for private school vouchers will leave districts with less money to pay those bills.

Other Consequences of School Vouchers

Racial Isolation

Supporters of voucher programs argue their plans could increase racial integration in American schools. They argue that because private schools recruit young people from larger geographic areas than public schools, the private institutions, especially those with religious affiliations, have more diverse student populations than public schools. Availability of vouchers will make it possible for more minority parents, disproportionately represented among the poor, to choose private schools. Thus, they conclude, parental choice through voucher programs will result in more integrated schools.

However, research does not support this belief. Studies in the United States as well as other countries indicate that family choice programs, including voucher programs, do not decrease racial segregation. In fact, the data from those studies suggest that the programs lead to less integrated educational settings. (Betts, 2006; Mickelson, Bottia, and Southworth, 2008).

In Milwaukee supporters claimed the voucher plan resulted in more integration in private schools that participate in the program (Fuller and Mitchell, 1999). Ironically, however, the increased racial balance at those schools may have been the result of a form of "white flight." The study's own data showed that the number of minorities in private schools accepting vouchers increased over the life of the program. However, the same data showed the number of white students in those schools decreased even more. So the greater diversity in those private schools may not have been the result of a happy and peaceful process of integration. On the contrary, it could represent a trend toward increasing segregation in schools that previously were more integrated than the public schools (Wolf, 2008).

The possibility that educational choice programs such as vouchers could result in increased racial isolation should not be shocking. After all, some of the first attempts in this country to protect families' rights to choose their children's school occurred during periods of racial unrest. In the Jim Crow era in the South, a dual educational system was developed to support white parents' right to choose not to educate their children side by side with black ones. During the early days of court-ordered desegregation in those same states, white parents created networks of segregated private schools to protect that same right and lobbied state officials to provide financial aid to the new schools. In some situations, they successfully pressured governors and state legislatures to shut down public school systems rather than integrate them, leaving black families with few, if any, educational choices. In the North during periods when urban schools were required to integrate by the courts, white parents attempted to remove their children from public schools and enroll them in nearby Catholic ones. Many bishops in northern cities were forced to issue orders preventing schools under their control from registering such "refugees" from integration. Pressure for public taxpayer aid to parochial schools began to reemerge during this same period.

"Racial animosities and fears provided the soil in which many of the earliest proposals for vouchers and school choice took root. It would be comforting to believe that we have severed our ties to the unflattering past, but it would be naïve as well" (Henig, 1994, p. 114). Supporters of voucher programs rarely suggest, for example, that we maintain the public school system but allow students greater choice among districts. They usually do not advocate that students who attend underperforming urban schools, and for whom they claim to be concerned, should be able to use their vouchers to transfer to successful schools in nearby suburban districts.

Supporters of voucher programs seem able to ignore the way racial and class prejudice would affect the educational "marketplace" they are trying to create. Parents most often measure school quality by the quality of the students. In the minds of many, that "quality" is most often found in white, middle-, and upper-class children (O'Shaunessy, 2007). There is no reason to believe that a single factor such as vouchers will change consumers' perception of what makes a school "good." There will continue to be greater competition for places in schools where the student body's racial and economic makeup matches families' perceptions of what guarantees a quality school (Mickelson, Bottia, and Southworth, 2008). In a voucher school system, owners and administrators would be competing for students and their money. School officials would be pressured to create student bodies that appeal to families' beliefs about what kind of people attend "good" schools. These pressures easily could result in admissions practices limiting the number of students of color, students with special needs, and students with histories of poor academic performance. It would be highly unlikely that such policies would result in more integrated schools. Voucher programs would require parents to be well informed about educational options available for their children. Already privileged families would be better able to investigate possibilities and advocate for their children, putting them in a better position to compete for admission to schools most in demand. There is increasing evidence that a lack of information and social networks limits parents' ability to find public schools that are better than the ones their children attend, even when the law mandates provision for such help (Bernstein, 2006). There is little reason to believe that private schools would do more within a competitive market where the presence of racial diversity is not considered an incentive for choosing a particular school.

Selecting a child's kindergarten or elementary school would come to replicate the current competition for admission to colleges with prestigious reputations. There would be winners and losers, and our experience tells us something about the racial, ethnic, and socioeconomic backgrounds of each. In addition, parents who are members of a minority group often have had experiences of discrimination and bigotry that, in some cases, result in feelings of distrust, disillusion, and resentment toward social institutions perceived as being controlled by majority group members. Those feelings could cause parents to remove their children from the competition to attend prestigious schools. The parents might assume, for example, that their children also would have hurtful experiences in such settings. There is nothing in the voucher plans being proposed by educational free marketeers to diminish these social realities. Consequently, there is no reason to believe those same plans will not maintain or increase current social inequalities and isolation.

Questions of School Accountability

Proponents argue that vouchers will hold schools accountable to the market—that is, to the preferences of parents with children who have more or less power and information depending on their socioeconomic status. However, there are several forms of accountability to which schools receiving public funds must be held. They must be answerable for the academic performance of their students, compliance with laws protecting the rights of all students—including those with disabilities—and ensuring that teachers meet professional standards. Vouchers do not appear to provide the public that pays for them with accountability in those areas (Garn and Cobb, 2008; General Accounting Office, 2007). Another reason to reject voucher plans is because it is almost impossible to construct them in ways that would guarantee private schools were truly accountable to the public from whom they would be receiving their funding. If we regulate publicly funded private schools, we will have to introduce governmental interference in religious schools in a way that has never before happened in the United States. We would be asking those schools to compromise their independence in areas that many members of those communities would see as crucial to their mission. For example, religious schools currently are able to admit on a preferential basis those students whose families are members of the religious organization with which the school is affiliated. They also can decide to use textbooks supporting the beliefs of their faith communities even in subjects other than religion. They can require all students, regardless of their own traditions, to participate in religious instruction and ceremonies. They control their curriculum, teacher hiring, and most other aspects of school operation. It is questionable whether these practices could continue if governmental regulation was a condition of their receiving vouchers. Taxpayers paying the costs of private schools would have a right to hold such schools accountable and responsible. That is done best through government regulation.

All private schools, religious or nonsectarian, would have to rethink their admissions policies under governmental regulation. Currently, such schools can require test scores, written applications, interviews, and recommendations as part of the admissions process. They can set standards for these criteria as well as for prior academic and behavioral performances. Private schools can refuse to admit students who do not meet these standards. Based on that free-dom, private schools are under no obligation to admit or provide services for students with special needs. In addition, private schools currently are able to expel students who fail to follow their policies. Private school deliberations of budget and contracting are private, as are most business items. These rights and privileges are not extended to public schools and, if private schools were to come under governmental regulation, they might lose them as well.

One other difficulty could emerge with voucher programs for schools that are not publicly accountable. Without careful oversight, the enormous amounts of money at stake in voucher plans may tempt unscrupulous people. Even when no dishonesty is intended, private schools, especially new ones, may have very short lives, especially under plans in which vouchers would be worth less than the amounts being spent in public schools. The difficulty of providing qual-ity education at bargain basement prices would be insurmountable in many cases. Schools would go out of business, perhaps in midyear, leaving young people and their families without options. Both situations have happened in Milwaukee (Carr, 2005). Without governmental oversight, vouchers leave the neediest families vulnerable. That is not a responsible choice for parents.

However, requiring governmental oversight of voucher schools would result in increased costs that taxpayers would have to absorb. Ironically, it also would result in an educational bureaucracy even larger than the one voucher proponents believe is already too big. The difficulties in creating a system of accountability for publicly funded private schools make voucher programs unworkable.

Vouchers' Impact on Academic Achievement

Proponents of voucher programs claim that a major benefit will be improved academic achievement. Children who can use vouchers to leave schools where students fail to meet achievement standards will be able to find programs in which they can succeed. If supporters of vouchers could prove vouchers guar-anteed such success, it might make sense to initiate them across the country. However, claims of increased academic achievement are, at best, overblown and at worst, simply untrue.

Thirty years of research on the differences between private and public schools have demonstrated that private school students have a slightly higher average academic achievement than their public school counterparts. However, that same research indicates that most differences between students can be attributed to factors beyond schools' control such as the amount of education a student's parents completed and income levels of the student's family. The fact that public schools are required to take all legitimate students, while private schools can be selective, also makes one wonder about research that compares the academic achievement of private and public school students. The "private school effect," the amount of the difference in achievement between public and private school students that can actually be attributed to attending private school, is very small indeed (Coleman, Hoffer, and Kilgore, 1982; Alexander and Pallas, 1985; Hoffer, 2000). Despite this research, proponents of voucher programs still insist that providing an opportunity for underachieving students to attend private schools will help them reach higher academic standards.

However, research on the two largest voucher programs, those in Milwaukee and Cleveland, continue to demonstrate that attending a private school does not in and of itself guarantee higher academic achievement. Evaluations by researchers under contract to Wisconsin and Ohio have found "little or no difference in voucher and public school students' performances" in Cleveland and Milwaukee (Miron, 2008; Placker et al., 2006). These findings are not surprising in light of the earlier research on comparisons between student achievement in private and public schools. Students in both the public and private schools in the Milwaukee and Cleveland studies live in similar economic situations in the same communities. Factors shown to be most significant are just about the same for each group of students. The "private school effect" is minimal. A researcher in Milwaukee found that making changes in public school settings so the number of students in those classrooms was comparable to the number of students in private school classrooms eliminated the "private school effect" (Rouse, 1998).

There simply is no evidence voucher programs allowing students to attend private schools will improve children's academic performance. Proponents also argue that the competition from high-achieving private "voucher" schools will improve public schools in the same metropolitan areas. However, there is little evidence that market forces have such results (Arnsen and Ni, 2006; Costrell, 2008). Making reforms we know work—such as decreasing class size and implementing curricula proven successful in a variety of settings—will. Voucher supporters may try other arguments to make their case. Increasing academic achievement should not be one of them.

Voucher programs are not good public policy. They threaten to dismantle a system of education that has provided America's children with schools where they could meet people who were different from them, who had other beliefs, languages, customs, and opinions. In the public schools of this country, young people have learned to get along with one another despite those differences. They have become citizens of this democracy.

Voucher programs would cost taxpayers more money than they currently pay for education. In exchange for that increased expense, they would get schools accountable only to their "customers" and vulnerable to dishonest and scheming profiteers. In addition, by all indications, they would get schools that would not increase the academic achievement of the most needy students. We risk losing our public schools—some of the strongest centers of democratic community life—if we allow vouchers to drain them of funds and students. Vouchers would be a very bad bargain indeed for the American public.

For Discussion

1. The Supreme Court has ruled that providing parents with governmental funds to pay for their children's education is constitutional even if they use the money to pay for tuition at a school sponsored by a religious organization. How can you

reconcile that ruling with the constitutional guarantee of the separation of church and state?

2. Sponsors of vouchers have argued that allowing schools to become part of the "free market" competition is the only way to improve the quality of public education in the United States. Do you agree with the idea of allowing market forces to operate on schools? Are there any characteristics of the free market system that would prevent competition among schools from achieving the goal of equality? Does freedom of choice alone guarantee that all consumers have an equal chance in the marketplace? Do other protections need to be in place?

3. Imagine that a voucher program has been created in your state, and you have been asked to create the "accountability" regulations for private schools receiving such payments. Create a set of rules and develop a "white paper" explaining your rationale.

4. Design a proposal for a charter school you'd like to create. Explain the mission of the school, its organizational structure, and the ways it would differ from a traditional public school. Investigate your state and local school district's regulations concerning charter schools and be sure your proposal complies with those rules.

References

Agostini v. Felton. (1997). 522 U.S. 803.

AHMAD, I. AND SZPARA, M. (2003). "Muslim Children in America: The New York City Schools Experience". *Journal of Muslim Minority Affairs*, 23(2): 295–302.

ALEXANDER, K. L., AND PALLAS, A. M. (1985). "School Sector and Cognitive Performance: When is a Little a Little?" *Sociology of Education.* April: 115–128.

APPLE, M., AND BEANE, J. (1995). *Democratic Schools.* Alexandria, VA: ACSD.

ARNSEN, D. AND NI, Y. (2008). "The Competitive Effect of School Choice Policies on Performance in Traditional Public Schools." East Lansing MI: Great Lakes Center for Education Research and Practice. www.greatlakescenter.org/docs/Research/2008charter/policy_briefs/09.pdf

BETTS, J. ET AL. (2006). *Does School Choice Work? Effects on Student Integration and Achievement.* San Francisco: Public Policy Institute of California.

BIRCHARD, K. (2007). "Campuses Should Meet Unmet Needs of Muslim Students, Report Says." *Chronicle of Higher Education,* March 21. http://chronicle.com/news/article/1842/campuses-should-answer-unmet-needs-of-muslim-students-report-says

BLACK ALLIANCE FOR EDUCATIONAL OPTIONS. (2008) (http://www.baeo.org/)

Boy Scouts of America v. Dale. (2000). 530 U.S. 640.

BORSUK, A., "MPS Budget Forecast Grim; Closings Possible As Principals Cope With Dwindling Resources." *Milwaukee Journal Sentinel*, Dec. 27, 2007.

———. "Next year, MPS budget just grows tougher; More cuts, another tax increase loom for schools." *Milwaukee Journal Sentinel*, Nov. 14, 2007.

BRADY, E., "For Muslim Students A Drive to Deem Holy Days as Holidays." *New York Times*, April 29, 2007.

BROUGHMAN, S.P., AND SWAIM, N.L. (2006). *Characteristics of Private Schools in the United States: Results From the 2003–2004 Private School Universe Survey* (NCES 2006–319). U.S. Department of Education. Washington, DC: National Center for Education Statistics.

BROWNSTEIN, R. (2003). "Locked Down." *Education Next*, 3(3), 40–46.

CANADIAN FEDERATION OF STUDENTS. (2007). "Final Report of the Task Force on Needs of Muslim Students." Toronto: Canadian Federation of Students. www.cfsontario.ca/mediareleaselinks/TaskForce-Final.Report.pdf

CARR, S., "State Seeks Fraud Inquiry into Two Voucher Schools." *Milwaukee Journal Sentinel*, Feb. 11, 2005.

CENTER FOR EDUCATIONAL REFORM. (2008). "Charter Connection: Working together for the Community." www.edreform.com/parentpower/charter_schools/mountain_view.htm.

———. (2005). "Nine Lies About School Choice: Proving the Critics Wrong". www.edreform.com/index.cfm?fuseAction=document&documentID=825

CHILDREN'S SCHOLARSHIP FUND. (2008). "About CSF: Facts." www.scholarshipfund.org/index.asp

COLEMAN, J., HOFFER, T., AND KILGORE, S. (1982). *High School Achievement*. New York: Basic Books.

COSTRELL, R. (2008). *The Fiscal Impact of the Milwaukee Parental Choice Program in Milwaukee and Wisconsin, 1993–2008.* Fayetteville, Arkansas: School Choice Demonstration Project, University of Arkansas.

DEWEY, J. (1916). *Democracy and Education.* New York: Macmillan.

ENROW, R. (2008). "Grading School Choice: Evaluating Choice Programs by the Friedman Gold Standard." Indianapolis: The Friedman Foundation for Educational Choice.

FORSTER, G. (2008). "Lost Opportunity: An Empirical Analysis of How Vouchers Affected Florida Public Schools." Indianapolis: The Friedman Foundation for Educational Choice.

———. (2006). "Segregation Levels in Cleveland Public Schools and the Cleveland Voucher Program." Indianapolis: The Friedman Foundation for Educational Choice.

GARN, G. AND COBB, C. (2008). "School Choice and Accountability." East Lansing MI: Great Lakes Center for Education Research and Practice. www.greatlakescenter.org/docs/Research/2008charter/policy_briefs/04.pdf

GENERAL ACCOUNTING OFFICE (2007). District of Columbia Opportunity Scholarship Program Additional Policies and Procedures Would Improve Internal Controls and Program Operations. Washington, D.C.: General Accounting Office. www.gao.gov/new.items/d089.pdf.

GOOD, T., AND BRADEN, J. (2000). *The Great School Debate: Choice, Vouchers and Charters.* Mahwah, NJ: Lawrence Erlbaum.

GREENE, J. AND WINTERS, M. (2006). "An Evaluation of the Effect of D.C.'s Voucher Program on Public School Achievement and Racial Integration After One Year." Manhattan Institute Working Papers, No. 10, SCDP-06-01. www.manhattan-institute.org/html/ewp_10.htm

HARRISON, M. (2005). "Public Problems, Private Solutions: School Choice And Its Consequences." *CATO Journal*, 25(2) 197–216.

HENDRIE, C. (2004). "*Friedmans'* Foundation Rates Voucher Plans." *Education Week*, 23(27), March 17.

HENIG, J. (1994). *Rethinking School Choices: Limits of the Market Metaphor.* Princeton: Princeton University Press.

HOFFER, T. (2000). "Catholic School Attendance and Student Achievement: A Review and Extension of the Research," In *Catholic Schools at the Crossroads*, eds, J. Youniss and J. Convey, New York: Teachers College Press.

Hurley v. Irish American Gay, Lesbian, Bisexual Group of Boston. (1995). 515 U.S. 557.

KEWALRAMANI, A., GILBERTSON, L., FOX, M., AND PROVASNIK, S. (2007). *Status and Trends in the Education of Racial and Ethnic Minorities* (NCES 2007-039). National Center for Education Statistics, Institute of Education Sciences, U.S. Department of Education. Washington, DC.

KOZOL, J. (2007). "The Single Worst, Most Dangerous Idea" [Excerpted from Letters to a young teacher]. *Principal* 87(1): 56–59.

KROW, L. (2008). "Learning Curve." *JTNews. Net.* February 8. www.jtnews.net/index .php?/news/item/3949/C22/

LEWIN, N. (1999). "Are Vouchers Constitutional?" *Policy Review.* Heritage Foundation. Jan.–Feb., no. 93. (www.heritage.org/policyreview/jan99/lewin.html)

LINDSEY, D. (2000). "Vouchers and the Law." *Salon.* March 27. (www.salon.com/new/ feature/2000/03/27/vouchers)

LIPS, D. (2007). "Reforming No Child Left Behind by Allowing States to Opt Out: An A-PLUS for Federalism." *Backgrounder.* Washington DC: Heritage Foundation.

MACFARQUHAR, N., "Many Muslims Turn to Home Schooling." *New York Times,* March 26, 2008.

MANZI, J. (2008) "A More Equal Capitalism." *National Review,* February 25: 40–43.

MCDONALD, D. (2008). "United States Catholic Elementary and Secondary Schools 2006–2007: The Annual Statistical Report on Schools, Enrollment and Staffing." Washington, D. C.: National Catholic Education Association. www.ncea.org/news/AnnualDataReport.asp#tuition

MICHOS, L AND AUD, S. (2006). *Spreading Freedom and Saving Money: The Fiscal Impact of the D.C. Voucher Program.* Washington, DC: Cato Institute.

MICKELSON, R., BOTTIA, M, AND SOUTHWORTH, S. (2008). "School Choice and Segregation by Race, Class, and Achievement." East Lansing MI: Great Lakes Center for Education Research and Practice. www.greatlakescenter.org/docs/Research/2008charter/policy_ briefs/08.pdf.

MIRON, G., EVERGREEN, S. AND URSCHEL, S. (2008) "The Impact of School Choice Reforms on Student Achievement." East Lansing MI: Great Lakes Center for Education Research and Practice. www.greatlakescenter.org/docs/Research/2008charter/policy_briefs/10.pdf.

MOGRA, I. (2007). "Moral Education in the Makatib of Britain: A Review of Curriculum Materials." *Journal of Moral Education,* 36(3): 387–398.

Mueller v. Allen. (1983). 463 U.S. 388.

NATIONAL ASSOCIATION OF INDEPENDENT SCHOOLS. (2008). NAIS Facts at a Glance. www .nais.org/resources/statistical.cfm?ItemNumber=14671.

O'SHAUNESSY, T. (2007). "Parental Choice and School Quality when Peer and Scale Effects Matter." *Economics of Education Review,* 26(4): 501–515.

PATERSON, F. (2000). "Building a Conservative Base: Teaching History and Civics in Voucher-Supported Schools." *Phi Delta Kappan.* Oct: 150–155.

PEOPLE FOR THE AMERICAN WAY FOUNDATION. (2005). "Flaws and Failings: A Preliminary Look at the Problems Already Encountered in the Implementation of the District of Columbia's Federally Mandated School Voucher Program." www.pfaw.org.

PLACKER, J. ET AL (2006). *Evaluation of the Cleveland Scholarship and Tutoring Program 1998–2004.* Bloomington, IN: Center for Education Evaluation and Policy. http:// ceep.indiana.edu/projects/PDF/200602_Clev_Tech_Final.pdf.

READ, T. (2008). "Exploring Quality Choices: Vouchers." *Closing the Achievement Gap: A Series of Stories, Results, and Lessons Learned from Seven Years of Investing by the Annie C. Casey Foundation. http://www.aecf.org/KnowledgeCenter/Publications.aspx?pubguid ={B60E9AE0-5F6B-48CA-B0A5-732413FD287B.*

Roberts v. United States Jaycees. (1984). 468 U.S. 609.

ROSE, L., AND GALLUP, A. (2007). "The 39th Annual Phi Delta Kappan/Gallup Poll of the Public's Attitudes Toward the Public Schools." *Phi Delta Kappan,* 89(1): 33–49.

ROUSE, C. (1998). "Private School Vouchers and Student Achievement: An Evaluation of the Milwaukee Parental Choice Program." *Quarterly Journal of Economics.* May: 553–602.

SALISBURY, D. (2003). "Lesson from Florida." Cato Institute Briefing Papers, No. 81. March 20.

SHAW, L., "Parents Taking Issue with Forfeits When Boys Don't Join Girls on Mat." *Seattle Times,* May 7, 2005.

SLATER, J. (2005). "Christian Schools Fail Test of Tolerance." *Times Educational Supplement,* 4618, Jan, 21; p.1.

STROM, R. (2005). "Presbyterians: Pull Kids From Public Schools." *World Net Daily,* June 15 www.worldnetdaily.com/news/article.asp?ARTICLE_ID=44770.

U.S. CHARTER SCHOOLS. (2008). "Overview." www.uscharterschools.org/pub/uscs_docs/o/index.htm.

U.S. DEPARTMENT OF EDUCATION. (2003). The Conditions of Education, 2003." Washington, DC: National Center for Education Statistics. www.nces.ed.gov.

———. (2004). *America's Charter Schools: Results from the NAEP 2003 Pilot Study.* (NCES 2005–456). Washington, DC: National Center for Educational Statistics. www .nces.ed.gov.

———. *(2005). NAEP 2004 Trends in Academic Progress: Three Decades of Student Performance in Reading and Mathematics: Findings in Brief* (NCES 2005–463). Washington, DC: National Center for Education Statistics. www.nces.ed.gov.

———. (2007). *A Brief Profile of America's Private Schools.* Washington, DC: National Center for Educational Statistics. www.nces.ed.gov.

———. (2007a) *Education Options in the States: State Programs That Provide Financial Assistance for Attendance at Private Elementary or Secondary Schools.* Washington, DC: Office of Innovation and Improvement. http://www.ed.gov/parents/schools/choice/educationoptions/educationoptions.pdf.

———. (2008). "Choices for Parents." http://www.ed.gov/nclb/choice/index.html.

———. (2008a) "Number and Types of Open Enrollment Policies," Washington, DC: National Center for Educational Statistics. http://nces.ed.gov/progrms/statereform/ssco_tab1.asp.

———. (2008b). *Digest of Education Statistics 2007.* Washington, DC: National Center for Educational Statistics. http://nces.ed.gov/programs/digest/d07/index.asp.

———. (2008c). "Private School Questionnaire," 1999–2000. Washington, DC: National Center for Educational Statistics. www.nces.gov.

WASHINGTON SCHOLARSHIP FUND. (2007). "D.C. School Choice Program Again Sets Record for Enrolled K-12 Students." www.washingtonscholarshipfund.org/news/news/pr_09_26_07.html.

WITTE, J. , WOLF, P., COWEN, J., FLEMING, D., LUCAS-McLEAN, J. (2008). *MPCP Longitudinal Growth Study: Baseline Report.* Fayetteville, Arkansas: School Choice Demonstration Project, University of Arkansas.

Witters v. Washington Department of Services for the Blind. (1986). 474 U.S. 481.

WOLF, P. (2008). *The Comprehensive Longitudinal Evaluation of the Milwaukee Parental Choice Program: Summary of Baseline Reports.* Fayetteville, Arkansas: School Choice Demonstration Project, University of Arkansas.

WOLF, P. ET AL (2007). *Evaluation of DC Opportunity Scholarship Program: Impacts after One Year.* Washington DC: U.S. Department of Education.

Zelman v. Doris Simmons-Harris. (2002). 536 U.S. 639.

ZINE, J. (2007). "Safe Havens or Religious Ghettos? Narratives of Islamic Schooling in Canada." *Race, Ethnicity, and Education.* 10 (1): 71–92,

Zobrest v. Catalina Foothills School District. (1993). 509 U.S. 1.

CHAPTER 3

Financing Schools: Equity or Disparity

Is it desirable to equalize educational spending among school districts within a state or across the nation?

POSITION 1: FOR JUSTICE IN EDUCATIONAL FINANCE

At every level of government, policymakers give more resources to students who have more resources, and less to those who have less. These funding disparities accumulate as they cascade through layers of government, with the end result being massive disparities between otherwise similar schools.

—Carey and Roza, 2008, p. 1.

Some Consequences of Inequitable School Funding

In 1991, Jonathan Kozol described the "savage inequalities" American children faced in public school. Ten years later, activists around the country were still uncovering similar conditions (Oakes, 2002; Campaign for Fiscal Equity, 2001). Almost twenty years later, differences among schools within a state or among schools within a district remain because of how we finance public education and allocate those funds (Roza, Guin, Gross, and DeBurgomaster, 2007). The shocking disparities among school facilities and resources constitute unequal educational opportunities for our young people. The differences among schools within a state or even a district result from the way we finance public education in the United States since a fundamental injustice is built into that system. (Carey and Roza, 2008).

The conditions of underfunded schools make the best argument for why changes in school financing were and remain necessary. For the most part, those children in the United States whom fate has placed in middle- or upper-class families attend schools that are well equipped, safe, and clean. They have science labs and the necessary supplies for conducting experiments. They have access to up-to-date technology, which often is housed in libraries stocked with reference materials. Their textbooks are relatively new and, more importantly, each student has one. The schools of the "lucky" have art rooms and gyms, pools and playing fields, auditoriums and music rooms. When these districts spend money to improve facilities, the funds go to improvements—such as new science labs or computer equipment—intended to enhance learning directly (Greifner, 2006).

In the urban schools that many children from poor families attend, conditions are dramatically different. Principals of the schools report that 20 percent of those schools are overcrowded—37 percent when 50 percent or more receive free or reduced lunches. Forty-three percent of those schools hold classes in temporary buildings; 63 percent have no science lab; 50 percent, no art room; 35 percent, no music room; and 33 percent, no gym (Chaney and Lewis, 2007).

In many states, these differences in facilities are directly attributable to the dollars spent on each pupil. In New York State, for example, the wealthiest districts spend almost $15,000 per student; New York City spends approximately two-thirds as much and the poorest districts spend a little more than half of what the richest districts do (New York State Department of Education, 2008). Similar differences are found across the country. It is no small wonder that students experiences vary so widely. Teachers' salaries are significantly lower in the poorer districts, resulting in fewer experienced teachers, more teachers who are temporarily certified, and greater teacher turnover (Carey and Roza, 2008).

Student achievement varies among the districts and is correlated with pupils' need level and amount of money spent on their education. Twice as many students in low-need, highly funded districts score at the highest levels on fourth-grade state exams as in New York City. The ratio was the same for achieving passing grades on the first-level high school mathematics exam (New York State Department of Education, 2008b). High school graduation rates were also significantly lower. Although many factors may have contributed to the students' achievement levels, surely the correlation between low spending and low test scores is hard to ignore.

Causes of Inequitable School Funding

The Property Tax

U.S. public schools have long been a beacon of hope for the residents of this country. From the early 1800s, education offered the promise of social mobility. Schooling would help to equalize opportunities for all young people to better their lot in life. When reformers encouraged taxpayers to accept the responsibility of paying for schools, they promised that by doing so they would be providing young people with the chance to increase their own wealth and that of the nation as a whole. Tax dollars spent on schools would help to eliminate the potential for conflict between rich and poor by decreasing the numbers of the poor. Horace Mann expressed the belief this way: "Education, then, beyond all other devices of human origin, is the great equalizer of the conditions of men—the balance-wheel of the social machinery" (Mann, quoted in Cremin, 1957, p. 87).

Although many Americans came to believe that education should not be a luxury only the wealthy could afford, they worried about how publicly funded schools would be controlled. As compromises built into the Constitution suggest, having secured their independence from England, Americans in the early Republican period wanted to limit the power of centralized governments. In establishing public schools, they did not want local communities to lose control over what children would learn and who would teach them. States authorized local governments to impose property taxes on their citizens and to use those funds for the support of schools. Because these revenues came from local communities, rather than state or federal governments, primary control of schools remained with municipalities themselves. Through elected boards of education, the community maintained control of curriculum, hiring of teachers, and allocation of funding. Despite the growing oversight of schools by state agencies and centralization of teacher preparation and, sometimes, curriculum, nineteenth-century Americans were reassured local funding guaranteed that ultimate control of their schools would remain in their hands (Tyack, 1974; Katz, 1975; Urban and Wagoner, 2000).

The system remained in place, essentially unchanged, until the 1930s. When a local school district ran out of money, they had nowhere to turn for help. Most often they closed their doors until additional revenues were available. During the Depression, cities, towns, and villages faced tremendous financial difficulties. School districts across the country had trouble meeting payrolls and maintaining their buildings. Many states were able to provide assistance through their income and sales tax collections (Mackey, 1998). State-level financial contributions more than doubled for public education between 1930 and 1950, finally averaging approximately 40 percent of school budgets (Mackey, 1998). That percentage has continued to increase slowly. Nationally, states contribute almost half of school districts' revenue. Local funding is slightly less than half. A small contribution from federal tax dollars (roughly 7 percent) makes up the remainder (Zhou, 2008).

So if states are providing almost half of school districts' resources, why do disparities among districts still exist? Can't states provide enough money to equalize the resources available to each child regardless of his or her parents' income? To a certain extent states' contribution to school funding has helped lessen the differences among schools (Arroyo, 2008; Glenn and Picus, 2007). However, continued reliance on local property taxes to fund almost half of a district's budget still leads to large disparities in the amount of money available to educate students. Here's how it happens.

A local school district is authorized to levy property taxes and, through their votes, citizens have some voice in the rate at which they will be taxed. Let's imagine two districts—one urban and one suburban—that adopt the same property tax rate of 2 percent. In the suburban community, District A, the total value of property that can be taxed averages out to be $250,000 per child enrolled in the district's schools. In the inner-city community, District B, the property tax base is $50,000 per pupil. When taxpayers in each community pay the same rate, 2 percent, District A raises $5,000 to spend on each student in its schools. District B raises only $1,000. To achieve equality with District A in the amount they could spend on their children's education, taxpayers in District B would have to agree to a tax rate of 10 percent. When you consider that most taxpayers in District B have dramatically lower incomes than those in District A, you can see how much of a hardship such a high tax rate would be. People who already are poor would be forced to pay a much higher percentage of their income to fund their schools than their wealthier neighbors do. The higher rates of taxes in District B would make it less attractive to homeowners and business owners.

Despite the sacrifices involved in creating such higher tax rates, that is what many urban and rural school districts have been forced to do. However, political and economic realities put a ceiling on how much they could raise the tax rate and how much of the funds could be allocated to school expenses. As a result, even though residents of those communities pay a higher share of their income to fund their schools, they never raise enough money to equal resources available to schools in wealthier communities (Noguera, 2004). This pattern creates fundamental inequalities of educational opportunity in the United States, and in those states that rely most heavily on property taxes for educational funding the disparity between revenues available for students in high- and low-poverty schools is the greatest (Arroyo, 2008).

Limited Federal Role in School Finance

Although most Americans believe that public schools in the United States are well funded, the country actually ranks fifth in average expenditure per student among the thirty most democratic, market-based countries. Despite complaints about how much is spent on schools, Americans spent only 12 percent of the country's Gross National Product on K–12 education—22nd among the thirty OECD nations. "Ironically, but predictably, this measure appears to closely track the rank of the United States in test scores when compared with other OECD countries. Thus, one can argue with some confidence that within the realm of education the people of the United States get about what they pay for. Alongside the international test scores that rank the United States low among the thirty OECD countries, we also find a nation with low fiscal effort" (Alexander and Salmon, 2007, p. 220).

In most other nations, the national government—not the state, province, or town—provides most school funding; the U.S. federal government provides less than 10 percent (Organisation for Economic Cooperation and Development, 2007). As a result, students depend on state and local governments to pay for their schools. Even when adjusted for differences in the cost of living among the states, real disparities among available funds for schools remain. States like New Jersey, New York, Connecticut, and Rhode Island spend two or three times as much per student as do Utah, Mississippi, Louisiana, and Tennessee (Zhou, 2008).

Many of the federal school funding programs, such as Title I—a provision of No Child Left Behind—were originally designed to subsidize states' efforts to provide equal opportunity for the country's poorest students. However, since its inception in 1965, Title I has been inadequately funded. In every year since 2002, when No Child Left Behind was passed, the actual appropriation for Title I funding has been less than the level authorized by the original bill—that is, the amount determined to be necessary to meet the mandates of the bill (Rendell, 2005).

"Currently, the U.S. Department of Education appropriates Title I funds by multiplying the state average per-pupil expenditure by only 40 percent of children in each county over five years old living below the federal poverty guidelines. This means that only 40 percent of extremely poor children in each county are considered for funding, and districts do not receive that entire amount" (Brown, 2007). So if a district chooses to serve all the children living in poor families, it faces a challenge—how to utilize inadequate funding equitably and effectively. The task is even more complicated due to new regulations that are designed to advance other political agendas, such as requiring districts to set aside some of their Title I funds for transportation to charter and private schools. In addition, 4 to 7 percent must be used for professional development, after school and summer school programs, incentives for parent involvement, and aid to private schools (Brown, 2007). Furthermore, a "hold harmless" clause in No Child Left Behind prevents schools from losing Title I funds even when their low-income population decreases. This clause intersects with the requirement that 4 percent of Title I funds are set aside to improve "failing" schools—often those with the fewest material resources and least experienced teachers, but with the most students living in poverty. Since the "hold harmless" clause means districts cannot lose Title I funding, the money for failing schools comes by withholding increases that schools with increases in the number of poor children should receive. Thus, the lowest-performing schools do not receive the funds that they need to improve student performance.

Other provisions of No Child Left Behind have constituted unfunded mandates from the federal government. States and school districts have been required to develop and revise curriculum; develop, administer, and score standardized tests; provide professional development and increased staff to schools where students do not perform well on tests; provide additional supports, such as tutoring or summer school, for students in those schools; and recruit and retain teachers who have qualifications prescribed by the bill. However, the federal government has failed to provide states and districts with the money they need to complete those tasks—and states and districts have had to draw on their own resources to comply. Increasing and redirecting federal funds for K–12 education is necessary to ensure equity in the resources available to all American students. ". . . Kids do not go to school in America to be the citizens of Sacramento or Albany or Boston. They don't go to school to be citizens of California or North Dakota either. They go to school to be citizens of the United States. . . . All the money spent for public education in America ought to come from federal taxes that are equitably distributed with adjustments only for greater or lesser costs of living in various sections of the nation and the greater educational needs of certain children" (Kozol, 2006).

Legal Challenges to Inequitable School Financing

Since 2000, court cases in at least thirty-six states challenged school funding inequities. These changes, however, did not come easily. In some states there was vociferous and politically powerful opposition to them.

In New Jersey, for example, the state fought the court's decision for more than twenty years. Parents, school staff, and elected officials from wealthier districts mounted vigorous campaigns against implementation of the court's order to equalize spending in public schools.

> [There was] stubborn, hard-bitten opposition to distributing public resources equitably. Many individuals and groups fought publicly and zealously to continue to use the public schools and the public purse to maintain advantages for wealthy white communities, families and children at the expense of poor nonwhite communities, families and children. . . . Many of the participants felt no sense of shame as they argued to maintain an inherently unequal system of public education in which public money was used to confer private privilege to students in their well-appointed suburban schools while basic health and safety standards were routinely violated in their underfinanced urban counterparts. (Firestone, Goertz, and Natriello, 1997, p. 159)

This opposition should not have been unexpected. The authors of a comprehensive report on financing American schools found that conflicts involved in providing equity in school financing are rooted in competing values.

> Most Americans believe in equality of opportunity, but they also believe in the right of parents to choose to spend their money for the benefit of their own children. Most Americans believe that every child has a right to a good education in a publicly funded common school but they also believe in freedom of mobility in a way that allows affluent Americans to live together in locales able to easily support good schools and that tends to concentrate poverty and disadvantage, often in urban areas. . . . None of these commitments is unworthy and each has a claim for attention. But given these conflicting values, no model of either the finance system or of the education system as a whole could ever be consistent with all of them. (Ladd and Hansen, 1999, p. 264)

This opposition did not take place in political isolation. In the last thirty years in their unyielding pursuit of less governmental involvement in our lives, conservative politicians and their supporters have shifted the balance of power in such conflicts in favor of the rights of individuals and away from the common good. For example, in the last three decades, many Americans came to resent efforts made by the government to achieve equality of opportunity for all citizens. They believed these efforts unfairly penalized hardworking people who have achieved a measure of success through their own labor and sacrifice. They believed these governmental attempts to create a just society were fundamentally unfair and rewarded those who had not worked as hard as they did and who had come to expect handouts. They believed their tax dollars were "theirs" and did not belong to the community at large. They expected returns on those payments that directly benefited them and their families.

This attitude played out in a special way with regard to property taxes. Connected as they are to the value of the homes they have struggled to provide for their families, property taxes represent, for many people, an investment in their children's future. They believe they should be used for their own school districts and not applied to those of children whose parents are unwilling to support education in their locality.

Those who adopt the "me-first" attitude justify it by making claims about their own success that are not completely accurate. They attribute their achievements only to hard work and ignore advantages race and socioeconomic status of their own parents may have given them. Consciously or unconsciously they appear to want to maintain advantages with which their children come into the world, even if doing so means other children are seriously disadvantaged. Correct or not, however, these attitudes are translated into powerful political forces when citizens who hold them exercise their right to vote. They result in opposition to proposals that school funding be centralized at the state or federal level.

The genius of the American system of government, however, helps us work through these conflicts of values in unique ways. The system of checks and balances built into our political system protects us from impulses to sacrifice our commitment to equality in the name of individual freedom. In the case of school financing, the courts have provided the much-needed check to legislative and executive policies that unfairly limit the educational opportunity and achievement of poor and/or minority students. By holding states accountable to their constitutional obligations to provide adequate schooling for all their children, the courts ensure that the Fourteenth Amendment, providing equal protection under the law for all citizens, is safeguarded even from understandable desires of loving parents to care first and foremost for their own children.

"Adequacy" and School Funding

The earliest school funding equity case established *fiscal neutrality* as the litmus test for the constitutionality of school financing in various states (*Serrano v. Priest*, 1971). States were ordered to reduce disparities among districts by providing low-wealth communities with additional funds or tax relief, as long as the municipality made a good-faith effort to contribute to schools. It was a fairly straightforward, dollar-for-dollar equality; it was easily measured, if not so easily achieved. However, other court decisions have pointed us toward more complex, and ultimately more just, definitions of equity when the term is applied to school funding.

Later cases changed the criteria from *fiscal neutrality* to *adequacy*. State constitutions guarantee the right to "thorough and efficient," "sound, basic," or "suitable" public education systems (Campaign for Fiscal Equity, 2001; Imber, 2004). "When a service is constitutionally mandated, it becomes the duty, not the prerogative of the legislature to provide that service and the job of the judiciary to ensure that the service is being provided in a constitutionally acceptable manner" (Imber, 2004, p. 46). Lawsuits that challenge the way schools are financed have been filed in forty-five states (Access Quality Education, 2008). Courts are ruling that states are required to provide enough resources to their school districts to ensure the children under their care receive an education "adequate" to fulfill their constitutional mandate.

The shift from fiscal equity to adequacy has gotten a push from the national movement to raise educational standards. The No Child Left Behind Act of 2001 laid out ambitious goals and held states and districts accountable for meeting them. As a result, thirty states have had adequacy studies conducted to define what constitutes an acceptable level of academic achievement for their students, determine what resources are needed to see each child meets those standards, and then to create funding formulas providing those resources to every student in the state (Rebell, 2007).

A consensus definition of what constitutes an "adequate" education has emerged from state court rulings: "The preparation of students to function productively as capable voters, jurors, and citizens of a democratic society and to be able to compete effectively in the economy" (Rebell, 2008a, p. 432). To be effective citizens and workers students need literacy and oral fluency in English; mathematical and scientific knowledge; fundamental understanding of geography, history, and political and economic systems; critical thinking skills; social and communication skills; and sufficient intellectual or vocational skills to move forward in educational or employment settings. To develop such knowledge and skills schools need teachers and administrators qualified to provide academic instruction and to create a safe and orderly learning environment; adequate school facilities; appropriate class sizes; supplemental and remedial programs for students from high-poverty backgrounds, students with disabilities, and English language learners; and resources such as textbooks, libraries, laboratories, and computers (Rebell, 2008a). However, the cost of providing an "adequate" education varies, depending on the needs of students and the historic, social, and political contexts that have shaped their schools. Schools and districts whose populations include more poor, disabled, or non-English speaking students require more financial resources to achieve the same results as their wealthier, non-disabled, and English-speaking peers. Translating those differences in need into funding formulas is called "costing-out."

A variety of costing-out methods have been used around the country. Some states have relied on the judgment of experienced educators; some, on educational researchers. Others have built on the analysis of the resources that successful school districts have and determine how much it would cost to replicate those resources in less-successful schools. The most successful processes of determining adequacy in school funding—those that are approved by the courts—appear to share some characteristics, regardless of the specific method they use. These characteristics are carefully articulated outcomes or goals; rigorous attention to the needs of poor, disabled, and non-English speaking students; minimizing the political manipulation of the process; and a high degree of openness and public engagement in the process (Rebell, 2007). Whatever process is used, once a state has determined the basic cost of providing a sound education, it can guarantee every student that amount of funding and then provide additional resources to those districts that serve large numbers of poor, disabled, or non-English-speaking students.

Adequacy litigation has had significant success in reducing inequity in school financing in Alaska, Arkansas, Connecticut, Maryland, Minnesota, New Jersey, New Mexico, New York, Ohio, and Wyoming. However, sixteen states still spend less per student in districts with high populations of students receiving free and reduced lunches; twenty-one spend less per student in districts with high populations of students of color; and in the eight states where more than 10 percent of the students are English language learners, five spent less per student in districts with high concentrations of those students (Arroyo, 2008).

Centralizing School Funding

Money does matter when it comes to education. Despite early studies emphasizing the influence of nonschool factors, such as family background and neighborhood environment (Coleman, 1966; Hanushek, 1996), growing evidence shows student achievement is affected by the amount of money schools spend on their education (Bray, 2003). If schools have enough financial resources to create small classes, employ experienced and well-educated teachers, provide ongoing professional development for those teachers, buy enough textbooks and other curricular materials, repair and maintain their buildings, then student achievement is positively affected (Barth and Nitta, 2008; Bray, 2003; Rebell, 2008b).

A commitment to providing high-standard adequacy in education means all schools have those resources. It is clear that differences in local communities' abilities to raise revenue through property taxes means that overreliance on mixed funding streams for schools will always result in unfair disparities among schools. The courts have attempted to remedy the injustice by creating new obligations for the states to ensure that all districts within their borders have the income to provide adequate education for all. However, these remedies can not fully correct the problem. What is needed instead is a radical rethinking of school funding.

Instead of dividing the fiscal responsibility for schools between the state and local governments, equality would be better served if the states had access to all tax dollars collected to support education and could distribute them "unequally." That is, if the amount of money currently being collected through property taxes could go to the state instead of to local governments, then each district—and each school—could receive the amount of money it had been determined was needed to provide "adequate" education for its children. Districts with more educationally needy students—English-language learners, young people with disabilities, or children living in poverty—would receive higher per-pupil allotments. Providing schools with resources that were matched to the needs of their students would, for the first time in American history, really ensure that the conditions of a child's birth did not determine his or her opportunities.

Of course adequate oversight by federal, state, and local government is needed to ensure resources are being spent appropriately and honestly; such accountability is difficult, but not impossible to achieve, and the requirements of No Child Left Behind are pressuring states to create such systems. Convincing residents of affluent communities to support state based systems of school funding will not be easy. Their resistance could be overcome, however, if states collected revenue for schools in ways that could be perceived as equitable—such as sales, use or income taxes, or revenue from recreation activities such as lotteries or casinos. Currently, few legislators had the courage to propose such radical reform. However, less dramatic changes have been suggested or enacted across the country (Raffaele, 2008; Schencker, 2008; Sigo, 2008; Walton, 2008). The limitations of these proposals has become apparent, however. When states and municipalities share the cost of schools, one party may back out of an agreement, claiming that their revenue did not match projections on which the settlement was based. When that happens, as it has recently in New York State, students lose resources they need to learn while a long, intractable political argument takes place. If there were only one government body responsible for school funding, voters would be better able to hold their leaders accountable and ensure that all students were adequately and justly served. Equity in school finance is a matter of justice. The courts have ruled that all children in this country have constitutionally guaranteed rights to equal treatment. Clearly, they are currently not receiving that protection under the present system of paying for schools. Issues of individual freedom, local control, and overinvolvement by government in our daily lives certainly deserve consideration. They do not, however, automatically outweigh the rights of all children to receive an education that will empower them to be competent to take up their duties as citizens, members of society, and workers. Centralizing the funding for public schools will ensure that all children in a state have the resources they need to meet its learning standards, regardless of where they live or their families' socioeconomic status. Every other educational funding formula is designed to maintain the privilege of wealthier families at the expense of the rights of less affluent ones.

POSITION 2: AGAINST CENTRALIZATION IN EDUCATIONAL FINANCING

The hitch is that in most states . . . funds come with strings attached. As states have funded public education, state lawmakers have used their funding formulas to exert their own influence on what is purchased and how resources are deployed within districts.

—Timar and Roza, 2008

Those suggesting we centralize funding for American public schools in an attempt to ensure equal opportunity for children are well meaning but misguided. They demonstrate a concern for justice for some but almost completely ignore the rights of others. In the concern to provide what they call equal educational opportunity for children, they forget to consider taxpayers' freedom to exercise the maximum possible control over the use of their money. They deny those footing the bill the opportunity to see their funds are spent efficiently, wisely, and honestly; they ignore strong reasons for allowing parents and other taxpayers to support their own children's schools to the full extent of their ability; and they dismiss strong arguments in favor of supporting academic achievement for more able students who will be able to make significant returns on public funds spent on their education.

The Missing Connection between School Finances and Academic Achievement

Those who support centralized educational funding schemes believe we should allow federal or state governments to collect taxes and distribute them equally among all school districts. In doing so, they say, we will provide schools in poorer districts with needed resources to help students improve their academic performance. It sounds as if the plan has possibilities for addressing the persistent problem of underachievement by students from low socioeconomic backgrounds. It would if a link could be made between a school's material resources and its students' academic achievement. However, in over four decades, scholars have been unable to demonstrate conclusively that such a link exists.

The first of these research efforts, the famous "Coleman study," took place in the mid-1960s. It was the era of President Johnson's War on Poverty, and many Americans were convinced schools could be a primary tool in winning that battle. James Coleman and his colleagues conducted a large-scale national survey of thousands of schools. They calculated the resources they assumed would be connected to student achievement—teacher education and experience, number of books in the library, laboratory equipment, and so on. In other words, they counted the things money can buy. The results were surprising, even to them. They concluded that a school's material resources had little effect on student achievement. Instead they found that "family background differences account for much more variance in achievements than do school differences" (Coleman, 1966, p. 73). Other researchers have reached the same conclusion. "There is no strong system relationship between school expenditures and student performance" (Hanushek, 1989, p. 46). Those researchers who claimed their studies indicated that a few factors related to funding do affect school performance could not definitively show that providing more resources to schools serving children from poor or uncaring family backgrounds improved those children's academic achievement (Hedges, Laine, and Greenwald, 1994). Even recent experiments in increased school funding have not conclusively defined the relationship between money and student success (Costrell, Hanushek, and Loeb, 2008).

Many factors other than financial resources affect students' academic achievement. Students who grow up with no educated role models often are unable to see school success as a real possibility. At least one study indicated that young people who are members of minority groups actually have rejected school success, believing that to achieve good grades they would have to "act white." They decided that the price of separating themselves from their poor communities, troubled parents, or indifferent peers was too high in return for the chance to participate more fully in a capitalist system (Fordham and Ogbu, 1986). Adding resources to such students' schools will not necessarily result in academic achievement. All the money in the world cannot resolve their ambivalence about academic success; that is up to them and their families (Wilson, 2003; Ogbu, 2003).

Even when poor parents want their children to succeed in school and encourage them to do so, their efforts will fall short. Mothers and fathers living in poverty are not able to prepare young people for challenges they will face in schools. They do not have the money to buy them books or computers; they cannot take them to museums or concerts. They have so many other problems and demands on their time that they cannot even give their children the attention they need to grow and develop. So poor children come to school less prepared than those whose parents have more time and money to share with them (Gershoff, 2003). No matter how hard teachers try, no matter how much money is spent on education, it does not seem to make up completely for all that was lost in their preschool years (Payne, 2008).

Let's face it—if more money led to better academic performance, we would have it by now. In the last three decades of the twentieth century, we spent more money for each child's education than most other industrialized countries did (Organisation for Economic Cooperation and Development, 2004). Within that period (controlling for inflation) educational funding rose 60 percent and spending per pupil tripled (National Center for Education Statistics, 2003). Some children, however, are still less successful than others. Despite all our efforts, for example, children from minority groups still score substantially lower on standardized tests than do white children (Carey, 2005; National Center for Education Statistics, 2005a). It may simply be, as some scholars have suggested, that members of some racial and ethnic groups are, on average, less intellectually gifted than those of other groups (Jensen, 2003; Rushton and Rushton, 2003). It is not "justice" to spend large sums of other people's money on their education when the return will be smaller than if we invested those same dollars on children who have a better chance of succeeding. Taxpayers have a right to insist their hard-earned money be spent in the most efficient way possible. Proponents of centralized school funding who argue that it is the only way to ensure all children receive an "adequate" education can't even agree on a definition or measure of adequacy (Costrell, 2008; Rebell, 2007). How can we hope that they will understand how to provide such an education efficiently?

Instead of diverting other people's money to schools with large numbers of failing students, it would be a wiser use of public funds to provide poor children and their families with social services they need to create better lives.

We need to change the realities of their homes and neighborhoods if children are going to be able to take advantage of what schools have to offer. We should channel tax dollars to fight crime, provide recreational facilities, and create jobs, rather than waste money on schools, and ensure that every child has adequate health care—both physical and mental—and lives in a safe home and neighborhood. Only then will they come to school ready to learn. Spending money to solve their economic and social problems directly will be a better choice than putting more money into school districts that are often corrupt and mismanaged (Alexander and Salmon, 2007; Rothstein, 2008).

Historical Misuse of Public Funds in Urban School Districts

Proponents of centralized educational funding claim to be most concerned about children in failing urban schools. Some of their advocates even argue that all the factors we have been discussing mean these students need and deserve more of the public resources than those students whose backgrounds better prepare them for school success (Hansen, 2001). According to these advocates, federal and state government should turn over to poor children's schools even larger sums of taxpayer money than they do now (Halstead, 2000, 2002). It is a strange suggestion—to reward failing schools and punish successful ones.

Increased funding to failing school districts will indeed reward some people; however, it will not necessarily help students. For example, increasing teachers' salaries will further enrich professionals who are already middle class. Requiring more professional development for teachers will increase the income of consultants who provide teacher training. Prepackaged instructional programs many districts are encouraged to buy bring profits to their creators. However, there is no guarantee such expenditures will help children in any way (Merritt, 2004; Olson, 2005).

Urban schools have long been used to better the lives of some city residents at the expense of children's education. Urban school districts historically have been a source of patronage jobs politicians could hand out in exchange for votes. Members of various ethnic communities have, in their turn, assumed control of the districts and provided salaries to members of their constituencies—sometimes without requiring work in return (Connors, 1971). ". . . [T]he history of patronage is a method by which city residents without access to other political and economic resources have taken care of themselves and their friends" (Anyon, 1997, p. 159). In the 1980s one critic charged that in a city in the Northeast, "The political patronage has been so widespread that those filling district positions of responsibility have no idea of their actual duties. Positions were created to be filled by cronies. Routine hiring, evaluating and record keeping were not only bypassed but not even expected" (Morris, 1989, p. 18). The situation has not dramatically improved. "[T]he patronage system in large cities has been responsible for the appointment of many unskilled, educationally marginal school administrators. The history of patronage has also been partly responsible for those inner-city teachers who are ineffective" (Anyon, 1997, p. 158).

In many school districts patronage jobs have resulted in bureaucracies that hamper teachers' abilities to meet students' needs. Employees within these bureaucracies are sometimes involved in corrupt and illegal activities. Administrators and employees in large urban districts are routinely arrested for taking bribes and diverting public funds for their private use (Dugan, 2008; Hernandez, 2008; Waldman, 2008). Any scheme to increase funding to these districts would have to ensure new monies did not create more ineffective administrative positions. In addition, oversight procedures would need to be in place to prevent misappropriation of new funds.

As part of their legacy of providing patronage jobs, urban schools also employ a large number of paraprofessionals. These jobs are an excellent source of income for local community members. Cafeteria workers, teachers' aides, attendance assistants, special education aides, bus drivers, transportation aides, and sentries are all positions that ordinarily require no education beyond high school. They are jobs members of the neighborhoods around the schools seek out. Getting one's name on "the list" is often a matter of *who,* not *what,* you know. In many cities these paraprofessionals have unionized and command far higher wages in the school system than they would be able to earn in similar private sector jobs.

In the past, teachers who were hired in urban schools were often better "connected" than "prepared." Union contracts protect under-qualified teachers who entered the system under pre-existing patronage arrangements under the guise of "seniority" privileges and often prevent principals from hiring less experienced but more committed teachers. The problem is magnified when money becomes tight and layoffs are required. Less effective teachers maintain their jobs while more effective, newly hired ones lose theirs (De Wys and Hill, 2008).

Providing services to urban schools has been a lucrative business for many. Because of the enormous sums of money involved, urban schools are especially vulnerable to the greed of vendors and the moral weakness of their employees. In New York City, four employees of the Department of Education, responsible for school bus safety, were indicated on charges of soliciting bribes from bus companies that serve thousands of students with disabilities (Greenhouse, 2008). As New Orleans schools struggled to recover from Hurricane Katrina, the president of the school board accepted $140,000 in bribes for a software contract award (Nossiter, 2008). And in Chicago, school officials accepted bribes from companies that provide tires for buses and other vehicles (Secter and Coen, 2008).

Those who demand, in the name of justice, that hardworking taxpayers provide more funds to these mismanaged districts need to rethink their priorities. No such increases in funding should take place until appropriate personnel, accounting, and management policies and practices are in place. Fairness to those paying the bills demands no less. No taxpayer should be asked to sacrifice to provide opportunities for "fat cats" to get richer by skimming money from school budgets or providing jobs for those who keep them in power. School finance equalization plans would do just that.

The Consequences of Centralizing School Finance

Lower Student Achievement

Those who propose we centralize school funding at the state or federal level seem oblivious to what happens when such attempts are made. The "equalizers" have been successful in some states, often with disastrous results. There are two options for creating equalization plans for school spending. The financing can be "leveled up" or "leveled down." In leveling up, the state funds all schools at the same per-pupil rate as the wealthiest districts. In leveling down, all schools receive a per-pupil amount equivalent to that being spent in middle-class or poorer districts in the state. In most leveling-down schemes, a limit is placed on what a district can spend above the state subsidy. Leveling up is an expensive proposition. It requires an increase in taxes across a state; people pay higher taxes but only a few of them see increased services to their communities as a result of those rate hikes. As a result, leveling-up schemes are unpopular and rarely are implemented fully.

In 1971, the California Supreme Court heard the first legal challenge to differences in school financing. In that case, *Serrano v. Priest,* the court held that inequalities in district per-pupil funding violated the equal protection clauses of the state and federal constitution. Those who supported equalization of school spending believed they had won a victory. They assumed the changes resulting from the court order would improve education for all California's students. They were wrong. Taxpayers revolted against any plan to increase state taxes in order to equalize school spending (Fischel, 1989, 1996). They passed Proposition 13, which placed a "cap" on taxes and effectively limited funds for all California districts. The result is the schools that educate high-poverty students receive only $13 more per student than do their counterparts serving wealthier students (Timar and Roza, 2008). Despite claims that centralizing the funding of their schools would improve their academic chances, California's students are performing below national averages on the National Assessment of Educational Progress in mathematics and reading (U.S. Department of Education, 2007, 2006). Five states, Oklahoma, South Carolina, Hawaii, Michigan, and Kansas, provide more than 90 percent of public schools' funding—a greater centralization of funding than in California (Hoxby, 2003). In two of those states, Kansas and Michigan, the average test scores were slightly higher than the national average; in the other these three, they were somewhat lower (U.S. Department of Education, 2007, 2006). In other words, funding schools almost exclusively at the state level is no guarantee that academic achievement will improve.

Decreases in Local Support

Research into other instances of equalization attempts shows court-ordered increases in state financial support for schools often were accompanied by decreases in local support. In other words, schools did not experience a real increase in resources. Municipalities sometimes saw the increased state aid as an opportunity to reduce the local tax burden on residents instead of a chance to provide better schools for their children (Driscoll and Salmon, 2008). These decisions made sense politically and economically for those cities and towns. They also reflected the antagonism often generated by decisions imposed on people by judges. It is not only local financial support for schools that suffers as a result of centralizing finance. When the state exercises a high degree of control over schools' fundings, "it necessarily means that local parents and residents have less control. Parents and neighbors can find this alienating." They are less likely to be involved in schools if they feel they have no real power over educational decisions. They are also less likely to make the additional contributions of time and material resources if they have little say in how those commodities are used (Hoxby, 2003). No school district can afford to lose the parents who are most interested in their children's school success.

Loss of Local Control

One of the most unique aspects of the U.S. school system is the fact that schools historically have been designed to meet the needs of individual areas. In the late nineteenth and early twentieth century, for example, different courses of study were taught in rural schools than in urban ones. Each local school district, working with concerned members of the community, was able to create schools that met their children's needs (Cremin, 1961). Schools were able to hire and fire teachers and could do so based on criteria established locally. A teacher needed to live up to an individual community's standards, not just ones created by some state bureaucrats with little or no sense of the municipality's needs or values.

Even in the late twentieth century, local control of schools remained an important aspect of their governance. Taxpayers could accept or reject school boards' proposed budgets. They could elect or throw out of office school board members. In doing so, they ensured that their ideas for their children's education would be carried out in the schools. In addition, taxpayers could select those elected officials who set property tax rates for funding schools, and thus could work to see their tax burden would not be unduly high. Because most people in a town, city, or village had attended a local school or had children who did, interest in a local school district was high. The added dimension of locally controlling school funding increased taxpayers' involvement in the schools. People are willing to pay if they can see their money is being spent on something of value and that they have something to say about what constitutes that value.

When school funding is substantially centralized—when states take over most of the task of paying for education—taxpayers lose a substantial amount of the control over the schools for which they are paying. When local control is lost, administrators' flexibility is also sacrificed. Local school and civic leaders can no longer respond effectively to the needs of their community and their students. Some schools may, for example, want after-school programs; others may want to provide very small classes; still others may want to create accelerated programs. When funding is centralized and its distribution mandated by the state, programmatic decisions are no longer theirs to make (Hoxby, 2003). For example, in many states where the state's share of school funding has increased, so have rules and regulations. States across the country are establishing standards for student performance. These standards are often innocuous statements of general academic achievement. For example, in New York the standards for academic achievement in languages other than English are Standard 1: students will be able to use a language other than English for communication and Standard 2: students will develop cross-cultural skills and understanding (New York State Department of Education, 1996).

Who could argue with such bland proposals? On the other hand, who can, with a straight face, argue that they represent adequate guidance for schools struggling to measure student performance. Indeed such standards usually are backed up by systems of evaluating students through tests prepared by the states' departments of education. School districts and individual teachers have little say in the curriculum they are expected to deliver and even less input into tests their students will take. While state taxpayers may have a right to see their money is being well spent, the procedure for doing so takes away large amounts of local influence over what young people learn and how they are evaluated.

In centralized funding schemes, local taxpayers also experience diminished authority over how their money will be spent because decisions about school finance are made in a state legislature instead of by a district's school board. When school taxes are collected by the state instead of municipalities, the money from a locality goes into a big pot. Interest groups from all across the state want to use that money for their pet projects. The money must be divided in many more ways than if it were allocated locally. The number of people involved in the process increases when funding is centralized. It takes longer to decide on state budgets, and passing them requires a level of compromise that would be unheard of in a local process. Imagine the chaos if every school in the country was forced to wait for state budgets before the local districts would know how many teachers or administrators they would be able to afford! Local control is not only a matter of convenience; it is a matter of efficiency and, therefore, justice. Every taxpayer has the right to expect the funds they provide will be available in a speedy way for the services for which they had been collected.

Good Schools Are a Reward for Hard Work

Whether proponents of centralized educational funding like it or not, we live in a capitalist society. We have an economic system that thrives on full and fair competition among businesses and workers. If you produce a product or provide a service that members of society value, you are more highly rewarded than those who do not. It is a system that has created a standard of living in the United States that is the envy of the rest of the world. We provide safety nets for those who cannot participate in the free market; we do so even for the children of those who *will* not take part.

However, one reason this economy works so well is because people can enjoy the fruits of their labor. Those who "crack the system" and figure out what the public will buy can reap monetary rewards they then can translate into assets, one of the most cherished of which is a home. One of the factors that most influence those homebuyers is the opportunity to provide better schools and safer neighborhoods for their children. In turn, the quality of schools is an important factor in determining the market value of a home. Equalizing funding for schools and ensuring that all students receive the same advantages will remove one of the primary reasons why one house is worth more than another.

The American economic system is based on competition and on the idea that some things are "better" than others. These perceived advantages provide an incentive for most Americans to work hard, to save and spend their money. If we centralize school spending and equalize the education children receive, we remove one of the greatest incentives for adults to make sacrifices of time and money this economy requires. It may not seem "fair" but, in general, the system works and it is foolish to think about making dramatic changes to it.

Kozol (2006) laments the fact that children in poorer school districts perceive the differences between their schools and those in wealthier districts. He suggests this awareness makes young people bitter, and that as a result they eventually drop out of the competition that is at the heart of the American economic system. There is, however, another way of looking at the children's awareness. We can see it as the same kind of knowledge that has propelled so many others in this country to work harder than they ever imagined possible. We can see it as providing the same kind of motivation possessed by the pioneers who crossed this country in search of a better life. Some who currently live in municipalities that provide more resources for their schools started out in neighborhoods such as those that Kozol and others describe. Their hard work, determination, and perseverance enabled them to provide a better life for their children. We should not assume that today's young people are incapable of the same kind of effort and success. We need to hold out the promise of rewards for the kind of behavior that most benefits this society. Centralizing and equalizing school funding takes away one of the primary reasons people choose to act in ways that will build up this great country. We cannot risk the consequences of removing that motivation.

Local control of school funding is an important aspect of American public life. In the last twenty-five years, the U.S. electorate has made clear their preference for public policies that reflect the fundamental principles of federalism and decentralization. They want less interference in their lives by governmental officials—legislative, executive, or judicial. They want to control their own destinies, in their own cities and towns and villages. Proposals to centralize school funding run counter to this preference. Even though they may reflect their supporters' desire to create more equitable educational opportunity, in the long run, the plans will not succeed. "We now have sufficient evidence that some policies that look good at first sight have unfortunate consequences" and centralized funding for schools "is particularly likely to have negative long-term consequences" (Hoxby, 2003, p. 36). " . . . decentralization may . . . appear to be messy and inefficient" but it is still superior to the "benevolent dictatorship" of state control over education (Rossell, 2003, p. 30).

For Discussion

1. Research your own state. Have there been lawsuits pursuing equity in educational funding? What were the arguments, pro and con? What were the courts' decisions? Have they been implemented? What have been the results?
2. Some proposals for reducing school financial inequity rely on a shift from property tax revenue to sales tax revenue. Discuss the pros and cons of such a shift. Remember to consider questions such as the reliability of each revenue source in times of economic difficulty.
3. Consider how increased state contributions to school districts may affect local control of schools. Research your own state's policies with regard to the level of independence school districts have in the areas of curriculum, testing, personnel, and length of the school year.
4. For a moment, turn the whole question of school financing on its head and consider whether governments have the right to tax citizens to pay for schools. Discuss whether such taxation violates individual rights of those citizens who do not have children in public schools. In doing so, you might try to support the arguments that only parents have the right and obligation to provide their children with education they deem appropriate and government has no right to interfere in their decisions. What might be some effects on the country of implementing such a school financing policy?

References

Access Quality Education (2008). "Litigation." www.schoolfunding.info/litigation/litigation.php3.

ALEXANDER, K, AND SALMON, R. (2007). "Warranting Failure: The System That Breeds Poverty and Starves Public Schools." Journal Of Education Finance. 33(2): 203–221.

ANYON, J. (1997). *Ghetto Schooling.* New York: Teachers College Press.

ARROYO, C. (2008). "The Funding Gap." Washington, DC: The Education Trust. www2.edtrust.org/NR/rdonlyres/5AF8F288-949D-4677-82CF-5A867A8E9153/0/FundingGap2007.pdf.

ASBY, C. (2008). "No Child Left Behind Act: Education Actions Could Improve the Targeting of School Improvement Funds to Schools Most in Need of Assistance. Report to Congressional Requesters." Washington, DC: General Accounting Office (GAO-08-380).

BARTH, J. AND NITTA, K. (2008). *Education in the Post Lakeview Era.* Little Rock: Arkansas Advocates for Children and Families. www.schoolfunding.info/states/ar/ARAdvocates-AchievementGap08.pdf.

BROWN, C. (2007). "Are America's Poorest Children Receiving Their Share of Federal Education Funds? School-Level Title I Funding in New York, Los Angeles, and Chicago," *Journal of Education Finance.* 33(2): 130–146.

CAREY, K. AND ROZA, M. (2008). "School Fundings' Tragic Flaw." Seattle: Center on Reinventing Public Education.

CHANEY, B., AND LEWIS, L. (2007). *Public School Principals Report on Their School Facilities: Fall 2005* (NCES 2007–007). U.S. Department of Education. Washington, DC: National Center for Education Statistics.

COLEMAN, J. (1966). *Equality of Educational Opportunity.* Washington, DC: U.S. Department of Health, Education, and Welfare, Office of Education.

CONNORS, R. (1971). *A Cycle of Power: The Career of Jersey City Mayor Frank Hague.* Metuchen, NJ: Scarecrow Press.

COSTRELL, R., HANUSHEK, E. AND LOEB, 2008. "What Do Cost Functions Tell Us About the Cost of an Adequate Education," *Peabody Journal of Education,* 83(2): 198–223.

CREMIN, L. (1961). *The Transformation of the School: Progressivism in American Education 1876–1957.* New York: Random House.

CREMIN, L., ED. (1957). *The Republic and the School: Horace Mann on the Education of Free Men.* New York: Teachers College Press.

DEWYS, S. AND HILL, P. "Putting Students First," *Seattle Post Intelliger,* Feb. 29, 2008. http://seattlepi.nwsource.com/opinion/353294_focus02.html.

DRISCOLL, L. AND SALMON, R. (2008). "How Increased State Equalization Aid Resulted in Greater Disparities: An Unexpected Consequence for the Commonwealth of Virginia." *Journal of Educational Finance* 33(3); 238–261.

DUGGAN, P., "Ex-official Sentenced in Embezzlement," *Washington Post,* May 8, 2008. Final Report on the National Assessment of Title I: Summary of Key Findings. Washington, DC: U.S. Department of Education, Institute of Education Sciences, 2007.

FIRESTONE, W., GOERTZ, M., AND NATRIELLO, G. (1997). *From Cashbox to Classroom: The Struggle for Fiscal Reform and Educational Change in New Jersey.* New York: Teachers College Press.

FISCHEL, W. (1989). "Did Serrano Cause Proposition 13?" *National Tax Journal.* December: 465–474.

_____. (1996). "How Serrano Caused Proposition 13." *Journal of Law and Politics* 12:607–645.

FORDHAM, S., AND OGBU, J. (1986). "Black Students' School Success: Coping with the 'Burden of Acting White.'" *The Urban Review.* 18(1), 176–206.

GLENN, W. AND PICUS, L. (2007). "The *Williams* Settlement and the Prospects for Future School Finance Adequacy Litigation in California," *Journal of Education Finance* 32(3): 382–394.

GOTTLOB, B. (2003). "The Results of the New Hampshire Education Funding Reform," The Josiah Bartlett Center for Public Policy.

GREENHOUSE, S. "School Bus Safety Officials Are Accused of Soliciting Bribes," *New York Times,* May 14, 2008.

GREIFNER, L. (2006). "Facilities Spending Criticized as Uneven," *Education Week,* November.18: 1.

HALSTEAD, T. (2000) "The National Debate Over School Funding Needs a Federal Focus." *Los Angeles Times.* Oct. 8, p. M2.

_____. (2002). "Rich School, Poor School." *The New York Times.* Sec. A, Jan. 8, p. 19.

HANSEN, J. (2001). "21st Century School Finance: How is the Context Changing?" Education Commission of the States. ECS Issue Paper. Education Finance in the States: Its Past, Present and Future. www.ecs.org/clearinghouse/28/04/2804.htm.

HANUSHEK, E. (1989). "The Impact of Differential Expenditures on School Performance." *Educational Researcher.* May, pp. 45–51.

_____. (1996) "School Resources and Student Performances." In G. Burtless, ed., *Does Money Matter?: The Effect of School Resources on Student Achievement and Adult Success.* Washington, DC: Brookings Institution.

HEDGES, L., LAINE, R., AND GREENWALD, R. (1994). "Does Money Matter? A Meta-Analysis of Studies of the Effects of Differential School Inputs on Student Outcomes." *Educational Researcher.* 23(3), 5–14.

HERNANDEZ, C. "A Lucky Return," *Newsday,* March 20, 2008.

HOXBY, C. (2003) "Achievement, Efficiency and Centralization in California Public Schools," Prepared for *Williams v California*. www.decentschools.org.

IMBER, M. (2004). "Adequacy in School Funding," *American School Board Journal*, November, 46–47.

KATZ, M. (1975). *Class, Bureaucracy and Schools: The Illusion of Educational Change in America*. New York: Praeger.

KNOEBBEL, R., VERSTEGEN, D., AND RINEHART, J. (2007). "What Is the Relationship Between Resources and Student Achievement? A Canonical Analysis," *Journal of Education Finance* 33(2): 183–202.

KOZOL, J. (2006). "Jonathan Kozol Takes on the World," *District Administration*, January. www.districtadministration.com/viewarticle.aspx?articleid=37&p=1#0.

LADD, H. AND HANSEN, J., EDS. (1999). *Making Money Matter: Financing America's Schools*. Washington, DC: National Academy Press.

MACKEY, S. (1998). "The School Money Puzzle." *Government Finance Review*. (2), 39–42.

MERRITT, J. (2004). "A Syllabus Way Beyond the SATs," *Business Week*, April 26.

MORRIS, G. (1989). "The Blackboard Jungle Revisited." *National Review*. 41(8), 18–19.

NEW YORK STATE DEPARTMENT OF EDUCATION. (1996). *Learning Standards for Languages Other Than English*. Albany: Author.

———. (2008a). *New York: The State of Learning (Chapter 655 Report)*. www.oms.nysed .gov/faru/PDFDocuments/2007_Analysis.pdf

_____.(2008b) *New York State School Report Cards*: Accountability and Overview Report 2006-2007 www.nystart.gov/publicweb/.

NOGUERA, P. (2004). Racial Isolation, Poverty and the Limits of Local Control in Oakland. *Teachers College Record,* 106(11), 2146–2170.

NOSSITER, A. "Louisiana: Lawmaker's Brother Indicted," *New York Times*, April 3, 2008.

OAKES, J. (2002). " Education Inadequacy, Inequality, and Failed State Policy: A Synthesis of Expert Reports Prepared for *Williams v. State of California*. www.decentschools. org/experts.php.

OGBU, J. (2003). *Black American Students in an Affluent Suburb*. Mahawah, N.J.: Lawrence Erhlbaum Associates.

ORGANISATION FOR ECONOMIC COOPERATION AND DEVELOPMENT. (2007)). *Education at a Glance: OECD Indicators 2004 Edition*. Washington, DC: Author.

PAYNE, R. (2008) "Nine Successful Practices," *Educational Leadership.* 65(7); 48–52.

RAFFAELE, M., "District-by-district details on property-tax breaks released," Associated Press, May 1, 2008. www.philly.com/philly/wires/ap/news/state/pennsylvania/ 18453849.html.

REBELL, M., (2008a). "Sleepless in Seattle: There's Still Hope for Equal Educational Opportunity." *Education Week*, February 13: 32–33.

_____. (2008b). "Equal Opportunity and the Courts," *Phi Delta Kappan* 89(6): 432–439. www.pdkintl.org/kappan/k_v89/k0802reb.htm.

_____. (2007). Professional Rigor, Public Engagement and Judicial Review: A Proposal for Enhancing the Validity of Education Adequacy Studies. *Teachers College Record* 109(6): 1303–1373.

RENDELL, E. (2006). "Amicus Curiae Brief of the Governor of the Commonwealth of Pennsylvania in *Pontiac v Spellings*." www.nea.org/lawsuit/images/rendellbrief.pdf.

ROZA, M., GUIN, K., GROSS, B. AND DEBURGOMASTER, S. (2007). "Do Districts Fund Schools Fairly?" *Education Next*, 7(4). www.hoover.org/publications/ednext/9223676.html.

ROTHSTEIN, R. (2008). "Whose Problem is Poverty?" *Educational Leadership*, 65(7):8–13.

SCHENCKER, L. "Property-Tax Cut, Sales-tax Hike Proposed," *The Salt Lake Tribune*, February 20, 2008, n.p.

SECTER, B. AND COEN, J. "Levine Weaves Tawdry Tale," *Chicago Tribune,* March 19, 2008

SIGO, S , "Plan OK'd to End Florida-Mandated School Property Taxes," *The Bond Buyer,* April 28, 2008 p. 3.

TIMAR, T. AND ROZA, M. "A False Dilemma: Should Decisions about Education Resource Use Be Made at the State or Local Level?" Paper presented at University of Californa, Davis, Center for Applied Policy in Education Symposium, April 18, 2008.

TYACK, D. (1974). *The One Best System: A History of American Urban Education.* Cambridge: Harvard University Press.

U.S. Department of Education, National Center for Education Statistics. (2007). The Condition of Education 2007 (NCES 2007-064). Washington, DC: U.S. Government Printing Office.

_____. (2006). The Condition of Education 2006, NCES 2006-071, Washington, DC: U.S. Government Printing Office.

URBAN, W., AND WAGONER, J. (2000). *American Education: A History.* 2nd Ed. New York: McGraw-Hill.

WALDMAN, S. "Missing Funds Reach $303,000," *Albany Times Union,* Sept. 11, 2007.

WALTON, V., "Suit Contests State Property Tax Claims that Tax Revenue for Schools Not Enough, Not Equal," *Birmingham News,* March 18, 2008 p. 1B.

WILSON, J. (2003). "Convincing Black Students That Studying Hard is Not Acting White," *Journal of Blacks in Higher Education,* 38, 85–88.

ZHOU, L. (2008). *Revenues and Expenditures for Public Elementary and Secondary Education: School Year 2005–06 (Fiscal Year 2006)* (NCES 2008-328). National Center for Education Statistics, Institute of Education Sciences, U.S.Department of Education. Washington, DC. http://nces.ed.gov/pubsearch/pubsinfo.asp?pubid=2008328.

CHAPTER 4

Gender Equity: Eliminating Discrimination or Accommodating Difference

Is it ever necessary to create schools or classroom settings that separate students by gender?

POSITION 1: ELIMINATING DISCRIMINATION

Creating sex-segregated schools and classrooms is a waste of time and effort that diverts resources from initiatives that actually will improve the education of both boys and girls—such as reducing class sizes and increasing teacher training. Moreover, these sex-segregated classes deprive students of important preparation for the real, coeducational worlds of work and family. Rather than offering choice, sex-segregated programs limit the education of both boys and girls.

—American Civil Liberties Union, 2008

The ongoing struggle for civil rights in the United States has included efforts to end gender discrimination in schools. The attempt to ensure equal educational access, opportunity, and achievement to both men and women faces new challenges. Recent revisions to federal law, allowing the creation of single-sex classes and the reintroduction of gender discrimination in educational funding threaten the progress made. Perhaps these changes are sincere efforts to meet young people's needs. However, they will result in a return to discriminatory policies and practices that privilege one gender over another in schools.

Gender Roles and Education

Debates about gender equity always have been inextricably connected to society's understanding of gender roles—that is, the social roles men and women were assigned shaped Americans' view of appropriate education for boys and girls. Of course, race and social class also have affected equity between males

97

and females in schools. In some ways, however, notions of what men and women are expected to be and do have transcended those other categories. So, ending discrimination in schools has depended on changes in gender roles—especially for women.

In colonial America gender roles were rooted in a biblical understanding that women were subservient to men. Yet colonial Christianity also required each believer, male or female, to be able to read and interpret the Scriptures and to provide their children with the same skills. As a result most boys and girls gained limited access to education through education at home or in "dame" schools. Because males were thought to have the responsibility to work in the public sphere, boys with the potential to become leaders in the community were allowed to pursue more education. Girls, however, were provided with the opportunity to learn only enough to perform private religious and domestic duties (Tyack and Hansot, 1992; Spring, 1997; Urban and Wagoner, 2000; Tozer, Violas, and Senese, 2002).

After the American Revolution, gender roles were rooted in a political, not religious, ideology. In the fledgling country, men continued to have public responsibilities. They were expected to be moral neighbors, informed voters, and responsible businessmen. Schooling was designed to help boys develop manly virtues such as obedience to authority, respect for the rights of others, an appreciation of "fair play," and patriotism, as well as to provide opportunities to develop appropriate skills in literacy, natural science, history, and mathematics (Tozer, Violas, and Senese, 2002).

Women's responsibilities in the republic remained primarily in the private sphere. They were expected to provide homes in which their sons and daughters learned to be responsible citizens and in which their husbands could find respite from the cares of the world (Douglas, 1977; Evans, 1989; Tyack and Hansot, 1992; Zinn, 1995). Schooling prepared girls for those domestic duties. Believing both men and women's contributions were vital to the country's well-being, Americans in general supported gender equity in access and, to some degree, in curriculum (Kaestle, 1983; Evans, 1989; Tyack and Hansot, 1992; Zinn, 1995). Coeducational elementary schools became the country's norm (Tyack and Hansot, 1992; Sklar, 1993).

Equality of access and opportunity in secondary education was, at first, more contentious (Tyack and Hansot, 1992). By the early nineteenth century, upper- and middle-class boys increasingly went beyond elementary school, attending "grammar" schools that prepared them for college or for occupations such as business, surveying, and teaching (Tozer, Violas, and Senese, 2002). Pioneers such as Catharine Beecher, Emma Willard, and Mary Lyon argued the country's well-being required women to extend their duties as "Republican mothers" by taking their "natural" aptitude for teaching into schools. As a result of their arguments and their fund-raising, private "academies" for women opened, allowing girls to continue their educations to prepare for careers as teachers and, eventually, nurses. By the early twentieth century, the academies were replaced by public high schools that admitted boys and girls on a relatively equal footing (Rury, 1991; Tyack and Hansot, 1992; Spring, 1997; Urban and

Wagoner, 2000). The belief that both men and women had some role in public life resulted in greater equity in schooling.

However, educational opportunity remained rooted in the belief that men and women had distinct gender characteristics, suiting them for different work. Despite the increased availability of secondary schools and the long struggle to grant women access to colleges and universities (Horowitz, 1984; Solomon, 1986), few women had the opportunity to pursue education preparing them for professions. The right to work in the law, business, medicine and ministry belonged almost exclusively to men (Horowitz, 1984; Solomon, 1986; Tozer, Violas, and Senese, 2002).

Even at the high school level, despite equality of access, gender stereotypes began once again to result in discrimination. During the Progressive Era, girls were tracked into programs that prepared them to be teachers, nurses, secretaries, receptionists, and clerks. In home economics courses they learned how to be good wives and mothers (Rury, 1991). At the same time, boys took college preparatory courses in larger numbers than girls and participated in vocational programs preparing them for "manly" jobs in industry and the trades (Rury, 1991; Tyack and Hansot, 1992; Ravitch, 2000). The introduction of the "girls' electives" such as cooking, sewing, typing, and stenography increased segregation by gender in high school and decreased women's participation in more "academic" courses (Rury, 1991). For more than thirty years, gender differences in educational opportunity remained part of American secondary and higher education with serious consequences. Although a higher percentage of women completed four years of high school between 1940 and 1965, fewer women than men completed four years of college during that same period (U.S. Census Bureau, 2008a).

In the last half of the twentieth century, the relationship between society's view of gender roles and the kind of education appropriate for males and females was renegotiated once again. This time dramatic progress was made in ending educational gender discrimination. During World War II, women took on industrial jobs previously considered too "masculine" for them to perform (Evans, 1989). Universities and professional schools opened their doors to women when prospective male students were in the military. Despite efforts to restore the previous gender order during peacetime (Evans, 1989), once the genie was out of the bottle, there was no going back.

The 1960s saw a renewed commitment to the position that biological differences should not affect the kind or quality of education men and women received. Many argued the differences between men and women actually were more social than biological (Miller, 1976; Chodorow, 1978; Gilligan, 1982; Segal, 1990; Connell, 1995). Scholars investigated the policies, practices, curriculum, and student–teacher interactions in schools for explanations for differences in school achievement between boys and girls and reported many gender in equities (U.S. Department of Health, Education and Welfare, 1978; Mac an Ghaill, 1994; Sadker and Sadker, 1982, 1994).

Feminists who did the earliest of this research argued that discrimination supported the inferior social status of women. Women and their accomplishments were missing from textbooks. Girls were still tracked into courses of study associated with traditionally female—and lower-paying—occupations like nursing, teaching, secretarial work, or homemaking. Instructional materials virtually ignored women's contributions and experiences in other areas. Boys received more teacher attention than did girls. Their learning was supported in more positive ways. In addition, discrimination existed in admission practices, financial aid, counseling, athletics, and access to programs and courses (Frazier and Sadker, 1973; Howe, 1984; AAUW, 1995; Biklen and Pollard, 1993; Sadker and Sadker, 1994).

Gender discrimination in education was linked to the larger civil rights movement, which had awakened the country to the social and economic costs of denying any citizen their individual freedoms. Passage of the Civil Rights Acts in the late sixties legislated an end to policies and practices blocking racial equality. Advocates of gender equity argued that discrimination on the basis of sex was an equal violation of the Fourteenth Amendment. For the first time in American history, the struggle for gender equity in education was grounded not in arguments that men' and women's unique gender roles required a particular type of educational access or opportunity. Instead it was based on the idea that they shared equally in the "unalienable rights" named by the Declaration of Independence and guaranteed by the Constitution.

In that spirit, in 1972, Congress passed Title IX of the Educational Amendment Act. Although most closely identified with efforts to make athletic programs more equal, Title IX actually bans discrimination on the basis of sex in *any* educational program or activity receiving federal financial assistance. Course-taking opportunities, participation in extracurricular activities, eligibility for awards, and college and university admission policies no longer could be determined by a student's gender. In 1974, the Women's Educational Equity Act (WEEA) was passed. It required the Secretary of Education to promote gender equity in schools, especially for women and girls who suffer multiple types of discrimination based on sex, race, ethnic origin, limited English proficiency, disability, or age. Funding is allocated under WEEA for model equity programs, education for teachers and other school personnel, leadership training for women and girls, school-to-work and vocational programs, assistance for pregnant and parenting students, sexual harassment prevention programs, and research and development of nondiscriminatory curricula, resources, and standardized tests (U.S. Department of Education, 2008a). Title IX provided the framework for ending gender discrimination; WEEA provided the financial assistance that enabled schools to do so. These laws have resulted in dramatic progress toward equalizing achievement—the third aspect of educational equity—as identified by indicators such as standardized test scores, course-taking, participation in sports and extracurricular activities, and educational attainment. These results are reasons for continued commitment to eliminating gender discrimination in schools.

Improvements

Since Title IX outlawed gender discrimination in college admissions policies, scholarships, and financial aid, women have made remarkable progress in completing their studies. In 1970, among Americans 25 years old or older, only

FIGURE 4.1 Percentage of Bachelor's Degrees Conferred on Women in Selected Fields of Study

	1970	2006
Engineering	0.7	17.9
Agriculture	4.1	47.7
Business	9.0	49.8
Computer Science	12.9	41.8
Mathematics	37.4	45.1
Physical Science	13.6	41.8

Source: U.S. Department of Education. (2008b). *The Condition of Education, 2008.*

8.2 percent of women had bachelor's degrees, compared with 14.1 percent of men. Almost four decades later, 28 percent of women and 29.5 percent of men had attained those degrees (U.S. Census, 2008a).(See Figure 4.1.) More women than men hold master's degrees, and women are making gains in professional and doctoral degrees as well (U.S Census, 2008b). (See Figure 4.2.)

These remarkable developments resulted, at least in part, from efforts to end discriminatory practices in elementary and secondary schools. For example, since Title IX was passed, girls have adjusted their high school course-taking patterns. More girls than boys now take advanced science and mathematics courses (U.S. Department of Education, 2007). Eleven percent of girls are completing a rigorous curriculum that typically includes physics and calculus (Corbett, Hill, and St. Rose, 2008). Their GPAs in mathematics and science are higher than those of boys (U.S. Department of Education, 2007). These gains have brought them much closer to equality with their male counterparts. As they have taken more math courses, girls' scores on the math sections of the SATs have increased. In 2007, their average score was 502 (Corbett, Hill, and St. Rose, 2008). In addition,

FIGURE 4.2 Percentage of Graduate Degrees Awarded to Women in Selected Fields

	1970	2005
Law (L.L.B., J.D.)	5.4	48.6
Medicine (M.D.)	8.4	47.3
Dentistry	0.9	43.7
Computer Science (Ph.D.)	1.9	21.7
Engineering (Ph.D.)	0.7	20.2
Physical Sciences (Ph.D.)	5.4	30.0
Business (M.B.A.)	1.6	42.9

Sources: U.S. Department of Education (2008b). *The Condition of Education, 2008* and U.S. Department of Educaton (2004). "Trends in Educational Equity of Girls and Women."

more young women are prepared to take Advanced Placement tests. Those who do so are achieving scores almost equal to those of their male peers—and earning college credits and preferential treatment in the admissions process as well (U.S. Department of Education, 2004).

As a result of pressure to treat girls equitably, teachers now differentiate instruction within classrooms to meet individual students' complex educational needs. They have developed a repertoire of instructional strategies to more effectively help each child achieve her or his full potential. Ending gender discrimination for girls has improved the chances of success for boys as well (Corbett, Hill, and St. Rose, 2008). Spurred by the No Child Left Behind Act, the movement to standards-based education also has reduced gender discrimination in schools. Almost all the subject-based professional associations for teachers require members to demonstrate competency in providing instruction that addresses gender issues (National Council on the Accreditation of Teacher Education, 2008).

The provisions of Title IX legislation have been applied most noticeably to athletics. Although gender differences still remain, more equitable distribution of resources has dramatically increased girls' participation in scholastic sports programs in the last thirty-five years. In 1972, approximately 30,000 women participated in college or university sports programs; in 2002, over 205,500 women did. Women have made good use of these opportunities. By 2007, 71 percent of Division I female athletes finished college within 6 years, compared with 68 percent of all female students (Women's Sports Foundation, 2008). In the days before Title IX, athletic scholarships for women were nonexistent. Women now receive 45 percent of the available scholarship money for sports. (Cheslock, 2007). Before Title IX fewer than 300,000 girls played high school sports. In 2007, that number was over 3 million (Women's Sports Foundation, 2007).

The benefits of gender equity in sports have been significant. The increasing number of athletic scholarships for women has made it possible for more of them to attend college than ever before. Participation in sports also leads to healthier lifestyles and less risk-taking behavior among adolescents. Student athletes are less likely to smoke or use drugs; female adolescent athletes are less likely to engage in premarital sex or become pregnant during high school (Women's Sports Foundation, 2008). Girls who play sports are less likely to consider suicide (Women's Sports Foundation, 2008). In addition, there are long-term health benefits from women's participation in athletics. Women who take part in rigorous exercise such as provided by sports are less likely to develop heart diseases, osteoporosis, and breast cancer over the course of their lives (Tuoker Center for Research on Girls and Women in Sports, 2007). Increased gender equity in sport participation provides benefits that, like academic achievement, are long-lasting.

What Remains to Be Done

Despite gains in creating equality of educational access, opportunity, and achievement, gender discrimination remains an issue in American schools. Although Title IX has been somewhat successful in increasing equity in college sports, men and women's teams do not always have the same access to practice time, facilities, and faculty support. "Female college athletes receive only 38 percent of sports operating dollars, which is $1.17 billion less than male college athletes; 45 percent of college athletic scholarship dollars, which is $148 million fewer scholarship dollars than male college athletes; and 33 percent of athletic team recruitment spending, which is $43 million less for recruiting female athletes than male athletes" (Women's Sports Foundation, 2008). In addition, schools, colleges, and universities have played the "blame" game with Title IX. They continue to fund expensive male sports such as basketball, football, and ice hockey, stretching their athletic budgets to the breaking point. Then, prevented by Title IX from discriminating against women's athletics, they cut smaller men's teams and blame the law for needing to do so. Yet nothing in the law requires that men's teams be cut. In fact, under Title IX, men's opportunities to participate in school athletics, the number of them doing so, and the budgets for their sports have all increased (National Coalition for Women and Girls in Education, 2007). The inequity continues because for many years the law has not been enforced in any meaningful way.

If enforcement is lax at the college and university level, it has been almost nonexistent in K–12 schools. Only 42 percent of high school and college varsity athletes are female, even though they constitute more than 50 percent of the students (Women's Sports Foundations, 2007). Girls' teams suffer discrimination in practice sites and times, transportation, and revenues. In one case when the coach of a girls' high school basketball team notified school officials that such actions were violations of Title IX, he was fired. It took a decision by the Supreme Court to restore his rights and those of his players (*Jackson v. Birmingham Board of Education,* 2005). Without the legal framework provided by Title IX, there would have been no way to prevent or remedy the injustices.

The failure to monitor compliance with Title IX goes beyond athletics. Researchers report that in colleges and universities, women professors in science experience discrimination (Settles, Cortina, Malley, and Stewart, 2007) and that, overall, women faculty are paid lowers salaries and promoted less often than their males counterparts (Cooperstein, 2008).

At the K–12 level, ending gender discrimination may also mean going beyond compliance with the letter of the law. Reviewing guidance materials and practices, educating and involving parents, introducing students to nontraditional career options, providing role models and mentors, and conducting recruitment efforts targeted to increase comfort with course-taking options all produce greater gender equality in schools (Lufkin, 2005). When school personnel take Title IX seriously, good things happen for students.

New Challenges to Ending Discrimination

The 1975 guidelines for Title IX's implementation prohibited public schools from segregating students according to gender, even for part of the day. However, since the 1990s, the regulation has been ignored or violated by many school districts (Stowe, 1991; Perry, 1999; Streitmatter, 1997, 1998, 1999). In 2004, the Department of Education issued new Title IX regulations that permitted single-sex schools and classes in publicly funded schools and imposed few limitations on such projects (*Federal Register*, 2002). In 2006, the Department went even further by actually inviting and encouraging school districts to create single-gender classes and schools (*Federal Register*, 2006). Shockingly, unlike laws governing racially segregated schools, these new policies allowed "separate" without requiring "equal" opportunities (American Civil Liberties Union, 2008). The growth of these discriminatory settings has been phenomenal. A decade ago, there were only four single-sex public schools in the country; today, there are approximately 100 that admit students of only one gender and more than 300 that offer segregated classes (National Association for Single Sex Public Education, 2008a). It is particularly disturbing that so many charter schools provide this option. The law allows them to operate in a gender-segregated way without requiring that similar opportunities be guaranteed to the other sex (American Civil Liberties Union, 2008; National Association for Single Sex Public Education, 2008c).

Arguments supporting single-sex educational projects generally have been based on public schools' failure to meet students' needs. For example, feminist concerns that sexism in schools creates unequal opportunity for girls are the driving force in the creation of many single-sex classes and schools for young women. Advocates for classes exclusively for African American boys often cite their failure to succeed in coeducational settings (Gewertz, 2007). In fact, a thorough review of scientifically based research on the topic revealed that the findings are inconclusive with regard to the single-sex "factor" (U.S. Department of Education, 2005d). Even more recent studies suggest that there is no evidence that girls' motivation to learn is improved in single-sex settings (Chouinard, Vezeau, and Bouffard, 2008). Most studies suggest that factors other than gender explained whatever academic advantages were found in single-sex settings. Single-sex schools tend to be smaller, have more personal social relations among school community members, and teaching strategies that allow more student activity. In addition, parents who send their children to single-sex schools have made a "pro-academic choice," which itself may explain students' higher academic achievements (Weil, 2008).

Since they cannot prove the effectiveness of single-sex education, proponents simply provide reasons why it *should* work—arguments often based on a pseudo-science of gender differences (Guerian, 2007a, 2007b; Sax, 2006, 2007). Sometimes advocates of single-sex education even argue that gender differences in the size of the brain make a difference in how young people learn, even when the studies to which they refer make no such claim (Lenroot et al., 2007; National Association of Single Sex Public Schools, 2008b). They also argue that schools routinely mis-educate boys as a result of the movement for gender equity, suggesting that girls' and women's gains have come at boys' expense (Sommers, 2000; Sax, 2007). However, recent studies have disproven the existence of a "boys' crisis" in education (Corbett, Hill, and St. Rose, 2008; Klein et al., 2007). "From standardized tests in elementary and secondary school to college entrance examinations, average test scores have risen or remained stable for both girls and boys in recent decades. Similarly, both women and men are more likely to graduate from high school and college today than ever before" (Corbett, Hill, and St. Rose, 2008, p. 2–3).

Policies allowing publicly funded single-sex educational settings run counter to the law. In 1996 the Supreme Court ruled the single-sex admission policy at state-funding Virginia Military Institute was unconstitutional (*United States v. Virginia,* 1996). According to the Court, government agencies such as schools must have "an exceedingly persuasive" reason, based in research, to establish programs that make distinctions based on gender. The single-sex program must have social and educational outcomes related to that reason, and evidence that the program will achieve those goals and protect gender equity. With such a shaky research base, the policy to establish single-sex schools or classes lacks the fundamental justification demanded by the Court's ruling (Salamone, 2006).

Even if well-intentioned, this policy is dangerous. Many of those who advocate single-sex schools or classes may be doing so to advance another agenda. They often insist that providing such options increases "parental choice" with regard to children's education (Meyer, 2008). Those who use the language of choice often support privatization of education—they are often in favor of charter schools, vouchers, and other proposals that provide public funds for nonpublic schools. Currently, most single-sex schools are private schools. If proponents of gender-segregated settings can convince the public of their value, it might become easier to convince voters to allow students to choose to attend one outside the public school system. After all, they will argue, wouldn't it be easier just to give students the tuition money to attend an already existing school than go to all the trouble and expense of creating one? Once that door has been opened, it will be difficult to close and could be pushed open even farther by those who want to dismantle the American public school system completely.

The struggle to achieve gender equity in American public education has been long and difficult. It has required commitment to the quintessentially American principle that accidents of fate, such as gender, do not limit a person's fundamental right to equal treatment under the law, define ability, or determine destiny. Any retreat from that commitment with regard to equality of educational access, opportunity, or achievement risks reinforcing sexual stereotypes and traditional gender roles and has the potential to create the kind of segregated educational settings ruled unconstitutional in *Brown v. Board of Education* (1954). In education, separate is never equal and unequal is never legal. Eliminating gender discrimination in education is the best way to guarantee individual rights and that is the best way, ultimately, to create a more just country.

POSITION 2: ACCOMMODATING DIFFERENCES

Co-ed schooling imposes the need for sex-blind instruction material and uniform testing and standards of behavior. As a result, on the way to a perfectly balanced sexual universe in our schools, "equal to" was turned into "the same as." But there's a problem when you bleach out gender differences: boys and girls are not the same.

—Gilbert, 2007

There is no question that the efforts of many Americans to end educational gender discrimination have resulted in some important gains, especially with regard to access to schools. All phases of public education—from kindergarten to graduate school—are open to members of both genders. However, there are real differences between males and females that deserve accommodation in schools. Rigid policies of "sameness" instead of making legitimate distinctions actually limit opportunities for students. We have ample evidence that boys and girls do not experience school in the same way.

Gendered Experiences in Schools

The recent generation-long effort to eliminate discrimination from schools began with analyses of the way gender affected students' educational experiences. Researchers found preschool boys played with tools, simple machines, balls, and blocks much more often than girls (Kahle, in AAUW, 1995). Teachers encouraged boys to be assertive and independent, discouraged girls from taking risks, and rewarded them for being "timid, cooperative and quiet" (Tozer, Violas, and Senese, 2002, p. 392).

In elementary schools, teachers worked with boys more often and gave them more attention and affection than they provided girls. They prompted boys to think through projects or answer difficult questions on their own and were more likely to give girls the answers or show them how to do a task. When boys answered a question by calling out, teachers paid attention to what they said. When girls did the same thing, teachers more often ignored the content of the comment and scolded them for not following classroom rules (Sadker and Sadker, 1994). Boys were more likely than girls to be regarded as "trouble-makers," have their teachers contact parents about behavioral problems, repeat a grade, and be labeled as learning disabled (U.S. Department of Education, 2000).

By the time they got to middle school, girls were struggling with messages about their academic competency and had become tentative about speaking up in class (Brown and Gilligan, 1993). By high school, many girls were quite good at "doing school"—that is, presenting their work neatly, turning it in on time, and regurgitating information on tests. They did not, however, excel in independent or critical thinking and rarely took risks in choosing courses or assignments (Brown and Gilligan, 1993; AAUW, 1995). Boys were more likely to take higher-level math, science, and computer classes. They were also more likely to drop out. Boys faced peer pressure to take part in sports and their masculinity was judged on their ability to compete. They encouraged one another to engage in drug and alcohol use and other risky behaviors. Expressions of emotion were mocked (Kindlon et al., 1999; Pollack, 1999). Acting as if they had power through posturing and violence was rewarded. Interest in "feminine" things such as reading and the arts was ridiculed (Kimmel, 2000).

Textbooks contributed to sex discrimination in schools by not deeply challenging traditional understandings of gender. Curricular materials did not affirm differences between members of the same gender or integrate the experiences, needs, and interests of both sexes in their material (AAUW, 1995). Vocational education programs reflected and reproduced traditional gender expectations. Females were overwhelmingly directed or allowed to enter "training programs for historically female—and traditionally low wage—jobs" in cosmetology, child care, and practical nursing (Brake, 1999, p. 10). Boys took courses designed to get them ready for high-paying work as carpenters, electricians, or plumbers.

Four out of five students reported that they had been the victim of sexual harassment. One-quarter said it happened to them "often" (AAUW, 1993). Sexual harassment took many forms in secondary schools: comments, jokes, gestures, and looks. Students were touched, grabbed, or pinched. They were subjected to mooning, flashing, and genital exposure. Students became targets of sexual rumors or written graffiti, had their clothes pulled at or off, were spied on in locker rooms, were shown or given unwanted sexual pictures or notes, and were blocked or cornered in sexual ways. They were forced to kiss someone when they did not want to, and in some cases do something even more sexual than kissing. It seemed that no school space was entirely safe. Students reported harassment took place in classrooms, hallways, gyms, cafeterias, locker rooms, parking lots, playgrounds, and buses (AAUW, 1993). Advocates railed against the impact of these behaviors. "The consequences can be devastating, as young women struggle to survive in a learning environment they often experience as toxic. When so much of a female student's day is spent fending off diminishing comments, sexual innuendoes and physical pestering, how can she be expected to thrive at school?" (Larkin, 1997, p. 14).

Finally, researchers found schools discriminated against young women who were pregnant or parenting, doing little to accommodate their special needs. Few schedules were adjusted to allow for the extra time mothers might need to transport their babies to child care. Even fewer provided such centers on-site. These young women were more likely to drop out of school than other female students (U.S. Department of Education, 2000).

The research made a compelling case that boys and girls had different experiences in schools—and that each group was being shortchanged because of gender discrimination. However, the policies and practices developed to address these issues seem disconnected from the reality they described.

One-Size-Fits-All Regulations

During the 1970s, feminists and other civil rights advocates tried to equate racism and sexism. They lobbied for passage of an Equal Rights Amendment (ERA) that would have prohibited all discrimination on the basis of gender. However, the decade-long national debate on the ERA made it clear to most Americans that treating people differently based on their gender was far different from discriminating on the basis of race. They understood it sometimes was necessary to make legitimate distinctions between the genders in order to serve the best interests of women and their children.

A determined campaign by those who saw the dangers to women inherent in the ERA convinced Americans that the amendment would prevent the courts from allowing legitimate distinctions to be made in public policies such as child custody, alimony, and workforce accommodations. After 1977, no state legislature could be persuaded to ratify the amendment. By 1982, even the most ardent feminists declared the effort to pass the ERA to be at an end (Blair, 1997).

However, efforts to use one-size-fits-all policies to address gender discrimination did not end with the death of the ERA. In 1972, Congress passed Title IX, which required more equitable distribution of educational resources and opportunities among males and females. When Title IX has been applied in rational and thoughtful ways, the consequence has been a more just educational system. However, the problems inherent in ruling out all legitimate distinctions between treatment of the sexes has also created situations in which Title IX's consequences have been unjust—and absurd.

The limitations and resulting failures of the attempt to create gender equity by relying solely on ending discrimination are particularly obvious in the application of Title IX regulations to athletics. The legislation originally was intended to end discrimination in school sports programs. Over time, however, it has created a "quota system" in colleges and universities' athletics programs that actually limits opportunity for some students. Through the efforts of feminists and others who support rigid policies of "nondiscrimination," the law has been interpreted as requiring strict "proportionality" between the percentage of women in a school's student body and the percentage of women participating in varsity sports. That is, if 55 percent of the students at a given institution are female, then 55 percent of the athletes also must be female. Schools are considered in violation of the law and face loss of government aid if they fail to comply (Kennedy, 2007).

Despite girls' increased participation in sports, fewer young women than men make the commitment to take part in intercollegiate athletics. Since they ignore the element of individual choice in the creation of gender identities and the influence of those choices on gender equity in educational settings, proponents of rigid nondiscrimination policies blame schools for the differences in student involvement in sports. When colleges cannot entice or coerce enough women to participate in sports, they are forced to achieve proportionality by cutting men's teams. Sports like track, golf, tennis, rowing, swimming, gymnastics, and wrestling have experienced the greatest decline. There are nearly 1,000 more women's than men's teams in the NCAA. The average number of male athletes on NCAA college campuses has dropped from 253 to 199. As the percentage of men in college drops, the number of male teams will drop as well, eliminating even more male NCAA athletes (College Sports Council, 2008). Proponents of absolute "equality" in sports have now turned their attention to high school athletics. There is every reason to expect that the results will be "equally" devastating to male athletes who want, need, and deserve an opportunity to compete (Gavora, 2007). The absurdity of the claim that this policy helps achieve justice is obvious. Committed male athletes are being deprived of their right to participate in sports and to have that choice supported by their schools. The law never authorized discrimination against men through a policy that does not take into account individual freedom. It was meant to ensure equal opportunity for males and females.

School textbooks have also suffered from efforts at social engineering. Diane Ravitch has documented how publishers have responded to Title IX.

Quotas have been imposed on examples, test questions, and illustrations; males and females must appear in 50:50 ratios. Words like "actress," "heroine," "brotherhood," and "forefathers" are banned. Women cannot be shown doing household tasks or taking care of children. Men cannot be portrayed in traditional jobs like plumbers or carpenters. Boys cannot express anger; girls cannot be frightened (Ravitch, 2003). Sanitizing textbooks does not create equality. In fact, demanding "political correctness" in texts can hurt efforts to make real progress toward justice. Critics find such efforts easy targets of ridicule and dismiss real concerns as "more of the same." Those who proposed changes to textbooks may have begun with the laudable aim of creating an equal playing field for girls and boys by opening their minds to possibilities that transcended traditional gender roles. However, the result is a system that polices the language and images young people see—hardly the soil in which freedom of choice can grow.

Perhaps the most absurd consequence of efforts to eliminate all discrepancies in treatment of boys and girls in schools is their effect on school dress codes. According to the most rigid interpretation of the law, districts can make no distinctions between males and females with regard to wearing clothing, jewelry or makeup to school. Surely, creating equality of educational opportunity for male and female students does not require the creation of policies that equate sameness with fairness. The time has come to explore strategies that recognize and respond appropriately to the learning needs of both boys and girls. Policies and practices that do so will, in the long run, result in more equity for men and women.

Real Differences Require Real Accommodations

There is certainly no denying that biological differences between males and females really exist. Women conceive, gestate, give birth, and suckle new members of the human race. Men do not. But reproductive differences are only one way in which men and women are not the same. Male and female brains also differ. Scientists have known for more than a hundred years that men's brains are larger than women's. However, they have recently discovered that females have almost 20 percent more gray matter than males in their brains. "The female brain is more densely packed with neurons and dendrites, providing concentrated processing power—and more thought-linking capability" (Marano, 2003). Men's brain structures allow them to perform better than women when attempting visual or spatial tasks. Women's brain structures help them do better than men on verbal- or language-oriented tasks (Burman, Bitan, and Booth, 2008). "The areas of the brain associated with language appear to work harder in girls during language tasks, and boys and girls rely on different parts of the brain when working on these tasks" (Science Daily, 2008). We may not understand completely how physical differences between males and females are related to thinking and learning. We know enough, however, to realize schools and teachers must be responsive to those differences if children are going to have equal educational opportunity. For example, boys need brightly lit classrooms and teachers who speak in loud, enthusiastic tones. They need exercise periods during the day, more confrontational disciplinary practices, and learning activities that engage them in quests for answers. Girls do better in quieter classrooms where cooperation and bonding are encouraged (Sax, 2006, 2007). Obviously, coeducational settings make it impossible to respond adequately to both sets of needs—they are, to a large degree, mutually exclusive. Single-sex classes and schools are not discriminatory—they are necessary accommodations that produce real and significant results.

It may be too early to understand completely how the physical differences between men and women are related to thinking and learning. However, such differences do exist and schools need the freedom to explore ways to accommodate them.

Single-Sex Settings

For many years, only those children whose families could afford private schools were able to experience the benefits of single-sex schools (Meyer, 2008). Fortunately, recent changes to the No Child Left Behind Act have made it possible for public schools also to meet the real needs of students. The results have been overwhelmingly positive. All across the country, teachers and administrators report fewer discipline problems, higher test scores, and more time on tasks. Parents say their children are more eager to go to school and more interested in what happens there. Students say it is easier to learn (Conklin, 2008; Gerwetz, 2007; Holleran, 2007; Jan, 2008; Meyer, 2008; Weil, 2008).

It may be that single-sex settings are successful not only because they accommodate learning differences between boys and girls. They also present students with alternatives to gender stereotypes and, more importantly, with spaces in which it is safe to challenge them. For example, in single-sex schools, in addition to acquiring knowledge that will result in increased choices about future education and careers, it also is considered within the range of acceptable femininity for a girl to learn how to work hard, discover what kinds of efforts are successful for her, and develop time-management and problem-solving skills. Most importantly in such a setting, young women can come to believe that they have tremendous control over the course of their lives and still be considered feminine. Teachers and administrators also expand the definition of acceptable gender behavior for girls in most single-sex schools. Students see women teaching subjects such as chemistry, physics, and advanced mathematics that traditionally have not been considered "feminine" (Meyer, 2008; Weil, 2008).

Research on the effects of single-sex settings on boys provides some evidence that in such spaces traditional gender roles are challenged as well. There is a greater range in the definitions of masculinity in schools for boys than in coeducational ones. So, many boys and young men take part in activities traditionally defined as "feminine" such as the arts and community service (Excellence Charter School, 2008; National Association for Single Sex Public Schools, 2008d).

In many ways, in single-sex educational settings students no longer have to match their behavior or attitudes to gender stereotypes. It is ironic that advocates of educational equity oppose them.

The effort to create educational gender equity is laudable and rightly has been pursued throughout U.S. history. Eliminating truly discriminatory policies and practices has been a necessary part of that process. It has not, however, proven to be a sufficient one. Eliminating the possibility of making legitimate distinctions between educational needs of males and females has prevented the struggle for educational equality from being as successful as justice demands it be.

Educational gender inequity remains a fact of life in American schools. It will continue to do so until educators are allowed to create settings addressing the total process by which gender differences in schools are produced. By ignoring the tendency of coeducational settings to reproduce society's dominant gender prescriptions, and refusing to permit educators to create settings that resist those stereotypes, we perpetuate pressures that result in students' choices to conform to them. What is needed is a commitment to make public education better able to meet the needs of all the students it serves. Young people deserve nothing less than having an equal right to education that recognizes the complexity of the problem of gender.

For Discussion

1. Although the positions in this chapter allude to the effects race, class, and ethnicity might have on an individual's creation of his or her gender identity, they do not discuss those effects in any detail. Consider how the other facets of a person's identity or situation in life might affect the choices they make about how much or how little to conform to various forms of masculinity or femininity. That is, does a person's race, class, or gender affect how free people feel they are to deviate from gender stereotypes? Depending on your answers, what kinds of changes to the proposals in this chapter do you think are necessary to create gender equity in schools that takes race, class, and ethnicity into consideration?

2. Access information about gender differences in test scores from the Educational Testing Services website, www.ets.org/research. (For example, the report by Richard Coley cited in the references is available there.) In light of the discussions in this chapter, how do you explain such differences? How do you explain the fact that there appears to be little variance among gender differences from one racial/ethnic group to another? What does that suggest to you about ways to remedy gender inequity?

3. Research your college or university's athletic program. Do they seem to be in compliance with Title IX regulations? Have any male teams been cut to achieve "proportionality"? Interview male and female athletes and coaches to get their views on gender issues in the program and to determine for yourself if any discrimination exists.

4. Advantages of single-sex schools are discussed in Position 2. Can you think of any disadvantages of attending such schools? Are they academic or social in nature? Interview friends or classmates who attended single-sex high schools. How do their experiences confirm the arguments made in the chapter? How do their experiences confirm your speculated disadvantages?

References

AMERICAN ASSOCIATION OF UNIVERSITY WOMEN (AAUW). (1993). *Hostile Hallways: The AAUW Survey of Sexual Harassment in America's Schools.* Washington, DC: Author.
———. (1995) *How Schools Shortchange Girls.* New York: Marlowe.

American Civil Liberties Union (2008). "Sex Segregated Schools: Separate and Unequal." www.aclu.org/womensrights/edu/30129res20070614.html.

BIKLEN, S., AND POLLARD, D., EDS. (1993). *Gender and Education.* Yearbook of the National Society for the Study of Education. Chicago: NSSE.

BROWN, L., AND GILLIGAN, C. (1993). *Meeting at the Crossroads.* Cambridge: Harvard University Press.

Brown v. Board of Education of Topeka, Kansas. (1954). 347 U.S. 483.

BURMAN, D., BITAL, T. AND BOOTH, J. (2008). "Sex Differences In Neural Processing Of Language Among Children." *Neuropsychologia* 46(5): 1349–1362.

CHESLOCK, J. (2007). "Whose Playing Sports? Trends in Participation." East Meadow, NY: Women's Sports Foundation.

CHODOROW, N. (1978). *The Reproduction of Mothering.* Berkley: University of California Press.

CHOUINARD, R., VEZEAU, C., BOUFFARD, T. (2008). "Coeducational or Single-Sex School: Does It Make a Difference on High School Girls' Academic Motivation?" Educational Studies 34(2): 129–144.

College Sports Council. (2008). "Facts." www.collegesportscouncil.org/about/facts.cfm.

Conklin, M, "Single-sex Classes Tried in Janeville", *Wisconsin State Journal,* May 4, 2008.

COOPERSTEIN, D. (2008). "The Long Road to Pay Equity for Women at Adelphi." *Academe* 94(1):34–36.

CORBETT, C., HILL, C. AND ST. ROSE, A. (2008). *Where the Girls Are: The Facts About Gender Equity in Education.* Washington, D.C.: American Association of University Women.

DOUGLAS, A. (1977). *The Feminization of American Culture.* New York: Avon Books.

EVANS, S. (1989). *Born for Liberty: A History of Women in America.* New York: Free Press.

Excellence Charter School. (2008). "Our Program." www.uncommonschools.org/ecs/aboutUs/programAndValues.html.

FEDERAL REGISTER. (2006). "Nondiscrimination on the Basis of Sex in Education Programs or Activities Receiving Federal Financial Assistance; Final Rule." October 25: 62529.

———. (2002) "Nondiscrimination on the Basis of Sex in Education Programs or Activities Receiving Federal Financial Assistance: Notice of Intent to Regulate." May 8: 31098.

FRAZIER, N., AND SADKER, M. (1973). *Sexism in School and Society.* New York: Harper and Row.

GAVORA, J. (2007). "Sex Games: Coming To A High School Near You." *National Review.* June 20. http://article.nationalreview.com/?q=NTgxOTlmZmMzYTgwMWZkZWY1NDA1YjkxZWE5MTU0Yjc=.

GEWERTZ, J. (2007). "Black Boys' Educational Plight Spurs Single-Gender Schools: New Federal Rules Seen as Chance for Innovation." *Education Week* 26(42):1.

GILBERT, M. (2007). "Single Sex Schools Help Children Thrive." *Christian Science Monitor,* September 20. www.csmonitor.com/2007/0920/p09s01-coop.html.

GILLIGAN, C. (1982). *In A Different Voice: Psychological Theory and Women's Development.* Cambridge: Harvard University Press.

GUERIAN, M. (2007a). *Nurture the Nature.* New York: Jossey-Bass.

———. (2007b). *The Minds of Boys: Saving Our Sons From Falling Behind in School and Life.* New York: Jossey-Bass.

HOLLERAN, K., (2007). "Educators Report Benefits from Gender-Segregated Teaching," *Charleston Daily Mail,* November 7.

HOROWITZ, H. (1984). *Alma Mater.* New York: Knopf.

HOWE, F. (1984). *Myths of Coeducation: Selected Essays.* Bloomington: Indiana University Press.

Jackson v Birmingham Board of Education. (2005). 125 S. Ct. 1497

JAN, T., (2008). "Keeping the Boys Away from the Girls," *Boston Globe,* May 9.

KAESTLE, C. (1983). *Pillars of the Republic: Common Schools and American Society 1780–1860.* New York: Hill and Wang.

KENNEDY, C. (2007). "The Athletics Directors' Dilemma: $$$ and Women's Sports." *Gender Issues* 24: 34–45.

KIMMEL, M. (2000). "What About the Boys?" *WEEA Digest,* Nov. 1, 1–2, 7–8.

KINDLON, D., ET AL. (1999). *Raising Cain: Protecting the Emotional Life of Boys.* New York: Ballantine.

KLEIN, S., RICHARDSON, B., GRAYSON, D., FOX, L., KRAMARAE, C., POLLARD, D. AND DWYER, C. (Eds.). (2007). *Handbook for achieving gender equity through education* (2nd ed.). Mahwah, NJ: Lawrence Erlbaum Associates.

LARKIN, J. (1997). *Sexual Harassment: High School Girls Speak Out.* Toronto: Second Story Press.

LEE, V. (1998). "Single Sex Secondary Schooling: A Solution to the Problem of Gender Inequity?" In *Separated by Sex.* Washington, DC: AAUW.

LENROOT, R., et al. (2007). "Sexual Dimorphism Of Brain Developmental Trajectories During Childhood And Adolescence." *Neuroimage.* 36(2007): 1065–1073. www.boysadrift.com/2007Giedd.pdf.

LUFKIN, M. (2005). "Taking the Road Less Traveled." *School Counselor Magazine* 41(5), n.p.

MAC AN GHAILL, M. (1994). *The Making of Men: Masculinities, Sexualities and Schooling.* Buckingham: Open University Press.

MARANO, H. (2003). "The New Sex Scorecard," *Psychology Today,* July/August, n.p. www.psychologytoday.com/articles/pto-20030624-000003.html.

MEYER, P. (2008). "Learning Separately: The Case for Single Sex Schools." *Education Next* 8(1): 10–21.

MILLER, J. (1976). *Toward A New Psychology of Women.* Boston: Beacon Press.

National Association for Single Sex Public Education. (2008a). "Single-Sex Schools/Schools with single-sex classrooms/what's the difference?" www.singlesexschools.org/schools-schools.htm.

———. (2008b) "Brain Differences." www.singlesexschools.org/research-brain.htm.

———. (2008c). "The Legal Status of Single Sex Public Education." www.singlesexschools.org/policy-legalstatus.htm.

———. (2008d). "Single Sex Schools." http://www.singlesexschools.org/home.php.

National Coalition for Women and Girls in Education. (2007). *Title IX Athletics Policies Issues and Data for Education Decision Makers.* Washington, DC: author.

National Council on the Accreditation of Teacher Education. (2008). "Program Standards and Report Forms." www.ncate.org/public/programStandards.asp?ch=4.

POLLACK, W. (1999). *Real Boys.* New York: Dimensions.

RAVITCH, D. (2000). *Left Back.* New York: Simon and Schuster.

———. (2003). *The Language Police: How Pressure Groups Restrict What Students Learn.* New York: Alfred A. Knopf.

RURY, J. (1991). *Education and Women's Work.* Albany: SUNY Press.

SADKER, M., AND SADKER, D. (1982). *Sex Equity Handbook for Schools.* New York: Longman.

———. (1994). *Failing at Fairness: How Schools Cheat Girls.* New York: Touchstone.

SALAMONE, R. (2006). "Single-Sex Programs: Resolving the Research Conundrum," *Teachers College Record* 108 (1). (n.p.)

SAX, L. (2006). *Why Gender Matters: What Parents and Teachers Need to Know about the Emerging Science of Sex Differences.* New York: Broadway.

———. (2007). *Boys Adrift: The Five Factors Driving the Growing Epidemic of Unmotivated Boys and Underachieving Young Men.* New York: Basic Books.

SCIENCE DAILY (2008). "Boys' And Girls' Brains Are Different: Gender Differences In Language Appear Biological." *Science Daily*, March 5.

SETTLES, I.; CORTINA, L.; MALLEY, J. AND STEWART, A . (2007)."The Climate for Women in Academic Science: The Good, the Bad, and the Changeable." *Psychology of Women Quarterly* 30(1): 47–56.

SKLAR, K. (1993). "The Schooling of Girls and Changing Community Values in Massachusetts Towns 1750–1820." *History of Education Quarterly* 33(4), 511–542.

SOLOMON, B. (1986). *In the Company of Educated Women.* New Haven: Yale University Press.

SOMMERS, C. (2000). "The War Against Boys." *Atlantic Monthly. Digital Edition.* www .theatlantic.com/issues/2000/05/sommers.htm.

SPRING, J. (1997). *The American School 1642–1996.* New York: McGraw-Hill.

STOWE, L. (1991). "Should Physics Classes Be Single-sex?" *Physics Teacher* 29(6), 380–381.

STREITMATTER, J. (1997). "An Exploratory Study of Risk-Taking and Attitudes in a Girls Only Middle School Math Class." *Elementary School Journal* 98(1), 15–26.

———. (1998) "Single-sex Classes: Female Physics Students Make their Case." *School Science and Mathematics* 98(7), 369–375.

———. (1999). *For Girls Only.* Albany: SUNY Press.

TOZER, S., VIOLAS, P., AND SENESE, G. (2002). *School and Society: Historical and Contemporary Perspectives.* 4th Ed. Boston: McGraw-Hill.

TUCKER CENTER FOR RESEARCH ON GIRLS AND WOMEN IN SPORT. (2007). *The 2007 Tucker Center Research Report, Developing physically active girls: An evidence-based multidisciplinary approach.* University of Minnesota, Minneapolis, MN: Author.

TYACK, D., AND HANSOT, E. (1992). *Learning Together: A History of Coeducation in American Public Schools.* New York: Russell Sage Foundation.

United States v Virginia. (1996). 518 U.S. 515, 533.

URBAN, W., AND WAGONER, J. (2000). *American Education: A History.* New York: McGraw-Hill.

U.S. CENSUS BUREAU. (2008a). "Percent of People 25 Years Old and Over Who Have Completed High School Years 1940 to 2007. (Table A-2)" www.census.gov/population/ www/socdemo/educ-attn.html.

———. (2008b). "Educational Attainment of the Population 25 Years and Older by Selected Characteristics". www.census.gov/population/www/socdemo/education/ cps2007.html.

U.S. DEPARTMENT OF EDUCATION. (2008a). "Women's Educational Equity." www.ed.gov/ programs/equity/index.html.

———. (2008B). *The Condition of Education, 2008.* Washington DC: National Center for Education Statistics. http://nces.ed.gov/pubsearch/pubsinfo.asp?pubid=2008031.

———. (2007). *The Nation's Report Card: America's high school graduates: Results from the 2005 NAEP high school transcript study,* by C. Shettle, S. Roey, J. Mordica, R. Perkins, C. Nord, J. Teodorovic, et al. (NCES 2007-467). Washington, DC: U.S. Government Printing Office. http://nces.ed.gov/nationsreportcard/pdf/studies/2007467.pdf.

———. (2005). *Single-Sex Versus Secondary Schooling: A Systematic Review.* Washington, D.C: author. www.ed.gov/rschstat/eval/other/single-sex/single-sex.pdf.

———. (2004). "Trends in Educational Equity of Girls and Women." Washington, DC: National Center for Education Statistics. NCES 2005-016.

WEIL, E. (2008). "Teaching Boys and Girls Separately," *New York Times*, March 2.

Women's Sports Foundation. (2007). "Mind the Gap: Women Still Underrepresented in High School Athletics." www.womenssportsfoundation.org/Content/Articles/Issues/Participation/M/Mind-the-Gap-Women-Still-Underrepresented-in-High-School-Athletics.aspx.

————. (2008). "2007 Statistics - Gender Equity in High School and College Athletics: Most Recent Participation and Budget Statistics." www.womenssportsfoundation.org/Content/Articles/Issues/General/123/2007-Statistics--Gender-Equity-in-High-School-and-College-Athletics-Most-Recent-Participation--Budge.aspx.

ZINN, H. (1995). *A People's History of the United States.* New York: Harper.

CHAPTER 5

Standards-Based Reform: Real Change or Political Smoke Screen

Will the standards-based reform movement improve education or discriminate against poor and disadvantaged students?

POSITION 1: STANDARDS-BASED REFORM PROMISES QUALITY EDUCATION FOR ALL STUDENTS

We have a responsibility as a nation to take bold steps to close the achievement gaps that plague our nation's schools and to ensure that all students are properly prepared for successful and productive lives after high school. Failing to take sustained action will not only result in the continued tragedy of unfulfilled potential, but will also threaten our nation's economy and competitiveness in the world.

—Commission on NCLB, 2007, p. 9

Public education always has been the focus of one reform impulse or another. Earlier generations of school reformers were concerned with *access* to education, and for good reason. One hundred years ago, only 10 percent of Americans attended secondary schools, and barely 2 percent received degrees (Gardner, 2002). Fewer still could think realistically about college. Before the twentieth century, race, gender, and economic circumstances combined to make it unlikely many students would continue their education beyond elementary school. Previous reforms focused on making schools affordable and accessible to all students, and those efforts were largely successful. Today's reformers have turned their attention to school *quality*, kindergarten through high school, and this too is for good reason. Americans now ask schools to do more than enroll large numbers of students and pass them along from one grade to another. For citizens to thrive personally and for the nation to prosper as a whole, schools must ensure students have an adequate command of math, science, and language arts. Our economic and political well-being depends on what is learned in schools. Educational quality is now the focus of national reform.

Under the American system of government, legislative powers not expressly given to the federal government are reserved for the states or the people therein. The U.S. Constitution does not give the federal government any specific authority to regulate or control education, and therefore the United States has developed fifty state systems of education administered by 15,000 school districts. Local control of schooling is part of the American tradition of education. Nevertheless, the federal government has played an increasingly important role in education since the founding of the nation. Grants of federal land were used to create public schools, and the Morrill Act of 1862 helped support the development of over sixty land-grant colleges. Nowhere has the federal government's role in education been felt more powerfully than in the 1954 Supreme Court decision known as *Brown v. Board of Education*, which held that segregated public schools were a violation of the Constitution. *Brown* was a significant assertion of federal authority in education, guaranteeing equal treatment before the law for all children in public schools. *Brown* addressed the issue of *equality* in schooling. Forty-seven years later, the No Child Left Behind (NCLB) legislation extended the role of the federal government to the related issue of *quality* in schooling for all children. As Chubb (2005, p. 29) argues, in addition to shouldering more of the costs of public schooling, the federal government has expanded its role and taken the high moral ground, "becoming the leading advocate for equality— for racial minorities, special education students, English language learners, and girls. . . ."

Standards-Based Reform and America's Underachieving Schools

The 1983 publication of *A Nation at Risk* was the catalyst for NCLB, today's standards-based reform movement. A short 63-page book, written in direct, simple language without academic jargon or confusing statistics and tables, it called public attention to serious deficiencies in schools. "Our nation is at risk," the report begins. "Our once unchallenged preeminence in commerce, industry, science, and technological innovation is being overtaken by competitors throughout the world. . . . What was unimaginable a generation ago has begun to occur—others are matching and surpassing our educational attainments. If an unfriendly foreign power had attempted to impose on America the mediocre educational performance that exists today, we might have viewed it as an act of war" (National Commission on Excellence in Education, 1983, p. 5).

A sobersided panel of educators, which included college presidents and public school administrators, brought together by the secretary of education, used intentionally alarming language to describe the state of K–12 education and shake Americans from their quiescence and self-satisfaction. The panel found a host of problems in schools. Among other things, achievement scores on standardized tests were down and international comparisons were embarrassing. Thirteen percent of all seventeen-year-olds were functionally illiterate, and many of their literate peers could not "draw an inference from written material, write a persuasive essay, or solve a math problem that required more than one or two steps." The report's directness attracted attention of parents, educators, and elected officials. Recommendations for public education were straightforward: (1) improve education for all students, and (2) develop higher standards. The report urged those in charge of the nation's schools to chart a more rigorous course and measure student progress more systematically.

In the 1980s, President George H. W. Bush recognized that states by themselves were not able to bring about necessary national changes. President Bush believed the nation needed to establish world-class national standards in core subject areas, and to make sure that students were meeting these standards, his administration called for voluntary testing in grades four, eight, and twelve. In 1989, at a conference in Charlottesville, Virginia, President Bush and the nation's governors agreed to six national goals for education. "America 2000," as the goals became known, stipulated that by the year 2000,

1. All children will start school ready to learn.
2. The high school graduation rate will increase to at least 90 percent.
3. All students in grades four, eight, and twelve will demonstrate competency in English, math, science, civics, foreign language, economics, arts, history, and geography.
4. U.S. students will be first in math and science achievement.
5. Every adult will be literate.
6. Every school in the U.S. will be free of drugs and violence, and the unauthorized presence of firearms and alcohol. (Jennings, 1998, p. 14; Ravitch, 2005)

In 1994, Congress added additional goals designed to improve the quality of teacher education and increase parental involvement in schools. These proposals would take standards-based reform in a new direction. America 2000 encouraged high standards and high national expectations for all students. The federal government would not intrude on the states' control of education, but it could urge them to raise the academic bar. The standards proposed by President Bush were not designed to serve as a national curriculum. Instead, they were to be academic models state and local school districts could adopt to raise expectations for teachers and students. Improved state standards promised national reform. Variations would continue to be found across state lines, but students, parents, and teachers in every state would know what was expected of them. Schools of education were asked to equip prospective and in-service teachers with the skills needed to help students meet the new standards. Test makers were asked to develop examinations keyed to the standards. By design, all students were to benefit.

Although the timetable proved to be overly optimistic, President Bush's call for high national standards and assessment of student performance set the stage for substantive reform in the quality of education. In 1992, Bill Clinton was elected president. Mr. Clinton, as governor, had been active in the 1989 education conference. A year later, President Clinton proposed "Goals 2000," a legislative package that, if it had been enacted, would have set into law the six national goals for education agreed to by George Bush and the nation's governors. Under President Bush, the Department of Education provided grants to national organizations of scholars and teachers to develop voluntary national standards in important school subjects. President Clinton's administration provided funds for states to develop standards of their own at about the same time national standards were being released. The issue grew murky with both states and national organizations developing academic standards simultaneously. President Clinton tried to help by agreeing to support state standards as long as states volunteered to go along with national testing. However, the ensuing confusion between state and national standards and difficulty of assessing fifty state systems through one national test hindered the progress of school reform until 2001.

"No Child Left Behind Act," 2001

The No Child Left Behind legislation, supported by large majorities of Democrats and Republicans in both houses of Congress and signed by President George W. Bush, is designed to create a stronger, more accountable education system. It does not call for national standards or national tests, as Presidents Bush and Clinton had advocated. NCLB legislation shifts the action back to the states. Under the new law, states are required to develop their own standards for what students should know at every grade level in math, English/ language arts, and science. When the specific standards were put in place— stipulating the level at which a child should be reading by the end of third grade, for example—the states began to assess every student's progress with exams aligned with state standards. All states must administer academic assessments in reading and mathematics to students in grades three through eight and once more in high school. Beginning in 2007–2008, NCLB required states to conduct assessments in science at least once in grades three to five, six to nine, and ten to twelve.

States are required to develop a "single statewide accountability system" to ensure schools and school districts—not individual students—are making "adequate yearly progress" in math, English/language arts, and science. Progress is to be demonstrated for all students, with "separate measurable annual objectives" for (1) economically disadvantaged students, (2) students from major racial and ethnic groups, (3) students with disabilities, and (4) students with limited English proficiency. By 2014, twelve years from the enactment of the legislation, "all students were to meet the proficient level on state tests." The legislation requires each school, school district, and state to make "adequate yearly progress"[1] toward meeting state standards. Parents with children in failing schools are given the right to have them transferred to better-performing schools. Students who have been victims of violent crimes and those who attend persistently unsafe schools

---

[1]As defined on the NCLB website (2008), adequate yearly progress is "an individual state's measure of progress toward the goal of 100 percent of students achieving state academic standards in at least reading/language arts and math. It sets the minimum level of proficiency that the state, its school districts, and schools must achieve each year on annual tests and related academic indicators."

also are allowed to transfer schools (No Child Left Behind, 2008). NCLB legislation focuses on all children, from all races and social classes. The legislation recognizes that the nation increasingly depends on the academic success of minority children, and that their poor academic performance—the achievement gap between white and black and Hispanic students—is not only an affront to American values but also a threat to the nation's economic future (Reyna, 2005).

Three presidents, two Republicans and one Democrat, established the priorities for the school reform agenda in the early twenty-first century. They agreed that to improve the nation's schools, the United States should develop a system of high state standards and rigorous state testing. The standards movement will help *all* students. This is a significant policy shift in itself. Currently U.S. schools sort students into various categories by academic ability, and treat different groups of students differently. The most able students are provided college-preparatory curricula of reasonably high quality. For all other students—in many cases, the vast majority of students—the curriculum is watered down, ineffective, and unlikely to equip them with the skills and knowledge needed for economic success and the common store of knowledge necessary for informed civic participation. The standards movement is designed to bring all students up to higher levels of academic performance, no matter where they begin (Tucker and Codding, 1998). An education built around academic standards serves students from poor as well as wealthy homes, and it will be especially valuable to students who, in the course of their education, move from school to school or district to district. It should be self-evident that students are likely to learn more when there is common agreement about what they are supposed to learn and high expectations for their achievement. In fact, the logic of standards-based school reform is so obvious and compelling that one may wonder why it is referred to as a *reform movement* (Bennett et al., 1999, p. 586). As Diane Ravitch (2005) notes, "Teachers, sports teams, and business leaders have long realized that measuring performance matters. Incentives matter. The absence of incentives also matters. These ideas would be considered axiomatic in any other profession or line of endeavor. This is why the principles embedded in NCLB are not likely to go away" (p. 50).

Support for the standards movement rests on the assumption that the subject matter students learn in school is important: content counts. The store of knowledge possessed by individuals operates to determine success or failure in school and, to a large measure, success or failure in life (Hirsch, 1996). That is to say, individuals who know more, those who have a greater store of knowledge, are more successful in school and tend to be more successful in getting into college, securing employment, and earning higher-than-average salaries. Subject matter knowledge is the very essence of education. It is important to be able to read, but it is more important what is read. Students who study and understand Dickens, Shakespeare, and Virginia Woolf are more likely to succeed than students who read less important, less challenging works. It is not enough for schools to pass students along from grade to grade simply because they attend regularly and are taught so many hours of reading and mathematics. States must establish content standards appropriate for success, and students must demonstrate command of subject matter and academic skills at the

FIGURE 5.1 Four Pillars of NCLB

Accountability: States must describe how they will close the achievement gap among all children and make sure all students achieve academic proficiency. States must produce annual report cards that inform parents of the academic progress made by the state and the various school districts within the state.

More local freedom: States and school districts have unprecedented flexibility in how they use federal education funds. Districts can use these funds for their particular needs, such as hiring new teachers, increasing teacher pay, and improving teacher training and professional development.

Encouraging proven methods: Federal funding is targeted to support programs that have been proven effective in increasing student learning and achievement. Reading programs are an example. NCLB supports scientifically-based instruction in the early grades under the new Reading First Program and in preschool under the Early Reading First Program.

Choices for parents: NCLB allows parents to choose other public schools or take advantage of free tutoring if their child attends a school that needs improvement. Also, parents can choose another public school if the school their child attends is unsafe.

Source: NCLB, 2008.

level described in the standards. Schools should not focus on "library skills" and "keyboarding," or other warm and fuzzy objectives. It is the content of education that matters.

When schools focus on content-free goals—for example, self-esteem exercises, discovery techniques, cooperative learning strategies—all students suffer because they learn less subject matter content (Hirsch, 1996; Bennett et al., 1999). Any approach to learning that emphasizes a process approach limits the futures of children by denying them access to intellectual capital—that is, the store of knowledge needed to do well in school and life. All children are harmed by a content-light approach, but children of the poor will be affected the most. Children from middle-class homes can count on their parents to compensate for schools' inattention to subject matter. They are likely to benefit from the company of literate adults, family trips, and private tutors to help them with foreign language acquisition, music and art, and mathematics. The negative effects of watered-down content, low standards, and low expectations fall hardest on the poor and students from less well-educated families. For these students, standards reform can produce dramatic improvements.

Consider one example, from Mount Vernon, New York, a working-class, suburb with a predominantly minority population. Following the national model, New York developed standards and assessment tests for all children, and initially the tests proved to be an embarrassment to the state's cities. Only 36 percent of Mount Vernon's fourth graders, for example, passed the English Language Arts (ELA) test. Instead of rolling over and playing dead or blaming the tests, Ronald Ross, a newly appointed school superintendent, decided to tackle the problem head-on. Ross examined the test and decided that it asked reasonable things of students and encouraged the teaching of worthwhile content. For example, fourth graders were expected to read stories and poems, chart the chronology of each, understand their imagery, and write an essay using the content from both the story and the poem. Ross decided that the ELA test was of educational value and teaching to the test would help students learn more skills and content than they had in the past. Teaching to the test would lead students and teachers along a higher curricular path. Children took books home every night and read for at least thirty minutes; they wrote every day; teachers drilled them and prepared them to meet state standards. The following year, the fourth graders at the lowest-achieving school improved their passing rate from 13 to 82 percent (Taub, 2002, p. 49).

In the world of education, a phrase such as "teaching to the test" sounds like heresy, and stressing content over process may seem like a renunciation of the progressive pedagogical creed. For decades, teachers have been told to "teach the individual child" and build content around the "interests of each child"—mantralike aphorisms offered by people who are well-meaning but misinformed. Unfortunately, the "child-centered" approach led to the "dumbing down" of the school curriculum, and test results indicate students were not learning enough of value. The standards-reform movement asks states and school districts to develop high standards and reasonable tests that hold schools accountable for teaching worthwhile material. It may not be as much fun for students as a child-centered approach to learning, and may not sound lofty and inspiring, but will be more beneficial for children in the long run.

Standards and Test Items: Examples from Mathematics

> To keep America strong in the 21st century, we must improve the way we teach math and we must give more students the chance to take advanced math and science courses in high school. (Margaret Spellings, Secretary of Education, quoted on NCLB website, 2008.)

The standards movement is well under way. The effort to develop academically appropriate standards has been ongoing for more than a decade. Some disciplines are ahead of others, and some states are further along the path to standards-based teaching and assessment, but changes are occurring everywhere. The field of school mathematics offers a good example of progress made in one K–12 discipline. Since 1989, the National Council of Teachers of Mathematics (NCTM) has released a series of documents that have paved the way for high-quality, thoughtful reform (NCTM, 2008). Based on NCTM recommendations, states developed their own math standards and curriculum frameworks. State standards usually are written by experts in the field—mathematicians, math educators and math teachers—and cover the range of content knowledge students need to know.

The website of one state explains its math standards are designed "to enable all of [the state's] children to move into the twenty-first century with the mathematical skills, understandings, and attitudes they will need to be successful in their careers and daily lives."[2] This very general math objective then is fleshed out, organized by topics, and applied appropriately to various grade levels in the

---

[2] Our examples, typical of the field, are taken from the New Jersey standards in mathematics (New Jersey Department of Education, 2008).

form of sixteen separate "standards" designed to define and illustrate "what is essential to excellent mathematics education." Consider the standard for "probability and statistics," a subset of the state's more general math objective. It reads,

> All students, will develop an understanding of statistics and probability and will use them to describe sets of data, model situations, and support inferences and arguments.

Most states have developed between five and twenty global standards in mathematics, and to make them understandable to students and their parents, and workable for teachers and administrators, each state has developed "substandards," sometimes in the form of indicators and activities by grade level that offer specificity and practical classroom guidance. Consider one indicator that has established expectations for what students in grades three to four should know and be able to do in the area of "statistics and probability." It requires students to:

> *Understand and informally use the concepts of range, mean, mode, and median.*

The indicator provides teachers with a clear picture of what they are expected to teach and what their students should know. The following sample activity offers teachers a practical teaching strategy for helping their students develop understandings of the concepts:

> Before counting the number of raisins contained in each of twenty-four individual boxes of raisins, students are asked to estimate the number of raisins in each box. They count the raisins and compare the actual numbers to their estimates. Students discover that the boxes contain different numbers of raisins. They construct a frequency chart on the blackboard and use the concepts of range, mean, median, and mode to discuss their situation.

In grades seven to eight, one standard for statistics and probability requires students to:

> *Select and use appropriate graphical representations and measures of central tendency (mean, mode, and median) for sets of data.*

A sample teaching strategy asks the teacher to have students work on problems like this one:

> A set of test scores in Mrs. Ditkof's class of twenty students is shown below:
>
> | 62 | 77 | 82 | 88 | 73 | 64 | 82 | 85 | 90 | 75 |
> | 74 | 81 | 85 | 89 | 96 | 69 | 74 | 98 | 91 | 85 |
>
> Determine the mean, median, mode, and range for the data. Suppose each student completes an extra-credit assignment worth five points, which is then added to his or her score. What is the mean of the set of scores now if each student received the extra five points? Explain how you calculated your answer.

While math may not become fun for every student, at the very least on a statewide basis, more math will be taught at a higher level to all students. Teachers will know what they are expected to teach; parents will know what their children are expected to learn; and the state math test will measure what is being taught in math classes. All students will receive higher-quality instruction thanks to standards-based reform. The NCTM believes that mathematics is a subject matter for every student, not just the few who may have the unusual talents needed by future engineers or scientists. All students deserve a high-quality mathematics education. The NCTM argues,

> We live in a mathematical world. All students deserve an opportunity to understand the power and beauty of mathematics. Students need to learn a new set of mathematics basics that enable them to compute fluently, and to solve problems creatively and resourcefully (NCTM, 2008).

The Logic of Standards-Based Reform

Advocates of standards-based reform in education offer several arguments to support their position, and they encourage you to think about the issue with these points in mind:

- Standards-based reform of education offers the best current remedy for reducing the achievement gap experienced by schools and districts serving economically-disadvantaged students (Gamoran, 2007).
- Content matters in education. For personal economic success and for the civic well-being of the nation, students should possess a reasonable command of a common store of agreed-upon content in math and literature, and the social, natural, and biological sciences (Hirsch, 2006).
- For too long, schools have permitted teachers to use methods based on fad, fancy, and personal preferences, without sufficient evidence of their effectiveness. NCLB emphasizes classroom practice based on rigorous, replicable, scientific research (Yell and Drasgow, 2005; Lyon, 2005).
- High standards work. The Commission on No Child Left Behind reported, "More progress was made by 9-year-olds in five years than in the previous 28 years combined. Reading and math scores for fourth-graders have reached all-time highs" (2007, p. 14).
- Schools will be better places for all children when curriculum planners stipulate in the clearest language possible what students should know and be able to do.
- Students are advantaged when schools test what is taught. The goal of assessment is to ensure that students have learned what is contained in the curriculum.
- To help students reach high standards, NCLB schools must hire "highly qualified teachers." Academic research demonstrates that the cognitive abilities of teachers (as measured by objective tests) and their command of subject matter are strong determinants of student achievement (Moe, 2005, pp. 176–177).
- Testing is an essential component of standards-based reform, necessary to gauge the extent to which standards have been followed and achieved (Phelps, 2004).

- Teacher-led instruction and other forms of explicit instruction are among the most effective methods for leading students to a consideration of subject matter. Book learning, memorization, and drill are part of successful instruction (Evers, 2001).
- The evidence suggests that common curriculum standards and curriculum-based tests increase academic achievement and decrease the achievement gap between rich and poor students (Hirsch, 2001, p. 201; Hoxby, 2005; Commission on NCLB, 2007).
- Standards-based reform is more than making sure students do better on tougher tests. The standards-reform movement is less about imposing rigor than it is a program for ensuring academic and personal success for all students (Paige, 2006).

NCLB, the most far-reaching reform of public education ever enacted in the United States, made a commitment that no child would be ignored and left behind in the nation's schools. The evidence thus far is that it is working to raise the achievement of all children of every race and family background. It is a long-overdue reform and it holds every promise of success.

POSITION 2: STANDARDS-BASED REFORM IS A POLITICAL SMOKE SCREEN

After six years, there is overwhelming evidence that the deeply flawed "No Child Left Behind" law (NCLB) is doing more harm than good in our nation's public schools. NCLB's test-and-punish approach to school reform relies on limited, one-size-fits-all tools that reduce education to little more than test prep. It produces unfair decisions and requires unproven, often irrational "solutions" to complex problems. NCLB is clearly underfunded, but fully funding a bad law is not a solution (FairTest, 2008).

Advocates of the standards movement argue they are responding responsibly to a crisis in education. *A Nation at Risk* (National Commission on Excellence in Education, 1983), the much-cited instigator of standards-based reform, describes a national danger brought about by anemic academic standards and poor student performance. The report argues teachers are not teaching well, and students are not learning very much of value in schools. International comparisons of student achievement reflect so poorly on U.S. students that the result is considered a potential tragedy for all Americans. The authors of the report argue that Americans face a crisis, economically and politically. They claim schools have let the nation down, and the nation is now in peril. If this were all true, an academic call to arms would be in order. The data and arguments of the report, however, defy common sense and do not stand up to even modest scrutiny. It's been twenty years since the publication of *A Nation at Risk*. In that time, and despite terrorist attacks and natural disasters, the United States continues to experience prosperity and economic growth. American achievements in science, technology, and medicine are the envy of the world. When Nobel Prize winners are announced, you can bet half your SAT score that Americans will figure prominently among the winners. There is also solid evidence to indicate that the American students do quite well in international comparisons. Reviewing the results of six international achievement assessments conducted over a ten-year period, two researchers conclude that "U.S. students have generally performed *above average* in comparisons with students in other industrialized nations" (Boe and Shin, 2005, p. 694).

Everything is not perfect in education, but it is not crumbling and certainly not in crisis. The jeremiads are not to be believed. *A Nation at Risk* helped promote the myth of a failing public school system, and it is used for political purposes with little if anything to do with academic quality. Berliner and Biddle (1995) argue that the authors of the report distorted the picture of American schools. While there are still too many poor and failing schools, there is no evidence of systemic collapse, and overheated rhetoric and questionable comparisons do not match the facts. The charges, the authors say, are "errant nonsense."

> If we go by the evidence, despite greatly expanded student enrollment, the average American high school and college student is now doing as well as, or perhaps slightly better than, that student did in previous years. Indeed, not only is student achievement remaining steady or rising slowly across the land, but so also is student intelligence. (p. 64)

Errant nonsense or not, *A Nation at Risk* focused attention on school reform for the first time in a generation. The report, widely publicized by journalists, made Americans suspicious of their schools. While some politicians and school reformers saw this as an honest opportunity to create sounder academic standards, others seized the report and used it to attack schools and advance their own agendas. Those on the far right in religion and politics used the "manufactured crisis" as an opportunity to take control of schools and ban ideas they found ideologically distasteful. Only with national and statewide curricula could ultraconservatives be assured that disquieting local voices—advocates of gay rights, abortion rights, and birth control, for example—could be kept out of schools. Other more centrist conservatives wanted schools to return to the "good old days," before they had been captured by "social experimentalists," advocates of whole language, new math, and sex education in schools (Berliner and Biddle, 1995). The report also serves the political agenda of homeschoolers, voucher supporters, and other advocates of alternatives to public schools (Bracey, 2003; Gardner, 2002). The publication of *A Nation At Risk* fueled the myth of failing schools and paved the way for NCLB and a conservative school agenda that has little to do with real reform.

Privatization and Other Risks of a Business Rationale in Education

McNeil (2000) and Horn and Kincheloe (2001) provide instructive histories of the Texas standards movement, a statewide effort and a national model for standards-based reform influenced by Ross Perot, the highly successful businessman and unsuccessful presidential candidate in 1992 and 1996. Perot, appointed head of a state commission on education reform, argues that if something is proved to be effective in business management, it must be good for education. Many in Texas were persuaded by this argument, as well as by Mr. Perot's record of business success and his folksy straight-talking personal style. Perot distrusts middle management—a lesson he learned from business. Mr. Perot likes to control things from the top, and he had found mid-level managers an obstacle to change and champions of the status quo. Middle managers in business like things the way they are, he argues, and he believes this also is true in education. Perot places the blame for Texas's education problems at the doorsteps of school administrators, education's middle managers, and he is convinced they are opponents of reform and incompetent. He endears himself to teachers by exempting them from blame and deriding their bosses. He argues that school administrators do not have the ability to lead or the sense to get out of the way. "Half of them," Perot said, poking fun at their backgrounds in coaching, "still have whistles around their necks." (Thomas Toch quoted in McNeil, 2000, p. 179).

The consequences of Perot's reforms have been profound and largely negative. Ross Perot and the school reform committee he chaired advocate top-down management and a centralized system designed to bypass Texas school administrators and hasten school reforms. Schools have to be changed quickly and all at once. Otherwise, he says, middle managers, "the good ol' boys at the local level, would incrementalize them to death" (McNeil, 2000, p. 186). Following Mr. Perot's advice, the Texas legislature tried to reform schools as if they were a large, foundering business. Linda McNeil argues that school reform failed in Texas because what works for a business does not necessarily work in education. Texas legislators, she writes, tried to simplify and standardize everything about classroom processes: planning, teaching, and assessment. They attempted to "teacher-proof" the curriculum with a checklist for teacher behaviors and tests of students' minimum skills. This might be an effective way to reform a production-line industry, but it is the wrong approach for education and is particularly damaging to the brightest and most thoughtful teachers.

By mandating certain forms of instruction and curriculum, Texas school officials made schools exceedingly comfortable for mediocre teachers who like to teach routine lessons according to a standard sequence and format, who like working as de-skilled laborers not having to think about their work. They made being a Texas public school teacher extremely uncomfortable for those who know their subjects well, who teach in ways that engage their students, who match their teaching to reflect their own continued learning (McNeil, 2000, p. 187).

A business focus on schools distorts an understanding of teachers' work and the critical role teachers play in education. It fails to take into account teachers' ability to encourage or discourage students, to bring out their potential or thwart it, to open students to new worlds of understanding or to close them off. Business solutions are overly simple, with an emphasis on uniformity of outcomes and achievement measured along a single plane. Success in business is determined by profits and growth. According to a business model, school success could be measured by test scores and increases in the number of test-takers who improve. The emphasis on scores and statewide achievement measures is too narrow a measure for schools. It is, McNeil (2000) writes, as if the multiple dimensions of a well-rounded, well-educated child had been reduced to a "stick figure." The narrowness of statewide testing fails to capture important dimensions of learning. While testing may indicate whether children can indent paragraphs or reduce fractions, it does not begin to capture a student's social awareness, civic responsibility, creativity and imagination, and emotional development. Learning reduced to the measurable leaves out more than it can report.

In 2007, the Gallup organization asked the public if they believed NCLB was hurting or helping the public schools in their community. Twenty-six percent reported that NCLB was helping; 27 percent reported it was hurting schools; and 41 percent responded that it made no difference. On the same poll, 52 percent of the respondents indicated that NCLB's emphasis on English and math had reduced the instructional time spent on science, health, social studies, and the arts (Rose and Gallup, 2007).

Education's embrace of business models is unwarranted but it is not surprising. First of all, American business, measured by profits and losses, is both an unqualified success and easy to understand. *A Nation at Risk* (National Commission on Excellence in Education, 1983) tied education and business together and frightened readers with threats to their economic comfort. Schooling must attend to the "new basics" or the American system was at risk. According to the report,

> The risk is not only that the Japanese make automobiles more efficiently than Americans and have government subsidies for development and export. It is not just that the South Koreans recently built the world's most efficient steel mill, or that American machine tools, once the pride of the world, are being displaced by German products. It is also that these developments signify a redistribution of trained capability throughout the globe. Knowledge, learning, information, and skilled intelligence are the new raw materials of international commerce. . . . (pp. 6–7)

Think about the best teachers you have had in school. It is quite likely they all had high standards for your work, but did they simply take someone else's standards off the shelf and apply them? Did they use prepackaged lessons or did they craft standards based on what they knew about you and your classmates and what they imagined you would like to read, explore, and think about? Were your best teachers the efficient managers of someone else's plan for your education or were they the personal planners and evaluators for you and others in your class? How would you describe your best teachers? Jonathan Kozol says the best teachers he knows are poets at heart who love the unpredictable aspects of teaching and uniqueness of every child in their classes. That's why, he argues, they are drawn to teaching children and not to business school. Teaching to standards that are not their own will make teachers technicians, and the classroom will lose its best teachers. Kozol writes, "If we force them to be a little more than the obedient floor managers for industry, they won't remain in public schools. The price will be too high. The poetry will have turned to prose: the worst kind too, the prose of experts who know every single thing there is to know except their own destructiveness" (Kozol in Cohen and Rogers, 2000, p. xii).

NCLB is not just a wrong-headed business plan. It has become increasingly clear that NCLB has become a "stalking horse" for privatization (McKenzie, 2003; Kohn, 2004; Borkowski and Sneed, 2006). NCLB requires that by 2014, the test scores of *all students* must be at proficiency standards in state tests on reading and math, a level never before attained. Most schools will not meet the unrealistic demands imposed by the law, and it is likely that no school serving children from the poorest financial situations will clear these arbitrary hurdles (FairTest, 2008). Low test scores are likely to set off new accusations that the public schools are not able to do the job entrusted to them. Teachers will be criticized; teacher education will be taken to task; and the school administrators will be excoriated, if not fired. All this will, by design, fan public outrage and feed a desperate enthusiasm for vouchers and the privatization of public schools.

The stage is now being set for the privatization agenda. Long before 2014, public education is likely to come under fire. An important aspect of NCLB accountability is the parental option that allows students to transfer from a school that has failed to make "annual yearly progress" for at least two consecutive years. Parents, as President Bush has said, can opt to send their children to public schools, or charter schools, or church-related schools that have been approved by the state. Funds that have gone to public schools are likely to be shifted to free-market schools of highly varied quality. As one former school superintendent notes, NCLB is an assault on the public education system rather than a well-intentioned reform effort. It is more about abandonment, punishment, and privatization than reform (McKenzie, 2003).

Costs of High-Stakes Testing

No Child Left Behind is fundamentally flawed. Despite the word "progress" in the phrase Adequate Yearly Progress, the law doesn't give enough credit for improvement. Instead it requires schools and districts to meet arbitrary and unreasonable benchmarks (American Federation of Teachers, 2007).

In the 1980s, the nation was deluged with reports critical of public education.[3] The standards movement recommended testing as a quick-fix solution, and like all quick fixes, it is overly simplistic and accompanied by problems. State accountability systems tied to common standards place students and school

[3]For examples written during the same period that were equally critical of public education, see: Adler, M. J. (1982). *The Paideia Proposal;* Boyer, E. L. (1983). *High School: A Report on Secondary Education in America;* Goodlad, J. L. (1984). *A Place Called School: Prospects for the Future;* Twentieth Century Fund. (1983). *Making the Grade: Report of the Twentieth Century Fund Task Force in Federal Elementary and Secondary Education;* and Sizer, T. R. (1984). *Horace's Compromise: The Dilemma of the American High School.*

personnel in thralldom to testing companies. Multiple-choice tests have become the assessment tool of choice for most states, and they involve high stakes. Students who do poorly on state tests may not be promoted or graduate. The building principal's salary and his or her job continuation may depend on the school's scores (FairTest, 2002). Art and music, typically not part of standards assessments, tend to disappear from many schools, and upper-level science electives, such as marine biology or biochemistry, also may fall victim to the standards movement because they are not tested. In many school districts, a good part of the school year is now given over to test preparation. When teachers take weeks and months from the regular curriculum to teach students test-preparation skills, it cannot be known for certain if subsequent gains in test scores result from real advances in learning and improvements in the quality of education, or if higher scores reflect the impact of drill and repetition and an improvement mainly in test-taking skills (McKeon, Dianda, and McLaren, 2001).

High-stakes multiple-choice tests have few fans in the education community. Practitioners and researchers in education believe that to capture the full range of a student's skill and knowledge, it is necessary to use an array of techniques, designed by classroom teachers, and administered over time. In addition to standardized tests, assessments should use classroom-based student assessments, portfolio reviews, and essay exams that measure academic subtleties and the complexities of thinking (Janesick, 2001; FairTest, 2008). The education research community has opposed single "high-stakes" measures. Consider Figure 5.2, the position statement on "high-stakes" testing of the American Educational Research Association, the nation's largest organization dedicated to the scientific study of education. NCLB reliance on high-stakes testing ignores the experience and recommendations of testing researchers and other experts.

In some states, the major problem with the standards movement is the poor alignment among its three elements: the standards themselves, resources available to the school for helping students reach the standards, and instruments used to assess learning. Often, the rush to develop assessment instruments outpaced the development of new curricula and teaching approaches necessary to implement new high-standards learning (McKeon, Dianda, and McLaren, 2001, p. 5). It has proved to be a far easier process to write multiple-choice tests than to revamp curriculum and instruction. Teachers and administrators, buried in the work of developing new, more rigorous programs, looked up from their curriculum work only to find that evaluation instruments were already in place. As has happened all too frequently in education, the tests were completed and ready to go before the curricula and matching teaching strategies had been designed. The tests were driving the reform, and in many cases the new curricula did not match the new tests. The tests were measuring content and skills that had not been introduced to students. The result has been confusion known as "misalignment": accountability systems not matched to the curriculum or classroom instruction. One set of skills and knowledge is being taught and another set of skills and knowledge is being tested.

FIGURE 5.2 High-Stakes Testing in Pre K–12 Education Position Statement of the American Educational Research Association (excerpted). Adopted July 2000.

---

1. Protection Against High-Stakes Decisions Based on a Single Test

Decisions that affect individual students' life chances or educational opportunities should not be made on the basis of test scores alone. . . . [W]hen there is credible evidence that a test score may not adequately reflect a student's true proficiency, alternative acceptable means should be provided by which to demonstrate attainment of the tested standards.

2. Adequate Resources and Opportunity to Learn

[I]t must be shown that the tested content has been incorporated into the curriculum, materials, and instruction students are provided before high-stakes consequences are imposed for failing examinations.

3. Validation for Each Separate Intended Use

Test valid for one use may be invalid for another.

4. Full Disclosure of Likely Negative Consequences of High-Stakes Testing Programs

Where credible scientific evidence suggests that a given type of testing program is likely to have negative effects, test developers and users should make a serious effort to explain these possible effects to policy makers.

5. Alignment Between the Test and the Curriculum

Both the content of the test and the cognitive process engaged in taking the test should adequately represent the curriculum. High-stakes tests should not be limited to that portion of the relevant curriculum that is easiest to measure.

6. Careful Adherence to Explicit Rules Determining Which Students Are to Be Tested

When schools, districts, or other administrative units are compared to one another or when changes in scores are tracked over time, there must be explicit policies specifying which students are to be tested. . . .

7. Sufficient Reliablility for Each Intended Use

Reliability refers to the accuracy or precision of test scores. It must be shown that scores reported for individuals or for schools are sufficiently accurate to support each intended interpretation.

8. Ongoing Evaluation of Intended and Unintended Effects of High-Stakes Testing

---

Source: www.aera.net/about/policyandprograms (2008).

Equity

> Because it is unrealistic to expect improvements in the educational system to fully offset the disadvantages faced by historically lower performing groups of students, we need to complement these programmatic and systemic reforms with out-of-school interventions, such as high quality preschool services, and programs that address nonschool conditions such as housing, poverty, health care and safety (Sunderman, 2008, p. 225).

Students come to school with various backgrounds and differing sets of academic advantages and disadvantages. More than 10 percent of children come from homes where English is not the primary language. One in five children lives in poverty. These children typically test poorly and have trouble with math, science, and language arts (Janesick, 2001; McKeon, Dianda, and McLaren, 2001). The nation may well be in crisis, Deborah Meier argues, but it's not the crisis described by the authors of *A Nation at Risk*. The real crisis, she says, is one of equity and justice for our most vulnerable citizens: the children of the poor. The United States spends "less on child welfare—baby care, medical care, family leave—than almost every foreign counterpart," and in the United States, the gap between rich and poor is greater than in other advanced industrial countries, while "our high rate of and investment in incarceration places us in a class by ourselves" (Meier, 2000, pp. 12–13). The size and costs of America's prison system have soared. In 2008, the Pew Center on the States reported that, for the first time in American history, more than 1 in every 100 adults was in prison, at a cost to the states of more than $49 billion a year. The incarceration rate for black men ages twenty to thirty-four was 1 in 9. The rate for all black men was 1 in 41; the rate for all white men was 1 in 245 (Pew, 2008).

The real crisis facing the United States is social, not academic. Children who come to school hungry and poor are not likely to be helped by more rigorous standards. Children with children of their own and children from abusive homes are unlikely to see their lives improve through statewide accountability plans. The real national risk is more appropriately measured not by test scores but by dropout rates, unemployment statistics, and the juvenile incarceration rate. By itself, the standards-based reform movement will not affect deeper social problems. The standards movement can be thought of as a new kind of discrimination. Under the guise of fairness, offering all students the same curriculum, same forms of instruction, and same objective assessments, students from less wealthy homes with less well-educated parents are denied the education they need. With its emphasis on drill and repetitive practice for the exams, the standards movement has increased classroom tedium and time spent on numbing routine. High-stakes testing has added stress and the threat of failure. The negative impact of standards reform has fallen hardest on poor and minority students. In Texas, the graduation rate for minority students has decreased since the beginning of the standards movement (McNeil, 2000). Increasing numbers of poor-performing students have been pushed out of schools made less pleasant by the changes brought by standards reform.

This is not a new phenomenon. Variables of class and race have always had high correlations with the dropout rate. SAT scores, for example, of both white and black students are influenced by social class. Low parental income predicts low SAT scores, and the higher the family income, the higher the scores for both races. The black-white test gap narrows at the highest income levels. It helps to have wealthy parents if you want to score well on standardized tests (Lemann, 1999). The relationship between achievement and social factors should not be a surprise in a society where race and class weigh so heavily in so much of life. Supporters of the standards movement pretend that academic achievement is more important than anything else in securing a job. However, educational attainment is less likely to predict who will get into college or land a good job than race and class (Bowles, Gintis, and Groves, 2005; Douthat, 2005). The standards movement is a smoke screen. Under competitive economic systems, not everyone is expected to prosper equally. Supporters of standards pretend to sort winners and losers by academic achievement, as if academic achievement were not proxies for race and class, the real variables that determine who will succeed and who will fail in life.

Standards Alone Cannot Solve the Problems of Schooling

Everyone wants to improve schools and raise the levels of learning. No one is opposed to standards, but higher standards alone are not likely to offer help for the range of school-based problems. We have argued a number of points: (1) the so-called crisis in education that gave rise to the standards movement is largely manufactured; (2) the key to better schools is not likely to be realized through imposition of more rigorous standards; (3) standards-based reform makes inappropriate use of a model borrowed from business; (4) the standards approach to school reform discourages the best teachers; (5) the standards movement has been confusing to everyone involved because of the misalignment of standards, teaching practices, and the means of assessment; (6) high-stakes testing puts unnecessary stress on students; (7) standards ignore issues of equity; and (8) standards-based reformers rarely mention the real problems of schools: poverty and social injustice, and national inattention to these issues. In addition, the standards movement has many unresolved issues and questions that should make you cautious. Look carefully at these issues before you jump on the standards bandwagon.

Unresolved Issues and Needed Changes in NCLB

- *Where is teacher and administrator involvement?* Teachers and administrators should be involved in developing local standards for their students. The people at the school level know best what is needed in the community and what will work in classes. To exclude them is to deny their knowledge and skills. As Gerald Bracey notes, the problem with NCLB is that "too many people who spend little or no time in schools created too much of our legislation and reform policy" (2007, p. 128).
- *Can coerced reform produce positive changes?* Top-down school reform is arrogant and unwarranted. The failure to bring teachers and administrators into the reform effort decreases the likelihood that standards reform will be effective. Excluding parents and other community members is undemocratic, insulting, and irresponsible (Kohn, 1999).
- *One standard fits none.* Outside of a very few core standards, there is no compelling reason that all students of a state should be held to the same standards. Such uniformity penalizes the highest-achieving students as well as those who have the most difficulty in school.
- *Beware of the promise of "school choice."* This might well prove to be a phoney promise. According to NCLB legislation, "Parents with a child enrolled in a failing school will be able to transfer their child to a better performing public school or public charter school. Charter Schools are independent public schools designed and operated by educators, parents, community leaders,

educational entrepreneurs, and others. They are sponsored by designated local or state educational organizations, who monitor their quality and effectiveness but allow them to operate outside of the traditional system of public schools" (No Child Left Behind, 2008). However, the promise of school choice may well be an illusion. Few seats may be available in better-performing schools, and it is unlikely that poor students will magically improve merely by transferring schools (Borkowski and Sneed, 2006).

- *Testing is only one aspect of assessment.* NCLB equates learning with performance on standardized tests of content knowledge, Such tests are only one dimension of assesssment and insufficient to capture other aspects of learning, including processing abilities, affect, and beliefs (Alexander and Riconscente, 2005; Sunderman, 2008).
- *Attend to social measures of poor performance.* The United States trails other industrialized nations in its ability to limit the percentage of citizens living in poverty and reduce the infant mortality rate, measures directly related to educational achievement. It is not likely educational achievement will rise until these statistics decline.
- *Don't shortchange the poor.* Students with good test scores in well-funded schools will continue to benefit from a full range of curriculum options, such as art and music, and elective courses and programs. Students from poor neighborhoods will have fewer options, more drill, and a leaner diet of basic skills (McKenzie, 2003, p. 2).
- *NCLB is not working!* According to the Congressionally mandated evaluation, Reading First, the $1-billion-per-year initiative designed to help all children read at or above grade level by the end of the third grade, did not improve students' reading comprehension (Gamse et al., 2008).

Reform movements with so many problems and so many unresolved issues should be greeted with suspicion. Who will be served by standards-based reform? Who will be disadvantaged? Is this real reform or the smoke and mirrors of sham reform? Standards-based reform is taking schools in the wrong direction and ignoring the real problems. It seems likely to discourage teachers and administrators while doing little to improve education for most students. We are puzzled how NCLB can be referred to as "reform."

For Discussion

1. In late 2007, a leading education journal printed a petition addressed to the U.S. Congress calling for the dismantling of the No Child Left Behind Act and arguing that the law is too destructive to salvage. Among the sixteen points against NCLB were the following:
   - Misdiagnoses the causes of poor educational development, blaming teachers and students for problems over which they have no control.
   - Assumes that competition is the primary motive of human behavior and market forces can cure all educational ills.
   - Neglects the teaching of higher-order thinking skills, which cannot be evaluated by machines.

- Drives art, music, foreign language, career and technical education, physical education, geography, history, civics, and other nontested subjects out of the curriculum, especially in low-income neighborhoods.
- Rates and ranks public schools using procedures that will gradually label them all "failures," so when they can fail to make adequate yearly progress, as all schools eventually will, they can be "saved" by vouchers, charters, or privatization (Phi Delta Kappan, 2007, p. 273).

Do you support these arguments? If you do, would you sign the petition?

2. John Chubb (2005) recommends a revision of NCLB to encourage qualified college graduates to become teachers without going though a teacher-education program. According to Chubb, to be "qualified," prospective teachers must (1) have a college major in the subject they will teach; (2) pass a subject matter competency test, and (3) demonstrate effectiveness as teachers by the achievement scores of their students on state tests. Do you support Chubb's recommendations and his defintion of a "qualified teacher"? Are there merits to his arguments?

3. The Tenth Amendment to the U.S. Constitution states that, "The powers not delegated to the United States by the Constitution, nor prohibited by it to the States, are reserved to the States respectively, or to the people." As a result of this division of legislative authority, the United States has developed a system of local rather than national control of education. By contrast, Great Britain has moved toward national control, and France has long had a national system of education. Leaving aside Constitutional issues, do you think that education in the United States would benefit if it were to move in the direction of national standards and national examinations? What, if anything, would be lost?

References

ALEXANDER, P. A., AND RICONSCENTE, M. M. (2005). "A Matter of Proof: Why Achievement ≠ Learning." In J. S. Carlson and J. R. Levin, eds., (2005). *The No Child Left Behind Legislation: Educational Research and Federal Funding.* Greenwich, CT: IAP.

AMERICAN FEDERATION OF TEACHERS. (2007). www.aft.org/topics/nclb

BENNETT, W. J., FINN, C. E., AND CRIBB, J. T. E. (1999). *The Educated Child: A Parent's Guide from Preschool through Eighth Grade.* New York: Free Press.

BERLINER, D. C., AND BIDDLE, B. J. (1995). *The Manufactured Crisis: Myths, Fraud, and the Attack on America's Public Schools.* Reading, MA: Addison-Wesley.

BOE, E. E., AND SHIN, S. (2005). "Is the United States Really Losing the International Horse Race in Academic Achievement?" *Kappan* 86: 688–695.

BOWLES, S., GINTIS, H, AND GROVES, M. O., eds. (2005). *Unequal Chances: Family Background and Economic Success.* Princeton, NJ: Princeton University.

BORKOWKI, J. W., AND SNEED, M. (2006). "Will NCLB Improve or Harm Public Education?" *Harvard Educational Review* 76:503–525.

BRACEY, G. W. (2003). *What You Should Know About the War Against America's Public Schools.* Boston: Allyn and Bacon.

———. (2007). "The 17th Bracey Report on the Condition of Public Education; The First Time 'Everything Changed.'" *Kappan* 89: 119–136.

BROWN V. BOARD OF EDUCATION, 1954, 347 U.S. 483.

CARLSON, J. S., AND LEVIN, J. R., eds. (2005). *The No Child Left Behind Legislation: Educational Research and Federal Funding.* Greenwich, CT: IAP.

COHEN, J., AND ROGERS, J., EDS. (2000). *Will Standards Save Public Education?* Boston: Beacon.

CHUBB, J. E., ed. (2005). *Within Our Reach: How America Can Educate Every Child.* Lanham, MD: Rowman and Littlefield.

COMMISSION ON NO CHILD LEFT BEHIND. (2007). *Beyond NCLB: Fulfilling the Promise To Our Nation's Children.* Washington, DC: The Aspen Institute.

DOUTHAT, R. (2005). "Does Meritocracy Work?" *The Atlantic* 296, November, 120–126.

EVERS, W. M. (2001). "Standards and Accountability." In T. M. Moe, ed., *A Primer on America's Schools.* Stanford, CA: Hoover Institution.

FAIRTEST. (2002). "Initial FairTest Analysis of ESEA as passed by Congress, Dec. 2001." www.fairtest.org/nattest/ESEA.html

———. (2008). www.fairtest.org/NCLB-After-Six-Years.

GAMORAN, A., ed. (2007). *Standards-Based Reform and the Poverty Gap: Lessons of No Child Left Behind.* Washington, DC: Brookings Institution.

GAMSE, B. C., ET AL. (2008). READING FIRST IMPACT STUDY: INTERIM REPORT. WASHINGTON, DC: Institute of Education Science, National Center for Education Evaluation and Regional Assistance. http://ies.ed.gov/ncee/pdf/20084016.pdf

GARDNER, H. (2002). "Too Many Choices?" *New York Review of Books.* April 11, 51–54.

HIRSCH, E. D. (1996). *The Schools We Need and Why We Don't Have Them.* New York: Doubleday.

———. (2001). "Curriculum and Competence." In T. M. Moe, ed., *A Primer on America's Schools.* Stanford: Hoover Institution.

———. (2006). *The Knowledge Deficit.* Boston: Houghton Mifflin.

HORN, R. A., AND KINCHELOE, J. L., eds. (2001). *American Standards: Quality Education in a Complex World.* New York: Peter Lang.

HOXBY, C. M. (2005) "Adequate Yearly Progress." In J. E. Chubb, ed., *Within Our Reach: How America Can Educate Every Child.* Lanham, MD: Rowman and Littlefield.

JANESICK, V. J. (2001). *The Assessment Debate: A Reference Handbook.* Santa Barbara, CA: ABC-CLIO.

JENNINGS, J. F. (1998). *Why National Standards and Tests? Politics and the Quest for Better Schools.* Thousand Oaks, CA: Sage.

KOHN, A. (1999). *The Schools Our Children Deserve: Moving Beyond Traditional Classrooms and "Tougher Standards."* Boston: Houghton Mifflin.

———. (2004). "Test Today, Privatize Tomorrow: Using Accountability to 'Reform' Public Schools to Death." *Kappan* 85:569–577.

LEMANN, N. (1999). *The Big Test: The Secret History of the American Meritocracy.* New York: Farrar, Straus and Giroux.

LYON, G. R. (2005). "Why Converging Scientific Evidence Must Guide Educational Policies and Practices." In J. S. Carlson and J. R. Levin, eds., (2005). *The No Child Left Behind Legislation: Educational Research and Federal Funding.* Greenwich, CT: IAP.

MCKENZIE, J. (2003). "Gambling with Children." http://www.nochildleft.com

MCKEON, D., DIANDA, M., MCLAREN, A. (2001). "A National Call for Midcourse Corrections and Next Steps." National Education Association. http:// www.nea.org/accountability/advancing.html

MCNEIL, L. M. (2000). *Contradictions of Reform: The Educational Costs of Standardized Testing.* New York: Routledge.

MEIER, D. (2000). "Educating a Democracy." In J. Cohen and J. Rogers, eds., *Will Standards Save Public Education?* Boston, MA: Beacon.

MOE, T. M. (2005). "A Highly Qualified Teacher in Every Classroom." In J. E. Chubb, ed., *Within Our Reach: How America Can Educate Every Child.* Lanham, MD: Rowman and Littlefield.

NATIONAL COMMISSION ON EXCELLENCE IN EDUCATION. (1983). *A Nation at Risk: The Imperative for Educational Reform.* Washington, DC: U.S. Department of Education.

NATIONAL COUNCIL OF TEACHERS OF MATHEMATICS. (2008). "Overview of Principles and Standards for School Mathematics." http://standards.nctm.org

NEW JERSEY, DEPARTMENT OF EDUCATION. (2008). "New Jersey Mathematics Curriculum Framework." http://state.nj.us/education/frameworks/math

NO CHILD LEFT BEHIND. (2008). www.ed.gov/nclb.

PAIGE, R. (2006). "No Child Left Behind: The Ongoing Movement for Public Education Reform." *Harvard Educational Review* 76: 461–473.

PEW CENTER ON THE STATES. (2008). *One in 100: Behind Bars in America* 2008. www.pewcenteronthestates.org

PHELPS, R. P., ed. (2004). *Defending Standardized Tests.* Mahwah, NJ: Lawrence Erlbaum.

PHI DELTA KAPPAN. (2007). "A Petition Calling for the Dismantling of the No Child Left Behind Act." *Kappan* 89:273.

RAVITCH, D. (2005). "A Historical Perspective on a Historic Piece of Legislation." In J. E. Chubb, ed., *Within Our Reach.* Lanham, MD: Rowman and Littlefield.

REYNA, V. F. (2005). "The No Child Left Behind Act and Scientific Research: A View from Washington, DC." In J. S. Carlson and J. R. Levin, eds. (2005). *The No Child Left Behind Legislation: Educational Research and Federal Funding.* Greenwich, CT: IAP.

ROSE, L. C., AND GALLUP, A. M. (2007). "The 39th Annual Phi Delta Kappa/Gallup Poll of the Public's Attitudes Toward Public Schools."*Kappan*: 89:33–48.

SUNDERMAN, G. L., ed. (2008). *Holding NCLB Accountable; Achieving Accountability, Equity and School Reform.* Thousand Oaks, CA: Corwin.

TAUB, J. (2002). "The Test Mess." *New York Times Magazine.* April 4, Sec. 6, 46–51, 60, 78.

TUCKER, M. S., AND CODDING, J. B. (1998). *Standards for Our Schools: How to Set Them, Measure Them, and Reach Them.* San Francisco: Jossey-Bass.

YELL, M. L. AND DRASGOW, E. (2005). *No Child Left Behind: A Guide for Professionals.* Upper Saddle River, NJ: Pearson.

CHAPTER 6

Religion and Public Schools: Unification or Separation

How do schools find a balance between freedom of religious expression and the separation of church and state?

POSITION 1: FOR RELIGIOUS FREEDOM IN SCHOOLS

Congress shall make no law respecting an establishment of religion or prohibiting the free exercise thereof. . . .

—U.S. Constitution, First Amendment

Take out a dollar bill. Turn it over to the back. What do you see when you look beneath the heading "The United States of America"? Printed on the dollar, as on every other denomination of American paper currency, is the motto "In God We Trust." Will we soon have to add the phrase "Except in Public Schools"? Students, public school teachers, and administrators who attempt to discuss the God on whom Americans supposedly rely, face disciplinary action and lawsuits. Court decisions and pressure from special interest groups have whittled away at religious freedom in schools. This situation can be remedied, and full freedom of religious expression can be restored to all citizens in America's public schools without violating the Constitution. Public schools can protect the basic human right of religious liberty and still maintain the separation of church and state.

The First Amendment

The First Amendment to the Constitution was carefully crafted by the Founding Fathers to protect what they considered "inalienable rights" of American citizens. For example, they wanted to protect their countrymen's right to practice the religion of their choice without fear. Aware of British history, they knew one of the greatest impediments to religious freedom was state support of one denomination. To these early Americans, breaking away from England meant, among other things, putting an end to religious conflicts. Therefore, they believed prohibiting governmental support for any individual faith was the best policy for their new republic (Wood, 1969; MacLeod, 2000; Tozer, Violas, and Senese, 2002).

To protect religious freedom, the founders included two clauses in the First Amendment. The first, called the Establishment Clause, decrees that religions and the state should be kept separate so that no religion has more rights than any other. The second clause, the Free Exercise Clause, prevents the government from limiting Americans' expressing religious beliefs in ways that seem right to them. Reading these two clauses carefully is important in understanding that current attempts to banish religion from public schools violate the founders' intention.

The Establishment Clause says, "Congress shall make no law respecting *an* establishment of religion." Many people, when referring to the clause, quote it incorrectly as saying, "Congress shall make no law respecting *the* establishment of religion." The difference is crucial. The first, and accurate, reading clearly shows the intent was to prevent any one religious denomination from receiving governmental support or protection not available to all others. In fact, one of James Madison's original drafts of the religious section of the amendment said, "The civil rights of none shall be abridged on account of religious belief or worship, nor shall any national religion be established" (Robb, 1985, p. 7). His purposes, however, were clear. The establishment of any religion through governmental support was to be prohibited because it would negatively affect individuals' freedom of religious expression. The fact that many states already had done exactly that added a sense of urgency to the task of the Constitutional Convention. Madison and others wanted to prevent a repeat of the religious wars in England that resulted from royal support of different Christian denominations (Wood, 1969; MacLeod, 2000).

The Founding Fathers had no intention of barring all mention of God from American public life—almost all professed belief in God although many did not identify themselves as members of any religious denomination. They routinely began assemblies with prayers for guidance and inspiration. They asked God's blessing on themselves and their countrymen in their foundational documents. Their language in such settings went beyond the traditional words used in different denominations. They spoke of a God who had created all and maintained the world, a God who was bigger than the claims of any individual group of believers (Farrand, 1986).

For most of American history, the Supreme Court did not interfere in state laws regarding religious practices in schools (Batte, 2008). Any act on the part of government supporting one religious denomination at the expense of others was considered unconstitutional. Any act of the government limiting an individual's right to free expression of his or her religious beliefs was equally illegitimate. Recently, however, the balance between the needs expressed in the two clauses has been reinterpreted.

The Supreme Court and Religion in Public Schools

Contemporary court decisions have emphasized the Establishment Clause to the detriment of the Free Exercise Clause. The trend began in a decision that, on the surface, appeared to support religious freedom. In 1947 in *Everson v. Board of Education,* the Supreme Court ruled using state funds to reimburse parents for the cost of transporting children to religious schools did not violate the Establishment Clause. However, in writing the majority opinion, Judge Hugo Black interpreted that section of the First Amendment in a way that ignored its text. Black wrote that the Establishment Clause created "a complete separation between the state and religion" (*Everson v. Board of Education,* 1947). This interpretation was based on a letter Jefferson wrote ten years after ratification of the First Amendment in which he made his famous "wall of separation" statement (MacLeod, 2000). It reads in part: ". . . I contemplate with sovereign reverence that act of the whole American people which declared that their legislature should 'make no law respecting an establishment of religion, or prohibiting the free exercise thereof,' thus building a wall of separation between Church and State" (Koch and Peden, 1944, p. 307).

Those using this statement of Jefferson's to limit individual freedom of religious expression would do well to read the rest of the quote. He writes, "Adhering to this expression of the supreme will of the nation in behalf of the *rights of conscience,* I shall see with sincere satisfaction the progress of those sentiments which tend to restore to man all his natural rights, convinced he has no natural right in opposition to his social duties" (Koch and Peden, 1944, p. 307). Clearly, Jefferson's words about the strict separation between church and state were not meant to limit individual rights but rather to argue against the possibility that any one religious sect would become a "national religion" through government efforts. When understood in this light, Jefferson's "wall" should be seen as the protector of freedom of religious expression (Chadsey, 2008). Instead it has been used to remove religion from public schools in ways that neither he nor the other founders of this nation intended. Other court cases have followed, relying on the interpretation offered by Justice Black in *Everson*. One by one they have created a legal legacy that violates the intentions of our founders.

In *McCollum v. Board of Education* (1948), the court ruled sectarian religious leaders were constitutionally forbidden from conducting voluntary, optional religious instruction in school buildings. Some years later the court held in *Engel v. Vitale* (1962) and *Abington Township School District v. Schempp* (1963) that neither classroom prayer nor Bible readings were constitutional even when students had the option of being excused from participation. Building on the misinterpretation of the Establishment Clause as presented by Justice Black in *Engel,* the Court took the serious step of defining governmental acts to accommodate religious freedom that could be deemed constitutional. In doing so, however, the Court created such narrow parameters that, since *Lemon v. Kurtzman* (1971), almost no religious practices in school have been declared constitutional. The "Lemon test," as the policy has come to be known, consists of three standards that must be met if the action of a school district can be established as protecting religious freedom rather than endorsing religious practices. To be constitutional, a policy or activity supported by a school must (1) have a secular purpose, (2) not have the effect of advancing or inhibiting religion, and (3) avoid excessive entanglement between government and religion (ACLU

Legal Bulletin, 1996; MacLeod, 2000). Applying the "Lemon test" in other cases has resulted in even more limitations on religious practices in schools.

For example, in *Stone v. Graham* (1980) the Court declared that a state law requiring public schools to post the Ten Commandments was unconstitutional. *Wallace v. Jaffree* (1985) struck down a state law requiring a moment of meditation or silent prayer. In *Lee v. Weisman* (1992) the Court ruled that, even when offered by a private individual with no formal connection to the school or government, prayer at public school graduation is unconstitutional. Apparently, asking students to bow their heads, remain silent, and show respect during such a prayer violates the rights of students who do not believe in God. They are, according to the Court, compelled to participate and in so insisting on their participation, the school is "conveying a message that religion or a particular religious belief is favored or preferred" over unbelief (*County of Allegheny v. American Civil Liberties Union, Greater Pittsburgh Chapter*, 1989).

Finally, in *Santa Fe Independent School District v. Jane Doe* (2000) the Court ruled student-led prayer at football games was unconstitutional. Even though participation in such games is purely voluntary, the fact that the school district sponsors and pays for the games makes them governmental actions. So prayers at the games also are government-supported activities that must pass the "Lemon test." The Court says they do not because there is no secular purpose for the prayers, which have the effect of advancing religion because they will be "perceived by adherents . . . as an endorsement, and by nonadherents as a disapproval, of their individual religious choices" (*School District of the City of Grand Rapids v. Ball*, 1985). In 2002 a federal court ruled that the phrase "under God" in the Pledge of Allegiance also fails the "Lemon test" (*Newdow v. U.S. Congress*, 2002).

Consequently, students are prevented from leading prayers at high school graduation ceremonies, even when members of the senior class want to include such devotions. Student athletes are forbidden from praying at sporting events, even in their own locker rooms. School board meetings cannot be opened with prayer or a moment of silent meditation. Teachers cannot discuss their own religious experiences with children, even if they believe their religion commands them to do so. They cannot use such expressions as "God Bless You" in communications with students or parents. Children cannot read Bible stories to classmates as part of oral communication lessons, nor can they express religious beliefs during a class presentation. In addition, they should not expect to see drawings they've made of religious figures or symbols hanging on the walls of their classrooms or schools. Bibles may not be distributed in public schools during regular operating hours. Teachers and students may not celebrate the religious aspects of such holidays as Thanksgiving, Christmas, or Easter (Pew Forum, 2007).

History of American Education

Banishing religion from all but the most innocuous aspects of U.S. public school life is truly ironic. The very first schools in the English colonies that would become the United States were instituted for religious reasons. The leaders of the Pilgrims, living in the Massachusetts Bay Colony, passed a law establishing schools that would teach children to read their Bibles. Their literacy would protect them from "that old deluder Satan."

In the early days of the Republic, American schools were, for the most part, privately funded and religious practices considered an essential part of the curriculum. Early public schools taught religion from a perspective shared with others influenced by the Enlightenment. For them a shared belief in God was necessary to create the moral discipline required for living in a democratic society (McConnell, 2000). The *McGuffey Readers*, the most popular textbooks for most of the nineteenth century, built on a presumption that Americans shared a belief in God to teach children what behavior was expected of them. Concern for the needs and rights of others, honesty, and perseverance despite difficulties were presented as the responsibility of all God's children in America. "It was almost universally accepted that American democracy drew its strength from the general conviction that there was a divine power, the author of the rights of man defined in America's first political document" (McCluskey, 1967, p. 237). Children were taught that each citizen derived his or her rights from their Almighty Father and that no human being had the right to take away those rights. In that era most Americans believed the majority could, on the basis of their religious beliefs, determine basic community norms including the place of religion in the public school curriculum and activities (McCarthy, 1983, p. 7). "Nonsectarian did not mean nonreligious. . . . Nondenominational Christianity was assumed to be 'nonsectarian'" (McConnell, 2000, pp. 1263, 1264). Protestant Christian beliefs and practices were incorporated into public schools. Teachers led children in daily prayer. The Bible, usually the King James Version, was read in schools. Religious holidays were celebrated (Goodman and Lesnick, 2001). State laws not only permitted such practices, they mandated them (McCarthy, 1983). So what happened?

The loss of balance between protecting both clauses of the First Amendment's statements on religion began in the first half of the nineteenth century. Immigrant children from Ireland, Germany, and, later, Italy and Eastern Europe swelled American public school enrollment, especially between 1840 and 1924. Most of these children were Catholics. Catholic religious leaders objected to what they saw as the Protestant character of religion being taught in public schools. They did not understand that the religious dimensions of public school life actually were designed to help their children become part of American life (Kaestle, 1983; Goodman and Lesnick, 2001). Their leaders protested strenuously and began a campaign to create schools that socialized children to their own religious beliefs (Cross, 1965; Sanders, 1977; Tozer, Violas, and Senese, 2002). To many Protestant Americans, these early immigrants seemed to reject becoming part of the very country to which they had turned as a refuge from political and economic oppression (Kaestle, 1983).

Despite the conflict, several factors made compromise possible. Immigrants perceived that public education would contribute to their social mobility. Native-born citizens believed schools would Americanize the newcomers. To achieve both ends, schools made reasonable accommodations. Some districts eliminated Bible readings altogether to end the Catholics' objections to using the Protestant version of the scriptures (Wright, 1999, p. 18).

A kind of neutrality among religious denominations was maintained in public schools that preserved the freedom of students and teachers to exercise their religious freedom (Goodman and Lesnick, 2001). Prayers were offered in "theistic" rather than "Christian" language, and holidays from both traditions were celebrated. Catholics and Jews who could not make this accommodation sent their children to schools in which their own beliefs could be practiced more freely (Cross, 1965; Sanders, 1977; Zeldin, 1986). As some historians see it, by the end of the nineteenth century, sectarian religious practices had been eliminated from public schools. However, schools were still faithful to the project of assimilating children, especially immigrant children, into the American way of life.

In the last half of the twentieth century, public schools were faced with new challenges to that Americanization obligation. Immigrant children from nonbiblical faith traditions began to appear in public schools. Among those who believe in God or seek divine assistance, compromises on language and practices have been achievable. For example, many schools have found ways to accommodate Muslim students' religious obligation to pray five times during the day (Dorrell, 2007). In other instances, dress code regulations have been modified to allow students to dress according to the norms of their religious traditions.

However, in the last sixty years, the delicate balance required to enforce both clauses of the First Amendment has been upset by the growth of a more secular belief system. The United States, like many other Western countries, saw an expansion of agnostic, atheistic, and antireligious philosophies. Those who shared these beliefs were concerned about what they perceived to be the vulnerability of children in schools. They worried that schools, by openly supporting free expression of religious beliefs—indeed by mandating them in some cases—were creating situations in which young people were being taught that religious beliefs were normative. They argued such tacit approval of religious faith would pressure young people to profess such beliefs themselves without being given the opportunity to evaluate them.

Most Americans—approximately 90 percent—believe in God (Gallup Organization, 2007). Only a very small number of Americans totally reject the existence of a divine being. However, that very vocal and powerful minority brought many of the lawsuits that have had such negative effects on the free exercise of religion by students and teachers (*McCollum v. Board of Education,* 1948; *Zorach v. Clauson,* 1952; *Engel v. Vitale,* 1962; *Abington Township School District v. Schempp,* 1963; and *Murray v. Curlett,* 1963). These "nonbelievers" actually have a belief system that is derived from the secularization of liberal political thought. For secularists, investigation, rather than religious teachings, is the source of answers to important human questions (Council for Secular Humanism, 2008). Even the Supreme Court has affirmed that secular humanism is a religious belief and that the rights of those who share that belief to practice their religion are protected by the free exercise clause of the first amendment (*Torcaso v Watkins,* 1961; *U.S. v Seeger,* 1965).

Most Americans who believe in God have come to accept that sectarian religious education no longer is possible in American public schools. Nonbelievers, however, want to impose their ideology in schools in ways that closely resemble the sectarian projects of nineteenth-century school reformers. They argue their beliefs actually are neutral regarding religion. In many ways, however, they are hostile to it. They contend any expression of belief in God is unconstitutional in public settings because, by being exposed to such activities, their children are coerced into accepting the beliefs from which they spring. In most cases the Supreme Court has accepted their arguments. The result is that the most privileged belief system in public schools is secularism. The rulings against common prayer, moments of silence, and celebrations of religious holidays in schools give privilege to secular beliefs. As Mitt Romney said during his unsuccessful bid for the 2008 presidential nomination, "In recent years, the notion of the separation of church and state has been taken by some well beyond its original meaning. They seek to remove from the public domain any acknowledgment of God. Religion is seen as merely a private affair with no place in public life. It is as if they are intent on establishing a new religion in America—the religion of secularism. They are wrong" (2007).

Of course such a policy clearly is unconstitutional. Several Supreme Court justices have explained what neutrality with regard to religion in public schools really means. Writing in *Everson v. Board of Education* Hugo Black stated, "State power is no more to be used so as to handicap religions than it is to favor them" (1947). In *Abington v. Schempp*, Tom Clark wrote, "The state may not establish a 'religion of secularism' in the sense of affirmatively opposing or showing hostility to religion, thus 'preferring those who believe in no religion over those who do believe'" (*Abington Township School District v. Schempp*, 1963, p. 225). In *Lynch v. Donnelly,* Sandra Day O'Connor argued, "What is crucial is that the government practice not have the effect of communicating a message of endorsement or disapproval of religion" (1984, p. 692). It would seem these warnings were ignored. The public school environment has increasingly become hostile to believers, limiting their freedom of expression while allowing secularists and nonbelievers license to incorporate their beliefs into the curricula. In doing so, the role of religious belief in American culture has been overlooked (Gateways for Better Education, 2008).

Religion and American Culture

While U.S. laws have prevented the establishment of a state sect, religious belief has influenced its culture. From its beginnings, America has been a nation that integrated political and religious understandings of the value of human life and the nature of freedom. According to Supreme Court Justice Anton Scalia, the secular model of the relationship between church and state, requiring that religion be strictly excluded from the public forum, "is not, and never was, the model adopted by America" (*McCreary County v. ACLU*, 2005, p. 74).

As Scalia and others argue, religion has and continues to contribute to the culture of the United States in positive ways. For example, a democracy requires moral citizens who are able to practice self-restraint, put the needs of others above their own interests, and sacrifice for the sake of the common good. Americans have seen religion as one of the most significant teachers of that kind of morality (*McCreary County v. ACLU*, 2005). In fact our history—distant and recent—demonstrates that the government has affirmed society's belief in God to strengthen us in difficulty, to guide us in perplexity, to comfort us in sorrow, and to express gratitude for the benefits of our shared life. "Historical practices thus demonstrate that there is a distance between the acknowledgement of a single Creator and the establishment of religion" (*McCreary County v. ACLU*, 2005, p. 89). A small minority of believers in impersonal gods, polytheists, and atheists may feel excluded when God is called upon in public settings. However, so long as they are not coerced into joining in the invocation, their rights to private belief are maintained (Feldman, 2005).

In fact "public expressions of religion even hold out the possibility of enabling religious minorities to participate fully in the American public sphere." If we allow the public acknowledgement and celebration of religious holidays, we enable Jewish, Hindu, Buddhist, and Muslim traditions to become part of a traditionally Christian culture. In doing so we validate the "sense of belonging" in a greater number of citizens and may generate more national loyalty from them (Feldman, 2005).

Curricular Consequences

Integrating religion in U.S. public life and culture is an admittedly difficult and delicate process. Chief Justice William Rehnquist has suggested that in doing so, the courts must be like Janus, the Roman god who was depicted with two faces looking in opposite directions. "One face looks toward the strong role played by religion and religious tradition throughout our Nation's history. . . . The other face looks toward the principle that governmental intervention in religious matters can itself endanger religious freedom" (*Van Orden v. Perry*, 2005, p. 11).

Public schools no longer balance these two aspects of the First Amendment. The perspectives of religious believers have almost been eliminated from public school curricula. In general, fear of controversy has led textbook publishers to neglect the study of religious influences on thought or historical events (Tolson, 2007). In fact, antagonism to religious approaches exists in most subjects. One of the most serious examples of this conflict takes place daily in science classes when students study the origin of life. Any perspective that does not support the Darwinian theory of natural selection is at best ignored and, at worst, ridiculed. Evolution is presented as fact even though there is convincing evidence that randomness and material forces alone cannot explain the complexity of the world in which we live.

The theory of intelligent design is a scientific approach to the origins of life that presents such a challenge to the theory of evolution (Beckwith, 2003; Dembski, 2004; Dembski and Wells, 2007). Opponents of intelligent design fail to distinguish intelligent design science from creationism—the belief that the universe was created in six days as described in the book of Genesis in the Hebrew Bible. However, intelligent design is rooted in the principles of science, not religion. For example, biochemist Michael Behe argues that natural selection cannot explain "irreducibly complex systems"—systems composed of a variety of parts that interact with one another to carry out the system's task. In systems like the flagella of bacteria, the flow of proteins in cells, and the mechanisms that cause blood to clot, the removal of any one part causes the whole to stop working

(Behe, 2007). The theory of evolution argues that these systems were produced by a series of small changes to prior systems, taking place in succession. However, that is impossible because if an irreducibly complex system were missing any one of its parts, it would simply not work. There would be no system from which the new one could evolve. Similarly, no known scientific "law" can explain the specific sequence of the four nucleotide bases found in DNA. William Dembski has established a reliable scientific method for identifying designed objects or systems from those that result from chance or the laws of nature (Dembski and Wells, 2007). Even theorists who accept evolution have acknowledged that many organisms seem to be the result of an intelligence beyond the organism itself—an intelligence with a purpose. Some of the most honest among them questioned their own theories. "As a result an increasing number of scientists have begun to argue that organisms *appear* to be designed because they actually *are* designed" (Buell, 2007, p. xvi). However, the law prevents teachers from presenting students with opportunities to hear about this alternative to the theory of evolution (*McLean v. Arkansas Board of Education*, 1982; *Edwards v. Aguillard*, 1987; *Webster v. New Lenox School District*, 1990; *LeVake v. Independent School District 656, et al.*, 2002; *Dover*, 2008; *Kitzmiller v. Dover*, 2008).

School districts are not even allowed to alert students that evolution is not a fact. For example, Cobb County school district officials in Georgia attempted to place stickers on science books that said: "The textbook contains material on evolution. Evolution is a theory, not a fact, regarding the origin of living things. This material should be approached with an open mind, studied carefully, and critically considered" (Selman Injunction, 2005, p. 13). A federal court judge ruled that doing so would violate the First Amendment because a "reasonable, informed observer" would interpret the stickers as endorsing the religious beliefs of the citizens who opposed the adoption of a textbook that endorses evolution, even though the stickers contained no reference to God or religious belief (Selman Injunction, 2005). Although the Cobb County stickers represented a good-faith effort to provide quality education without violating the Constitution, those who brought suit prevented a compromise that accommodated both believers and nonbelievers, imposing instead a solution that favored nonbelief.

Ironically, by not allowing young people to explore alternative explanations, schools—backed by the Supreme Court and acting under the protection of "scientific objectivity"—actually require young people to accept the theory of evolution "on faith." This refusal has serious consequences for young people and for the country. It means the American educational system relies solely on materialistic interpretations of reality. As William Dembski argues, "as you go through the educational programs of this country, through grade school, high school and then college, what you find is that education is a subversion, an indoctrination into a materialistic mindset where what should be evident and plausible becomes increasingly implausible, so that in the end, if you go through this education and buy it, you will not accept that there is design in the world. What you will accept is just material forces" (Dembski, 2004). Indoctrination is not education. A free and open debate of this and other controversies is.

Health classes are another area of the curriculum in which governmental neutrality toward belief and nonbelief has been violated. Students, regardless of their religious beliefs, are compelled to hear presentations in which their traditions' teaching about abortion, premarital sex, homosexuality, masturbation, and other topics are dismissed as unscientific and irrational. Students are invited to create their own code of ethics instead of being educated in the rich Western tradition of philosophical and religious thinking about moral topics (Zenit.org, 2007). Nonbelievers have convinced the courts and the courts have convinced school boards that including religious perspectives on such topics constitutes breaches in the separation between church and state. In doing so, however, they set up a situation in which schools, governmental institutions, indicate that nonbelief is the stance preferred by the school. That endorsement is, in fact, the kind of action that violates the First Amendment. (LaHaye, 2007).

The First Amendment religious clauses clearly establish two duties for government regarding freedom of religion. Government must not favor one religion over others and must not prevent citizens from expressing their religious beliefs. The founders assumed that religion would have a vital place in the private and public lives of Americans. When courts ignored that fundamental reality and the historic role of religion by requiring governmental neutrality between belief and nonbelief, they created an unsolvable problem. In protecting a minority of students from hearing religious speech that is "offensive" to them, they have provided inadequately for the rights of students who are religious. "In a country of many diverse traditions and perspectives—some religious, some secular—neutrality cannot be achieved by assuming that one set of beliefs is publicly more acceptable than another . . . religious citizens and religious ideas can contribute to the commonweal along with everyone and everything else" (McConnell, 2000, p. 1264). Certain practices, such as prayer in public gatherings or reference to God in discussions of moral issues, are part of a long-standing American tradition and have enjoyed historical acceptance. If administrators, teachers, and students ensure that no one is coerced to participate in such activities or accept the beliefs on which they are based, the First Amendment can be protected in public schools to a greater degree than it currently is.

POSITION 2: AGAINST VIOLATING THE SEPARATION BETWEEN CHURCH AND STATE

The Civil Rights of none shall be abridged on account of religious belief or worship, not shall any national religion be established, nor shall the full and equal rights of conscience be in any manner, or on any pretence, infringed.

—James Madison (Original Wording of the First Amendment; Annals of Congress 434, June 8, 1789)

To hear members of the religious right complain, you'd think that all religious expression had been totally banned in American public schools. Actually, teachers and students enjoy a great deal of freedom to engage in religious speech and practices. The No Child Left Behind Act of 2001 "Guidelines on Constitutionally Protected Prayer in Public Schools" reminded school officials that "The First Amendment forbids religious activity that is sponsored by the government but protects religious activity that is initiated by private individuals" (Paige, 2003, p. 2). The document does enumerate teachers and administrators' actions that are prohibited: leading classes in prayer, reading devotionally from the Bible, persuading or compelling students to participate in prayer or other religious activities, and including prayer at school-sponsored events. However it also contains an impressive list of students' rights, including reading scriptures, saying grace before meals, and discussing religious views in informal settings such as cafeterias and hallways. Students may also speak to and try to persuade other students about religious topics, participate in prayerful gatherings before and after school, and express their religious beliefs in homework, artwork, and other written and oral assignments—as long as their beliefs cannot be attributed to the school. Their prayer groups or religious clubs must be given the same right to use school facilities as is extended to other extracurricular groups. They can be dismissed for off-premise religious instruction and excused briefly from class to enable them to fulfill religious obligations such as prayer (Pew Forum, 2007). A school can limit these expressions of free speech only to the same degree it limits other comparable words or activities. So, for example, students have the right to distribute religious literature, hold prayer gatherings on school grounds, and discuss their religious beliefs to the same extent that they could engage in similar activities on comparable topics—such as politics or social issues.

Sounds good, doesn't it? It appears that students who want to engage in religious activities or speak about their faith have lots of freedom to do so. It sounds fair and reasonable—an all-American compromise that respects every student's right to religious liberty. So what's the problem?

Some believers want to break down the separation between church and state. They think schools ought to sponsor religious activities and coerce students to attend those events. For example, they believe school officials should be able to organize or mandate prayer at graduation ceremonies or, alternatively, to organize religious "baccalaureate" ceremonies for graduates, their friends, and their families. They believe it should be acceptable for teachers or principals to encourage students to participate in prayer gatherings before or after school, want teachers to be able to speak openly about their own religious beliefs in classroom settings, and advocate celebrating religious aspects of holidays in school. Even the federal government's guidance on constitutionally protected prayer seems to agree. It advises school officials on how to allow such activities, suggesting that when student speakers at assemblies, sporting events, or graduation are selected "on the basis of genuinely neutral, evenhanded criteria and retain primary control" over their speech, then the content can be religious, even prayerful, in nature (Paige, 2003, p. 3). However, that interpretation violates the law. The rationale of the courts has been that prayers of all kinds at such events violate the First Amendment's prohibition against the support of religion by government, no matter how much the majority of participants would like to include them.

When protecting the right to attend free public schools in which the government does not promote religion is juxtaposed with the need to accommodate freedom of religious expression, complex legal issues arise. Religious liberty in America means all are free to express their beliefs but may not impose them on others. Public schools are governmental agencies and, as such, are bound by the First Amendment not to take any action that would favor one religion over another—or belief over nonbelief. Engaging in sectarian behavior at taxpayer expense and preaching one's religion to others in publicly funded schools violate the constitutionally required separation of church and state.

Establishing Religion in Public Schools

Supporters who argue for greater freedom of religious expression in schools argue that they want the same protection for believers as for nonbelievers. There is evidence, however, that their real intent is to re-establish Christianity as a state-sponsored religion. Members of the religious right often suggest that public schools promote amoral values, are antireligious, and threaten the health and well-being for Christian children and youth (Christian Parents, 2008). Some leaders have gone so far as to suggest that parents remove their children from public schools, establish Christian alternatives, or home school (Exodus Mandate Project, 2008). Others see public schools as "gardens to cultivate" in the effort to promote their religious beliefs. For example, members of the group Gateways to Better Education "envision public schools as learning communities enriched by the appropriate and lawful expression of Christian values and ideas, and educators teaching about the contribution Christians and Christianity have made and continue to make to America and the world." The group calls on educators to become "Campus Partners" in the effort, provides curricular resources for teachers, and offers materials to begin a local campaign to restore celebrations of religious holidays to schools (Gateways to Education, 2008).

"Good News Clubs," organized by the Child Evangelism Foundation, are tools believers hope to use to create these witnesses. At the club meetings, children sing hymns, memorize scripture verses, and act out Bible stories. Since 2001, with the blessings of the Supreme Court, they have been able to meet in public schools after classes (*Good News Club v. Milford Central School*). Leaders have also demanded that administrators allow them to use official school communications to advertise their meetings and, in cases where secular groups have been allowed to advertise sports clubs or child care centers, the courts have ruled that the religious groups be given the same access to "customers."

Not satisfied with these gains, Christian leaders campaign to include Bible study in public school curriculum itself. Groups like the National Council on Bible Curriculum in Public Schools (NCBCPS) distribute course syllabi in school districts around the country, claiming they "convey the content of the Bible as compared to literature and history" (Ridenour, 2007). However, reviews of the curriculum by scholars find "various editions of this curriculum have been filled with factual errors, fringe scholarship, and plagiarism.

With its promotion of a fundamentalist Protestant understanding of the Bible and a revisionist history of the United States as a distinctively (Protestant) Christian nation, the curriculum appears not to pass legal muster" (Chancey, 2007, p. 554). "Students have been taught one religious interpretation of the Bible. That's not only violating the Constitution, it's also giving students a bad education" (People for the American Way, 2008). It has taken sustained political pressure—and lawsuits—to remove the curriculum from schools and prevent it from being implemented by even more districts.

Another way that some religious believers have attempted to ensure that public schools endorse their religious beliefs is by regulating sex education. Because their religious beliefs prohibit sexual intercourse outside of marriage, groups like Focus on the Family, Concerned Women for America, and the American Family Association oppose education about birth control or sexually transmitted infections. As a result of heavy lobbying from the Christian Right, since 1996, the federal government has provided funding for sex education programs only to school districts that have "abstinence only" sex education. The regulations governing these programs ensure that the beliefs of certain religious groups are embodied in the programs. For example, they require that students be taught that a mutually monogamous relationship in the context of marriage is the expected standard for human sexual activity and that sexual activity outside of marriage is likely to have harmful physical or psychological effects. Heterosexuality is also considered the norm, and efforts to address sexual orientation are condemned as part of "the homosexual agenda" (Society for Adolescent Medicine, 2006).

These "standards" are the beliefs, rooted in religious faith, of a minority of Americans. The dramatic increase in funding for these programs that has taken place since 1996 is a governmental stamp of approval for them that clearly violates the separation of church and state. Supporters argue they are merely attempting to preserve an atmosphere of intellectual and religious freedom in the face of nonbelievers' efforts to substitute their "science" for "moral values." In fact, sex education programs that go beyond abstinence only are more likely to offer students a chance to explore thoughtfully their own and their family's religious values. Abstinence-only programs provide direct instruction on what those values should be.

The effects of this violation of the Establishment Clause have been chilling. Public schools in many states now hold "chastity" events in which students are invited to promise that they will refrain from sexual intercourse until they are married. In some cases, these pledges are made directly to God. Textbooks are censored; crucial information about AIDS and other sexually transmitted diseases is omitted from sex education courses; teachers are harassed by parents and disciplined by school authorities for answering students' questions that go beyond the scope of the abstinence-only curriculum (Planned Parenthood, 2005). Research studies have consistently shown that abstinence-only sex education programs do not prevent young people from engaging in intercourse (Stepp, 2007). They also indicate that young women who have not learned about birth control in their health classes are 50 percent more likely to become pregnant when they become sexually active than are their peers who received more comprehensive sex education (Song, 2008). Apparently, for some, promoting their religious beliefs is a more important goal. Government support of these "education" programs constitutes an establishment of religion that violates the Constitution.

The Creationism/Intelligent Design Debate

Similar efforts to infuse a particular religious perspective into public school curricula have taken place with regard to science courses. The theory of evolution is one of the most important contributions ever made to our understanding of the connections between all living things, and is fundamental to genetics, biochemistry, physiology, and ecology. "Biological evolution is one of the most important ideas of modern science. Evolution is supported by abundant evidence from many different fields of scientific investigation. It underlies the modern biological sciences, including the biomedical sciences, and has applications in many other scientific and engineering disciplines" (National Academy of Sciences, 2008, p. 47). An earth science or biology course that does not include evolution shortchanges students. "Science and technology are so pervasive in modern society that students increasingly need a sound education in the core concepts, applications, and implications of science. Because evolution has and will continue to serve as a critical foundation of the biomedical and life sciences, helping students learn about and understand the scientific evidence, mechanisms, and implications of evolution are fundamental to a high-quality science education" (National Academy of Sciences, 2008, p. 47). Yet, after eighty years, the teaching of evolution is being disputed once more in school districts across the country. Some people are convinced that, unless the "theory" of evolution is challenged in science classes, then the state is violating their right to religious liberty and perpetuating intellectual fraud. What is going on?

Some people object to the teaching of evolution because they believe that the world was created 6,000 years ago by a divine being acting purposefully. Beginning with the Scopes trial in 1925, creationists have attempted to protect their children from what they see as the evil influences of the teaching of evolution. Consequently, they have lobbied to have textbooks removed from schools if authors do not give "equal time" to creationism and convinced legislators and departments of education to remove evolution from state science standards that strongly influence the curriculum taught in public schools. They have had all mention of evolution removed from statewide tests, thus giving school districts the green light to ignore the topic in their classes without fear that students will suffer.

However, the courts repudiated their efforts (*Edwards v. Aguillard*, 1987). So creationists repackaged their argument and attempted to seize the intellectual high ground. Instead of lobbying for creationism, they now argue for "intelligent design" theory and want schools to present it to students as an alternative to natural selection—despite the lack of scientific evidence to support their ideas. They argue that science teachers should be required to suggest that it is quite possible that the process of evolution is the work of an "intelligent designer." That is, they want students to be taught that the existence of God is supported by scientific evidence. However, the "anti-evolutionary" forces would have to redefine science in order to justify that claim.

"The formal scientific definition of theory is quite different from the everyday meaning of the word. It refers to a comprehensive explanation of some aspect of nature that is supported by a vast body of evidence" (National Academy of Sciences, 2008, p. 11). In *McLean v. Arkansas Board of Education*, the Supreme Court noted five characteristics of science: "(1) It is guided by natural law; (2) It has to be explanatory by reference to natural law; (3) It is testable against the empirical world; (4) Its conclusions are tentative; (5) It is falsifiable" (1982). Neither creationism nor intelligent design meets such criteria. The "scientific" explanation for creationism, that the universe came into being from "nothingness," cannot be explained in reference to natural law, does not establish its own scientific hypotheses, and is neither testable nor falsifiable. Similarly, intelligent design's claim that there is a plan for the universe does not lead to predictions that are testable, nor results that can be verified or reproduced. It is not rooted in natural law but explains the origins of life with reference to a supernatural force. Creationism and intelligent design are, in fact, religious beliefs and their claims don't need to be tested in order to be accepted as *religious* truths. A person can accept on faith any explanation they choose for the origin of the world or the relationships between its living things. People can draw on statements based on revelation or religious authority. They can take great comfort from such faith and can be profoundly inspired by its explanations. They can study different expressions of those beliefs, comparing and contrasting them—sifting among them for the one that is most convincing. But what they can't do is call them "science."

In contrast, evolution is an explanation for the facts that have been collected through the scientific tools of observation and experimentation (Alberts, 2005). It is a prime example of the way scientific knowledge is constructed: "natural explanations, logically derived from confirmable evidence" (Alberts, 2005). The theory of evolution has been built up through facts such as "the presence and / or absence of particular fossils in particular strata of the geological column. From these confirmed observations we develop an explanation, an inference, that what explains all of these facts is that species have had histories, and that descent with modification has taken place" (Scott, 2001, p. 6). Scientists no longer debate whether evolution has taken place because the data from experimentation and observation is too strong.

Nevertheless, supporters of intelligent design portray themselves as victims of discrimination, unable to exercise their First Amendment free speech rights. They create slogans such as "Teach the controversy," and "Go where the evidence leads" (Thomas, 2008). They argue for fairness, tolerance for diversity, individual choice, and opposition to censorship, which are powerful arguments in a society committed to those core values. The problem is that there is no controversy, at least no scientific controversy. Instead, adherents of one faith tradition are attempting to alter school curriculum and teaching methods because they cannot be reconciled with their religious beliefs.

Lately, supporters of intelligent design have avoided any mention of religious motivations or intentions in their efforts to limit the teaching of evolution. They have created what some scholars call "mini-Intelligent Design." They no longer argue that the Intelligent Designer must be supernatural. They know that the Supreme Court has ruled that mention of a creator in public schools violates the separation of church and state. So they stick with arguments that adaptations in organisms "scientifically" prove the poverty of evolution as an explanatory theory and hope that Americans, whose own science education has often been limited, will be impressed and lobby for "fairness" (Sober, 2007).

What's the Big Deal?

What's wrong with majority rule in regard to curriculum and religious practices in public schools? Ninety percent of Americans indicate they believe in God (Gallup, 2007); 82 percent believe that Jesus is God or the son of God (Gallup, 2007); 81 percent support prayer at school-sponsored events; and 61 percent believe that the creation story in Genesis is literally true (Ellison, 2008). What's the harm in bringing those beliefs into public school? Some argue that America is a nation founded by men with Judeo-Christian beliefs, and religion provides a moral compass for individuals and society. Public prayer and other rituals serve "in the only ways reasonably possible, the legitimate secular purposes of solemnizing public occasions, expressing confidence in the future, and encouraging the recognition of what is worthy of appreciation in society" (*Lynch v. Donnelly*, 1984, p. 693). Only a few people object to them and, in schools, no one is forced to participate; they can remain silent while others pray. Why should most citizens be denied their preferences because they would offend a minority of non-Christians or nonbelievers?

While it might prove satisfying in the short term, breaking down the barrier between religion and the state in schools—even in the name of majority rule—is in no one's best interests. It hurts individuals by making full acceptance as a member of the school community dependent on sharing the majority's religious beliefs. It harms the school and, ultimately, society by minimizing the need for religious tolerance and making it difficult to maintain peace in a pluralistic society. Finally, it undermines religion itself by making religious languages, symbols, and practices so bland that they lose all spiritual significance (Warren, 2003).

When the separation of church and state is violated in schools—for example, by a prayer at a graduation ceremony or a football game, or by the introduction of creationist arguments in a science class—students receive the message that belief is favored over nonbelief. So, young people who are atheists or members of nonmonotheistic traditions are plunged into crises of conscience by these school practices. They must either risk their acceptance in the school community or take part in religious activities with which they do not agree. The Establishment Clause was meant to prevent the development of such dilemmas in public spheres. Under its protection, religious belief or nonbelief should be irrelevant in one's ability to participate fully in schooling. Even though members of the majority find the practices untroubling, the situation upsets the delicate balance between individual and collective rights that the Constitution preserves (Warren, 2003).

Violating the separation of religion and state in schools also harms society. Favoring the beliefs of one religious tradition over others, or belief over disbelief, creates tensions that pose a threat to the cohesiveness of our very pluralistic society. For example, when "nonsectarian" prayers are said at school events, they reflect the Judeo-Christian tradition. Members of nonmajority religious groups get the message that their beliefs are not really "American"—they are both overlooked and excluded (Warren, 2003). The result is a society in which individuals and groups are assigned social status on the basis of how closely their beliefs adhere to the preferred religion. That kind of social stratification can have serious results. Jews, Hindus, Muslims, Sikhs, other non-Christians, and nonbelievers may isolate themselves from public schools if they feel their rights are not protected in them. That separation could exacerbate differences and cause resentments and misunderstandings. We can look into the past—recent and ancient—and discover the harm that such divisiveness has caused. The struggles of Shiite and Sunni Muslims in Iraq, and Protestant and Catholic Christians in Ireland are but two recent examples. In each case, one group's religious beliefs and practices were sanctioned by the government; members of that group enjoyed social and economic privileges that members of the other did not. The results were tragic for both societies.

Although believers argue that religion exerts a good influence by encouraging people to act morally, that opinion overlooks historical reality. Religion has been used to justify slavery, war, terrorism, imperialism, and genocide. Systems of belief suggesting they have answers to every question can threaten fundamental aspects of democracy. When government endorses religious belief, it limits the necessarily critical discourse about the impact of faith on society (Warren, 2003).

Finally, breaching Jefferson's wall between church and state jeopardizes religion itself. When one chooses freely to believe, religion has the power to provide comfort, guidance, and a sense of community. When spiritual practices are mandated in public schools, the voluntary nature of religious observance is sacrificed. When participation in spiritual practices is mandated in schools, individual conviction in religion may be lost. As a consequence, people's commitment to a religion may be dependent on the social setting, rather than on their own belief. When they leave school, they may leave religious practice behind them as well. Rather than strengthening religion, mandating its practice in school may actually weaken it. In addition, justifying prayer or other religious observances in public schools on the ground that they are merely "secular" denies their spiritual integrity. Christians would be shocked and offended to hear that a Christmas scene is acceptable in school because it is merely a historical symbol of a winter holiday. Jews would have difficulties with similar uses of a Menorah.

"The text of the First Amendment is only ink on centuries-old paper; its power lies in the people who give it practical meaning throughout this religiously diverse nation. Were this an easy task, the Supreme Court would not have heard over ninety cases on religious liberty since 1815" (Branch, 2007).

For Discussion

1. The National Academy of Sciences (NAS) has argued that creationism does not meet the criteria for a scientific theory. Investigate the NAS definition further and determine whether creation scientists could gather facts that would support their theory regarding the origin of life on earth and what type of evidence they would need. Can you find other definitions of scientific knowledge that might be expansive enough to include creation science?
2. The courts have ruled that teachers may not communicate their own religious beliefs to students. What do you think is the basis for those rulings? Research other legal limitations that have been placed on teachers' individual freedoms. Do they reflect society's attempt to balance the rights of individuals and needs of a democratic society? Do you agree with the way that balance has been achieved? What would you do differently?
3. Read or watch a film or video version of *Inherit the Wind*, the dramatization of the Scopes trial. Research the actual event as well. What role did the historical and geographical setting play in the case? Would the case have been brought to court in a different location—even during the same period? Speculate on whether geographic differences might exist today regarding the question of religious freedom in public schools. What implications might these differences have for those entering the teaching profession? On what grounds would you base your guesses? How could you verify your thesis?
4. The U.S. Department of Education has issued guidelines for religious expression in public schools. Using those guidelines, take the role of a school superintendent and prepare a set of rules for your school district. Assume that they will need to be approved by your school board and create an explanation for each of the regulations you propose.

References

Abington Township School District v. Schempp. (1963). 374 U.S. 203.

ACLU Legal Bulletin. (1996). "The Establishment Clause and Public Schools." (www.aclu.org.issues/religion/pr3.html)

ALBERTS, B. (2005). "Intelligent Design." *New York Times.* February 12.

BATTE, S. (2008). "School Prayer Decision." The Constitutional Principle of Church and State Website. http://members.tripod.com/candst/pray2a.htm.

BECKWITH, J. (2003). *Law, Darwinism, and Public Education: The Establishment Clause and the Challenge of Intelligent Design.* Lanham, MD: Rowman and Littlefield.

BEHE, M. (2007). *The Edge of Evolution: The Search for the Limits of Darwinism.* New York: Free Press.

BOSTON, R. (2007). "Revised Standard Bunk: Religion Scholar Dissects Religious Right's Flawed Bible Course." Americans United for Separation of Church and State. http://blog.au.org/2007/09/14/revised-standard-bunk-religion-scholar-dissects-religious-rights-flawed-bible-course/

BRANCH, C. (2007). "Unexcused Absence: Why Public Schools in Religiously Plural Society Must Save a Seat For Religion in The Curriculum," *Emory Law Review.* 56 Emory L.J. 1431.

BUELL, J. (2007). "Preface," in Demski, W. and Wells, J. *The Design of Life: Discovering Signs of Intelligence in Biological Systems.* Dallas: Foundation for Thought and Ethics.

Brown v. Board of Education of Topeka, Kansas. (1954). 347 U.S. 483.

CHADSEY, M. (2007). "Thomas Jefferson and the Establishment Clause." *Akron Law Review,* 40 Akron L. Rev. 623.

CHANCEY, M. (2007). "A Textbook Example of the Christian Right: The National Council on Bible Curriculum in Public Schools." *Journal of the American Academy of Religion* 75(3): 554–581.

CHRISTIAN PARENTS. (2008). "Worst Enemy of Christian Children is not Dope or Pornography." http://www.christianparents.com/worst1.htm.

County of Allegheny v. American Civil Liberties Union, Greater Pittsburgh Chapter. (1989). 492 U.S. 573.

COUNCIL FOR SECULAR HUMANISM. (2008). "The Affirmations of Humanism: A Statement of Principles." http://secularhumanism.org/index.php?section=main&page=affirmations.

———. (2004). "Brief of the Council for Secular Humanism as *Amicus Curiae* in Support of Respondent Michael A. Newdow." http://supreme.lp.findlaw.com/supreme_court/briefs/02-1624/02-1624.mer.ami.sechum.pdf

CROSS, R. (1965). "Origins of Catholic Schools in the United States." *The American Benedictine Review,* XVI. June, 1965.

Daubert v Merrell Dow (1993). 516 U.S. 869.

DEMBSKI, W. (2004). "Intelligent Design: Yesterday's Orthodoxy, Today's Heresy," http://www.designinference.com/documents/2005.04.ID_Orthodoxy_Heresy.htm

DEMSKI, W. AND WELLS, J. (2007). *The Design of Life: Discovering Signs of Intelligence in Biological Systems.* Dallas: Foundation for Thought and Ethics.

DORRELL, O., "Some Say Schools Giving Muslims Special Treatment," *USA Today,* July 25, (2007).

ELLISON RESEARCH. (2008). "Liberals and Conservatives Both Want Freedom of Religious Expression and Practice." www.ellisonresearch.com/releases/20080110.htm.

Edwards v. Aguillard. (1987). 482 U.S. 578.

Engel v. Vitale. (1962). 370 U.S. 421.

Everson v. Board of Education. (1947). 330 U.S. 855.

EXODUS MANDATE PROJECT. (2008). "Exodus Mandate, Phyllis Schlafly and a Coalition of Christian and Pro-family Organizations Endorse Call for 'Exodus' From California Schools." www.exodusmandate.org/art_20080207-call-for-exodus-from-california-schools.htm.

FARRAND, M. (1986). *The Records of the Federal Convention of 1878.* New Haven: Yale University Press.

FELDMAN, N., (2005). "A Church State Solution," *The New York Times,* July 3, Section 6, p. 28.

FREEDOM FORUM. (2005). *Education for Freedom.* (http://www.freedomforum.org/packages/first/curricula/educationforfreedom/index.htm)

THE GALLUP ORGANIZATION (2008). Easter Season Finds a Religious, Largely Christian, Nation. March 21.

———. (2007) The Gallup Poll, May 10–13. (http://www.pollingreport.com/religion.htm)

GATEWAYS FOR BETTER EDUCATION. (2008). "Keeping the Faith in Public Schools." http://www.gtbe.org.

GENERAL ACCOUNTING OFFICE. (2006). *Abstinence Education: Efforts to Assess the Accuracy and Effectiveness of Federally Funded Programs.* www.gao.gov/new.items/d0787.pdf

GOODMAN, J., AND LESNICK, H. (2001). *The Moral Stake in Education.* New York: Longman.

KAESTLE, C. (1983). *Pillars of the Republic.* New York: Hill and Wang.

Kitzmiller v Dover. (2005). 400 F. Supp. 2d 707.

KOCH, A., AND PEDEN, W. (1944). *The Life and Selected Writings of Thomas Jefferson.* New York: Random House.

LAHAYE, T. (2007). "Godless Society." *The Atlantic.* November. www.theatlantic.com/doc/200711/lahaye-godless.

Lee v. Weisman. (1992). 505 U.S. 577.

Lemon v. Kurtzman. (1971). 403 U.S. 602.

Lynch v. Donnelly (1984) 465 U.S. 668.

MACLEOD, L. (2000). "School Prayer and Religious Liberty: A Constitutional Perspective." Washington, DC: Concerned Women for America. www.cwfa.org/library/freedom/2000-09-pp_school-prayers.html.

MCCARTHY, M. (1983). *A Delicate Balance: Church, State and the Schools.* Bloomington, IN: Phi Delta Kappan Educational Foundation.

MCCLUSKEY, N. (1967). "The New Secularity and the Requirements of Pluralism." In T. Sizer, ed., *Religion and Public Education.* Boston: Houghton Mifflin.

McCollum v. Board of Education. (1948). 333 U.S. 203.

MCCONNELL, M. (2000). "Religion and Constitutional Rights: Why is Religious Liberty the 'First Freedom'?" *Cardozo Law Review,* February, 21 Cardozo L. Review 1243.

McLean v. Arkansas Board of Education. (1982). 529 F. Supp. 1255.

McCreary County v ACLU. (2005) 2005 U.S. LEXIS 5211.

Murray v. Curlett. (1963). 371 U.S. 944.

NATIONAL ACADEMY OF SCIENCES. (2008). *Science, Evolution and Creationism: A View from the National Academy of Sciences.* Washington, DC: National Academy Press.

Newdow v. U.S. Congress. (2002). 293 F. 3d. 597; 328 F.3d 466.

PAIGE, R. (2003). "Guidance on Constitutionally Protected Prayer in Public Elementary and Secondary Schools." U.S. Department of Education. www.ed.go/policy/gen/guid/religionandschools/prayer_guidance.html.

PEOPLE FOR THE AMERICAN WAY. (2008). "Texas School Board Agrees To Stop Teaching Unconstitutional Bible Class in Public Schools." http://www.pfaw.org/pfaw/general/default.aspx?oid=25063.

PEW FORUM ON RELIGION AND PUBLIC LIFE. (2007). "Religion in the Public Schools." Washington, DC: The Pew Forum. http://pewforum.org/church-state-law/religion-public-schools.pdf.

PLANNED PARENTHOOD. (2005). "Abstinence-Only Sex Education." http://www.plannedparenthood.org/pp2/portal/files/portal/medicalinfo/teensexualhealth/fact-abstinence-education.xml

RIDENOUR, E. (2007). "It's Coming Back and It's Our Constitutional Right." http://www.bibleinschools.net/.

ROBB, S. (1985). *In Defense of School Prayer.* Santa Ana, CA: Parca Publishing.

ROMNEY, M., "Romney's Faith in America Address," *New York Times,* Dec. 6.

SANDERS, J. (1977). *Education of an Urban Minority.* New York: Oxford University Press.

Santa Fe Independent School District v. Jane Doe. (2000). 530 U.S. 290.

School District of the City of Grand Rapids v. Ball. (1985). 437 U.S. 373.

SELMAN INJUNCTION. (2005). *Selman v Cobb County School Dist,* Civ. No 1 02-CV 2325-CC, 005, U.S. Dist LEXIS 432).

SEWALL, G. (1999) "Religion Comes to School." *Phi Delta Kappan,* 81(1), 10–16.

SOBER, E. (2007). "What's Wrong With Intelligent Design." *The Quarterly Review of Biology.* 82(1): 3–8.

SOCIETY FOR ADOLESCENT MEDICINE. (2006). "Abstinence-only education policies and programs: A Position Paper of the Society for Adolescent Medicine." *Journal of Adolescent Health* 38: 83–87.

SONG, K., (2008). "UW researchers say comprehensive sex ed cuts teen pregnancies," *Seattle Times,* March 20.

STEPP. L., (2007). Study Casts Doubt on Abstinence-Only Programs. *Washington Post,* April 14.

Stone v. Graham. (1980). 449 U.S. 39.

THOMAS, D. (2008). "President's Message," *The Beacon: News from the Coalition for Excellence in Science and Math Education."* www.cesamenm.org/download/beacon/03_2008beacon.pdf.

TOLSON, J. (2007). "In America, An F in Religion," *US News and World Report,* 142 (12): 28.

Torcaso v. Watkins. (1961). 367 U.S. 488.

TOZER, S., VIOLAS, P., AND SENESE, G. (2002). *School and Society.* New York: McGraw-Hill.

U.S. v Seeger. (1965). 380 U.S. 163.

Van Orden v Perry. (2005).2005 U.S. LEXIS 5215.

Wallace v. Jaffree. (1985). 472 U.S. 38.

WARREN, C. (2003). "No Need To Stand On Ceremony," *Mercer Law Review,* Summer, 54 Mercer L. Rev. 1669.

WOOD, G. (1969). *The Creation of the American Republic 1776–1787.* New York: W. W. Norton.

WRIGHT, E. (1999). "Religion in American Education: A Historical View." *Phi Delta Kappan* 81(1), 17–20.

ZELDIN, M. (1986). "A Century Later and Worlds Apart: American Reform Jews and the Public School-Private School Dilemma, 1870–1970." Paper presented at the Annual Meeting of the American Educational Research Association, San Francisco.

ZENIT.ORG. (2007). "What Abstinence Education Gets Right". http://www.zenit.org/article-20109?l=english.

Zorach v. Clauson. (1952). 343 U.S. 306.

CHAPTER 7

Privatization of Schools: Boon or Bane

What criteria are most suitable for deciding whether schools are better when they are operated as a public or private enterprise?

POSITION 1: PUBLIC SCHOOLS SHOULD BE PRIVATIZED

Charter schools continue to be the largest example of school privatization with more than 4,000 schools holding contracts with government agencies . . . serving more than one million children.

—Snell, 2007, p. 5

Changing the way government operates opens the door for entrepreneurs to offer innovative and cost-effective solutions to today's problems. Outsourcing provides numerous benefits—economies of scale, greater expertise in diverse fields, and much needed flexibility in this new changing world.

—Bush, 2008, p. 12

Public schools are prime candidates for privatization. Privatization involves changing services once operated by governmental agencies to private ownership or operation—"the transfer of assets or service delivery from the government to the private sector" (Reason Foundation, 2008). This cuts the high cost to taxpayers, government bloat, and the typical inefficiencies of governmental activities and monopolies. Public education is one of the most tax costly, bloated, and inefficient enterprises of government. It is also largely monopolistic, but has not consistently produced sound education (*The Economist*, 2005). For these and other reasons, public education has not fulfilled its social purpose of providing high-quality education at reasonable cost. With no competition and a tradition of inefficiency, public schools have become the major burden on, and frustration for, the local taxpayer. Privatization offers market efficiency, accountability, professional design, and choice.

There are three main types of privatization: (1) transfer or sell state-owned enterprises to private individuals, corporations, or organizations, (2) contract out for services formerly done by government to a private company, and (3) deregulate the public enterprise to offer opportunities for private industry to enter and compete (Emmons, 2000).

School privatization has mainly occurred in the second category contracting with a private enterprise to provide better education for less money. Public school districts are unlikely candidates for a public sale to private companies in the way that nations have divested themselves of governmentally owned telecommunication and transportation systems. Also, a strong private school movement in the United States already exists. Instead, most public schools recognize the values of private operation of some or all of their work. Many states and districts are developing charter or other parental-choice schools, which represent the deregulation approach in education.

Increased privatization of public education is going on worldwide. Adnett (2004) identifies several reasons for this governmental interest in privatizing public schools:

> Increased concern with student outcomes from public schooling;
>
> Increased dissatisfaction with rising costs while quality is stagnant;
>
> Frustration from their inability to find incentives that change schools.

Among the powerful arguments for privatizing schools is that the government can design contracts for very specific performance objectives within a stuctured budget and private companies who agree are bound to deliver. That is not the current case for United States public schools. The No Child Left Behind Act attempts to hold schools accountable, but it has yet to prove itself and adds more government bureaucracy. Contracting for private operation of schools offers hope.

Reasons for the Privatization of American Public Schools

1. Improving Schools for Our Children

The most important reason to involve private enterprise in schools is to benefit our children. They deserve the best schools we can provide. The bureaucracy created for government-operated schools overwhelms local budgets and does not respond to complaints. Private enterprise could not survive with that approach; its success is linked to increasing efficiency and customer satisfaction. Privatization increases accountability, making school staffs responsible for meeting performance standards for the benefit of children. Accountability, a keystone of private enterprise, offers a way to clearly identify problems and reward good performance in schools. Instead of weak, vague educational jargon that hides poor school practices, private enterprise sets specific goals and measures how well schools meet them. Schools that work will be rewarded; those that don't will be changed or closed.

The Edison Schools, an innovative approach to school privatization, contracts with public schools to operate them with no increase in costs, but with better results.

In addition, Edison offers opportunity for stockholders to participate while providing a public good. The Edison purposes are clear and direct: "to offer the best education in the world," "to welcome all students," and "to operate at an affordable price" ("An Invitation to Public School Partnership: Executive Summary," the Edison Project, www.edisonschools.com, undated). This puts the focus on student achievement. Edison includes strict performance conditions in its contracts, which can be terminated on short notice if results are not satisfactory. The improving quality of schooling in Edison-operated schools is documented (Chubb, 1998; Edison Schools, 2005, 2008); academic scores of students are improving under Edison leadership. Private contractors put performance conditions in their contracts. What public school operation gives the public the same guarantee?

2. Providing Democratic Choice—Breaking the Public School Monopoly

A second reason for privatizing schools is to break the monopoly public education has in the United States. Privatizing schools offers choices to parents concerned about their children's education. School choice is certainly in the best interest of children and their parents, but it also forces schools to compete to attract students and financial support.

John Coons (1988) describes the U.S. education system as a "state-run monopoly." He argues that state-run schools strip families of authority to choose their children's schools by limiting them to local public school boundaries. The comparatively few private and parochial schools in the nation currently are prohibited from receiving taxpayer money. As a result, they serve a different and more selective clientele than their public counterparts; they don't compete for taxpayer dollars.

The public schools have had a monopoly for far too long and suffer from lack of competition. They have institutional hardening of the arteries, bloated and inefficient operations, and slow bureaucratic response to public concerns. There is little reason to provide better public service, increase efficiency, require higher standards, or eliminate layers of bureaucracy. Privatization can bring customer satisfaction and state-of-the-art efficiency to such schools. Of course, public schools do not welcome privatization, and their unions continue to fight it (Snell, 2005; *The Economist,* 2005; Murphy, 2004).

3. Increasing Productivity in Education

Privatizing increases productivity in public schools, a place where productivity has not changed for a century. Most public school districts operate in much the same manner as when our grandparents were students. Expensive, labor-intensive public schools with inflated administrations sap local and state finances. Improvements in technology and communications have revolutionized U.S. business and provided manifold increases in productivity, but virtually not changed public schools. Computers and other technology speed up industry, but schools, even with many computers, continue the same costly approach. Most school administrators come through the ranks of education and lack the business background and discipline needed to develop and implement sound strategic planning, efficient resource allocations, monitoring and accountability control, and effective management in schools. That may explain their lack of interest in improving productivity (Hentschke et al., 2004).

In high-cost, high-maintenance buildings, students attend classes about six hours a day for about one-half of the calendar year. Teachers teach about twenty-five students per hour in separate classrooms using multiple copies of costly printed textbooks, similar to school life at the beginning of the twentieth century. Those teachers, no matter how good or bad, are paid on a standard scale, earning about $30,000 to $75,000 per year for only nine months' employment. The one-size-fits-all teacher pay scale depends on seniority, not on how well each teacher teaches or how well students learn. This compromises good teachers and forces many away from teaching as a career. Competitive schools will change that.

4. Meeting Global Competition

Schools exert great influence on the future of the United States and its role in the global marketplace. International competition requires the United States to remain on the cutting edge of innovation or suffer future decline. If public schools are not up to the task, we need to find other approaches. Privatization of schools is an idea whose time has come. The resounding collapse of the Soviet Union illustrated defects in economic structures that depend on government operation. Now we are in a race to see which nation will provide leadership in private development.

As democracy and capitalism increase across the globe, privatization will continue to be a strong movement in public life during the twenty-first century. Government-run operations show weaknesses that private enterprise can overcome. Worldwide, leaders recognize private enterprise as the key vehicle for improving citizens' lives while making government more efficient with available funds and resources. Nations from differing economic traditions are moving toward private operation of a variety of public services. Schools are among the social institutions increasingly undergoing privatization in many nations. England and New Zealand provide excellent examples of this process; the public in each of these nations recognizes the value of private enterprise in more effectively and efficiently operating schools. The United States is actually lagging behind other nations in this global movement.

A Variety of Approaches to School Privatization: Charter Schools to Food Operations

Complete privatization offers some distinct advantages, such as allowing districts to hold private managers accountable for student learning, but it is also possible to identify limited segments of current school operations that private contractors could handle to the benefit of students and taxpayers. In public-private partnerships, the school board hires private managers to run the public schools under a multiyear contract that specifies performance standards and allows the board to fire the managers with ninety days' notice.

Educational management organizations, similar to HMOs for medical care, are emerging to improve schools. Sylvan Learning Systems, Nobel Learning Communities, Edison Schools, and Knowledge Universe are current examples of private management of education. The twenty-first century should see expansion of school privatization from 13 percent in 2000 to 25 percent by 2020 (Hentschke et al., 2004).

Under complete privatization, rigorous contracts with the local board of education guarantee performance. Included in complete privatization would be all activities from managing the school(s), hiring, and evaluating staff, to developing the curriculum, evaluating student learning, communicating with parents and the community, and providing custodial and ancillary maintenance. These individual items also are excellent candidates for partial privatization of school operations.

Public schools now contract for selected services that are too costly or too cumbersome to handle under public control. Districts contract payroll and accounting services. Others find that contracting with popular fast-food companies, such as McDonald's and Pizza Hut, to provide school lunch service is more cost-effective, more acceptable to students, and sometimes more nutritious than the standard school cafeteria food. Private contracts for specific services, from the provision of food to managing all school operations, have proved their value to students, school officials, and taxpayers. Piecemeal privatization of school services has been working well for years in many schools. Now private operation of individual schools, and even entire city school districts, is developing. Charter school programs, in which the state grants specific charters to groups to organize or take over schools, now are legal in many states.

The Massachusetts charter school law allows profit-making companies to apply for charters. Edison, developed by business entrepreneur Chris Whittle, recently won three charters to operate public schools in Massachusetts as part of its original plan to establish up to 200 public, but for-profit, schools nationwide. Whittle's Channel One, the privately sponsored television channel for schools, has been operating successfully in a number of school districts—another example of the privatization of schools. The Edison Project has about 130 schools under its management, educating 330,000 students (Steinberg, 2002; Edison, 2006), with low costs and good results.

Revitalizing the Public Sector: Improving Schools

Privatization is a valid idea for any public sector enterprise that has become stagnant. Public agencies provide needed services where private enterprise can't. Public agencies, however, must meet the standard: whether the quality of service they provide is the best we can get for the price we pay. If public agencies don't measure up against their counterparts in the private sector, we should replace them. That is the essence of privatization. Public agencies can outlive their purposes and become a drain on public funds. Doyle (1994), submits that police departments and the issuance of currency must remain in public hands, but that construction of public roads, buildings, and bridges can be performed (and already is) mainly by private contractors, as are trash collection and maintenance in many cities. Contracting out for services is good business for many public agencies. Doyle singles out public schools as places where entrepreneurship is needed to provide innovation and confront unproductive and conformist traditions: "The uniformity of the school system, once thought to be a virtue, is clearly a liability in the modern era" (p. 129).

Schools consume more taxes than any other agency in local communities, and account for the largest part of most state budgets. That favored financial position should make U.S. schools the best in the world, but this is not the case. Public schools spend increasing amounts of taxpayer money while becoming more and more mediocre. Privatizing schools is one strong alternative to the spend-and-decline model we have seen in education during the latter half of the twentieth century (Snell, 2005).

Historically, public schools made a contribution to the nation by providing access to education for many and literacy and Americanization to immigrant children. Mass education is important in this modern and globally competitive age, but there is no reason that government must own and operate schools. The government school is an anachronism, held over because of romantic ideas about tradition. We will look back on one day and wonder why it lasted so long and cost so much to maintain.

Obstacles to Privatization of Schools

When people understand that, for less cost, they can have better service and more accountability, they quickly become supporters of the shift to private operation. Other, more difficult, obstacles remain.

Public employee labor unions lobby against privatization of public services—obvious self-interest. Teacher unions have been particularly active opposing school privatization and are among the largest, best-financed, and most active organizations in state legislatures. Many state legislators fear their power. Teacher unions filed suit against school vouchers in Milwaukee, against school management contracts in Baltimore; Hartford, Connecticut; and Wilkinsburg, Pennsylvania; and against school janitorial contracts in California (Eggers and O'Leary, 1996). The teachers union actively, but unsuccessfully, opposed the shift to privatization of schools in Philadelphia (Steinberg, 2002; Snell, 2005).

Government bureaucracies also present obstacles to private enterprise, since bureaucracies may lose some of their power. Charter schools are not subject to some of the bureaucratic regulations that have kept the public school establishment so entrenched. They may establish teacher accountability without tenure requirements, develop a curriculum without contending with state mandates, and organize classes and provide instruction without meeting some of the trivial specifications that have petrified public education. The public education bureaucracy built a massive fortress of regulations. It is the IRS of the school business. Deregulation is a fearful event to some agency bureaucrats whose influence and positions are in jeopardy.

Privatization Is in America's Interest

The President's Commission on Privatization recommends the transfer of selected public services to the private sector (*Privatization: Toward More Effective Government*, 1988).

With regard to education, the commission found that:

> The recent record of educational achievement has fallen far short of the basic goals that Americans set for their schools. . . . Despite substantial public spending on education—at all levels of government—the nation's schools were not producing commensurate results—educational report cards have turned the 1980s into a decade of dissatisfaction with schools. (p. 85)

The commission reported that taxpayer spending on public schools doubled during the prior two decades, but educational results have been less impressive than expected. Expenditures per student in private education are about two-thirds the per-student costs of public education. Although the nation spends heavily on public schools, average SAT test scores declined in the 1980s. These scores have only haltingly started to increase, and a massive infusion of tax dollars over the past decades has not had any effect on them. The National Assessment of Educational Progress (NAEP) and other tests show that U.S. students perform poorly. In the international arena, comparative studies of test scores show that U.S. students rank at the bottom among industrialized democracies (Finn, 1995; Mandel et al., 1995; *The Economist*, 2005). Pumping more taxpayer money into those schools is not likely to alter their long-term deficiencies. Feistritzer (1987) reports that no apparent correlation exists between education spending and student achievement. At no additional cost, privatization can improve schools, increase teacher motivation, and enhance student learning.

Public schooling can be improved through expertise in management, cost control, and performance. Schools are a public service that the private sector can help.

Privatization and the Public School Crisis: What Can Privatization Provide for Schools?

There are many reasons to seriously question the continuation of public education as it is presently organized and operated (Geiger, 1995; Murphy, 2004).

Public schools are a lockstep system, out of touch with contemporary business management. Current school management follows an archaic and costly pattern, under regulations the education establishment set up early in the twentieth century. Many small schools have separate administrations and budgets for providing essentially the same services. New Jersey, for example, has more than 600 separate school districts. In some states, even tiny schools are mandated to employ a school principal, and often a superintendent and other staff. In large districts, multiple, well-paid school administrative officers never teach a student and seldom visit the district's schools. Organizational structures of schools are more similar to those of inefficient early factories than to structures of modern corporations.

Public schools use an old-fashioned political system for more tax money, elaborate and expensive lobbying in state legislatures to improve teacher salaries and keep teacher unions in power, and coziness with state education agencies to maintain the status quo. Increasing state regulation serves only to further bloat school administrations without accountability. Schools are mired in bureaucracy and self-protective traditional thinking. They are not efficient institutions. Instead of attempting to keep costs down while improving quality, a standard that business sets, schools simply obtain increased tax funds without improving productivity.

There are numerous places to increase productivity and improve school performance in this antiquated system of education. The school day and school year are expensive links to our agricultural past. Most industrialized nations keep students in school for longer days and for more days of the year. Traditional small-group instruction, with one well-paid teacher for each class of twenty-five students, does not take advantage of striking advances in communication technology or flexible management. Interactive computers linked with major libraries and scholars would make better use of limited resources. The lack of merit-based salary recognition for teachers limits teachers' motivation. The inertia of low productivity is built into the current public schools; private enterprise offers a fresh approach.

The Privatization Movement: A Global Context

A worldwide privatization movement is already in progress, rapidly improving services in many other areas, such as transportation and communication. Schools are an important part of this movement, and the effort to privatize them should be viewed in the larger context.

The global political economy has changed since the end of the cold war, as the world increasingly recognizes the values inherent in free-market enterprise. Privatization is consistent with the realization that communism and socialism are defective political systems. Communism robs people of their individuality, and socialism robs them of their personal motivation. The former communist and socialist nations of the old Soviet bloc realize that privatization of state-owned industries will improve their economies and the lives of their people.

Economic analyses (Vickers and Yarrow, 1991; van Brabant, 1992; Earle, Frydman, and Rapaczynski, 1993) describe the difficulties such nations as Hungary, Poland, Czechoslovakia, and Russia encountered in their massive efforts to restructure a failed system, but economists generally recognize the need to privatize to compete in the global market. Earle, Frydman, and Rapaczynski, for example, note:

> After decades of experience with malfunctioning command economies and unsuccessful attempts to improve their performance through moderate "market socialist" reforms, the countries of Eastern Europe and the former Soviet Union are struggling to radically transform their economic systems. (p. 1)

In 1990, formerly communist East Germany had almost 14,000 state-owned businesses, and just four years later, the number was fewer than 150 (Protzman, 1994). Private enterprise and marketplace competition are replacing inefficient government-controlled business enterprises.

Other nations engage in massive privatization of publicly owned industries. Great Britain recently privatized many publicly owned and operated industries. The British economy has improved significantly as a result. Privatization is an idea taking hold for industries in many nations. Water and waste treatment, for example, are 100 percent privatized in England, while the United States has privatized only about 15 percent (Farazmand, 2001).

Competition is a hallmark of private enterprise and requires efficient operation and consumer satisfaction—two elements lacking in government monopolies. Under privatization, it is possible to maintain and improve public services while cutting taxes. Private enterprise is built on the human desire to succeed and get credit for succeeding. This system motivates people to achieve more and rewards those who show improved work.

We should not be content with old structures and their myths if those structures are no longer efficient. An old car must be replaced when it costs more to repair it than it is worth; we need to review social agencies to see if they are as efficient as alternatives.

Schools are basic to the national interest and to international competition. America's leadership depends on top-quality, well-educated people—successful students from achievement-driven schools. The talents and vision of such people are limited by cookie-cutter schools that offer less than the most current and efficient approaches to education. The private sector of the U.S. economy, which demands innovation and efficiency to survive, offers to reshape U.S. schools to meet the demands of global competition. For many good reasons, privatization of schools is the wave of the twenty-first century.

POSITION 2: PUBLIC SCHOOLS SHOULD BE PUBLIC

In short, privatization cannot replace governmental functions; indeed it cannot even replace a portion of these functions in society. There are areas in which government does better and best, such as in policy making and management, regulation, control, social equity, prevention of discrimination and exploitation, protection of individual rights and citizenship, provision of security and stability in governance and administration, social control and cohesion, and more.

—Farazmand, 2001, p. 15

The public is losing its sense of ownership of its schools, which threatens democracy itself.

—Mathews, 2008, p. 560

The idea that private operation of public services is superior is a socially destructive myth. Schrag (1999) points out that "the pattern in our society is toward withdrawal from community into private, gated enclaves with private security, private recreational facilities, private everything, even as the public facilities deteriorate." Self-serving myths—promoted in the corporate world and corporate-oriented mass media—are that private enterprise offers superior services, efficiency, competition, and management.

Krugman (2002) shows that privatization by governments record does not support claims of improving efficiency. Typically, private contractors submit low bids to get a contract, then move prices up—or have cost-overruns—after government workers have been eliminated and are no threat to the contractor.

There is no solid evidence of superior performance, higher quality, lower costs, or better management in schools by the private sector. Evidence demonstrates the opposite. Edison Schools, the largest of private corporations running schools, can produce no substantial data of improvements in academic performance by students (Miron and Applegate, 2000; Bracey, 2002, 2008; Henriques and Steinberg, 2002a, 2002b; Holloway, 2002; AFT, 2003; Lubienski and Lubienski, 2004; Ratchford, 2005).

Henry Levin, an economist of education who directs the Center for the Study of Privatization in Education at Columbia University, summarizes research on claims about private operation of public schools:

> ". . . studies of EMOs [for-profit Educational Management Organization, like Edison Schools] have found greater administration costs than comparable public schools. EMO contracts have also been more costly than funding received by similar public school sites. Moreover, there is little evidence that EMO-run schools outperform public schools with similar students." (Levin, 2006. pp. 11, 12)

Uncritical reporting by mass media on charter schools describes them as innovations to improve education, but hides their lack of academic performance. Not all charter schools are private, but many are and there is a false presumption that they are somehow better than public education. A vast, 2.5-year study by researchers at UCLA finds little support for claims that charter schools improve learning; charter schools neither fulfill their promises nor improve student achievement (Magee and Leopold, 1998). Some charter schools, relieved from many state regulations, have serious problems in finances, student achievement, and operations. A Brookings Institute Brown Center report on American education (2002), examining academic achievement in charter schools in ten states from 1999 to 2001, concludes: "in a nutshell, charter schools performed about one-quarter standard deviation below comparable regular public schools on these three years of state tests" (Brown Center Report, 2002, p. 1). Privatizing schools is not improvement or progress, just another avenue for private wealth to gain more control.

Since private companies are supposed to be good in the area of management, look at how well Edison Schools manages itself: This corporation often faces financial crises, issuing new stock to finance continuing operations and borrowing immense amounts of money. Edison gets substantial funds from public school district money for, ironically, contracting to manage public schools in a cost-effective way. In 2001, Edison reportedly had to pledge $61 million as collateral to obtain a loan of only $20 million—a demonstration of the company's financial problems. No public school would be permitted to do such shaky financing. In addition, Edison sometimes gets subsidies from private charities for running its schools—raising questions about the corporate claim that they can run schools at less cost per pupil than public schools (Henriques and Steinberg, 2002a). Bracey (2002) and Saltman (2005) detail a long series of Edison difficulties, both financial and educational, suggesting Edison used questionable political arrangements to obtain contracts in such places as Philadelphia, prompting investigations of Edison's efforts to provide private schooling in such places as New York, Georgia, Massachusetts, Connecticut, Texas, and Kansas.

Is privatization of public services good public policy or just corporate propaganda? Do corporations do things better than public agencies, or are they just better at PR? Are Enron, WorldCom, and sub-prime mortgage bundlers good examples of how privatization might work for education? Should we work out a system for privatizing public schools that would handsomely reward the school CEO and a chosen few insiders, penalize the workers and general stockholders, and allow a failing corporation to walk away from the schools with little responsibility for their failure?

Social Purposes and Private Goals

In a capitalistic democracy, some activities fit private enterprise and some deserve public operation and oversight. Kozol (*Rethinking Schools*, 1998) finds no evidence that "a competitive free market, unrestricted, without a strong counterpoise within the public sector will ever dispense decent medical care, sanitation, transportation, or education to the people" (p. 1).

Privatizing public schools exemplifies a myth, a siren song of lower costs and better scores. Significantly, this shifts attention from the fundamental social purposes of public education in a democracy. A shift may serve those advocating privatization, but basic social purposes must be the centerpoint of any substantial debate over privatization. A major test of the public/private balance lies in the fundamental social purposes of an activity. Thus, we can measure public and private operation of schools against the broad social purposes of schooling. Any debate over privatizing public schools should focus on whether public or private control is more likely to move us toward fulfilling those large social purposes.

The clamor to privatize, and a long-term campaign to demonize public schools, has stifled the more significant debate on social purposes. Lacking is the necessary long-range social perspective in the pressure to privatize schools (Hunter and Brown, 1995). Shortsighted goals of achieving higher test scores and saving money are simply insufficient reasons for privatizing, even if private schools could ensure these results. Of course, they can't; and short-term test score improvement has been shown to be the result of manipulation, not superior schooling. The privatization myth magnifies social and economic problems plaguing public schools for over a century, while it hides significant historical defects of private enterprise.

Despite a century-long tradition of excellent public service in difficult social and financial conditions, public schools have been subjected to a relentlessly negative campaign during the past two decades. Ironically, the privatization myth has protected private enterprise from similar attacks for its many failures and its significant threat to democracy. The history of private enterprise—with its questionable ethics, cavalier treatment of employees and the public, financial manipulation of the political process, and escapes into bankruptcy or taxpayer bailout when in trouble—goes unmentioned in reporting and public discourse on privatization. Much support for privatization of public schools revolves around shallow advertising that capitalizes on negative images of public schools, unsupported claims of potential cost savings, and a paternalistic aura that corporations know best. The evidence does not support the claims. A Brookings Institution study of privatization in public schools, especially big city schools, found that most arguments for school privatization are based on wishful thinking (Ascher, Fruchter, and Berne, 1996). Other studies have shown for-profit schools do not have innovative practices, curriculum, or management programs (Kaplan, 1996; Zollers and Ramanathan, 1998).

The rush to privatization demands a serious look at rationales, practices, and potentials. In certain situations and under strict and open public regulation and school district supervision, it is reasonable to provide some aspects of public services, such as food service in school lunchrooms, through private contracts. But wholesale privatizing of schools, where a private corporation controls the management, curriculum, and instructional decisions of a whole school or school district, is an extremely hazardous approach to dealing with public services. In areas as important to society's future as education, privatizing may destroy the soul of democratic life (Saltman, 2000; Sudetic, 2001).

Two major points stand out: (1) public schools serve significant public purposes, and (2) privatization is being championed under a number of myths that hide its unpleasant characteristics. Our conclusion in advance: that public schools must not be sacrificed to private profiteering.

Privatizing and the Democratic Purpose of Public Education

A democracy requires a well-informed, active, and free populace. The primary ideals of democracy in the United States include justice, equality, and freedom. Within those high social ideals, the overriding purpose of public education is to prepare students for active and knowledgeable participation in society. In schools, that preparation involves development of language and number facility, social knowledge, ethical conduct, and critical thinking—all in the context of the accumulated wisdom of the arts and sciences. Standardized test scores, of course, reveal relatively little about this significant curriculum or about the social purposes public schools serve. The root purpose of education is improving civilization by ensuring and expanding justice, equality, and freedom. To lose sight of that grand democratic ideal by a narrow focus on costs and test scores undercuts the fabric of American society.

This relationship between a democratic society and the need for publicly operated schools has been widely recognized throughout history. Aristotle (1988), the first Western political philosopher, clearly recognized the public need to provide schooling for all citizens to preserve a democracy. Among the most compelling statements for public education in a democratic society is John Dewey's *Democracy and Education* (1916). In recent years, leading political theorists and education scholars have reiterated the significance of public education to democracy (Gutmann, 1999, 2008; Saltman, 2000; Kadlec, 2007).

The goals of improving justice, equality, and freedom are central to the idea of a public school, but not to private enterprise. We have a long way to go in public education to meet these high standards; minorities and women have not had equal opportunities or freedom in schools. But we are improving significantly in this area, and we continue to pursue those goals in public education. Privatizing, with its attendant emphasis on cutting costs and improving test scores, is less likely to expand opportunities for the weakest or most disadvantaged. When you take seriously the need to educate the whole society, and not merely the elite, you improve society—but you may not increase average test scores or cut the school budget.

Schools should also offer freedom of inquiry needed to fulfill the claim of democracy. Education for knowledgeable self-governance liberates us from ignorance, including that perpetuated by propaganda and censorship. Public education for all citizens requires student and teacher freedom of inquiry and critical thinking about social problems. But free, critical study of social problems may not be a goal in corporation-operated schools. Open examination of controversial topics, necessary in democratic society, may conflict with corporate agendas in an ethos in which business knows best. How many corporations encourage criticism, especially public criticism, of their purposes and practices? Saltman (2000, 2005) condemns the utter commercialization of public education as a major threat to democracy.

The common schools tradition in the United States been a keystone of democratic society by offering individuals the opportunity to develop skills and knowledge needed to self-govern. Schools also have provided a community-centered service responsible to the community in a variety of ways. Privatization threatens that tradition. Dayton and Glickman (1994) point clearly to one aspect of the threat:

> A fundamental problem with the privatization movement is that it views public education as merely another individual entitlement and ignores the vital public interests served by common public schools. Public education is democratically controlled by the elected representatives of the People. Ultimately it is the People who decide how public education funds are expended. Privatization systems use public funds, but limit public control. Allowing private control of public funds circumvents the democratic control and interests of the People. (p. 82)

Is private management likely to view justice, equality, and freedom as schools' most important purposes? Public education may have some difficult problems, but its purposes are clear and positive. Can the private sector be trusted to foster these democratic ideals?

Example of School Privatization: Reasons for Resistance

The two most prominent efforts to privatize public schools in the United States have already frayed, engaging in questionable practices that should arouse the public's skepticism about the whole process (Saks, 1995; Toch, 1995; CUPE Report, 1998; Shrag, 1999; Breslau and Joseph, 2001; Shrag, 2001; Bracey, 2002; Henriquez and Steinberg, 2002a, 2002b; Saltman, 2005).

The Edison Project/Schools

The Edison Project, the most widely advertised effort to take over and profit from operation of public schools, was established by Christopher Whittle in 1991. Whittle, a strong advocate of free-market economics, was known for comments that were "unbelievably hostile to the public school world" (*New York*, 1994, p. 53).

The Edison Project began by proposing to build new schools. That idea changed quickly to an effort to contract for the complete operation of existing public schools. Whittle predicted that the Edison Project would be operating 200 private schools by 1996, and would be educating 2 million children by the year 2010. He also pledged to personally finance the education of 100 "Whittle Scholars" for a year at the University of Tennessee (Stewart, 1994). The widely publicized project now appears unable to meet any of its initial projections. Edison reportedly was operating a few for-profit schools with a record of high teacher turnover because of organizational disarray, lack of materials and support, and other related problems (CUPE Report, 1998; Breslau and Joseph, 2001; Shrag, 2001; Bracey, 2002; AFT, 2003; Moberg, 2004; Glassman, 2005; Snyder, 2007).

Privatization means even lower pay and higher workloads for teachers and counselors, increased savings on textbooks and materials, cutting or elimination of other services, to help finance higher salaries for executives. This corporate model—excessively paid executives over underpaid workers—benefits an elite few, but does not benefit society in general.

Can private business show how to better finance schools with public funds, make a profit, and preserve educational quality? By 1994, Whittle Communications had reached a state of financial collapse. The *New Yorker* magazine (1994) featured a long story detailing this collapse under the title "Grand Illusion," and subtitled with the line, "But the biggest surprise may be that it took so long for anyone to know that things had gone so wrong" (p. 63). The story described Whittle's reputation on Madison Avenue as a "legendary salesman" and one whose "most striking quality may be his charm" (p. 63). This charm has not made the Edison stock worthwhile; it declined precipitously from $37 to 14¢ per share amid concerns about its profitability and an SEC investigation (Steinberg and Henriques, 2002). Edison went private.

Whittle earlier established Channel One, a private television channel that "gave" TV equipment to schools on the condition that students be required to watch the channel and its commercials daily. Needing capital to try to save his other ventures, Whittle sold Channel One to K–III Communications. K–III owns *Seventeen* magazine and the *Weekly Reader*, a school newspaper, and is itself under the control of the same corporate body that controls RJR Nabisco. That relationship raised some concerns about corporate interests and influence when the *Weekly Reader* carried a story on "smokers' rights" (*Wall Street Journal*, 1994). But the larger concern is about the broad effort to commercialize public education.

Edison's financial difficulties illustrate some defects inherent in the privatization scheme. Venture capital, with its high risks and potentially high rewards for a few, is not the best model for organizing public schools in a democracy. Public schooling's long-term goals of providing knowledge and encouraging ethical conduct based on justice, equality, and freedom are socially constructive. A public education system based on charm and advertising is inconsistent with the democratic purposes of education.

Privatization and Private Enterprise: Beyond Schooling

In areas where private enterprise is supposed to afford the best leadership (efficiency, financial acuity, accountability, and performance), these private ventures do not measure up. Instead, evidence of financial manipulation, wastage and inefficiency, and insufficient public accountability crops up (Sheppard, 1998). Further, private enterprise has offered no demonstration that instruction actually was improved and at a lower cost when private groups take over. The social purposes of public education, of course, are not addressed in these examples.

Private entrepreneurship is one of the values American society holds dear. We prize the brave individuals who risk their financial security to bring new ideas and products to the public marketplace. Private entrepreneurs encourage innovation, experimentation, and development. But private entrepreneurship also is marked by unethical and illegal practices, including fraud and scams, graft and corruption, "Let the buyer beware" as a common corporate philosophy, and irresponsible pollution of the environment. The robber baron mentality permeates much of private enterprise, where payoffs and hidden conspiracies for fixing prices or controlling the market are simply ways of doing business. The primary value is personal greed. In these ways, private enterprise has shown little regard for social responsibility. Incompetent private operation and lack of adequate governmental regulation have cost taxpayers billions in government bailouts and subsidies of Chrysler, Lockheed, the savings and loan associations, and subprime mortgage financiers. Yet private enterprise maintains an aura of respectability that implies it is better than public operations.

Challenging the Privatization Myth

Striking examples of improvements and declines in the quality of human life can be attributed to both private and public enterprise; neither has an automatic superiority in economic, ethical, or social terms. In addition to lack of clear supportive evidence about the extraordinary claims of privatization advocates, questions arise about the ideology of privatization and its consequences for society.

Inherent in privatization mythology is the presumption that if something makes a profit, it must be good for us. How can a democracy sustain the idea that greed offers more to society than social responsibility? Privatization encourages privateering over the public good. Standard Oil's manipulation of the public trust was so massive it resulted in antitrust laws supposed to protect us from further fleecing by private enterprise (Tarbell, 1904). Unfortunately, we have suffered a long history of corporate corruption, fraud, and manipulation of the public even with some protections resulting from antitrust legislation (Adams, 1990; Calavita et al., 1997; Mitchell, 2001; Sherman, 2001; Palast, 2002).

Enron and WorldCom showed us that the corporate world remains ready and eager to gain excessive, some say obscene, profits on public necessities without accepting public responsibility. A pattern of Enron political action, including gifts, contributions, and extraordinary lobbying, gave Enron executives access to top politicians. These Enron executives became leaders of the effort to deregulate the energy industry, a necessary public commodity. Their substantial contributions to both political parties assured Enron of a more than equal opportunity to have their side heard in the halls of government. The resulting deregulation, a form of privatization, permitted manipulation of the system of electricity and gas provided to the public, creating manufactured crises, shortages, and windfall profits to companies like Enron. Enron had not been entirely without public blame before the debacle of 2002; three years earlier, Human Rights Watch published a dark story of Enron's involvement in human rights violations (Human Rights Watch, 1999). While other examples of corporate greed are not as large or public as Enron's, there are many others. WorldCom's hidden losses were, apparently, the largest of any corporation in history and were taken largely by shareholders and employees—not the key executives. We need to exercise great caution in accepting the myth that corporations will look out for the public good.

Exposing the Myths of Privatization

Clever packaging in a period when people distrust government and are concerned about rising taxes has made privatization popular. There are, however, several presumptions that privatization is based on, and they are simply false or at least seriously questionable. The popular media have not challenged these presumptions. They are myths of private enterprise, and deserve to be fully examined before the public purse is opened even wider to private operations.

Myths about privatization include the ideas that privatization is:

- efficient, so it can save tax money while providing quality services.
- market-driven, so it is responsive to the consumer.
- performance-based, rewarding the productive and cutting out the incompetent.
- a success as a worldwide movement.

Myth: Efficiency

Efficiency is the main claim of private enterprise. It is almost an article of faith, but the claim collapses under scrutiny.

Efficiency is a means, not a goal; the mere act of being efficient is inadequate as a rationale for social policy. There has to be a purpose for striving to make human activities efficient. In a democratic society that respects the environment and aspires to equity for its members, efficiency can be a worthwhile pursuit, but effectiveness is more important. Efficient use of resources, human and other, should aim to preserve and improve the environment. That is a worthy goal, and efficiency is an appropriate means to reach it; but environmental improvement by efficiency is not in the interests of many industries. Efficient operation of social services should have the purpose of improving the lot of society as a whole, not just of one class of people.

The superficial type of efficiency used in the private sector is found wanting. The profit motive defines efficiency as a cost-saving way to increase corporate income. Saving time by requiring dangerous shortcuts may appear to be efficient, but may simply be foolhardy. Efficient slaughter of wild animals, once a pastime of the wealthy and a business enterprise, sped endangerment of many species. Wild animal wall trophies and exotic meat dishes are not worth the price of those forms of efficiency.

Efficient manufacturing has created toxic waste, workplace accidents, worker health problems, overproduction, and waste. Actual social costs of this type of efficiency are seldom calculated. Environmental and human costs of industrial efficiency are hidden in the search for profit. In addition, the public often subsidizes the private sector through corporation-friendly policies on taxes and use of natural resources.

A related concern is whether captains of industry are themselves efficient and productive. Do they lead lives that model efficiency and social improvement? Some wealthy people make significant contributions to the improvement of society and strive for efficient and productive lives; that is not standard. Large homes, expensive cars, servants, yachts, exclusive clubs, private planes, and legal and financial assistance to take advantage of tax loopholes typify those who gain the most from private enterprise. These are not accoutrements normally found among public school educators, whose lives are devoted to public service. Conspicuous consumption is a characteristic of private enterprise, not of public employment.

Myth: Market-Driven and Consumer-Responsive

Another myth is that the private sector competes in the open marketplace and pleases its customers. However, there is no free and open market in the current economy. Price-fixing, monopolistic trusts, special interest legislation, weak regulatory agencies, and other corporation-protective practices skew the market to benefit the biggest corporations and most politically adept businesspeople. Lobbying, graft, buyouts, control of regulating authorities, and an "old boys' network" combine to deny newcomers equal marketplace opportunity. Most corporate strategies aim to gain control of the market to keep others out, not to encourage free competition. When that doesn't work well, corporations appeal to the government for special treatment or subsidies, or undergo bankruptcy, which hurts small investors but leaves executives wealthy. The free market does not exist.

Public bailouts of failed corporations have enormous public costs, but somehow they are not classified as failures since they were successful at getting taxpayers to cover the cost. Publicly funded bailouts of failed corporations could be called publicization, but they were not made public enterprises—they remained profit-making entities with taxpayers taking the loss. The term used for using public funds to shore up failing or weak private corporations is *corporate welfare.* Destruction of the myth that business leaders have superior wisdom, skill, or ethics would help to allay the rush to privatize schools; in many respects, public schools show superior wisdom, skill, and ethics in providing good mass education at a remarkably low cost over a long time with relatively few ethical lapses.

Consumer responsiveness is another figment of the imagination. Marketing to increase consumerism is a high priority in the private sector, but the primary purpose is to increase profits, not to please customers. Enticing consumers to buy things they do not need is one of the purposes. Consumer protection and satisfaction is a public, not a private, concern, fostered by decades of consumer manipulation by private businesses. Every consumer has experienced traumatic confrontations with corporations; they make errors, furnish poor-quality goods or services, are unwilling to correct or replace items, use bait-and-switch tactics, provide weak warranties, list conditions of sale in unreadable fine print on contracts, and inflate credit charges.

Myths: The Performance-Based Corporation, Rewarding Merit, and Cutting Incompetence

Another myth about private enterprise is that it is rigorous about performance, expecting increased productivity and eliminating incompetence. But performance, in business terms, is merely selling more products at less cost with more profit. This goal has nothing to do with quality. Business news is filled with stories of chief executive officers (CEOs) whose corporations underperform, but who still receive large salary increases and bonuses. Incompetence occurs regularly and at high levels, office politics is more important than quality of work, and you can't challenge higher-level decisions even when these decisions obviously are wrong.

If U.S. businesses are so committed to performance, why was there a decline in its quality of manufacture and share of the world marketplace? Why are corporation stockholder meetings a façade while good ideas from ordinary stockholders essentially are excluded? Why is the business of consumer advocate offices increasing? Why are the most meritorious employees often forgotten, while the well-connected earn quick promotions? These and other points suggest that performance is not always the corporation's focus, and is not a major principle in big business.

Myth: The Successful Worldwide Movement

The vaunted privatization of public services in many nations has been unraveling. Britain's problems with the privatization of public services illustrate public loss for private gain. After World War II, Britain moved to public ownership of many enterprises to provide better accessibility to education, health care, and social services. Fifteen years of the Thatcher and Major governments produced privatization, and public services found themselves under assault.

Ellingsen (1994a) examined this privatization program and found: "Britain's passion for privatization has produced no payoff for the public . . . the public is starting to realize not only that the sell-offs have made millionaires of those who run former state enterprises, but have cost consumers something like $9 billion" (p. 21).

London Electricity executives saw their salaries rise from averages well below those in the private sector—to over $4 million annually for each of the twelve top officers. Public utilities were sold at excessively low prices that allowed quick profits, and executive income was linked to those profits in a charade claim of performance—all essentially at taxpayer expense. The greed of privatization has transformed the benevolent post–World War II British welfare state into a nation plagued by increased separation between the social classes, illegal child labor, hidden sweatshops, and crime and drugs (Ellingsen, 1994b).

Gillard (2008) examined England's experiment with "creeping privatization" of taxpayer-financed schools and noted there were "many failures," which he compared to similar results in privatized charter schools in the U.S. The English failures included schools with academic performance among the worst in the nation, lack of accountability, ghettoized school communities, increased bullying, poor staff morale, no coherent educational strategy, an increase in separation by social class, and more teaching of religious dogma.

Australia's experience with privatization also is problematic. Although studies concluded that a Sydney harbor tunnel was not economically viable, a private firm was proposed to build and operate one. After two years of private operation, taxpayers learned they will pick up a previously unreported tab of $4 billion to cover extra expenses during the thirty-year life of the private contract. Following that disclosure, alarms were sounded about other privatization efforts because of secrecy, hidden costs, and lack of scrutiny of private contracts for public services, such as building and operating hospitals, prisons, airports, railroads, and water services (*Sydney Morning Herald,* 1994a, 1994c, 1994d; The Center for Public Integrity, 2003). A new cross-city tunnel as a private tollway has similar problems of public accountability for expenses (*Sydney Morning Herald,* 2006).

Citizens of other nations also have suffered under privatization. In Eastern Europe and the former Soviet Union, privatization created high unemployment, extraordinary inflation, pyramid schemes that enriched a few and caused financial disaster for many, and social unrest (van Brabant, 1992; Earle, Frydman, and Rapaczynski, 1993). Canada is among the nations that have a series of problems with privatization of public services, including the outsourcing of some in education. (Public Services International, 2006).

The Privatization Barometer, an independent agency that tracks privatization efforts around the world, reports that privatization in "Europe is fading, China is surging, Russia is resting, and India becalmed" and that nations may be at a turning point, with "support for revising privatization high" (PB Annual Report, 2007, p. 3, 5). A survey of 28,000 people in twenty-eight European countries showed 80 percent want such things as renationalization or more realistic sale prices and taxes on the privateers. These findings are consistent with discontent about privatization in Latin America (Panizza and Yanez, 2006).

These myths of privatization should become part of the public debate before we take irretrievable actions to dismantle public schools. Privatizing public schools is another example of mythology, a siren song of lower costs and better scores.

Ideology or Sound Thinking?

Sclar (1994) dismisses the claim that privatizing would save money while improving services. He found this promise to be ideological hype, a starkly conservative agenda unsupported by research or practice. Sclar suggests that real competition in the global marketplace will require an improved public infrastructure, not its decimation by privatization. Undercutting public services, increasing in actual total costs, and raking in windfalls for the well-connected do not offer a quality of life that encourages global leadership. Sclar concludes: "Finally, it is the public sector that is the dispenser of social justice. It is difficult to envision America sustaining itself as a progressive democracy with that role impaired" (p. 336).

In a system of democratic capitalism, where the relationship between public and private sectors is delicate, there are many tensions. Private enterprise has some virtues and advocates, but it creates severe economic disparity among people and carries a history of exploitation. Similarly, public enterprise offers virtues and has supporters, but creates tax burdens and opens itself to bureaucratic bungling. Each sector serves different needs of individuals and society at large. Increasing the proportion controlled by the private sector comes at a cost to the public. For a democracy, the cost of privatizing public education is too high.

For Discussion

1. Table 7.1 shows categories and examples of government services that are candidates for privatization.
   a. What are the advantages and disadvantages of privatization in regard to each of the examples?
   b. What criteria should be used to determine the advantages and disadvantages?

Table 7.1 Government Services and Privatization

Category of Service	Example Activities for Privatization
Defense	military support, training
Health	public hospitals, FDA operations
Transportation	airports, Amtrak, FA, urban mass transit
Recreation	parks service, public land development
Justice	crime control, prisons
Communication	public radio, monitoring airwaves
Taxes	collection enforcement, IRS audits

    c. How do these criteria fit a discussion of privatizing schools?

    d. Who should be empowered to make the decisions about privatization?

2. Dialogue Ideas: Even if we find that it costs more to educate children under private operations, this clearly would show the public the need to better finance schools. Either way, it benefits education. What are the implications of this position?

3. The Government Accounting Office (1996) found five studies that compared public and private prisons in California, Texas, Washington, Tennessee, and New Mexico on the criteria of operational costs and quality of service provided. The GAO drew no conclusions from these studies because they found little or no differences in operational costs or in quality of service provided. How does this report support public or private operation of prisons? How does it relate to schools?

4. The Milwaukee parental-choice program, a voucherlike plan that uses state funds for sending a small group of children from poor families to private schools, has been evaluated in three independent studies. Evidence shows parents in the privatization program are more satisfied with school than those not in the program, but evidence also shows no difference between public and private schools in actual student achievement. What could account for these findings? What implications can we draw from the evidence? What does this say about privatization?

References

ADNETT, N. (2004). "Private-Sector Provision of Schooling: An Economic Assesment." *Comparative Education* 40 (3):384–399.

AMERICAN FEDERATION OF TEACHERS. (2003). "AFT Report on Edison Schools Finds Achievement Worse Than Edison Claims." Washington, DC: AFT

APPLEBOME, P., "A Venture on the Brink: Do Education and Profits Mix?" *New York Times,* Oct. 30, 1994.

ARISTOTLE. (1988). *The Politics,* ed. S. Everson. Cambridge: Cambridge: University Press.

ASCHER, C., FRUCHTER, N., AND BERNE, R. (1996). *Hard Lessons: Public Schools and Privatization.* Washington, DC: Brookings Institution Press.

BRACEY, G. (2002). "The 12th Bracey Report on the Condition of Public Education." *Kappan* 84(2):135–150.

———. (2008). "Who's out to Get Public Education?" *Huffington Post.* www.huffingtonpost.com January 30.

BRESLAU, K., AND JOSEPH, N. (2001). "Edison's Report Card: Problems in San Francisco and Elsewhere." *Newsweek* 138(1):48, 49.

BROWN CENTER ANNUAL REPORT ON EDUCATION IN THE UNITED STATES—CHARTER SCHOOLS. (2002). Brookings Institute Website: www.brook.edu/gs/brown/bc.

BUSH, J. (2008). "Improvement Requires Willingness to Change." *Privatization Watch* 31(5) 3, 12. www.reason.org

CALAVITA, K., ET AL., eds. (1997). *Big Money Crime.* Berkeley, CA: University of California Press.

THE CENTER FOR PUBLIC INTEGRITY. (2003). *The Water Barons.* February. www.publicintegrity .org.

CHUBB, J. (1998). "Edison Scores and Scores Again in Boston." *Phi Delta Kappan* 80(3): 205–213.

COONS, J. (1988). "Testimony, Hearings on Educational Choice. December 22." Cited in *Privatization: Toward More Effective Government.* Washington, DC: U.S. Government Printing Office.

CUPE REPORT. (1998). Canadian Union of Public Employees. www.cupe.ca.

DAYTON, J., AND GLICKMAN, C. D. (1994). "American Constitutional Democracy: Implications for Public School Curriculum Development." *Peabody Journal of Education* 69:62–80.

DEWEY, J. (1916). *Democracy and Education.* New York: Macmillan.

DOBEK, M. M. (1993). *The Political Logic of Privatization.* Westport, CT: Praeger.

DOYLE, D. (1994). "The Role of Private Sector Management in Public Education." *Kappan* 76:128–132.

EARLE, J., FRYDMAN, R., AND RAPACZYNSKI, A. (1993). *Privatization in the Transition to a Market Economy.* New York: St. Martin's Press.

The Economist. (2005). "The Missing Rungs in the Ladder." 376(8435):17.

EDISON SCHOOLS. (2005). Seventh Annual Report on School Performance 2003–04. "Student Achievement Data." www.edisonschools.com.

———. (2008). Edison Schools Overview. www.edisonschools.com.

———. (2008). "Welcome to Edison Schools." www.edisonschools.com

EGGERS, W., AND O'LEARY, J. (1996). "Union Confederates." *American Spectator.* March.

ELLINGSEN, P., "Making Profit in Private," *Sydney Morning Herald,* Nov. 26, 1994a.

———. "Rule Britannia—A Nation of Despair," *Sydney Morning Herald,* Oct. 29, 1994b.

EMMONS, W. (2000). *The Evolving Bargain.* Boston: Harvard Business School Press.

FARAZMAND, A., ed. (2001). *Privatization or Public Enterprise Reform?* Westport, CT: Greenwood Press.

FEISTRITZER, E., "Public vs. Private: Biggest Difference Is Not the Students," *Wall Street Journal,* Dec. 1, 1987.

FINN, C. (1995). "The School." *Commentary* 99:6–10.

GEIGER, P. E. (1995). "Representation and Privatization." *American School and University* 67:28–30.

GIBBS, N. (1994). "Schools for Profit." *Time.* Oct. 17:48–49.

GILLARD, D. (2008). "Blair's Academies: The Story So Far." *Forum* 50(1), 11–22.

GLASSMAN, J. K. (2005). "An Entrepreneur Goes to School." *Wall Street Journal.* Sept. 7.

GLANZ, J. (2008). "Iraq Spending Ignored Rules, Pentagon Says." *New York Times.* May 23. www.nytimes.com.

GLAZER, J. (1994). "The New Politics of Education: Schools for Sale." *Education Week* 14:44–ff.

GOVERNMENT ACCOUNTING OFFICE. (1996). "Private and Public Prisons: Studies Comparing Operational Costs and/or Quality of Service." Report GCD-96-158. Report to the Subcommittee on Crime, Committee on the Judiciary, House of Representatives. Washington, DC: August.

GUTMANN, A. (1999). *Democratic Education.* 2nd Ed. Princeton, NJ: Princeton University Press.

———. (2008). "Educating for Individual Freedom and Democratic Citizenship," in Siegel, H. ed., *Oxford Handbook of Philosophy of Education.* Oxford: Oxford University Press.

HASTINGS, S., AND LEVIE, H., eds. (1983). *Privatisation?* Nottingham, England: Spokesman.

HENIG, J. R. (2008). *Spine Cycle—How Research is Used in Policy Debates: The Case of Charter Schools.* New York: Russell Sage Foundation.

HENRIQUES, D. B., AND STEINBERG, J., "Woes for Company Running Schools," *New York Times,* May 14, 2002a. www.nytimes.com.

———. "Operator of Public Schools in Settlement with SEC," *New York Times,* May 15, 2000b. www.nytimes.com.

HENTSCHKE, G., ET AL. (2004). "The Rise of Education Management Organizations" *Privatization Watch* 28(7):13.

HOLLOWAY, J. H. (2002). "Research Link: For-Profit Schools." *Educational Leadership* 59(7): 84, 85.

HUMAN RIGHTS WATCH. (1999). The Enron Corporation: Corporate Complicity in Human Rights Violations. New York: Human Rights Watch.

HUNTER, R. C., AND BROWN, F., eds. (1995). "Privatization in Public Education." *Education and Urban Society* 27:107–228.

JEFFERSON, T. (1939). *Democracy.* New York: Greenwood Press.

JUDSON, G., "Hartford Hires Group to Run School System," *New York Times.,* Oct. 4, 1994.

KADLEC, A. (2007). *Dewey's Critical Pragmatism.* Lanham MD: Rowman and Littlefield.

KAPLAN, G. (1996). "Profits R Us." *Kappan* 78(3):K1–12.

KRUGMAN, P., "Victors and Spoils," *New York Times,* Nov. 19, 2002. www. nytimes.com.

LESLIE, C. (1994). "Taking Public Schools Private." *Newsweek.* June 20:7.

LEVIN, H. (2006). "Why Is Educational Entrepreneurship So Difficult?" Unpublished paper: National Center for the Study of Privatization in Education. January.

LUBIENSKI, C., AND LUBIENSKI, S. J. (2004). Re-examining a Primary Premise of Market Theory. National Center for the Study of Privatization in Education. New York: Teachers College, Columbia University.

MAGEE, M., AND LEOPOLD, L. S., "Study Finds Charter Schools Succeed No More Than Others," *San Diego Union-Tribune,* Dec. 4, 1998.

MANDEL, M., ET AL. (1995). "Will Schools Ever Get Better?" *Business Week.* April 17:64–68.

MATHEWS, D. (2008). "The Public and the Public Schools." *Kappan* 89(8) 560–564. April.

MIRON, G., AND APPLEGATE, B. (2000). *An Evaluation of Student Achievement in Edison Schools Opened in 1995 and 1996.* Kalamzaoo, MI: The Evaluation Center, Western Michigan University.

MITCHELL, L. E. (2001). *Corporate Irresponsibility: America's Newest Export.* New Haven, CT: Yale University Press.

MOBERG, D. (2004). "How Edison Survived." *The Nation.* 278(10) March 15.

MOLNAR, A., ET AL. (2005). Profiles of For-Profit Education Management Organizations: 2004–2005. 7th Annual Report of Commercialism in Education Research Unit. Tempe: Arizona State University. www.asu.edu/educ/epsl.

MURPHY, R. (2004). "What Is the Proper Way to Run a School?" Ludwig Von Mises Institute. May. www.mises.org.

NEALE, J. (2004). *What's Wrong With America?* London: Vision Books.

New York. (1994). "Has Benno Schmidt Learned His Lesson?" Oct. 31:49–59.

PALAST, G. (2002). *The Best Democracy Money Can Buy.* London: Pluto Press.

PANIZZA, U. and Yanez, M. (2006). "Why are Latin Americans So Unhappy About Reforms?" Report, Research Department, Inter-American Development Bank. pp 1–29, July.

PB Report 2007. Privatization Barometer. www.privatizationbarometer.net

Privatization: Toward More Effective Government. (1988). Report of the President's Commission on Privatization. Washington, DC: U.S. Government Printing Office.

PROTZMAN, F., "East Nearly Privatized, Germans Argue the Cost," *New York Times,* Aug. 12, 1994.

PUBLIC SERVICES INTERNATIONAL. (2006). *Developments in Privatization of Public Services.* March. www.cupe.ca.

RATCHFORD, W. (2005). "Going Public with School Privatization." *The Abell Report.* 18(3). Sept./Oct.

REASON FOUNDATION. (2008). "What Is Privatization?" www.privatization.org.

Rethinking Schools. (1998). "The Market Is Not the Answer: An Interview with Jonathan Kozol." www. rethinkingschools.org.

SAKS, J. B. (1995). "Scrutinizing Edison." *American School Board Journal* 183:20–24.

SALTMAN, J. (2000). *Collateral Damage: Corporatizing Public Schools—A Threat to Democracy.* Lanham, MD: Rowman and Littlefield.

———. (2005). *The Edison Schools: Corporate Schooling and the Assault on Public Education.* New York; Routledge.

SCHIPKE, A. (2001). *Why Do Governments Divest?* Berlin: Springer.

SCHMIDT, P. (1994). "Hartford Hires E.A.I. to Run Entire District." *Education Week* 14:1, 14.

SHRAG, P., "Private Affluence and Public Squalor." *San Diego Union-Tribune,* Jan. 8, 1999.

———. (2001). "Edison's Red Ink Schoolhouse." *The Nation* 272(25):20–24.

SCLAR, E. (1994). "Public-Service Privatization: Ideology or Economics?" *Dissent,* Summer: 329–336.

SHAFER, G. (1999). "The Myth of Competition and the Case Against School Choice." *The Humanist* 59(2):15–ff.

SHEPPARD, R. (1998). "A School Failure." *MacLeans* 111:52–53.

SHERMAN, M. (2001). *White Collar Crime.* Washington, DC: Federal Judiciary Center.

SNELL, L. (2005). "Unions Try to Discredit Education Outsourcing." *Privatization Watch* 29(1):12,13.

———. (2007). "Charter School Enrollment Swells." *Privatization Watch* 31(2) www .reason.org.

SNYDER, S. (2007). "Report: How Managers Fall Short in Philadelphia Schools." *Philadelphia Inquirer.* May 27.

SOLOMON, M. (2004). "Privatization Zealotry." Education News.Org. Dec. 13. www .educationnews.org.

STEINBERG, J. "Private Groups Get 42 Schools in Philadelphia," *New York Times,* April 18, 2002. www.nytimes.com.

STEINBERG, J., AND HENRIQUES, D., "Edison Schools Gets Reprieve," *New York Times,* June 5, 2002. www.nytimes.com.

Sydney Morning Herald, "Auditor Criticises Secrecy on Public Works Contract," October 8, 1994a.

———. "Competition May Kill Utilities: ACTU," October 29, 1994b.

———."Public Funds, Public Works," October 18, 1994c.

———."Why Parlt [Parliament] Must Scrutinize Projects with Private Sector," October 18, 1994d.

———."Let the Public See the Full Deal," April 5, 2006.

SUDETIC, C. (2001). "Reading, Writing, and Revenue." *Mother Jones* 26(3):84–95.

STEWART, J. B. (1994). "The World of Business: Grand Illusions." *New Yorker.* Oct, 31:64–81.

TARBELL, I. M. (1904). *The History of the Standard Oil Company.* New York: McClure, Phillips and Company.

TOCH, T. (1995). "Taking Public Schools Private: A Setback." *U.S. News and World Report* 117:74.

U.S. GENERAL ACCOUNTING OFFICE. (2003). Public Schools: Comparisons of Achievement Results for Students Attending Privately Managed and Traditional Schools in Six Cities." Washington, DC: U.S. General Accounting Office.

VAN BRABANT, J. V. (1992). *Privatizing Eastern Europe.* International Studies in Economics and Econometrics, No. 24. Boston: Kluwer Academic Press.

VICKERS, J., AND YARROW, G. (1991). "Economic Perspectives on Privatization." *Journal of Economic Perspectives* 2:111–132.

Wall Street Journal, "A KKR Vehicle Finds Profit and Education a Rich But Uneasy Mix." Oct. 12, 1994.

WEISLAK, L. J., AND LAFAIVE, M. D. (2004). "Privatize the University of Michigan." Michigan Privatization Report. Mackinak Center for Public Policy. www.mackinac.org.

ZOLLERS, N., AND RAMANATHAN. A. (1998). "For-Profit Charter Schools and Students with Disabilities." *Kappan* 80(4):297–315.

CHAPTER 8

Corporations, Commerce, and Schools: Complementing or Competing Interests

Does school support become corporate support?

POSITION 1: BUSINESSES ARE SCHOOL PARTNERS

The schools are the central public institution for the development of human resources. Tomorrow's workforce is in today's classrooms; the skills that these students develop and the attitudes toward work that they acquire will help determine the performance of our businesses and the course of our society in the twenty-first century. The case for business involvement not only centers on the benefits business derives from education, but also on what business can contribute.

—Committee for Economic Development, 1985, p. 5

The United States cannot succeed in the international economy without a well-educated, well-trained workforce. The United States needs a strong education system to prepare the next generation of workers for the ever-changing economy.

—Business Roundtable, 2008, p. 2

Educating for Employment and the Economy

The health and vitality of our economy and our society depend on schools. Businesspeople understand this principle. For many years, corporations and local businesses have been among the strongest supporters of education. Business enterprises provide substantial financial contributions, internships and scholarships, guest speakers and teaching materials, advisors and consultants, fundraising assistance, and employment for parents, students, and other taxpayers. Leaders of the business community recognize the significant benefits that good schools offer, and they are active advocates of improvements in education.

Businesspeople, from the owners of local enterprises to the executives of major international corporations, know that there may be no more important work in American society than the improvement of schools. Good schools are simply good business.

Schools are important in preparing people for productive lives in society and in various occupations, and important in the continuing development of our economy. Schools have a fundamental responsibility for providing increased communication, math, civic, technical, and workplace skills for a variety of purposes. Improved cognitive and workplace skills are required for employment, higher education, and civic life; they are also necessary in America's continuing competition in the global business world. A correlated expectation is for schools to adequately educate students about our free-market economy and the importance of consumers (National Council on Economic Education, 2008). The majority of high school students do not understand basic economic concepts (National Council on Economic Education, 2005). Businesses assist schools by providing resources and encouraging educational improvements. Schools support businesses by providing well-educated people. If the skills or attitudes of students seeking employment are unsatisfactory, or if their grasp of basic economics is insufficient to maintain our standard of living, we all suffer.

Democracy, Capitalism, and the Business of Education

The strength of U.S. society lies in the fortuitous combination of democracy and capitalism. We not only offer freedom and opportunity in politics (the democratic concept), but also in economics. The freedom to engage in enterprise without obstructive interference provides opportunities and incentives for everyone. Free enterprise is a basic condition for releasing the entrepreneurial spirit in humans, and entrepreneurs built and developed this great nation. The United States has moved from being a minor colony to a world power because of this spirit of freedom and ingenuity. The free marketplace for which the United States has become respected globally requires continual improvement— that directly incorporates education. Schools are key to the future development of the American economy (Business Roundtable, 2008).

Our success causes many other nations to emulate American entrepreneurship. That is complimentary, but it is also a challenge. The breakdown of most communist countries at the end of the 1980s illustrates the flawed nature of socialism. The death of communism finds the early twenty-first century a world of competing capitalist nations. This new scenario requires even more U.S. commitment to an education-business partnership. Schooling that will maintain our leadership in international business competition is a top priority. Business must enter into new and more intertwined partnerships with schools to ensure that the United States keeps its competitive edge in global markets.

Our economy thrives when commerce thrives. In order to have a well-functioning economy, we must have a well-educated populace. The United States was among the first nations to recognize this necessary parallel between mass education and a sound economy. Now competition among nations goes beyond industrial production and gross domestic product; it necessarily includes competition in education. Nations are in a race in terms of expanding and improving their educational systems.

As DeLong and others (2003) write:

> The twentieth century can thus be thought of not only as the "American century" but as the "human-capital century." The twentieth century became the human-capital century because of wide-ranging changes in business, industry, and technology that increased the demand for particular cognitive skills. The early twentieth century rise of big business and of large retail, insurance, and banking operations, for example, generated increased demand for literate and numerate office workers. (p. 20)

Human capital is an important concept in economics and social thought. The premise of human capital is that investments in humans can be at least as valuable to the economy as investments in plants and equipment. This leads immediately to the concept that education is a key investment strategy. Gary S. Becker (2005), whose Nobel Prize in 1992 was partly for his work on human capital, writes that "Education and training are the most important investments in human capital" (p. 1). His Nobel Lecture of 1992 includes: "The human capital approach considers how the productivity of people in market and non-market situations is changed by investments in education" (Becker, 1992). This approach uses schooling as an investment rather than as a vague cultural exercise; it posits that people decide about education in terms of costs and benefits. Becker (2005) notes a continuing condition: "The earnings of more educated people are almost always well above average . . ." (p. 1).

These points are elaborated in many of the most significant writings on education and economics (Schultz, 1971; Mincer, 1974; Keeley, 2007). They form one of the rationales for the strong interest that business enterprises have in schooling. Education is directly linked to increased economic development, productivity, and individual reward. Jac Fitz-Enz (2000), noting the returns from investment in human capital, puts it: "In the American economy, where over half of the gross national product is allocated to the information sector, it is obvious that knowledgeable people are the driving force" (p. 1).

The U.S. government considers human capital to be a concept important enough to (1) be a focus of the U.S. Office of Personnel Management, (2) establish national standards for improvements in agencies, and (3) include a requirement in the Homeland Security Act that government agencies designate a Chief Human Capital Officer (http://apps.opm.gov/HumanCapital.2008; www.chcoc.gov). Schools are key elements in human capital: developing and distributing knowledge, providing skills and attitudes, continuously improving. This is needed for a strong economy.

Meeting the Competition of the Twenty-First Century

The connection between increasing education and improvements in national economies has stimulated nearly all governments to provide, actually mandate, elementary and secondary schooling for most of their citizens. That is a recent development in educational history. During the first half of the twentieth century, most industrialized nations required attendance only in primary schools as the way to provide basic literacy, while academic secondary education was limited to members of elite classes. After primary school, the other children usually went into apprenticeships, other vocational training, or took jobs. The United States, however, has long been an international leader in public support for expanding mandatory education for all students through high school, and also for increasing the opportunities for access to higher education.

This twentieth-century leadership by the United States in education has been accompanied by a parallel development—a significant increase in our per capita income and one of the highest standards of living in the world by the end of the century. Rapid changes in technology, business, finance, and industry fueled the need for employees with more than basic literacy skills. As other nations came to recognize this link between expanded educational opportunity and the national economy, they have actively pursued increased schooling for their people (The World Bank, 2006). As the twenty-first century unfolds, data show that the United States is actually losing its international leadership, slowing down in its rate of school completion while other nations are accelerating. For America, this decline "threatens to retard future economic growth" (DeLong et al., 2003, p. 21).

More Than Quantity of Schooling

Beyond problems created by a decrease in the rate of school completion by American students, there is a more significant international competition over the quality of schools. Our students do not do as well on internationally comparable tests of knowledge as our historic investment in education would suggest. American students usually rank near the bottom of test scores in math and literacy when compared with the scores of students in other industrialized democracies.

Language and math skills are an obvious requirement in modern business and social life, and schools must emphasize them. Many who are already employed are illiterate, substandard in language or math, or lack good work habits. United States corporations, in addition to directly supporting schools (Business Roundtable, 2008), spend billions of dollars annually on remedial education for their own employees. The extensive school focus on writing skills helps, but American corporations still invest about $3 billion annually to upgrade the writing skills of their employees after schooling is finished (*Education Week,* 2004). Calculation skills are also among the most emphasized by schools and still augmented later by corporations. Serious problems confront the United States when students do not leave school with solid skills and workplace values. Those who seek employment without adequate skills or attitudes are in for a shock in the workplace. Both the individuals and the society suffer when people are not prepared for work.

The United States risks losing its competitive advantage because the workforce is undereducated. This situation is particularly harmful in a time of rapid technological change, and especially when workers' skills are improving in other nations. Outsourcing of jobs to other nations occurs partly because American corporations find that countries like India and China have well-educated citizens with good work habits and attitudes. A dramatic shift has already occurred in the production of electronics, automobiles, furniture, and other consumer goods: High-quality products are now manufactured in China, India, Japan, Taiwan, Korea, and other places. Similarly, there is a shift in the service and information industries from the United States to other nations; this is directly related to improved education in those nations.

Commerce needs people who are competent in basic skills, who can understand technical manuals and operations, and who can work with management in a cooperative effort to strengthen the nation's economy. In far too many schools, students have trouble following simple written forms and directions, understanding low-level technical information, and maintaining interest in their work.

Business Interest in Partnerships with Schools

It is this competition for school completion and school quality that demands the joint interests of businesspeople, corporations, and school people. Consistent with these beliefs, business leaders are in the forefront of efforts to reform schools (Ramsey, 1993; Aaron et al., 2003). The Business Roundtable, an organization of the CEOs of the 200 most prominent U.S. corporations, was an early and strong supporter of the No Child Left Behind (NCLB) Act of 2002. The Roundtable website (www.businessroundtable.org) contains links to various Roundtable school reform activities and forums that follow up on the implementation of NCLB legislation. The companies with membership in the Roundtable employ about 34 million people. That constitutes a very sizable and influential group of corporate people with educational interests.

Corporate support for school improvement goes far beyond that in earlier days and now includes leading businesses in virtually all segments of the economy. These corporate-sponsored school activities focus on such diverse areas as academic instructional improvement, career awareness, civic and character education, drug abuse prevention, dropout prevention, and programs for the disadvantaged. The U.S. Chamber of Commerce, the National Alliance of Business, and the Business Roundtable joint statement, "A Common Agenda for Improving American Business" (1997), stems from a concern that "the graduates of America's schools are not prepared to meet the challenge posed by global economic competition . . . business continues to have trouble finding qualified workers" (p. 1).

Much of the NCLB support came from the Goals 2000 national strategy to improve schools. Goals 2000 emerged from state governors with strong interests in education. It identifies the business community as essential to such improvements. After major national reports detailed problems with the quality of American education, the Business Roundtable made a ten-year commitment to reform the public education system. Business leaders spearheaded the establishment of the Education Excellence Partnership, a coalition including the

Business Roundtable, the U.S. Department of Education, the American Federation of Teachers, the National Education Association, the National Governors Conference, and the U.S. Chamber of Commerce.

School-Business Partnerships

The president of the National Education Association, in announcing a new form of responsible unionism, stated: "Despite the political rhetoric, public schools and business are natural allies" (Chase, 1998). This allied position bodes well for dramatic improvements in schooling, and offers opportunities for school-business partnerships to provide leadership and support. There are some good examples of this allied effort.

Almost all of the member corporations of the Business Roundtable belong to school partnerships for educational improvement. A new Council for Corporate and School Partnerships, established by Coca Cola in 2001 (www .corpschoolpartners.org), offers support and rewards for schools engaged in partnership activities. This council is headed by a former U.S. Secretary of Education and governor of South Carolina, and includes school administrators, leaders of the national PTA and administrator and school board associations, and chief executive officers of major corporations on its board. The purpose for the council is to encourage school-business partnerships that improve the academic, social, or physical well-being of students. The council presents six large awards per year to model school-business partnerships. There are now several hundred such partnerships, representing nearly every state, competing for the awards.

The Boston Compact established a partnership between Boston's schools and the Boston Private Industry Council. Businesses promised students jobs if the schools were able to raise test scores and decrease dropout rates. This alliance has provided jobs for over a thousand graduates, and reading and math scores have improved (www.bostonpic.org).

Through such partnerships, business leaders can come into the schools to teach, to talk with students, and to help teachers and guidance counselors develop programs to improve student skills and attitudes. Students can visit places of employment and gain understanding of the economy and business interests and concerns. Partnerships can establish work-study arrangements for students, produce teaching materials, and provide financial support for all aspects of schooling from teacher seminars to improving school technology and career guidance. Many businesses participate in "Adopt-a-School" programs that enrich the school's ability to prepare students for employment. Other businesses invite teachers to visit, provide summer employment and other opportunities for teachers to learn about their operations, and prepare free teaching materials. Business-to-school financial support by direct grants, special project sponsorship, advertising in school media, discounted purchase arrangements, equipment and resource acquisition, and a variety of other avenues provides much-needed money for school uses.

Corporations help schools in these key areas because they recognize the value of helping students reach their full potential. This is not a new role for business leadership in U.S. schools; business-education relations have a long and positive history. Mann (1987) examined school-business partnerships and concluded that "partnerships between businesses and the schools have made positive contributions to the public schools . . . [they] have offered concrete assistance to the schools in a number of ways" (p. 228). These contributions included cash, services, sympathy, and assistance in political and economic coalitions. Mann notes a few problems with school-business alliances as well, but cites a large number of examples where businesses have been particularly helpful in improving local schools. There are many varieties of school-business partnerships; the most effective ones provide for mutual respect and participation, with each partner satisfied with the results (Hann, 2008; Daniels Fund, 2008).

Education and the Changing Nature of Employment in the United States

Prominent changes in the nature of employment in American society have had major implications for schools. Historically, the shift was from agricultural to manufacturing jobs; now the shift is from manufacturing to service and information. In the short space of the last fifty years, the proportion of farmers and farmworkers has declined from almost 20 percent of the workforce to only 3 percent; manufacturing jobs have declined from about 32 percent to 27 percent of total employment, whereas service jobs have increased from about 53 percent to 69 percent. The service sector has grown primarily in social and producer services (for example, health and medical technology), rather than in personal services (for example, hairdressing or domestic work) or distributive services (sales and delivery). The most prominent change has been in the kinds of jobs available. White-collar jobs rose from about 45 percent of the labor force in 1940 to over 70 percent by the mid-1980s and about 80 percent by 2000. Blue-collar jobs declined from about 42 percent to about 20 percent over the same period (U.S. Census Bureau 2000, 2007).

In educational terms, this means students need more and better schooling. Many agricultural jobs no longer demand just sheer physical labor, but involve technical work that requires strong academic skills. White-collar jobs typically require increased education. The data that show how the level of education relates to income are compelling. Education influences the kind of job and the level of income people have. This has been true for many years.

In earlier times, basic literacy could be recommended purely for its inherent values; it had no special relation to people's work requirements. In a period when most citizens lived rural, agricultural lives, reading, writing, and calculating were nice to know, but not necessary for securing and keeping employment. Even in those times, however, obvious links existed between education and employment. A study conducted in 1867 by the Commonwealth of Pennsylvania, for example, showed that income was related directly to literacy: Those who could not read earned an average of $36 per month; those who could read, but were otherwise poorly educated, earned an average of $52 a month; and those who were well-educated earned an average of $90 a month (Soltow and

FIGURE 8.1 Education and Earning Power

Education Attainment	Average Annual Earnings	Expected Lifetime Earnings	Unemployment Rate
Less than High School	$20,000	$1,000,000	6.8%
High School Graduate	30,600	1,200,000	4.3
Some College	35,600	1,500,000	3.9
Associate Degree	37,900	1,600,000	3.0
Bachelor's Degree	53,500	2,100,000	2.3
Master's Degree	67,350	2,500,000	1.7

Annual Earning data based on 2004 income data, U.S. Census Bureau, rounded. Lifetime earnings extrapolated.

Source: U.S. Census Bureau. (2005). *Current Population Survey, 2005 Annual Social and Economic Supplement.* June 24, Business Roundtable, 2008.

Stevens, 1981). But literacy for business purposes does not mean just proficiency in reading and writing. As Soltow and Stevens (1981), in examining the history of literacy in the United States, note, "To be literate, as we have seen, did not simply mean to be competent at a specific level of reading mastery. It meant, perhaps more importantly for the employer, exposure to a set of values compatible with a disciplined workforce" (pp. 127–128).

There is a correlation between education and income, between education and national development, and between education and "the good life." In the United States, average annual earnings for college graduates are over twice as much as earnings of high school dropouts. Lifetime earnings average $2.5 million with a college degree, and $1.4 million for those with a high school diploma (see Figure 8.1). Nations with the highest levels of education also have the highest levels of wealth, innovation, and achievement (Isaak, 2005).

Social class and occupational experience are also considered influential in employment status, but education had the greatest effect. More recently, a U.S. Census Bureau report from the 2000 Census demonstrates that those who do not complete high school earn less than 50 percent of the average income college graduates earn, and those who graduate from high school earn about 62 percent of the incomes of degree holders (U.S. Census Bureau, 2003). Figure 8.1 shows the value of education in the workforce, with increasing earnings as school level rises.

Consumers and Schools

In addition to the business interest in education for developing the economy, investing in human capital, and preparing good employees, there is an obvious interest in the schools as a location of consumers. Consumers, of course, are one of the driving forces of our economy; our economy depends upon consumers. Just check stock market reports on TV or in newspapers and note how much of our market is determined by consumer actions. It is not only the earnings of retail stores that rise and fall according to consumer choices. Manufacturers of electronics, clothing, appliances, and vehicles, and their suppliers of raw materials, are also examples of industries subject to consumer selections. Banks and other financial institutions, gas and oil companies, house construction and repair agencies, food producers and suppliers, entertainment industries, and a myriad of other consumer-driven corporations exist and change because of what people buy.

Consumer confidence is one of the major indicators of economic activity, one closely examined by Wall Street firms and market watchers worldwide. The monthly national survey conducted by the University of Michigan Survey Research Center, the Index of Consumer Sentiment (www.sca.isr.umich.edu), is among the most widely used and accurate indicators of the future direction of the U.S. economy. It tracks how consumers feel about their personal financial ability to make purchases, and how they feel about short- and long-term prospects for the whole economy. Another example is the Conference Board's Consumer Confidence Index (www.conference-board.org). The Conference Board is an international independent group of concerned business leaders, formed in 1916. The Michigan and Conference Board reports influence stock markets, manufacturers and retailers, and other economic news.

We are a consumer society. A free market gives us competition that provides choices among quality, prices, and variety. An important part of the economic process in a consumer society is getting information to the consumer about new or improved products and services, places to obtain them, reminders about trade names, and ways to obtain competitive prices or opportunities. This is a place for corporate notices, news releases, advertising, and other uses of media to convey information. Although we may complain at times about some advertising, we recognize that much of the information that ads contain is valuable. Through advertising we learn of innovations, modifications, and opportunities that make our lives easier or happier. We can find better prices, products, and services for things we want. We can find standards against which we can measure products and services. Advertising provides us with important ideas and information, necessary to our roles as consumers. The marketplace adjusts according to the decisions made by consumers; advertising adjusts according to the market and how consumers respond to ads.

Consumer life does not stop at the school door. After all, students are consumers and they influence consumer decisions in families. They deserve to know about products and services available. The school setting is an appropriate location for some of that information. Schools employ teachers and administrators to develop curricula and classroom practices designed to help students gain an adequate understanding of life. Certainly, student life outside of school involves advertising and commerce. Schools should provide education that reflects the society, and societies depend upon commerce. Businesses know that children and adolescents are a very significant segment of buyers, among the most important in many areas of retail purchases. Within this context, the provision of corporate-sponsored school material offers information for students, and it gives financial support for schools. Students can learn from the material, and schools are relieved from the extra burden of paying for it.

Business Approaches to School Operation

Schools could also benefit from the use of business models in school organization and operation. Schools are often inefficient. Their organization and operation did not change much during the twentieth century, and show little alteration in the twenty-first, while corporations have made remarkable progress in becoming more efficient and more productive. If U.S. industry had been as stultified as the schools, it would have failed long ago. In fact, those businesses that have not updated and improved their efficiency and productivity have failed; private enterprise cannot survive stagnation. Yet we have protected our schools from this necessary competition. The No Child Left Behind legislation provides motivation to improve and standards to hold schools accountable.

School budgets represent one of the biggest expenses in most communities. Improved technology and productivity could increase school efficiency considerably. For example, if innovative technologies come into play, the teacher could present more interesting material to larger groups in less time, individual students could work more extensively on computers under the general guidance of the teacher or a teacher's aide, the school day and curriculum could be more varied, parents could get up-to-date information on their child's progress, early warning systems could limit student failures, and teachers could identify their own and their students' peak performance data. Schools would be organized very differently, but that is what we need. Businesses are constantly reorganizing to achieve better productivity because competition demands it. Schools should not be exempt from similar requirements.

Another businesslike approach that could bring great benefits to schools is in the use of incentives and rewards for good performance. Currently, schools pay teachers on the basis of nineteenth-century ideas that all teachers are the same and that only increased experience should provide increased income. This levels down the performance of many teachers and schools to the lowest common denominator. There is no incentive for individual teachers to perform in a superior manner. That limits the best teachers and their students. With teacher pay based on performance, the most talented teachers will get better salaries and other teachers will have a very good reason to start measuring up. That would make the salaries for the best teachers competitive with salaries for other professionals, and would attract more of the topflight college graduates into teaching.

Another place to bring incentives for performance is in school administration. There is a bit of that now in schools since teachers often find they have to go into administration to get higher salaries, but often the administrator salaries are also limited by job title and excellent performance is only rewarded by having to change jobs. One idea would be to tie administrator income to accountability standards, like those in the No Child Left Behind Act. When administrators lead their schools forward to better student achievement, as determined by NCLB standards, they get increased income through bonuses or other rewards.

Business thinking can help education in other areas. School buildings are often large, inefficiently utilized, and costly to build and maintain. In districts where student enrollment has declined, expensive school buildings have been sold, destroyed, or renovated at great public financial loss. Some school build-ings are used less than half of the year and then for only one-third of the day. The practice of issuing bonds has passed the debt for building these behemoths on to future generations. Many small schools, with separate buildings and school staffs, could be reorganized into less costly regional districts if we applied busi-ness concepts. Individual school districts purchase millions of dollars' worth of books, equipment, and teaching materials at high cost, when a coordinated effort could decrease such expense considerably.

Businesses have shown that they can train large numbers of employees by using video and computer systems, lectures, programmed materials, self-study, and other devices that do not consume the high levels of precious human resources that schools use. Furthermore, this training occurs in facilities used extensively for the whole of each year.

This is not a time for schools to continue their course—it is a time to change schools, and business-proven techniques can effect the changes. The structure of business based on a competitive marketplace has withstood the most severe tests of war, depression, and dislocation. We need to introduce contemporary business management—management concerned with improved efficiency and productivity—into education.

It is a social and educational necessity that we reorder our schools to give stu-dents solid grounding in academic skills and good, positive workplace values. It is an economic necessity that we reorganize school operations to more closely approximate good business practices. All in all, business has much to offer edu-cation, much more than just providing money for school projects (Feulner, 1991; Mandel et al., 1995; Oravitz, 1999; Aaron et al., 2003). Financial support alone cannot confront the crisis in education. To develop basic and advanced skills, to improve workplace attitudes and values, to increase the productivity of U.S. business, to enhance our competitive stance in international markets, and to make schools more efficient are goals business and the schools share. For the good of our young people and for our future as a nation, we need to encourage schools to form strong alliances with business to reach these shared goals.

POSITION 2: COMMERCIALIZING THE SCHOOL

Schools have become integral to the marketing plans of a vast array of cor-porations as commercial interests—through advertising, sponsorship of curriculum and programs, marketing of consumer products, for-profit priva-tization, and fund-raising tied to commercial entities—continue to influence public education.

—Molnar, 2004, p. 1

During the last two decades, the invisible hand of the corporation has sought to capture and control the most pivotal institutions in the determination of culture, consciousness, and individual freedom. Among these are the justice system, the educational system, and the public spaces that define community.

> Until the 1980s, these areas were strictly the province of a civic culture deter-
> mined by individuals and their work. The individual was not routinely asked
> to waive her legal rights as a condition of commerce, as mandatory binding
> arbitration agreements demand today. Corporations did not interject com-
> mercial messages into the public school classroom. . . .
>
> —Court, 2003, p. 89

Kids as Commodities; Schools as Agents

The commercialization of education is one of the most unfortunate developments in modern society. Schools and corporations may share some general
social interests, but they have incompatible goals. The major purpose of corporations is to make profits for shareholders and executives; corporations are
not concerned with social well-being unless that stance happens to suit their
profit-seeking purpose. The major purpose for schooling, however, is social
well-being; schools are social institutions intended to transmit and expand
knowledge and to develop critical thinking. Corporations are not interested in
the search for truth, justice, or democracy—and they are certainly not interested
in developing critical thinking among the population. They usually prefer docile and easily-manipulated consumers and workers. Schools offer a tempting
morsel for business influence: the potential of properly trained employees and
a captive market of buyers of their products. As an additional incentive for commercialization, schools have a continuing need for more finances and corporations have funds to use for corporate purposes.

Corporate strategy in regard to schools is to see students as commodities
and schools as advertising agents. The pattern of this work is to offer induce-
ments to have schools become partners in endeavors that bear direct or subtle
business imprints. These endeavors are not always as obvious as teaching materials and school TV programs that display company logos or school stadiums
named after corporate sponsors (Lewin, 2006; Weissman, 2007). Some sponsored resources involve "free enterprise" educational programs or corporate
speakers on environmental or governmental policies. Others involve efforts to
improve the basic skills and work ethic of students—future employees. Seldom
does corporate sponsorship come with no strings or only with a proviso that
schools stimulate creative or critical thinking.

Companies are necessarily interested in self-preservation and expansion
of marketshare. That perspective necessarily colors the corporate approach
to education; corporation efforts in schools reflect their interest in the pursuit
of commercial enterprise (Apple, 2004; Boninger and Molnar, 2007). Schooling,
however, is too important to leave to corporations.

But, sadly, as David Korten (2001) states:

> In modern societies, television has arguably become our most important insti-
> tution of cultural reproduction. Our schools are probably the second most
> important. Television has already been wholly colonized by corporate inter-
> ests, which are now laying claim to our schools. The goal is not simply to sell

products and strengthen the consumer culture. It is also to create a political culture that equates the corporate interest with the human interest in the public mind. . . . Corporations are now moving aggressively to colonize the second major institution of cultural reproduction, the schools. (pp. 151, 157)

Extensive Evidence of Commercialization

Commercialization of schools is evident in many areas. Commercial Alert (2008), a campaign to stop companies from exploiting "captive audiences of school children for commercial gain," is one of several watch-dog groups that identifies many of the avenues used by corporations to impose on those children:

- Channel One, Bus Radio, CNN Student News
- Naming rights for school buildings and facilities
- Exclusive contracts for vending machines, soft drinks, snacks
- Field trip sponsorship
- "Free" teaching materials
- Advertisements on school buses, school equipment, school materials
- Computer programs that track school student website visits for marketers
- Sponsorship of sports and school events
- Seminars, meals, events for teachers
- Corporate speakers, temporary company-paid teachers, curricular designs
- Contests and incentive programs

    (www.commercialfreechildhood.org; Commercialism in Education Research Unit, www.epicpolicy.org; Deardorff, 2007; www.commercialalert.org)

Channel One is a commercial channel designed to be used in schools as an advertising device. Contracts with Channel One usually stipulate that schools show it to 90 percent of the students on 90 percent of the school days each year, without teacher interruptions. The channel presents about 10 minutes of "news" and 2 minutes of commercials each day. In return, those schools are to receive loaner "free" TV equipment. Such disparate progressive and conservative leaders as Ralph Nader and Phyllis Schlafly agree that Channel One is a wrong way for schools to go. Nader (1999) says that "Channel One corrupts the integrity of public schools and degrades the moral authority of schools and teachers." Schlafly (1999), president of the right-wing Eagle Forum, says "Channel One is a 12 minute a day television marketing device forced on a captive audience of teenagers."

A GAO report also found that some 200 schools had exclusionary contracts with soda bottling companies, contracts that provide funds for schools in return for limiting sales of on-campus soda to one corporation (Hays, 2000). One school in Georgia actually suspended a student who wore a T-shirt with a Pepsi logo on the school's "Coke Day" (Hertz, 2001). Another place for corporate intrusion on schools when school funding is desired, is in selling the right to name schools and school facilities. One high school in West Philadelphia has its name for sale, for $5 million, and naming rights to classrooms can be bought for $25,000 each (Snyder, 2004). "Naming" of school facilities and events for to other individuals" (p. 113). Robert Putnam (2000) studied what he called "social capital" over a twenty-five year period at the end of the twentieth century and found great declines in our participation in social activities:

    having family dinners down 33%

    attending club meetings down 58%

    having friends come over down 45%

Putnam argues that school and local neighborhoods don't succeed when social capital declines and that is a threat to our democracy, our economy, and our health and well-being.

Another consequence of the human capital view is the differentiation between management and worker, where management knows what skills and attitudes are needed and provides them to workers. Thus, education is more like training. Students are perceived as commodities and the school as a processing plant. Schools are supposed to take incoming students, stamp them with previously approved ideas and attitudes, shape them to conform and to pass tests, and give them credentials useful to businesses. In that process, schools are expected to weed out those who don't "fit," who cause trouble, who challenge authority, who make critical evaluations, and who are not business-oriented. Henwood (2003) finds that "employer surveys reveal that bosses care less about their employees' candlepower than they do about 'character'—by which they mean self-discipline, enthusiasm, and responsibility. Bosses want underlings who are steadfast, dependable, consistent, punctual, tactful, and who identify with their work. . . ." (p. 76). Employees who are considered "creative" or "independent" are given low ratings (Henwood, 2003).

School Reform and Business Interests

Reform movements in education in the United States have often victimized the underclasses on the pretext of making them "fit for work and for citizenship." Schools tell students to be obedient, punctual, frugal, neat, respectful, patriotic, and content with their lot in life. The work ethic, drawing from Puritan views, is of great value to industrialists who desire uncomplaining and diligent workers. This ethic has become the school ethic in far too many locations. Employment has become the curriculum of the schools, enabling business to sustain a receptive workforce. An opposing view is that of social responsibility, where human rights, dignity, and democratic citizenship are more important than profit. The carrot of democratic citizenship, however, is mythological, since the economic facts of life are that the elite remain in power while others do the work. Education for democratic participation, in the pursuit of justice and equality, is still in the rhetoric of school literature, but is not acted on in all schools—that would be bad for business. A duality can exist between what is good for business and what is good for society.

This disparity in the schools' purposes—preparing students to participate as workers versus preparing them to participate as equal citizens in striving for justice in society—is overlooked in much of the reform literature. As historian Barbara Finkelstein (1984) notes:

> Nineteenth-century reformers looked to public schools to instill restraint in increasingly large numbers of immigrants and native children, while at the same time preparing them for learning and labor in an industrializing society. . . . They saw no contradiction in the work of schools as economic sorting machines and enabling political institutions. . . . Contemporary calls for reform reflect a retreat from historic visions of public education as an instrument of political democracy, a vehicle of social mobility, a center for the reconstruction of community life. . . . Rather, the educational visions of contemporary reformers evoke historic specters of public schools as crucibles in which to forge uniform Americans and disciplined industrial laborers. (pp. 276–277)

Finkelstein also discusses how corporate leaders expand their influence on public education in order to assure a competent and compliant workforce. She illustrates this with examples from a business-education alliance at George Washington Carver High School in Atlanta, where business conducts the daily activities of the school by providing work-study in semiskilled jobs in local businesses, making moral pronouncements to promote industrial discipline in students, and establishing public rituals, such as "Free Enterprise Day" and "passports to job opportunity." This, and other business intrusions into schools, leads to "an effective transfer of control over education policy from public school authorities to industrial councils. . . . For the first time in the history of school reform, a deeply materialistic consciousness seems to be overwhelming all other concerns" (Finkelstein, 1984, p. 280).

The current period shows the truth of Finkelstein's insight (McNeal, 1992; Molnar, 1996, 2004; Boutwell, 1997; Court, 2003; Berger, 2004; Saltman, 2004; Commercial Alert, 2008). We have become very good at teaching students to be avaricious, greedy, selfish, and conniving. Academic students are especially eager to get good grades in order to get into the right colleges and get high-paying jobs. Many seem uninterested in intellectual development unless it pays off in employment and salaries. They seem uncaring about the homeless, the starving, and others who are disadvantaged, as well as the rest of the world outside of the United States. They are excessively competitive with each other and press for competitive advantage over other groups. Ethical considerations, including the pursuit of justice, do not seem to pose an obstruction to their efforts. Cheating, buying term papers, using parental influence, taking drugs to temporarily enhance performance, paying someone to take a college admission test, and falsifying a résumé may be part of the process.

Is Business a Good Model for Schools?

Consider the defects of permitting business to "catalyze" educational reform. This idea assumes that business knows what needs reform in schools and how to do it. Most of the negative statements corporate leaders make about schools refer to lacks in basic skills and workers' values. Students certainly need basic skills, but who should decide which skills? Must they be employment-related?

And the idea of educating students to develop workers' values imposes a misguided and improper burden on schools. Human values and ethical conduct are proper goals of education, but employer values often contradict human and ethical values. Schools are not the place to insist on "worker" values.

Business executives advocate using national test scores as the main criterion in hiring workers. This is little more than a simplistic and bean-counting method for pressuring schools into using and reporting the tests, demeaning the more important evaluation approaches that better express the complexities of human knowledge. Executives whose lives are determined by "the bottom line" seize on a single test score as the essence of each worker's talents and abilities. Test scores are likely to become even more oppressive, covering up the interesting multifaceted personalities of students and employees. Business could also insist on significantly influencing the construction of the tests themselves. As Carnegie and other notorious industrialists showed us, whoever controls all elements of an industry also controls prices and profits. The same can happen with industry-controlled schooling. Those who control test design and usage can manipulate employment levels, wages and benefits, labor contracts, and profits. They would also come to control the school curriculum through the tests.

Imagine allowing U.S. corporations to design the new models for schools of the twenty-first century. What values would they express? We would not expect to see humane values, protection of the environment, caring and mutual support, skeptical consumerism, health and safety, and positive images of labor unions in that curriculum. Business control could also lead to severe limits to teacher and student freedom. Studying opposing views about society, the environment, science, economics, politics, and history could be very discomforting to corporations. Would you expect to see the full examination of robber barons, Enron and mortgage manipulation scams, environmental and personal health costs of industrial pollution, unjustifiably high salaries for corporate executives, corruption in corporations, and related negative information about business operations be part of the curriculum in these corporate-influenced schools? Reclaim Democracy (2006) proposes to "return corporations to their intended (and useful) role: business. Corporations were never intended to engage in education, politics or many other realms of civic society."

Big business "sweetheart" contracts negotiated with current and former government officers have fattened business profits while increasing taxpayer costs exorbitantly. Halliburton's no-bid contract arrangements for the war in Iraq are a good example. The Pentagon's extravagant contracts for military supplies are other obvious examples, but many other federal, state, and local government contracts also overpay and underexpect for work and supplies. Widely publicized government and corporate corruption scandals and no-bid contracts to favored companies are not the only examples of questionable alliances between big business and government (Court, 2003; Huffington, 2003; Palast, 2002; Korten, 2001; Drutman and Cray, 2004; Center for Corporate Policy, 2006). The mass media, now largely under corporate control, report on some of the worst cases, but certainly not all.

The big business of professional athletics has apparently ignored, condoned, or supported performance-enhancing drug use by athletes. Fraud, misrepresentation, cheating, using or peddling improper influence, falsifying or hiding records, and abusing drugs for business purposes appear to be acceptable ethical standards for many in business. This nefarious curriculum is one many students have chosen.

This pattern of greedy beliefs is drawn from big business. Wall Street companies have engaged in securities fraud, insider scandals, and various scams. Follow the latest examples of corporate greed and deceit at such Internet sources as the Center for Corporate Policy (www.corporatepolicy.org) and www.corpwatch.org. Unethical operations of business are manifold, and we hear about them often enough to suggest that business is not the place to look for educational views on ethics. Investigative reporter Greg Palast (2002), in *The Best Democracy Money Can Buy*, identifies a large number of corporations with deceptive and socially destructive actions that undermine American democracy. Mitchell (2001) uses the title *Corporate Irresponsibility* for his book on how corporations contribute to the greed of "an attitude of grab and get" and to the "suppression of any impulse to care about the welfare of others" (p. 30).

Even if one grants that unethical conduct is not the standard but the exception in business, there remains a serious concern about the business view of social justice and responsibility. Industrial waste pollutes the land, water, and air, but industry does not accept the responsibility to clean it up. Heavy political influence by the corporate world has been effective in slowing and stopping the public regulation to ensure worker health and safety, consumer protection, and improvement in public utilities and services.

The Notorious Contributions of Business to Civilization

As noted, the record of U.S. business in its own domain has not been exemplary. While there are many fine and humane businesspeople, there are also many whose interests are inconsistent with social improvement. There is a stark and dark side of American business—our history is replete with evidence of it. A partial list includes sweatshops, child labor, virtual slavery of migrant workers, unhealthy and unsafe workplaces, pollution, linkages with corrupt politicians, secret coalitions to set falsely high prices, anticonsumer tactics, deceptive advertising, dissolution of pension funds, bankruptcy laws that permit executives to retain major assets while middle-class stockholders lose their life savings, taxpayer subsidies to cover up inept corporate management, and corporate lawyers and corporation-influenced laws that absolve corporations from accountability or responsibility for their wrongdoing. Huffington (2003) writes: "The excesses of corporate America have become more than just a social crime; they are a direct threat to the well-being of our society" (p. 14). Are these the ideas and values we want to emulate in schooling?

Unfortunately, students in U.S. schools have been shortchanged, and American society has been deluded by the imposition of business views on education for the past century (Apple, 1984, 2004; Callahan, 1962; Finkelstein, 1984;

Court, 2003; Landau, 2004; Molnar, 2004). It is deceptive to train the masses to conform to business interests while providing the elite with increased privileges. This is the most insidious educational trick in the new reform movement. Millions of students are relegated to nonthinking, menial work as preparation for poor jobs, and the schools are expected to make them think they are happy and well-educated.

Historian Christopher Lasch (1984) says the system of industrial recruitment is centered on the school. The modern system of public education, remodeled in accordance with the same principles of scientific management first perfected in industry, has replaced apprenticeship as the principal agency of training people for work. The transmission of skills is increasingly incidental to this training. The school habituates children to bureaucratic discipline and to the demands of group living, grades and sorts them by means of standardized tests, and selects some for professional and managerial careers while consigning the rest to manual labor. A willingness to cooperate with the proper authorities offers the best evidence of "adjustment" and the best hope of personal success, while a refusal to cooperate signifies the presence of "emotional problems" requiring more sustained therapeutic attention (pp. 48–49).

American schools have been dominated by the values of business and industry since the beginning of the twentieth century, and schools have lost their primary purpose: enlightenment for the improvement of social justice. Rather than being liberating, schools are now indoctrinating institutions. They provide docile and hardworking employees that business can rely on to gain a profit. Further, these future employees are taught an ideology that supports business regardless of ethical considerations and conditions them to unquestioningly accept the authority of a managerial elite.

Educational and Social Consequences of a Corporate Takeover

The corporate takeover of schooling affects everyone, but the greedy and already advantaged stand to benefit the most. Those who are not going to college, and who are less likely to share the American business dream of success, are subjected to second-class treatment in schools and in careers. The industrial curriculum is designed to give them skills, not the ability to think, intended to make them believers, not thinkers. Industrial education increases the gap between these groups and is meant to produce workers willing to be manipulated.

Business leaders criticize the schools because new employees do not possess basic skills and do not have proper work attitudes. The basic skills business wants do not include critical judgment or the persuasive skills that could be useful in reconstituting the moribund union movement or in challenging management dictates. Rather, the basic skills business wants students to learn are fundamental reading and computation skills that make one more efficient in carrying out management's policies. A job candidate who demonstrates the ability to read radical left-wing literature and to raise questions about worker safety, environmental hazards, and excessive salaries and disparate benefits provided to owners and executives is not likely to be hired. A candidate who can calculate the differences in value between the worker's effort and the pay received, or between labor and management perks in health care and leisure provisions, is not likely to be hired. It is the moral curriculum rather than the academic that is of most interest to business. Managers want workers who believe that what is good for business is good for the nation, and who agree that management knows what is good for business.

Several states now require a high school course in "free enterprise," instead of a solid course in economics. Obviously, a course in free enterprise is not neutral; it is an advocacy course intended to indoctrinate youth to the idea that corporate practices, under the label of free enterprise, are good for the nation. In English class, students fill out job application forms and answer "help wanted" ads. Math is preparing students to work in stores and make change. History classes incorporate myths about the virtues of American business leaders, the appropriate power of corporations, and the threat of governmental interference in business. Business has been a major influence on education for a long time, yet it still complains about the product of an institution and a curriculum dominated by its ethos. Raymond Callahan (1962) conducted a historical study of what most influenced the development of contemporary public education in its formative period in the early twentieth century:

> At the turn of the century, America had reason to be proud of the educational progress it had made. The dream of equality of educational opportunity had been partly realized . . . the basic institutional framework for a noble conception of education had been created. . . . The story of the next quarter-century of American education—a story of opportunity lost and of the acceptance by educational administrators of an inappropriate philosophy—must be seen . . . the most powerful force was industrialism . . . the business ideology was spread continuously into the bloodstream of American life. . . . It was, therefore, quite natural for Americans, when they thought of reforming the schools, to apply business methods to achieve their ends. (pp. 1, 5)

Callahan considered this business influence tragic for education and society because it substituted efficiency for effectiveness: We got cost control at the sacrifice of high-quality schooling for all. The business dominance stuck, and in the first decades of the twenty-first century, schools are still controlled by a corporate value system. This explains the factory mentality of schools. It explains why teachers are so poorly paid and badly treated—they are considered laborers. It explains why students are treated as objects in a manufacturing process on school assembly lines. It explains the conformity and standardization, the excessive testing, and the organization and financing of schools. It also explains the lack of concern for social justice and ethics, issues the schools were making progress on until business gained influence.

Upton Sinclair's devastating criticism of the meatpacking industry for ignoring public health and worker safety (*The Jungle,* 1906, 1938) helped spur federal legislation to found the FDA and regulate food products. Sinclair also published two books about schools that showed the detrimental effects of business influence. *The Goose Step* (1922) detailed how major industrialists determined educational policies and controlled appointments and promotions to professorships in the most important universities in the United States. Leaders of big business dominate the boards that govern most colleges and universities—a point Thorstein Veblen (1918) made long ago. Veblen found that business practices and values detracted from the primary purpose of academic institutions: to liberate students. Sinclair also spent two years studying the public schools, finding heavy-handed control by business leaders over school policies and practices across the United States. In *The Goslings* (1924), he stated, "The purpose of this book is to show you how the 'invisible government' of Big Business which controls the rest of America has taken over the charge of your children" (p. ix).

There is considerable evidence that things may have gotten much worse in the seventy-five years since Sinclair wrote about schools and business. Schools often teach what business wants them to teach, but they should teach what society needs and justice requires them to teach. We need to return to the civilizing purposes of schooling—justice and ethics—and to wrench control of the schools away from those who see the school as just another agency to support the interests of big business. Hartman (2002) points out that increasing dominance of the society by corporations has lead to a decline in human rights. This constitutes a broad social concern, not just a matter of education policy. Schools should exist to reflect, represent, and challenge the society to uphold its ideals and improve its conditions. Schools should not be another pawn in the corporate chess game to control the world. The school should be the place where commercialization and corporatization are critically examined, not merely imposed. The role of business in society and in schools, positive and negative, deserves study and critique.

Schools have enough work to do in trying to educate the young without adding the temptations and dangers of commercialization. Students are not commodities, and schools should not be business agents. Society should have strong doubts about the wisdom of allowing business leaders to influence how students are educated. Corporate altruistic rhetoric about supporting good schools for all children is clouded by their self-interest in profit. Corporations would like the taxpaying public to pay for the kinds of education they want their employees to have, and they would like schools to convey a positive view of business, no matter what its defects. Businesses will serve their own interests if they can gain control of the schools. But schools exist for society's benefit; society is not served by having business interests dominate the schools (Marina, 1994; Buchen, 1999; Korten, 2001). Business seeks profit, not enlightenment.

The business community should mind its own business first. If businesses could demonstrate a clear tradition of quality, ethics, social responsibility, and efficiency in their own operation, then they might be in a position to claim that schools should follow that example. Schools have many problems, but they will not be remedied by thoughtlessly adopting business practices or following the dictates of the corporate world.

Business has a grasping and greedy history, whereas education serves essentially civilizing purposes. Among the schools' most positive goals is to enable students to improve society by increasing justice and expanding social ethics to incorporate a stronger concern for others. This ensures the future of

American democracy and poses a significant challenge to schools to strive continually for social development. And that requires knowledge, critical thinking, cooperative endeavor, and a set of values based on justice.

Critical examination of business values and practices, in terms of social justice and human ethics, are of great import. We need to invert the current situation, in which business controls schools, to one in which education influences business values and practices, encouraging responsibility and enlightenment. This would put education in its proper role, monitoring the improvement of society by examining various social institutions, including business. It would certainly improve education, and it might improve business.

For Discussion

1. Bill Gates delivered the keynote address at the National Summit on High Schools. The conference was sponsored by Achieve Inc., an organization created by state governors and business leaders to improve school standards and achievement so that graduates are prepared for "college, careers, and citizenship" (www.achieve.org). Gates suggested that the American public schools are obsolete, and that America is falling behind in developing "knowledge workers."

   Philip Kovacs (2005), in Commons Dreams (www.commondreams.org), argues that the underlying reason for Gates' view is corporatization. He comments that "raising standards" is tied to corporate interests in obedient workers, that IT outsources for cheaper labor no matter the quality of American schools, and that active citizenship may conflict with corporate interests because citizens may question why corporations have so much influence.

   a. Select one of these positions, or propose a different position on this topic, and present an argument in its support. Provide school examples to illustrate the position you select. Discuss the results in class.

   b. How would you define "knowledge workers"? Does teaching fit? Does librarianship? Does automobile repair? Does orthopedic surgeon?

   What criteria are useful in making this definition? Is this corporatization in schools?

2. Do you recall examples of commercialization at schools you attended? Were they generally positive, supportive of the school's mission, or generally negative, distracting from the school's mission?

   What school policies would you recommend for use in considering proposals from businesses for sponsorship, partnerships, or other activities in schools?

3. What would you change in the current K–12 school curriculum to produce graduates more satisfactory as

   a. employees in U.S. business enterprises?

   b. consumers of goods, services, and advertising?

   c. fellow members of society?

4. Figure 8.1, in this chapter, shows a relationship between educational attainment and average annual income, lifetime earnings, and unemployment.

   a. What other factors, besides education, could account for an increase in income and unemployment?

   b. These are general data. How do they account for some relatively low-paying fields that usually require college and a graduate degree—for example, librarians, teachers, and social workers?

   c. How do such data inform the debate over business involvement in schools?

References

AARON, H., ET AL., eds. (2003). *Agenda for the Nation.* Washington, DC: Brookings Institution Press.

America 2000. (1991). Washington, DC: U.S. Department of Education.

APPLE, M. (1984). *Education and Power.* New York: Routledge and Kegan Paul.

———. (2004). *Ideology and Curriculum.* 3rd Ed. New York: Routledge.

BATES, S. (1998). "Building Better Workers." *Nation's Business* 86:49.

BAUMOL, W., ET AL. (1970). *A New Rational for Corporate Social Policy.* New York: CED.

BECKER, G. S. (1992). "The Economic Way of Looking at Life." Nobel Lecture. In *Nobel Lectures, Economics 1991–95.* (1997). Singapore: World Scientific Publishers.

———. (1993). *Human Capital.* Chicago: University of Chicago Press.

———. (2005). "Human Capital." *The Concise Encyclopedia of Economics.* Library of Economics and Liberty. www.econlib.org.

BERGER, A. A. (2004). *Ads, Fads, and Consumer Culture.* 2nd Ed. Lanham, MD: Rowman and Littlefield.

BONINGER, F. AND MOLNAR, A. (2007). *Adrift.* 10th Annual Report on Schoolhouse Commercialism Trends. www.epicpolicy.org

BOUTWELL, C. E. (1997). *Shell Game: Corporate America's Agenda for Schools.* Bloomington, IN: Phi Delta Kappa.

BUCHEN, I. (1999). "Business Sees Profit in Education." *The Futurist* 33(5):38–44.

BUSINESS ROUNDTABLE. (1997). "A Common Agenda for Improving American Education." Washington, DC. July 2.

BUSINESS ROUNDTABLE. (2005). "K–12 Education Reform, Education and the Workforce Task Force." April 11. www.businessroundtable.org.

———. (2008). Prospering Together. www.businessroundtable.org Feb.

CALLAHAN, R. (1962). *Education and the Cult of Efficiency.* Chicago: University of Chicago Press.

CENTER FOR CORPORATE POLICY. (2006). "Cracking Down on Corporate Crime." April. www.citizenworks.org.

CHASE, R. (1998). "Changing the Way the Schools Do Business." *Vital Speeches of the Day* 64:444–446.

COMMERCIAL ALERT, (2008). Homepage. www.commercialalert.org

COMMITTEE FOR ECONOMIC DEVELOPMENT (1985). *Investing in Our Children.* New York: CED.

COURT, J. (2003). *Corporateering.* New York: Putnam.

CULLEN, L. T. (2004). "Brand Name Field Trips." *Time.* June 28.

DANIELS FUND, (2008). *School Business Partnerships.* www.danielsfund.org

DAWKINS, J. (2003). "The State of Partnerships Between Schools and Businesses." Paper presented at Partners in Citizenship conference, February.

DEARDORFF, J. (2007). "Fast Food Gets Its Greasy Hands on Report Cards." *Chicago Tribune.* Dec 16.

DELONG, J. B., ET AL. (2003). "Sustaining U.S. Economic Growth," in *Agenda for the Nation,* ed. Aaron, H., et al. Washington, DC: Brookings Institution.

DRUTMAN, L., AND CRAY, C. (2004). *The People's Business: Controlling Corporations and Restoring Democracy.* Williston, VT: Berrett-Hoehler.

Education Week. (2004). "American Corporations Invest About $3 Billion Annually to Upgrade Writing Skills of Employees." 24(5):11.

FEGE, A. (2008). "Commercialization of Schools." www.commercialfreechildhood.org June.

FEULNER, E. J. (1991). "What Business Leaders Can Teach the Educators." *Chief Executive,* September: 16–17,

FINKELSTEIN, B. (1984). "Education and the Retreat from Democracy in the United States, 1979–1980." *Teachers College Record* 86:276–282.

FITZ-ENZ. J. (2000). *The ROI of Human Capital.* New York: American Management Association.

FLOWERS, L. F. (2008). "Naming Rights May Provide Districts with Funding," *Morning News,* Northwest AR. Jan 26.

HANN, L. W. (2008). "Profit and Loss in School Business Partnerships." *District Administration.* www.districtadministration.com April.

HARTMAN, T. (2002). *Unequal Protection: The Rise of Corporate Dominance and the Theft of Human Rights.* New York: Rodale Press.

HARTY, S. (1980). *Hucksters in the Classroom.* Washington, DC: Center for Responsive Legislation.

———. (1989). "U.S. Corporations: Still Pitching After All These Years." *Educational Leadership* 47:77–79.

HAYS, C., "Commercialism in U.S. Schools Is Examined in New Report," *New York Times,* Sept 14, 2000.

HENWOOD, D. (2003). *After the New Economy.* New York: New Press.

HERTZ, N. (2001). *The Silent Takeover: Global Capitalism and the Death of Democracy.* New York: Free Press.

HUFFINGTON, A. (2003). *Pigs at the Trough.* New York: Crown.

ISAAK, R. (2005). *The Globalization Gap.* New York: Prentice-Hall.

KEELEY, B. (2007). *Human Capital.* Paris: OECD Publications.

KORTEN, D. C. (2001). *When Corporations Rule the World.* San Francisco: Berrett-Koehler Publishers.

KOVACS, P. (2005). "Bill Gates and the Corporatization of American 'Public' Schools," *Common Dreams.* www.commondreams.org.

LANDAU, S. (2004). *The Business of America.* New York: Routledge.

LASCH, C. (1984). *The Minimal Self.* New York: Norton.

LEWIN, T., "In Public Schools, the Name Game as a Donor Lure," *New York Times,* January 26, 2006.

MANDEL, M., ET AL. (1995). "Will Schools Ever Get Better?" *Business Week,* Apr. 17:64–68.

MANN, D. (1987). "Business Involvement and Public School Improvement, Part 2." *Kappan* 69:228–232.

MARINA, A. (1994). "Can the Private Sector Save Public Schools?" *NEA Today* 12:10–12.

MCNEAL, R. U. (1992). *Kids as Customers.* New York: Lexington Books.

MINCER, J. (1974). *Schooling, Experience, and Earnings.* New York: Columbia University Press.

MITCHELL, L. E. (2001). *Corporate Irresponsibility.* New Haven, CT: Yale University Press.

MOLNAR, A. (1996). *Giving Kids the Business.* New York: Harper/Collins.

———. (2004). "Virtually Everywhere: Marketing to Children in America's Schools. Seventh Annual Report on Schoolhouse Commercializing Trends, 2003." Arizona State University Commercialism in Education Research Unit. www.asu.edu/educ/eps/ceru/htm.

NADER, R. (1999). Testimony, U.S. Senate Committee on Health, Education, Labor, and Pensions Hearing. May 20.

NATIONAL COUNCIL ON ECONOMIC EDUCATION. (2005). "What American Teens and Adults Know About Economics." NCEE-Harris Poll. April 26. www.ncee.cet.

———. (2008). "Voluntary National Content Standards in Economics." www.ncee. org.

ORAVITZ, J. V. (1999). "Why Can't Schools Be Operated the Way Businesses Are?" *Education Digest* 64(6):15–17.

PALAST, G. (2002). *The Best Democracy Money Can Buy*. London: Pluto Press.

PARMET, S., "Reading, Writing and Retail Tours," *San Diego Union-Tribune*, May 2, 2005.

PUTNAM, R. D. (2000). *Bowling Alone*. New York: Simon and Schuster.

RAMSEY, N. (1993). "What Companies Are Doing." *Fortune* 128:142–150.

RECLAIM DEMOCRACY. (2006). Mission Statement. April. www.reclaimdemocracy.org.

SALTMAN, K. J. (2004). "Coca-Cola's Global Lesson." *Teacher Education Quarterly* 31(1): 155–172.

SCHLAFLY, P. (1999). Testimony, U.S. Senate Committee on Health, Education, Labor and Pensions Hearing. May 20.

SCHULTZ, T. W. (1971). *Investment in Human Capital: The Role of Education and of Research*. New York: Free Press.

SHILLER, R. J., "How Wall Street Learns to Look the Other Way," *New York Times*, February 8, 2005. www.nytimes.com.

SINCLAIR, U. (1906, 1938). *The Jungle*. London: Cobham House.

———. (1922). *The Goose Step*. Pasadena, CA: Sinclair.

———. (1924). *The Goslings*. Pasadena, CA: Sinclair.

SNYDER, S., "West Philadelphia High School's Name Is Up for Sale," *Philadelphia Inquirer*, Nov. 11, 2004.

SOLTOW, L., AND STEVENS, E. (1981). *The Rise of Literacy and the Common School in the United States: A Socioeconomic Analysis to 1870*. Chicago: University of Chicago Press.

U.S. CENSUS BUREAU. (2000, 2007). "Employment, Work Experience, and Earnings by Age and Education." Table 1. Washington, DC: Government Printing Office.

———. (2005). *Current Population Survey, 2005 Annual Social and Economic Supplement*. June 24.

VEBLEN, T. (1918). *The Higher Learning in America*. New York: Heubsch.

WEISSMAN, R. (2007). "Revisiting the Commercialization of Public Schools." *Counter Punch*. www.counterpunch.org. June.

THE WORLD BANK GROUP. (2006). "Education for All: Fast Track Initiative." February. www.worldbank.org.

CHAPTER 9

New Immigrants and the Schools: Unfair Burden or Business as Usual

Should schools offer free opportunity to all children of new immigrants?

POSITION 1: SCHOOLS SHOULD OFFER EDUCATIONAL OPPORTUNITIES TO ALL CHILDREN OF NEW IMMIGRANTS.

Many of the first Settlers of these Provinces, were Men who had received a good Education in Europe, and to their Wisdom and good Management we owe much to our present Prosperity . . . The present Race are not thought to be generally of equal Ability: For though the American Youth are allow'd not to want Capacity; yet the best Capacities require Cultivation, it being truly with them, as with the best Ground, which unless well tilled and sowed with profitable Seed, produces only ranker Weeds.

—Franklin, 1749

In an anonymously written pamphlet, Benjamin Franklin identified deficiencies in the education of the young men of Pennsylvania and proposed remedies for their academic "misfortunes." Franklin recommended a practical education, gained though work and apprenticeships, and an abstract education, learned through reading, writing, and debate. For young men to prosper in their social and political worlds, Franklin urged the cultivation of a sound and thorough command of the English language. English was not the only language spoken in the colony. By Franklin's own estimate, one-third of Pennsylvanians traced their homeland to the German states and spoke German as a first language. Franklin worried about the colony's future without a common language, and he proposed that English serve as the only language of instruction. He advised that the academy hire a teacher, or rector, who was "a man of good Understanding, good Morals, diligent and patient, learn'd in the Languages and Sciences, and a correct Speaker and Writer of the *English* Tongue" (Franklin,

1749). The University of Pennsylvania would eventually become the institution to carry out Franklin's education plan, although it did not adopt all of his ideas about teaching or curriculum (Spring, 2001, p. 25).

In Franklin's time, language diversity varied from colony to colony, and the first census in 1790, coincidentally the year of Franklin's death, provides an interesting picture of national diverse origin. Roughly half the population of the United States was of English decent. Another 15 percent were English speakers from Scotland and Ireland. People of Dutch, French, and Spanish origin made up about 14 percent of the population; and 19 percent were of African heritage (Wiley, 2007). A great many people, including many enslaved Africans and Native Americans, uncounted in the first census, did not speak English as their first language. By 1890, immigrants represented 14.8 percent of the total U.S. population and very few of the new arrivals of that time were from English-speaking counties.

Record-high immigration rates are projected for the year 2050, when one in five people in the United States is expected to be foreign born (Passel and Cohn, 2008). In the late nineteenth and early-twentieth centuries, immigrants tended to settle in urban areas, but twenty-first century immigrants are settling in cities, suburbs, and small towns. Schools everywhere are being directly affected by immigration, and teaching students whose primary language is not English is becoming commonplace. (See Figure 9.1: "US Immigration, 1960–2050.")

FIGURE 9.1 U.S. Immigration, 1960–2050 (in millions)

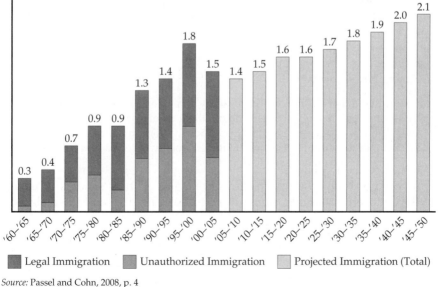

Source: Passel and Cohn, 2008, p. 4

The children of immigrants[1] are transforming American schools by their unprecedented numbers and sheer diversity. Forty percent of newcomer children are from Mexico, the largest sender nation. The remaining 60 percent come from all over the world, with the greatest number arriving from the Caribbean, East Asia, Europe, Canada, and Australia (10 to 11 percent each), and significant populations from Central and South America, Cambodia, Laos, Thailand, and Vietnam (5 to 7 percent each) (Hernandez et al., 2007, p. 2). Immigrant diversity extends beyond numbers and national origins to include the newcomers' level of education and social experience in their home counties. As one team of researchers notes, "On one end of the spectrum, we find children from middle-class urban backgrounds who have been preparing in their countries since early childhood for high-stakes, competitive exams . . . In sharp contrast are those children from strife-ridden countries with little or no schooling" (Suarez-Orozco and Suarez-Orozco, 2001, p. 128).

Language Rights

> Prof. Adolphe Cohen of Columbia University, in discussing the teaching of French and German in public schools, said the attitude of a good many people on that subject was explained to him very aptly by a remark he had once overheard in a streetcar. Two elderly Irish women were talking about their children, when one remarked: "I won't let my children be taught French."
> "Why not?" inquired the other.
> "Sure," replied the first. "If English was good enough for St. Paul to write the Bible in, it's good enough for me." ("Man in the Street," 1905)

American free public education developed in the period between 1830 and 1850, known as the era of the Common School. Schooling at public expense was viewed as broadly beneficial, contributing academic, social, and political value to daily life. Faced with a new and large number of newcomers from Ireland and Germany, advocates of the Common Schools urged the government to provide public-supported education to develop in the new immigrants the language, habits, and values of the old immigrants (Kaestle, 1983). The schools were seen as the most appropriate agency for advancing a common culture. As Joel Spring notes, in advocating for Common Schools,

> It was argued that if children from a variety of religious, social-class, and ethnic backgrounds were educated in common, there would be a decline in hostility and friction among social groups. In addition, if children educated in common were taught a common social and political ideology, a decrease in conflict and social problems would result (2001, p. 104).

It was no doubt challenging for nineteenth-century schools to encourage the children of German immigrants to learn English and the children of

---

[1] "Children of immigrants" refers to U.S.-born and foreign-born children of recent immigrants who are or will be attending U.S. schools. It includes "first-generation" foreign-born immigrants, U.S.-born "second-generation" immigrants (Suarez-Orozco and Suarez-Orozco, 2001, p. 1), and the so-called 1.5 generation, children arriving in the U.S. who are not yet of school age (Suarez-Orozco, Suarez-Orozco, and Todorova, 2008, p. 6).

Irish-Catholic immigrants to adopt Protestant values, but today's schools contend with students from everywhere in the world and of every religious belief. Forging a common social and political ideology would be impossible, even if it were desirable. Consider language alone: According to one estimate, within the next two years, over 30 percent of children in public schools will come from homes with limited English proficiency or where English is not the first language. Today, in New York City, more than 100 languages are spoken, and in Rochester, Minnesota, a city of about 86,000 people, there are sixty spoken languages (Bank Street, 2008). Although 82 percent of English Language Learners (ELLs) in schools come from Spanish-speaking homes, surveys have identified over 350 different first languages spoken among ELLs (NCTE, 2006, p. 1).

The education of immigrant children has always been a function of public schools, and it is not a responsibility today's schools could shirk, even if they wanted to. U.S. courts have ruled that the children of immigrants—documented or undocumented—have a right to a free, public education. Take the case of *Plyler v. Doe* (1982), a Supreme Court decision about the constitutionality of a Texas education statute: Texas law allowed local school districts to charge a "tuition fee" for the education of children who were not "legally admitted" into the United States. A class action lawsuit was brought on behalf of the children of Tyler, Texas, who could not demonstrate that they or their families had been legally admitted to the United States and were required to pay tuition to attend public school. A lower federal court had ruled that the Texas law violated the "Equal Protection Clause" of the Fourteenth Amendment of the U.S. Constitution, which reads, ". . . Nor shall any State deprive any person of life, liberty, or property, without due process of law; nor deny *to any person within its jurisdiction* the equal protection of the laws" (italics added). The State of Texas appealed the decision to the U.S. Supreme Court.

Justice William Brennan, delivering the majority opinion of the Supreme Court, wrote, "Aliens, even aliens whose presence in this country is unlawful, have long been recognized as 'persons' guaranteed due process of law by the Fifth and Fourteenth Amendments . . . The American people have always regarded education and [the] acquisition of knowledge as matters of extreme importance . . . [E]ducation provides the basic tools by which individuals might lead economically productive lives to the benefit of all of us. In sum, education has a fundamental role in maintaining the fabric of our society . . . Denial of education to some isolated group of children poses an affront to one of the goals of the Equal Protection Clause: the abolition of governmental barriers presenting unreasonable obstacles to advancement based on individual merit . . . This law imposes a lifetime of hardship on a discrete class of children not accountable for their disabling status" (*Plyler v. Doe*, 1982).

Plyler is still the law of the land, despite attempts by various states and Congress to reverse its effects. The lofty, well-reasoned arguments of the Court notwithstanding, undocumented students are still a vulnerable school population because of their precarious status outside of the school and their struggles with English in the classroom (Rabin, Combs, and Gonzalez, 2008).[2]

Language Matters

The U.S. Congress has been responsive to the role schools play in teaching increasing numbers of English language learners in the classroom. In 1967, Senator Ralph Yarborough of Texas introduced legislation to help school districts create programs for students who did not speak English as a first language at home. Senator Yarborough's bill, aimed at Spanish-speaking students, was designed to teach English as a second language while strengthening the students' heritage language skills and knowledge of their cultural past. Students would be assisted in the development of English, the language essential for their economic security and social integration, and this new learning would not come at the expense of losing their cultural history and original language. The legislation was merged with over thirty other bills and became known as Title VII of the Elementary and Secondary Education Act or the Bilingual Education Act of 1968. Although the legislation did not explicitly require bilingual instruction or teaching in the students' heritage language, it supported innovative multicultural curricula and multilingual instruction (Stewner-Manzanares, 1988).

Adjusting to American schooling is no easy matter for many children of immigrants. Multiple social forces influence the academic success of the children of newcomers, including the difficulties associated with the stress of migration, the separations from long-standing cultural traditions, and for many immigrants, the complex interplay of poverty, racism, social segregation, and identify formation with new cultural rules (Suarez-Orozco and Todorova, 2003). The education of ELLs has been the center of controversy, and it is not surprising that misconceptions have developed about the programs. You may have heard some or all of the following comments about bilingual education:

- Learning two languages, especially during the early childhood years, confuses children and delays the acquisition of English.
- Total English immersion is the most effective way for ELLs to acquire English.
- Native speakers of English suffer academically if they are enrolled in dual language programs.
- Spanish-speaking Latinos show social and academic delays as early as kindergarten (Espinosa, 2008).

---

[2]U.S. Courts have been very sympathetic to the language rights of students who do not speak English as a first language. In 1974, for example, the Supreme Court ruled that the City of San Francisco violated the Civil Rights Act of 1964, which bans discrimination based on "race, color, or national origin," when it had failed to offer appropriate bilingual education to children of Chinese ancestry (*Lau v. Nichols*, 1974). Another case, decided in 1981, found that in order to comply with the Lau decision, schools must serve English-language learners through programs that follow "sound educational theory" and established principles of good teaching (*Castaneda v. Pickard*, 1981).

These are all examples of popular myths that do not stand up to academic scrutiny. As Crawford (2007) writes, "A generation of research and practice has shown that developing academic skills and knowledge in students' vernacular supports their acquisition of English" (p. 146). In fact, bilingualism is an asset to all children in a multicultural society, and research reviewed by Espinosa and others demonstrates that young children are capable of learning two languages (Espinosa, 2008, NCTE, 2007). Researchers have also found that instruction in both English and the heritage language can effectively introduce newcomer children to the success patterns of the dominant culture without denigrating or destroying the home culture, while the loss of home languages has negative consequences for student learning (Adams and Kirova, 2007; Crawford, 2007; Faltis and Coulter, 2008).

Despite these research findings, the federal No Child Left Behind legislation, aimed at promoting accountability, equity, and school reform, neither prohibits nor encourages the development of native language skills and dual-language acquisition; bilingualism and biliteracy are not among its goals (NABE, 2007).

ELLs and NCLB

"What do you call a person who speaks two languages?"
"Bilingual."
"Okay, and what do you call a person who knows only one?"
"American."

The No Child Left Behind Act of 2001 was designed to hold all learners to high academic standards and ensure that specific subsets of the student population were not ignored or allowed to fall between the cracks of public education. NCLB focuses attention on all categories of student learners, including the historically neglected population of language-minority learners. This is all to the good. Students are generally considered to be advantaged when schools are held accountable for the achievement gains of all learners. Few argue with the spirit of NCLB, but problems abound in this legislation, particularly with the ways in which ELLs are to be assessed (Kieffer et al., 2008; NABE, 2007; Solorzano, 2008).

In 2007, the Executive Director of TESOL (Teachers of English to Speakers of Other Languages), wrote a letter to the Chairman and the Ranking Member of the Education and Labor Committee of the House of Representatives expressing his organization's concern about the validity and reliability of NCLB testing—the accuracy of state tests and the consistency of the test measurements. The letter notes that, while NCLB allows a student with limited English language proficiency to take assessment exams in the student's native language, "it is important to understand that in order for an assessment to be valid and reliable, the language of the assessment must match the language of instruction. Thus, while a native language assessment will be helpful in many cases, it may not be the most valid assessment for the majority of English language learners who receive instruction in English . . . The use of a single assessment for accountability purposes is not a valid, reliable, or fair method to determine academic progress, especially for English language learners" (Amorosino, 2007, pp. 1–2).

TESOL's objections to NCLB's reliance on single high-stakes exams resonates with the arguments of other anti-testing educators (see Chapter 5: Standards-Based Reform: Real Reform or Political Smoke Screen?), but the well-intentioned goals of NCLB may have especially negative consequences for English language learners. As noted, ELLs are not likely to do well on subject-matter tests in a language that is not the language in which they were introduced to the academic discourse of the subject, that is, the language of instruction. To make matters worse, it is hard, if not impossible to determine whether poor student performance is attributable to the student's difficulties with the content or with the language of the exams. In a real sense, every test of content is also a test of language skills (Kieffer et al., 2008).

English language learners, similar to other subgroups labeled under NCLB, must score in the "proficient" range on state exams by 2014, or the schools they attend will face sanctions. NABE (National Association for Bilingual Education) argues that NCLB will ultimately harm schools and ELL programs: "Virtually all schools with significant ELL enrollments will soon be in the 'failing' category. It is hard to see how such an indiscriminate 'accountability' system . . . has anything to do with improving schools" (NABE, 2007). NCLB threatens the schools attended by ELLs. Referred to by some researchers as its "diversity penalty," the NCLB legislation "requires the largest gains from lower-performing schools, although these schools serve needier students and generally have fewer resources than schools serving wealthier students" (Darling-Hammond, 2008, p. 164).

NABE has joined with more than thirty education and civil rights organizations calling for the overhaul and reorganization of NCLB. Among other elements, NABE recommends that NCLB legislation allow States and school districts to:

- Develop alternative assessments, in both English and the student's native language, to measure more accurately the student's content knowledge;
- Promote the student's native language;
- Guarantee that all ELLs, independent of English language proficiency, have access to the full range of school services and educational programs (NABE, 2007).

Cultural Challenges: Teaching More Than Language Skills

> Great achievements were the product of [the immigrants'] labors; without their contributions the country could not have taken the form it did. But they paid a heavy price, not only in the painful process of crossing and resettlement but also in the continuous ache of uprootedness . . . And to the extent that the process succeeded, a widening gulf developed between the immigrants and their children (Handlin, 1966, pp. xiii, xiv).

Immigration has always been a difficult and stressful experience for newcomer families. Immigrants leave behind friends and familiar ways, and older family members often forfeit esteemed community roles and assume lower social status and lesser-valued employment in the United States. Children of immigrants may struggle in schools as they wrestle with the different culture and unfamiliar language of their new home (Gaytan et al., 2007). Americans have always celebrated the success stories of this nation of immigrants. Today, as in the past, many immigrants do very well in school and life, but many more are at risk of failure. As Suarez-Orozco and Gardner write, "Our research indicates that while some [children of immigrants] will end up as the beneficiaries of life in the new land, too many others are unable to cope with the global dislocations. As we have come to put it, the life options become Yale or Jail, Princeton or Prison" (2003, p. 3).

Schools can help expand the range of successful options. Schooling is central to the processes by which the children of immigrants are taught to survive and prosper and forge a better life in their new country (Suarez-Orozco, Suarez-Orozco, and Todorova, 2008). In schools, the children of immigrants learn the skills necessary for academic success. Newcomers also experience schools as cultural sites where they are introduced to the social "rules" of American society, and they meet teachers, typically members of the dominant culture, who help them understand their new country and find their way in it. Because of their experience with formal schooling and, typically, their greater language facility, children of immigrants are often asked to play the role of "culture brokers" for their parents and families. These young people, with a foot in each of two worlds, are often called upon to mediate the conflicting expectations and experiences of host and heritage cultures while trying to honor both (Adams and Kirova, 2007). Informed teachers, sensitive to immigration issues, can help students navigate between the two worlds.

Success in schools has always been important to the children of newcomers, but it may be more important today than any time in our history. Given the nature of the American economy, doing well in school is central to economic survival and social integration. In the earlier days of high migration to the United States, schooling certainly figured prominently in individual success, but today, when the U.S. economy has few meaningful jobs for those who do not complete high school, school success matters more than ever (Suarez-Orozco, Suarez-Orozco, and Todorova, 2008). The children of immigrants are literally America's future. Today's newcomers will inherit tomorrow's political and economic systems, and the future of American democracy and its economic well-being rest in their hands. Schools can help the children of immigrants achieve academically without uprooting them from the traditions of their families. Schools and teachers can help the children of new immigrants preserve their heritage language and culture and maintain their own historical identity while mastering English and the values and skills necessary for economic and social advancement in the United States (Adams and Kirova, 2007; Suarez-Orozco and Qin-Hilliard, 2004; Suarez-Orozco, Suarez-Orozco, and Todorova, 2008). Schools are in a unique position to help the children of new immigrants and their families successfully adjust to life in the United States. American schools have been able to help previous generations of immigrants, and they can serve new immigrants. Helping all the children of immigrants is business-as-usual for American schools. It is what schools have done well in the past and what they should do today.

POSITION 2: BAD POLICY OVERBURDENS SCHOOLS

The average immigrant comes to this country much poorer and far less edu-cated than Americans and consumes far more per capita in public services. Economically, immigrants are a net burden on the nation. . . . We are on a treadmill we will never get off if we do not get control of immigration.

—Buchanan, 2006, pp. 43, 46.

This cultural struggle over the future of America—and the very definition of America—underlies the immigration fight. The gap between the leftist elites and the rest of America could hardly be broader.

—Gingrich, 2008, p. 129.

Education Problems from Immigration, Legal and Illegal

The relation of new immigrants to schools is complex. Historic, political, legal, and cultural issues surround the question of how immigration influences edu-cation. Current massive problems in legal and illegal immigration demonstrate our nation's lack of intelligent control, identification, and law enforcement, as well as a lack of adequate funding for the additional social services required. Schools bear much of the brunt of this predicament. Educational problems that stem from weak and ineffective immigration policies and practices should be examined within that larger context (Brimelow, 2008).

American immigration policies and practices continue as divisive and con-troversial social issues. A history of mostly dysfunctional approaches to immi-gration purposes, control, balance, and enforcement haunts us. Schools share in the results. Since before our nation's founding, we have argued about immigra-tion, and the relation of education to that process. Benjamin Franklin, in 1753, noted that bad immigration policies may create "great disorders" among us. He concluded that if the new German immigrants were distributed equally and mixed well with the English, *with English schools established in immigrant neigh-borhoods,* then there could be some benefit (Abbott, 1969, cited in Borjas, 1999, emphasis added).

Inconsistent policies and disparate practices create special problems and expenses for schools with immigrant populations. Legal immigration is now at record levels in the United States, and illegal immigration produces large, but uncharted, numbers. The Census Bureau calculates net immigration between 2000 and 2007 at almost 8 million, not accounting for illegal immigrants. In 2007, the official number receiving legal permanent residency (green card) was over 1 million; Migration Policy Institute (2006) estimates the actual number of legal immigrants to be over 1.8 million annually. Illegal immigration, for obvious reasons, is much more difficult to determine. One source, using U.S. Census data, estimates the total number of illegal aliens at over 21 million (www.immigrationcounters.com, 2008). Other organizations estimate illegals at between 12 and 14 million. Uncontrolled future immigration will cause

82 percent of the projected increase in U.S. population between 2005 and 2050, from about 300 million to 438 million. (Pew Research Center, 2008).

Large scale legal and illegal immigration presents severe problems for society and schools. The sheer numbers of immigrants, necessary screening and record-keeping, expensive special provisions to meet their divergent needs, and potential policing-enforcement-social welfare requirements to maintain American qualities all impose costs on social services. Buchanan (2006) put the added social costs for schooling, health care, welfare, social security, and prisons at about $400 billion per year, far more than the taxes immigrants pay, plus the costs of extra "pressure on land, water, and power resources" (p. 35).

Illegal immigration causes higher net costs for schools and other social services than legal immigration. Two-thirds of illegal aliens have not graduated from high school, thus earning less income and contributing less in taxes—while requiring more from U.S. public education and social services. These findings are consistent with a National Research Council study (Smith and Edmonston, 1997) showing that immigrant educational level is the "key determinant of their fiscal impact." ("The High Cost of Cheap Labor," Center for Immigration Studies, 2008, p. 1).

Questions surround American immigration policies in regard to education. Do current American immigration policies and practices help or hinder schools? Should schools be responsible, and accountable, for the education of all immigrants, legal and illegal? Should this all be taxpayer financed? Should that include taxpayer-subsidized higher education? Should the proportion of immigrant students be grounds for differential rating in terms of national test score standards and graduation rates? Should we encourage immigration by people who have certain specialized education that America desires, or should we place no educational barriers on those who want to enter our nation? Should we be concerned about disparities between the levels of schooling of some immigrant groups and others, and as compared with levels of regular citizens? Should we require demonstrated fluency in English, knowledge of American history and government, and allegiance to America before immigrants are granted permanent status? These are not easy questions to answer, and they are politically thorny.

School Responsibilities, Immigrant Needs, and Who Pays

In 1982, the Supreme Court split five to four in a decision that the equal protection clause of the Constitution required public schools to admit illegal alien children (*Plyler v. Doe*, 1982). The specific conditions that led to that decision could change. The court determined then that admission of illegals would not damage the educational opportunities of citizens' children, and that there was no solid evidence that the United States actually intended to deport the illegal parents. If those conditions change, or Congress legislates a school exclusion for these illegal students, there could be a different outcome (FAIR, "Immigration and School Overcrowding," 2002). For now, that is the law.

Schools are expected to provide basic knowledge, skills, and corrective educational assistance to immigrant children, as well as to help Americanize and integrate them into society. Schools also offer their parents and other immigrant

	%			LEP	No High School
State	Population	Source	%	%*	Diploma
California	27%	Latin America	53%	59%	37%
New York	21	Latin America	53	46	26
Texas	16	Latin America	74	62	47
Florida	19	Latin America	73	49	25
Illinois	14	Latin America	48	56	31
New Jersey	20	Latin America	46	46	22
Washington	12	Asia	31	49	28
U.S. Average	**21%**			**52%**	**32%**

Table 9.1 Selected Characteristics of Immigrants by State, 2006

*LEP – Limited English Proficiency
Source: Migration Policy Institute (2008). "2006 American Community Survey and Census Data on the Foreign Born by State," "States With the Largest and Fastest Growing Foreign Born Populations." www.migrationinformation.org

adults avenues to self-improvement and preparation for citizenship. Immigrants from a variety of nations show wide differences in their educational attainment, skills, attitudes toward American traditions and values, English language fluency, and requirements for public assistance.

The gap between regular citizen-student academic achievement and that of immigrants is growing. Organization for Economic Co-operation and Development (OECD) data show that U.S. immigration caused high school graduation rates in the United States to drop from being the best in the world to being lower than that of sixteen other nations (Federation for American Immigration Reform, 2002). For a school district, these incoming immigrant educational differences create multiple problems with corollary extra costs. For example, the New York City schools recently identified about 175 different languages among its students. The extra costs and difficulties finding and keeping well-prepared teaching and school staffs to provide appropriate school and other services for this diversity are immense. Table 9.1 shows some characteristics of immigrants by selected states in 2006.

For most states, the current source of the majority of immigrants is Latin America. The percentage of immigrants who have Limited English Proficiency (LEP) is very high in many of these states; the national average LEP is 52 percent, an increase of 25 percent between 2000 and 2006. The proportion of immigrants who have not completed high school is also high and climbing in these states. The national average is 32 percent, a 50 percent increase in the past ten years. For illegals, the numbers without high school diplomas and with more limited English proficiency are much higher, with higher associated educational costs.

The Federation for American Immigration Reform (FAIR) Report shows annual national extra educational cost to taxpayers for illegal immigrant students is more than $7.4 billion (Collins, 2008; FAIR Report, 2008). Schooling costs from illegal immigration are usually without compensatory funds. Former

California Governor Pete Wilson tried to get federal funds to pay, but the case was not adjudicated. Among individual states, California spends about $2.2 billion extra per year. Texas spends over $1 billion annually, Florida spends about $308 million, Georgia about $231 million, and Illinois about $484 million each year (Collins, 2008; FAIR Report, 2008).

More Than Direct Cost

Poorly controlled immigration gives more than just money problems to schools. Immigrants from highly diverse cultural, tribal, religious, and economic backgrounds, when mixed in the schools, create conditions for significant misunderstandings and potentially explosive environments. Differences stimulate the development of school-disruptive behaviors like gangs, bullying, ethnic slurs, extortion, violence, and threats. They also contribute to student segregation by immigrant group, intimidation, and necessarily restrictive school rules with enforcement officers. This is not consistent with the idea of school as a safe place to gain knowledge and develop positive attitudes toward the nation.

The special teaching, curricular, and staff needs created by an influx of immigrants distract schools from their primary purposes for local citizens, requiring additional care and effort. Immigrants are more likely to need other social services, like school nurses and social workers, draining funds from regular school activities.

How did we reach this position where legal and illegal immigration cause such problems for our schools?

Immigration Policies: A Study in Turmoil

Immigration is America's great tradition and glory; it is also its great peril. We are a nation founded by immigrants, and we remain prideful of immigrant contributions to culture, industry, technology, and life. Immigrants are us, or better, are U.S. This extraordinary tradition is honored as we eat Italian or Thai or Mexican meals, use computers and TVs invented and enhanced by Irish-Americans and Japanese-Americans, buy furniture and clothing designed by French-Americans and Swedish-Americans, and use an imported English language enlarged by contributions from many other languages.

Immigration, if it can be intelligently controlled, balanced, and enforced, helps the United States. But despite periodic public alarm, we have failed to control immigration. Our immigration policies veered from open door to restrictions by nationality and personal history, then to allowing increasing numbers and amnesty for some. Presumably restrictive laws have not been followed up with serious enforcement and actual control.

The current large-scale immigration wave is the fourth in our history (Leonhardt, 2008). Political reaction to each of the previous great waves—in the 1850s, 1880s, and 1900s—was intense and restrictions ensued. Anti-immigration movements developed as each wave became more threatening to Americans. Laws were passed to limit immigration with modest results in attempts to bring more

Table 9.2 Average Annual Immigration per 1,000 Citizens							
1.3	12.1	10.5	11.0	4.0	.6	4.8	5.1
1820–30	1850–60	1880–90	1900–1910	1920–30	1940–50	1980–90	2000–2010

Source: Pew Research Center, *New York Times*, March 2, 2008.

orderliness to the process. Table 9.2 shows the main waves of immigration, per 1,000 American citizens, by decade since the early 1820s.

The United States was concerned about risks in naturalizing immigrants from unfriendly nations too quickly in the 1790s, but until the 1870s we encouraged immigration as helpful to build the society. Then, in 1875, we barred immigration by convicts and prostitutes, adding paupers and "mentally defectives" to the immigrant ban in 1882, when we also halted Chinese immigration for ten years, extending that ban until 1943. Congress passed laws for two decades to require a literacy test of immigrants, but these laws were vetoed by three presidents before Woodrow Wilson's second veto was overridden in 1917 and all adult immigrants had to be able to read in some language. Immigration laws in the 1920s limited annual streams to 150,000, plus immediate families, and imposed a quota system favoring immigrants from northern and western Europe.

These quotas were eliminated in 1965, and later modifications increased the total annual immigrant limits. Immigration reform laws in 1986 tried to restrict illegal immigration by penalizing employers and offering amnesty to some illegals who came forward. Enforcement has been very uneven, even nonexistent, and illegal immigration expanded to our current estimates of 12 to 21 million, but no exact figures exist. Legislation in the 1990s increased the annual number of legal immigrants from 270,000 to 675,000, and doubled the number of visas for economic and employment purposes to 140,000 (Cornelius, 2004; Meilander, 2001; Morris, 2007; Leonhardt, 2008), and we now have record numbers.

America's Great Peril

The peril to America is not from the idea of immigration. We have an immigrant tradition, but that immigration occurred over a long time and smaller scale. One aspect of the peril is simply the relative size of immigrant groups. Buchanan (2006) points out that there are 36 million foreign-born now in the United States—three times the number that immigrated in the so-called Great Wave of 1910—and that "the Border Patrol catches as many illegal aliens every month as all the legal immigrants who came to America in the 1920s" (p. 10). Such large numbers produce dislocations, suspicions, economic uncertainty, and fear among existing citizens. The size of immigrant groups creates difficult assimilation conditions, taxes social services, and undermines local employment arrangements and social conditions.

A second important aspect of the peril to America is the disorderly, disruptive, and potentially dangerous illegal acts of people who come into America without proper authorization, or who stay longer than their visas permit. The main threats of unfettered and uncontrolled immigration include the obvious: crime, disease, national security, undercutting American workers, dislocation in low-income communities, and overloading social services like health and education. One-third of all patients treated in the Los Angeles Health system each year are illegal aliens (FAIR, 2008).

Between 2000 and 2005, about 4.5 million illegals were caught trying to break into the United States, and more than 300,000 of them had criminal records (Buchanan, 2006). That is one criminal in every twelve immigrants, and that is only among illegals who were caught. The current immigration issue differs significantly from those in the past in that a large number of immigrants have come illegally or overstayed their visas and have become illegal. We have done little to fully identify these illegal immigrants or to enforce the laws which they have broken. Simply coming over our borders without official permission or overstaying an authorized visa is a crime. Those who intentionally engage in these activities are criminals. It is illegal for good reason. Open access to public schools should not be a reward for illegal activity.

A third aspect of the peril for America by uncontrolled immigration is more esoteric but important: challenges to American values, national unity, social relations, and commonalities of spirit that define the United States. Finding and nurturing common grounds for social life is a long and often grueling process; it can easily be fractured by competing ideologies from immigrant groups.

Our national security, national integrity, and economy depend upon controlling our borders and developing clear and reasoned policies to limit immigration. We welcome immigrants who follow the rules. Most of our immigrant ancestors endured long and difficult journeys to come here. They applied for permission to enter and those who desired citizenship fulfilled requirements that included good health, a law-abiding history, learning English, and passing a test of American history and government. They understood the needs for national security and border integrity that require laws, rules, and regulations regarding immigration. They desired opportunities and rights that American citizenship provides, and they used their time, energy, intelligence, and commitment to fulfill those requirements. They were often leaving places where those opportunities and rights did not exist.

True, some legal immigrants also have criminal records, serious health problems, or antipathy to American ideals, but they were often weeded out through the application, waiting, educational, and testing process for citizenship. And we had records for them. Rules and regulations worked in these cases to protect America. Orderly immigration and legitimate educational requirements well serve those who have properly immigrated.

Needed Basic Immigration Policies: Immigration Policy in the National Interest

America needs a thorough and vigilant border protection system, as a beginning point. In an age of terrorism threats, fast transportation, and massive population shifts, a sound immigration policy has to start with full control of our borders (Auster, 2003). That can mean fences, electronic monitoring, active and frequent land and air patrols, night vision imaging, lighting, and similar screening devices. They work (von Drehle, 2008). It can also mean personal identification that cannot be compromised, coordinated international verification and tracking systems, and speedy deportation arrangements.

We also need improved control over legal entry as visitors, workers, and scholars. This requires complete and verifiable application data, with continuing full information on travel and contact locations for all entrants to improve our ability to find them when their authorized visitation time is nearing completion. Our visa limits must be stringently enforced, with severe and enforced penalties for overstaying without permission.

We need clear and simple federal procedures for immigration and for illegals. Employers and sponsors should be legally responsible for checking positive identification for legality, with verification from government agencies, before employment. We should strengthen all bans on the hiring of illegal immigrants, with serious penalties that increase if the offense is repeated. In the meantime, we should do better enforcement of existing laws governing immigrant employment, identification, and supervision. The European Union recently passed tougher laws on immigration, with longer detention and easier expulsion (Brothers, 2008).

Our immigration system should be tuned primarily to improving our nation, with humanitarian and other purposes next in order. More intelligent and limited immigration policies are necessary to coordinate our national needs for well-educated people in particular fields. We must cut the sheer numbers of immigrants to assure the continuation of American values and traditions, and we must encourage the best and brightest of those who want to come to the United States and who have skills complementary to our national interests. At a minimum, we should require at least high school graduation for all adult immigrants.

We must require demonstrated fluency in English as basic to permanent residency or citizenship, and we should provide government information, except for tourist purposes, only in English. A knowledge of American history, government, and economics, and agreement with values should also be required of anyone applying for naturalization. Schools have responsibilities for this education; smaller numbers of and mandated minimal education requirements for immigrants can mitigate the costs and problems.

Summary

Some immigrants have made major contributions to American education, and to our culture. Many have used our open educational system as a springboard to a better life. Escaping oppression and finding freedom are educational, and so is trying to better oneself financially. But those may not be sufficient grounds for a national policy that only limits legal immigration by numbers, and weak immigration practices that have allowed 12 to 21 million illegal immigrants to remain—and to remain unidentified.

It is only with intelligent immigration reform and consistent enforcement practices that we can hope to deal with the educational problems that flow from the current immigration situation.

Immigration and education are linked. Lack of control and coordination of immigration creates problems for schools and society. Mass immigration threatens the basic fiber of the nation and overloads the schools. Illegal immigration has exploded, is hidden, and is a peril to our country. Immigration reform is not only necessary for national security and to promote our national interest, but it will also help schools refocus on their primary purposes for American citizens.

For Discussion

1. A Pew Research Center report (Passel and Cohn, 2008), covering U.S. population projections until 2050, contains the following key points:
   - Almost 20% of the U.S. population in 2050 will be immigrants;
   - The elderly population will increase by more than double, and the working-age group will decline as a percentage of population;
   - Hispanics, currently the largest minority group, will triple in size, becoming about 29% of the population.

   If this develops,
   a. What would you identify as the most important positive and negative consequences from this?
   b. What are the likely impacts of each point on schooling by 2050?
   c. What recommendations would you make to help the schools prepare for each of those potential impacts?
   d. What social, cultural, and economic impacts would you expect from this change?

   If you think this projection is negative for the United States,
   a. What would you propose for changing immigration policies and practices?
   b. How would your proposals affect schools?
   c. How would your proposals affect social and economic conditions in the United States and in the world?

2. Drachman and Langran (2008) state that "Language has become one of the most important and contentious problems in the United States. A major reason is that it is interlaced with a number of other highly controversial issues such as politics, immigration, civil rights, citizenship, equality of educational opportunity, and American culture and national identity. . . . Historically, the public schools have been the great Americanizing force, with the teaching of English their major tool" (p. 65).
   a. What evidence supports, and what evidence is in opposition to, their view about the level of controversy about language in the United States?
   b. Identify and evaluate some examples of how language is, or is not, interlaced with the list of other factors (e.g., politics, immigration, civil rights) noted in the quote above. Pay special attention to examples involving immigration.
   c. If the authors are correct about language as one of the most problematic current issues, what does that say about the effectiveness of the public schools in its Americanizing role over history?
   d. Discuss how schools have attempted to meet their role in Americanizing, and how English language instruction is related to that role.
   e. Develop a proposal for how schools could better address any language issues, with a focus on new immigrants.

3. Over 550,000 foreign students come to study each year in colleges and universities in the United States, but only a small proportion (65,000 in 2009) are able to obtain special visas, known as H-1B visas, to stay on for work in the United States. And these visas are awarded in a lottery system that is oversubscribed each year. The United Kingdom's immigration policy, however, is to welcome those they identify as most likely to make contributions to the British nations, with no lottery.
   a. What are the main arguments for and against the policies in the United States and the United Kingdom?
   b. Whose interests are served under each policy?
   c. What would you expect to be the long-term results of both policies?
   d. If one policy is seen as a thesis, and the other an antithesis, what would be a suitable synthesis?

References

ADAMS, L. D. AND KIROVA, A. eds. (2007). *Global Migration and Education.* Mahwah, NJ: Lawrence Erlbaum.

AMOROSINO, C. S. (2007). Letter to The Honorable George Miller and The Honorable Howard P. McKeon, U.S. House of Representatives. September 5. http://www.tesol.org

AUSTER, L. (2003). "Erasing America: Politics of the Borderless Nation." Monterey, VA American Immigration Control Foundation. www.aicfoundation.org

BANK STREET. (2008). *Literacy Guide.* http://bnkst.edu/literacyguide

BRIMELOW, P. (2008) "Mass Immigration and Education." www.commonsenseonmassimmigration.us?articles/art-brimelow

BORJAS, G. J. (1999). *Heaven's Door: Immigration Policy and the American Economy.* Princeton, NJ: Princeton University Press.

BROTHERS, C. (2008). "EU Passes Tough Migrant Measures." *New York Times,* June 19. www.nytimes.com

BUCHANAN, P. J. (2006), *State of Emergency.* New York: St. Martin's Press.

Castaneda v. Picard 448 F.2d 989; 1981 U.S. APP Lexis 12063, June 23, 1981 http://stanford.edu/~kenro/LAU/IAPolicy/IA1bCastaneda

CENTER FOR IMMIGRATION STUDIES. (2008). "The High Cost of Cheap Labor." April 15. www.cis.org

COLLINS, D. (2008). "Failing to Reform Immigration Threatens Education." *Pittsburgh Tribune-Review.* Sept. 8. p. 1.

CORNELIUS, W. A., et al., eds. (2004) *Controlling Immigration.* Stanford: Stanford University Press.

CRAWFORD, J. (2007). "Hard Sell: Why Is Bilingual Education So Unpopular with the American Public?" in *Bilingual Education,* ed. O.Garcia and C. Baker. Clevedon, England: Multilingual Matters.

DARLING-HAMMOND, L. (2008). "Improving High Schools and the Role of NCLB," in *Holding NCLB Accountable; Achieving Accountability, Equity and School Reform,* ed. G.L. Sunderman. Thousand Oaks, CA: Corwin.

ESPINOSA, L. M. (2008). *Challenging Common Myth About English Language Learners.* NY: Foundation for Child Development. http://www.fcd-us.org/resources.

FALTIS, C. J. AND COULTER, C. A. (2008). *Teaching English Learners and Immigrant Students in Secondary Schools.* Boston, MA: Allyn and Bacon.

FEDERATION FOR AMERICAN IMMIGRATION REFORM (FAIR). (2002) "Immigration and School Overcrowding." www.fairus.org

_____. (2005). "What's Wrong With Illegal Immigration." March. www.fairus.org

FRANKLIN, B. (1749). *Proposals Relating to the Education of Youth In Pennsylvania, 1749.* http://www.archives.upenn.edu/primdocs/1749proposals.

GAYTAN, F. X. et al. (2007). "Understanding and Responding to the Needs of Newcomer Immigrant Youth and Families." *The Prevention Researcher* 14: 10, 11–13.

GINGRICH, N. (2008). *Real Change.* Washington, DC: Regnery.

HANDLIN, O. ed. (1966). *Children of the Uprooted.* New York: George Braziller.

HERNANDEZ, D. J., DENTON, N. A., AND MACARTNEY, S. E. (2007). "Children in Immigrant Families — The U.S. and 50 States: National Origins, Language, and Early Education." Albany, NY: Child Trends and the Center for Social and Demographic Analysis, University at Albany, SUNY: 2007 Research Brief Series, 2007-11, April. www.childtrends.org.

IMMIGRATION COUNTERS. (2008). "Real Time Data." April. www.immigrationcounters.com

KAESTLE, C. (1983). *Pillars of the Republic: Common Schools and American Society, 1780–1860.* NY: Hill and Wang.

Lau v. Nichols, 414 U.S. 563 (1974). http://supreme.justia.com/us/414/563/case.

LEONHARDT, D. (2008). "The Border and the Ballot box." Mar 2, pp 1–3 *New York Times.* www.nytimes.com

"Man in the Street." (1905). *New York Times*, January 15. http://www.nytimes.com/archive

MEILANDER, P. C. (2001*). Toward a Theory of Immigration.* New York: Palgrave.

MIGRATION POLICY INSTITUTE. (2006). "Annual Immigration to the United States: The Real Numbers." www.migrationinformation.org

_____. (2008). "2006 American Community Survey and Census Data on the Foreign Born by State." www.migrationinformation.org

MORRIS, D. AND MCGANN, E. (2007) *Outrage.* New York: Harper Collins.

National Association for Bilingual Education (NABE). (2007). *NABE Principles on the Reauthorization of NCLB.* Washington, DC: NABE http://www.nabe.org/advocacy/nclb

NCTE ELL TASK FORCE. (2006). *NCTE Position Paper on the Role of English Teachers in Educating English Language Learners (ELLs).* National Council of Teachers of English. http://www.ncte.org

PASSEL, J. S. AND COHN, D. (2008). *U.S. Population Projections 2005–2050*, Washington, DC: Pew Research Center http//pewhispanic.org/files.reports/85.

Pew Research Center. (2008). U.S. Population Projections: 2005–2050. Feb 11. (Passel, J.S. and Cohn, D.) http://pewsocialstrends.org

Plyler v. Doe, 457 U.S. 202 (1982) http://supreme.justia.com/us/457/202/case.

PORTES, A. AND RUMBAUT, R. G. (2006). *Immigrant America, A Portrait.* Berkeley, CA: University of California.

RABIN, N., COMBS, C., AND GONZALEZ, N. (2008). "Understanding Plyler's Legacy: Voices from Border Schools." *Journal of Law and Education* 37:15–82.

ROBERTS, S. (2004). *Who We Are Now.* New York: Henry Holt.

SMITH, J. P. AND EDMONSTON, B. eds. (1997). The New Americans: Economic, Demographic, and Fiscal Effects of Immigration. Washington, DC: National Academy Press.

SOLORZANO, R. W. (2008). "High Stakes Testing: Issues, Implications, and Remedies for English Language Learners." *Review of Educational Research* 78:260–329.

SPRING, J. (2001). *The American School: 1642–2000, 5th ed.* NY: McGraw-Hill.

STEWNER-MANZANARES, G. (1988). *The Bilingual Education Act: Twenty Years Later.* Washington, DC: National Clearinghouse for Bilingual Education. http://www.nclea.gwu/pubs/classics

SUAREZ-OROZCO, C., SUAREZ-OROZCO, M., AND TODOROVA, I. (2008). *Learning a New Land; Immigrant Students in American Society.* Cambridge, MA: The Belknap Press.

SUAREZ-OROZCO, M. AND GARDNER, H. (2003). "Educating Billy Wang for the World of Tomorrow." *Education Week* 8:43, 34. October 22.

SUAREZ-OROZCO, M. AND QIN-HILLIARD, D. B. (2004). *Globalization: Culture and Education in the New Millennium.* Berkeley, CA: University of California Press.

SUAREZ-OROZCO, M. AND SUAREZ-OROZCO, C. (2001). *Children of Immigration.* Cambridge, MA: Harvard University Press.

VON DREHLE, R. O. (2008). "A New Line in the Sand." *Time*17:28–35.

WILEY, T. G. (2007). "Accessing Language Rights in Education: A Brief History of the U.S. Context," in *Bilingual Education*, ed. O.Garcia and C. Baker. Clevedon, England: Multilingual Matters.

What Should Be Taught?

Knowledge and Literacy

About Part Two: School curriculum battles are the outward sign of competing social forces. Curriculum control is the result of power and politics. Decisions on what should be taught are political decisions, involving questions about the definitions of knowledge, intelligence, literacy, and learning. These terms are complementary concepts—but they often have differing definitions and interpretations (Coiro, 2008). Schools are necessarily involved with definitions of these four terms and with disputes over them. Topics covered in Part Two include disparities in academic achievement, values and character development, multicultural education, technology, and testing. Each issue involves both theoretical and practical concerns; what does it mean to know something and how should schools undertake that activity?

This introductory essay examines the idea of knowledge and its corollaries, political and philosophic contexts for school curriculum decisions, and

ideological and practical contexts of curriculum control. School curriculum is controversial. Raskin (2004) points out:

> Throughout the twentieth century, brutal fights were waged about the content in education, what educators thought it proper to teach, analyze, and question. Hidden behind these struggles were issues of class, cultural homogenization, propaganda as knowledge, the abstract versus the concrete, and, of course, race, sex, and leisure. (p. 103)

INTRODUCTION

From the testing of selected knowledge as mandated under the NCLB Act to school board arguments over evolution or intelligent design as appropriate content for science classes, curriculum debates abound. Whose history should be studied and tested, and which interpretations? Which literature should be required and which censored? How important are the arts and humanities, physical education, home economics, commercial subjects, mathematics? Should all students take the same courses?

Teaching is, of course, more than telling or testing. And learning is more than listening and recalling. Good education requires more thought about what should be taught and why, and consideration of what is to be learned and how. We may all think we are well educated, so it is easy to assume that what should be taught is what we were taught—and learned as we did. That self-congratulatory response answers a question about the central purpose for schools—what should be taught?—but not satisfactorily (Ippolito et al. 2008).

If the best education is simply what we learned and recall, then teaching could be only telling and testing of what we already think we know. There would be no sense trying to make changes in schools, curriculum, or teaching. Education would be static. There would also be no reason for a book on educational issues—there would be no issues. But there are enormous and important issues about schooling, and what should be taught is one of the most enormous and important. What we were taught, or what our parents and grandparents were taught, represented ideas of important school knowledge in those times. But knowledge changes—and so do our conceptions of intelligence, literacy, and learning. Noble (2004) comments: "As fashionable as it is to decry the woeful state of American schooling, and to mock students who can't locate one or another country on a map, the great mass of American citizens are probably better informed than they were one hundred or even fifty years ago, when formal school stopped for most people at or before high school, and the curriculum was designed to teach the children of farmers and factory workers how to keep still and take orders" (p. 157).

Schools, from day care to graduate school, exist to determine, examine, convey, question, and modify knowledge. That responsibility is the root of issues surrounding what should be taught. Communicating knowledge, most people agree, is the core purpose of schools. That interactive communication depends upon our definitions (Coiro, 2008).

Issues arise because of major disagreements over how knowledge is to be defined, whose ideas of knowledge should prevail in the schools, how to package that knowledge, and how to organize and teach knowledge (Rosenberg, 2002; Rose, 2008). In addition to disputes about the nature, value, and expression of knowledge, are disagreements about how to define and measure human intelligence and literacy, and how to identify and stimulate the best kinds of learning. Disputes this complex are often at the center of various school wars, since the control of knowledge is the control of society.

- What knowledge should we teach, in what sequence, and who gets to decide?
- Which knowledge should be required study, which should be elective, and which should be censored?
- Who should get access to which kinds of knowledge?

• How do we know if and when that or other knowledge is learned?

These are not only theoretical concerns linked directly to decisions about school curriculum, they are also practical concerns basic to teaching and learning, success and failure.

Schools should provide teaching in the most valuable knowledge, but that begs the questions of who decides what is worth knowing and on what grounds. The struggle to control what is accepted as valued knowledge is inevitably a struggle for power (Cherryholmes, 1978; Popkewitz, 1987; Sizer, 2004; Moran, 2005). Control of people's minds is control of their expectations, behavior, and allegiance. Deciding which students get access to which knowledge has a powerful impact on social policy and politics, with results that can lead in opposite directions: more social egalitarianism or more elitism, more social-class separation or more social integration (Rose, 2008). Such decisions can enable or restrict individual achievements and enhance or detract from democracy.

Should schools aim to produce broadly educated people, specialists in academic subjects, social critics, book learners, industrial workers, college material, athletes, consumers, patriots, or something else?

NONSCHOOL KNOWLEDGE AND UNINTENDED SCHOOL LEARNINGS

School, of course, is not the only place where knowledge is gained, intelligence developed, literacy honed, and learning produced. Glynda Hull and Katherine Schultz (2002) summarized the large volume of research on learning in and out of school, commenting:

> During the last two decades researchers from a range of disciplines have documented the considerable intellectual accomplishments of children, adolescents, and adults in out-of-school settings, accomplishments that often contrast with their poor school-based performances and suggest a different view of their potential as capable learners and doers in the world . . . school has come to be such a particular, specialized institution with its own particular brand of learning. . . . (pp. 575, 577)

All of us experience nonschool settings where we gain significant knowledge; families, friends, peers, work groups, and media are but a few examples. We learn from our earliest days to the last, and formal schooling accounts for less than 10 percent of that learning period for most people.

Some wisdom we gain comes in school, but is not what the school intended for us to learn—this is the hidden curriculum of schooling. Some students learn dishonesty and cheating as a result of experiences in school life, but the school did not intend that result.

Learning in nonschool settings and through the hidden curriculum in schools challenges many of our limited conceptions about school as the prime location for knowledge, intelligence, literacy, and learning. Schooling is but one dimension of this process of development, but school is the organized agency given responsibility for defining, transmitting, and changing knowledge deemed important in a society. Our focus, in this section, will be on disputes over what should be taught in schools, but we must not mistake that for the whole of knowledge or intelligence.

Knowledge, of course, depends on intelligence since it is only through intelligence that we gain, interpret, and use knowledge. Yet, there are as many disputes about intelligence as there are about knowledge. As Ken Richardson (2000), notes:

> There has probably been a concept of intelligence, and a word for it, since people first started to compare themselves with other animals and with one another. We know this at least since thinkers first began to theorize about the nature of the mind. . . . the existing ground does not offer a firm foundation for anyone seeking to answer the question: "What is intelligence?" Indeed, it is a complex confusion. (pp. 1, 20)

Psychologist Howard Gardner (1993, 1999, 2000, 2003) argues that we really have multiple intelligences, not just a single form. He suggests that intelligences are actually potentials for people to develop processes to solve problems or create things; they are not completed events, nor are they clearly observable or testable, and they are relatively independent of each other. Some kinds of intelligence (such as logical-mathematical and linguistic) are especially useful in satisfying school academic requirements, and others (such as intra- and interpersonal, musical, and bodily-kinesthetic) are more useful in other settings in and

out of school. This level of complexity makes "intelligence" testing and other efforts to standardize and measure schooling more difficult, if not impossible. As Gardner puts it, "intelligence is too important to be left to the intelligence testers" (1999, p. 3).

Similarly, we have multiple literacies and multiple learning processes (Hull and Schultz, 2002; Coiro, 2008). Literacy can be defined in many ways: as basic reading/writing skills, as computer skills, as economic ability, as cultural capabilities, as historical cognizance, or as artistic or critical literacy (Gee, 1996, 2000). Critical literacy provides a way to use basic school knowledge to identify and correct significant power disparities between haves and have-nots (Freire, 1970; Freire and Macedo, 1987; Comber and Simpson, 2001).

Multiple learning processes are obvious to anyone who observes children acquire walking, speaking, reading, creative, and interpretive abilities. This sophisticated concept of multiple intelligences, literacies, and learning processes not only makes definitions of knowledge, intelligence, literacy, and learning very problematic, it also raises important questions about school curriculum, national and state standardized testing, and teaching.

THE SCHOOL CURRICULUM: KNOWLEDGE AND POLITICS

The school curriculum of each society reflects the definitions of formal knowledge and literacy prevalent in that society and in that time—and they reflect political decisions. These definitions often conflict—arts versus sciences, practical versus theoretical, socialization versus individual independence. In an age of witchery, a literate, intelligent person is one who shares the language and values of the sorcerer's form of knowledge. In an age of technology, a literate and intelligent person may be defined as one who shares the language and values of technological knowledge. Thus, the term *literate* may be thought of as a verbal badge given to those who possess knowledge considered socially valuable. Schools provide literacy credentials in the form of diplomas, degrees, and various types of professional certificates. When magic and witchcraft were socially credible, sorcerers enjoyed great power and status (Moran, 2004). Their pronouncements often became laws and policies. Only a select few had the opportunity to learn their secret rites. When knowledge of witchcraft came to be viewed as evil, sorcerers were burned. In modern societies where scientific knowledge is prized, "sorcerers" are considered interesting eccentrics. The postmodern society suggests new definitions and a new school curriculum for meeting the needs of the twenty-first century (Stanley, 1992; Greene, 1994; Ippolito et al., 2008).

Typically, traditional school subjects coexist in the curriculum until new topics or arguments arise challenging that emphasis. In our seventeenth-century secondary schools, classes were taught in Latin, and Greek was required along with moral philosophy. In the last decades of the twentieth century, when test scores revealed deficiencies in the basic skills of reading, writing, and arithmetic, most elementary schools decreased the curriculum time spent

on science, social studies, and the arts and shifted it to reading and arithmetic. When computers became more socially valuable, schools made space to fit computer study into a crowded school curriculum. Other additions such as driver's education, physical education, drug education, and character education illustrate curriculum changes based on redefinitions of knowledge and the politics of schools. The specific mix of courses and emphasis within the curriculum depend on prevailing visions of the "good" individual and the "good" society. In every age, people hold disparate views on what kinds of individuals and society are most desirable. Some want individuals to be free, independent, and critical; others advocate behavior modification to control deviation and ensure social conformity. Some demand prescribed moral values and beliefs; others demand release from moralisms and prescriptions. Some desire respect for authority; others prefer challenges to authority.

PRACTICAL, THEORETICAL, AND MORAL SCHOOLING

The literature is filled with disputes over how school should develop the good individual and the good society. Aristotle considered the state the fulfillment of our social drives and saw education as a state activity designed to provide social unity. He said that "education is therefore the means of making it [the society] a community and giving it unity" (Aristotle, 1962, p. 51). In *The Politics*, Aristotle discussed the controversy over whether schools should teach practical knowledge, moral character, or esoteric ideas.

Contemporary curriculum debate continues to focus on the relative emphasis schools should give to practical, theoretical, and moral schooling.

Contemporary comprehensive public schools offer some useful applied educational programs, such as reading, music, wood shop, home economics, computer operation, physical education, and vocational training. They also offer the study of theoretical concepts in English, math, social studies, the arts, and science. And schools provide various forms of moral education; students study materials conveying ideas of the good person and the good society, and learn from school rules and teachers to be respectful, patriotic, loyal, and honest. The exact mix of these forms of education varies as different reforms become popular and as local communities make changes.

Curricular reforms between 1980 and 2010 are seen by many as essentially mechanistic and "top-down." The president, governors, legislators, and national commissions tell the schools what and how to teach to correct educational ills. Their prescriptions—for increased course requirements, longer school days and school years, more homework, more testing, and force-feeding knowledge to students in factory-like schools—do not prove their curative abilities.

Most schools teach a relatively standard curriculum. States mandate certain courses, such as English, American history, and drug and alcohol education. Accrediting agencies examine schools periodically, and review the curriculum for conformity. Publishers, aiming at a national market, produce teaching materials for a national curriculum. And school district curriculum coordinators and department heads attend national conferences and read journals that stress standard curricular structures. Thus, a broad outline exists for a general national curriculum based on common practices, even though specific curricula in each state differ.

In the twenty-first century, external forces still largely determine the formal curriculum in American schools. We have national and state standards, increasing external accountability for student learning, and more complex ideas of socially expected literacy. Since colonial times, the curriculum has evolved from a narrow interest in teaching religious ideals to multiple, and often conflicting, interests in providing broad knowledge, skills, and values relevant to nearly every aspect of social life. In U.S. schools, the medieval curriculum of "seven liberal arts"— rhetoric, grammar, logic, arithmetic, astronomy, geometry, and music—has given way to a list of subjects too long to enumerate. And the formal curriculum is certainly not all that students are expected to learn in school.

THE HIDDEN CURRICULUM

The hidden curriculum of unexpressed and usually unexamined ideas, values, and behaviors conveys subtle, often unintended, things to students (and teachers).

A few brief examples illustrate the hidden curriculum at its simplest level. Teachers tell students to be independent and express their own ideas, but they often chastise or punish the student who actually exhibits independence and expresses ideas the teacher doesn't like. In history courses, students hear that justice and equality are basic American rights, yet they see that compliant and well-dressed students earn favored treatment. In school, students are told that plagiarism is an academic sin; then the news shows prominent and award-winning historians (probably quoted in the high school history textbook) who plagiarized from others. Students are told to not smoke, by teachers who do. The hidden curriculum is a vast, relatively uncharted domain often much more effective than the formal curriculum in shaping student learning and knowledge.

At a deeper level, discrepancies between what schools say and what schools do may raise a more significant concern about competing ideologies. The hidden curriculum conflicts with the stated purposes of the visible curriculum. The stated curriculum may value diversity; the hidden curriculum expects conformity. The stated curriculum advocates critical thinking; the hidden curriculum supports docility. The visible curriculum emphasizes equal opportunity; the hidden curriculum separates students according to social-class background, gender, race, or other factors.

Critical literature examines the hidden curriculum and its ideological bases (see, for example, Young, 1970; Cherryholmes, 1978, 1988; Anyon, 1979, 1980; Giroux and Purpel, 1983; Popkewitz, 1987; Giroux, 1988; Apple, 2000; Aronowitz, 2008; Stanley, 1992, 2004). From this critical view, the "great debates" about schooling

extensively covered in the media and mainstream educational literature are actually narrowly constructed differences between liberals and conservatives. At bottom, public debates do not raise ideological concerns about the control of knowledge and its social consequences. Tinkering with the stated curriculum leaves the powerful hidden curriculum intact. Superficial school reforms do very little to change schooling, and neither mainstream liberals nor conservatives really want much change.

At the surface level, where much school reform debate occurs, a discussion about whether to spend more school time on computers, math, and English and less on the arts and social studies is a comparatively trivial matter; it hides more fundamental disputes about whose interests are served and whose are maligned. Shallow arguments about whether the curriculum should stress the basics, provide vocational courses, allow electives, or emphasize American values should lead to deeper, more critical examinations of who controls the school curriculum and consequences of that control. In mainstream discourse, those basic issues are hidden.

A central issue in the struggle for control of knowledge is whether traditional knowledge provides enduring wisdom or promotes social oppression. In opposition to the traditional use of literacy as a tool of the dominant class to separate and control the masses is the idea of literacy as a tool for liberation, Paulo Freire's revolutionary concept (Freire and Berthoff, 1987). Freire, born in one of the most impoverished areas of Brazil, came to know the plight of the poor. He vowed to dedicate his life to the struggle against misery and suffering, and his work led him to define the "culture of silence" he saw among the disadvantaged.

Freire realized the power of knowledge and recognized that the dominant class used education to keep the culture of silence among the victims—the poor and illiterate. He taught adults to read in order to liberate them from their imposed silence. As a professor of education in Brazil, he experimented to erase illiteracy, and his ideas became widely used in private literacy campaigns there. Freire became a threat to the government and was jailed after a military coup in 1964. Forced to leave his native country, he went to Chile to work with UNESCO, came to the United States, and then joined the World Council of Churches in Geneva as head of its educational division. Freire's program involves the development of critical consciousness, using communication to expose oppression. Teacher and student are "co-intentional," sharing equally in dialogues on social reality and developing a critical understanding that can liberate them from the culture of silence.

Henry Giroux, citing Freire, argues that we need a redefinition of literacy to focus on its critical dimensions. Mass culture via television and other electronic media is under the control of dominant economic interests, and offers only immediate images and unthoughtful information. This creates a "technocratic" illiteracy that is a threat to self-perception, critical thought, and democracy. Giroux (1988) states:

Instead of formulating literacy in terms of the mastery of techniques, we must broaden its meaning to include the ability to read critically, both inside and outside one's experiences, and with conceptual power. This means that literacy would enable people to decode critically their personal and social worlds and thereby further their ability to challenge the myths and beliefs that structure their perceptions and experiences. (p. 84)

CURRICULUM CONTROL

Control of knowledge, and the school curriculum, is a product of both prevailing social goals and prevailing social structures. During the United States' formative years, religion was the basis. Differences existed among the colonies, but most people expected all young children to be taught religious precepts at home or at dame or writing schools. The purpose was to thwart the efforts of "that ould deluder, Satan," who sought to keep human beings from knowledge of the scriptures. After learning to read and write, however, most girls were not permitted further education. They returned home to learn the art of homemaking, while boys from more affluent homes continued their schooling at Latin grammar schools. African Americans and Native Americans were virtually excluded from schools.

Historically, the struggle for the control of knowledge has paralleled social-class differences (Anyon, 1980, 2005; Spring, 1998). The assumption was that workers needed practical knowledge, the privileged class needed higher knowledge, and both needed moral knowledge, but with great disparity in the kinds of moral knowledge they required. Craft apprenticeships to acquire practical knowledge were for the masses. Formal schooling to learn critical thinking and study philosophy, science, and the arts was for the aristocratic class. In terms of moral instruction, the masses were to gain the moral character to obey, respect authority, work hard and be frugal, and suffer with little complaint. Members of the privileged class were supposed to gain the moral character to rule wisely, justly, and with civility.

One of the central purposes of schooling is to prepare future leaders of society. When the powerful class controls education and decides what is to be taught, the essential curricular question is: What should members of the ruling class know? In more democratic societies, involved in mass education, the curricular questions revolve around what all members of the society need to know to participate fully and actively.

Even in democratic societies, however, curricular needs of those identified as potential leaders receive special attention. We can see this in the higher academic tracks and honors programs characterizing many modern high schools. The correlation between social expectations, social-class structure, and what schools teach deserves ongoing examination.

R. H. Tawney (1964), criticized the elite "public boarding-school" tradition of the wealthy in England, and advocated improvements in the developing system of free schools for the working classes. The very nature of the elite

system was a part of the hidden curriculum, teaching the sons of the wealthy "not in words or of set purpose, but by the mere facts of their environment, that they are members . . . of a privileged group, whose function it will be, on however humble a scale, to direct and command, and to which leadership, influence, and the other prizes of life properly belong" (1964, p. 83).

Social class is not the only major factor lying behind curricular decisions. Race, gender, national origin, and religion are other conditions that influence decisions about which people receive what knowledge in a society. The concept of privilege, and the education that privilege brings, has been linked to racism and sexism in American and other national histories. Educational discrimination against racial minorities, women, Jews, Catholics, Native Americans, Eskimos, and others is a sorry tradition in a democratic society.

About half a century ago, psychologist Kenneth Clark, whose studies were a significant factor in the Supreme Court decision that found segregated schools unconstitutional (*Brown v. Board of Education*, 1954), put the case clearly:

> The public schools in America's urban ghettos also reflect the oppressive damage of racial exclusion. . . . Segregation and inferior education reinforce each other. . . . Children themselves are not fooled by the various euphemisms educators use to disguise educational snobbery. From the earliest grades a child knows when he has been assigned to a level that is considered less than adequate. . . . "The clash of cultures in the

classroom" is essentially a class war, a socioeconomic and racial warfare being waged on the battleground of our schools, with middle-class and middle-class-aspiring teachers provided with a powerful arsenal of half-truths, prejudices, and rationalizations, arrayed against the hopelessly outclassed working-class youngsters. (Clark, 1965, pp. 111–117)

Similar condemnations of educational discrimination based on religion, nationality, and gender are common in the critical literature (Hofstadter, 1944; Clark, 1965; Katz, 1971; Feldman, 1974; Spring, 1976, 1998; Apple, 1979, 1990; Sadker and Sadker, 1982; Walker and Barton, 1983; Grimshaw, 1986; Giroux, 1991; Lather, 1991; Weiler, 1991). As Rosemary Deem (1983) comments: "Women have had to struggle hard against dominant patriarchal power relations, which try to confine women to the private sphere of the home and family, away from the public sphere of production and political power" (p. 107). Weiler (1991) essentially agrees in a critique of the Western system of knowledge, arguing that feminist pedagogy is rooted in a critical, oppositional, and activist vision of social change. Schooling that provides different types of knowledge and skills to students who differ only in race, gender, class, religion, or nationality contributes to continued inequality of treatment and stereotypes.

SOCIAL EXPECTATIONS

Should schools concentrate on subject knowledge of historic and socially approved value, or on material encouraging critical thinking and student interest? If individual students are expected to develop independent and critical judgment so they can participate actively in improving the democratic society, we should expect schooling that leads to that goal, and can expect educated individuals to have an impact on society. If society values a structure where only a few people have power and most people are expected to be docile and conform to social norms, we should expect schooling that leads to that end, and the resulting society.

Those two hypothetical statements seem to suggest the choice is simple; it is not. There are complex and changing relationships between the kinds of individuals we desire, the society we want to develop, and schooling we provide. These relationships often send conflicting signals to schools, and the conflicts become enshrined in the school curriculum. Society wants students to become self-sufficient individuals—but not too self-sufficient too early, so students have little latitude in deciding what to study until they reach college. We desire a society that is democratic and inspires voluntary loyalty, but we do not trust open inquiry, so we require courses stressing nationalistic patriotism.

Prior to the American Revolution, religion was waning as the primary social glue. National political interests emerged. After the Revolution, and into the nineteenth century, nationalism replaced religion as an educational force. Literacy became important not for religious salvation, but for patriotism, preservation of liberty, and participation in democracy. The political-nationalistic tradition remains strong in U.S.

schools, with a call for renewed emphasis each time social values seem threatened (Westheimer, 2007). The War on Terrorism is a prime contemporary example; there is a redoubled effort to require allegiance pledges, patriotic exercises, and U.S. history.

There are many other examples of political uses of schools. During the period of overt racism in the United States, and as a reaction to the abolition of slavery, some regions used literacy tests to restrict voting rights. Since slaves had been prohibited, by law in some states, from receiving an education, these tests were intended to keep former slaves and the poor from voting. Their proponents also used them to limit participation of immigrants. David Tyack (1967) quotes an imperial wizard of the Ku Klux Klan as saying, "Ominous statistics proclaim the persistent development of a parasitic mass within our domain. . . . We have taken unto ourselves a Trojan horse crowded with ignorance, illiteracy, and envy" (p. 233).

The "Red Scare" of the 1920s, McCarthyism in the 1950s, and anticommunist political rhetoric in the 1980s were also periods when people perceived social threats; the effect was to strengthen a nationalist viewpoint in history, government, literature, and economics curricula. International competition in technology and trade threatens Americans today and translates into an increased curricular emphasis on mathematics, science, technological subjects such as computers, and foreign languages.

The formal curriculum is one of the most visible parts of a school, indicating the relative value schools put on various forms of knowledge, and definitions of intelligence and literacy. There is far more to knowledge and literacy than what schools organize and teach, but schools provide legitimacy to the knowledge they select and teach, and credentials to those students who are successful in school.

Some people enjoy mathematics. For others, reading history or literature is a great joy. Some like to dissect white rats in biology class, saw wood in shop, or exercise in gym. Others are completely baffled or utterly bored by textbooks and teachers. Different strokes, as they say, for different folks. But aren't there some things that everyone should know, whether they enjoy it or not? Is there a set of skills that all should master? Should we require that anyone who graduates from high school be literate? Who should decide the criteria for literacy? What does it take to be educated in this beginning decade of the twenty-first century?

The chapters of Part Two examine some of the current curriculum disputes that have emerged as part of reform movements in education. These disputes illustrate the question of what knowledge is most valuable in our society, a question that, in turn, relates to our differing visions of what constitutes the good individual and the good society.

References

ANYON, J. (1979). "Ideology and U.S. History Textbooks." *Harvard Educational Review* 7:49–60.

———. (1980). "Social Class and the Hidden Curriculum of Work." *Journal of Education* 162:67–92.

————. (2005). *Radical Possibilities.* New York: Routledge.

APPLE, M. (1979, 2004). Ideology and Curriculum. 3rd Ed. New York: Routledge.

————. (2000). *Official Knowledge.* London: Routledge.

ARISTOTLE. (1962). *The Politics of Aristotle,* translated by E. Barker, Oxford: Oxford University Press.

ARONOWITZ, S. (2008). *Against Schooling: Toward an Education that Matters.* Boulder: Paradigm Publishing.

BERNSTEIN, B. (1977). *Class, Codes, and Control,* Vol. 3. London: Routledge and Kegan Paul.

BOURDIEU, P., AND PASSERON, J. (1977). *Reproduction in Education, Society, and Culture.* London: Sage.

BOWLES, S., AND GINTIS, H. (1976). *Schooling in Capitalist America.* New York: Basic Books.

BOYER, E. L. (1983). *High School.* New York: Harper and Row.

BRAUNGER, J., AND LEWIS, J. P. (1997). *Building a Knowledge Base in Reading.* Newark, DE: International Reading Association.

BROADFOOT, P., ED. (1984). *Selection, Certification and Control: Social Issues in Educational Assessment.* London: Falmer Press.

Brown v. Board of Education of Topeka, Shawnee County, Kansas, et al. (1954). 74 Sup. Ct. 686.

BUTTS, R. F. (1955). *A Cultural History of Western Education.* New York: McGraw-Hill.

CARNOY, M. (1975). *Schooling in a Corporate Society: The Political Economy of Education in the Democratic State.* 2nd Ed. New York: McKay.

CARNOY, M., AND LEVIN, H. (1985). *Schooling and Work in America.* Stanford, CA: Stanford University Press.

CHENG, L. (1998). "Beyond Multiculturalism," chapter in Pang, V., Cheng, L., *Struggling to Be Heard.* Albany, NY: State University of New York Press.

CHERRYHOLMES, C. (1978). "Curriculum Design as a Political Act." *Curriculum Inquiry* 10:115–141.

————. (1988). *Power and Criticism: Poststructural Investigations in Education.* New York: Teachers College Press.

CLARK, K. (1965). *Dark Ghetto.* New York: Harper and Row.

COIRO, J., et al., (2008). *The Handbook of Research in New Literacies.* Mahwah, NJ: Erlbaum.

COMBER, B., AND SIMPSON A. (2001). *Negotiating Critical Literacies in Classrooms.* Mahwah NJ: Erlbaum.

CROUSE, J., AND TRUSHEIM, D. (1998). *The Case Against the SAT.* Chicago: University of Chicago Press.

DEEM, R. (1983). "Gender, Patriarchy and Class in the Popular Education of Women," *Gender, Class and Education,* ed. S. Walker and L. Barton. London: Falmer Press.

EDELSKY, C., ALTWERGER, B., AND FLORES, B. (1991). *Whole Language, What's the Difference?* Portsmouth, NH: Heinemann.

EGGLESTON, J. (1984). "School Examinations—Some Sociological Issues," in *Selection, Certification and Control,* ed. P. Broadfoot. London: Falmer Press.

FELDMAN, S. (1974). *The Rights of Women.* Rochelle Park, NJ: Hayden.

FISKE, E. B. (1991). *Smart School, Smart Kids.* New York: Simon and Schuster.

FORD, P. C., ED. (1962). *The New-England Primer: A History of Its Origin and Development.* New York: Teachers College Press.

FREIRE, P. (1970). *Pedagogy of the Oppressed,* translated by M. B. Ramos. New York: Herder and Herder.

FREIRE, P., AND BERTHOFF, D. (1987). *Literacy: Reading and the World.* South Hadley, MA: Bergin and Garvey.

FREIRE, P., AND MACEDO, D. (1987). *Literacy.* South Hadley, MA: Bergin and Garvey.

GARDNER, H. (1983, 1993). *Frames of Mind.* New York: Basic Books.

————. (1999). *Intelligence Reframed: Multiple Intelligences for the 21st Century.* New York: Basic Books.

————. (2000). *The Disciplined Mind.* New York: Penguin.

————. (2003). "Multiple Intelligences After Twenty Years." Presentation at American Educational Research Association meeting, April 23.

GEE, J. P. (1996). *Social Linguistics and Literacies.* 2nd Ed. London: Falmer Press.

————. (2000). "The New Literacy Studies," in *Situated Literacies,* ed. D. Barton et al. London: Routledge.

GIROUX, H. (1981). *Ideology, Culture, and the Process of Schooling.* Philadelphia, PA: Temple University Press.

————. (1988). *The Teacher as Intellectual.* South Hadley, MA: Bergin and Garvey.

————, ed. (1991). *Postmodernism, Feminism and Cultural Politics.* Albany, NY: SUNY Press.

GIROUX, H., AND PURPEL, D. (1983). *The Hidden Curriculum and Moral Education.* Berkeley, CA: McCutchan.

GOODLAD, J. (1999). "Flow, Eros, and Ethos in Educational Renewal." *Kappan* 80(8): 571–578.

GREENE, M. (1994). "Postmodernism and the Crisis of Representation." *English Education* 26:206–219.

GRIMSHAW, J. (1986). *Philosophy and Feminist Thinking.* Minneapolis: University of Minnesota Press.

HANSON, F. A. (1993). *Testing, Testing: Social Consequences of the Examined Life.* Berkeley: University of California Press.

HOFSTADTER, R. (1944). *Social Darwinism in American Thought.* Philadelphia: University of Pennsylvania Press.

HULL, G., AND SCHULTZ, K. (2002). *School's Out: Bridging Out-of-School Literacies with Classroom Practice.* New York: Teachers College Press.

IPPOLITO, J., STEELE, J., and SAMSON, J. (2008). "Introduction: Why Adolescent Literacy Matters Now." *Harvard Education Review.* 68(1), 1–5, Spring.

KATZ, M. B. (1971). *Class, Bureaucracy, and Schools.* New York: Praeger.

KINCHELOE, J. L. (2005). *Critical Constructivist Primer.* New York: Peter Lang.

LANGER, J., ed. (1987). *Language, Literacy and Culture: Issues of Society and Schooling.* Norwood, NJ: Ablex.

LATHER, P. (1991). *Getting Smart: Feminist Research and Pedagogy Within the Postmodern.* New York: Routledge.

LEMANN, N. (1997). "The Reading Wars." *The Atlantic Monthly,* November: 128–134.

MEHRENS, W. A., AND LEHMANN, I. J. (1987). *Using Standardized Tests in Education.* 4th Ed. New York: Longman.

MORAN, B. T. (2005). *Distilling Knowledge.* Cambridge, MA: Harvard University Press.

NATIONAL COMMISSION ON EXCELLENCE IN EDUCATION. (1983). *A Nation at Risk.* Washington, DC: U.S. Department of Education.

NELSON, J., CARLSON, K., AND LINTON, T. (1972). *Radical Ideas and the Schools.* New York: Holt, Rinehart and Winston.

NOBLE, C. (2004). *The Collapse of Liberalism.* Lanham, MD: Rowman and Littlefield.

OAKES, J. (1985). *Keeping Track: How the Schools Structure Inequality.* New Haven, CT: Yale University Press.

OWEN, D. (1985). *None of the Above.* Boston: Houghton Mifflin.

POPKEWITZ, T. (1977). "The Latent Values of the Discipline-Centered Curriculum." *Theory and Research in Social Education* 13:189–206.

————. (1987). *The Formation of School Subjects.* New York: Falmer Press.

PRITCHARD, R. (2005). *Epistemic Luck.* New York: Oxford University Press.

RASKIN, M. (2004). *Liberalism: The Genius of American Ideals.* Lanham, MD: Rowman and Littlefield.

REICH, R. B. (2004). *Reason: Liberals Will Win the Battle for America.* New York: Alfred Knopf.

RICHARDSON, K. (2000). *The Making of Intelligence.* New York: Columbia University Press.

ROCKMORE, T. (2005). *On Constructivist Epistemology.* Lanham, MD: Rowman and Littlefield.

ROSE, M. (2008). "Intelligence, Knowledge, and the Hand/Brain Divide." *Kappan.* 89(9), 632–639. May.

ROSENBERG, J. F. (2002). *Thinking About Knowing.* Oxford, United Kingdom: Clarendon Press.

SADKER, P., AND SADKER, D. M. (1982). *Sex Equity Handbook for Schools.* New York: Longman.

SHANNON, P. (1989). *Broken Promises: Reading Instruction in Twentieth-Century America.* Granby, MA: Bergin and Garvey.

SIZER, T. (2004). *The Red Pencil.* New Haven, CT: Yale University Press.

SPRING, J. (1976). *The Sorting Machine.* New York: McKay.

———. (1998). *American Education.* 8th Ed. New York: McGraw-Hill.

STANLEY, W. (1992). *Education for Utopia: Social Reconstructionism and Critical Pedagogy in the Postmodern Era.* Albany, NY: SUNY Press.

TALLIS, R. (2005). *The Knowing Animal.* Edinburgh: Edinburgh University Press.

TAWNEY, R. H. (1964). *The Radical Tradition.* London: Allen and Unwin.

TEN ELSHOF, G. (2005). *Introspection Vindicated.* Burlington, VT: Ashgate.

TRAVERS, R. M. W. (1983). *How Research Has Changed America.* Kalamazoo, MI: Mythos.

TYACK, D. (1967). *Turning Points in American Educational History.* Waltham, MA: Blaisdell.

WALKER, S., AND BARTON, L. (1983). *Gender, Class and Education.* London: Falmer Press.

WEILER, K. (1991). "Freire and a Feminist Pedagogy of Difference." *Harvard Educational Review* 61:449–474.

WERKMEISTER, W. H. (1968). *The Basis and Structure of Knowledge.* New York: Greenwood Press.

WESTHEIMER, J., ED., (2007). *Pledging Allegiance.* New York: Teachers College Press.

YOUNG, M. F. D., ed. (1970). *Knowledge and Control.* London: Collier-Macmillan.

CHAPTER 10

The Academic Achievement Gap: Old Remedies or New

Are already existing policies and practices reducing the academic achievement gap or are new measures needed?

POSITION 1: FOR MAINTAINING EXISTING PROGRAMS

By passing this bill, we bridge the gap between helplessness and hope for more than 5 million educationally deprived children. We put into the hands of our youth more than 30 million new books, and into many of our schools their first libraries. We reduce the terrible time lag in bringing new teaching techniques into the nation's classrooms. We strengthen State and local agencies which bear the burden and the challenge of better education. And we rekindle the revolution—the revolution of the spirit against the tyranny of ignorance.

—Johnson, 1996

The Academic Achievement Gap

If you were an African American or Latino teenager in the early 1960s, you probably were prevented from attending an integrated high school (Weinberg, 1977). The laws of your state might have specifically mandated separate schools for black and white students. In other areas school districts enforced regulations prohibiting students from enrolling in schools outside their neighborhoods—and those neighborhoods were segregated by race. There was only a fifty-fifty chance you would graduate from high school. Your chances of finishing college were about four in one hundred (Orfield and Eaton, 1996).

Tests designed to measure academic achievement also documented the gap between students of color and their white counterparts. The National Assessment of Educational Progress (NAEP) testing program was established in 1969 "to monitor the academic achievement of nine-, thirteen-, and seventeen-year-olds currently enrolled in school" (Jencks and Phillips, 1998, p. 152). NAEP annually tests 70,000 to 100,000 students in reading, math, science, and writing. It is influential and credible enough to be called "The Nation's Report Card." In the early 1970s the NAEP demonstrated dramatic differences between white students and those of color. In all subjects, across all grade levels, white students outperformed African American and Latino students by 12 to 20 percent (Campbell, Hombo, and Mazzeo, 2000).

In the first half of the twentieth century, the common wisdom was that some students simply were incapable of mastering the standard curriculum. If most were students of color, that was to be expected; they simply were genetically or culturally inferior. Southerners justified segregated schools on that basis (Tyack, 1974). In the North, school districts created vocational and industrial educational programs. Many students of color were automatically assigned to them—and not to schools with college preparatory courses (Tyack, 1974; Angus and Mirel, 1999). Education reflected the reality that America was a racially segregated society. In housing, employment, and social relations, people of color and whites lived separate, and definitely not equal, lives. For the most part, those racial arrangements were not challenged in American public schools (Tyack, 1974; Anyon, 1997; Taylor, 1998; Angus and Mirel, 1999). Faint rumblings, however, could be heard heralding a revolution in American life (Tushnet, 1987).

After World War II, racial attitudes in America began at long last to change. Soldiers of African American and Latino descent had risked their lives for the United States and were unwilling to continue to accept second-class citizenship. Civil rights organizations such as the NAACP and LULAC began to challenge segregation and inequality in the courts. Inevitably attention turned toward schools (Kluger, 1975; Tushnet, 1987; Taylor, 1998; Wilson, 2003). Members of these groups "rejected earlier diagnoses of the problem of poor [school] performers, especially those that located the trouble in the defects of individuals (whether of character or chromosomes)" (Deschenes, Cuban, and Tyack, 2001, p. 533). Instead they believed discrimination prevented students of color from having access to the kind of schools, instructions, and resources white students had. And they had every intention of changing that situation.

Thanks to pressure from members of marginalized communities and their white allies, changes began that were nothing short of revolutionary. Over the last thirty-five years, we developed laws and programs designed to make equal educational opportunity a reality. The courts declared that laws mandating segregation in schools are illegal. Congress enacted legislation creating Head Start and Title I, which allocates funds to schools with high concentrations of low-performing students. The executive branch of government established affirmative action programs to remedy historic discrimination against people of color. Some of these programs faced tremendous opposition. It took many legal, political, and social struggles to put them into place. It was a fight well worth having; the combined consequences of these policies and programs have been revolutionary.

While estimates vary, according to the most recent research, approximately 74 percent of African American students and Latino adolescents receive "regular"

FIGURE 10.1 Long-Term Trend NAEP Reading. Differences between Average Test Scores of Whites, Black, and Hispanics (ages 17, 13, 9)

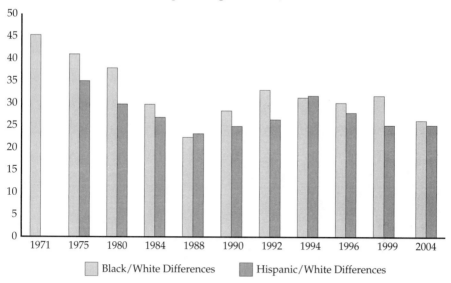

Black/White Differences   Hispanic/White Differences

Source: U.S. Department of Education, National Center for Educational Statistics, National Assessment of Educational Progress. (2004). Long-Term Trend Assessment Data. (Note: Data not available for Hispanic students until 1975.)

high school diplomas. An additional 10 to 12 percent of students of color who drop out go on to earn a GED (Roy and Mishel, 2008). Almost four times as many African American students and five times as many Latino American students take the SATs as did in 1996 (College Entrance Examination Board, 1996; 2008). In the last thirty years, the number of African American students attending college has doubled. In the same period, the number of Latino American students attending college has quadrupled. The gap between the scores of white and African American children on the National Assessment of Educational Progress (NAEP) in reading has decreased by almost half; the gap between white and Latino American students, by 38 percent. The gap in NAEP scores in math has decreased by 45 percent for African Americans and by 40 percent for Latino Americans (Kewal Ramani, Gilbertson, Fox, and Provasnik, 2007). See Figures 10.1 and 10.2.

Societal gains in eliminating some of the harshest forms of racial and ethnic discrimination have resulted in increased economic possibilities for African and Latino Americans who complete college. Now, on average, men of color earn almost 80 percent as much as white men; women of color earnings equal those of their white counterparts (Kewal Ramani, Gilbertson, Fox, and Provasnik, 2007). However, between one quarter and one third of children of color live in poverty; only 10 percent of white children do. By the time children from low-income families come to school, they already lag behind wealthier children socially, academically, and physically. Schools should close those gaps—and can, if all levels of government provide appropriate resources and support.

FIGURE 10.2 Long-Term Trend NAEP Mathematics. Differences between Average Test Scores of Whites, Blacks, and Hispanics (ages 17, 13, 9)

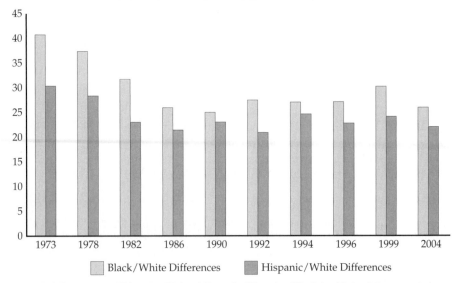

Black/White Differences   Hispanic/White Differences

Source: U.S. Department of Education, National Center for Educational Statistics, National Assessment of Educational Progress. (2004). Long-Term Trend Assessment Data.

If we want to eliminate poverty and the "underclass" in American society, we need to ensure that every child has equal educational opportunity. The academic achievement gap is the most important civil rights issue of the new century. Integration, affirmative action, Title I, and Head Start are legacies from those who knew school achievement was key to creating a more just society. Maintaining, extending, and even expanding these programs and policies is the best way to close the gap that prevents people of color from taking their rightful place in the United States.

Integration

In 1954 the Supreme Court ruled in the landmark case, *Brown v. Board of Education of Topeka, Kansas,* that laws assigning students to school based on their race were unconstitutional. Segregated schools could never be equal, the Court declared in its unanimous ruling. The laws violated the Fourteenth Amendment's guarantee that the rights of all Americans deserved equal protection. Being separated from white students engendered feelings of inferiority in students of color and jeopardized their futures. The desegregation struggle for Hispanic Americans began differently. In many parts of the country, their segregation from Anglo students was not based on their "race," for the courts had declared them "white." States passed laws requiring that all instruction be conducted in English. Children of Spanish heritage were presumed to be "deficient" in English. So, without being evaluated, they were placed in separate classes or schools. There were 28 lawsuits brought by Mexican Americans between 1925 and 1985. One of them, *Mendez v. Westminster* (1946), used a framework that would later be articulated in *Brown* (Wilson, 2003). Mexican American lawyers came to understand that the power of *Brown* could be utilized for their own struggle. In *Cisneros v. Corpus Christi ISD* and in *Keyes v. School District Number One, Denver,* the courts ruled that Hispanics could suffer the same kind of discrimination as blacks and were, therefore, eligible to receive the same kind of remedies—namely, desegregated schools (Wilson, 2003).

The struggle to carry out the Court's ruling was difficult—at times even violent. Two centuries of belief in white superiority did not disappear overnight and could not be "court-ordered" away. In the South, governors turned students away from schools they attempted to integrate. State troopers protected crowds of angry whites while leaving black schoolchildren vulnerable to expressions of hatred. School districts closed down rather than integrate. Many whites attended newly created private schools exempt from desegregation orders. Children of color were completely shut out. It took almost two decades for every state in the South to begin to comply with court orders to desegregate. In the North, the problem was different, but equally difficult. There, most metropolitan areas were segregated by economics. Schools reflected housing patterns of communities and de facto segregation developed. Courts began to order school districts to assign students to schools outside their neighborhoods to desegregate them and transport them to their new schools. Many urban whites already felt "left behind" in the movement to the suburbs their wealthier neighbors began in the 1930s and 1940s. Taking away their neighborhood schools was the last straw. In the 1970s, the "busing" issue heated up and sometimes violent protests took place in large cities outside the South. The federal courts' uncompromising commitment in the early desegregation period meant, however, there was no turning back. All across the country school districts attempted to comply with desegregation orders. Creative opportunities for all students resulted including magnet schools whose innovative programs were designed to attract white students to attend integrated schools (Lewis, 1965; Sarratt, 1966; Cecelski, 1994; Taylor, 1998; Orfield, 2001).

Even though it was a tremendous struggle, desegregation was worth the effort. The integration era was a period of dramatic changes in the academic achievement gap. The difference in standardized tests scores between students of color and whites decreased dramatically in the years when integration plans were being implemented (National Center for Education Statistics, 2005). Students of color who attended desegregated schools, especially if they began to do so in the early grades, had educational achievement levels one grade higher than they would have attained in a segregated school (Mahard and Crain, 1984). African American and Latino students who attended desegregated schools were less likely to become teenage parents or delinquents. They also were more likely to graduate from high school, enroll in and be successful in college (Liebman, 1990; Orfield and Eaton, 1996; Orfield, 2001). "Racially integrated schools prepare students to be effective citizens in our pluralistic society, further social cohesion, and reinforce democratic values. They promote cross-racial understanding, reduce prejudice, improve critical thinking skills and academic achievement, and enhance life opportunities for students of all races. These benefits are maximized when schools are structured in ways that optimize intergroup contact. Communities also benefit from a potential work-force that is better prepared for a global economy, reduced residential segregation, and increased parental involvement in schools—all of which increase the stability of communities" (Orfield, Frankenburg, and Garces, 2008).

Despite its success, integration has become increasingly difficult to maintain. Relying only on the limited power of the courts to sustain this policy has had disastrous consequences. The Supreme Court has narrowly defined the role of the judicial branch in creating desegregated schools. The courts can intervene only in cases where segregation results from previous governmental policies. If, for example, a school district constructed schools in racially isolated neighborhoods, then it can be held responsible for the resulting segregation. In such a case, the courts can order integration (*Keyes v. School District No. 1, Denver, Colorado,* 1973). If, however, the segregation is the result of individuals' choices—such as living in a more expensive suburb rather than the city—school districts cannot be forced to remedy the resulting segregation (*Milliken v. Bradley,* 1974). In addition to these understandings of when the courts can order integration, the increasing absence of whites in urban public schools also has caused a decrease in integration efforts. Once a school district has demonstrated it has done everything to desegregate schools and programs, it can be declared "unitary" and released from desegregation orders. School districts then can return to neighborhood school policies, even if they result in resegregation. The Supreme Court has even ruled that municipalities cannot protect the gains of the desegregation era by student assignment polices that maintain a racial balance comparable to that of the community—even when the voters and their elected officials deem those policies to be absolutely necessary to providing equal opportunity for every child in their school district (*Parents Involved in Community Schools Inc. v. Seattle School District, 2007; Meredith v. Jefferson County (Ky.) Board of Education,* 2007).

The combination of court rulings, school district decisions, and white flight does not mean the effort to integrate American schools has been lost. It does mean that a renewed commitment at the local level to create schools with diverse student populations is required. States could provide extra funds to urban and suburban municipalities that create consolidated, metropolitan school districts. Such systems could create extraordinary magnet schools that students of all races and ethnicities would be eager to attend. If communities became convinced once again of the value of integrated schools for all children, they could pressure legislatures to authorize and fund such efforts. They could use the political process and create constitutionally viable policies and practices that would support a new mandate for integration.

Head Start

In 1965, Congress funded an innovative program for preschoolers based on the belief that children born to poor families faced disadvantages that translated into school difficulties. Head Start goes far beyond traditional preschool programs. It attempts to address a multitude of factors affecting poor children and their families. It offers opportunities for three- and four-year-old children to become "school-ready" through a variety of programs (U.S. Department of Health and Human Services, 2008). The bill authorizing the program stated, "It is the purpose of this subchapter to promote school readiness by enhancing the social and cognitive development of low-income children through the provision, to low-income children and their families, of health, educational, nutritional, social, and other services that are determined, based on family needs assessments, to be necessary" (Head Start Act, 2007).

Head Start is a remarkably effective program. It may well be the most researched social service program in our history, and the conclusions are impressive. Assessments show that Head Start children go to school more ready to learn, like school, try to do their best, and get along well with their teachers and peers (U.S. Department of Health and Human Services, 2005). Unlike other poor children, Head Start graduates enter kindergarten meeting national norms in early reading and writing and close to those norms in math and vocabulary. They are healthier in general and have fewer health-related absences from school. Even siblings of children who attend Head Start programs appear to benefit, even if they themselves do not participate in the program (Garces, Thomas, and Currie, 2002).

For more than forty years, the Head Start program received bipartisan support in Congress and was a relatively uncontroversial program. It was underfunded; only about half of the eligible children and families were enrolled. Because the income guidelines for eligibility were lower than any other federal program—including the Women, Infant, and Children (WIC) and the school lunch programs—one million of the poorest children in the country never received the proven benefits of Head Start. In 2003, however, when the Head Start law was due to be reauthorized by Congress, the Bush administration and Republican members of Congress were opposed unless burdensome new requirements were met. The political battle continued for four years. The agenda was clearly ideological. Advocates of privatization schemes such as vouchers and charter schools testified in favor of similar programs for preschoolers. The emphasis on testing that has characterized K–12 education under No Child Left Behind was proposed for two-, three-, and four-year-olds, as well (Klein, 2007). As the battle continued, funding for Head Start was frozen for six years, and hours of operation, transportation services, and support staff were cut in centers across the country. By 2008, only 40 percent of eligible children were enrolled. A reauthorization bill was finally passed late in 2007, but although income eligibility requirements were raised making more children eligible, the funding for the program was cut by $10 million and no catch-up monies were allocated (Jacobson, 2008; National Head Start Association, 2008). Politicians who are serious about closing the academic achievement gap need to stop kidding themselves and the American people. They need to fund the program fully so that all eligible children can take part. Anything less is simply political smoke and mirrors, not good public policy.

Title I

In 1965, as a follow-up to the Civil Rights Act of the previous year, Congress passed the Elementary and Secondary Education Act. The bill was based on the understanding that inequalities in educational opportunities were responsible for the academic achievement gap between poor and privileged children and between whites and students of color. The federal government, through this legislation, began to provide financial assistance to school districts with large numbers of low-income families. In addition, it provided money for library improvement, instructional materials, educational innovations, and research. It has been revised and reauthorized every five years since. Over time it has come to include funding for bilingual education, drug education, school lunch and breakfast programs. The federal government has also, through this law, increased resources for the education of Native Americans (Sadker and Sadker, 2002). The aspect of this legislation that most directly affects students in schools where families have low incomes is usually referred to as Title I.

In the 1980s when Title I experienced high levels of growth in its funding, it enabled schools to address the needs of their students. The increase in Title I money occurred at the same time as the increase in the average test scores of children of color. The differences between white and both African American and Latino students narrowed steadily until 1988 (Campbell, Hombo, and Mazzeo, 2000). Title I was an important factor in reducing the academic achievement gap in the 1970s and 1980s (Center on Educational Policy, 2005).

When progress made in closing the achievement gap stalled in the early 1990s, Title I was revised to reflect increasing knowledge of what kinds of programs actually benefit children. We have moved, for example, away from "pull-out" programs in which disadvantaged students were taken from their classrooms and given extra help to whole school reform programs. Research had shown that the remedial instruction children received was not enough to close the achievement gap between students in high- and low-poverty schools. Studies have found that expectations were lower overall in high-poverty schools and that students who attended them achieved less than students in low-poverty schools, no matter what their own family income level might be (Chait et al., 2001). Now, efforts funded by Title I go toward setting high standards for all children in poor schools and for providing instruction that enables them to meet those goals.

Title I has been critical in reforming high-poverty schools and promoting achievement. However, the No Child Left Behind Act has set the bar higher for students and school districts, and funding for Title I has not kept pace with those demands. In 2004, the Congress Research office reported appropriations for Title I provided only half the funds needed to serve all the children eligible for such help under NCLB (Center on Educational Policy, 2005). Approximately two-thirds of states reported the funding they received from the federal government was inadequate to pay for the services they were required to provide under the law (Center on Educational Policy, 2007). Federal district courts have ruled that states and district courts cannot be required to spend taxpayers' money to comply with a federal law. Yet, recent education appropriations bills have failed to provide the necessary funds. Over the life of the bill, No Child Left Behind has been underfunded by $70 million federal dollars—funding that state and local governments had been forced to attempt to provide (National Education Association, 2008). School districts are being forced to "earn" federal aid by increasing test scores, at the same time as funding for the programs that produce such results has become unreliable. Title I works—even in the highly politicized atmosphere created by No Child Left Behind. However, if the avowed aim is to close the academic achievement gap, mandating state and local government action without providing financial assistance is a recipe for failure.

Affirmative Action

Closing the academic achievement gap also requires a commitment to remedying past discriminatory practices through affirmative action policies. They are the most controversial of all the political legacies of the civil rights era—perhaps because they have been so effective at disturbing structures of racial and ethnic privilege. They have not always been implemented perfectly and certainly have not ended prejudice and discrimination.

For forty years Americans have attempted to deal with the effects of discrimination—for almost two centuries people of color were denied employment and educational opportunities because of race or ethnicity while white males received preferential treatment. Before affirmative action, for example, it once was legal to pay white workers more than people of color for doing the same job and to have separate sections in the "want-ads" for each group. Employers could refuse to hire people because of the color of their skin or the place they or their parents were born. Even private schools, colleges, and universities could refuse to admit students based on race or ethnicity. Schools could set "quotas" limiting their number of nonwhite students. Colleges and universities insisted students abide by segregated housing policies or would transfer a roommate simply because of race or ethnicity. White Americans didn't wake up one morning and decide such practices were unfair and had to be eliminated. It took a long, slow process in which people of color and their allies demanded everyone be given the equal protection the Fourteenth Amendment guaranteed (Tierney, 2007).

Even when it became illegal to continue such practices, their consequences lingered and adversely affected people of color. "The disadvantages to people of color and the benefits to white people are passed on to each succeeding generation unless remedial action is taken" (Kivel, 1996, p. 2). Discrimination people's ancestors faced continues to affect them generations later. Because one family faced little prejudice, its members may have, through contacts with their friends, obtained well-paying jobs, purchased a home in a neighborhood with good schools, learned about cultural events and institutions, and gone to college. A family that faced more discrimination would have few of those advantages. Their friends would have been as shut out from information about jobs, culture, and education as they were. The cycle would perpetuate itself for many years.

Affirmative action is meant to break this cycle by outlawing prejudice in favor of whites in hiring and admission policies, and starting a larger process of creating equal opportunity. If a person of color is qualified for a job or a school, neither an employer nor an admissions officer can turn them down simply because of race or ethnicity. If two equally qualified people seek the same benefit, affirmative action requires the job or college placement be offered first to the person of color. The law also allows employers or schools to choose a person of color whose qualifications are roughly comparable, but not exactly equal, to those of a white person. By providing such opportunities for members of groups who experienced previous discrimination, we started to end the cycle described before. Now people of color have access to jobs or education, can begin to accumulate both material and cultural "wealth" to pass on to their descendants, and have a chance to experience the "rising tide that lifts all boats" in America.

Clearly, affirmative action policies have helped to narrow the academic achievement gap. Since discriminatory admission policies are illegal, qualified African American and Latino students now can seek admission to any college or university and entertain reasonable expectations of success. Young people condemned by society to attend inferior public schools but who demonstrate commitment and academic potential can be admitted to many schools, even if their test scores are lower than those of their white counterparts.

Opponents of affirmative action protest that it's not fair. The question is, not fair to whom? There are few, if any, complaints about higher education policies that are equally "unfair." Colleges have preferential recruiting and admission policies for veterans, children of alumni, athletes, and students whose families are wealthy enough to afford the tuition with no financial help from the school. Members of these groups do not have to have exactly the same test scores as other applicants to be admitted. These policies represent honest attempts by colleges and universities to create winning teams, balance budgets, and reward school loyalty and patriotism. Many argue that these goals are no more morally acceptable than efforts to eliminate and compensate for institutional effects of racism and ethnic prejudice (American Association for Affirmative Action, 2008).

A compelling case can be made that affirmative action in educational settings has benefits for all students, not just those of color. There is a growing body of evidence that students educated in universities, colleges, and graduate programs where there is a diverse population actually experience academic gains. They learn to think in more complex ways. Diversity on a college campus directly increases the numbers of interactions among members of racial and ethnic groups typically isolated from one another. These interactions indirectly lead to greater understanding of people whose backgrounds are different from students' own (Pike, Kuh, and Gonyea, 2007). A recent survey of 1990–1994 graduates of the University of Michigan showed that more than a decade after graduation, they still believed being a member of a diverse undergraduate student body had helped them professionally and personally. Researchers found that alumni identified specific benefits such as being able to relate to diverse groups of patients, clients, and students as a result of being part of a heterogeneous student body (Pluviose, 2008). The Supreme Court recognized the need for leaders who, through their educational experiences, are prepared to understand the ideas and cultures of those whose backgrounds differ from their own. This interest is serious enough to justify the use of race as one of a range of factors a college or university can consider in admissions decisions, so long as the institution does not establish a quota system and does not make an applicant's race or ethnicity the defining factor in the acceptance (*Grutter v. Bollinger*).

Those who attack affirmative action need to reflect carefully before using slogans such as "reverse discrimination." Quite often what they describe is not discrimination but a loss of privilege. Saying you favor equal opportunity but opposing every effort society makes to ensure that equality is hypocritical. "Color-blind policies will treat individuals equitably when the community no longer has any vestiges of racism. Where race continues to play a major role in the ability of all citizens to participate fully in the public sphere, then color-conscious policies need to remain in place" (Tierney, 2007).

We must continue to work to eliminate the last effects of discrimination in elementary and high schools, so that race is no longer a factor in a young person's opportunity to become prepared for higher education. As we engage in that long struggle for a better future, however, we must keep faith in the present and maintain our commitment to providing short-term remedies through affirmative action policies.

Social change takes place slowly, and closing the academic achievement gap between students of color and their white counterparts constitutes a dramatic change in American society. Some advocates for reform argue that minimizing government's role in schooling will produce better results than the programs described in this chapter. However, the results of their experiments are not convincing. Students of color are isolated in schools with the least experienced and qualified teachers—and with the lowest test scores. Charter schools have been successful at controlling students but not in raising their academic achievement. The elimination of affirmative action programs has decreased the numbers of students of color in colleges and universities. Hesitancy about enforcing those programs has also resulted in fewer African American and Latino American faculty members. Linking Title I funds to results of high-stakes tests has caused large numbers of public schools to be ranked as "failing"—even though the funds needed to produce the required results have been absent. Making the reauthorization of Head Start into an ideological battle has caused the loss of staff and limited the number of children who can be served. Arguing that programs are not effective when they have been starved for funds, misrepresented in the media, handcuffed by decisions made by right-wing activist district judges and Supreme Court justices is disingenuous and deprives millions of American children of equal opportunity for academic achievement. Knowingly or unknowingly, these policies weaken Head Start, racial integration, Title I, and affirmative action and secure advantages for already privileged white children while limiting the prospects of students of color. The consequences of abandoning the remedies of the past will fall on all of us. Knowing the possibilities for success are extremely limited, young people lose faith in education. Such hopelessness is a breeding ground for social alienation. Without a stake in society, people have no reason to obey its laws or support it against its enemies. The nation's security demands we maintain our commitment to providing programs that promote educational equality. Fully funding and supporting Head Start, Title I, desegregation, and affirmative action are the best ways to fulfill that obligation.

POSITION 2: FOR INNOVATIVE SOLUTIONS

On education, we must trust students to learn if given the chance, and empower parents to demand results from our schools. In neighborhoods across our country, there are boys and girls with dreams—and a decent education is their only hope of achieving them. Six years ago, we came together to pass the No Child Left Behind Act, and today no one can deny its results. Last year, fourth- and eighth-graders achieved the highest math scores on record. Reading scores are on the rise. African American and Hispanic students posted all-time highs. Now we must work together to increase accountability, add flexibility for states and districts, reduce the number of high school dropouts, provide extra help for struggling schools.

—Bush, 2008

Reconsidering the Academic Achievement Gap

A decade of differences in academic achievement between young white Americans and their African American and Latino counterparts was a nagging, persistent reminder of just how ineffective large, bureaucratic governmental programs actually are. On the National Assessment of Educational Progress— "The Nation's Report Card"—students of color made progress in closing the gap between them and their white counterparts during the 1970s and 1980s. Then, for almost a decade, progress stalled. At all ages and in all subjects, the gap was larger in 2000 than it was in 1988—in some cases by as much as 50 percent (Campbell, Hombo, and Mazzeo, 2000). The average SAT scores of African Americans were 195 points lower than the average scores of white test-takers; for Latinos, the difference was 100 points less. Although the gap narrowed, African American and Latino students still had lower rates of college entrance and completion and lower grades than did white students (Steele, 1992; Campbell, Hombo, and Mazzeo, 2000; Haycock, 2001).

These statistics painted a gloomy picture. Some gains made through older strategies were lost and others too small to be meaningful. The remedies applied in the 1970s and 1980s suited the causes of the achievement gap as we then understood them; our national culture and the political climate has changed. There is great pessimism about government's ability to solve problems and more irritation with the ways it interferes with individual freedom. These attitudes are dramatically different from those of the 1960s and 1970s when a liberal optimism pervaded the country, promising that with enough regulation and tax dollars we could fix anything that was wrong with America.

Blaming the Victims

Clearly, there is no one easy answer to the question of why African American and Latino children continue to have lower scores on standardized tests and generally experience less academic success than white students. The reasons are complex and fluid and probably interact with one another in ways we have yet to understand. We can, however, think of them in two categories: sociocultural and school related.

For most of the last thirty years, we emphasized sociocultural causes, believing segregation, discrimination, and effects of poverty were mostly to blame for the low levels of achievement among students of color. Our thinking about these causes resulted in national soul-searching and in making necessary corrections to laws and policies—for example, putting an end to racially separate and unequal schools.

We also focused on what we perceived to be "lacks" in the children and families we hoped to serve. We believed parents' low level of educational achievement, lack of financial resources, and child-rearing practices all contributed to their children's low levels of academic achievement. We thought by creating antipoverty programs such as Head Start, Food Stamps, Job Training, and Medicaid, and finding ways of connecting poor people to them, we'd improve children's chances of succeeding in schools.

We thought children of color were themselves partly to blame for their educational difficulties. Linguistic differences between them and the school communities created problems, but the young people were unwilling to give up their unique ways of speaking. They used drugs, became parents themselves in their teens, and appeared to prefer the culture of the streets to the promise of entrance into mainstream America. So we introduced drug and sex education into school curricula, introduced bilingual education, and attempted to teach the values of hard work and perseverance.

The solutions we created in response to our understandings, however, were only partially effective and, in some cases, actually have worsened the problems they were intended to correct. For example, thirty years ago, we believed the academic achievement gap was caused by segregation and discriminatory practices. Segregation isolated children of color and convinced them that they were inferior to whites (*Brown v. Board of Education*, 1954). If we could only get them into integrated schools, then their success rates would soar. So the government mandated desegregation programs all across the country. Most of the policies involved busing children around cities, increasing their time away from home and their studies, removing many urban children from their neighborhoods. In many cases, such policies destroyed the work of generations of city-dwellers who had painstakingly built up connections between their schools and communities (Cecelski, 1994; Taylor, 1998). Parent involvement became more difficult and involved long treks to schools in unfamiliar areas of the city. Eventually, those who could—admittedly, most often whites—voted with their feet and left the cities and "integrated" public schools. As a result, in most cities the majority of the population overwhelmingly consists of people of color. Suburbs are equally segregated; it's just that whites are the majority there.

Consequently, schools are becoming increasingly racially isolated (Orfield, Frankenburg, and Garces, 2008). There are many reasons for these changes in school populations. Some are relatively benign, such as people seeking the more relaxed lifestyle of the suburbs. Some are more troubling. Forced integration did not change people's minds and hearts; racial prejudice still exists and some whites have expressed their preferences by moving away from neighborhoods with diverse populations. Court-ordered desegregation of schools did not prevent the continued residential isolation between white people and those of color.

The end of Court-mandated integration actually may be a good thing. There was a kind of racial superiority implicit in the frantic efforts to get children of color into "good" schools—schools whose populations historically had been white (*Parents Involved in Community Schools Inc. v. Seattle School District*, 2007). The same sense permeated attitudes toward African American and Latino American parents; middle-class European-American practices were set as the norm and the cultural differences among parenting styles were deemed "deficits" that had to be corrected (Gosa and Alexander, 2007; Guilamo-Ramos et al., 2007; Mandara, 2006). Similarly, affirmative action programs also contained a hidden belief in the inferiority of some groups of people: they are simply less able and, without special treatment, cannot compete with those who are more competent (Townes, 2008). Even the way young people of color dressed and talked, the music they liked, the foods they ate, and the recreational activities they enjoyed were seen as "improper" and as hindrances to their future success. They were placed on notice that were obliged to "act white" in order to be successful and, forced to choose between their identity and academic success, they often chose membership in their primary community over acceptance by teachers (Ford, Grantham, and Whiting, 2008; Freyer and Torelli, 2005).

Analyses of the academic achievement gap between children of color and their white counterparts that focus on cultural differences between the groups but ignore socioeconomic ones are incomplete. Nearly 2 million of the 5.6 million American children living in extreme poverty are black; 1.6 million are Latino. In the first decade of the twenty-first century, government funding decreased for housing, health, and nutrition programs, while the number of children living in poverty rose dramatically (Children's Defense Fund, 2008). The interaction between these background characteristics and school-related factors—such as the quality and experience of teachers, standards of instruction and accountability, and relations between family, community, and educational personnel—are the most likely explanation for the academic achievement gap (Orfield and Lee, 2005; Rothstein, Jacobsen, and Wilder, 2008). Explanations that "blame the victim" of discriminatory policies and practices miss the mark.

School-Related Causes of the Academic Achievement Gap

In the past decade, researchers have identified several school-related causes of the academic achievement gap. In many public schools, children of color encountered teachers who had low expectations of them and viewed them through a lens of prejudice. Teachers did not search aggressively for instructional strategies to help African American or Latino American students who were having difficulty, having already concluded that those children had limited potential. In turn, students of color internalized these low expectations and did not see themselves as capable of succeeding in school (Diamond, Randolph, and Spillane, 2004). Children of color were less likely than their white counterparts to attend schools with experienced teachers, more likely to have teachers without college preparation in subjects they were teaching, and twice as likely to have teachers without state certification (Clotfelter, Ladd, Vigdor, and Wheeler, 2007; Peske and Haycock, 2006). All these factors negatively affected student performance.

In schools that served these students, policies and practices too often accepted and contributed to the achievement gap. Students of color were more likely than their white peers to attend schools that prepared them for industrial jobs that no longer existed (Haycock, 2003). Students of color were less likely than their white peers to attend schools that offered advanced math and science or be prepared to take advantage of them if such opportunities were presented. They too often had been tracked into "general" or "basic" courses where the curriculum was simplified and teachers covered less material, gave less homework, and rewarded low-level performance with high grades. This failure to take high-level coursework resulted in lower scores on standardized tests and lower likelihood of college enrollment—and so, contributed greatly to the achievement gap (Tyson, Lee, Borman, and Hanson, 2007). By opting out or being forced out of the most challenging curriculum, the futures of students of color were being limited.

Teachers and administrators complained that African American and Latino American parents were not involved enough in schools. Yet, most research showed that African American and Latino parents wanted to be involved in their children's schooling but were often prevented from doing so by school policies and practices. School personnel often failed to take the most elementary steps to increase parent involvement. For example, when Latino parents came to school, they often encountered a staff that spoke only English and interpreters were rare (Wong and Hughes, 2006).

School districts that serve students of color have high mobility rates. Children routinely move from one to school to another in the district *within* a school year. Yet urban districts did little to respond to that reality. They did not standardize curriculum, textbooks, or instruction. Students who moved found themselves repeating material they already had learned or being challenged to do work for which they had not been prepared. They often lost heart and stopped trying (Smith, Fien, and Paine, 2008).

Policies and practices that ignored or disparaged children's cultural lives also contributed to low academic achievement. Students who believed their teachers did not value their communities or background felt alienated from school. They found it difficult to respect the requests or suggestions of such adults—even when they were well-intentioned and, if taken, might have led to improvements in the students' life chances. Instead, the students resisted, rebelled, were often disciplined and suspended. Their performance on high-stakes tests suffered and perpetuated the academic achievement gap (Fenning and Rose, 2007).

Closing the Academic Achievement Gap: New Solutions

Studying and coming to understand the socioeconomic and school-related causes of the academic achievement gap and the intersection between them has resulted in new solutions, which, although relatively recent, have already proven to be effective.

In 2002, Congress reauthorized federal assistance to elementary and secondary schools in the No Child Left Behind Act (NCLB). The descendant of the original Elementary and Secondary Education Act (ESEA) passed in 1965 during the heyday of the War of Poverty, NCLB has a dramatically different approach to the academic achievement gap. It is true that some teachers and administrators accomplished a great deal with the funding ESEA provided. The drill and practice approach to remediation most often subsidized by the legislation did improve basic skills of many students of color. Test scores rose in the 1970s and 1980s but then stalled as the solutions of the 1960s proved insufficient to help students master higher level skills such as analyzing, not merely decoding, what they were reading and using critical-thinking skills to solve complex mathematical problems. No Child Left Behind was an attempt to use the influence of the federal government to help all students meet the more challenging standards of a new century.

One of the most significant aspects of NCLB with regard to closing the achievement gap is the emphasis on state and local accountability for the progress of all students. Each state must specify what children are to learn, when they are to learn it, and how their learning will be assessed. Teachers, administrators, and school districts are held accountable for their students' progress through an in-depth, appropriate, and on-going testing system developed by each state for students in grades three to eight. In addition, a group of fourth- and eighth-graders in each state must participate in the National Assessment of Educational Progress (NAEP) each year. In reporting the results of both the state tests and the NAEP, states must disaggregate the scores. That is, they must be reported by students' race, ethnicity, and poverty status. If a school fails to make "Adequate Yearly Progress" toward the goal of having 100 percent of students meet state standards in literacy and math by 2014, it suffers serious consequences. Students immediately must be allowed to transfer to a school within the district that *has made* progress; after three years without satisfactory improvement, districts must provide supplementary tutoring options for all students; if in five years, the goals are not met, the school can be closed, reorganized, and reopened with new administrators, faculty, and staff (U.S. Department of Education, 2002).

The accountability provisions in NCLB was accompanied by greater freedom for innovation. The bill has promoted the creation of educational settings where students can receive the instruction, attention, and support they need to meet high standards, score well on standardized tests, and graduate from high school prepared to attend college. These include "small schools" and "charter schools." Both types of schools serve around 400 students, allowing a personal setting where every student is known by several adults who serve as advisers and confidants. Families are seen as members of the school community—teachers, administrators, and family members work together to ensure student success. They are relatively autonomous, even though they are still part of the school district; the school community is able to make decisions about its direction. They have a distinctive and focused curriculum and use multiple types of assessments (Center for Education Reform, 2008; Small Schools Project, 2008).

NCLB also requires that each child has a "highly qualified" teacher in every class and every grade, one who has a bachelor's degree, state certification, and knowledge of the discipline in which he or she teaches. Recruiting and retaining such teachers in urban and rural areas has been historically difficult. Now, states have been forced to utilize every effective strategy to attract good teachers in order to meet NCLB requirements. Teacher education programs have been strengthened and streamlined. Alternative routes to teacher certification have been established. Notable among these are "Fellows" programs in major cities that have in the past had chronic shortages of qualified teachers (Chicago Teaching Fellows, 2008; D.C. Teaching Fellows, 2008; New York Teaching Fellows, 2008; Philadelphia Teaching Fellows, 2008). These programs recruit people with experience in business, research, engineering, and other professions to become teachers. In addition, privately funded programs such as Teach For America (TFA) have enticed graduates from elite colleges and universities to work for several years in high needs schools. TFA "corps members" and Fellows receive a seven-week-long summer training before becoming classroom teachers. Generally, they make a two-year commitment, during which time they receive the same salary as other beginning teachers in the district and complete a certification or graduate degree program at a deeply discounted price. Although most TFA corps members generally leave teaching after two years, some continue to work for educational equity in other ways. Districts tend to have somewhat better retention with Teaching Fellows.

The connection between families and schools is another area in which new responses to the academic achievement gap have been developed. NCLB allows federal funds to be used to improve communications with parents, make child care available at school events, and provide literacy instruction to family members. It even respects parents' rights to use funds designated for supplemental tutoring services in faith-based and other community organizations whose values and cultures match the family's own. Instead of viewing parents as impediments to improving student performance, this new generation of remedies sees parents as full partners in the reform effort (Small Schools Project, 2008; Center for Education Reform, 2008).

These new approaches to closing the academic achievement gap are producing promising results. More students in low-poverty schools are being taught by highly qualified teachers (U.S. Department of Education, 2008b). Parents are reporting high levels of satisfaction with their children's schooling even in urban areas where problems were rampant in the past (New York City Department of Education, 2008). Graduation rates are improving (U.S. Department of Education, 2008a).

The achievement gap, as measured on the long-term trend National Assessment of Education Progress (NAEP), is closing. "The average reading and mathematics scores of Black and Hispanic nine-year-olds in 2004 were the highest of any assessment year. For Black thirteen-year-olds, reading and mathematics scores were higher in 2004 than the scores in the early 1970s, and the 2004 mathematics score was higher than in any previous assessment year. For Hispanic thirteen-year-olds, mathematics scores were higher in 2004 than in any previous assessment year. In contrast to the overall national results, the average scores of Black and Hispanic seventeen-year-olds were higher in 2004 than in the early 1970s. Black seventeen-year-olds improved 25 points in reading between 1971 and 2004, and 15 points in mathematics between 1973 and 2004 on a 0–500 point scale. Hispanic seventeen-year-olds improved 12 points in reading between 1975 (the first year the reading achievement of Hispanics was specifically measured) and 2004, and 12 points in mathematics between 1973 and 2004 (26 vs. 32 points)" (U.S. Department of Education, 2008a, Indicators 16 and 17).

We have entered a new era in American public education. The remedies of the past are no longer suitable. While government programs and attempts at social engineering reaped some benefits, their usefulness is over. There is no longer any room for promises without proof. The new solutions for the academic achievement gap more effective because they are data-driven, rely on market forces, and provide teachers, students, and parents with choices—not mandates. These fresh remedies focus attention where it belongs—on schools and what happens in classrooms. Time and lives would be wasted by perpetuating inadequate ideas from the past. We cannot champion the cause of equal opportunity by spending large sums of money without holding anyone accountable for results, by forcing families to send their children to schools they do not choose, or by making unjust allowances for past discrimination. We must continue to experiment with solutions—keeping those that work, discarding those that do not—until we have achieved a new kind of justice—good schooling for all children, regardless of their race or ethnicity.

From that perspective, researchers have begun to show that school reform alone is not sufficient. The "equity gap" between white students and those of color encompasses not only differences on test scores; it also includes "basic academic skills, critical thinking and problem solving skills, social skills and work ethic, readiness for citizenship and community responsibility, a foundation for lifelong physical health, foundation for lifelong emotional health, appreciation of the arts and literature, and preparation for skilled work for those youths not destined for academic college" (Rothstein, Jacobson, and Wilder, 2008, p. 12). With regard to these outcomes, white students' average rating exceeds that of their African American counterparts by almost 20 percent. It would appear that Systemic Standards Based Reform (SSBR) must be supplemented with other resources in order to secure educational equality. "Achieving this goal may require an intervention strategy that acknowledges and addresses out-of-school factors that significantly influence student performance. School-linked services and the more extensive full-service community schools provide a wide range of services to students and their families through partnerships with local organizations, thereby attempting to mitigate the numerous pathologies that undermine good outcomes for poor and minority children. The services, which include parent education, after school programs, health services, mental health services, preschool, and on-site assistance from social welfare services, are funded by reallocating resources from various child and family programs. We posit that the combination of fully funded SSBR and school-linked services/community schools would improve student performance and reduce the achievement gap to a greater extent than either of these strategies could alone." (Kirst and Rhodes, 2007).

For Discussion

1. We might assume Latino children would face many academic challenges due to limited English language proficiency. However, the gap between their test scores and those of white students usually is less than the difference between black students' scores and those of whites. (See Figures 9.1 and 9.2.) How would you account for these findings? What factors might account for the differences?
2. The No Child Left Behind Act of 2002 requires states to report on student performance on standardized tests and to disaggregate that data by "race, gender, and other criteria to demonstrate not only how well students are achieving overall but also progress in closing the achievement gap between disadvantaged students and other groups of students" (U.S. Department of Education, 2002). Will the requirement to provide such data pressure school districts to improve instruction for children of color? Discuss why or why not.
3. Talk to an admissions counselor in your college or university about the institution's policy regarding affirmative action and admissions. Critique the policy from the point of view of its effectiveness in closing the academic achievement gap.
4. Using the NAEP database (http://nces.ed.gov/nationsreportcard/naepdata/search.asp), research the achievement gap in your state. Speculate on factors that may influence conditions in your state. Using databases and other sources of information, research and evaluate your state's efforts to close the gap.

References

American Association for Affirmative Action. (2008). "Statement of the American Association for Affirmative Action on the American Civil Rights Institute's Anti-Affirmative Action Campaign." www.affirmativeaction.org/news.html.

ANGUS, D., AND MIREL, J. (1999). *The Failed Promise of the American High School 1890–1995.* New York: Teachers College Press.

ANYON, J. (1997). *Ghetto Schooling.* New York: Teachers College Press.

Brown v. Board of Education of Topeka, Kansas. (1954). 347 U.S. 483.

BUSH, G. (2008). "State of the Union Address." www.whitehouse.gov/news/releases/2008/01/20080128-13.html.

CAMPBELL, J, HOMBO, C., AND MAZZEO, J. (2000). NAEP 1999 Trends in Academic Progress: Three Decades of Student Performance. National Assessment of Educational Progress. http://nces.ed.gov/nationsreportcard/pubs/main1999/2000469.asp.

CECELSKI, D. (1994). *Along Freedom Road.* Chapel Hill: University of North Carolina Press.

Center for Education Reform. (2008). "Charter School Laws." www.edreform.com/index.cfm?fuseAction=document&documentID=60.

Center on Educational Policy (2005). "Title I Funds: Who's Gaining, Who's Losing and Why?" Washington, DC. www.cep-dc.org/index.cfm?fuseaction=document.showDocumentByID&DocumentID=84&varuniqueuserid=00302986781.

———. (2007). *Reauthorizing the Elementary and Secondary Education Act of 1965: Recommendations from the Center on Education Policy.* Washington, DC: author.

CHAIT, R., et al. (2001). "High Standards for All Students: A Report from the National Assessment of Title I on Progress and Challenges Since the 1964 Reauthorization." Washington, DC: U.S. Department of Education. ERIC Document, ED 457280.

Chicago Teaching Fellows. (2008). "Chicago Teaching Fellows." www.chicagoteachingfellows.org.

Children's Defense Fund. (2008). "Trends in Child Poverty and Extreme Child Poverty." www.childrensdefense.org/site/PageServer?pagename=research_family_income_2006childpovertytrends.

College Entrance Examination Board. (1996). "1996 Profile of College-Bound Seniors." http://professionals.collegeboard.com/data-reports-research/sat/archived/1996

———. (2008). "2007 Profile of College-Bound Seniors." www.collegeboard.com/prod_downloads/about/news_info/cbsenior/yr2007/nationalreport.pdf.

D.C. Teaching Fellows. (2008). "D.C. Teaching Fellows." http://www.dcteachingfellows.org.

DESCHENES, S., CUBAN, L., AND TYACK, D. (2001). "Mismatch: Historical Perspectives on Schools and Students Who Don't Fit Them." *Teachers College Record* 103(4), 525–547.

DIAMOND, J., RANDOLPH, A., AND SPILLANE, J. (2004) "Teachers' Expectations and Sense of Responsibility for Student Learning: The Implications of School Race, Class, and Organizational Habitus." *Anthropology and Education Quarterly,* 35(1): 75–98.

FENNING, P. AND ROSE, J. (2007). "Overrepresentation of African American Students in Exclusionary Discipline The Role of School Policy." *Urban Education* 42(6): 536–559.

FORD, D., GRANTHAM, T. AND WHITING, G. (2008). "Another Look at the Achievement Gap." *Urban Education* 43(2): 216–239.

FRYER, R. AND TORELLI, P. (2005). "An Empirical Analysis of 'Acting White,'" National Bureau of Economic Research Working Paper 11334. http://post.economics.harvard.edu/faculty/fryer/papers/fryer_torelli.pdf.

GARCES, E., THOMAS, D., AND CURRIE, J. (2002). "Longer Term Effects of Head Start." *American Economic Review* 92 (4), 999.

GOSA, T. AND ALEXANDER, K. (2007). "Family (Dis)Advantage and the Educational Prospects of Better Off African American Youth: How Race Still Matters." *Teachers College Record* 109 (2): 285–321.

GUILAMO-RAMOS, V. et al. (2007). "Parenting Practices among Dominican and Puerto Rican Mothers." *Social Work* 52(1): 17–30.

HAYCOCK, K. (2001). "Closing the Achievement Gap." *Education Leadership,* 58(60). www.ascd.org/readingroom/edlead/0103/haycock.html.

———. (2003). "A New Core Curriculum For All: Aiming High For Other People's Children." *Thinking K-16* 7(1): 1–2.

Head Start Act. (2007). Sec. 636. [42 U.S.C. 9801]. http://eclkc.ohs.acf.hhs.gov/hslc/Program%20Design%20and%20Management/Head%20Start%20Requirements/Head%20Start%20Act/HS_Act_2007.pdf.

JENCKS, C., AND PHILLIPS, M., eds. (1998). *The Black-White Test Score Gap.* Washington, DC: Brookings Institution.

JOHNSON, L. B. (1996). *Public Papers on the Presidents of the United States: Lyndon B. Johnson, 1965.* Vol. I. Washington, DC: U.S. Government Printing Office. Entry 181, pp. 412–414.

KEWAL RAMANI, A., GILBERTSON, L., FOX, M., and PROVASNIK, S. (2007). *Status and Trends in the Education of Racial and Ethnic Minorities* (NCES 2007-039). National Center for Education Statistics, Institute of Education Sciences, U.S. Department of Education. Washington, DC.

Keyes v. School District No. 1, Denver, Colorado. (1973). 413 U.S. 189.

KIRST, M. AND RHODES, L. (2007). "Two Alternative Yet Complementary Conceptual Frameworks For Financing American Education." Seattle: Center on Reinventing Public Education, Working Paper No. 22. www.crpe.org/cs/crpe/view/csr_pubs/182.

KLEIN, A. (2007). "Head Start Measure Expected to Launch New Era for Program," *Education Week,* November 28.

KLUGER, R. (1975). *Simple Justice: This History of Brown v. Board of Education and Black America's Struggle for Equality.* New York: Knopf.

LEWIS, A. (1965). *Portrait of a Decade.* New York: Bantam Books.

LIEBMAN, J. (1990). "Desegregating Politics: All-Out School Desegregation Explained." *Columbia Law Review* 90, Column L, Rev. 1463.

MANDARA, J. (2006). "The Impact of Family Functioning on African American Males' Academic Achievement: A Review and Clarification of the Empirical Literature." *Teachers College Record* 108(2): 206–223.

MAHARD, R., and CRAIN, R. (1984). "Research on Minority Achievement in Desegregated Schools." In C. Rossell, and W. Hawley, eds., *The Consequences of School Desegregation,* Philadelphia: Temple University Press.

Mendez v. Westminister School District of Orange County. 64 F. Supp. 544 (D.C.CAL. 1946).

Meredith v. Jefferson County (Ky.) Board of Education (2007). 127 US 575.

Milliken v. Bradley. (1974). 419 U.S. 815.

National Education Association. (2008). "Stand Up For Children: *Pontiac v. Spellings.*" www.nea.org/lawsuit/index.html.

National Head Start Association. (2008). "Head Start Leaders Have High Hopes for New President and Congress." www.nhsa.org/press/News_Archived/index_news_061908.htm.

New York City Department of Education. (2008). "Learning Environment Survey 2007–2008." http://schools.nyc.gov/NR/rdonlyres/F3D9A118-C51E-4E23-841C-3DB5B24C87DC/40757/les2008citywide.pdf.

New York City Teaching Fellows. (2008). "New York City Teaching Fellows." www.nycteachingfellows.org.

ORFIELD, G. (2001). "Schools More Separate: Consequences of a Decade of Resegregation." The Civil Rights Project University of California at Los Angeles. www.civilrightsproject.ucla.edu/research/deseg/separate_schools01.php

ORFIELD, G., AND EATON, S. (1996). *Dismantling Desegregation.* New York: New Press.

ORFIELD, G. AND LEE, C. (2005). *Why Segregation Matters: Poverty and Educational Inequality.* Cambridge: Civil Rights Project.

ORFIELD, G., FRANKENBURG, E. AND GARCES, L. (2008). "Statement of American Social Scientists of Research on School Desegregation to the U.S. Supreme Court in Parents v. Seattle School District and Meredith v. Jefferson County." *Urban Review* 40:96–136.

Parents Involved in Community Schools Inc. v. Seattle School District. (2007). 127 US 2738.

PESKE, H. AND HAYCOCK, K. (2006). "Teaching Inequality." Washington, DC: Education Trust. www2.edtrust.org/NR/rdonlyres/010DBD9F-CED8-4D2B-9E0D-91B446746ED3/0/TQReportJune2006.pdf.

PIKE, G., KUH, G. AND GONYEA, R. (2007). "Evaluating the Rationale for Affirmative Action in College Admissions: Direct and Indirect Relationships between Campus Diversity and Gains in Understanding Diverse Groups." *Journal of College Student Development* 48 (2): 166–182.

PLUVIOSE, D. (2008). "American Association for Affirmation Action Conference Highlights Policy Action Themes." *Diverse: Issues in Higher Education* 22:28.

ROTHSTEIN, R., JACOBSEN, R., and WILDER, T. (2008). *A Report Card on Comprehensive Equity: Racial Gaps in the Nation's Youth Outcomes.* Washington, DC: Economic Policy Institute.

ROY, J. AND MISHEL, L. (2008). "Using Administrative Data to Estimate Graduation Rates: Challenges, Proposed Solutions and their Pitfalls." *Education Policy Analysis Archives* 16(11):1–34. www.epaa.info/ojs/index.php/epaa/article/view/EPAA_v16n11/13.

SADKER, M., and SADKER, D. (2002). *Teachers, Schools and Society.* New York: McGraw-Hill.

SARRATT, R. (1966). *The Ordeal of Desegregation.* New York: Harper and Row.

SMALL SCHOOLS PROJECT. (2008). "What are Small Schools?" www.smallschoolsproject .org/index.asp?siteloc=whysmall&section=whatss.

SMITH, J., FIEN, H., AND PAINE, S. (2008). "When *Mobility* Disrupts Learning." *Educational Leadership* 65(7): 59–63.

TIERNEY, W. (2007). "Merit and Affirmative Action in Education: Promulgating a Democratic Public Culture." *Urban Education* 42(5):385–402.

TAYLOR, S. (1998). *Desegregation in Boston and Buffalo.* Albany: SUNY Press.

TOWNES, G., (2008). "Affirmative Action A Hot Issue In 2008 Election," *The Amsterdam News,* April 17.

TUSHNET, M. (1987). *Segregated Education, 1925–1950.* Chapel Hill: University of North Carolina Press.

TYACK, D. (1974). *The One Best System: A History of American Urban Education.* Cambridge: Harvard University Press.

TYSON, W., LEE, R, BORMAN, K., AND HANSON, M. (2007). "Science, Technology, Engineering, and Mathematics (STEM) Pathways: High School Science and Math Coursework and Postsecondary Degree Attainment." *Journal Of Education For Students Placed At Risk,* 12(3), 243–270.

U.S. Department of Education. (2002). "No Child Left Behind Act." http://www.ed.gov/ policy/elsec/leg/esea02/index.html.

―――. (2008a). *The Conditions of Education, 2008.* Washington DC: National Center for Education Statistics. http://nces.ed.gov/pubsearch/pubsinfo.asp?pubid=2008031.

―――. (2008b). "Mapping Educational Progress, 2008." www.ed.gov/nclb/ accountability/results/progress/index.html

U.S. Department of Health and Human Services.(2005). "Head Start Impact Study: First Year Findings." Washington, DC: author. www.acf.hhs.gov/programs/opre/hs/ impact_study/reports/first_yr_execsum/first_yr_execsum.pdf.

―――. (2008). "About Head Start." http://eclkc.ohs.acf.hhs.gov/hslc/About%20 Head%20Start.

CHAPTER 11

Values/Character Education: Traditional or Liberational

Which and whose values should public schools teach, and why?

POSITION 1: TEACH TRADITIONAL VALUES

There is no more destructive force in your children's lives than American popular culture. It promotes the worst values in people and disguises them all as entertainment . . . Additionally, popular culture is pervasive, dominating virtually every part of our lives.

—Taylor, 2005, p. 4

Throughout history, and in cultures around the world, education rightly conceived has had two great goals: to help students become smart and to help them become good.

—Character Education Partnership, 2008, p. 8

American public schools, echoing the moral defects in American popular culture, commonly operate without an ethical compass. Schools should provide a firm education in ethical principles that help youth sort, analyze, and evaluate behaviors and values expressed in popular culture. This is character education, designed to instill and inspire good character—morally grounded behaviors and attitudes.

Unfortunately, schools are subject to the relativism that underlies much of life today. Relativism in schools reflects the ideas that (1) all values are relative, with none superior; (2) there is no enduring set of ethical standards; and (3) personal character is a matter of individual choice and particular situations. It incorporates situational ethics and egotistical rationalization to justify any values or actions. Relativism keeps such schools and their students adrift in a sea of personal and social temptations.

Sommers (1998) summarizes this position: "The last few decades of the twentieth century have seen a steady erosion of knowledge and a steady increase in moral relativism" (p. 33). She demonstrates the link betwen a host of other school problems and the fact that Johnny can't read, write, or count; continuing: "it is also true that Johnny is having difficulty distinguishing right from wrong. . . . Along with illiteracy and innumeracy, we must add deep moral confusion to the list of educational problems" (p. 31). This is a very serious problem that will continue to haunt American society until it is adequately addressed. Hansen (2001) notes, "Studies suggest that teaching is inherently a moral endeavor" (p. 826). Morality cannot be escaped by pretending schools are outside its sphere.

We are not born with a set of values, they are all—good and bad—learned. Although we learn values in many places, from many people, and through many media, schools form a particularly significant institution for imparting values. Blackburn (2001) points out, Aristotle "emphasized that it takes education and practice in order to become virtuous" (p. 113). Former Secretary of Education William Bennett (1992) highlights the tradition of common schools as the basis of common values, with leaders of the common school movement coming mainly from people who "saw the schools as upholders of standards of individual morality and small incubators of civic and personal virtue; the founders of the public schools had faith that public education could teach good moral and civic character from a common ground of American values" (p. 58).

Yet, as Bennett documents, schools lost this central purpose in a contemporary welter of value-neutral, value-relative, and anything-goes approaches to values education. The former position of schools was to be stalwart conveyors of good values and sound character, with exemplary moral and ethical modelling by school teachers and administrators. That has been replaced by an institutional blind eye to values and educator disinterest in, or fear of, maintaining high standards of morality and ethics for themselves and their students. Far too many public schools lack a central core of fundamental morals and give students no ethical basis for guidance through life. Instead, secular domination of education mistakenly keeps religious values at bay, while self-absorption becomes a primary focus for students. Is it any wonder that society is crumbling, violence is increasing, families are in disarray, and civility has disappeared?

Education emphasizing selfishness, personal freedom, and permissiveness is a major contributor to the significant decline in social and family values (Sowell, 1992; Shapiro, 2005). Increased crime and abuse is a natural outcome of schooling that preaches self-indulgence. Where can one gain a deep respect for other people, property, and social traditions if schools assume the relativist stance that these things do not matter?

Liberalism and Moral Decline

The liberal view of education—that traditional values don't matter and students should decide basic value questions for themselves without guidance from educators, religious leaders, or parents—has an eroding effect on the cornerstones of American society. Liberalism itself is a culprit; in education it does significant damage to American morality (Falwell, 1980; Bennett, 1993; Bork, 1996;

Himmelfarb, 1999; Charen, 2004; Coulter, 2004, 2007; Sowell, 2007; Hannity, 2004; Frank, 2005; Savage, 2005). It does not take a rocket scientist to recognize that common values undergirding civility, manners, and courtesies once dominant in the United States have given way to self-indulgent values of greed, destruction, consumption, and distrust of authority. This erosion has been the companion of permissive attitudes fostered in schools since progressive education concepts enveloped schools in the 1930s.

Family values have declined in the face of a long-term educational philosophy based on individualism and libertine lifestyles (Rafferty, 1968; Anderson, 1994; Roberts, 1994; Gallagher, 2005; Shapiro, 2005). Evidence of moral disaster surrounds us: extraordinarily high divorce rates, child and spouse abuse, lack of ethics in business and government, drug and alcohol addiction, out-of-control teenage pregnancy rates, excessive reliance on child care outside the home, acceptance of immorality on television and in the arts, cheating scandals and explosive violence in schools (Colson, 1994; Bouza, 1996; Jacobs, 2004).

Schools have lost their moral focus and, thus, their ability to educate youth in the most important of areas—morality. Without a moral focus, other learnings are shallow.

Christensen (1991) raises important questions about teachers who presume to supersede parents in implanting moral values in children. Further, he cites the work of Vitz and Levin, who document an aggressive feminist bias in school texts and teachings—a feminist bias in opposition to traditional American family values. Traditional parenthood and family life are virtually censored from school materials, while available teaching materials convey romantic images of adventurous single women. Similarly, reports Christensen, traditionalist parents have good reason to worry about amoral messages in literature, music, and arts that denounce religion and espouse adultery or other antifamily values.

Radical feminism is not the only culprit in the theft of morality from schools; it is just one of several modern amoral attitudes. Similar attacks on American family values have appeared under the banners of "diversity," "multicultural-ism," and "sexual orientation." These banners share the root idea of moral relativism, the idea that all views are equally valid in the classroom—from killing by euthanasia or abortion to gay and lesbian advocacy. As it destroys traditional values, moral relativism substitutes amorality or immorality as a guide to life. Even in this, there is rank logical inconsistency in the advocacy of value neutrality by many liberals. While claiming that no values are more important than any others, liberal advocates still propose a set of special interests they claim deserve special treatment in classrooms and textbooks: minorities, women, disabled, gay and lesbian (Charen, 2004; Gallagher, 2005; Savage, 2005). This special treatment constitutes a set of values they consider more valuable. Further, they accept mercy killings, abortions, and homosexuality as examples of perfectly acceptable topics of study and conduct, while praying in school is not. This is hypocrisy.

Lickona (1991, 1993, 2004, 2005) outlined the kinds of problems that demonstrate a decline in values among youth. He includes violence, vandalism, bad language, sexual promiscuity, peer cruelty, stealing, and cheating. He linked this decline to a series of factors, including:

> Darwinism and the relativistic view that springs from it,
>
> A philosophy of pseudo-scientific logical positivism that separates "facts" from "values,"
>
> Personalism, emphasizing individual rights over social responsibilities and moral authority,
>
> Pluralism, suggesting multiple values and raising a question of which ones we should teach, and
>
> Secularization, which falsely separates church and state and offers no religious guidance.

Traditional Values Can Be Restored to Schools

There is a tight relationship between good families and good schools in a society based on common values. Efforts to bring schools and society back to their moral base can yield positive results (Institute of Education Sciences, 2007). Although we can differentiate among definitions of values, ethics, morals, and character, school programs bearing labels such as "values education," "ethics education," "moral education," and "character education" often use the same principles, purposes, and general practices. We will treat them equally unless the terms are used as covers for value-free or value-neutral programs. The best of the good programs restore traditional values to schools and students; and these good programs work. The Center for the 4th and 5th Rs (respect and responsibility) shows much promise in restoring "good" character to its historic place at the center of schooling. Leming and Silva (2001) report excellent results from a five-year study on teaching a special Heartwood Foundation ethics curriculum to fifth-graders; the program produced more caring and respectful actions and fewer disciplinary referrals, and the teachers' approach to ethics teaching changed in a positive way.

Other indicators of success include the increasing number and quality of educational materials available for teachers and parents. Teaching materials are aimed at instilling universal values in students: honor, honesty, truthfulness, kindness, generosity, helpfulness, courage, convictions, justice, respect, freedom, and equality.

Internet sites offer assistance (see www.goodcharacter.com; www.character .org; www.aimcenter.com; www.ethicusa.com). The Character Education Partnership, developed and maintains a database at www.character.org, which includes ideas, materials, and descriptions and analyses of various instruments that can be used to assess character education.

Among the agenda items in the new movement for family values is the restoration of religion and patriotism to U.S. schools. (see www.freedomalliance.com).

Model centers and special programs for character education are under way in a number of states, including North Carolina, California, Iowa, New Mexico,

Utah, Connecticut, Maryland, Washington, Missouri, Kentucky, New Jersey, and South Carolina. The centers sponsor such activities as programs devoted to creating safe and orderly school environments, encouraging students to take responsibility for their conduct and for others, preventing violence, and reinforcing efforts to curb drug abuse and weapons in school. Character education is developing quickly into one of the most important new projects in the schools (Thorkildsen and Wallberg, 2004; Nucci and Narvaez, 2008).

What Should Be Taught: Traditional Values as the Focus

Clearly, schools need to rediscover their proper role and function in a moral society. The United States was founded on Judeo-Christian ideals. They form the basis of our concepts of justice and democracy. Schools were established to transmit those values to the young to preserve values and society. Support for traditional values gave early American schools a clarity of purpose and a solid direction. Children did not receive mixed messages about morality and behavior, and did not get the impression they could make up and change their values on a whim.

Renewing character education should include a prominent focus on traditional values at all levels. In elementary school, reading material should emphasize ideals (Anderson, 1994; O'Sullivan, 2002; Bennett, 2008). Stories of great heroes, personal integrity, resoluteness, loyalty, and productivity should dominate. The main emphasis should be on the positive aspects of U.S. history and literature, showing how individuals working together toward a suitable goal can succeed. Teachers should stress and expect ethical behavior, respect, and consideration (Lickona, 1991, 2004). Classes should study various religions with the purpose of understanding their common values and how those values apply to life. Providing time in school for children to reflect on personal religious beliefs would be appropriate.

Signs and symbols in school should reinforce American values. Pictures, displays, and assemblies on morality offer students a chance to see how important those values are to society and school. Inviting speakers into classes, showing films, and taking students to see significant monuments to American values are techniques that can help. Teachers can emphasize good values by providing direct instruction on moral precepts and rewarding students for good citizenship.

At the secondary level, emphasis on traditional values should continue with more sophisticated materials and concepts. There is no need for a special course on sex education if family values are covered in other courses and at home. A student honor roll, citing acts of outstanding school citizenship, might be as prominently displayed as athletic trophies. Libraries are good places for displays of books featuring the kinds of thoughts and behaviors we seek to encourage.

Literature classes should teach U.S. and foreign literature portraying rewards of moral behavior and negative consequences of immorality. American history classes should express ideals for which we stand and our extraordinary historical achievements. Science courses should feature stories of hard work and perseverance in making scientific discoveries, as well as stories of how basic values and religious views have guided many scientists in their work.

The arts are a rich place to show values through study of paintings, compositions, sculptures, and other art forms that express the positive aspects of human life under a set of everlasting ideals. Religious music and art can be a part of the curriculum, as can nonreligious art idealizing such values as the golden rule and personal virtue. Vocational subjects afford numerous ways to present good attitudes toward work, family, responsibility, loyalty, decency, and respect. Sports are an especially important place in which to reaffirm these same values; numerous professional and college teams pray together before matches, and many players are leading figures in setting high standards of moral conduct.

We need teachers who demonstrate a strong personal commitment to traditional values and whose behaviors and lives exhibit that commitment. Obviously, determining a teacher's moral beliefs goes beyond examining his or her college transcripts, since the subjects a person studies bear little relation to his or her moral conduct.

States have a right to require high moral standards from those who obtain state licenses to teach in public schools. Colleges preparing teachers should examine potential students' records and deny entry to those with criminal or morally objectionable backgrounds (for example, a history of cheating, dishonesty, or sexual misconduct). Applicants for teaching credentials should be expected to submit references that speak to their moral character. Since we ask this of lawyers who take state bar exams, why shouldn't we expect it of people going into teaching? Schools should require applicants to prepare essays discussing their values. Clearly, student teaching and the first few years of full-time teaching provide opportunity to screen young teachers to ensure they uphold moral standards. If these criteria are clearly and publicly stated, they have fair warning. Teachers found wanting should find employment in some other occupation. They should not be retained in positions where they can influence young people's ideals.

How Schools Destroy Values: Values Clarification and Moral Obfuscation

In many schools, children are taught that values they learn at home or church are a matter of choice. Through teachings such as "values clarification," children are led to believe that right and wrong are purely matters of individual opinion. There is no moral guideline for conduct or thought. In values clarification, teachers may ask children to publicly identify situations when their father or mother was wrong and to present their own view of what the parent should have done. Teachers ask children personal questions about their family lives and private thoughts. There are no criteria children can use to weigh right and wrong. Instead, teachers encourage children to determine their own set of values. Bennett (1992), describes values clarification:

> Schools were not to take part in their time-honored task of transmitting sound moral values; rather, they were to allow the child to "clarify" his own values

(which adults, including parents, had no right to criticize). The "values clarification" movement didn't clarify values, it clarified wants and desires. This form of moral relativism said, in effect, that no set of values was right or wrong. (p. 56)

In class discussions on values, children who present their personal opinions with conviction can influence other children, and the teacher is not to intercede for fear of impeding the "clarification" of values. An entire class can agree that tying cans to a cat's tail, euthanizing people who are old or ill, or remaining seated during the salute to the flag may be acceptable behavior. Children also learn to report on their parents and to ridicule those who support traditional values concerning discretion and privacy. Obviously, without clear and consistent standards of acceptable behavior and belief, our society is doomed to ethical destruction. Can one argue seriously that a life of dishonesty and cheating is morally equal to a life of honesty and integrity? How can schools adopt a position of neutrality regarding values and character development? Yet that absurd view is behind values clarification and other relativistic approaches to dealing with values in schools.

Confusing Values in the Current Curriculum

School curriculum and textbooks currently present a wide array of relativistic values that only confuse children. Secular humanism, relativism, and liberalism are not defined as school subjects, and schools offer no courses with those titles. Instead, these insidious ideas filter into nearly all courses and often go unrecognized, even by teachers. Because no specific curriculum stresses traditional morals and values, teachers and courses easily present differing views, leading students to believe there are no eternal or universal values, only personal ones. If courses and teachers do not attest to a common core of morality, students are left morally rudderless. This spawns confusion or self-indulgence at best, and scorn for morality at worst.

Teaching materials children learn from often are either vapid, without any connection to moral thought and behavior, or confusing, displaying multiple values of supposedly equal weight. Current school reading materials include trash directing attention to the values of the worst elements of society, and adult stories well beyond children's moral development. In civics and history, the focus is on political power, not virtue. Children are taught how to manipulate others and how interest groups get their way. History texts are bland and noncommittal concerning basic values and treat religion with disdain. Sex education instruction tends toward the belief that students will engage in promiscuity and sexual freedom, not exercise abstinence and responsibility (Shapiro, 2005). Science ignores religious views and substitutes the "value-free" ideas; any scientific experiment is okay. Instead of protecting and encouraging innocence, schools savage and debase it.

Results of this permissive and selfish education are apparent. We are subject to increasing abuse in contemporary life. We have seen a startling increase in child abuse, so prevalent we now have twenty-four-hour telephone hotlines to report it. Spousal abuse is another item featured almost daily in newspapers.

Animal abuse is so common it no longer makes news. And sex and drug abuse have become epidemic.

Other abuses currently abound. We abuse our ideals, respect, heroes, national honor, and religious base. Political and business leaders abuse the public trust through cheating and corruption. Young people no longer understand why we fought wars to protect our liberties. Some children refuse to recite the Pledge of Allegiance or to sing the "Star-Spangled Banner." Graffiti covers many of our national monuments and our statues of heroes. Children no longer honor their parents or respect their elders.

Schools Are Rooted in Moral Values

Schools in America were founded to provide a moral foundation, and they were effective. Colonial schools had as their core a firm commitment to morality, ethics, and traditional values. The first school laws, passed in Massachusetts in 1642 and 1647, mandated that communities provide schooling for young people and that those schools preserve religious and social values. The *New England Primer,* the colonial schoolbook used to teach the alphabet and reading, incorporated moral virtues in its teaching of basic skills. All schoolbooks followed this pattern for many generations. Early Americans clearly recognized the link between a good society and solid religious, family, and school values. Religion continues to be a firm foundation for teaching traditional values, and should not be kept out of public school classrooms.

From the *New England Primer* through *McGuffy's Readers,* the content studied in school was consistent with America's traditional values. We can learn much from the moral stories these old works present. Children learned it was wrong to misbehave at home, in the community, and at school. They learned the consequences of affronting the common morality, reading about what happened to those who did. They gained respect for proper authority in families, churches, society, and school. We need to reject permissiveness and valuelessness of current schools and return to emphasizing moral precepts and proper behavior. The crisis in education has the same origin as the crisis in society: a decline in basic values. Correction in schools is the main avenue to correction in society.

Religion affords a good moral base for young people, but isn't the only source of traditional values. Ethical personal behavior also derives from deep-rooted family and social values. The good society depends on citizens who have developed keen concern for others, awareness of personal responsibility, and habits of moderation. Etzioni (1998) argues that values education has broad and deep support among the American public, and he proposes "we just teach the values that most Americans agree upon" (p. 448). Sommers (1998) presents a clear case for classical moral education for students, the "core of noncontroversial ethical issues that were settled long ago. . . . We need to bring back the great books and the great ideas" (pp. 33, 34).

The obvious decline in values among the young results from a number of factors. Foremost is that schools have forsaken the responsibility to teach solid values, instead, substituting highly relativistic opinions that undermine parental and religious authority. Children are taught all values are equal, so whatever they value is fine. We can't hold children responsible for this rejection of common morality because their natural tendency is to be selfish. Parents must teach children to share and to respect traditional social values. Historically, we relied on schools to reinforce and extend the basic ethical code families, churches, and other religious institutions teach. When parents are unable, or refuse, to teach children right from wrong, schools usually have supplied this important function. Those who now run the schools have forgotten their history, and people who forget will repeat mistakes of the past.

With current high divorce rates and parental lack of attention to their children's moral development, schools should play an even more significant role in conveying American values to children. In times of family and social stress, schools should exert expanded influence to ensure continuation of our heritage. Many of our young parents grew up during the 1960s and 1970s, when there was a sharp decline in religious participation and a significant increase in immorality. Without the value base provided by strong religious and national traditions, the United States will be in trouble. Schools must assume an increased responsibility for training students in traditional values.

We must restore basic American values to schools and to our young people, and it is possible. But a potential opportunity is not enough. It is crucial that we move quickly to reinvigorate our school leaders with the resolve to do it. We are facing a crisis of values in society, and the crisis is reflected in our schools. Our society is extremely vulnerable. Schools must reassume their original responsibility for moral teachings.

POSITION 2: LIBERATION THROUGH ACTIVE VALUE INQUIRY

The great majority of character education programs consist largely of exhortation and directed recitation . . . Most character education programs also deliver homilies by way of posters, banners, and murals throughout the school . . . The children are passive receptacles to be filled—objects to be manipulated rather than learners to be engaged.

—Kohn, 1997, p. 158

. . . "character" is an archaic, quasi-metaphysical term, more related to horoscopes than any scientific concept. It is a term with no agreed upon definition, even among proponents of character education . . . character education is part of an agenda to introduce conservative ideology, alone, into the minds of . . . students.

—Cornwall, 2005, p. 1

School is not a neutral activity. Decisions to provide and to participate in education are based on a set of values. Everything schools do and decide not to do reflects a set of values. We educate and are educated for some purpose we consider good (Purpel, 2003; Spring, 2008). We teach what we think is a valuable set of ideas. How else could we construct education? It would be absurd to have schools without goals, teaching without purpose, curriculum without objectives.

Schools, then, are heavily involved in a series of value-based decisions. Schools provide values and character education through a variety of forms, whether intended and thoughtful or not. Thoughtful education about values incorporates society's primary ideals expressed and examined by students in a rational, respectful approach. That requires teachers to encourage intelligent and critical examination that reflects the ethical dimensions of education (Giroux, 2004; Kohn, 2008). It respects student learning and maturity, as well as disagreements. Rather than preach morality and goodness, it expects students to develop reasoned appreciation of core civilizing values and correlated ethical behavior.

Students come to school with a collection of values and opinions on good and bad; these have been acquired from family, TV, friends, and other experiences (Aronowitz, 2008). Students do not come to school as empty moral vessels, waiting for proper values to be poured in. Even primary-grade children have a pretty clear sense of right and wrong; in fact, they are almost too clear in their determination of what is fair and what is not and who should get punished and for what infractions. There are few gray areas. Try playing a game with young children and see how rules are interpreted. Maturity brings a more sophisticated sense of justice, morality, ethics, and values—much of which is honed among families, friends, media, and such institutions as formal religion and schools.

Good character is a work in progress, exhibited in actions in situations where morals, values, and ethics are tested. Values education should critically examine traditional and contemporary moral ideas, and test and refine a set of personal beliefs about ethical conduct. Attempted indoctrination by slogans, moralisms, and dogmatic piety does not meet that high standard and can result in nonthinking knee-jerk reactions. Examples of unethical and immoral actions by some clergy and corporate executives over the recent past show that moral righteousness can be spoken by everyone, but moral action requires a higher level of principles and fortitude. There are no guarantees, but more likely good results from value inquiry than from programs of moralisms and authoritarian pronouncements. Sociologist J. S. Victor (2002) points out that "It is much more useful to offer our children a path to follow than a battery of abstract values . . . a way of thinking rather than a code of rules to follow" (p. 31).

Liberation = Education

Education's primary purpose is liberation. Liberation from ignorance is the foundation beneath freedoms from slavery, dictatorship, and domination. Freedom to know underlies the freedom to participate fully in a democracy, enjoy and extend justice and equality, live a healthy and satisfying life, and provide the same opportunities to others. These are all solid values students can examine and relate to their own lives. But that inquiry requires freedom. Freedom to think and freedom to act are based on freedom to know. Any society intending to be free and democratic must recognize an elemental equation: liberation = education. Schools that restrict and contort the minds of the young oppose that principle, and democratic civilization is the victim. Since students learn a lot about values by observing the operation of values in the world about them, unreasonably authoritarian schools convey antidemocratic values inconsistent with many basic moral principles, in addition to being disrespectful of student intelligence (Kessler, 2000; Kincheloe, 2004).

Clearly, this is not an essay in favor of abandoning the civilizing character-istics of human society, including decency, respect, responsibility, courage, and magnanimity. Indeed, it is the opposite—a plea in favor of values inquiry that offers to empower students to develop and enhance civilization without hypoc-risy. We cannot impose traditional values on schoolchildren and not allow criti-cism of those values. Students, in traditional values indoctrination courses, learn conformity to authority, not thinking. Value inquiry into basic values of civiliza-tion will yield stronger, more realistic convictions among students than mere sloganeering and student conformity. Often, as a result of student passivity and obedience, such moral problems as social injustice and inequality are ignored. Instead of questioning and acting to improve society, students are expected to sponge up moralisms and be quiet. Greene (1990) argued moral choice and ethi-cal action should be products of careful and critical thought. That occurs when the community provides freedom and encouragement for individual students and teachers to engage in such thinking.

Limits and Conditions

There are, of course, reasonable limits and conditions to this concept of freedom, as there are to all freedoms. Very young children require guidance and direc-tion in basic good habits. And the small number of people whose development has been arrested at an equivalent level of infancy or young childhood may require some caring control for their own safety and well-being over much of their lives. We should expect the vast majority of children and school students, however, to mature in terms of intellect and values, progressing beyond fixed habits and adopting a reasoned understanding and independent judgment of suitable values and ethical conduct.

That maturing requires the opportunity to question, challenge, and critically examine moral pronouncements within the context of a considered view of right and wrong. Does that mean we support a school approach to values as anything goes? Absolutely not. It means students need to fully comprehend social mores and values and recognize and take responsibility for the consequences of their actions. It also means they must understand and reason through moral princi-ples undergirding adequate ethical conduct and values.

Such principles as humanity and human rights, justice, equality, freedom, and civilization deserve considerable and rational deliberation in terms of how they can be used as standards against which to weigh ethical conduct and val-ues in given situations. Confronted with a choice between rational deliberation and emotional outburst, few thinking students will pick emotion. They want to reason, even as emotion plays some role in their decisions. Given a choice between freedom and slavery, most will pick freedom—and for good reasons. Value inquiry involves the thinking through of fundamental moral principles, testing those principles in the cauldron of value conflicts in society and daily life, providing opportunity to rationally criticize, and developing a more consistent set of values and operational ethics (Singer, 2002). This is not license to do whatever one wants, and it is clearly not blind obedience to authority.

Wolfe (2001) found in interviews across the United States that a concept of moral freedom is evolving. Moral freedom draws from ideas similar to those political, economic, and religious freedom ideas flowing from the revolutionary ideas in the founding of this society—a recognition that freedom and democracy are necessary cohabitants. Wolfe notes that previous ideas of character formation required unthinking obedience to institutional authoritarianism, based on the idea that individuals were basically evil and needed correction:

> "... character formation involved the alchemist task of making something good (virtue) out of something bad (human nature) ... the process of character formation, premised on individual weakness, always sits uncomfortably in a liberal democratic society. ... Highly structured systems of moral authority require that we repress our instincts and needs for the sake of authority. But if we believe ourselves to be inherently good people—or at the least neither good nor bad— why can't we trust ourselves more and learn to trust institutions, which are capable of abusing the power they have, less?" (Wolfe, 2001, pp. 179, 180)

We have certainly seen enough authoritarian institutions who have abused their power in the past decades. From churches to government to corporations, there are plenty of examples of abuse. Some who preach morality, ethics, and responsibility have been found to be wanting in exactly those areas. But this new moral freedom from such authoritarianism does not lead to personal anarchy or irresponsibility, with no central values. Many key traditional moral precepts remain, but, as Wolfe points out for those he interviewed: "In an age of moral freedom, moral authority has to justify its claims to special insight" (p. 226). Legitimacy and credibility are necessary conditions for sound moral authority. Wolf found respondents had strong feelings supporting such traditional values as loyalty, self-discipline, honesty, and forgiveness. They had consulted authorities and institutions, but did not simply obey them, in arriving at these values. They were struggling with how to apply them to everyday life in a variety of situations, but felt free to do that and question them at the same time. This is a form of value inquiry based on the concept of liberation, consistent with the research of Coles (1997) and Piaget (1997) on how moral reasoning develops. Eisgruber (2002) comments,

> One of the defining characteristics of liberal democracy is that persons must give reasoned justification for the power they seek to exercise; they behave undemocratically insofar as they rely only on personal status or authority ... the liberal democratic state teaches most powerfully by example, not by sermonizing. (pp. 72, 83)

Principles of liberation and education operate whether students are learning basic skills and knowledge, or values, ethical conduct, morality, and character development. While it may be possible to develop basic skills and rote information in dogmatic and dictatorial schools, that denies the concept of independent thinking necessary to a democracy. It is, therefore, undemocratic to teach academic subjects in that system. Similarly, it is possible to indoctrinate students with values and ethical standards, but that approach is inconsistent with democracy and independent thinking. In addition to being undemocratic, teaching values and ethics in authoritarian settings also is counterproductive. The purpose of values education is to get students to understand, examine, derive, and thoughtfully adopt a set of socially positive values that can be translated into ethical behavior. Authoritarianism is in opposition to that purpose; it requires only obedience, blindly.

School Decisions about Values Education

The issue is not whether schools should be engaged in values education, since all are by their very nature. Rather, the issues are what kinds of values should be central to schoolwork, and how should they best be taught and learned. Teachers, textbooks, and schools in general all teach some set of values to young people. Schools can be organized and operate in ways that develop conformity, obedience to external authorities, and passive, docile behavior. Schools also can work to develop thoughtful critics of society's problems, students who are willing to challenge social norms and pursue continued improvement of humankind into the future (Kidder, 1994; Haydon, 1995; Kohn, 1997, 2008; Purpel, 2003; Anyon, 2008). There are many variations on these purposes of either socializing students to conform to social values or liberating them to engage in social improvement.

Unfortunately for those who believe schools have more significant social purposes, much contemporary school activity is devoted to producing docile, passive students who will be unlikely to challenge the status quo or raise questions even in the face of unreasoned authoritarianism. Current materials for teaching values and character in schools often are intended to protect the status quo, make students vessels for conformist behavior, and offer a noncritical perspective on religious views. Kohn (1998), for example, provides ample evidence that "conventional character education rests upon behaviorism, conservatism, and religious dogma" (p. 455). Even more unfortunately for students and society, schools often are successful in this purpose. School life focuses far too much on conformity, placing extreme pressure on all students to think, behave, and view life in the same way. This not only is hypocritical, since many adult citizens and educators do not adhere to the moralistic standards prescribed, but it destroys our young people's creativity and energy. It also leads to passivity in civic life—a serious malady in a democracy.

John Stuart Mill (1859/1956) defines the commonplace conformist education of his time:

> A general State education is a mere contrivance for moulding people to be exactly like one another; and as the mould in which it casts them is that which

pleases the predominant power in the government—whether this be a monarch, a priesthood, an aristocracy, or the majority of the existing generation—in proportion as it is efficient and successful, it establishes a despotism over the mind, leading by natural tendency to one over the body. (p. 129)

Mill's comments still are appropriate today. Sadly, many schools aim to produce obedient citizens to assure social control, not critical thinking to enhance the society.

In traditional schools, students are force-fed moralisms and value precepts inconsistent with what they see in society. Poorly paid teachers preach honesty while wealthy financiers, bankers, and politicians loot the public. Well-heeled or well-connected people who commit so-called white-collar crimes seldom are punished, although a few may be sent to luxurious detainment centers for brief stays. However, people from lower-social-class backgrounds who commit nonviolent crimes often receive long and debilitating sentences in standard prisons, where they learn more criminal behavior. Even recent U.S. presidents who engage in questionable ethical behavior are given credibility, as though the behavior is acceptable. These obvious disparities in our concept of justice, and in our other values, is evident to students. Similar examples of disparity in equality, justice, honesty, and citizenship abound in our national life. Students are well aware of these inequities. A moralistic slogan or required reading in school does not hide the defect.

Liberation Education and Critical Pedagogy: Values Inquiry

Liberation education offers an opportunity to examine social problems and conflicting values. It is linked well with ideas of critical pedagogy, a program to assist teachers to engage students in this examination (Shor, 1987; Burbules and Berk, 1999; Kincheloe, 2004, 2008; see www.perfectfit.org; www.csd.uma.org). Liberation education is not a prescribed set of teacher techniques, a specific lesson plan, or a textbook series for schools to adopt. There is no mechanistic or teacher-proof approach that will produce liberation. Critical pedagogy is anything but mechanical and teacher-proof; it is dynamic and teacher-oriented. Liberation is the emancipation of students and teachers from the blinders of class-dominated ignorance, conformity, and thought control (Shor, 1987; Clark, 1990; Ahlquist, 1991). Its dynamic quality views students and teachers as active participants in opposing oppression and improving democracy (Giroux, 1991, 2004, 2008). Applied to values, it proposes students inquire into basic moral concepts, apply them to disparities in society's values, examine alternative views, and arrive at a valid and usable set of ethical guidelines. It is grounded in reason, based on well-examined beliefs. A very popular ethics course at Harvard appropriately includes work on liberation education (www.ethics.harvard.edu).

Liberation education is complex, because the social forces it addresses are complex. The central purpose is to liberate the individual and society and to broadly distribute liberating power (Freire, 1970; Glass, 2001). It requires a set of values, including justice and equality, to serve as ideals in opposition to oppression and authoritarianism, and a critical understanding of the many cultural cross-currents in contemporary society and mechanisms of manipulation that hide ideological purposes. Liberation education and critical pedagogy uncover myths and injustices evident in the dominant culture. They also embrace the expectation that the powerless can, through education, develop power. This requires us to recognize that forms of knowledge and schooling are not neutral, but are utilized by the dominant culture to secure its power.

Schools must become sites where we examine conflicts of humankind in increasing depth to understand ideological and cultural bases on which societies operate. The purpose is not merely to recognize those conflicts or ideologies, but to engage in actions that constrain oppression and expand personal power. This profound, revolutionary educational concept goes to the heart of what education should be. Schools themselves need to undergo this liberation, and we should take actions to make them more truly democratic. Other social institutions also merit examination and action. Obviously, liberation education, a redundant term, is controversial in contemporary society. Liberated people threaten the traditional docility and passivity schools now impose.

What Should Be Taught

Liberation education for values inquiry requires us to blend curriculum content with critical pedagogy. We cannot separate what students study from how they study it. The basis of this approach to schooling is to engage students in critical study of the society and its institutions with the dual purpose of liberating themselves from blinders that simply reproduce old values that continue such ethical blights as greed, corruption, and inhumanity; and liberating society from oppressive manipulation of people by government, corporate, and institutional propaganda (Yu, 2004; Baker and Heyning, 2004; Blau, 2005).

Critical study involves both method and content. It expects an open examination and critique of diverse ideas and sees the human condition as problematic. That places all human activity within the scope of potential curriculum content and makes all activity subject to critical scrutiny through a dynamic form of dialectic reasoning.

Obviously, students cannot examine all things at all times. Thus, selection of topics for study depends on several factors, including what students previously have studied, and the depth of those investigations; which contemporary social issues are significant; students' interests and maturity level; and the teacher's knowledge. There is no neatly structured sequence of information all students must pass through and then forget. Students should examine the nature of knowledge itself. That can lead to liberation. And liberation develops strong character.

Among topics of early and continuing study should be ideologies. Students need to learn how to strip away layers of propaganda and rationalization to examine root causes. Ideology, in its most literal sense, is the study of ideas. Those ideas may be phrased in a language intended for mystification, or designed to persuade people. Racism and sexism are not considered acceptable public views in the United States, and yet they often lie behind high-sounding pronouncements and policies. Test scores from culturally biased tests are rationalized to segregate students for favored treatment in neutral-sounding nonracist and nonsexist terms, but basic causes and consequences are still racist or sexist. Imperialism is not considered proper in current international relations, but powerful nations do attempt to control others through physical or political-economic means while labeling their actions defensive or even "freedom fighting." Ideological study can help students situate events in historic, economic, and political settings deeper and richer than surface explanations.

Mainstream Mystification

Too little in popular educational literature speaks to liberation, opposition to oppressive forces, and improvement of democracy. Most mainstream educational writing raises no questions about the context schools sit within; the writers seem to accept the conservative purposes of schools and merely urge us to "fine-tune" them a bit. Standard educational writing does not examine our schooling system to the depth of its roots, ideologies, and complexities. Instead, teachers and teachers-in-training read articles on implementing teaching techniques and making slight modifications in curriculum. There is nothing critical in these pieces, and no liberation of the mind from strictures of a narrow culture. The dominant concern is to make schools more efficient, mechanical, factory-like, and conformist.

Mainstream educational literature rests on a mainstream of thought in American society. This thought is bound by a narrow band between standard conservative and liberal ideas. Those who go outside this band are labeled radical or "un-American" and viewed with suspicion. Outside ideas and criticisms have no public credibility. Neither conservatives nor liberals are pleased to see schools critically examine American democracy.

Conservatives and liberals do seem to agree that U.S. schools should support democracy. Numerous platitudes about schools preparing citizens for democracy, or about schools as a minidemocracy, fill mainstream literature. This literature can be classified as mystification because it uses high-sounding phrases to cover its ideology, a continuation of status quo and power of the already dominant class. It is not active democracy, with its liberation values, that this literature commends. The real purpose of this line of thought is to keep the masses content as uncritical workers who believe themselves to be free but actually are bound and powerless. The function of mainstream writing, in other words, is to mystify readers with a rhetoric of freedom while maintaining domination of the powerful.

Current educational terms, such as *excellence, standards, humanistic,* and *progressive,* fill mainstream periodicals. Although the terms may be useful in discussing education, they often serve as camouflage. Conservatives use the terms excellence and standards to mask the interests of the dominant classes in justifying their advantages and the interests of business in production of skilled but docile workers. Liberals use the terms humanistic and progressive to hide a soft, comfortable individualism that ignores society's basic problems and conflicts (Giroux, 2008). Together, the terms combine the business ideology dominating schools and society and narcissism preventing groups from recognizing defects in that ideology. That is *mystification*—an effort to mystify the public and hide the real school agenda.

That agenda is to maintain what Joel Spring (1976) calls a "sorting machine," sorting different social classes into various categories of citizenship. Raymond Callahan (1962) documents this agenda as a business orientation in schools, designed to prepare the masses to do efficient work and the elite to manage. Jean Anyon (1980) exposes the actual curriculum of docility and obedience taught to the lower classes. Henry Giroux (1988) describes the hidden curriculum imposing dominant class values, attitudes, and norms on all students. And Aronowitz and Giroux (1991) identify the need for a strong schooling in criticism to buttress students against crippling effects of traditional values society imposes.

The mass media amplify conservative and liberal arguments about schooling, but, in fact, little separates them. Schools can and do, by making slight modifications every few years, accommodate each side for a while. The pendulum swings in a narrow arc from the center, but schools remain pretty much the same, with only cosmetic changes. When conservatives are in power, people express more concern about competition, grading, passing tests, and knowing specific bits of information. Liberals try to make students feel happy, allow more freedom in the curriculum, and offer more student activities.

With regard to democracy and schooling, differences between conservative and liberal views lie in how narrowly democracy is defined and at what age students are to begin practicing democracy. Conservative rhetoric calls for a narrower definition and inculcation of good habits and values among students at an early age. Liberals call for a somewhat broader definition and for establishment of schools as places where students pretend to practice a form of democracy.

Neither conservative nor liberal mainstream views raise questions about democracy's basic nature or the means we use to achieve it. Neither view is critical of existing class domination over knowledge and schools. Neither sees democracy as problematic, deserving continuing critical examination to improve it. Both views assume there is a basic consensus on what democracy is, and that schools are an agency for achieving it. As a result, conservative and liberal views about schooling in a democracy differ very little. The two groups express only shallow differences over what subjects schools should emphasize and how much freedom students should have. Those may sound like important differences, but debates over such matters as how tough grading practices should be or whether students need extra time for reading drill do not address serious, significant issues of democratic life. Ideologically, conservatives and liberals share basic beliefs. Their form of values education is devoted to the status quo to avoid confronting more serious social problems of injustice and inequality.

Reactionary Indoctrination and Cultural Reproduction

Right-wingers are open advocates of indoctrination and censorship. If you know the truth, why would you present other ideas? Dissent, of course, should be stifled because it confuses children of all ages, and deviation cannot be tolerated. This view has potentially disastrous consequences for any democracy and its schools (Yu, 2004; Noddings, 2003).

Interestingly, both conservatives and liberals expect indoctrination, but are loath to tell anyone because it sounds undemocratic. Instead, since they control schools and society, they can impose their dominant views by more subtle means. Through state laws, this coalition controls school curriculum, textbook selection, school operation, and teacher licensing. State agencies monitor schools and prescribe limits. The news media, which also are dominated by mainstream conservative and liberal forces, persuade the public that democracy is working relatively well. Basic ideological disputes on social values are not confronted because no real disputes arise between standard conservative and liberal views (Chambers and Kymlicka, 2002; Giroux, 2008).

So schools are expected to indoctrinate students into mainstream culture, and the mainstream has the power to require conformity. "Cultural reproduction" means each generation passes on to the next the dominant cultural ideology that was imposed on it. In the United States, this cultural reproduction takes two forms: (1) a set of positive beliefs that the United States is a chosen country, with justice and equality for all and the best of economic systems; and (2) a set of negative beliefs that any views raising troubling questions about American values are automatically anti-American. This twofold reproduction ensures teachers and students will not engage in serious critical thinking, but will merely accept dominant ideologies. Thus, the very nature of democracy, and means for improving it, are perceived as naturally existing and beyond the school's scope of inquiry.

In school, students read mainstream literature, hear mainstream views from teachers and peers, see mainstream films, listen to mainstream speakers, and engage in mainstream extracurricular activities. The school library carries only mainstream periodicals and books. Finding an examination of highly divergent ideas is virtually impossible. When students are not in school, they read the mainstream press, watch mainstream TV, and live in families of people who were educated in the same manner. Teachers prepare in colleges where they study mainstream views of their subjects and the profession of teaching. No wonder schools are prime locations for cultural reproduction; they contain no other sources of ideas. To have mainstream ideas broadly represented in schools is certainly not improper, but to suppress critical examination of those ideas, and limit students to such a narrow band of ideas, is not liberating.

Students often are surprised to stumble on a radical journal or book legitimately challenging basic assumptions about capitalism and U.S. politics and their impact on justice and equality. Those students rightfully are concerned about an education that did not permit them to consider opposing values and ideologies. Unfortunately, the vast majority of students never come across radical materials, or they automatically and unthoughtfully reject any divergent views because schools have effectively sealed their minds—hardly character building.

Mainstream Control of Knowledge

Not only do schools sort and label students and limit the range of views that undergo examination, but they also provide class-biased knowledge to differing groups of students. Michael F. D. Young (1971), a British sociologist, has argued that "those in positions of power will attempt to define what is taken as knowledge, [and] how accessible to different groups knowledge is. . . ."

Essentially, those in power in schools guard knowledge they consider high status and use it to retain power and differentiate themselves from the masses. Although some auto mechanics, for example, must use complex skills and knowledge, it is not considered high-status knowledge. Law and medicine, which also utilize complex skills and knowledge, are considered high status. Apple (1990) notes a relationship between economic structure and high-status knowledge. A capitalist, industrial, technological society values knowledge that most contributes to its continuing development. Math, science, and computer study have demonstrably more financial support than do the arts and humanities. A master's degree in business administration, especially if from a "prestigious" institution, is more valuable than a degree in humanities. Technical subjects, such as math and the sciences, are more easily broken into discrete bits of information, and are more easily testable than are the arts and humanities. This leads to easy stratification of students, often along social class lines. The idea of school achievement is to compete well in the "hard" technical subjects where differentiation is easiest to measure. Upper-class students, however, are not in the competition, since they are protected and usually do not attend public schools. The upper middle class provides advantages for its children; the working-class child struggles to overcome disadvantage.

Separation of subjects in the discipline-centered curriculum serves to legitimize the high status of hard subjects and academic preparatory sequence. Few critically examine the organization of knowledge or understand it as class-based or problematic. Instead, schools present information in segments and spurts, testing on detail and ranking students on how well they accept the school's definitions. We pretend that knowledge is neutral, that numerous subject categories and titles are merely logical structures to assist understanding. This separates school learning from social problems, reinforces the existing authority's domination over what is important to know, and maintains students as dependent and uncritical thinkers.

The Dynamic Dialectic

Liberation education requires teachers and students to engage in a dynamic form of dialectic reasoning to uncover ideological roots of significant values. A dynamic dialectic opens topics to examination. It does not impose a set of absolutes with a known truth, but operates more like a spiral, digging deep into rationales. It examines the topic in its total social context, not in segments as in the discipline-centered curriculum. And it requires a vision of liberation allowing students to dig beneath the topic's surface to uncover its basic relationships to society's structure and to dominant interests. The purpose of the dialectic is to encourage students to transcend their traditional nonactive, sterile roles and accept active roles as knowledgeable participants in the improvement of civilization. In theory, the dialectic is never-ending, since civilization is in continual need of improvement. In practice in the schools, the dialectic is limited by time, energy, interest, and topics under study.

These divergent ideas must be examined in a setting where they can be fully developed and are perceived as legitimate, rather than strange or quaint. Adequate time and resources must be available, and censorship and authoritarianism kept at bay.

To ensure a truly liberated society, one cannot expect less of schools than education for liberation. Critical pedagogy offers a major opportunity to move in that direction. An emancipatory climate in schools will regenerate students and teachers to fully use their intellects and creativity. Those are fitting and proper goals for schools, unachievable under restricted mainstream forms of schooling our society now practices. This is values inquiry for liberation.

For Discussion

1. Values and character are two very important dimensions of education. If indoctrination is one view of how values should be imparted—a thesis—and relativistic open inquiry is another—an antithesis—what are some possible school approaches that could represent a synthesis view? How do you justify your proposal?
2. You have been asked to recommend ten members to a local advisory council on Values and Character Education. The council's charge is to identify how schools should approach teaching values and character development.
    a. What process would you go through to find the best people?
    b. What kinds of people would you select, and how many of each? Why?
    c. What educational background should be required?
    d. What occupations should be represented, and in what proportions?
    e. What groups or agencies should be represented, and in what proportions?
    f. What age, gender, or ethnic categories should be represented, and in what proportions?
    g. What other characteristics would you look for?
    h. What kinds of people would you want to exclude? Why?
3. Paulo Freire, a major advocate of liberation education, claims that traditional teaching is fundamentally "narrative," leaving the subject matter "lifeless and petrified." Freire writes:

> The teacher talks about reality as if it were motionless, static, compartmentalized, and predictable. Or else he expounds on a topic completely alien to the existential experience of the students. His task is to "fill" the students with the contents of his narration—contents which are detached from reality. . . . The more completely he fills the receptacles, the better a teacher he is. The more

meekly the receptacles permit themselves to be filled, the better students they are. (1970, pp. 57, 58)

Does this description fit your experience in schools? What evidence can you provide? Criticize Freire's view of this "banking" form of education. Has he properly characterized what happens in schools? Should it happen? What are the social costs of changing to liberation education? What are the costs of not changing? What would be an example of an antithetical position to Freire's?

4. Many agree we should teach values in school, but disagree about which values and who makes that choice. Some propose everlasting universal values; others propose utilitarian short-term values; some propose general and vague social values; and still others propose values based on individual or immediate circumstances. What is a reasonable way to determine what kind of values education we should teach in U.S. schools? What possible social consequences can you foresee for the various forms of values education? Who should decide on which values should be taught?

References

AHLQUIST, R. (1991). "Critical Pedagogy for Social Studies Teachers." *Social Studies Review* 29:53–57.

ANDERSON, B. C. (2005). *South Park Conservatives*. Washington, DC: Regnery.

ANDERSON, D. (1994). "The Great Tradition." *National Review* 46:56–58.

ANYON, J. (1980). "Social Class and the Hidden Curriculum of Work." *Journal of Education* 162:67–92.

———. WITH DUMAS, M. et al. (2008). *Theory and Educational Research: Toward Critical Social Explanation.* New York: Routledge.

APPIAH, A. (2005). *The Ethics of Identity*. Princeton, NJ: Princeton University Press.

APPLE, M. (1990). *Ideology and Curriculum.* 2nd Ed. London: Routledge and Kegan Paul.

ARONOWITZ, S. (2008 *Against Schooling*). Boulder, CO: Paradigm Publishers.

ARONOWITZ, S., AND GIROUX, H. A. (1991). *Postmodern Education: Culture, Politics, and Social Criticism.* Minneapolis: University of Minnesota Press.

BAKER, B. M., AND HEYNING, K. E. (2004). *Dangerous Coagulations?: The Uses of Foucault in the Study of Education.* New York: Peter Lang.

BENNETT, W. J. (1992). *The De-Valuing of America.* New York: Summit Books.

———. (1993). *The Book of Virtues.* New York: Simon and Schuster.

———. (1994). "America at Risk." *USA Today* 123:14–16.

———. (2008). *Book of Virtues for Boys and Girls.* New York: Aladdin Paperbacks.

BLACKBURN, S. (2001). *Being Good.* Oxford: Oxford University Press.

BLAU, J. R. (2005). *Human Rights: Beyond the Liberal Vision.* Lanham, MD: Rowman and Littlefield.

BORK, R. (1996). *Slouching Toward Gomorrah: Modern Liberalism and American Decline.* New York: Regan Books.

BOUZA, A. V. (1996). *The Decline and Fall of the American Empire*. New York: Plenum Press.

BURBULES, N., AND BERK, R. (1999). "Critical Thinking and Critical Pedagogy," in *Critical Theories in Education,* ed. T. Popkewitz and L. Fendler. New York: Routledge.

CALLAHAN, R. (1962). *Education and the Cult of Efficiency.* Chicago: University of Chicago Press.

CHAMBERS, S., AND KYMLICKA, W., eds. (2002). *Alternative Conceptions of Civil Society.* Princeton, NJ: Princeton University Press.

CHARACTER EDUCATION INSTITUTE. (1998). www.charactereducation.com.

CHARACTER EDUCATION PARTNERSHIP. (2008) Performance Values. Position Paper, www.character.org April.

CHAREN, M. (2004). *Do-Gooders: How Liberals Hurt Those They Claim to Help.* New York: Sentinel.

CHRISTENSEN, B. (1991). "Pro: The Schools Should Presume That Parents Have the Primary Authority to Determine the Cultural Traditions to Be Transmitted to Pupils." Debates in Education. *Curriculum Review* 31:6–10.

CLARK, M. A. (1990). "Some Cautionary Observations on Liberation Education." *Language Arts* 67:388–398.

COLES, R. (1997). *The Moral Intelligence of Children.* New York: Random House.

COLSON, C. (1994). "Begging for Tyranny." *Christianity Today* 38:80–81.

CORNWALL, W. (2005). "The Problem with Character Education." *Patriotism for All.* www .members.cox.net/patriotismforall/ April.

COULTER, A. (2004). *How to Talk to a Liberal (if you must).* New York: Crown Forum.

———. (2007). *Godless: the Church of Liberalism.* New York: Three Rivers Press.

DALAI LAMA. (1999). *Ethics for the New Millenium.* New York: Riverhead Books/Penguin Putnam.

DIAMOND, S. (1999). *Not by Politics Alone: The Enduring Influence of the Christian Right.* New York: Guilford Press.

EISGRUBER, C. L. (2002). "How Do Liberal Democracies Teach Values?" in *Moral and Political Education,* ed. S. Macedos and Y. Tamir. New York: New York University Press.

ETZIONI, A. (1998). "How Not to Discuss Character Education." *Kappan* 79:446–448.

FALWELL, J. (1980). *Listen, America!* Garden City, NJ: Doubleday.

FRANK. J. (2005). *Left Out!: How Liberals Helped Reelect George W. Bush.* Monroe, ME: Common Courage Books.

FREIRE, P. (1970). *Pedagogy of the Oppressed.* New York: Herder and Herder.

GALLAGHER, M. (2005). *Surrounded By Idiots: Fighting Liberal Lunacy in America.* New York: William Morrow.

GIROUX, H. (1988). *Teachers as Intellectuals.* Granby, MA: Bergin and Garvey.

———. (1990). "Curriculum Theory, Textual Authority, and the Role of Teachers as Public Intellectuals." *Journal of Curriculum and Supervision* 4:361–383.

———. (1991). "Curriculum Planning, Public Schooling, and Democratic Struggle." *NASSP Bulletin* 75:12–25.

———. (2004). "Critical Pedagogy and the Postmodern/Modern Divide." *Teacher Education Quarterly* 31(1):31–47.

———. (2008). Against the Terror of Neoliberalism. Boulder, CO: Paradigm Publishers.

GLASS, R. D. (2001). "On Paulo Freire's Philosophy of Praxis and the Foundations of Liberation Education." *Harvard Education Review* 20(2):15–25.

GOLDBERG, B. (2005). *100 People Who Are Screwing up America.* New York: Harper Collins.

GREENE, M. (1990). "The Passion of the Possible." *Journal of Moral Education* 19:67–76.

———. (1991). "Con: The Schools Should Presume that Parents Have the Primary Authority to Determine the Cultural Traditions to Be Transmitted to Pupils." Debates in Education. *Curriculum Review* 31:6–10.

HANNITY, S. (2004). *Deliver Us From Evil: Defeating Terrorism, Despotism, and Liberalism.* New York: Regan Books.

HANSEN, D. T. (2001) "Teaching as a Moral Activity," in *Handbook of Research on Teaching,* ed. V. Richardson. 4th Ed. Washington, DC: American Educational Research Association.

HAYDON, G. (1995). "Thick or Thin: The Cognitive Content of Moral Education." *Journal of Moral Education* 24:53–64.

HETHERINGTON, M. J. (2005). *Why Trust Matters.* Princeton, NJ: Princeton University Press.

HIMMELFARB, G. (1999). *One Nation, Two Cultures.* New York: Knopf.

HOFSTEDE, G. H. (2001). *Culture's Consequences: Comparing Values, Behaviors, Institutions, and Organizations Across Nations.* Thousand Oaks, CA: Sage Publishers.

HUNTER, J. D. (2000). *The Death of Character: Moral Educaiton in an Age Without Good or Evil.* New York: Basic Books.

INSTITUTE OF EDUCATION SCIENCES, (2007). "What Works: Character Education." Washington, DC: U.S. Department of Education. June 4

JACOBS, J. (2004). *Dark Age Ahead.* New York: Random House.

KESSLER, R. (2000). *The Soul of Education.* Alexandria, VA: ASCD.

KIDDER, R. (1994). "Universal Human Values." *The Futurist* 28:8–14.

KINCHELOE, J. (2004, 2008). *Critical Pedagogy Primer.* New York: Peter Lang.

KOHN, A. (1997). "The Trouble with Character Education," chapter in *The Construction of Children's Character,* ed. A. Molnar. Chicago: National Society for the Study of Education.

———. (1998). "Adventures in Ethics Behavioral Control." *Kappan* 79:455–460.

———. (2008). "Progressive Education: Why It's Hard to Beat, but Also Hard to Find," *Independent School.* Spring.

LATHER, P. (1991). *Getting Smart: Feminist Research and Pedagogy Within the Postmodern.* New York: Routledge.

LATHROP, A. (2000). *Student Cheating and Plagiarism in the Internet Era.* Englewood, CO: Libraries Unlimited.

LEMING, J. (2002). Assessment Database. Character Education Partnership. www.character.org.

LEMING, J., AND SILVA, D. (2001). "A Five Year Follow-up Evaluation of the Effects of the Heartwood Ethics Curriculum on the Development of Children's Character." Character Education Partnership. www.character.org.

LICKONA, T. (1991). *Educating for Character.* New York: Bantam.

———. (1993). "The Return of Character Education." *Educational Leadership* 51(3):6–11.

———. (2004). *Character Matters.* New York: Simon and Schuster.

MILL, J. S. (1859/1956). *On Liberty,* ed. C. V. Shields. Indianapolis: Bobbs-Merrill.

MURCHISON, W. (1994). *Reclaiming Morality in America.* Nashville: Thomas Nelson.

NODDINGS, Nel. (2003). *Happiness and Education.* Cambridge: Cambridge University Press.

NUCCI, L. AND NARVAEZ, D. (2008). *Handbook of Moral and Character Education.* Mahwah, NJ: Lawrence Erlbaum.

O'SULLIVAN, S. (2002). *Character Education Through Children's Literature.* Bloomington, IN: Phi Delta Kappa Foundation.

PAIGE, R. (2002). "An Overview of America's Education Agenda." *Kappan* 83(9):711–714.

PIAGET, J. (1997). *The Moral Judgment of the Child.* New York: Free Press Paperbacks.

PURPEL, D. (2003). "The Decontextualization of Moral Education." *American Journal of Education* 110(1):89–95.

RABKIN, J. (1995). "Let Us Pray." *The American Spectator* 28:46–47.

RAFFERTY, M. (1968). *Max Rafferty on Education.* New York: Devon-Adair.

READ, L. (1968). *Accent on the Right.* Irvington-on-Hudson, NY: Foundation for Economic Education.

ROBERTS, S. V. (1994). "America's New Crusade." *U.S. News and World Report* 117:26–29.

SAVAGE, M. (2005). *Liberalism is a Mental Disorder.* Nashville, TN: Nelson Current.

SHAPIRO, B. (2005). *Porn Generation: How Social Liberalism is Corrupting our Future.* Washington, DC: Regnery.

SHOR, I. (1987). *Pedagogy for Liberation.* South Hadley, MA: Bergin and Garvey.

SINGER, M. G. (2002). *The Ideal of a Rational Morality.* Oxford: Oxford University Press.

SINGER, P. (2000). *Writings on an Ethical Life.* New York: Ecco Press/HarperCollins.

———. (1989). "Developing Student Autonomy in the Classroom." *Equity and Excellence* 24:35–37.

SOMMERS, C. H. (1998). "Are We Living in a Moral Stone Age?" *Current* 403:31–34.

SOWELL, T. (1992). "A Dirty War." *Forbes* 150:63.

———. (2007). *Conflict of Visions.* New York: Basic Books

SPRING, J. (1976). *The Sorting Machine: National Educational Policy Since 1945.* New York: McKay.

SPRING, JOEL. (2008). *American Education. 13th ed.,* Boston: McGraw-Hill.

TAYLOR, J. (2005). *Your Children Are Under Attack.* Napeville, IL: Sourcebooks.

THAYER, V. T. (1947/1998). "The School as a Character-Building Agency." *The Humanist* 58:42–43.

THORKILDSEN, T. A., AND WALLBERG, H., eds. (2004). *Nurturing Morality.* New York: Kluwer Academic Press.

THURMOND, S. (1968). *The Faith We Have Not Kept.* San Diego, CA: Viewpoint Books.

TOWNS, E. T. (1974). *Have the Public Schools "Had It"?* New York: Nelson.

TYACK, D., AND HANSOT, E. (1982). *Managers of Virtue: Public School Leadership in America, 1820–1980.* New York: Basic Books.

VICTOR, J. S. (2002). "Teaching Our Children About Evil." *The Humanist* 62(4):30–32.

WEILER, K. (1991). "Freire and a Feminist Pedagogy of Difference." *Harvard Educational Review* 61:449–474.

WOLFE, A. (2001). *Moral Freedom: The Search for Virtue in a World of Choice.* New York: W. W. Norton.

YOUNG, M. F. D. (1971). *Knowledge and Control.* London: Collier-Macmillan.

YU, T. (2004). *In the Name of Morality: Character Education and Political Control.* New York: P. Lang.

CHAPTER 12

Multicultural Education: Democratic or Divisive

Should schools emphasize America's cultural diversity or the shared aspects of American culture?

POSITION 1: MULTICULTURALISM: CENTRAL TO A DEMOCRATIC EDUCATION

One of the guiding questions within the field of education is a deceptively simple one: What knowledge is of most worth? Over the past four decades, an extensive tradition has grown around a restatement of that question. Rather than "What knowledge is of most worth?" the question has been reframed. It has become "Whose knowledge is of most worth?"

—Michael W. Apple's introduction in Buras, 2008, p. ix

The population of the United States is expected to rise from 296 million in 2005 to 438 million by 2050, and most of the increase will come from new immigrants and their descendants. According to the Pew Research Center, nearly one in five Americans will be an immigrant in 2050; the Latino population will triple in size; the Asian population will continue to grow; and the non-Hispanic white population will increase more slowly than other groups, becoming a minority by 2050 (Passel and Cohn, 2008). The waves of "old immigrants" from Europe have been replaced by the arrival of "new immigrants" from Asia, India, Somalia, Mexico, and Central America.

Consider Figure 12.1. The foreign-born population of the United States is expected to swell every year, and the nation is becoming more racially and ethnically diverse. The census data paint a vivid picture of an increasingly multicultural nation. Not only will there be more Americans in the future, they will differ from one another more than ever before in history. The United States already

FIGURE 12.1 U.S. Population, 1960–2050.
Percentages by Racial and Ethnic Groups

Source: Passel and Cohn, 2008, p.1.

is multicultural, and it will become even more so. Multicultural approaches to education are not an option; the only question concerns the form they will take.

Multicultural education can take many forms. Some scholars in the field, for example, believe multicultural education should focus mainly on the concept of culture and problems resulting from the clash of cultures. They believe students should examine the conflicting demands of home versus school culture, as well as the conflict between cultures of the powerful and the powerless, and unequal treatment afforded certain groups because of race, gender, and sexual preference (Spring, 2000). For other scholars, multiculturalism is less about the study of culture than a vehicle for change. It is the method for critiquing and reforming society that includes political and moral correctives to assist working-class and nonwhite students in attaining social and economic advancement (Sleeter, 1996; Giroux, 1997; Willett, 1998; Steinberg and Kincheloe, 2001; McLaren, 2006).

Some critical multiculturalists consider their approach as a way to challenge "Eurocentric" ways of thinking and as a means to question the taken-for-granted assumptions about "meritocracy, objectivity, knowledge construction and individualism" (Sleeter and Delgado Bernal, 2004, p. 246). Other critical multiculturalists see multiculturalism as a remedy for the ills of "global capitalism" and "state repression" (McLaren and Farahmandpur, 2005, p. 117). The National Association for Multicultural Education website (2008) defined multicultural education as a "process that permeates all aspects of school practices, policies, and organizations. . . .

It prepares all students to work actively toward structural equality in organizations and institutions by providing the knowledge, dispositions, and skills for the redistribution of power and income among diverse groups. Thus, school curriculum must directly address issues of racism, classism, linguicism, ablism, ageism, heteroism, religious intolerance, and xenophobia" (www.name.org). Nieto and Bode view multiculturalism as a strategy to confront educational inequality and advance social justice. It is not enough, they argue, that multiculturalism seeks to help students get along, feel better about themselves, and to be more sensitive to one another. "If multicultural education does not tackle the far more thorny questions of [social] stratification and inequity . . . these goals can turn into superficial strategies that only scratch the surface of educational failure" (2008, p. 10).

Taking a conservative approach to multiculturalism, Glazer (1997) argues that "we are all multiculturalists," because whether you may favor or oppose it, multiculturalism is here, necessary, and unavoidable. All groups—ethnic, religious, racial—belong in any study of American culture because of their unique contributions and perspectives. Glazer argues that some groups have been denied appropriate recognition. "Multiculturalism," Glazer writes, "is the price America is paying for its inability or unwillingness to incorporate into its society African Americans, in the same way and to the same degree it has incorporated so many groups" (p. 147). Multiculturalism is a complex field, with multiple definitions and varied teaching approaches reflecting the many definitions. As one educator notes, even "Crayola crayons offer what it calls a 'multicultural' crayon set purportedly with hues that represent various skin colors" (Ladson-Billings, 2004, p. 52).

Although there are many approaches to multicultural instruction in schools, this section draws upon Professor James Banks's definition, who writes

> [Multiculturalism is a] reform movement designed to change the total educational environment so that students from diverse racial and ethnic groups, both gender groups, exceptional students, and students from social-class groups will experience equal educational opportunities in schools, colleges, and universities. (Banks and Banks, 2007, p. 474)

Professor Banks argues that the successful implementation of multicultural curricula requires schools to recognize the multiple dimensions of multicultural education (see Figure 12.2). Schools should not assume that multicultural education is the responsibility only of social studies and language arts teachers. Multiculturalism has to be defined broadly so everyone in every school discipline can embrace it appropriately.

The Best That Is Thought and Known?

Multiculturalists agree that people construct knowledge from slightly different perspectives. Everyone brings understandings to events based on their personal and academic experiences and on other interpretive lenses through which they view the world. Women, minorities, and new immigrants, for example, may see the world from a different vantage point than men, majority-group members, and

FIGURE 12.2 Dimensions of Multicultural Education*

Content Integration:
Teachers use examples from many cultures and groups in their teaching.

Equity Pedagogy:
Teachers organize their teaching to encourage the academic success of students from diverse racial, cultural, and social-class groups.

The Knowledge Construction Process:
Teachers help students understand how knowledge is constructed as part of cultural processes.

Prejudice Reduction:
Teachers use materials and methods to modify students' racial attitudes.

An Empowering School Culture and Social Structure:
The school culture is examined and analyzed to empower students from diverse racial, ethnic, and cultural groups.

---

*Banks, 2007, pp. 20–22.

long-established American families. Everyone develops separate frames of reference and different perspectives for interpreting the social and political world. No one frame of reference is more "true" than others, and all deserve to be heard and understood. Multiculturalism may be considered as part of the struggle to incorporate a wider range of perspectives into the way we make meanings in school (Takaki, 1993; Gordon, 1995). As Banks notes, "Individuals who know the world only from their own cultural and ethnic perspectives are denied important parts of the human experience and are culturally and ethnically encapsulated" (Banks, 2002, p. 1).

Multicultural education provides appropriate representation in the school curriculum to groups previously marginalized or excluded because of gender, class, race, or sexual orientation. Public schools should be places where students hear the stories of many different groups. The curriculum should present the perspectives of women as well as men, the poor as well as rich, and should celebrate the heroism not only of conquering generals but of those who are victorious in the struggles of everyday life. In a multiculturally reconfigured curriculum, the voices of all Americans would find legitimacy and academic consideration (Spring, 2000; Banks and Banks, 2007). Multiculturalism is not about pitting one group against others or claiming that any one perspective is more valid or more valued. Multicultural education is about fairness and justice. In the past, schools have done a disservice to students by assuming a single view of truth and ignoring students' need to create their knowledge of the world by considering multiple truths and multiple perspectives. A multicultural society will inevitably have competing views of truth and multiple sources of knowledge.

Different Voices

If you were to believe the critics of multiculturalism, you might conclude that multiculturalists are bent on destroying not only the schools but the whole of Western civilization. Samuel P. Huntington castigates multiculturalism as an immediate and dangerous challenge to America's sense of itself. Multiculturalists, he writes, have "denied the existence of a common American culture and promoted racial, ethnic, and other subnational identities and groupings" (1996, p. 305).

Huntington is not alone. Other traditionalists see multiculturalism as a threat to national identity, one that will divide the nation. E. D. Hirsch (1987, 1996), for example, tried to convince his readers that the nation would disintegrate unless schools required all students to study a common curriculum. Allan Bloom (1987) warned that multiculturalism poses the threat of cultural relativism, a disease, he says, that regards all values as equally valid, and that would likely cause the decline of the West. Another critic of multiculturalism, Diane Ravitch, argues that multiculturalism would lead to the death of education and fragmentation of American society. Professor Ravitch touts the elementary school curriculum of what she believes was a better time, the first decade of the twentieth century, when children were exposed to a common culture and high expectations:

> Most children read (or listened to) the Greek and Roman myths and folklore from the "oriental nations." . . . The third grade in the public schools of Philadelphia studied "heroes of legend and history," including "Joseph; Moses; David; Ulysses; Alexander; Roland; Alfred the Great; Richard the Lion Hearted; Robert Bruce; William Tell; Joan of Arc; Peter the Great; Florence Nightingale." (Ravitch, 1987, p. 8)

This represents a rich literature, to be sure, but, like the canon championed by Huntington, Hirsch, and Bloom, it is skewed toward a white, Western, male orientation. No people of other races were represented in classroom readings during the "good old days," and for women to find their way into the curriculum, they either had to be burned at the stake or to pioneer as nurses! Multiculturalists find little that was good in the so-called "good old days" of schooling. Very few students experienced schools that had high standards and excellent teachers. The old days were good for only a privileged handful—the high-achieving children of English-speaking families of means. For most others it was a time of alienation caused by a denial of their ethnic heritages. Henry Louis Gates Jr. refers to the nostalgic celebration of the good old days as the antebellum aesthetic position, "when men were men, and men were white . . . when women and persons of color were voiceless, faceless servants and laborers, pouring tea and filling brandy snifters in the boardrooms in the old boys' clubs" (Gates, 1992, p. 17).

Multicultural Perspectives

What do the multiculturalists want? Are they a threat to schools and the social cohesion of the country? Are they trying to impose political correctness on all Americans? Take a look at some of the multiculturalist arguments for curriculum change in the schools and decide for yourself.

As noted earlier, multiculturalists are a diverse group that includes feminists, Afrocentrists, social critics, and many people who defy labels but who simply want to transmit the variety of American culture more faithfully to their children. The charge that multiculturalists want to purge the school curriculum of Western culture is simply false. Multiculturalism, as the term is used here, does not require schools rid the curriculum of stories of white males and substitute the experiences of women, gays, African Americans, and other exploited and disadvantaged persons (Sobol, 1993). Multiculturalism is not a euphemism for white-male bashing or an anti-Western movement. Multiculturalists ask only for a fair share of curricular attention, an honest representation of the poor as well as the powerful, and reasonable treatment of minority as well as majority culture perspectives. Whatever the outcome of the current struggle over cultural representation in the curriculum, the world American students know already is multicultural (Gates, 1992, p. xvi). The curriculum must change to reflect this society, or it becomes irrelevant to students' lives.

You might think of the multiculturalist reaction against the traditional curriculum as a "victims' revolution," a repudiation of the top-down approach to literature, art, music, and history. It demands change by those discounted and otherwise harmed by traditional approaches to schooling. Multiculturalists ask schools to tell the cultural tale in a way that weaves experiences of the disadvantaged and marginalized into the tapestry of the U.S. rise to prominence. Multiculturalism is a call for fairness and a better representation of the contributions of all Americans. Multiculturalists do not disparage the school's role in developing a cohesive, national identity. At the same time, however, they recognize schools must ensure *all* students preserve, as well, their individual ethnic, cultural, and economic identities (Banks, 2004; Nieto, 2004; Pang, Kiang, and Pak, 2004).

Schools are obligated to teach multiple perspectives in the name of academic fairness and historical accuracy. Few events of significance can be understood considering only one perspective, and viewing any event from diverse, competing viewpoints leads to a fuller, more complete representation of truth. For example, school textbooks typically emphasize the role nineteenth-century white abolitionists played and discuss how whites struggled to achieve integration in the twentieth century. This is, of course, appropriate; many whites have played and continue to play vital and significant roles in the struggle for social justice. But these same textbooks typically minimize the stories of African American resistance to slavery, as well as their efforts to achieve integration and equality (Asante, 1991). These omissions alienate young African American students and present an inaccurate picture to their white peers. The story of slavery must be told from many sides, including the perspective of African Americans as agents in their own history and not simply as people who were colonized, enslaved, and freed by others (Asante, 1995). A multiculturally educated person would be able to see the slave trade from the view of the white slave trader as well as from the perspective of the enslaved people. The point is not to replace one group's story with another, but to tell the whole story more fully. To include women, the poor, and minorities is simply a way to make history richer and more complete. Including reports of the powerless as well as the powerful allows students to examine the historic relationship among race, class, gender, and political power (Sleeter and Delgado-Bernal, 2004).

Multiculturalism Is Basic Education

> Critics of multicultural education . . . define the interests of dominant groups as the "public" interest and those of people of color such as African Americans and Latinos as "special" interests that endanger the polity. (Banks, 2008, p.132)

Curriculum change may come from the top down or from the bottom up, but it never comes easily. The goal of multiculturalists is to bend education around the lives of students so all students can experience a real chance at school success. Today's multiculturalism has been influenced by earlier ethnic studies and black studies movements (Banks, 2007), and the logic of those reforms continues to be convincing. Anyone familiar with schools knows the most effective way to teach is to make the curriculum relevant to students. Curricula have more meaning when students find characters like themselves in the books they read, and instruction has a better chance of engaging students when the subject matter speaks to their experiences. Exclusion of particular groups of students and their history from the literature alienates students and diminishes academic achievement. Children who find themselves and their culture underrepresented in the school curriculum cannot help but feel lost and resentful (Assante, 1991; Au, 2006).

Everyone benefits from multicultural education. Descendants of immigrants from northern and western Europe need to read stories and listen to tales that resonate with their experiences. They also need to learn about the narrative experiences and cultural perspectives of children and families different from their own (Phillion, He, and Connelly, 2005; Banks and Banks, 2007). Children of new immigrants from Asia and Latin America need to learn about the lands they left, their new home, and varied neighbors. They must examine their cultural histories and perspectives so they can better understand how they and their families fit into their new society. The stories told and read in schools must become richer and broader, reflecting the traditions of African Americans, Native Americans, as well as Europeans. Multicultural education reflects the multicultural realities of school children. Multicultural education is an essential component to a sound basic education, as indispensible as reading, arithmetic, writing, and computer literacy (Nieto and Bode, 2008). Students cannot be considered well-educated unless they are able to consider broadly inclusive content and multiple interpretations of events.

A Responsible Multicultural Curriculum

Multicultural education reform has spread to many states (Banks and McGee-Banks, 1995) and nations (Cornwell and Stoddard, 2001). The experience of New York State is an interesting example because of the state's ethnic complexity and its combination of urban, suburban, and rural school districts. In the late 1980s, the New York State Commissioner of Education invited scholars and curriculum writers to review the appropriateness of the state's K–12 social studies curriculum and recommend any needed changes.[1]

The report, A *Curriculum of Inclusion, 1989,* recognized New York's curriculum was not fairly representing minorities. Although the state had opened its doors to millions of new immigrants, their ways of life, foods, religions, and histories were not found in the curriculum. Instead, the new immigrants were socialized along an "Anglo-American model" (New York State Social Studies Syllabus Review and Development Committee, 1991). New York was asking new immigrants to exchange their families' habits and rituals for a homogenized American culture. The unstated curricular message asked new immigrants to abandon their forebears' cultures and learn to prize the literature, history, traditions, and holidays of the Anglo-American Founding Fathers.

This is a familiar model of cultural assimilation. Proponents of state-funded education in the nineteenth century encouraged schools to teach immigrants social behaviors and patriotic rituals designed to encourage "Americanization." Such assimilation worked reasonably well for white Europeans who came to this country in the nineteenth century, but it did not work for other immigrants. Now, in the face of new immigration patterns, it seems to be an untenable ideal. A significant demographic difference distinguishes today's immigrants from those of the past. In the nineteenth century, most of the nation's voluntary immigrants came from Europe, and socialization toward an Anglo-American model of behavior may not have been terribly discontinuous with their heritage. Now, the majority of immigrants are from Asia and South America. People newly arrived from Korea and Colombia are less likely to find resonance in the Anglo-American cultural ideal than those who came to the United States from Ireland, Germany, and Italy.

New York State curriculum planners and teachers debated the design and implementation of a multicultural approach for the better part of twenty years. The new curriculum acknowledges the importance of socialization and nation building for an increasingly diverse population, but also fosters respect for cultural diversity. The New York State curriculum recognizes that to teach the nation's history appropriately requires teaching from multiple perspectives. Classroom attention must be focused on a wide range of people, their culture, and perspectives that make up the nation. The website describing "multiculturalism and multicultural perspectives" recommends that the social studies, K–12,

> should go beyond the addition of long lists of ethnic groups, heroes, and contributions to the infusion of various perspectives, frame of reference, and content from various groups. . . . Effective multicultural approaches look beyond

---

[1]Task Force members were asked to examine the curriculum and address questions about its fairness and balance. Did this curriculum speak to the varied needs of female as well as male students, African Americans and Asian Americans as well as European Americans, the disadvantaged as well as the advantaged? On the basis of the reviewers' recommendations, New York developed a new curriculum promising a fresh focus on the treatment of all students in the state. To compare New York's approach with that of a more rural state, see the "Nebraska Multicultural Education Bill" (Banks, 2002, pp. 128–130).

ethnic particularism, examine differences in light of universal human characteristics, focus on multiple perspectives, and attend to the mutual influences
among groups within and across national boundaries. (New York State Education Department, 2008, p. 5)

The multiculturalist argument is not that Eurocentric views are wrong or
evil or that children of Asian or African descent should not learn about the
European cultural legacy. Multiculturalism asks schools to subscribe to one
simple educational truth: Tolerance cannot come without respect, and respect
cannot come without knowledge of others and their point of view (Gates, 1992,
p. xv). Multiculturalism begins by recognizing the cultural diversity of the
United States, and asks that the school curriculum explore that diversity. To be
well educated in a multicultural sense means to learn about the histories, literature, and contributions of the varied people who have fashioned the complex
tapestry of American life. All students should sample broadly from all of the
cultures and all of the ideas that have contributed to the making of the United
States.

POSITION 2: MULTICULTURALISM IS DIVISIVE AND DESTRUCTIVE

*The "Core Knowledge" movement is an educational reform based on the
premise that a grade-by-grade core of common learning is necessary to
ensure a sound and fair elementary education. The movement was started
by Professor E.D. Hirsch, Jr., author of* Cultural Literacy *and the Schools
We Need, and is based on a large body of research in cognitive psychology
as well as a careful examination of several of the world's fairest and most
effective school systems. Professor Hirsch has argued that, for the sake of academic excellence, greater fairness, and higher literacy, early schooling should
provide a solid, specific shared curriculum in order to help children establish
strong foundations of knowledge.*

—Core Knowledge, 2008

Schools and the Cultural Heritage

For the past 150 years, public schools have had three broad objectives: to educate
individual citizens for democratic participation; encourage individual achievement through academic competition; and promote, encourage, and teach the
values and traditions of the American cultural heritage. The United States has
been enriched by every ethnic and racial group to land on these shores, and the
immigrants, in turn, have been well served by the nation and the nation's schools.
The public schools have their share of detractors, to be sure, but the multiculturalists' attack on the schools' curriculum seems misguided. Any fair assessment
would find it difficult to fault the success schools have had in passing the common culture of the United States to new generations of Americans—immigrants

and native-born citizens alike. No mean accomplishment, the transmission of the cultural heritage requires an appreciation for the complex aspects of U.S. history, literature, and political traditions (Ravitch, 1990; Schlesinger, 1992; Ravitch and Viteritti, 2001). American culture is, after all, a hybrid—a mix of European, Asian, and African cultures—and the school's job is to transmit this cultural legacy faithfully in all its complexity. The school's role in cultural transmission has been one of brilliant success for well over a century.

Nineteenth-century proponents of public education recognized the United States was a dynamic nation, with succeeding waves of immigrants changing and invigorating American culture. The new arrivals came from every corner of the world, and brought energy, talent, and cultural variation never before gathered in one nation. When they arrived in the United States, they spoke different languages, were of many races, and practiced many religions. What they shared was an eagerness to succeed economically and politically, and to learn how to become "American," to fit into a unique, unprecedented cultural amalgam.

Nineteenth-century common schools, influenced by Western ideas of philosophic rationalism and humanism, were an expression of optimism about human progress and democratic potential. Advocates of mass public education saw schools as a vehicle of social progress, and shared a common belief in education, "an education, moreover, which was neither a privilege of a fortunate few nor a crumb tossed to the poor and lowly, but one which was to be a right of every child in the land" (Meyer, 1957, p. 143). The common schools succeeded beyond anyone's expectations. Children of the poor as well as the rich received a public education; children of immigrants read the same texts and learned the same lore as the children of native-born Americans. The mix of immigrants now coming to the United States is far richer and more diverse than the founders of the common schools could ever have envisioned. The need for schools to transmit the common culture has never been greater; the preservation of democratic tradition has never been more difficult.

The United States always has been a haven for those seeking political freedom and political expression. In the nineteenth century, millions of immigrants came to this country, in large measure, to enjoy the fruits and accept the burdens of participating in a democratic society. This still is true today, but unlike the immigrants of former times, today's new arrivals typically have had little or no direct experience with democratic traditions. For example, in the 1840s, after the collapse of the Frankfurt diet, immigrants from Germany flocked to America seeking the democratic political expression they had been denied in their homeland. Today's immigrants may want democracy, but when they come from autocratic regimes in Asia and South America, they have had no experience with the responsibilities of democratic living. They are less prepared for assuming a role in a democratic society than any previous generation of immigrants. Clearly, it is up to schools to induct the children of the new immigrants into the complexities of a democratic society.

Although schools should expose children to the common culture, they need not pretend to a cultural homogeneity or deny individual students' ethnic experiences. Schools are obligated to represent the range of cultural voices—male and female, African American, Asian American, and European American—but these voices must be trained not for solo performances but to be part of a chorus. Schools must encourage individual identification with one central cultural tradition, or the United States might fall prey to the same ethnic tensions undermining the sovereignty of Afghanistan and the nations of Eastern Europe and Africa. Students should learn about the common Western ideals that shaped the United States and bind us together as a nation: democracy, capitalism, and monotheism.

Particularism

What happens when people of different ethnic origins, speaking different languages and professing different religions, settle in the same geographical locality and live under the same political sovereignty? Unless a common purpose binds them together, tribal hostilities will drive them apart. Ethnic and racial conflict, it seems evident, will now replace the conflict of ideologies as the explosive issues of our times. (Schlesinger, 1992, p. 10)

The United States stands to benefit—economically, politically, and socially—from the infusion of talent brought by new immigrants, as it has in the past. Assimilated new immigrants pose no threat to U.S. growth or nationhood. Instead, the United States faces a threat from those who deny that schools should teach a common American tradition or that a common culture even exists! Diane Ravitch calls these people particularists; they argue that teaching a common culture is a disservice to ethnic and racial minorities. "Particularism," writes Ravitch, "is a bad idea whose time has come" (Ravitch, 1990, p. 346).

Particularists demand public schools give up trying to teach the commonalities of cultural heritage in favor of teaching a curriculum centering on the specific ethnic mix represented in a given school or community. Students in predominantly white schools would have one focus, children in predominantly African American schools another, and so on. It is not at all clear where the particularists would stop in the Balkanization of the curriculum. Would a school with a predominantly Asian population have an Asian-focused curriculum, or would they further divide the curriculum into separate strands of Korean, Chinese, Vietnamese, Filipino, and Cambodian culture (Fox-Genovese, 1991)?

The extreme arguments of the particularists do not lend support to the unifying and democratic ends that the founders of the common schools envisioned. Asante, for example, advocates an Afrocentrist curriculum that would teach young African American children about their African cultural roots at the expense of teaching them about Western traditions. He denounces those African Americans who prefer Bach and Beethoven to Ellington and Coltrane. African Americans, he believes, should center on their cultural experience; any other preference is an aberration. Asante argues majority as well as minority students are disadvantaged by the "monoculturally diseased curriculum." He writes that few Americans of any color "have heard the names of Cheikh Anta Diop, Anna Julia Cooper, C. L. R. James, or J. A. Rogers," historians who contributed to an understanding of the African world (Asante, 1991, p. 175). He is probably right, but for better or worse, the most enduring mainstream white historians—for example, Spengler, Gibbon, Macaulay, Carlyle, and Trevelyan—are not likely to enjoy greater recognition.

The cultural focus of the curriculum is a serious matter, and although petty and irrational arguments exist on all sides, the real issue is the role schools must play in transmitting the common cultural heritage. Schools must teach children that regardless of race, gender, or ethnicity, one can achieve great feats. This is the record of the past and promise of the future. The public school curriculum should allow all children to believe they are part of a society that welcomes their participation and encourages their achievements. As Ravitch (1990) writes, "In their curriculum, their hiring practices, and their general philosophy, the public schools must not discriminate against or give preference to any racial or ethnic group. . . . They should not be expected to teach children to view the world through an ethnocentric perspective that rejects or ignores the common culture" (p. 352).

Schools cannot fulfill their central mission to transmit the common culture if they cater to particularist demands for teaching the perspective of every minority group. Ravitch argues that in the past, generation upon generation of minorities—Jews, Catholics, Greeks, Poles, and Japanese—have used private lessons, after school or on weekends, to instill ethnic pride and ethnic continuity in their children. These may be valuable goals, but they have never been the public schools' province, nor should they be. Public schools must develop a common culture, "a definition of citizenship and culture that is both expansive and *inclusive*," one that speaks to our commonalities and not our differences (Ravitch, 1990, p. 352). The public school curriculum must not succumb to particularists' demands to prize our differences rather than celebrate our common good.

Anticanonical Assaults

> When multiculturalism was first promoted as an educational philosophy, its stress seemed to be on the positive contributions of minority groups in this country and on a balanced portrayal of a variety of cultures around the world. But over the years, multiculturalism acquired an additional meaning. Instead of emphasizing the positive contributions of America's minority groups and a balanced range of social groups from around the world, the version of multiculturalism now promoted . . . posits an animus against what are perceived as Western values, particularly the value placed on acquiring knowledge, or analytical thinking, and on academic achievement itself (Stotsky, 1999, p. xi).

Among the greatest absurdities the particularists have produced is their attack on the canon, denouncing it as racist, sexist, Eurocentric, logocentric, and politically incorrect. Before we put these distortions to rest, a few words about the nature of the canon: The term *canon* (from the Greek word *kanon*, meaning a measuring rod), which originally referred to the books of the Hebrew and Christian Bibles, meant Holy Scripture as officially recognized by the ecclesiastic authority. Today, it has taken on secular and political meanings. The canon represents, first of all, the major monuments to Western civilization, great ideas embodied in books forming the foundation of our democratic traditions. The "great books" of the Western tradition (for example, the writings of Plato, Aristotle, Machiavelli, and Marx, to name but a few) have shaped our political thinking, whether we trace our origins to Europe, Africa, or Asia; Homer, Sophocles, George Eliot, and Virginia Woolf inform our sense of literature whether we are male or female. Every major university offers courses in the Western canon, and as the late Alan Bloom notes, generations of students have enjoyed these works. He writes, "wherever the Great Books make up a central part of the curriculum, the students are excited and satisfied, feel they are doing something that is independent and fulfilling, getting something from the university they cannot get elsewhere. . . . Their gratitude at learning of Achilles or the categorical imperative is boundless" (Bloom, 1987, p. 344).

The particularists' attack on the canon is new and somewhat surprising. The value of the canon has long been taken for granted as the cornerstone of quality education. As the philosopher John Searle writes, educated circles accepted, almost to the point of cliche, that there is a certain Western intellectual tradition that goes from, say, Socrates to Wittgenstein in philosophy, and from Homer to James Joyce in literature, and it is essential to the liberal education of young men and women in the United States that they receive some exposure to at least some of the great works in this intellectual tradition; they should, in Matthew Arnold's overquoted words, know the best that is thought and known in the world (Searle, 1990 p. 34).

In the past, support for the canon was an article of faith, not belabored or examined at length. People considered these works and the ideas they contained to be of enduring worth, part of a timeless literary judgment—as Samuel Johnson spoke of it—and quite apart from the hurly-burly of politics. Canonical authors were acknowledged representatives of the evolution in the thought of ideas shaping Western civilization. No longer. Particularists and multiculturalists attack the canon at every turn. Searle writes that the cant of the anticanonicals runs something like this:

> Western civilization is in large part a history of oppression. Internally, Western civilization oppressed women, various slave and serf populations, and ethnic and cultural minorities, generally. In foreign affairs, the history of Western civilization is one of imperialism and colonialism. The so-called canon of Western civilization consists of the official publications of the system of oppression, and it is no accident that the authors in the "canon" are almost exclusively Western white males. . . . [The canon] has to be abolished in favor of something that is "multicultural" and "nonhierarchical." (Searle, 1990, p. 35)

The particularists and multiculturalists are trying to do to the public school curriculum what they tried unsuccessfully to accomplish at universities: to politicize and bias the curriculum. In the name of justice and equity, they encouraged universities to broaden the curriculum and include non-Western as well as Western authors. This might not be so offensive if school *could teach everything*, but curriculum is a zero sum game; that is, if a school adds something, it also must take something else out.

The case of Stanford University is instructive. In the late 1980s, Stanford proposed adding authors from developing countries and both women's and minority perspectives into the curriculum of the Western Culture course. These changes would come at considerable cost. Plato's *Republic* and Machiavelli's *Prince* would be replaced by works such as *I, Rigoberta Menchu*, the story of the political coming-of-age of a Guatemalan peasant woman, and Franz Fanon's *Wretched of the Earth*, a book that encouraged violent and revolutionary acts among citizens of third world countries (D'Souza, 1991). Although campus radicals demonstrated in support of the proposal, chanting, "Hey, hey, ho, ho, Western Culture's got to go," cooler heads won the day. The required course in Western Culture retained its reading list but added some optional assignments that provided a non-Western focus.

Stanford's approach to curriculum reform underestimated the value of Western literature, the ability of great books to capture the imaginations of majority as well as minority students, and the ability minority students have to appreciate Western classics. Sachs and Thiel, Stanford students during the time of the "great curriculum wars," argue that Stanford multiculturalists rejected the universalism of Western culture and the power of ideas. They write:

> There exist truths that transcend the accidents of one's birth, and these objective truths are in principle available to everyone—whether young or old, rich or poor, male or female, white or black; individual (and humanity as a whole) are not trapped within a closed cultural space that predetermines what they may know. (1995, p. 3)

Misguided Curriculum Change in the Name of Multicultural Reform

Stanford successfully resisted the multiculturalists' social engineering, as have most universities; public schools have been less successful. New York State barely survived an attempt to radicalize its schools. The curriculum was headed in a strident multicultural direction when reason prevailed and the radicals lost. New York State had plunged headlong into the maelstrom of multiculturalism in reaction to a report critical of the state's social studies curriculum. The New York proposal was filled with problems. Consider a few: One of the guiding principles of the report is that "[t]he subject matter content should be *treated as socially constructed* and therefore tentative—as is all knowledge." The document had gone on to assert: "Knowledge is the product of human beings located in specific times and places; consequently, much of our subject matter must be understood as tentative" (New York State Social Studies Syllabus Review and Development Committee, 1991, p. 29). Supporters of this view believe we should teach students all knowledge is socially constructed—made up, fabricated—and that there is no overarching and agreed-upon sense of truth or right moral action.

This is distressing. What are we passing on to succeeding generations if not the fruits of our culture's pursuit of truth? According to social constructionists, all concepts of "truth and falsehood," "right and wrong," and "good and bad" are products of the human mind, as varied as human experience, and equally valid. As Glazer (2001) notes, "As the absolute ground of truth and morality weaken, one will find students (and teachers) who will question the automatic disapproval of practices once considered abhorrent (human sacrifice among the Aztecs?) because they have been taught that every culture has its own standard, and that there are no absolute grounds for judgment (p. 174). The New York State curriculum proposal (*One Nation, Many Peoples: A Declaration of Cultural Independence,* New York State Social Studies Syllabus Review and Development Committee, 1991) would have taken the state in inappropriate directions. Its most extreme positions were beaten down by critics, and the current (2008) curriculum contains less of the inflammatory language and ratiocinations of previous drafts. Many educators joined together and successfully denounced the earlier plan for its intellectual dishonesty and potential for divisiveness.

Albert Shanker, the late president of the American Federation of Teachers, argued that "multiculturalism" is an appealing idea but is likely to degenerate into stereotyping about minority views when applied in the classroom:

> For a teacher presenting a historical event to elementary school children, using multiple perspectives probably means that the teacher turns to each child and asks the point of view about the event. To the African American child this would mean, "What is the African American point of view?" To a Jewish child, "What is the Jewish point of view?" And to the Irish child, "What is the Irish point of view?" (Shanker, 1991, p. E7)

Shanker pointed out that multiculturalism is, in practice, a racist approach: It assumes that every single African American child shares the same perspective, as do all members of any religious and/or ethnic group. The rhetoric of cultural relevance and a curriculum centered on the child's sociocultural experience is, on the surface, attractive. Such an approach, however, treats culture as a heritable or biological characteristic that lumps individuals together inappropriately and without their permission. As Welsh notes, "Americans now speak of the 'African American community,' the 'Asian American community,' the 'Latino community,' and the 'Native American community' as though these constitute fully integrated, fully homogenous whole that are fully distinctive from each other (Welsh, 2008, p.2).

* * *

Multicultural education serves to undermine the school's commitment to forging a single national identify. "Mexican children newly arrived in American public schools now frequently find themselves in classrooms where they are taught part of the day in Spanish, where they learn more about the achievements of Mayans and Aztecs than about the Puritans, where they are taught to revere Miguel Hidalgo and Emiliano Zapata on the same plane as George Washington or Thomas Jefferson, and to celebrate Cinco de Mayo with more fanfare than the Fourth of July" (Chavez, 2002, p. 387). The historian Arthur Schlesinger Jr. argues that the defining experience for Americans has not been ethnicity or sanctification of old cultures, "but the creation of a new national culture and a *new* national identity." It is foolish, he argues, to look backward in empty celebration of what we once were. Instead, schools need to look forward and blend the disparate experiences of immigrants into one American culture (New York State Social Studies Syllabus Review and Development Committee, 1991, p. 89). Schools should continue to serve the nation by passing on to children elements of the common culture that define the United States and bind its people together. This is not to say schools should be asked to portray the culture as unchangeable or force students to accept it without question. The culture of a nation changes as a reflection of its citizens; U.S. culture will continue to change. School curricula will of necessity expand and sample more broadly from the various influences that have shaped our culture. However, to turn the schools away from Western ideals of democracy, justice, freedom, equality, and opportunity is to renounce the greatest legacy one generation ever bequeathed to the next. No matter who sits in American classrooms—African Americans, Asian Americans, Latin Americans, or European Americans—and no matter what their religion or creed, those students and their nation have been shaped by democratic and intellectual traditions of the Western world, and they had better learn those traditions or risk losing them.

For Discussion

1. According to John Searle (1990), the following characteristics define a well-educated person:
   a. The person should know enough of his or her cultural traditions to know how they evolved.
   b. The person should know enough of the natural sciences that he or she is not a stranger in that world.
   c. The person should know enough of how society works to understand the trade cycle, interest, unemployment, and other elements of the political and economic world.
   d. The person should know at least one language well enough to read the best literature that culture offers in the original language.
   e. The person needs to know enough philosophy to be able to use the tools of logical analysis.
   f. The person must be able to write and speak clearly and with candor and rigor.
   Do you agree or disagree with Searle's characteristics of a well-educated person? Do you like Searle's approach to defining a well-educated person or do you prefer the approach of those who assemble long lists of supposedly significant dates, names, and events, such as *Cultural Literacy: What Every American Needs to Know* (Hirsch, 1987), or *Critical Literacy; What Literate Americans Ought to Know* (Provenzo, 2005)? Are there other ways to define a well-educated person?
2. Steinberg and Kincheloe identify five positions in the public discourse about multicultural education (2001, pp. 3–5). From these following excerpts, do you find yourself more comfortable with one or more of these positions than others? Does your teacher-education program adhere more closely to one or more of them?
   a. *Conservative multiculturalism or monoculturalism position:*
      believes in the superiority of Western patriarchal culture
      promotes the Western canon as a universal civilizing influence
      targets multiculturalism as the enemy of Western progress

    b. *Liberal multiculturalism position:*

        emphasizes the natural equality and common humanity of individuals from diverse race, class, and gender groups

        argues that inequality results from lack of opportunity

        maintains that problems individuals from divergent backgrounds face are individual difficulties, not socially structured adversities

    c. *Pluralist multiculturalism position:*

        exoticizes difference and positions it as necessary knowledge for those who compete in globalized economy

        contends the curriculum should consist of studies of various divergent groups

        avoids the concept of oppression

    d. *Leftist-essential multiculturalism position:*

        maintains that race, class, and gender categories consist of a set of unchanging priorities (essences)

        assumes that only authentically oppressed people can speak about particular issues concerning a specific group

    e. *Critical multiculturalism position:*

        grounds a critical pedagogy that promotes an understanding of how schools/education works by the exposé of student sorting processes and power's complicity with the curriculum

        makes no pretense of neutrality, as it honors the notion of egalitarianism and elimination of human suffering

        analyzes the way power shapes consciousness

3. Diane Ravitch argues that pressure groups from both the left and the right have persuaded textbook publishers to censor the words and ideas children are allowed to read. Ravitch compiled "A Glossary of Banned Words, Usages, Stereotypes, and Topics" to illustrate some of the "words, usages, stereotypes, and topics banned by major publishers of educational materials and state agencies" (Ravitch, 2003, pp. 171–202).

    Consider some examples of banned terms Ravitch uncovered. Does the conscious omission of these terms from textbooks constitute a reasonable or an unreasonable censorship of ideas? Are the terms so offensive that students should be protected from reading them or is this, as Ravitch claims, a form of censorship and little more than an exercise in "political correctness"?

        Able-bodies (banned as offensive, replace with *person who is nondisabled*)

        Black (banned as adjective meaning evil)

        Cowboy, cowgirl (banned as sexist, replace with *cowhand*)

        Dwarf (banned as offensive, replace with *person of short stature*)

        Eskimo (banned as inauthentic, replace with Inupiat, Inuit, Yupik, Yuit, or Native Arctic peoples or Innuvialuit; note: *Yupik* and *Yuit* are "not interchangeable."

        Fat (banned, replace with *heavy, obese*)

        Indian giver (banned as offensive)

        Slave (replace whenever possible with *enslaved person, worker,* or *laborer*)

        West, Western (banned as Eurocentric when discussing world geography, replace with reference to specific continent or region)

        White (banned as adjective meaning pure)

References

ASANTE, M. K. (1987). *The Afrocentric Idea.* Philadelphia: Temple University Press.

_____. (1991). "The Afrocentric Idea in Education." *Journal of Negro Education* 60:170–180.

_____. (1995). *African American History: A Journey of Liberation*. Maywood, NJ: The Peoples Publishing Group.

AU, K. (2006). *Multicultural Issues and Literacy Attainment*. Mahwah, NJ: Erlbaum.

BANKS, J. A. (1994). "Transforming the Mainstream Curriculum." *Educational Leadership* 51:4–8.

_____. (2002). *An Introduction to Multicultural Education*. 3rd Ed. Boston: Allyn and Bacon.

_____. (2004). "Multicultural Education: Historical Development, Dimensions, and Practice," in *Handbook of Research on Multicultural Education*, 2nd Ed., ed. J.A. Banks and C.A. McGee-Banks. San Francisco: John Wiley and Sons.

_____. (2008). "Diversity, Group Identity, and Citizenship Education in a Global Age." *Educational Researcher* 37:129–139.

BANKS, J. A., AND MCGEE-BANKS, C. A., eds. (2004). *Handbook of Research on Multicultural Education*, 2nd Ed. San Francisco: John Wiley and Sons.

_____. (2007). *Multicultural Education, Issues and Perspectives*, 6th ed. NewYork: John Wiley and Sons.

BLOOM, A. (1987). *The Closing of the American Mind*. New York: Simon and Schuster.

BURAS, K. L. (2008). *Rightist Multiculturalism; Core Lessons on Neoconservative School Reform*. New York: Routledge.

CHAVEZ, L. (2002). "The New Politics of Hispanic Assimilation," in *Beyond the Color Line: New Perspectives on Race and Ethnicity in America*, ed. A. Thernstrom and S. Thernstrom. Stanford, CA: Hoover Institution.

CORE KNOWLEDGE. (2008). (http://coreknowledg.org/CK/about?FAQ)

CORNWELL, G. H., AND STODDARD, E. W., eds. (2001). *Global Multiculturalism: Comparative Perspectives on Ethnicity, Race, and Nation*. Lanham, MD: Rowan and Littlefield.

CROW, T. (2008). "The Necessity of Diversity." *Journal of Staff Development* 29:54–58

D'SOUZA, D. (1991). "Illiberal Education." *The Atlantic Monthly*. March, 51–79.

FOX-GENOVESE, E. (1991). "The Self-Interest of Multiculturalism." *Tikkun* 6(4), 47–49.

GATES, H. L., JR. (1992). *Loose Canons: Notes on the Cultural Wars*. New York: Oxford University Press.

GIROUX, H. A. (1997). "Rewriting the Discourse of Racial Identity: Towards a Pedagogy and Politics of Whiteness." *Harvard Educational Review* 67:169–187.

GLAZER, N. (1997). *We Are All Multiculturalists Now*. Cambridge: Harvard University Press.

_____. (2001). "Problems in Acknowledging Diversity." In D. Ravitch and J. P. Viteritti, eds., *Making Good Citizens: Education and Civil Society*. New Haven: Yale University Press.

GORDON, B. M. (1995). "Knowledge Construction, Competing Critical Theories, and Education." In J. A. Banks and C. A. McGee-Banks, eds., *Handbook of Research on Multicultural Education*. New York: Macmillan.

GRANT, C.A., AND SLEETER, C.E. (2007). *Doing Multicultural Education for Achievement and Equity*. New York: Routledge.

HIRSCH, E. D., JR. (1987). *Cultural Literacy: What Every American Needs to Know*. Boston: Houghton Mifflin.

_____. (1996). *The Schools We Need, and Why We Don't Have Them*. New York: Doubleday.

HUNTINGTON, S. P. (1996). *The Clash of Civilizations: Remaking of the World Order*. New York: Touchstone.

JAFFE, J. (1994). "Flunking Bigotry." *The Newark Star Ledger*. June 22, p. 14.

LADSON-BILLINGS, G. (2004). "New Directions in Multicultural Education: Complexities, Boundaries and Critical Race Theory," in *Handbook of Research on Multicultural*

Education, 2nd Ed., ed. J. A. Banks and C. A. McGee-Banks. San Francisoco: John Wiley and Sons.

MAYES, C., CUTRI, R., ROGERS, P. C., AND MONTERO, F. (2007). *Understanding the Whole Student*. Lanham, MD: Rowan and Littlefield.

McLAREN, P. ed. (2006). *Rage and Hope*. New York: Peter Lang.

MEYER, A. E. (1957). *An Educational History of the American People*. New York: McGraw-Hill.

NATIONAL ASSOCIATION FOR MULTICULTURAL EDUCATION (2008/2003). Resolutions and Position Papers. (www.nameorg.org)

NEW YORK STATE EDUCATION DEPARTMENT. (2008). *Social Studies: Resource Guide with Core Curriculum*. Albany: The State Education Department. (www.emsc.nysed/gov/ciai/socst/pub)

NEW YORK STATE SOCIAL STUDIES SYLLABUS REVIEW AND DEVELOPMENT COMMITTEE. (1991). *One Nation, Many Peoples: A Declaration of Cultural Independence*. Albany: The State Education Department, State University of New York.

NIETO, S. (2004). "Puerto Rican Students in US Schools: A Troubled Past and the Search for a Hopeful Future," in *Handbook of Research on Multicultural Education*, 2nd Ed., ed. J. A. Banks and C. A. McGee-Banks. San Francisoco: John Wiley and Sons.

NIETO, S., AND BODE, P. (2008). *Affirming Diversity; The Sociopolitical Context of Multicultural Education, 5th* edition. Boston: Pearson.

PANG, V. O., AND CHENG, L. L. (1998). *Struggling to be Heard: The Unmet Needs of Asian Pacific American Children*. Albany: State University of New York.

PANG, V. O., KIANG, P. N., AND PAK, Y. K. (2004). "Asian Pacific American Students: Challenging a Biased Educational System," in *Handbook of Research on Multicultural Education*, 2nd Ed., ed. J.A. Banks and C.A. McGee-Banks. San Francisoco: John Wiley and Sons.

PASSEL, J. AND COHN, D. (2008). "Immigration to Play Lead Role in Future U.S. Growth." Washington, DC: Pew Research Center. (http//pewresearch.org/pubs/729/united- states-population-projections)

PHILLION, J., HE, M. F., AND CONNELLY, F. M., eds. (2005). *Narrative and Experience in Multicultural Education*. Thousand Oaks, CA: Sage.

PROVENZO, E. F. (2005). *Critical Literacy; What Every American Ought to Know*. Boulder, CO: Paradigm

RAVITCH, D. (1987). "Tot Sociology, Grade School History." *Current* (Dec.), 4–10.

———. (1990). "Multiculturalism, E Pluribus Plures." *American Scholar* (Summer), 337–354.

———.(2003). *The Language Police: How Pressure Groups Restrict What Students Learn*. New York: Alfred A. Knopf.

RAVITCH, D., AND VITERITTI, J. P. (2001). *Making Good Citizens: Education and Civil Society*. New Haven, CT: Yale University Press.

SACHS, D. O., AND THIEL, P. A. (1995). *The Diversity Myth, "Multiculturalism" and the Politics of Intolerance at Stanford*. Oakland, CA: The Independent Institute.

SCHLESINGER, A. M. (1992/1998). *The Disuniting of America*. New York: W. W. Norton.

Searle, J. (1990). "The Storm Over the University." *The New York Review of Books*. Dec. 6, pp. 34–41.

SHANKER, A. (1991). "Multiple Perspectives." *The New York Times*. Oct. 27, p. E7.

SLEETER, C. E. (1996). *Multicultural Education as Social Activism*. Albany: State University of New York Press.

SLEETER, C. E., AND DELGADO-BERNAL, D. (2004). "Critical Pedagogy, Critical Race Theory, and Antiracist Education: Implications for Multicultural Education," in *Handbook of*

Research on Multicultural Education, 2nd Ed., ed. J. A. Banks and C. A. McGee-Banks. San Francisoco: John Wiley and Sons.

SOBOL, T. (1993). "Revising the New York State Social Studies Curriculum." *Teachers College Record* (Winter), pp. 258–272.

SPRING, J. (2000). *The Intersection of Cultures: Multicultural Education in the United States and the Global Economy*. 2nd. Ed. New York: McGraw-Hill.

STEINBERG, S. R., AND KINCHELOE, J. L. (2001). "Setting the Context for Critical Multi/Interculturalism: The Power Blocs of Class Elitism, White Supremacy, and Patriarchy." In S. R. Steinberg, ed., *Multi/Intercultural Conversations*. New York: Peter Lang.

STOTSKY, S. (1999). *Losing Our Language: How Multicultural Classroom Instruction is Undermining Our Children's Ability to Read, Write, and Reason*. New York: Free Press.

TAKAKI, R. (1993). *A Different Mirror: A History of Multicultural America*. Boston: Little, Brown.

THERNSTROM, A., AND THERNSTROM, S. eds. (2002). *Beyond the Color Line: New Perspectives on Race and Ethnicity in America*. Stanford, CA: Hoover Institution.

WELSH, J.F. (2008). *After Multiculturalism: The Politics of Race and the Dialectics of Liberty*. Lanham, MD: Rowen and Littlefield.

WILLETT, C., ed. (1998). *Theorizing Multiculturalism, A Guide to the Current Debate*. Malden, MA: Blackwell.

CHAPTER 13

Technology and Learning: Enabling or Subverting

What technology deserves significant school attention and who should decide?

POSITION 1: TECHNOLOGY ENABLES LEARNING

The technology that has so dramatically changed the world outside our schools is now changing the learning and teaching environment within them. This change is driven by an increasingly competitive global economy and the students themselves, who are "born and comfortable in the age of the Internet."

—U.S. Department of Education, 2005

. . . when computers are integrated into the flow of classroom action, a qualitative transformation occurs regarding the ways teachers teach and students learn.

—Angeli, 2008

Technology is transformative. It changes as it is used and it changes those who use it. Ideas to improve technology arise from its use—and new technology leads further, spiraling in speed and complexity. As we employ new tools, like laser surgery or satellite communications, we alter our perceptions of technology and our environments—and we are changed. Changes occur in other areas of life with the advances in such areas as solar energy, radio, TV, microwave, medical imaging, satellite and telecommunication, and other modern conveniences. Romano (2003) writes, "At the beginning of the twenty-first century, how we live, work and recreate are being transformed by a powerful, pervasive, global force—technology" (p. 2).

Teaching and learning are also changing as a result of technology (ISTE, 2008b). Spiro (2006) argues that a revolution is happening but the pace in schools is too slow, that incremental school thinking should be replaced by "principled leaps" (p. 4). He identifies several themes emerging:

increasing complexity with cognitive understanding;

speeding up the acquisition of experiences;

newer ways to comprehend knowledge structures without traditional pedagogy;

changing the way people think and getting them to think for themselves.

Technology in schools is changing from relatively simple devices to more complicated, sophisticated, and engaging environments. Technology has moved from chalkboards and textbooks to complex interactive media, complete systems of distance learning, e-learning, and virtual schools with customized pacing for individual students (Rotherham, 2006; Livingston, 2008). Technology demonstrates daily its practical value in classroom instruction, teacher and student research, improved school design and operation, increasing student interest and teacher scope, and interlinking the school and the globe. Inherent in these illustrations is technology's obvious importance to education and to society. In education, technology has the potential to completely reconstruct what we normally think of as schooling, learning, and teaching.

Rainie (2006) reports data collected by the Pew Research Center about teenagers and technology. He finds that current teenagers, identified as "Millenials," have a unique relation with technology, are immersed in media and gadgets, adapt easily to highly mobile technology, have become multi-taskers, and are unknowing or indifferent to the consequences of their use of technology for recording, altering, and sharing music, videos, and various forms of entertainment. Pew data show that 99 percent of teenagers have a TV in the home, 98 percent have CD or tape players, 86 percent have computers, and 82 percent have Internet access. Rainie makes the point that, compared with older generations, teenagers are "digital natives in a land of digital immigrants" (p. 3).

The special role that the Internet plays for teenagers is demonstrated in the following Pew data:

89 percent use email

84 percent get information on movies and TV shows

81 percent play games

76 percent get news

57 percent hunt for schools

51 percent download music

43 percent buy products

31 percent download videos

Rainie comments that, despite the significant changes already evident in the world of technology, "radical change will occur in the next decade" (p. 14).

The implications for schools are enormous, as "learning and research tasks will be shaped by their new techno-world" (p. 15).

More Than Just Teacher Gimmicks

We can no longer treat technology in school as just a collection of devices occasionally used by teachers to illustrate a lesson. Educational technology and technological education are no longer merely peripheral to the basic knowledge students must have to survive and thrive in our society. Technological knowledge itself is fundamental and should be deeply incorporated into the main courses of study in schools (Edutopia, 2008; Smith and Throne, 2008). Writing is so important to individuals and society that it should not be limited to English courses, but should be emphasized in all areas studied by students. Likewise, technology has become so important that we must fully integrate it into the central purposes of schooling. Students rate technological knowledge and use as necessary (Oblinger and Oblinger, 2005).

Technology is knowledge, but it is also a major means to learning and to developing improved knowledge. Technology is one of the knowledge products of human minds; it is useful in conveying that knowledge to others, and it is used in conducting research to improve knowledge. Learning, as well as teaching, is enabled by technology (Bransford, Brown, and Cockling, 2000).

New Media Consortium (NMC), a group of major corporations, over 200 colleges, museums, and other organizations, is "transforming the way people teach, learn, and create" (http://nmc.org). The NMC Horizon Project (2008) is a research effort to identify emerging technologies likely to have a large impact on teaching, learning, and creative expression. Although it is pointed at higher education, much can be used in considering K–12 education. NMC advocates developmental work on six technologies:

Emerging Technology

User-created content

Social networking

Mobile phones

Virtual worlds

New scholarship and forms of publication

Multiplayer educational games

Many elementary and secondary schools are engaged in similar frontier efforts using technology to change learning and teaching, like the Virtual Learning Resources Center and 21st Century Connections (McKenzie, 2000, 2001; McCain, 2000; Kirsner, 2002; O'Neil and Perez, 2003; www.virtuallrc.com; Borja, 2005; Armstrong, 2007; Livingston, 2008).

Evidence That Learning from and with Technology Is Beneficial

Reeves (1998) finds that "50 years of educational research indicates that media and technology are effective in schools as phenomena to learn *from* and *with*" (italics in original, p. 1). Others are consistent in demonstrating the educational value of technology in schools, and of students learning from and with it (Prensky, 2006). Johnson and Barker (2002), examining studies of about 100 government-funded educational technology projects, show the positive results from using technology, including improved student outcomes in cognitive knowledge and information access, and improved teaching. Ringstaff and Kelley (2002) analyzed findings from a large variety of research studies on the use of technology in learning and teaching, finding substantial improvements in most subjects.

The Apple Classrooms of Tomorrow (ACOT) study concludes that "introduction of technology into classrooms can significantly increase the potential for learning—especially in collaboration, information access, and expression and representation of students' thoughts and ideas" (Apple Classrooms of Tomorrow Study, 2000; Sandholtz, Ringstaff, and Dwyer, 1997). Technology contributed to teacher improvement in classroom organization, increased level of teacher use of technology, and positive differences in personal philosophy toward teaching—more excitement, feelings of capability, and accomplishment. Increased student achievement, improved teaching, and more efficient and effective use of schools result from the integration of technology into schools.

The Importance of Technology in Schools

The relation between technology and learning is not lost on policymakers. Lemke (2005) writes:

> Today's education policymakers are seeing technology through the lens of the No Child left Behind (NCLB) Act, which is creating expectations for a "learning return" on all technology investments. (p. 1)

Local, state, and federal governments spend billions to place new technology in schools, and private support adds considerable amounts. The results are remarkable: In 1994 about 35 percent of public schools had Internet access; by 2005 at least 99 percent of public schools had access. And the ratio of students to computer has decreased, from 12 to 1 in 1998 to 5 to 1 (U.S. Department of Education, National Education Technology Plan 2004, 2005).

Gallup's national surveys for the International Technology Education Association (ITEA) find that 98 percent of respondents stated that technology should be in the school curriculum and identified topics for inclusion as shown in Table 13.1.

Not only is study from and with technology of great benefit to students, teachers, and the school curriculum, it also has benefits for the society. The economics and politics of international competition demand that the United States remain in the forefront of technological innovation and development. Through

Table 13.1 Gallup Survey on Important Technology Topics for Schools to Teach

Topic	Not Important	Important	Very Important
Relation among math, science, technology	2 %	19 %	79 %
Skills for using technologies	1 %	22 %	76 %
Effects of technology on society	2 %	27 %	71 %
Technology and the environment	2 %	29 %	68 %
Pros and cons of each technology	2 %	29 %	58 %
How technology products are designed	12 %	45 %	41 %

Source: Rose, L., Gallup, A. M., et al. (2004). A Report on the Second Survey Conducted by the Gallup Organization for the International Technology Education Association. www.iteaconnect.org.

technological innovation, we can put the best schooling in the hands of all children—rural, suburban, or urban. Children can have access to fine teachers, excellent culture, significant science, and interesting learning (*Toward a New Golden Age in American Education*, 2005; Salpeter, 2008).

Developing Technological Knowledge, Skills, and Attitudes

Technological *knowledge* involves a working understanding of technical and operational language, an understanding of common technological equipment and related software, a grasp of basic scientific and mathematical principles on which technology rests, and an understanding of the history of technology and its impacts on society. It also includes the use of technology to learn: to discover, analyze, test, and comprehend ideas.

Technological *skills* are the techniques useful in efficient and effective operation of various technical devices, from computers and telecommunication equipment to image reproduction and robotics, and the techniques useful in dealing with the results of that work. This incorporates skills used in learning, evaluating, reporting on, and correcting or repairing technological, academic, and creative material.

Technological *attitudes* include a curiosity about ideas and knowledge, an awareness of the need for continued technological innovation, an openness to change, a desire to improve technology, and an optimistic sense that recognizes the value of technology to social and individual lives. This functional set of knowledge, skills, and attitudes should be included in the basic education for all students.

The United States requires a populace well informed about new technologies, their use, and social value (Braun, 2007). Technological literacy is the beginning point and schools are the obvious place to start (Salpeter, 2008). No other institution in society has taken such broad responsibilities for the development of various literacies—the ability to read, write, speak, understand, and apply information—among the young. Schools have a long, proud tradition of providing a common curriculum in necessary and important learnings: language use, civic responsibility, computation skill, scientific and economic understanding, and appreciation of the arts. Each involves forms of literacy, with schools offering the means to student comprehension and use. Because of technology's obvious and increasing significance to human life and societal well-being, schools must assure basic education from and with technology (Edutopia, 2008; Prensky, 2008).

In addition to Internet connections, schools with state-of-the-art equipment and teaching materials, a suitable technology curriculum, and teachers well prepared in the use and value of various technologies are a necessity. Schools play a particularly important role in diagnosis, delivery, and development of technological learning. Qualified teachers diagnose the students' technical knowledge and skill in reference to national standards, deliver appropriate learning to improve student mastery, and develop innovative and interesting teaching materials and techniques for continuing improvement. Further, schools must provide a supportive, sustaining environment for technology, assisting teachers and other staff to acquire and improve their skills.

Papert (2002) thinks technology can:

1. Change the whole system of schooling to improve learning and teaching (e.g., show that knowledge is interdisciplinary with no need for separate, compartmentalized subjects; that the learning process has continuity without age segregation).
2. "Mobilize powerful ideas" (e.g., use virtual reality to try things out, offer immediate feedback from multiple sources).
3. Encourage "children to become a driving force for educational change instead of passive recipients" (e.g., students teach along with teachers, children's curiosity stimulates innovative uses for technology).

Technological knowledge goes beyond basic operations and information to expand and engage students and teachers in redesigning the very nature of schooling and learning. It is transformative.

Setting Standards for Technological Learning

National education standards have a major impact on schools, providing focus for curriculum and instruction and offering accountability to society. Any subject not included in approved national standards is destined to be marginalized in schools. The NCLB Act requires schools to meet standards.

The International Society for Technological Education (ISTE) established the National Educational Technology Standards (NETS) for schools. These now provide the basis for nearly every state's standards documents (www.cnets. iste.org). General standards for technology education are to enable students to become capable users, information seekers, problem solvers, communicators, analyzers, evaluators, and decision makers—thus, informed, responsible, and productive citizens (National Educational Technology Standards, 2002, 2008).

There are some problems. For many schools and teachers, after "50 years of costly trial and error, technology is still not an integral, routine part of what happens in the classroom . . . there is still no common, coherent vision of how technology is to be used in the classroom; there are only unrealized expectations" (Romano, 2003, pp. 2, 23).

Within the framework of the NCLB Act, the U.S. Department of Education presented its National Education Technology Plan 2004 (*Toward a New Golden Age in American Education*, 2005). The plan identifies the problem: "Over the past 10 years, 99 percent of our schools have been connected to the Internet with a 5:1 student to computer ratio. Yet, we have not realized the promise of technology in schools" (p. 5). The action steps proposed are:

1. Strengthen leadership on integrating technology in schools.
2. Do innovative school budgeting to be sure technology gets an adequate share.
3. Improve teacher education.
4. Support e-learning (online and multimedia) and virtual schooling.
5. Encourage broadband access.
6. Move toward more digital content—away from cumbersome textbooks.
7. Integrate data systems.

Obstacles to Technological Education

Some obstacles to adequate technological education are evident, including financing, adequate staffing, suitable curriculum, technological fear, and the traditional slow speed of educational change. Financing is an important issue, but must be weighed against the social costs of not preparing students for twenty-first century technical life. If funds are not provided, we expand the digital divide between the well-to-do and the poor. A ten-year national investment in wiring schools helps to close that divide (Edutopia, 2002), and Internet access in public schools increases each year, moving from less than one-third of all schools in the mid-1990s to virtually all schools now. Community Tech Centers offer a national network of over 600 affiliates and more than 4,000 locations. The National Urban League, Boys and Girls Clubs, YMCA and YWCA groups, and others, with help from the Bill and Melinda Gates Foundation, will technologically link over 7,000 libraries (Edutopia, 2002).

Internationally, only a handful of nations, such as Canada, Finland, and Slovenia, have arranged to have all schools connected to the Internet (Pelgrum, 2001); the most significant obstacles were the lack of computers (identified by 70 percent) and teachers' lack of knowledge or skills (66 percent). Table 13.2 shows the highest-ranking obstacles identified by school principals and school experts in technology in twenty-four nations surveyed.

Some teachers fear, or are reluctant about, technology, and are not prepared to properly educate students. This fear can prevent them from

Table 13.2 Obstacles to Information and Communication Technology Improvement*

Rank	Obstacle
1	Insufficient computers available
2	Teachers lack knowledge or skills
3	Problems integrating into curriculum
4	Getting computer time into schedule
5	Insufficient equipment or software
6	Insufficient teacher time available
7	Lack of supervisory staff and technical assistance
8	Outdated network
9	Insufficient training opportunities
10	Lack of adequate school space

*Identified by school principals and school technology experts in 24 nations.

Source: Pelgrum, W. J. (2001). "Obstacles to the Integration of ICT in Education." *Computers and Education* 37(2):173.

exploring its uses and benefits as instructional tools (Wise, 2005). Some teachers disparage new computer or telecommunications devices as useful only for "entertainment" or "self-indulgence." A sizable number of teachers see laptop computers merely as a "presentation" tool and "marginalize every aspect of the laptop" in their classrooms (Windschitl and Sahl, 2002, p. 197). Teacher-imposed classroom rules often prohibit students from bringing in technological equipment; school rules may limit use of such equipment in the building. McKenzie (1999) points out that "except for a hardy group of pioneers who have shown what is possible, the bulk of our teachers lack the support, the resources, or the motivation to bring these intruders [new technologies] into the classroom core" (p. 1). McKenzie's (1999, 2000, 2001) books are designed to assist schools and teachers in overcoming this obstacle with practical ideas.

Some schools make it difficult for students to get access to various devices, and experimentation is not permitted. School computer rooms are often separated from classwork areas, are limited to select students or times, are heavily controlled and monitored, and have too few computers that are often poorly maintained older models with creaky programs. Only certain students get special training on computers. Teachers and administrators often perceive technical equipment as expensive and separate from standard schoolwork. They don't trust the students, and they may be uncomfortable around the equipment themselves. Sometimes they suspect students are using computers and other equipment inappropriately, as in "surfing" the Internet and finding something interesting. That hardly ties them into the ongoing educational activity in classrooms. This is not a setting that encourages learning from or with technology.

Academic Problems

We need constantly improving math, science, and technology education. This is not only for students who want to go into careers in math, science, and technology; technological knowledge is needed in virtually all contemporary occupations. Long-distance truck drivers, building contractors, salespeople, government employees, lawyers, doctors, travel agents, and farmers use and rely on technological equipment for their work. Homeowners, renters, taxpayers, parents, and voters need technological knowledge.

Technological change happens faster and faster, but not school change (Prensky, 2008). The time gap between discoveries in science and their application in technology has been shortening at an increasing rate. While it took more than one hundred years to transform scientific discoveries about light in the eighteenth century into technology for photography, it took only sixty-five years between the science behind electric motors and the technology that provided them. For radios, the gap between discovery and technology was about thirty-five years. From disoveries in atomic theory to technology for atomic weapons was only six years, and from science to technology on transistors was only three years (Gleick, 1999).

But we have a continuing deficiency in U.S. scientific and technological education. Comparative tests of math and science achievement show American students well behind some European countries and Japan. Math, science, and technology are very significant subjects; the United States should not be behind in these areas. Friedman (2005) noted that one U.S. university tied for seventeenth place, the lowest ranking ever in the twenty-nine-year history of an international programming competition, and that no U.S. school had won since 1997. American colleges dominated this competition for years, but have been falling behind. He attributes it to a serious lack in math and science education in precollegiate schools.

Developing Technological Proficiency

Education occurs in a variety of locations, under a number of circumstances, at any time, and through uncountable individual interests. Technology not only is a necessary subject to be taught, it offers the means and variety to improve and expand all learning for twenty-first-century schools. Student research is incredibly enhanced via Internet, satellite telecommunications, laser, and other resources. Virtual situations and simulations approximate real life and provide extraordinary learning experiences not available from books and teachers. Distance learning programs allow students to stay at home, sit on a beach, wait in a line, sip some milk and eat cookies, or be anywhere and still connected for learning. Computer programs exist in all subjects: English literature and grammar, histories of all types, math beyond belief, philosophy, multiple combinations of sciences, any of the arts, foreign language and culture, homemaking and home construction, and any other topic deemed important or interesting. Appreciation for and participation in creative arts is stimulated through use of technologies. Health and physical education can be better designed to suit individual needs and monitored more effectively by teachers with technology.

Not only are available technological options for education more interesting and involving, they are lower in cost and time than many equivalent educational activities. A trip to Italy to use Italian and see art can be simulated by computer at far less than by plane and guide. Designing a building or city is more efficient by computer. Reconstructing historical events is possible and educationally entertaining by computer. Obviously, technology can't fully substitute for real experience, but it is far better than the unreality that typifies standard schooling, and is safer and more open to multiple tries and modification than real experience. It allows rapid rethinking with "what-if" possibilities, stretching student thinking and creativity.

Available technology in schooling also is intellectually stimulating, interactive, visually stunning, pleasing in sound, and engaging of mind. It is tuned to individual student interests, tastes, and levels of knowledge—it is customized education that can be reorganized and resorted to fit changes in interests or level of understanding. Such education can occur at various times in libraries, on laptops, in centers, at home, by handheld device, and multiple other means, locations, and times (O'Neil and Perez, 2003). In addition, there is evidence that introduction of technology into classrooms has many other educational benefits, including a significant increase in the potential for learning (Apple Classrooms of Tomorrow Study, 2000; Armstrong, 2008).

Some progressive schools try to provide a laptop computer for each student from the fourth to seventh grade, a move that will significantly alter how classrooms operate, if we can find able teachers (Windschitl and Sahl, 2002). Students can gain understanding, via technology, of the most theoretical and most applied knowledge. And that knowledge can be rerun as often as students desire until it is mastered or revised.

Good examples of school-related programs aimed at improving technological knowledge and skills include FIRST (For Inspiration and Recognition of Science and Technology), a national championship robotics competition among school students. Over 1,130 teams made up of almost 30,000 students from North and South America and Europe compete. Students design, build, and operate robotic devices of all types (FIRST, 2006). Virtual schooling is a real possibility; some twenty-two states have established virtual schools now, and more are on the way. Thousands of students are in virtual education with good results and lower costs; Florida has over 22,000 virtual schools already (Winograd, 2002; Borja, 2005; Rotherham, 2006; U.S. Department of Education, 2007).

Technological progress requires talented people, with solid educations, and substantial resources in funds, facilities, and encouragement. Schooling is the key to continuing scientific achievements. In the past century, expansion of public schooling, a shift toward science and technology, new attitudes among workers and management about technology in the workplace, government encouragement of research and development, improved patent systems, and incentives for innovation helped make America powerful. Bromley (2002) points out how we overtook European nations in new knowledge in science and technological innovation after World War II by effective use of technology, giving us a jump start on the emerging global economy.

There is no better way to assess the future development of American science and technology than by examining our educational system. The future of American enterprise exists in the schools. We can tinker with current technology for short-term improvements, but long-lasting development depends on new generations of scientists, inventors, business leaders, skilled workers, and knowledgeable consumers. If schools falter, we are likely to continue declining in society and in world leadership.

POSITION 2: TECHNOLOGY CAN SUBVERT LEARNING

. . . without a broader vision of the social and civic role that schools perform in a democratic society, our current excessive focus on technology use in schools runs the danger of trivializing our nation's core ideals.

—Cuban, 2001, p. 197

At a certain point, everyone—teachers and taxpayers, parents and policymakers—has the right to stop and invoke the famous ad line "Where's the Beef?" If computers are so great, why aren't we seeing great things by now in our schools?

—Oppenheimer, 2003, p. 346

Technology is the application of science for some practical purpose. Decisions about suitable applications of science and the evaluation of practical purposes, however, require serious scrutiny. Some technologies seem to be just good sense. Safety goggles for welders, testing equipment used to assure safe blood supplies, staplers, and gummed stamps are examples. But some technologies bring serious problems; technologies are also responsible for supplies of crack cocaine, torture machinery, surveillance systems that abrogate civil liberties, and pollution of air and water. We can use weapons technology to protect ourselves and maintain peace or to threaten others in belligerence. Lasers can be used to save lives or to take them.

Personal experiences in technology may also fuel belligerence. Fox (2004) states:

> One-third of computer users admit to physically attacking a computer. More than 70 percent confess they swear at them. Frustration, anger, and exasperation—minus the swearing and hitting—affect 67 percent. (p. ix)

Fox notes that this behavior is variously called tech rage, web rage, or CRAP (Computer Rage, Anxiety, and Phobia). The commonly identified remedy is that "people must, in other words, adapt to the machine" (p. x). But that is not the only answer, probably not even the best answer. Neither is the extreme Luddite response, nor are head-in-the-sand attitudes about all new technology. Technology does not automatically or inevitably help learning. In some cases it can be a detriment.

We need reasoned criteria, solid evidence, and critical skepticism to make adequate judgments about the relative value of technologies. Commercialism, politics, and ideology are commonly the pressures for or against certain technological uses—these forces are not consistent with the reasoned judgment needed. You don't have to be a knee-jerk advocate of technology to show you are modern, and you don't have to be Neanderthal in views against technology to show you resist being dragooned. Good critical judgment based on evidence and logic, along with some healthy skepticism, is pertinent. But that critical judgment is what is often lacking in discussions about technology in education.

Some advocates of technology in schools want students trained to use and love the latest device, and do not enjoy it when students or teachers use critical judgment to question the value or use. Bromley and Apple (1998), note that most writing in this area "implicitly assumes that technology is beneficent, sure to bring us a better tomorrow if we simply attend to a little fine-tuning now and then" (p. 3). Technology, in the form of more computer activity, is often treated as an inevitable happening in schools, a type of determinism that leads us to feel helpless to stop or modify expansion.

Pflaum (2004) states:

> Test scores would soar, or tests would disappear altogether, as newly engaged, motivated students acquired skills, problem-solving abilities and a newfound thirst for knowledge. That was technology's promise. The reality, so far, has fallen short. (p. 4)

Jamie McKenzie (2008), editor of *From Now On*, the online journal of educational technology, makes the point:

> Technology vendors and cheerleaders would have you believe this is a digital age, but. . . . shall we walk through a virtual rainforest or a real one? Hardly a choice unless you are addicted to the couch, the tube, and your headphones. . . . To accept the digital label uncritically is a form of surrender to cultural trends that should inspire dissent and apprehension. (p. 1)

Old and New Technologies: Teachers Find the Good Ones

Teachers have used technologies in schools for centuries, and schools are often the key location for inventing and developing new technologies. Elementary school teachers are well-known for inventing creative ways to improve their classrooms and their practice, and technologies are often a key ingredient. Universities house research centers and individual faculty members devoted to innovations in technology. So education is already well suited to technologies that can improve schooling; education is also the most suitable location to raise questions and challenge the use and value of various technologies.

Teachers have a long history of using technologies that they find useful in their work, and ignoring those that aren't. As Tyack and Cuban (2000) note:

> Many Americans relish technological solutions to the problems of learning. It has long been so . . . advocates of educational radio, film, television, and programmed learning predicted pedagogical Nirvanas that never materialized.

Reformers have turned to machines when they were concerned about the competence of teachers, or the high cost of schooling, or some external threat to American security or prosperity that gave special urgency to education. . . . Teachers have regularly used technologies to enhance their regular instruction but rarely to transform their teaching. (pp. 247, 248)

Teachers use, and alter, technologies that show value in assisting learning—but there is no good reason to "transform" or "revolutionize" teaching by replacing solid teaching practices. Good teachers, and not machines or devices, are the key to good education. Students recognize the value of teacher-mitigated technology: "Teachers are vital to the learning process. Technology is good, but it is not a perfect substitute" (Oblinger and Oblinger, 2005).

Teachers already help students learn how to use writing instruments, printed material, graphics, art and craft and physical education equipment, and myriad other technological means to help learning. Most of the pleas made for significant expansion of technology in schools are about computers—that computers improve the quality of learning, lower costs, and improve teaching—so those arguments should be addressed.

Raising Questions: Do Computers Improve Learning?

In terms of academic learning, there is little evidence that computers add much. Cuban (2001) studied classroom use of computers in the place most likely to be in the forefront of educational technology: Silicon Valley in Northern California. He found no strong, consistent evidence that students increased academic achievement by using information technologies. Computers did not become the classroom's central learning feature.

An Alliance for Childhood (2004) analysis found that "there is scant evidence of long-term benefits—and growing indicators of harm—from the high tech lifestyle and education aggressively promoted by government and business" (p. 4).

MacDonald (2004) reports on a mammoth research project at the University of Munich, sampling computer usage among 175,000 fifteen-year-old students in thirty-one countries. Findings are that "performance in math and reading had suffered significantly," that students seemed to benefit from limited computer use at school, and that academic performance fell significantly among students who used computers several times a week. A lead researcher noted that if computers are overused and substituted for other types of teaching, it actually "harms the student." This large study controlled for variables of parental education and economic position.

Landry (2002) notes, "Yet, after hundreds of exhaustive studies, there remains no conclusive proof that technology in the classroom actually helps to teach students. In fact, in some cases it hinders learning" (pp. 37, 38). When students are distracted from schoolwork by machines or programs, their academic learning suffers. There is more to good education than mechanical presentation, even when that presentation uses all kinds of eye-and-ear-catching accompaniments.

Economists Angrist and Lavy (2002) studied computer use in Israeli schools: "There is no evidence, however, that increased educational use of computers actually raised pupil test scores" (p. 3). Indeed, there was surprising evidence of negative effects from computer use regarding math scores at the fourth- and eighth-grade levels, more surprising since the fourth grade was where the computers were reported to have the largest impact on teaching methods. An explanation offered was that computer-assisted instruction (CAI) "may have consumed school resources or displaced educational activities, which, had they been maintained, would have prevented a decline in achievement" (p. 23). In contrast, the authors note that research has shown that reductions in class size and more teacher training do benefit student learning.

Healy (1998), in a work summarizing much of the research on computers and learning, says:

> It is less amusing to realize that research to be cited throughout this book demonstrates how computer "learning" for young children is far less brain-building than even such simple activities as spontaneous play or playing board games with an adult or older child. "Connecting" alone has yet to demonstrate academic value, and some of the most popular "educational" software may even be damaging to creativity, attention, and motivation. . . . Even for older children and teens, research has yet to confirm substantial benefits from most computer-related products at school or at home. (pp. 20, 21)

Reports of studies that seem to show there is some educational improvement by use of computers need to be examined carefully (McKenzie, 2007). Most are very short-term studies that rely heavily on specific test scores that don't represent comprehensive learning; many are sponsored by corporations with special interests in computer sales; some are by government agencies previously committed to expanding computer usage. All studies should be analyzed to see if they are narrowly structured and controlled to show computer advantages without adequate study of comparable noncomputer settings (Wenglinsky, 1998; Cordes and Miller, 2000; Oppenheimer 2003; Alliance for Childhood, 2004; McKenzie, 2007).

Raising Questions: Do Computers Expand the Quality of Learning?

Broad integrative learning, beyond acquiring bits of information, can be even less satisfying via computer. Learning involves much more than test-item information easily presented in workbook form, but educational computer programs often follow that format, wherein students try to find answers to posed questions by using signals in the computer program. Visuals, narratives, and data may be impressive, but most students realize that the whole of the material is contained in the program, and their work is not to think outside that box. A curriculum based on computers suffers a decline in time for critical thinking, humanities, arts, health, and exercise.

Computer technology conveys information to students very quickly, develops skills of machine and program usage, and has excellent visual and auditory features. But it does not encourage questioning or critical examination; certainly not examination of the technology itself. Papert (1993) has reservations about noncritical true believers, "Across the world children have entered a passionate and enduring love affair with the computer. . . . In many cases their zeal has such force that it brings to mind the word *addiction* to the minds of concerned parents" (p. ix).

Significant expansion of computers in schools often is accompanied by a blind and mistaken belief in technology and collateral decline in support for the academic work of schools. Stoll (1999) argues that computers do not even belong in schools for a number of reasons, including:

They distract from the more important thinking goals of education;

They have limited use in learning and excessive use in simple entertainment; and

They require only low-level skills of transitory value to operate them.

Students develop an inclination to get the quickest, most efficient right answer that they know is hidden in the program. Speed, not thought, becomes more important. This translates into a distaste for intellectual work that requires struggle or time, uses resources outside of the classroom, and may have no right answer. They lose the richer context of human issues not mathematically computable. It becomes easy just to let machines take over, giving instant gratification and demanding little in response.

School computer use is usually individual and lacks social involvement or ethical considerations (Healy, 1998; Alliance for Childhood, 2004). So-called interactive educational programs are actually highly programmed and provide a limited set of responses to predictable keyboard or mouse entries, with an air of unreality and superficiality. Imagine learning to play tennis using only the computer and not going outdoors to swing a racquet. The same occurs in learning chemistry, biology, physics, and many more subjects by computer without labs or outdoors for real experience. Learning by machine does not provide the quality of educational experience that a classroom or lab of live students offers in the various questions and interchanges and experiments.

The accumulation of memorization and simplistic, often useless information is anti-intellectualism dressed up in technology and corporate language (Siegel, 2008). A school curriculum heavily dependent on technology is unlikely to offer questioning or critical evaluation. Having individual students at separate machines for long hours of lesson-learning or surfing is not a prescription for an education in critical judgment. The educational needs of students and society are not met in such an environment. The strong commercial interest in having schools adopt a technology-heavy and noncritical school program is evident in the corporation support for technology in schools (Giroux, 2001; Bromley and Apple, 1998; Oppenheimer, 2003).

Raising Questions: Do Computers Cut Costs?

Distance learning is one example of a claim that technology lowers educational costs. Would you want to be educated like that over the course of several years?

Where students live vast distances from schools, as in Australia's outback or sparsely settled parts of the United States, there is a good reason to provide the highest-quality TV and computer courses that can be arranged. Similarly, continuing education for professionals and preliminary classes for students who just want to try out a subject for interest may be good places for electronic schooling. But for mass public education, it often is touted as a way to save money and standardize education. Neither of these is an adequate reason to limit our students by massive distance learning. School, of course, is more than a set of taped lectures, an interesting keyboard or mouse activity, some "interactive" homework, and answering questions on a keypad. This trade-off is not worth it.

Distance learning and other forms of technological replacement of schools will be shown, in the long run, to be neither efficient nor effective. Temple University started a prototype virtual college, but closed it after determining it would not make a profit (Ohman, 2002). At the precollegiate or collegiate level, well-done distance education takes more resources and money—not less. Large volume and cheaper distance learning may mean that only the rich can afford real schools and real teacher contact; the rest get terminals.

In their economic studies of computers placed in Israeli schools, Angrist and Lavy (2002) found that the cost of the computers was about $120,000 per school, equivalent to four teacher salaries. The annual depreciation rate of the computers and software was calculated at 25 percent; thus, Angrist and Lavy summarize, the flow cost of these computers is about one teacher per year. They conclude, ". . . the question of future impacts remains open, but this significant and ongoing expenditure on education technology does not appear to be justified by pupil performance results to date" (p. 27).

Further problems occur in the corporatization of schooling, technology providing an easy means to make corporations more influential in education by control over machines, software, faculty, and intellectual property (Giroux, 2001; Werry, 2002). Corporate control is not likely to lead to critical education. Who benefits? Those already in power gain more and the rest lose more. More than $5 billion per year is spent for computer technology in classrooms, providing great benefits to tech companies (Landry, 2002). Expensive equipment, programs, and maintenance divert scarce resources from other educational activities. Corporate intrusions into education are abundant, but few have been so successful and so generally supported by government and school officials as the effort to computerize all schools (Leistnya, 2008). Sofia (2002) states: "The computer is an educational technology that did not arise within the classroom, but was imported into it as a result of vigorous corporate and government efforts to commercialize and eventually domesticate a tool initially developed within military-industrial complexes" (p. 29).

The current expensive effort to wire all schools for the Internet and provide massive numbers of computers, supported by corporations and government, will cost much more in maintenance, updating, facilities, software, new equipment, staff and student time, and related expenses than most schools and taxpayers realize. Wiring of all schools costs billions, and school districts take on the burden of paying maintenance and improvement costs. The Northwest

Education Technology Consortium ("Equity Gap in Technology Access," 2002), noted that only 6 percent of all wired schools have trained personnel to put in the available curricular material.

Raising Questions: Do Computers Improve Teaching?

A significant problem resulting from the overselling of technology in schools is the deprofessionalization of teachers, a decline in respect for teachers, teaching skill, and the value of academic/professional judgment. This problem is exacerbated by the too-easy manipulation of students, teachers, and curriculum as a result of corporate pressures and institutional control of electronic educational sources and testing. If operation of a machine is all there is to good education, where does that leave teachers at any level? Academic knowledge, teaching experience, instructional theory and practice will come to mean less, leading to no need for credentialed teachers, no respect for the position, no tenure to protect academic freedom, and no security (Bromley and Apple, 1998; Oppenheimer, 2003).

Erosion of intellectual freedom for teachers and students is a very serious possibility, denying the open pursuit of knowledge because technology substitutes sterilized and canned material that is easily controlled and censorable. A related problem is the question of intellectual property: Who has economic and editorial rights to material produced for technology and who can change it? With increasing technological incursions into schools, administrators are more likely to become like corporate vendors and teachers will be less likely to make academic decisions about their courses or their students. Teachers will lose instructional freedom and responsibilities for actual education, but are likely to remain accountable for any test results and school failures.

Are teachers the problem? Technology advocates in earlier times proposed to "revolutionize" classrooms and eliminate teachers by the use of such new technologies as (1) printed textbooks, (2) educational films and filmstrips, (3) school-based radio, (4) classroom television, (5) programmed learning, and (6) computers and online learning. (Tyack and Cuban, 2000; Monke, 2001; Oppenheimer, 2003). Thomas Edison predicted in 1922 that "the motion picture is destined to revolutionize our educational system and that in a few years it will supplant largely, if not entirely, the use of textbooks" (Lee, 2000, p. 48). Movies have changed much of American life and influenced teaching, but they have not replaced books, libraries, or reading. Other "seers" have predicted at one time or another that radios, phonographs, audiotapes, television, video courses, programmed textbooks, teaching machines, and/or computers would each replace teachers and classrooms (Cuban, 1986; Light, 2001, Oppenheimer, 2003).

These devices help schools and teachers in their work, but have not replaced them. It is presumed that technological devices offer more variety and consistent quality, and are more efficient, cheaper, controllable, and generally better than teachers. Had those characteristics actually been demonstrated in use, teacher replacement would have occurred long ago with movies, radio, or TV. Most of these innovations have evolved into forms of entertainment, useful in, but not central to, education. Many of these former wonder devices now sit unused in school storage closets or have been tossed onto trash dumps.

Oppenheimer (2003) states:

> The message here is pretty plain. Education's opportunities lie primarily in the teacher's hands, not in technology. . . . It's a lethal combination, this alliance between education and technology, because it joins two domains in which people are particularly gullible. . . . American people are especially susceptible to idealistic pitches. (pp. 399, 402)

There is another, perhaps more important, toll on the teaching profession and on educational policy when public perception of good schools focuses more on technology than learning. Even some supporters of technology in education agree the focus should not be on technology; as McKenzie (2001) notes, ". . . it is wrong-minded and shortsighted to make technology, networking, and connectivity the goal" (p. i). This problem is illustrated by the current craze to get more computers into schools, without providing the well-prepared teachers, effective educational programs, and critical literacy elements that McKenzie and others advocate (Leistnya, 2008).

Technology and the Schools: The Digital Divide

Uncritical expansion of computer technology in schools spawns social and personal problems. One widely held assumption is that more computers means more democratic technological development. The digital divide, however, has not diminished. It separates high-income people from low, those living in urban or suburban locations from the rural, the young from the old, and the otherwise privileged from those who are not. It is sometimes hidden by the veneer of corporate advertising that implies their products are necessary for all people for a better life. Bill Gates predicted in 1995 that the Internet would assist rural people to stay in small communities, since they would have equal advantage with city dwellers in terms of their access; his foundation provided substantial support to wire and equip many small-town libraries. But recent evidence suggests new computers may aid the exodus from rural areas as people go online to find jobs in other locations (Egan, 2002).

Schools that can afford it add more technology and frills, and those that can't are separated even further. Another divide in the technological workforce also has an educational component. Most jobs created by technology actually will be low-paid and boring work in such areas as maintenance; fewer jobs will occur in well-paid high-tech positions, and these will require more-advanced education. Should schools be responsible for training workers for low-paid, boring corporate jobs and not provide all students with critical-thinking skills challenging that system? Education should work to provide equity by enhancing equality of opportunity. The digital divide seems to move schools in the opposite direction. It separates races and classes even more—producing a new class of poor, the technologically illiterate, with increased disparity between managers and workers.

Personal and Social Costs of Excessive Reliance on Technology

Schools are social institutions; they cannot ignore how technologies influence personal and social life. A dependence on technology contains the seeds of narcissism, with individuals losing connections to others' political, economic, social, and personal problems. Social responsibility is ignored in the rush for self-satisfaction. Technology can separate people and soften the reality of human suffering.

Technologies can threaten society and human decency, and contain threats to individual freedoms and privacy. Secret surveillance and invisible recording of personal information, buying habits, interests, and contacts with others now are easily possible. This capacity is more than just annoying; it abrogates basic rights to personal privacy and against illegal search and places an unnecessary caution on your exercise of rights to free speech, assembly, and association. Technology is used to steal your personal identity, alter your records, confound your credit, and cause you substantial misery and trouble. Further, censorship by electronic screening of material restricts your access to ideas. Whether by commercial, criminal, or governmental action, technological intervention has multiple implications for personal and, thus, school life.

In addition to the costs of technology in personal loss of independence, ingenuity, and intellectual stimulation, there are various social costs. When individualism overcomes social responsibility, we lose the contribution many people could have made to improve society. Much new technology fragments people's lives and adds to isolation and alienation. We expect increased speed in everyday life, have lost the patience and focused attention that thoughtful reflection or social interaction require, and have seen dissolution of the family and home setting for maintaining social values and attitudes. Social bonds have deteriorated and there are increases in violent and technology-based crime, technologically produced drug abuse, and noninvolvement in community affairs. Technology saps the core of culture, too great a loss for the limited benefits (Postman, 1992).

Technology has been used to monitor and help clean the environment, but has also created significant threats to the environment and ecosystem, including ozone depletion, various pollutions, and health hazards. Other threats include the possibility of inappropriate cloning and inadequate ethics for technological medical research; insufficient regulation of gene research; racist, sexist, or humanly degrading content on the Internet; and military development of laser, nuclear, or biological weapons making mass destruction simple and distant (Talbott, 2008). Other social costs from technology include the multiple health problems associated with it and related costs in life quality, time, energy, and money. For the users of computers and other equipment, we now have unusual muscle and eyestrain problems, headache, fatigue, crippling hand and arm pain, and the potential of other long-term problems from monitor radiation. Cell phones are being investigated for causing some new health problems. Workers in high-tech manufacturing are subject to safety problems from chemical and radiological materials along with many ailments related to that work.

In many industries, workers must have protective gear—but we don't know the longer-term results of that protection. Gleick (1999) points out, "Modern times have brought certain maladies that might be thought of as diseases of technology: radiation poisoning (Marie Curie's truest legacy); carpal tunnel syndrome (descendant of Scrivener's palsy) . . ." (p. 102). Beyond the examples suggested, there are many other personal and social costs to technology; school offers opportunity to consider them in critical examination of technology in society.

The Need for Critical Technological Education

We need *critical* technological education, where serious questions are raised about technologies and their multiple impacts on individuals, society, and schools. The addition of the word *critical* to the idea of technological education changes the concept in basic ways. This phrase connotes an analysis of technology that does not varnish over or ignore important negative implications. It does not simply accept excessive claims made for technical improvements, as though there were only benefits and no social, human, or educational costs. Critical technological education is the full examination of issues involving the use and value of technology in schools, and the many issues that arise in considering technology in the larger society. Critical technological education expects students to fully examine claims and evidence provided by advocates and opponents of more technology, measured in terms of supportable criteria derived from civilizing individual and social values (Leistnya, 2008).

A good life is far more than the ability to read manuals and operate new devices, and technological education is more than just recreational or vocational training to use machines. Education is rich and intellectually rewarding, entailing the posing of questions, examination of issues, and search for adequate evidence (Dewey, 1933). These are elements of critical thinking, needed in the study of technology in society and school. Technological issues, both social and educational, are suited to examination in classes because schools exist to help students comprehend and deal with aspects of their environment, and technology has certainly become a major player in all of our environments.

This position does not oppose all technologies; it is against the overselling of certain technologies with little critical examination. It also is against development of a school curriculum or school system where technology supplants teachers as a main ingredient. The headlong and uncritical plunge into electronic technology over the past decades has had mixed results. The deprofessionalizing of teachers and runaway computer budgets are examples in schools (Bromley and Apple, 1998; McKenzie, 2005). Has the wonder of technology caused our enchantment with it, or is it just extraordinarily good salesmanship?

Schools should be the best places for students to evaluate these kinds of questions without commercial or ideological interference or influence. The mass media, corporations, and those with strong linkage to technological development cannot be expected to provide both sides of this argument fairly; forces related to the marketplace and ideology limit media and business presentation of negative ideas about technology they like or in which they have huge investments. Current and future social impact of technology is directly related to the kind of instruction and questioning that goes on in technological education.

Good educators want good schools with students evaluating important ideas. Such teachers also want students to learn, use, and improve their critical thinking. Whether working with students on the study of technology or using technologies in the classroom to explore another topic, responsible teachers recognize the importance of critical thinking on significant ideas and issues. Where technological innovation serves those ends in classrooms, teachers will pursue technologies with relish. But educators realize educational technologies are not a panacea, and do not exist in a social vacuum. There are large-scale issues beyond the classroom use of machines, issues involving the use, value, and impact of technologies in society. Critical examination of the social context of technological innovation and the instructional use of technologies are both topics of importance to educators.

We should subject technologies to critical examination in terms of education and society. The essential question is this: Does a new technology improve or diminish the quality of life for most people? If it does, then we need to ask whether or not the technology is worth its various costs. Answering those questions involves dealing with many other questions about technology, history, social values, and making choices. We cannot expect students to use and improve their critical thinking if teachers don't think critically themselves about such issues as the role and impact of technologies.

The overpromise and underachievement of computer technology in schools represents a major concern for education, one that goes far beyond financing problems. It includes questions about the nature and quality of learning that results, unfortunate alterations in the culture of schools that deprofessionalize teachers and restrict intellectual freedom, and the corporatization of schools and increases in the digital divide. Critical technological education also provides for full study of multiple personal and social costs of technology.

For Discussion

1. In the following paragraph, substitute terms for those underlined, then follow the discussion points. For example, you can substitute "radio" or "microfilm" for the underlined term "chalkboard" and see how this may change the rest of the paragraph.

   "The use of new technologies now available in chalkboards will revolutionize education. It will replace teachers and make schools more efficient. This new innovation will permit students to just read material from the chalkboard in order to become educated."

   —Millard P. Smedley (1831)

   Discuss the impact on education of any of the various technologies you have identified. As a result of this technology, have schools been:
   a. revolutionized?
   b. permanently changed?

  c. altered in important ways?
  d. only fleetingly influenced?
  e. not changed at all?
  Provide justification for your opinion by citing references in educational history, personal experience in schools, or current commentary in books, periodicals, and on the Internet.

2. Dialogue Ideas: The essays in this chapter propose distinctly different projections about the possible social and educational consequences of a school curriculum heavily weighted toward technology. Select some examples of technology in schools, either from the essays or from your own experience, and present a discussion of your views of the projections. How likely are any of them to occur? Are the potential consequences mostly positive or negative? On what grounds do you determine they are positive or negative? Do you have some suggestions for enhancing the positives and diminishing negatives?

3. Technology, some argue, is neutral—it simply exists. The real question revolves around how the technology is used. From that perspective, draft a short statement that addresses these questions:
  a. How should schools organize their use of technology?
  b. What are the best criteria for judging the most educational use of technology?
  c. Should technological innovators be free to develop any technology?
  d. Should technology advertising be regulated to prohibit misleading or incomplete information?
  e. Should education about technology be changed? How?
  Now, draft a short statement of opposite positions, based on the perspective that technology is not neutral. This view would hold that every technology has some value orientation, from potato peelers to hydrogen bombs. For example, hydrogen bombs have a political purpose; new potato peelers involve value assumptions about the market, the users, and how time should be used. Contrast the two statements to see if you can find a workable synthesis.

4. Is there a digital divide? What evidence can you find that supports your contention? How do you define it?
    If you find a divide:
  a. What are its characteristics—those identifying elements like social class, race, gender, age?
  b. What would you propose doing about a divide?
    If you do not find a digital divide:
  c. What criteria and what resources did you use to get evidence?
  d. What policies would you propose to prevent a divide?

5. What would you think if a local school offered programs for students to:
      stay away from school for all courses and all years, with school-provided technology?
      have an implant to permit instant information transfer to the brain?
      get full school credit for Internet game scores?
      graduate only if they invent one important technological innovation?
      Using your sense of the development of technological education over the next thirty to fifty years, present your view of a school of the future. Include physical features and curriculum.

6. How would you define technological literacy? Interview several friends to see how they define it. Compare the definitions according to such criteria about the interviewees as:

   a. age and gender
   b. relative amount of technological expertise
   c. any other obvious differences
      Given the comparison of views, what tentative conclusions can you draw about
   the definition that schools should use in preparing students in this area?

References

ALLIANCE FOR CHILDHOOD. (2004). *Tech Tonic: Toward a New Literacy of Technology.* College Park, MD: Author. www.allianceforchildhood.org.

ANGELI, C. (2008). "Distributed Cognition," *Journal of Research on Technology in Education.* 40(3), 271–297 Spring.

ANGRIST, J., AND LAVY, V. (2002). "New Evidence on Classroom Computers and Pupil Learning." *The Economic Journal* 112:1–31.

APPLE, M. (1991). "The New Technology." *Computers in the Schools* 8:59–79.

APPLE CLASSROOMS OF TOMORROW STUDY. (2000). www.apple.com/education/k-12Leadership/ACOT.html2000.

ARMSTRONG, S. (2008). "Virtual Learning 2.0." *Technology and Learning.* www.techlearning.com Nov.

BORJA, R.R. (2005). "Cyber Schools' Status," *EdWeek.* May 5. www.edweek.org.

BRANSFORD, J. D., BROWN, A. L., AND COCKLING, R. R. (2000). *How People Learn.* Washington, DC: National Academy Press.

BRAUN, L. W. (2007) *Teens, Technology, and Literacy.* Westport, CT: Libraries Unlimited.

BROMLEY, H. (2002). "Science, Technology, and Politics". *Technology in Society* 24(1–2):9–26.

BROMLEY, H., AND APPLE, M., eds. (1998). *Education/Technology/Power: Computing as a Social Practice.* Albany, NY: SUNY Press.

BROWN, J. S. AND ADLER, R. D. (2008). "Minds on Fire," *Educause.* 43(1): 16–32.

BUCK, J. A., ET AL. (2000). "Communicating Science." *Science Communications* 22(1):73–87.

CALLAHAN, R. (1962). *Education and the Cult of Efficiency.* Chicago: University of Chicago Press.

CEO FORUM ON EDUCATION AND TECHNOLOGY. (2002). Five Year Project. www.ceoforum.org.

CEO FORUM POLICY PAPER. (2001). "Education Technology Must Be Included in Comprehensive Education Legislation." March. www.ceoforum.org.

CHAIKA, G. (1999). "Technology in the School: It *Does* Make a Difference." *Education World.* www.education-world.com.

CORDES, C., AND MILLER, E. (2000). *Fool's Gold: A Critical Look at Computers in Childhood.* College Park, MD: Alliance for Childhood.

CUBAN, L. (1986). *Teachers and Machines.* New York: Teachers College Press.

———. (2001). *Oversold and Underused: Computers in the Classroom.* Cambridge, MA: Harvard University Press.

DEWEY, J. (1933). *How We Think.* Lexington, MA: D.C. Heath.

EGAN, T., "Bill Gates Views What He's Sown in Libraries," *New York Times,* Nov. 6, 2002. www.nytimes.com.

"EQUITY GAP IN TECHNOLOGY ACCESS." (2002). April. Northwest Educational Technology Consortium website: www.netc.org.

EDUTOPIA. (2008). "Why Integrate Technology into the Curriculum?" www.edutopia.org. March 16.

"50 TRENDS SHAPING THE WORLD." (1991). *The Futurist* 25(1):13–18.

FIRST. (2006). "9,600 Students Converge on Georgia Dome." Press Release. April 5. www.usfirst.org.

Fox, N. (2004). *Against the Machine.* Washington, DC: Island Press.

FRIEDMAN, T., "Americans Are Falling Further Behind," *New York Times,* May 13, 2005.

GIROUX, H. A. (2001). *Stealing Innocence: Corporate Culture's War on Children.* New York: St. Martin's Press.

GLEICK, J. (1999). *Faster: The Acceleration of Just About Everything.* New York: Pantheon.

HEALY, J. M. (1998). *Failure to Connect: How Computers Affect Our Children's Minds—For Better and Worse.* New York: Simon and Schuster.

HUNTER, J. O. (1992). "Technological Literacy." *Educational Technology* 32:26–29.

INTERNATIONAL SOCIETY FOR TECHNOLGY IN EDUCATION. (2008a). *National Educational Technology Standards for Teachers.* 2d ed., www.iste.org.

———. (2008b). *Transforming Classroom Practice.* www.iste.org.

JACOBY, S. (2008). "The Dumbing of America." *Washington Post.* Feb 17, p. B01.

JOHNSON, J., AND BARKER, L. T. (2002). *Assessing the Impact of Technology in Teaching and Learning.* Ann Arbor: Institute for Social Research, University of Michigan. www.dlrn. org/star/sourcebook.html.

JOHNSON, M. AND LIBER, O. (2008). "The Personal Learning Environment and the Human Condition." *Interactive Learning Environments.* 16(1) 3–15. April.

KIRSNER, S., "High Schools Vie to Build a Robotic Champ." *New York Times,* April 18, 2002.

LANDRY, J. (2002). "Is Our Children Learning?" *Red Herring* 116:37–41.

LEE, L. (2000). *Bad Predictions.* Rochester, MI: Elsewhere Press.

LEISTNYA. P. (2008). Introduction: Teaching About and With Alternative Media. *Radical Teacher.* #81. www.radicalteacher.org.

LEMKE, C. (2005). "Measuring Progress with Technology in Schools." Special Report. T.H.E. Journal. April. www.thejournal.com.

LIGHT, J. (2001). "Rethinking the Digital Divide." *Harvard Educational Review* 71(4):709–733.

LIVINGSTON, P. (2008). "E-Learning Gets Real." *Technology Learning.* www.techlearning. com. May 22.

MACDONALD, G. J. (2004). "Contrarian Finding: Computers Are a Drag on Learning," *Christian Science Monitor.* Dec 6.

McCAIN, T. (2000). *Windows on the Future: Education in the Age of Technology.* New York: Corwin Press.

McKENZIE, J. (1999). *How Teachers Learn Technology Best.* Bellingham, WA: FNO Press.

———. (2000). *Beyond Technology.* Bellingham, WA: FNO Press.

———. (2001). *Planning Good Change with Technology and Literacy.* Bellingham, WA: FNO Press.

———. (2005). "Singular Displeasure: Technology, Literacy, and Semantic Power Plays." *From Now On.* 14(3): www.fno.org.

———. (2007). "Digital Nativism, Digital Delusions and Digital Depravation." *From Now On.* 17 (2). Nov www.fno.com.

———. (2008). "What Digital Age?" *From Now On.* 17 (5). May. www.fno.com

MEADE, S. D., AND DUGGER, W. E. (2004). "Reporting on the Status of Technology Education in the U.S." *The Technology Teacher.* October.

MONKE, L. (2001). *Breaking Down Digital Walls: Learning to Teach in a Post-Modern World.* Albany: SUNY Press.

NATIONAL EDUCATIONAL TECHNOLOGY STANDARDS. (2002). www.cnets.iste.org. October/ December.

NEW MEDIA CONSORTIUM. (2005). The 2005 Horizon Report. http://nmc.org.

NEW MEDIA CONSORTIUM (2008). *The Horizon Project:* Call to Scholarship. www.nmc.org.

OBLINGER, D. G., AND OBLINGER, J. L. (2005). *Educating the Net Generation.* Educause e-book. www.educause.edu.

OHMAN, R. (2002). "Computers and Technology." *Radical Teacher* 63:206.

O'NEIL, H., AND PEREZ, R., eds. (2003). *Technology Applications in Education.* Mahwah, NJ: Lawrence Erlbaum.

OPPENHEIMER, T. (2003). *The Flickering Mind: The False Promise of Technology in the Classroom and How Learning Can Be Saved.* New York: Random House.

PEARSON, G., AND YOUNG, A. (2002). *Technically Speaking: Why All Americans Need to Know More About Technology.* National Academy of Engineering. Washington, DC: National Academy Press.

PAPERT, S. (1993). *The Children's Machine: Rethinking School in the Age of the Computer.* New York: Basic Books.

———. (2002). "Technology in Schools: To Support the System or Render it Obsolete." Milken Exchange. Milken Family Foundation. www.mff.org/edtech.

PELGRUM, W. J. (2001). "Obstacles to the Integration of ICT in Education." *Computers in Education* 37(2):163–178.

PEW RESEARCH CENTER. (2002). Study of Student Use of Internet. www.pewinternet.org.

PFLAUM, W. D. (2004). *The Technology Fix.* Washington, DC: ASCD.

POSTMAN, N. (1992). *Technopoly: The Surrender of Culture to Technology.* New York: Knopf.

PRENSKY, M. (2006). *Don't Bother Me Mom—I'm Learning.* St. Paul, MN: Paragon

———. (2008). "The True Twenty-first Century Literacy is Programming." *Edutopia.* Feb.

PRENSKY, M. (2008). "Young Minds, Fast Times." *Edutopia Magazine.* www.edutopia.org June.

RAINIE, L. (2006). Life Online. Unpublished paper, presented to the Public Libraries Association. Boston. March 23.

REEVES, T. C. (1998). *The Impact of Media and Technology in Schools.* A Research Report for the Bertelsmann Foundation. Feb. 12. www.athenscademy.org.

RINGSTAFF, C., AND KELLY, L. (2002). "The Learning Return on Our Educational Technology Investment: A Review of Findings from Research." #IR021079. www.ERICIT.org.

RINGSTAFF, C., AND YOCAM, K. (1996). "Integrating Technology into Classroom Instruction." ACOT Report #22. www.apple.com/education/html.

ROMANO, M. T. (2003). *Empowering Teachers with Technology.* Lanham, MD: Scarecrow Press.

ROSE, L., GALLUP, A. M., ET AL. (2004). A Report on the Second Survey Conducted by the Gallup Organization for the International Technological Education Association. www.itea.org.

ROSENBLOOM, S. (2008). "Sorry Boys, This is our Domain." New York Times online. www.nytimes.com. February 21.

ROTHERHAM, A. J., (2006). "Virtual Schools, Real Innovation," *New York Times,* April 7, www.nytimes.com.

———. (2008). "Virtual Schools, Real Innovation," *New York Times* online. www.nytimes.com April 7.

SALPETER, J. (2008). "Make Students Info Literate." *Technology and Learning.* www.techlearning.com. May 22.

SANDHOLTZ, J. H., RINGSTAFF, C., AND DWYER, D. (1997). *Teaching with Technology.* New York: Teachers College Press.

SIEGEL, L. (2008). *Against the Machine: Being Human in the Age of the Electronic Mob.* New York: Spiegel and Grau.

SMITH, G. AND THRONE, S. (2007). *Differentiating Instruction With Technology in* K–12 *Classrooms*. www.iste.org.

SOFIA, Z. (2002). "The Mythic Machine," in *Education/Technology/Power*, ed. Bromley and Apple. Albany: SUNY Press.

SPIRO, R. J. (2006). "The New Gutenberg Revolution." *Educational Technology*. Jan./Feb.: 3–5.

STOLL, C. (1999). *High Tech Heretic: Why Computers Don't Belong in the Classroom*. New York: Doubleday.

TALBOTT, S. (2008). *Beyond Biotechnology: The Barren Promise of Genetic Engineering*. Lexington, KY: University of Kentucky Press.

TENNER, E. (1997). *Why Things Bite Back: Technology and the Revenge of Unintended Consequences*. New York: Vintage.

———. (2003). *Our Own Devices*. New York: Knopf.

Toward a New Golden Age in American Education. (2005). National Education Technology Plan. Washington, DC: U.S. Department of Education.

TUTTY, J. I. AND KLEIN, J. D. (2008). "Computer-Mediated Instruction." *Educational Technology Research and Development*. 56(2) 101–24. April.

TYACK, D., AND CUBAN, L. (2000). "Teaching by Machine," in *Jossey-Bass Reader on Technology and Learning*. San Francisco, CA: Jossey-Bass.

U.S. DEPARTMENT OF EDUCATION. (2004). National Education Technology Plan. Washington, DC. January 7. www.ed.gov.

U.S. DEPARTMENT OF EDUCATION. (2005). National Education Technology Plan. Washington, DC. www.ed.gov.

U.S. DEPARTMENT OF EDUCATION. (2007). *Connecting Students to Advanced Courses Online*. Washington, DC. www.ed.gov. Dec.

WARLICK, D. (2002). "New Century Schoolhouse." www.landmark-project.com.

WENGLINSKY, H. (1998). *Does It Compute?* Princeton, NJ: Educational Testing Service.

WERRY, C. (2002). "The Rhetoric of Commercial Online Education." *Radical Teacher* 63. Spring.

WILLIAMS, T. I. (1982). *A Short History of Twentieth-Century Technology*. Oxford: Oxford University Press.

WINDSCHITL, M., AND SAHL, K. (2002). "Tracing Teachers' Use of Technology in a Laptop Computer School." *American Educational Research Journal* 39(1):165–205.

WINOGRAD, K. (2002). "ABCs of the Virtual High School." The Technology Source. http://ts.mivu.org.

WISE, T. (2005). Personal Correspondence. June 13.

CHAPTER 14

Standardized Testing: Restrict or Expand

Should the use of standardized school tests be increased or decreased?

POSITION 1: FOR RESTRICTING TESTING

America's public schools administer more than 100 million standardized exams each year, including IQ, achievement, screening, and readiness tests. Much of the time and money devoted to testing is misspent. Multiple-choice questions cannot measure thinking skills, creativity, the ability to solve real problems, or the social skills we want our children to have. Moreover, many exams are biased racially, culturally, linguistically, and by class and gender.

—FairTest, 2007a

Vexing Tests

In a witty attack on standardized testing, Banesh Hoffmann (1962) recounted a debate played out on the pages of the London *Times*. A letter to the newspaper's editor asked for help in solving a multiple-choice problem from a battery of school tests the letter-writer's son had taken. At first glance, the question seemed to be straightforward and not surprising to anyone who has taken school tests. It asked, "Which is the odd one out among cricket, football, billiards, and hockey"?

The letter-writer believed the answer must be billiards because it is the only one of the four games played indoors. He admitted to being less than sure of his answer, and reported there was no agreement among his acquaintances. One of his neighbors argued the correct choice was cricket, because in all of the other games the object was to put a ball in a net. The writer's son had selected hockey because it was the only one that was a "girls' game." The letter writer asked readers of the *Times* for help. Ensuing letters and arguments succeeded only in muddying the waters, since the logic supporting one choice was no more compelling than the logic supporting any other. For example, billiards could be considered the odd one out because it is the only one of the four games listed that is not ordinarily a team game. It is the only one in which the color of the ball matters. It is the only one in which more than one ball is in play, and it is the only one played on a green cloth rather than a grass field. Unfortunately, equally convincing briefs could be submitted in behalf of the other choices.

Hoffmann fumed about the inherent bias in the question. He assumed the test was designed to measure reasoning ability and not sports knowledge, but he argued that the test-taker might be disadvantaged by too little experience with athletics; for example, not all students with good reasoning skills may know how cricket is played. Test-takers who know too much about sports also might be disadvantaged; they might choose hockey as the odd one out because it is really two different games that share the same name—in England and in several other countries, hockey is a game typically played on grass by players who receive no salary; elsewhere it is a game played on ice, often by professional athletes.

The language of this test item also may trip up students, preventing it from measuring reasoning ability. For example, many working-class students may not be familiar with either cricket or billiards. Items of this sort favor the language and culture of the middle and upper-middle classes, and low scores may reflect measures of social standing more than achievement or ability (Neill and Medina, 1989). Americans also could be disadvantaged by the test item wording, which asks test-takers to select the "odd one out." A similar test item in the United States probably would read, "Which of the following does not belong?"

Test questions of this sort seem silly. There is no readily discernible "right" answer, and test-takers have no opportunity to demonstrate the thought processes that led to their decisions. As Hoffmann noted, "What sense is there in giving tests in which the candidate just picks answers, and is not allowed to give the reasons for his choice?" (Hoffmann, 1962, p. 20). Multiple-choice questions are an unnatural problem-solving format incongruous with solving real-life problems. Rarely are life's dilemmas delineated by four answers, one of which is guaranteed to be correct. Good problem solvers in the real world seldom are locked away, deprived of books, computers, and human contact; they seldom are told to respond to a set of timed, multiple-choice questions with no practical meaning.

If multiple-choice questions, such as the one that vexed *Times* readers, were nothing more than a parlor game, a form of Trivial Pursuit played for amusement, few would object to them. Standardized testing, however, has serious consequences, and for public school students, the stakes are particularly high. Standardized test results help determine placement in reading groups, admission to the college-track programs in public high schools, entrance into selective colleges, scholarship awards, admission into medical and law schools, and licensing to practice a profession or trade.

If Testing Is the Answer, What Was the Question?

In the early twentieth century, defining "native intelligence" and attempting to measure it "scientifically" through standardized examinations instigated one of the most controversial legacies of the testing movement (Gould, 1981). Sir Francis Galton in England and Alfred Binet in France attempted to measure mental capacities through standardized tests (Cremin, 1961). Binet developed his test, at the request of the French government, to identify those children who were "mentally subnormal" and not able to function adequately in regular classrooms. Louis Terman translated Binet's tests into English for American students, and he and his colleagues adjusted the tests to comport with their own sense of how intelligence was distributed. For example, Terman believed men are more intelligent than women and rural people are less intelligent than urban dwellers. Therefore, when girls outscored boys, Terman changed the test items on which girls scored unusually well. He made no changes on items where urban children outscored rural children (Garcia and Pearson, 1994). Terman argued that intelligence tests make schools more efficient. He claimed the tests could be used to sort children into differentiated curricula designed to prepare them for their appropriate lot in life:

> Preliminary investigations indicate that an IQ below 70 rarely permits anything better than unskilled labor; the range of 70–80 is preeminently that of semiskilled labor; from 80–100 that of skilled or ordinary clerical labor; from 100–110 or 115 that of semiprofessional pursuits; and that above all of these are grades of intelligence which permit one to enter the professions or other large fields of business. (Terman, 1922, in Wolf et al., 1991)

Psychologists working for the United States government during World War I introduced the first wide-scale use of standardized intelligence tests. The army was interested in classifying all new recruits, giving special attention to two groups: those of exceptional ability and those unfit for military service. Binet and Terman had used individual IQ tests that were not well suited to large-scale testing; under the direction of American psychologists, the army developed the first mass-testing program in history (Gumbert and Spring, 1974, pp. 87–112). The army test came in two forms: The Army Alpha was a written, objective exam; the Army Beta was a pictorial exam designed for illiterate recruits and non-English speakers.

The army used the tests to answer questions about the placement of soldiers: Who would best fit where? Who should be discharged on the grounds of mental incompetence? How could the army best use the varied talents and abilities recruits brought with them? The results helped determine who should be in the infantry and who should go to the army language school.

> It is unclear to what extent the army actually acted on such recommendation. Nevertheless, some disturbing conclusions emerged from the army testing program. The average mental age of white Americans turned out to be 13 (barely above the level of morons). Test results revealed immigrants to be duller still (the average age of Russians being 11.34, Italians 11.01, and Poles 10.74), and Negroes came in last with an average mental age of 10.41. These findings fueled debates about immigration quotas, segregation, eugenics, and miscegenation for years to come. (Hanson, 1993, p. 212)

After the war, colleges and universities bought the surplus exams, and found the language of the army tests required only slight modification for use in schools. The original instructions given to soldiers read:

> Attention! The purpose of this examination is to see how well you can remember, think and carry out what you are told to do in the army. . . . Now in the army a man often has to listen to commands and carry them out exactly. I am going to give you these commands to see how well you carry them out. . . .

In schools, these instructions were changed to read:

> Part of being a good student is your ability to follow directions. . . . When I call "Attention," stop instantly what you are doing and hold your pencil up—so. Don't put your pencil down on the paper until I say "Go." . . . Listen carefully to what I say. Do just as you are told to do. As soon as you are through, pencils up. Remember, wait for the word "Go." (Gumbert and Spring, 1974, p. 94)

For many years, schools used IQ tests to track children based on their test performance. Intelligence was viewed as the "raw material" required for schooling, and students judged to have less intelligence received less education. This reliance on IQ tests was designed to make education more objective and more efficient; it produced the unintended result of limiting students' educational access (Darling-Hammond, 1994). Students performing at the lowest levels on IQ tests received an education designed to prepare them to be tractable, unskilled laborers. Only the highest-achieving students would be introduced to the most complex skills. Intellect was viewed as a biological trait much like height or eye color: It was thought to be inherited, measurable, and fixed. IQ tests allowed schools to sort students into appropriate curricula and thus into their later place in society (Callahan, 1962; Wolf et al., 1991). Too frequently, these tests excluded the majority of students from the best opportunities the school offered. More often than not, the best education and the most promising futures were reserved for those who performed well on high-stakes standardized tests, and standardized testing typically has worked to the disadvantage of most minority groups.

In the United States, African Americans score below 75 percent of Americans of European descent on most standardized tests, IQ tests, and achievement tests alike (Jencks and Phillips, 1998, p. 1). There also are significant gaps between standardized test scores of European Americans, Mexican Americans, and Native Americans. Some researchers claim the tests themselves are biased, arguing the tests "reflect the language, culture, or learning style of middle- to upper-class whites. Thus scores on these tests are as much measures of race or ethnicity and income as they are measures of achievement, ability, or skill" (Neill and Medina, 1989, p. 691). Furthermore, psychologists do not agree about the thing we call "intelligence"—whether it is fixed or changeable, measurable or only describable, singular or plural. For example, Gardner (1983, 1999) argues that children have multiple forms of "intelligence," and schools typically ignore all but two of these. To date, no single explanation successfully accounts for the gap between white and black scores on standardized exams. There are as many explanations as there are disciplinary orientations of the researchers

(Lee, 2002). Educators know one thing for certain: No matter how good their grades, students are at a disadvantage in school if they do not score well on standardized tests. And the higher the stakes, the greater the disadvantage. The negative consequences of testing are likely to fall hardest on the economically disadvantaged. The legacy of poor test performance is enduring, serving as painful memories of humiliation and a sense of inadequacy (Hanson, 1993).

Teachers of poor and minority children report they spend more time teaching to the test and are more likely to rely on data from standardized tests than do teachers of students from moderate- and high-income families (Garcia and Pearson, 1994). Poor and minority children spend more time on workbook exercises and busywork assignments. They are less likely than middle-class students to have access to classes where they can discuss what they know, read real books, write, or solve problems in mathematics, science, or other school subjects (Darling-Hammond, 1994). Students from poor families and children of minorities have been awarded an education of less substance because of their poor performance on standardized tests. As Madaus (1994) points out, "Clearly, the unintended negative outcomes brought about by the widespread policy use of IQ tests disproportionately disadvantaged minority populations. Despite Binet's original purpose to identify children in need of instructional assistance, the IQ test in this country led to blacks and Hispanics being disproportionately placed in dead-end classes for the 'educable mentally retarded'" (p. 86).

Misleading Test Results

Until the last few years, despite questions about the validity of individual items on standardized tests (Crouse and Trusheim, 1988; Hoffmann, 1962; Nairn and Associates, 1980; Owen, 1985), test-takers never were able to see a list of the "right" answers after they had taken the exams. The Educational Testing Service (ETS)[1] of Princeton, New Jersey, and other test developers published only a few sample questions, claiming full disclosure would compromise the tests. To make the tests reliable,[2] they argued, many items had to be repeated

---

[1] The Educational Testing Service of Princeton, New Jersey, is world's largest testing company. Formed in 1947 to develop and administer college entrance exams for returning World War II veterans, the company now administers more than 50 million assessments annually in over 180 countries. The ETS website reports company revenues in 2006 of $836 million (www.ets.org). For a critical view of standardized testing, consider the website of the National Center for Fair and Open Testing (FairTest) at www.fairtest.org. FairTest describes itself as an organization that "advances quality education and equal opportunity by promoting fair, valid, and educationally beneficial evaluation of students, teachers, and schools. FairTest also works to end the misuses and flaws of testing practices that impede those goals."

[2] Reliability in testing can be thought of as a synonym for stability, consistency, or dependability. Kerlinger's simile might be useful in understanding this concept. He writes: "A test is like a gun in its purpose. When we measure human attributes and abilities and achievements, we want to measure 'true' amounts of attributes that individuals possess. This is like hitting a target with a gun. With a test we want to hit the attribute. If a gun consistently hits a target—the shots cluster close together at or near the center of the target . . . we say it is reliable. Similarly with psychological and sociological measures. If they hit the target, they are reliable." (Kerlinger, 1979, p. 133)

from year to year, and the answers therefore must be held back from public scrutiny. The ETS acknowledged it was possible to construct new equivalent exams every year; however, it would be an expensive process, and test-takers ultimately would bear the costs.

Recognizing the power standardized exams have on the lives of individual test-takers, and failing to be persuaded by ETS's arguments, New York and California enacted legislation allowing test-takers to see the answers after they had taken the exams. These truth-in-testing laws revealed ambiguity in test items. In some instances, more than one answer was correct. The ETS and other test-makers took the issue to court, and in 1990 a federal district court judge in New York set aside the requirements of the test disclosure law on the grounds that it interfered with copyright laws. The truth-in-testing laws have cast doubt on the ability of tests to measure what they claim to measure, and have opened the issue of validity[3] to public examination.

There is good reason for public suspicion. Some people have intentionally used results of standardized tests to mislead the public. Take the case of the "magic mean," uncovered by a physician in West Virginia. Local newspapers reported students in his state were performing above the national average on standardized tests. This intrigued him, considering that West Virginia had one of the highest rates of illiteracy in the nation. Further checking revealed that no state using the test was reported to be below the mean. The tests compared student achievement with outdated and very low national norms. Therefore, the test results made even the worst test-taker (and the school systems that bought the tests) appear to be above average. As one testing critic notes, "standardized, nationally normed achievement tests give children, parents, school systems, legislatures, and the press inflated and misleading reports on achievement levels" (Cannell, 1987, p. 3).

Indeed, by the late 1990s, it was hard to find any school districts or states scoring below the mean on nationally normed standardized tests. These data have contributed to what has been termed the Lake Wobegon Effect, after the mythical Minnesota town created by Garrison Keillor in which "the women are strong, the men are good looking, and all the children are above average" (Fiske, 1988; Mehrens and Kaminski, 1989; Phillips, 1990). Testing designs of this type are not uncommon, and educators need to exercise caution before making inferences about quality of education based on data from standardized testing (Linn, 1993; Judson, 1996). For the past fifty years, psychometricians and companies that market tests have convinced the public that short-answer tests are objective, scientific measures deserving of public confidence and faith, when in fact these tests suffer from vagueness, ambiguity, imprecision, and bias. In

---

[3] Validity refers to the ability of a test to measure what the test-maker wants to measure. Kerlinger uses the following example: "Suppose a group of teachers of social studies writes a test to measure students' understanding of certain social concepts: justice, equality, and cooperation, for instance. The teachers want to know whether their students understand and can apply the ideas. But they write a test of only factual items about contemporary institutions. The test is then not valid for the purpose they had in mind." (Kerlinger, 1979, p. 138)

truth, there is nothing scientific or objective about these items; highly subjective human beings write, test, compile, and interpret each item (Owen, 1985).

Bias and Irrelevance

Standardized tests have long been part of the college admissions process. Testing held out the promise, now widely under attack, that admission to elite schools could be determined by achievement and merit rather than wealth or other factors. The now-familiar SAT exam was first developed in the late 1940s. Originally, the letters stood for Scholastic *Aptitude* Test, a form of intelligence test designed to sort students into various schools based on inherent ability. The name was changed to Scholastic *Assessment* Test, and today SAT is no longer considered an acronym but the name of the test itself. Make no mistake; the original SAT was designed by ETS (Educational Testing Service) to be a pure intelligence test, and it still is (Lemann, 2004).

Standardized testing programs discriminate against women, minorities, the poor, and English-language learners while failing to deliver on the promise of scientific measurement and prediction. Although class rank and high school grades are far better predictors of college success, testing advocates argue that exam scores are very useful in estimating first-year college grades. Consequently, SAT and ACT scores are often part of the data colleges use in making admission and scholarship decisions. According to test-preparation companies, students with higher standardized test scores earn higher grade point averages during their first year in college. In fact, SAT and ACT scores accurately measure how well a student is likely to do only about half of the time (Chenoweth, 1997; FairTest, 2007b).

For women, the SAT *underpredicts* their first-year grades. In one study, the gap between average male and female scores on the test is 61 points. Female test-takers scored 50 points lower on the math section and 11 points lower on the verbal section of the exam. If the SAT accurately predicted grade point average, males would have higher first-year grade point averages than female students. But this is not the case. Despite lower scores on the SAT, women earned higher grades than men (Rosser, 1987; Perez, 2004). The SAT does not predict what it is supposed to predict: success in college. The scores students get on SAT exams have less meaning than ETS has promised. Rosser concluded that because of sex bias on the SAT exam, women have less chance of receiving financial aid, being accepted to college, and being invited to join programs for the gifted. Because of an invalid exam, women are likely to earn less money and lose out on appointments to positions of leadership. In 1989, a federal district court ruled that New York State's Regents Scholarship, based on a student's performance on the SAT exam, discriminated against women. Women had previously won only 43 percent of the scholarships. After the decision, which required the State of New York to consider high school grades as well as standardized test scores, women won 51 percent of the awards (Arenson, 1996).

The problem of discrimination is made worse by "coaching"—the process of improving individual scores through test-preparation programs, some costing nearly $1,000. Unfortunately, college admissions officers cannot separate applicants who were coached from those who were not. It is not possible to know if an individual's test score was the product of his or her own effort or the work of one or more professional coaching companies. Coaching may raise a student's score by 150 points or more on the SAT (FairTest, 2007a), creating a clear but unfair advantage in admissions for those who can afford to pay.

Tests, Curricula, and Learning

Despite their problems, standardized tests continue to exert great influence on schools. Every teacher knows that testing drives the curriculum: What is tested is taught. No teacher wants his or her students to perform poorly on standardized achievement tests, and no school administrator wants his or her school to rank below others in the state or district. Everyone in education knows that, too often, newspapers report results of statewide testing in much the same way they report basketball standings. "We're Number One" or "County Schools Lowest in State" are not uncommon headlines in many local newspapers. To avoid such invidious comparisons, schools gear instruction to the test. Over time, material not tested tends not to be taught. If only math and language arts are tested, other subjects, such as art and music, science and social studies, are likely to be deemphasized or eliminated. Teachers and administrators fall victim to test-makers' promises and the public's misplaced faith in testing. In truth, there is no compelling reason to subject students to large-scale multiple-choice exams.

National testing has become a national obsession. In the 1990s, President George Bush encouraged the education community to develop "New World Standards" in each of five core subject areas. President Clinton, in his 1997 State of the Union address, urged states to adopt higher standards and implement testing programs to ensure the standards were met. The Elementary and Secondary Education Act passed in December 2001, during the presidency of George W. Bush, and referred to as the No Child Left Behind Act, requires each state to establish standards for all students in math and language arts. To measure the extent to which students are making "adequate yearly progress" toward meeting the standards, states must conduct academic assessments in grades three to eight and once in high school. The results of this legislation have been a bonanza for test-makers who have fallen over themselves in a mad scramble to rush standardized tests to market. Many believe few outside of test-makers benefit from this legislation. FairTest argues that states are destroying local curricula and individually crafted assessment through the implementation of mandated standardized tests. The results have sorted students into winners and losers rather than help all children get a high-quality education (FairTest, 2008a). Recent polls by the Gallup Organization suggest that the public has become disenchanted with increased reliance on standardized testing. Asked about the value of teaching to the test, 79 percent reported that it is a "bad thing" (Rose and Gallup, 2007, p. 37).

There is an antidote to standardized testing that does not sacrifice accountability. In every community, teachers, parents, and administrators should select appropriate content based on students' interests, experiences, goals, and needs. Teachers should teach that content with all the skill at their command, and evaluate the extent of student learning with a wide variety of instruments. Students should be encouraged to demonstrate their ability to think through written exercises, verbal expression, and informal papers, and should be given ample opportunity to demonstrate the reasons for their choices. Assessment of student learning requires educators to develop a broader, richer array of measures (Ardovino, Hollingsworth, and Ybarra, 2000; Janesick, 2001; FairTest, 2008b). State and federal legislation should not try to reduce student achievement to a single numerical score. Multiple-choice tests cannot tell the story of academic success. Many students simply do not test well, and all students should be given multiple ways to demonstrate what they have learned. Assessment programs should be designed to improve student learning, not measure one student against another or measure a student's progress against some arbitrary standard.

Assessment programs should focus on the individual student and examples of what they actually have produced. A student's record of school achievement should include a rich portfolio of papers, essays, videos, poems, photographs, drawings, and tape-recorded answers, not a series of test scores. When parents want to know how well their child is doing in school, they should be able to review a portfolio of their child's work with the teacher or at least receive a written narrative from the teacher. Good assessment requires schools to use multiple forms of evidence, both quantitative and qualitative, that is, numbers and human judgment. No important academic decision should be made on the basis of only one piece of information, such as a standardized test score, and scores from many standardized tests do not equal multiple forms of evidence (FairTest, 2008b). Parents should be suspicious of schools that confuse the scores on a norm-referenced examination with a child's progress in the classroom. Parents should not worry about a teacher who does not rely on standardized tests; they should worry more about teachers who believe standardized tests measure the ways in which a child's mind works (Kohn, 2000). Educational decisions should not be based solely on test scores. Testing alone cannot convey to students, parents, college admissions officers, or anyone else adequate information about individual achievement and ability. Standardized testing is a threat to educational improvement, and its use should be restricted.

POSITION 2: FOR EXPANDING TESTING

Reform in elementary and secondary education remains in the forefront of the public's mind . . . Most of these reforms rely on testing—testing to show increased rigor of school curricula, testing to determine if students advance and graduate, testing to judge the effectiveness of schools and teachers, and testing to compare districts, states, and nations.

—P. E. Barton, director of ETS Policy Information
Center, quoted in Bennett, 1998/2008, p. iii

Americans support public education, but they are not satisfied with the current quality of schooling. Only 11 percent of Americans say that their schools are working well today, and a solid majority supports reforms that include developing higher standards for student achievement and holding students accountable for learning through regular, objective assessments (Hart and Winston, 2005). Standardized tests may not be popular among everyone, but several decades of opinion research indicates that the public is quite comfortable with the contributions standardized tests make to the quality of education. As one testing expert notes, "The American people have consistently advocated greater use of standardized testing, preferably with consequences for failure (i.e., 'stakes'). The margins in favor have been huge. . . . Testing's strong popularity extends across most stakeholder groups, including parents, students, employers and teachers" (Phelps, 2003, p. 15; 2005).

Previous generations of education reformers concerned themselves with making education available to children of all classes and races, and to a large extent they were successful. By the 1990s, a higher percentage of students were completing high school than ever before. The issue is no longer *availability;* the current generation of reformers now is forced to consider the *quality* of school experiences. As Mortimer Adler (1982) argues, we cannot satisfy the legal mandates for education simply by guaranteeing all children access to education. In order to satisfy the educational responsibilities of a democratic society, public education must demonstrate that each student is acquiring requisite skills and knowledge. Schools must guarantee the education they offer has a demonstrably positive effect on a student's ability to read, write, and do mathematics, and that moving up the academic ladder from grade to grade is based on merit rather than social promotion. The issue of educational quality raises a broad range of questions about performance and accountability.

Answers to these questions must be based on high-quality hard data. Schools need quantifiable measures of student performance and documentation of teacher effectiveness if they hope to maintain public support. Policymakers must have objective information in order to make intelligent decisions. Although no single means of data collection is sufficient, data from well-designed standardized tests are crucial to an understanding of school outcomes. Good tests and good testing programs permit schools to gather information about curricula and students not available to them through other means. Without these data, schools cannot make appropriate decisions about curriculum quality or power of specific programs to enhance learning.

Standardized testing is part of the scientific base that supports the art of teaching. Scientific testing permits measurement of the teacher's art, complementing as well as assessing classroom practice. Standardized testing sometimes has a negative connotation. You no doubt have heard that the tests are biased or unfair or worse. The truth is that standardized tests are designed to promote fairness and ensure a level playing field. *Standardized* refers to the fact that the test content and the conditions for test-takers are always and everywhere the same. When students take the ACT or the SAT, for example, they are all taking the same tests under the same testing conditions, and they will be compared with students of similar age and years of schooling (Sireci, 2005). Formal testing programs were introduced into schools in the nineteenth century to counter charges of examiner bias and subjectivity.[4] Today, standardized testing programs also provide the yardstick society uses to chart the progress and shortcomings of education, and their results allow schools to report the status of education to public officials and parents. Test and measurement experts are often at odds with others in education, and have suffered abuse from critics skeptical about the power of testing and fearful of the testing agencies' power to influence public policy. The purpose here is not to answer the critics or submit a brief in support of the Educational Testing Service or the National Assessment of Educational Progress. Instead, we will argue that (1) standardized testing is an essential tool for examining the measurable dimensions of education; and (2) education has entered an era of accountability. School officials must demonstrate that the money taxpayers spend for education is paying dividends in quality.

Testing for the Good of Schools and Students

Standardized testing is an essential element of rational curriculum work. The data testing programs generate help curriculum planners determine whether the measured outcomes of a given set of instructional inputs match the intended goals. In other words, tests can help educators find out if a specific program is working the way it was designed to work. When taxpayers are asked to foot the bill for a new science program in high schools or a new math program in elementary schools, they should be informed of the anticipated effects of these programs and how the results will be measured. The public demands accountability. The public views education reform proposals as incomplete without the means to hold teachers and administrators accountable (Hart and Winston, 2005). This is a simple matter of cost accounting and fiscal responsibility.

Effective change does not occur by chance. Educational decisions must be made about student progress, rate of achievement of proximate goals, and the best choice among competing paths to the next objective. Educational planners need to choose appropriate measures of student attainment. Impressionistic data are not sufficient; anecdotal evidence is not scientific. It is not enough that a program "seems to be working" or teachers "claim to like" this method or that approach. Schools need to have better answers to direct questions about the curriculum and student learning. At what grade level are students reading? What do diagnostic and prescriptive tests tell us about a child's performance in academic skill areas? How much of the required curricula have students mastered?

---

[4] Nineteenth-century Britain, in the throes of an expanding domestic economy and of becoming an international empire, found it could not satisfy the demand for large numbers of middle-class managers through the traditional patronage appointments. There simply were not enough privileged males—the sons of civil servants, members of Parliament, or others of wealth and connections—to fill the vacancies worldwide. Competitive exams were introduced to open the civil service to a broader range of male applicants.

The United States also used testing to democratize the selection of government workers. Political abuse, through patronage, was rampant in the nineteenth century. Civil Service reform began with the Pendleton Act of 1883, which established competitive exams for prospective government employees.

Standardized testing should not be viewed only as a report card but as part of an assessment system that permits schools to make decisions about curriculum and instruction. Standardized achievement tests are objective measures of performance. Standardized tests are designed to measure the extent to which the nation is meeting its goals and responsibilities to provide educational quality to all children.

Shooting the Messenger

Since 1969, the federal government has financed an assessment program known as the National Assessment of Educational Progress (NAEP). Administered since 1983, by the Educational Testing Service of Princeton, New Jersey, NAEP's website (www.nces.ed.gov/nationsreportcard) describes the organization as "the only nationally representative and continuing assessment of what America's students need to know and can do in various subject areas"—mathematics, reading, science, writing, the arts, civics, economics, geography, and U.S. history. Among its other assessments, NAEP reports national test results for students in grades four, eight, and twelve, in both public and private schools. The data from the NAEP national assessments are reported for individual states, as well as the national averages and for specific student groups in the population; for example, reports are grouped by race, ethnicity, and gender.

Consider Figure 14.1. It contains a sample of the NAEP questions used in the mathematics assessment of 2007.

Much of what NAEP reported in 2007 is very quite positive. For example:

- The average mathematics score for eighth-graders was higher in 2007 than in any previous assessment year.
- In 2007, white, black, and Hispanic students scored higher in mathematics than they did in 2005.
- The white-black achievement score gap at grade 8 narrowed between 2005 and 2007.

Some of the data from the 2007 Mathematics Assessment is quite troubling. For example:

- In 2007, 30 percent of all eighth-graders were below the "basic" level of proficiency; 39 percent were at the basic level; only 31 percent were at the "proficient" level or above.
- The average scores for black students in the eighth grade trailed the average scores for Hispanic and white students in the same grade level.
- The average scores for eighth-grade public school students eligible for free or reduced price school lunch trailed behind classmates not eligible (Lee, Griggs, and Dion, 2007).

Reporting valid test results, good and bad, NAEP provides the nation with fair and accurate measures of achievement in important subject areas. It is perhaps the best national achievement program in the nation (Haladyna, 2002, p. 101). NAEP also collects significant demographic data from test-takers—such as race, gender, and the level of parental education—and these data permit an

FIGURE 14.1 2007 Mathematics Assessment. Sample Question (Grade 8).

1. Mr. Hardt bought a square piece of carpet with an area of 39 square yards. The length of each side of this carpet is between which of the following?
   A) 4 yards and 5 yards
   B) 5 yards and 6 yards
   C) 6 yards and 7 yards
   D) 7 yards and 8 yards
   E) 9 yards and 10 yards
   Content Area: Measurement (Low complexity)
   National Results: 49 percent correct

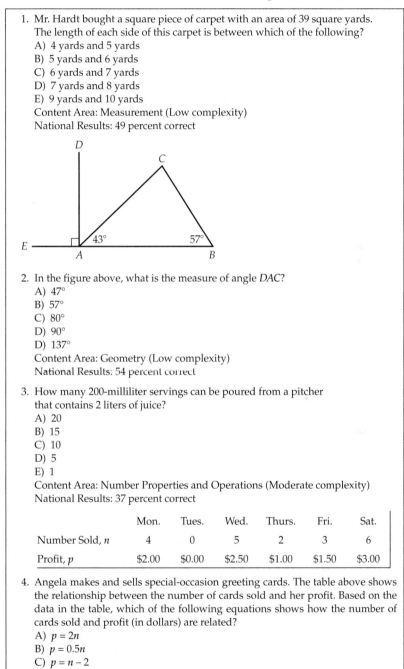

2. In the figure above, what is the measure of angle *DAC*?
   A) 47°
   B) 57°
   C) 80°
   D) 90°
   D) 137°
   Content Area: Geometry (Low complexity)
   National Results: 54 percent correct

3. How many 200-milliliter servings can be poured from a pitcher that contains 2 liters of juice?
   A) 20
   B) 15
   C) 10
   D) 5
   E) 1
   Content Area: Number Properties and Operations (Moderate complexity)
   National Results: 37 percent correct

	Mon.	Tues.	Wed.	Thurs.	Fri.	Sat.
Number Sold, *n*	4	0	5	2	3	6
Profit, *p*	$2.00	$0.00	$2.50	$1.00	$1.50	$3.00

4. Angela makes and sells special-occasion greeting cards. The table above shows the relationship between the number of cards sold and her profit. Based on the data in the table, which of the following equations shows how the number of cards sold and profit (in dollars) are related?
   A) $p = 2n$
   B) $p = 0.5n$
   C) $p = n - 2$
   D) $p = 6 - n$
   E) $p = n + 1$
   Content Area: Algebra (Moderate complexity)
   National Results: 54 percent correct

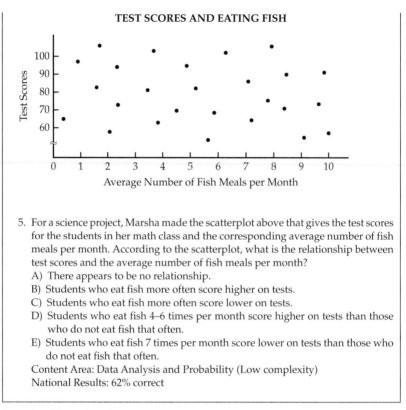

5. For a science project, Marsha made the scatterplot above that gives the test scores for the students in her math class and the corresponding average number of fish meals per month. According to the scatterplot, what is the relationship between test scores and the average number of fish meals per month?
   A) There appears to be no relationship.
   B) Students who eat fish more often score higher on tests.
   C) Students who eat fish more often score lower on tests.
   D) Students who eat fish 4–6 times per month score higher on tests than those who do not eat fish that often.
   E) Students who eat fish 7 times per month score lower on tests than those who do not eat fish that often.
   Content Area: Data Analysis and Probability (Low complexity)
   National Results: 62% correct

Source: http://nces.ed.gov/nationsreportcard/itmrls/itemdisplay.

examination of student scores in the context of the student's learning and home environments. For example, a long-term trand assessment asked students about the time they spent on homework and about computer access and use. The assessment also found that, "At age 13, the percentage of students spending less than 1 hour on homework increased from 36 percent in 1984 to 40 percent in 2004," and "The percentage of 13-year-olds with access to computers in school increased from 12 percent in 1978 to 57 percent in 2004" (Perie and Moran, 2005, pp. 1–5).

The point here is not to champion NAEP but to celebrate the contributions that standardized testing programs make to our understanding of educational outcomes, and to argue that without high-quality data from standardized tests, we would not be able to assess and understand the level of students' subject matter knowledge. What other measures are available? For example, would a comparison of students' grades over time tell us very much about achievement? Of course not. Research indicates the persistence of grade inflation, defying easy understanding of what an "A" means now and what it did 20 years ago (Woodruff and Ziomek, 2004a). Research also confirms another commonsense notion: the poor reliability of grades as a measure of student achievement. As everyone knows, a student's grades reflect not only the student's achievements, but also the grading climate of the school the student attended and whether the student's teachers were "tough" or "easy" graders (Woodruff and Ziomek, 2004b). By contrast, standardized test scores have the same meaning in all schools. No other forms of assessment can compete with standardized tests for gathering valid, reliable, and economical data about student performance.

Limits to Alternate Assessments

Most of us are familiar with tests that indirectly measure what we know. For example, a test-maker who wanted to determine students' woodworking ability might devise a test composed of a series of multiple-choice items. Students might be asked which of the following tools would be needed to make a wooden bowl: (a) a ball peen hammer, (b) a lathe chisel, (c) a screwdriver, or (d) a wrench? Other questions might probe the students' knowledge of various types of wood, appropriate procedures for using power tools, types of finishing materials, and safety procedures. These items taken together might indicate a student's knowledge of bowl making, but the student's score would tell the test-maker very little about the student's actual ability to fashion a wooden bowl. A more direct measure of that ability would entail taking students into a fully equipped woodworking shop to watch them set about making a bowl from a block of wood. This authentic measure of performance would allow the test-taker to demonstrate actual ability in a real-life situation, and would allow the test-giver to ask why students followed certain procedures or omitted others (Cizek, 1991).

However, authentic assessment is expensive, time-consuming, and impossible to implement on a large scale (Phelps, 2003). Standardized tests have unrivaled ability to deliver objective data that allow test-takers to know where they stand in relation to others and that permit policy-makers to gauge the progress of educational change. As the CEO of ETS notes, "When it comes to promoting standards, accountability, and student achievement, well-designed research-based assessments are fundamental. That's true whether they're measuring student learning at the end of a course of study or during a classroom lesson . . . [They] help identify a school's strength and weakness and point the way to improvement. They can ensure that higher standards mean something" (Landgraff, 2007).

Assessment of student learning always entails problems. Although policy-makers would prefer easy, accurate, and inexpensive assessments, their designs must be complex to account for variations among students, teachers, and curricula (Linn, 1993; Koretz et al., 1994). Charges that well-constructed, appropriately-standardized exams are guilty of ethnic and gender bias cannot be substantiated by the evidence of the research literature (Reynolds, Livingston, and Wilson, 2006). Psychometric test designers continue to produce better, more reliable testing instruments. Everyone interested in improving education would benefit from expanded use of standardized tests. They are both necessary and beneficial for schools and students.

For Discussion

1. Everyone agrees that good teachers are central to improving student learning. However, identifying good teachers has never been easy. In 2008, New York City Public Schools examined whether good teachers could be identified through the performance of their students on standardized tests. The teachers were to be judged by how much progress their students made in the course of a year and how the students' progress compared with similar populations of students taught by other teachers.

   Should teachers be evaluated by the performance of their students on standardized exams? Are there other/better ways to identify good teachers? Should the teachers of the highest performing students be paid more than other teachers?

2. Some research indicates parents want tests that produce information about how well their children are performing, how well they can solve problems, and where they need additional help. In one example, parents were asked to compare two sample items from a standardized test:

   a. How much change will you get if you have $6.55 and spend $4.32? (1) $2.23, (2) $2.43, (3) $3.23, (4) $10.87, and

   b. Suppose you couldn't remember what 8×7 is. How could you figure it out?

   Parents preferred the second question because they believed it to be more challenging and would likely lead teachers to a better understanding of children's thinking about mathematics (Kohn, 2000, p. 45).

   As a student do you prefer question a or b? Which is more common? Are both necessary?

3. Charles Murray of the American Enterprise Institute writes: "For most high school students who want to attend an elite college, the SAT is more than a test. It is one of life's landmarks" (2007, p.1). Once a supporter of the exam, Murray now believes that the exam should be abolished. Citing research evidence, he argues that the SAT does not predict college success any better than high school grades and it has become a negative force in American life. In 2008, FairTest reported that 755 four-year colleges did not use the SAT-1 or the ACT to admit a substantial number of undergraduates (www.fairtest.org).

   If you were designing the admission process for your college or university, what standardized tests, if any, would you use? In place of, or in addition to, standardized tests, how would you decide which students get the opportunity to attend your school? Would you use class rank, high school grades, interviews, records of extracurricular activities, or the academic rigor of the student's high school classes? Would you include the applicant's history of service or athletics, whether or not the applicant was first-generation college, or the socioeconomic status of the applicant's family?

References

ADLER, M. J. (1982). *The Paideia Proposal: An Educational Manifesto*. New York: Macmillan.

ARDOVINO, J. HOLLINGSWORTH, J. AND YBARRA, S. (2000). *Multiple Measures: Accurate Ways to Assess Student Achievement*. Thousand Oaks, CA: Corwin.

ARENSON, K. W. (1996) "College Board Revises Test to Improve Chances for Girls." *New York Times*, Oct. 2, www.nytimes.com.

BENNETT, R. E. (1998/2008). "Reinventing Assessment, Speculations on the Future of Large-Scale Educational Testing." www.ets.org/media/research.

CALLAHAN, E. (1962). *Education and the Cult of Efficiency*. Chicago: University of Chicago Press.

CANNELL, J. J. (1987). *Nationally Normed Elementary Achievement Testing In America's Public Schools: How All 50 States Are Above the National Average.* 2nd Ed. Daniels, WV: Friends for Education.

CHENOWETH, K. (1997). "A Measurement of What?" *Black Issues in Higher Education.* 14: 18–22, 25.

CIZEK, G. J. (1991). "Innovation or Enervation? Performance Assessment in Perspective."*Kappan* 72: 695–699.

CREMIN, L. (1961). *The Transformation and the School: Progressivism in American Education, 1876–1957.* New York: Knopf.

CROUSE, J. AND TRUSHEIM, D. (1988). *The Case Against the SAT.* Chicago: University of Chicago Press.

DARLING-HAMMOND, L. (1994). "Performance-Based Assessment and Educational Equity." *Harvard Educational Review* 64:5–30.

FairTest. (2007a)."The Testing Explosion." (www.fairtest.org/testing-explosion)

_____. (2007b). "The New SAT: A Better Test or Just a Better Marketing Ploy?" www.fairtest.org/new-sat-better-test?

_____. (2007c). SAT I: A Faulty Instrument for Predicting College Success." www.fairtest.org/facts/satvalidity.

_____ . (2008a). "No Child Left Behind After Six Years: An Escalating Track Record of Failure." www.fairtest.org/nclb-after-six-years.

_____. (2008b). ("Joint Statement On No Child Left Behind (NCLB) Act.") www.fairtest.org/node/30.

FISKE, E. B. (1988). "America's Test Mania," *New York Times*, Education Life, April 10.

GARCIA, G. E., AND PEARSON, P. D. (1994). "Assessment and Diversity," in *Review of Research in Education,* ED. L. Darling-Hammond. Washington, DC: American Educational Research Association.

GARDNER, H. (1983). *Frames of Mind: The Theory of Multiple Intelligences.* New York: Basic Books.

_____. (1999). *Intelligence Reframed: Multiple Intelligence for the 21st Century.* New York: Basic Books.

GOULD, S. J. (1981). *The Mismeasure of Man.* New York: W.W. Norton.

HALADYNA, T. M. (2002). *Essentials of Standardized Achievement Testing; Validity and Accountability.* Boston: Allyn and Bacon.

HANSON, F. A. (1993). *Testing Testing: Social Consequences of the Examined Life.* Berkeley: University of California.

HART, P. D., AND WINSTON, D. (2005). *"Ready for the Real World? Americans Speak on High School Reform."* Princeton, NJ: Educational Testing Service. www.ets.org

JANESICK, V. J. (2001). *The Assessment Debate: A Reference Handbook.* Santa Barbara, CA. ABC-CLIO.

JENCKS, C., AND PHILLIPS, M., EDS. (1998). *The Black-White Test Score Gap.* Washington, DC: Brookings Institution.

JUDSON, G. (1996). "What Makes the School Shine? Test Tampering, Officials Say," *New York Times*, May 1. www.nytimes.com.

KERLINGER, F. N. (1979). *Behavioral Research.* New York: Holt, Rinehart, and Winston.

KOHN, A. (2000). *The Case Against Standardized Testing: Raising the Scores, Ruining the Schools.* Portsmouth, NH: Heinemann.

KORETZ. D. ET AL. (1994). "The Vermont Portfolio Assessment: Findings and Implications." *Educational Measurement: Issues and Practice* 13:5–16.

LANDGRAFF, K. M. (2007). "Making Higher Standards Mean Something." http:www.ets. org/assessments.

LEE, J. (2002). "Racial and Ethnic Achievement Gap Trends: Reversing the Progress Toward Equity?" *Education Researcher* 31: 3–12.

LEE, J., Griggs, W. and Dion, G. (2007). *The Nation's Report Card: Mathematics* 2007 (NCES-2007-494). National Center for Education Statistics, Institute of Education Science, U.S. Department of Education, Washington, DC.

LEMANN, N. (2004). "A History of Admissions Testing," in *Rethinking the SAT: The Future of Standardized Testing In University Admissions*, ed. R. Zwick. New York: Routledge Falmer.

LINN, R. L. (1993). Educational Assessment: Expanded Expectation and Challenges." *Educational Evaluation and Policy Analysis* 15:1–16.

MADDAUS, G. F. (1994). "A Technological and Historical Consideration of Equity Issues Associated with Proposals to Change the Nation's Testing Policy." *Harvard Educational Review* 64:76–95.

MURRAY, C. (2007). "Abolish the SAT." *The American.* www.american.com/archive/2007/july-august.

MEHRENS, W. A., AND KAMINSKI, J. (1989). "Methods for Improving Standardized Test Scores: Fruitful, Fruitless, or Fraudulent?" *Educational Measurement: Issues and Practice* 8:14–22.

NAIRN, A. AND ASSOCIATES. (1980). *The Reign of ETS: The Corporation That Makes Up Minds.* Washington, DC: Nairn and Associates.

NEIL, D. M., AND MEDINA, N.J. (1989). "Standardized Testing: Harmful to Educational Health." *Kappan* 70: 688–697.

OWEN, D. (1987). *None of the Above.* Boston: Houghton Mifflin.

PEREZ, C. (2004). "Reassessing College Admissions: Examining Tests and Admitting Alternatives," in *Rethinking the SAT*, ed. R. Zwick, New York: Routledge Falmer.

PERIE, M., MORAN, R. (2005). "NAEP 2004 Trends in Academic Progress: Three Decades of Student Performance in Reading and Mathematics." www.nces.ed.gov/nationsreportcard/pubs/2005.

PHELPS, R. P. (2003). *Kill the Messenger: The War on Standardized Testing.* New Brunswick, NJ: Transaction.

_____. (2005*). Defending Standardized Testing*: Mahwah, NJ: Lawrence Erlbaum.

PHILLIPS, G.W. (1990). "The Lake Wobegone Effect." *Educational Measurement: Issues and Practice* 9:3,14.

REYNOLDS, C. R., LIVINGSTON, R.B. AND WILSON, V. (2006). *Measurement and Assessment in Education.* Boston: Pearson.

ROSE, L. C. AND GALLUP, A. M. (2007). "The 39th Annual Phi Delta Kappa/Gallup Poll of the Public's Attitude Toward the Public Schools." *Kappan* 89:33–45.

ROSSER, P. (1987). *Sex Bias in College Admissions Testing: Why Women Lose Out,* 2nd Ed. Cambridge, MA: FairTest.

SIRECI, S. G. (2005). "The Most Frequently *Unasked* Questions About Testing," in *Defending Standardized Testing*, ed. R.P. Phelps. Mahwah, NJ : Lawrence Erlbaum.

TERMAN, L. M. (1922*). Intelligence Testing and School Reorganization.* Yonkers-on-Hudson, NY: World Book.

WOLF, J. B. ET AL. (1991), "To Use Their Minds Well: Investigating New Forms of Student Assessment," in *Review of Research in Education*, ed. G. Grant. Washington, DC: American Educational Research Association.

WOODRUFF, D. J., AND ZIOMEK, R.L., (2004a). "High School Grade Inflation from 1991 to 2003." Iowa City, IA: ACT Research Report Series. www.act.org/research/reports/pdf/act_rr2004-4.pdf.

_____. (2004b). "Differential Grading Standards Among High Schools, 1998–2002." Iowa City, IA: ACT Research Report Series. www.act.org/research/reports/pdf/act_rr2004-2.pdf.

How Should Schools Be Organized and Operated?

School Environment

About Part Three: In Chapter 1, we argue that educational issues can be fully understood only by examining them against a larger social backdrop. Schooling and school policy are part of the political and economic context of society, and while issues in education may at first glance seem to concern only matters of instruction and learning and assessment, we believe schools are influenced by the social values of the communities in which they are located and the political systems that sustain them. Schools and society cannot be separated, and the influence flows in both directions. Schools influence society by how young children are educated and the values and content that are prized and passed on to them. Schools and society form a mutually-sustaining environment with obvious tensions.

Discipline and justice, unions and school leadership, academic freedom, inclusion and mainstreaming, and violence in schools are issues about the school environment you will be asked to consider here. The five chapters in this section focus on questions about the ways in which schools are organized and operated, and their relationship to justice and the just society.

PUBLIC EDUCATION AND PUBLIC PURPOSE

The link between society and the kinds of schools necessary to support it was described by Plato (427–347 B.C.E). Although Plato often is referred to as the "first philosopher of education," he was less interested in schools than their role in supporting the state. Plato's views of education came directly from his ideas about justice and the just society. For Plato, justice is so great a good that it is worth any cost, even the sacrifice of individual liberty. Plato believed democracy was dangerous and unnecessary, and beyond the intellectual grasp of most citizens. He argued that the great mass of people were not able to move beyond the enjoyment of bodily pleasure to the pleasure of honor, and only a few of the latter group were capable of enjoying the truest pleasure, that of the intellect (Curren, 2000, p. 51). For Plato, justice is the harmony achieved by everyone doing the work for which they were best suited and trained. Farmers farm; craftsmen build; philosophers rule. Democracy is dangerous to Plato's way of thinking; it could produce injustice and chaos by allowing people without good reasoning powers the freedom to choose their own direction in life as well as their own leaders.

Most contemporary definitions of justice involve the equal treatment of individuals and relationship among individuals within a fair and democratic system. That is, justice is related to the principle of each person getting what he or she is due—no more, no less—of all things, good and bad. Most modern writers try to situate justice in an individual context. They ask, what should the state do (or refrain from doing) to determine who should enjoy the benefits and shoulder the burdens of society when other citizens have equally good claims to them (Rawls, 1971; Nozick, 1974)? In America, we often think of justice both as a right of citizens and an obligation of the state. Justice demands certain actions by the state to ensure

fairness. By law, American citizens are to be treated equally. Their behavior, right or wrong, is to be judged independent of gender or race or social class. The just society treats everyone fairly. Of course we can all think of exceptions to this principle of justice. It is a safe bet there are always more paupers than millionaires on death row, and we can all name individuals who have escaped minor infractions of the law because of who they are or who they know. Our notion of modern justice, however, is rooted in the principle of fair treatment by the state for all individuals, and we are taught to accept no less.

In Part One, we argue that school is both the source of public disputes and a logical place for their thoughtful resolution. We encouraged you to consider the logic and evidence of competing views on six specific issues. We ask, whose interests should schools serve based on what is just and equitable. In Part Two, we ask you to consider what knowledge is of most value and what should be taught. The organization of this book reflects our belief that schools are social institutions and any notion of schooling begins with questions focusing on the expectations society has for student achievement and behavior and social justice. Plato's view of schools is similarly linked to social ends, but because we might not share his view of justice, we might not share his vision of the ideal school.[1] Of particular interest

[1]Karl Popper, the late British philosopher (1902–1994), argues Plato's sense of justice is not based on fairness for the individual or right action by the state to protect the individual, but is instead a justification for what is good for the state and the ruling aristocracy. Plato's justice, according to Popper, is designed to protect the state from any change and to hold firm the rigid class structure of Craftsmen, Guardians, and Rulers. Plato's justice is a property of the state necessary to ensure its own best functioning and ultimate survival. Citizens of Plato's state fall into social classes because of their natural talents and abilities, and are all expected to serve the state in different, fixed, and predetermined ways. Some men will naturally be weavers; others will be warriors; and a few will be selected to lead. Craftsmen will never become warriors; leadership will be left to the leaders. Justice is the harmonious and selfless toil of individuals in support of the state (Popper, 1966).

in Part Three is the job of teaching. One set of questions running through Chapters 15 through 19 asks you to consider the role teachers should play in schools. How is school discipline related to and affected by notions of justice? What should be the nature of teachers' work? How much decision-making authority should teachers have? How should the work of teachers be organized and managed to maximize student learning? How free should teachers be to select content and teaching methods?

Consider Plato's recommendations for teaching subject matter. In Book II of the *Republic,* Plato argues, "we must set up a censorship over the fable-makers, and approve any good fable they make, and disapprove the bad; those which are approved we will persuade the mothers and nurses to tell the children, and to mould the souls of the children by the fables even more carefully than the bodies by their hands. Most of those they tell now must be thrown away" (Plato, 1984, p. 174). Plato recognizes that stories have great influence on children's behaviors, and many childhood behaviors carry into adulthood. Plato advocates censorship of all stories that are either (a) false, or (b) true, if the truth of the story is not in harmony with the needs of the state. The poets and other storytellers, Plato tells us, are dangerous because their writing is so beautiful and engaging. The charm of their words, when false, could lead children to adopt the wrong attitudes, but even when they speak the truth, they could lead children astray (Copleston, 1993).

Plato argues public education "is necessary to a just city because it is essential to good order, consensual rule and human virtue, happiness and

rationality" (Curren, 2000, p. 53). For Plato, exercising censorship over what is taught helps to create a positive educational environment. It protects a vulnerable class of young citizens from dangerous effects of an inappropriate body of literature: stories that harm the individual and myths that undermine the state. Children are sheltered from stories in which the gods are portrayed as deceivers or dissemblers, changeable or fickle. In school, the gods always are represented as eternal simplicity and truth. To portray the gods in a bad light would harm the child and ultimately the state. It is nothing less than the duty of schools to prevent damage, as long as the methods of prevention are no more harmful than the evils they are to guard against (Copleston, 1993). Platonic education is to form character and judgments about good and evil in harmony with virtues of both the individual and the state. Education, according to Plato, is designed to "induce an admiration for what is admirable and hatred for what is shameful, and by means of this harmony with reason, as receptivity to reason which will mature into a capacity to grasp why some things are to be admired and others condemned" (Curren, 2000, p. 52).

Plato represents the authoritarian school tradition in which, a) society has an obligation to exclude from consideration in schools anything that may harm its interests, and b) teachers have no inherent right to teach; they are to be the obedient servants of the state. Plato prized tradition and recommended censorship of new ideas: "When the poet says that men care most for 'the newest air that hovers on the singer's lips,' they will be afraid lest he be taken not merely to mean new songs, but to commending a new style of music. Such innovation is not to be commended, nor should the poet be so understood. The introduction of novel fashions in music is a thing to beware of as endangering the whole fabric of society" (Cornford, 1968, p. 115).

Unlike Plato, most people today believe in the potential of progress and value of change. Few people would deny teachers the right to select appropriate teaching methods and be innovative in the classroom. Many believe, however, that control of the curriculum's subject matter remains the rightful province of the state or community and not the teacher. To empower teachers with authority over the curriculum is to disempower taxpayers, their elected community representatives (boards of education), and school administrators. Consider yourselves, for a moment, not as teachers or prospective teachers, but as taxpayers with children in public schools. Would you be comfortable paying school taxes while having little or no say in the education of your children? Would you be willing to leave decisions about curriculum, textbooks, teaching methodology, and evaluation to teachers who are not directly accountable to you? Or would you prefer to have these policy matters rest in the hands of school administrators and elected school boards who are responsible to you as a citizen and community resident? Clearly, a strong case can be made for community control of schools.

Others will argue with equal conviction that school reform has failed in the past largely because reformers have ignored the role teachers play. For today's schools to become more satisfying and more thought-provoking for children, they must first become better work places for teachers. Teachers must be allowed to assume their rightful place as professionals with genuine authority in schools; they should control matters of curriculum, instruction, and policy. Teachers should be able to assume a responsible role in shaping the purposes of schooling (Aronowitz and Giroux, 1985). How many thoughtful, creative people would teach in a school district that refused to listen to them about matters of curriculum and instruction?

Arguments about the organization and management of schools lie along a continuum of political thought. The left or liberal end of the continuum includes those who tend to be sympathetic toward the rights of workers and toward teacher empowerment. It also includes those with positive views of unions and union involvement in school policy matters, as well as those who champion academic freedom for public school teachers. The left also tends to be critical of discipline policies that fall most heavily on minorities and the poor. Instead of developing increasingly draconian punishments, they argue, schools should work to reduce the causes of disorder in schools. The right or conservative end of the continuum includes those more comfortable with the traditional exercise of authority in the schools. They tend to oppose any attempt to weaken community control of schools, such as granting greater power to teachers. Those on the right tend to be less sympathetic toward unions, often viewing them as the protectors of incompetent teachers and as unwise meddlers in local school management. Conservatives typically share a less than generous view toward extending academic freedom to public school teachers, regarding it as an overused shield for spreading ill-founded and even dangerous ideas in the classroom. Conservatives tend to support strict school disciplinary practices to maintain an orderly learning environment and zero-tolerance policies to punish those who cross the line from order to disobedience and dangerous behavior. Of course, we need to be cautious about painting with too broad a brush. Our goal is not to label school critics, but to make you more aware of competing perspectives in education. As you think about what teaching should be, look to the arguments of both left and right. Where do you find yourself along the spectrum of opinion on each issue? What evidence do you find most convincing? Is there a middle ground between any or all of the issues?

THE ISSUES OF INSTRUCTIONAL LEADERSHIP AND ACADEMIC FREEDOM

The public views teachers positively. A poll by Phi Delta Kappa and the Gallup Organization asked parents if they would like to see their child pursue a career as a teacher. Sixty-two percent of the parents said yes, the fourth highest total in the nine times the same question has been asked (Rose and Gallup, 2005, p. 19). This is not to say that all is well with the teaching profession. Teaching continues to be described as a "careerless profession," a good entry-level job that offers only

limited opportunity for promotion or increases in authority and salary (Etzioni, 1969; Lortie, 1975). Upon graduation from college, most people pursue a series of work experiences and job-related career moves that bring them additional responsibilities and greater compensation. A few teachers—mainly those who move from classroom teaching through the principalship to central office administration—follow a similar ascent. However, most teachers typically do not have access to a promotion path that includes a series of increasingly rewarding positions.

Beginning in the 1980s, researchers uncovered a variety of problems with public schooling. Educational expenditures had never been higher, but scores on standardized achievement tests were hitting all-time lows. Restive teachers demanded higher salaries, while the popular press delighted in printing stories of increases in school violence, crime, and the numbers of poorly educated students. Studies criticized everything from student learning to teacher preparation (Boyer, 1983; National Commission on Excellence in Education, 1983; Goodlad, 1984; Sizer, 1984; Goodlad, 1990; Archibold, 1998; Levine, 2006). Schools were said to be in crisis, and the nation was declared at risk because of the poor quality of teaching and learning. Teachers were held up to public scrutiny, and their work was weighed, measured, and assessed. Everywhere, researchers found dull, lifeless teaching; an absence of academic focus; bored, unchallenged students; and teachers mired in routine and paperwork. An inescapable conclusion of the 1980s research was that teachers were not doing, or were not able to do, the job expected of them. While some advocates of change seized on standards-based reform and championed NCLB legislation, others focused on teachers and teaching. The conditions of teaching were revisited as objects of policy reform, and teachers' work has been reopened for debate (Tye and O'Brien, 2002; Ingersoll, 2003; Smylie and Miretzky, 2004). Would student learning improve though a restructuring of teachers' work? Is there something wrong with the model of schools that separates teaching from school management? Would teaching be a more attractive career choice if teachers were allowed to play larger roles in school management and school reform? In short, should schools be organized to include classroom teachers as school leaders and managers, or are schools and students better off when leadership is left to others? Conservatives cite research evidence that finds little or no relationship between teacher leadership and student achievement. Liberals, on the other hand, argue that unions have had a positive effect on education, and collective bargaining and union influence should extend beyond wages and hours to include matters of school policy and reform. For those on the left, the success of school reform is directly linked to teachers, and they see no better way to involve teachers in school reform than guaranteeing them a formal role in running the schools.

Plato introduced the topic of censorship in education: Modern democracies pay less attention to school censorship than they do to the other side of the coin—-the right to inquire freely in schools. What place should academic freedom play in defining the teacher's role? If you view teachers as the leaders in education, then you are likely to believe they have a "right to teach," based on their special skills and knowledge, and this right should be supported and protected. If, instead, you see teachers as craftsmen or practitioners who merit little authority over the curriculum, then you may be less willing to grant them the same freedoms enjoyed by those who teach in colleges and universities. "Academic freedom," as commonly applied to higher education, is a contemporary term for the classical ideal of the right to teach and learn (Hofstadter and Metzger, 1955). Socrates, Plato's teacher, charged with impiety and the corruption of Athenian youth, defended himself by arguing that all wickedness is due to ignorance and that he and his students had the freedom to pursue truth. Socrates argued the freedom to teach and learn is essential to uncover knowledge and improve society. His fellow citizens were not persuaded and sentenced Socrates to death. Academic freedom has fared better; though regularly attacked and battered, it has survived. Academic freedom, as applied to American higher education today, typically refers to several related freedoms: (1) the freedom of professors to write, research, and teach in their field of special competence; (2) the freedom of universities to determine policies and practices unfettered by political restraints or other outside pressures; and (3) the freedom of students to learn.

Advocates argue that academic freedom ensures freedom of the mind for both students and scholars and therefore is essential to the pursuit of truth, the primary mission of higher education (Kirk, 1955; MacIver, 1955). The American Civil Liberties Union (ACLU) objects to limiting academic freedom to university settings. The ACLU claims academic freedom should extend to public schools, which they describe as the "authentic academic community" for young people. "If each new generation is to acquire a feeling for civil liberties," the ACLU argues, "it can do so only by having a chance to live in the midst of a community where the principles are continually exemplified" (ACLU, 1968, p. 4). The issue of academic freedom raises a series of difficult questions about the organization of the school environment: What is academic freedom and whom should it protect? Is it a right that can be extended to teachers at all grade levels? Does academic freedom clash with the community's right to determine what to teach its children? Can higher education continue to claim academic freedom as a special right reserved for university experts (Hook, 1953)? Or is this an essential right in all learning environments?

ORGANIZING SCHOOL ENVIRONMENTS FOR STUDENTS WHO ARE "HARD TO TEACH" AND MANAGE

Among the great debates about schooling is one that asks what schools should do with students who are hard to teach. Those on one side in the debate argue that schools are designed and organized to teach subject matter, and may weed out or exclude those students who do not show sufficient compliance or the ability to learn. The other side counters that schools are student-centered institutions, and therefore must bend subject matter and programs around all the students. The argument has been going on for over 100 years. It was central in the discussions about schools throughout the twentieth century, and so far has resisted resolution in the early twenty-first century. In 1902, John Dewey characterized the dispute as argument between two "sects." The subject-matter sect wanted to organize schools by academic topics, subdivided into separate lessons, with each lesson having its own set of facts for students to learn. Children were to proceed step by step in the mastery of individual facts until they had covered the prescribed academic terrain. The other sect, Dewey argued, focused on the individual child as the starting point, middle, and end of education. The academic terrain was irrelevant compared to the needs and interests of individual learners (Loveless, 2001, p. 1).

Among other things, we ask that you consider how school should provide the most appropriate education for students who have "special needs." Children with particular mental or physical disabilities, who are emotionally disturbed, or who have other specific needs fall into this category. Sometimes the term *exceptional* is applied to this group of children in educational literature; usually, this term also includes children identified as gifted and talented. The main reason for trying to identify and evaluate children with special or exceptional needs is to provide them with appropriate educational assistance. For children with physical disabilities, that may mean special equipment such as magnification devices for the children with visual impairment. For children with learning disabilities, it may mean specially prepared teaching materials. For gifted and talented children, it may mean artistic tutoring or advanced academic work. The fundamental question is one of degree: How much should school environments be modified to accommodate learners? When schools try to meet the needs of all students, do they run the risk of serving no student very well?

In the twenty-first century, public schools are asked to do more with a wider range of students than ever before. In the heavy-handed state idealized by Plato, citizens received an education limited by social class. In the *Republic,* justice was served when every citizen and every class of citizens functioned harmoniously, each being educated and performing according to his or her abilities and inclinations for the harmonious good of the state. Athenian education was not to produce citizens who were "to go their own way," as Plato put it. American society and its schools, along with others in the West, have adopted a different understanding of justice and relationships between the individual and the state. Influenced by philosophers who followed Plato (in particular, his student, Aristotle, and later, Immanuel Kant) justice has been identified less frequently as something that exists in the state and more often as something that resides within the individual. Education in democracies requires individuals make their own decisions about vocation and training and type of schooling to be received. Interests

of the individual are considered paramount, and the state is thought to be just only when the majority of citizens are served well. Public schools are designed to serve all students. Clearly, problems arise at the margins. How should schools tend to children with special needs, the unusually disaffected, the gifted as well as the troubled? We know students are at a terrible disadvantage if they are not graduated from high school, but what should be done with students whose very presence in school works to the academic detriment of others? Chapter 19 will ask you to look at the issue of school violence.

As you are no doubt aware, violence has become one of the most troubling problems facing American educators. Schools, once safe havens from the outside world, now must contend with acts of bullying and violence at every grade level. With school violence on the increase, experts continue to debate its causes and how schools should handle violent students. Many teachers and criminologists argue the time has come to crack down on the most violent offenders and expel them from school. They argue that the school's job is to teach academic subject matter to those who are at least minimally willing to cooperate. Others argue that educators are responsible for helping students with whatever problems they bring to school, even if this means expanding the role of schools into nonacademic areas.

Although this book is divided into three parts, we believe the parts are related to one another in important ways, and also believe you are better able to understand schools and issues surrounding education by considering the interrelationships. Part One focuses on the interests schools should serve; the chapters ask you to consider the nature of justice and equity and what they mean for people interested in public education. Justice is one of the oldest of the social virtues. If justice is about social fairness, with each getting what he or she is due, how is this related to the practical matters of education? The chapters in Part One ask you to examine competing perspectives about the interests schools should serve, and ask you to decide which positions seem to you to be the more just and offer greater equity.

Part Two asks what knowledge schools should teach. Those on one side of the debate argue that knowledge is neutral and American society in the early twenty-first century has an agreed-upon body of knowledge important for all citizens and should be taught in all schools. Not everyone believes there is or should be one uniform body of knowledge. Picking up a philosophic argument as old as Heraclitus, a pre-Socratic philosopher, and amplified by Friedrich Nietzsche and more contemporary philosophers, those on the other side of the argument claim that all truth is perspectival. For them, a single or absolute truth does not exist; what we call knowledge is the perspective or interpretations made by various groups and classes of people. There is no single truth but many truths based on individual factors such as age, race, nationality, religion, and gender. Men and women see the world differently; the young and the old rarely agree. No one perspective is considered to be more true than others. All have

an equal right to be heard. Schools, for those who subscribe to this view, should not pretend to teach knowledge as if it were an agreed-upon, objective, and neutral representation of reality. There are many competing realities, and schools must teach multiple perspectives of what is true. Joel Spring (2002a, 2002b), for one, argues that schools will always be places of conflict among those who hold competing notions of justice, equity, and forms of knowledge flowing from varied perspectives.

Part Three asks you to consider the human environment of schools, specifically the rights and roles of teachers and whether or not we can teach all students in public schools. These issues are likely to be related to your positions on the nature of knowledge, the content you believe schools should teach, and ultimately your views of justice and equity. We hope you will find the arguments on both sides convincing and engaging, and encourage your thoughtful deliberations and disagreements. Our goal is to present for your consideration competing perspectives on important issues. We again invite your understanding and encourage well-reasoned dialogues. As we wrote in Chapter 1, if you like arguments, you'll love the study of education.

References

AMERICAN CIVIL LIBERTIES UNION (ACLU). (1968). *Academic Freedom in the Secondary Schools.* New York: Author.

ARCHIBOLD, R. C., "Getting Tough on Teachers," *New York Times*, Nov. 1, 1998.

ARONOWITZ, S., AND GIROUX, H. A. (1985). *Education Under Siege: The Conservative,*

Liberal, and Radical Debate Over Schooling. South Hadley, MA: Bergin and Garvey.

BOYER, E. L. (1983). *High School: A Report on Secondary Education in America.* New York: Harper and Row.

COPLESTON, F. (1993). *A History of Philosophy, Vol. I: Greece and Rome.* New York: Doubleday.

CORNFORD, F. M., ed. and translator. (1968). *The Republic of Plato.* New York: Oxford University Press.

CURREN, R. R. (2000). *Aristotle on the Necessity of Public Education.* Lanham, MD: Rowan and Littlefield.

ETZIONI, A., ed. (1969). *The Semi-Professions and Their Organization: Teachers, Nurses, Social Workers.* New York: Free Press

GOODLAD, J. I. (1984). *A Place Called School: Prospects for the Future.* New York: McGraw-Hill.

———. (1990). *Teachers for Our Nation's Schools.* San Francisco: Jossey-Bass.

HOFSTADTER, R., AND METZGER, W. P. (1955). *The Development of Academic Freedom in the United States.* New York: Columbia University Press.

HOOK, S. (1953). *Heresy, Yes—Conspiracy, No.* New York: John Day.

INGERSOLL, R. M. (2003). *Who Controls Teachers' Work? Power and Accountability in America's Schools.* Cambridge, MA: Harvard University Press.

KIRK, R. (1955). *Academic Freedom: An Essay in Definition.* Chicago: Henry Regnery.

LEVINE, A. (2006). Educating School Teachers. www.edschools.org/pdf/ Educating_Teachers_Report

LORTIE, D. (1975). *Schoolteacher.* Chicago: University of Chicago Press.

LOVELESS, T., ed. (2001). *The Great Curriculum Debate: How Should We Teach Reading and Math?* Washington, DC: Brooking Institution.

MACIVER, R. M. (1955). *Academic Freedom in Our Time.* New York: Columbia University Press.

NATIONAL COMMISSION ON EXCELLENCE IN EDUCATION. (1983). *A Nation at Risk: The Imperative for Educational Reform.* National Education Association. Washington, DC: U.S. Government Printing Office.

NOZICK, R. (1974). *Anarchy, State, State and Utopia.* New York: Basic Books.

PLATO. (1984). *Great Dialogues of Plato.* W. H. D. Rouse, translator. E. H. Warmington and P. G. Rouse, eds. New York: Mentor.

POPPER, K. (1966). *The Open Society and Its Enemies.* Princeton, NJ: Princeton University Press.

RAWLS, J. (1971). *A Theory of Justice.* Cambridge, MA: Harvard University Press.

ROSE, L. C., AND GALLUP, A. M. (2005). "The 37th Annual Phi Delta Kappa/Gallup Poll of the Public's Attitudes Toward the Public Schools." www.pdkintl.org/ kappan/k0509pol.htm.

SIZER, T. R. (1984). *Horace's Compromise: The Dilemma of the American High School.* Boston: Houghton Mifflin.

SMYLIE, M.A., AND MIRETZKY, D., eds. (2004). *Developing the Teacher Workforce.* 103rd Yearbook of the National Society for the Study of Education, Part I. Chicago: University of Chicago Press.

SPRING, J. (2002a). *Political Agenda for Education: From the Religious Right to the Green Party.* 2nd Ed. Mahwah, NJ: Lawrence Erlbaum.

———. (2002b). *Conflict of Interests, The Politics of American Education.* Boston: McGraw-Hill.

TYE, B. B., AND O'BRIEN, L. (2002). "Why Are Experienced Teachers Leaving the Profession?" *Kappan,* 84:24–32.

CHAPTER 15

Discipline and Justice: Zero Tolerance or Discretion

What concept of justice should govern school and classroom discipline?

POSITION 1: ZERO-TOLERANCE DISCIPLINARY POLICIES PROVIDE JUSTICE IN PUBLIC SCHOOLS

In the end, those kids who receive less than firm, fair, and consistent discipline end up being taught that there are no consequences for inappropriate—and sometimes illegal—behavior as long as it occurs within the grounds of those schools having administrators who are often more worried about keeping their disciplinary and criminal incident reports down for the sake of their own career advancement.

—National School Safety and Security Services, 2008

Why We Need Zero-Tolerance Policies

Every day in American public schools, students and adults face disrespect, disruption, and disorder. Countless minutes and hours, which could be used for teaching and learning, are lost in classrooms each year as teachers struggle to control unruly students. Zero-tolerance policies assure that such students can and will be removed from the school setting. They protect the educational rights of the majority of students from being violated by undisciplined classmates. While these policies may at first appear harsh, in fact, they are an important tool for school personnel who seek to carry out their mandate to educate the next generation of responsible American citizens.

Discipline problems in public schools receive substantial attention when the rare, but devastating, acts of violence take place. However, once the media spotlight dims, the significant difficulties faced by teachers and students in thousands of schools continue. In the most recent government report regarding school safety, 28 percent of students reported being bullied at school (U.S. Department of Education, 2007, Figure 11.3); 37 percent saw hate-related graffiti in school (U.S. Department of Education, 2007, Figure 10.1); and 11 percent were the targets of hate-related comments (U.S. Department of Education, 2007, Figure 10.1). Twenty-four percent said there were gangs at their school (U.S. Department of Education, 2007, Figure 8.1). A quarter reported that drugs were available to them on campus (U.S. Department of Education, 2007, Figure 9.1). Almost 14 percent were involved in a physical fight (U.S. Department of Education, 2007, Figure 13.1). Seven percent reported carrying a gun to school (U.S. Department of Education, 2007, Figure 14.1).

School safety is an issue for teachers as well. A quarter of a million were threatened with injury by a student during the previous 12 months (U.S. Department of Education, 2007, Figure 5.1). Some students made good on their threats—127,500 teachers were physically attacked by a student (U.S. Department of Education, 2007, Figure 5.2). In all, there were 1.5 million violent incidents—rapes, sexual assaults, physical attacks, and robberies in American schools (U.S. Department of Education, 2007, Figure 6.2). A recent study indicated that almost half of teachers leaving the profession cited student discipline issues as one of the causes (Mississippi Youth Justice Project, 2008).

Removing disruptive students from class has become a Herculean task in some school districts. For example the discipline code for New York City schools is over 27 pages long. It includes a "range of possible disciplinary options" that leaves students and, to a large extent, teachers and administrators confused about what happens when a child or adolescent violates an element of the code. The infractions are categorized in five levels, with a set of possible consequences for each level. (See Table 15.1.)

There are thirteen possible consequences running the gamut from admonishment by school staff to expulsion. Each consequence can only be meted out by the appropriate bureaucrat. As the severity of the infraction increases, the authority to apply any consequence is reserved for personnel farther and farther removed from the student's action—and its impact on the learning environment. For example, a teacher can remove a student from her classroom for disruptive behavior, but only a regional superintendent can suspend a student for longer than five days. Principals who want to suspend a disruptive general education student must follow most of the following steps **every** time.

- Confirm that the teacher who originally removed the student from class has followed the applicable regulations.
- Determine that the student's behavior is so disruptive as to prevent the orderly operation of the school or represents a clear and present danger to the student, other students, or school personnel.
- Inform the student of the charges and evidence against him/her and listen to student's side of the story.
- Inform the student that he/she is suspended and for how long.
- Notify the parent or guardian to come and pick up the child.

Table 15.1 Levels of infractions and range of consequences—New York City schools

Level	Infractions	Examples	Range of Consequences
1	Insubordinate Behavior	Failing to wear uniform Being late to school Bringing cell phone to school Making excessive noise Wearing clothing that disrupts the learning process	Admonition by school staff to removal from classroom to principal suspension
2	Disorderly Disruptive Behavior	Smoking and gambling Using profane or obscene language Lying to school personnel Leaving school premises Causing school bus disruptions Cheating, plagiarizing Persistent level 1 behavior	Admonition by school staff to removal from classroom to principal suspension
3	Seriously Disruptive or Dangerous Behavior	Being insubordinate or disobedient Using hate speech Fighting Stealing Tampering with school records Committing vandalism Making false fire alarms or bomb threats Persistent level 2 behavior	Admonition by school staff to removal from classroom to 30 day Regional Superintendent's suspension
4	Dangerous or Violent Behavior	Engaging in intimidation, threats, extortion Engaging in risky, intimidating, bullying, gang-related or sexually harassing behavior Possessing illegal drugs or alcohol Participating in an act of group violence Committing arson Persistent level 3 behavior	Parent conference to one-year Regional Superintendent's suspension
5	Seriously Dangerous or Violent Behavior	Using force against school personnel or students Selling drugs Possessing or using a weapon	Regional Superintendent's suspension or expulsion

Source: NYC Department of Education, 2008. "Citywide Standards of Discipline and Intervention Measures."

- Reach the parent within twenty-four hours with a written notice that describes the event and the time and place of the suspension conference (which must be held within five days of the written notice).
- Write a second letter to parents explaining that the student is going to have a suspension conference, describing the alternative instruction arrangements and the hearing process, notifying them that they may bring a translator, and listing the parents' and student's rights to question witnesses at the hearing, be accompanied by advisors (including a lawyer), be returned to school at the end of the suspension, and appeal the process.
- Hold the suspension conference at a time convenient for the parents.
- Reschedule the conference if the parents cancel.
- Prepare and maintain a record of the conference.
- Notify the parents within ten days whether the suspension was ruled justifiable.
- Notify the parents within ten days of additional recommendations.
- Respond to the regional superintendent in writing within five days if student appeals the suspension.
- Respond to the chancellor if the student appeals to him.

(Common Good, 2008)

Dismissing a student with disabilities is even more complicated and time consuming. In that case, a hearing must be held to determine whether or not the behavior is a "manifestation of the student's disabilities" and if the school somehow failed to provide "appropriate" (and usually very costly) services. If such a determination is made, the administrator's options become even more limited.

Regulations like these limit administrators' effectiveness in almost every school district in the United States. Given these cumbersome processes, many principals simply do not have the time to suspend disruptive students. Instead, the youngsters are returned to classrooms and the cycle of disrespect and disorder continues. Without zero-tolerance policies that clearly spell out the inevitable consequences for inappropriate school behaviors and give administrators the freedom they need to apply them swiftly and consistently, students who wish to learn and teachers who want to teach are the ones being punished.

Emergence of Zero-Tolerance Policies

"From its inception in federal drug policy of the 1980s, zero tolerance has been intended primarily as a method of sending a message that certain behaviors will not be tolerated, by punishing all offenses severely, no matter how minor" (Skiba, 2000, p. 2). In the late 1980s, school districts across the country enacted disciplinary policies that promised "zero tolerance" for the possession of weapons in schools. At the federal level, the concept inspired the 1994 Gun-Free Schools Act (PL 103-227), which mandated a minimum one-year expulsion for a student who brought a gun (and later other weapons) to school. An amendment to the Elementary and Secondary School Act required that school districts or states develop disciplinary policies that conformed to the law or lose federal funding. Over time, the term has come not only to be applied to those infractions for which the consequence is expulsion or suspension. "Zero tolerance generally is defined as a school district policy that mandates predetermined consequences of punishment for specific offenses, regardless of the circumstances, disciplinary history, or age of the student involved" (Stader, 2004, p. 62).

States have taken advantage of the opportunity to create clear and definitive behavioral codes and initiated expulsion for possessing, selling, or using drugs or alcohol, fighting, and threatening students or staff (Skiba, 2000; Casella, 2003). They also created zero-tolerance policies to actions that, while ostensibly less dangerous, create an atmosphere that is not conducive to learning. These actions include open defiance of authority, disruptive or disorderly behavior, deliberate disobedience, sexual harassment, theft, threats, extortion, membership in a gang, the use of profane language, and defacing school property (Brady, Balman, and Phenix, 2007).

There is a clear and present danger in America's schools; children live in a society where the media creates "heroes" who are disdainful of legitimate authority and pursue their own interests at the expense of other people's safety. For those characters, revenge and retaliation for real or imagined injuries are justified. When young people accept the values of such role models, there are several results. At worst, they put the lives of others at risk. In less severe cases, they jeopardize the learning process. Since education leads to individual success and provides society with competent citizens and leaders, anything that interferes with schooling puts all of us at risk. Zero-tolerance policies are efficient responses to this crisis, and, by definition, they are fair—applied in the same way to each student. On the other hand, discretionary discipline policies have "great potential for idiosyncrasies" in the consequences students receive (Brown, 2007).

Zero Tolerance and Rational Choice

Zero-tolerance policies do allow schools to remove students who endanger the safety and well-being of others, but they are even more important as deterrents. They are designed to persuade young people not to engage in dangerous, disruptive, or disrespectful behaviors. Like other crime-prevention policies, they are meant to "head off trouble" before it begins (Casella, 2003b, p. 875). These policies are based on the theory of "rational choice," which is rooted in understandings of human behavior developed by classical economists, including Jeremy Bentham. These theorists assume that humans act in their own best interests, based on calculations they make about the costs and benefits inherent in a particular choice. People always choose the action that they believe will maximize their pleasure— and minimize their pain. Since punishment will result in increased pain, the perception that swift, severe consequences are inevitable deter individuals from choosing to behave in ways that violate the common good. If people do not fear being caught or punished for an act, there is little to deter them from engaging in whatever behavior enhances their own pleasure.

Zero-tolerance policies provide exactly the kind of punishment that acts as a deterrent. Young people are impetuous and often ill-equipped to judge the potential of their actions to cause serious harm to themselves or others. Indeed, if causing such injury interferes with the pursuit of their own pleasure, it may not even reach their "radar screen." They need the external, counterbalancing forces of swift, severe, and certain punishment to rein in their impulsiveness. Zero-tolerance policies provide that counterweight. They "heighten the consequence side of the crime and punishment balance, attempting to convince individuals that the consequences are not worth the risks" (Casella, 2003b, p. 877). When the policies are followed consistently, students calculate their choices differently. When they perceive school authorities as serious about discipline—and when they understand that no one is exempt from taking responsibility for their actions—they make choices that better contribute to the order of the schools, and ultimately to their own education.

The key component of zero-tolerance policies *is* the consistency with which the consequences are applied. Young people recognize that the only rules that really count are ones that apply equally to everyone. Many students regularly experience this kind of discipline outside of school. Children who play Little League baseball, for example, recognize that batters who swing and miss the ball three times are "out"—no matter whether they are the best or worst player on the team. The "punishment" is immediate, can have serious implications for the outcome of the game, and is absolute. Consequently, players practice batting for hours, learning how to make good choices about when to swing and when not to do so. Although parents and coaches may protest a strike-out call, they never bring lawyers into the argument and rarely hold up the game for very long. The rules are the rules; the umpire is the interpreter of the rules; and, if you want to play baseball, you abide by them.

Similar consistency in schools provides students with the "certainty" that they will not be able to escape punishment for inappropriate behavior. Giving administrators or school boards discretion in applying consequences dilutes the power of zero-tolerance policies. "Many educators tend to bend over backwards to give students more breaks than they will ever receive out on the streets of our society and in the workplace where we are supposed to be preparing them to function" (National School Safety and Security Services, 2008). Punishment is no longer "swift, severe, and certain," and, therefore, it loses its efficacy in controlling students' choices. Such an atmosphere does not encourage young people to set aside their own interests. The consistent application of consequences for actions that jeopardize the safety and freedom of others does.

Benefits of Zero-Tolerance Policies

Zero-tolerance school disciplinary policies are beneficial to students, teachers, parents, administrators, and taxpayers in several important ways. They are fair, position public schools to compete effectively with private schools, turn the job of law enforcement over to professionals, minimize time spent on discipline, and—most importantly—are effective at creating and maintaining orderly learning environments.

The orderliness of a school has a tremendous impact on whether or not parents allow their children to attend it. In the past, parents believed they were faced with choices between public schools that tolerate disruptive or disrespectful behavior and private schools that remove students whose actions endangers others' ability to learn. The ability of private school administrators to expel misbehaving students has been seen as one of their primary strengths (Casella, 2003a). Zero-tolerance policies provide administrators of public schools with that same freedom and reassure taxpayers their money is being well spent. The fact that disciplinary policies of charter schools more closely resemble those of private schools is a factor that parents cite as a reason for choosing those schools and for their high degree of satisfaction with them (Lips, 2008).

Disciplinary policies that mandate specific punishments can also preserve diversity in public schools. As mentioned previously, parents are unwilling to place their children in situations they perceive to be unsafe. When they became fearful of public schools, middle-class parents attempted to achieve "safety" by moving out of urban areas and into suburban school districts. The suburbs, however, provided "security by separation—the roomier house, fence, lawn, and distinct property lines" (Casella, 2003a, p. 132). The creation of the suburbs—and their accompanying school districts—resulted in a re-creation of cities (Anyon, 1997). What were once vibrant centers of life and hope for Americans became filled with run-down buildings and broken dreams. They were filled with people who were poorer and more hopeless. Drug trafficking and violence increased in the cities. "In circular fashion, what suburbanization helped to create in the form of desperation in cities became further evidence for the need of the middle classes to leave the city for safety's sake" (Casella, 2003a, p. 142). As a result of white flight, education in America has become increasingly isolated by race, ethnicity, and class. Students go to school with people who look like them and whose families have approximately the same income (Orfield and Lee, 2007). While it would be overly optimistic to suggest that confidence in schools could revitalize urban neighborhoods, it is reasonable to assume that it could make an important contribution to doing so.

In most states, zero-tolerance policies have resulted in the increased presence of law enforcement officers in school. The COPS in Schools program has awarded approximately $748 million in grants to provide funding for over 6,500 "school resource officers" (SROs)—trained, sworn in law enforcement officers (U.S. Department of Justice, 2004). Generally, when a student's behavior requires arrest, the on-site SRO is able to act quickly. Because they are known to students, their presence as the arresting officer minimizes any danger or disruption inherent to the process. The presence of School Resource Officers is also a strong deterrent to inappropriate or dangerous student behaviors. A great deal of their time is spent on preventative duties such as one-on-one counseling with students and coordinating extracurricular activities. They teach crime prevention in classes, help students deal with the presence of gangs in schools and neighborhoods, and help administrators develop policies and procedures that increase school safety. In addition, many SROs have developed expertise in dealing with bullying and internet related crime and harassment (U.S. Department of Justice, 2008; National Association of School Resource Officers, 2005).

Zero-tolerance policies are effective—they remove the troublemakers and deter impetuous students from becoming problems. Many of the indicators of order in schools—including the percentage of students who were bullied, involved in a fight, or reported being afraid, and the number of teachers who were threatened, have shown improvement in the last ten years (U.S. Department of Education, 2004, Figure 3.1, Table 5.1, Figure 6.1, Table 9.1, Table 11.1, Table 12.1). Zero tolerance has also been effective in achieving its primary goal—decreasing the number of weapons in schools by almost half (U.S. Department of Education, 2007, Table 14.1).

Civil Rights Protections under Zero-Tolerance Policies

Critics of zero-tolerance policies are quick to point out applications of the policy that they believe are fundamentally unfair. They argue that discipline codes conforming to the Gun-Free Schools Act and No Child Left Behind result in punishment of "good" kids who made one "mistake." They also suggest that students with disabilities forfeit some of their rights, as protected by the Individuals with Disabilities Acts (IDEA). However, such claims ignore the law's language, "The provisions of this bill shall be construed in a manner consistent with the Individuals with Disabilities Acts" and "State law shall allow the chief administering officer of a local educational agency to modify such expulsion requirement for a student on a case-by-case basis if such modification is in writing" (U.S. Department of Education, 2001, Sec. 4141 b, c). The Department of Education reports that such modifications have been utilized in an average of 35 percent of expulsions since the school year 1997–1998. Students with disabilities received almost 30 percent of those adaptations. In those rare instances where real miscarriages of justice have taken place, students have been successful in using the courts for recourse (*Seal v. Morgan*, 2000; *Butler v. Rio Rancho Public School Board*, 2002). Critics also argue that a disproportionate number of students of color are suspended or expelled under zero-tolerance policies. However, since the policies are designed to treat all students who misbehave without bias, the cause of the discrepancy between exclusionary discipline rates and racial or ethnic representation in a school community cannot be blamed on zero tolerance. In fact, such policies were designed to address earlier findings of discretionary applications of discipline policies that were skewed by the biases of those administering them (Billitteri, 2008). Worries that racial or class prejudices affect disciplinary actions can be addressed by carefully defining misbehavior and crafting a set of consequences that result for each and every student, regardless of ethnicity or socioeconomic status.

Providing such protection with regard to the application of the most serious consequences makes good sense. Insisting on complex and time-consuming procedures that ostensibly protect students' rights to "due process" for minor infractions with less serious consequences do not. When justice is invoked only for those members of society who fail to carry out their obligations and the rights of the majority of students to attend safe and orderly schools are violated, something is seriously wrong. When making "exceptions" becomes discipline policy, rules become meaningless to students. Then, learning does not happen and tax-payers' hard-earned money is wasted. Justice for all demands the better solution offered by zero-tolerance policies.

POSITION 2: ZERO-TOLERANCE DISCIPLINE POLICIES ARE FUNDAMENTALLY UNJUST

The zero-tolerance mania, which disproportionately affects students of color, is part of the pervasive punitive ideology and social policy that also includes trying minors as adults, deterrence theories, and mandatory sentencing.

—Stein, 2007, p. 31

The Social Context of Zero-Tolerance Policies

Fear and love do strange things to people. When Americans became frightened by drug related violent crime in the late 1980s, severe and non-negotiable penalties for illegal acts seemed to make sense. The passage of the Violent Crime Control and Law Enforcement Act of 1994 was evidence of these concerns. The bill made it possible to invoke the death penalty for large-scale drug trafficking, provided new and stiffer penalties for gang members found guilty of violent or drug-related crimes, and imposed mandatory life sentences without possibility of parole for those convicted of a third federal felony. Since approximately 6 percent of criminals are responsible for 70 to 80 percent of the illegal acts in this country, the provision was meant to "provide a method for society to attempt to capture this highly active and dangerous group of career criminal, thus reducing crime level substantially" (Jones, Connelly, and Wagner, 2001, p. 1). Since 1993, thirty-seven states have adopted similar laws. Studies about the laws' effectiveness have brought surprising results. Early research indicated little deterrent effect (Turner, 2000); more recent ones report that the laws have deterred some criminals but have the unintended consequences of increasing the violence of crimes that are committed—especially by offenders with "two strikes" (Shepherd, 2001; Iyengar, 2008). Three strike laws also exacerbate racial discrimination in the justice system. African Americans are thirteen times more likely to be incarcerated than whites for drug-related crime and almost twice as likely to be sentenced to life imprisonment (Beatty, Petteruti, and Ziedenberg, 2007). The laws have also increased the cost of imprisonment and clogged the courts and overcrowded prisons. They take away the discretionary power of judges—who, after all, are meant to weigh the circumstances of a case, the age, intellectual capabilities, and emotional state of the accused and to measure the impact of the crime and the victim and society when deciding guilt and imposing sentences (Jones, Connelly, and Wagner, 2001).

Despite evidence that mandatory sentencing policies are ineffective deterrents to crime, are racially discriminatory, and limit the decision-making authority of those closest to a situation, they have been adopted in the disciplinary policies of almost all school districts in the United States. They found their way into schools for seemingly valid reasons. Although incidents of gun violence in schools were relatively small in number, they prompted a desire to protect young people. The original "zero-tolerance" policy, the Gun-Free Schools Act was clear-cut—if you brought a *gun* to school, you were expelled. Over time, however, the concept was applied to more and more infractions that were less and less serious. Harsh discipline codes tied the hands of caring school professionals as surely as mandatory sentences limited options for judges and resulted in serious consequences for students who had no intention of causing harm to anyone. They have disproportionate impact on students of color and those with disabilities. They are costly in terms of money and time, taking both away from more pressing educational issues. They provide little return in deterring disruptive, disorderly, or disrespectful behavior in schools. In addition, they violate a basic democratic norm—that punishment should fit the crime.

Concern Run Amok

"While zero tolerance once required suspension or expulsion for a specified list of serious offenses, it is now an overarching approach toward discipline" (Advancement Project and The Civil Rights Project, 2005, p. 15). It is certainly true that students are suspended for the possession of potential, perceived, or imagined weapons and for fighting. However, they are also removed from school for behavior that is "subjectively labeled 'disrespect,' 'disobedience,' and 'disruption'" (Advancement Project and the Civil Rights Project, 2005, p. 15).

There are numerous reports of incidents in which zero-tolerance policies in schools have resulted in unfair—and sometimes bizarre, consequences.

- A thirteen-year-old boy in Arizona was suspended for three to five days for drawing a gun—on a piece of paper (KOLD News, 2007).
- A sixth-grader in Katy, Texas, was suspended for four months for writing "I love Alex" on a locker (Eriksen, 2007).
- Two students in Minnesota were expelled for buying replicas of swords as souvenirs on a school trip to England. The swords were never taken to school. They were never used to threaten anyone. Trip chaperones found them wrapped and secured with tape for shipping back to the United States (Lemagie, 2008).
- Three preschoolers, sixteen kindergartners, and twenty-two first-graders were among the 166 elementary students in Maryland who were suspended in 2007 for sexual harassment (Schulte, 2008).

Situations like these are the result of the "demonization" of young people (Giroux, 2003, p. 554). Children and adolescents are perceived as dangerous, requiring constant surveillance. Some are tested for drugs if they want to participate in extracurricular activities. Others submit daily to metal detector searches and the presence of armed guards and surveillance cameras in their schools. In the name of protecting them, young people have been unfairly singled out for societal sanctions. "Even harmless acts are now subject to citations (tickets) or arrests and referrals to juvenile or criminal courts. In fact, in many instances the charges (e.g. 'terroristic threatening' for playing cops and robbers, or assault for throwing a snowball) would never constitute a crime if an adult were involved" (Advancement Project and The Civil Rights Project, 2005, p. 15). A five-year-old boy in Queens, New York, was handcuffed and sent to a psychiatric ward after a temper tantrum in the principal's office (Sullivan, 2008). The number of police officers in schools has increased dramatically. In New York City, there are more than 4,600 School Safety Agents and 200 armed police officers in school. They are the tenth largest "police force" in the country, bigger than those in Washington, D.C., Detroit, or Boston (New York Civil Liberties Union, 2007).

In addition, students are being expelled under zero-tolerance policies that are overreactions and profoundly anti-democratic. In Pittsburgh, a fourteen-year-old boy was expelled for writing rap songs that described violent acts even though his songs were written at home and never brought to school. Students in California were suspended for organizing an anti-war rally at a school where military recruiters make announcements over the public address system. Young people around the country have faced similar punishments for wearing t-shirts with messages that school officials have deemed "dangerous" or anti-American (American Civil Liberties Union, 2005).

Disproportionate Impact on Students of Color

Zero tolerance proponents argue that such policies are just. However, nothing demonstrates their fundamental unfairness so much as the way they, like the mandatory sentencing policies from which they descend, are racially discriminatory. Such policies affect students of color in dramatically different ways from their white counterparts.

For the last thirty years, researchers have consistently shown that students of color are suspended at double to triple the rate of other students. In South Carolina, African American students are suspended five times more often than white children. In Minnesota, the rate is six to one; and in New Jersey, African Americans were sixty times more likely to be suspended than whites (Billeteri, 2008). Boys especially are at risk—usually twice as likely as girls to be excluded from school. Children of color are also overrepresented in lesser school disciplinary practices, such as referrals to the principal and reprimands by the teacher. If such disparities could be explained because children from minority groups actually were more violent or had higher rates of misbehavior, then the zero-tolerance policies themselves could not be faulted. However, that is simply not the case. Students of color receive harsher penalties than their white counterparts for the same offense (Fenning and Rose, 2007). In many schools, African American and Latino students are suspended most often for being "disrespectful," "defiant," or "loud" (Walsh, 2008). These terms are clearly subjective—and culturally specific. Teachers and administrators are as susceptible as the rest of the population to stereotypes about people of color. These stereotypes can affect educators' perceptions of students, causing them to see children of color as more threatening or dangerous than their white counterparts. When disruptive events occur in a classroom, for example, teachers become fearful that they will not be able to manage the event. When that fear intersects with racial stereotypes, that concern often results in a student of color being identified, removed from class, and suspended. Studies reveal "those singled out tended to be the 'spokespersons' for the class, and these interactions occurred in the midst of the teacher perceiving lack of control rather than an actual violent offense occurring"(Fenning and Rose, 2007). Students of color report feeling as though they are expected to act badly (New York Civil Liberties Union, 2007). So some young people respond by acting out in inappropriate ways, while teachers and administrators fail to reflect on their contributions to students' behaviors. Zero-tolerance policies do not require such introspection. In fact, they cloak prejudice with the mantle of impartiality and contribute to its perpetuation (Brady, Balmer, and Phenix, 2007; Fenning and Rose, 2007).

Discipline and Students with Disabilities

Most students come to school able to understand the rules and how to follow them. For students with disabilities, however, especially students with "behavioral disorders," coming to understand and being able to conform to expectations is a much more difficult task. The result is that students with disabilities are more likely to be excluded from schools. Approximately 20 percent of students with disabilities are suspended or expelled each year, compared with only 10 percent of their non-classified counterparts. The rate is higher for students with particular disabilities. Forty-four percent of students with emotional or behavioral disorders and 21 percent of students with other health impairments (usually Attention Deficit Disorder) are suspended each year (Achilles, McLaughlin, and Croninger, 2007). Students with conduct disorders ". . . come into the classroom with perceptions and beliefs . . . that may leave them less capable of recognizing and responding to the typical social curriculum of schools" (Skiba and Peterson, 2003, p. 3). They may have come from homes in which the most effective way to avoid being abused is to become aggressive themselves. Others, whose parents are inconsistent in their expectations, learn to behave inappropriately to find out what the limits truly are. Some students whose disabilities make the academic tasks of school extremely difficult become disruptive or disorderly in order to avoid doing work that is too hard. All these behaviors make sense to children in light of what they "know" and feel about the world and their place within it. Since teachers and administrators do not perceive the world in the same way, the students are viewed as disrespectful, disorderly, disobedient, defiant, and disruptive. Their behaviors simply make no sense to adults who do not share their experiences and disabilities.

Students with disabilities often have trouble making sense of peer relationships as well. Interactions with their school mates become difficult. Disagreements break out over misunderstandings resulting from the "failure"—that is, the inability—of students with disabilities to pick up on verbal and non-verbal cues. They continue talking when their classmates want to say something. They refuse to share toys, supplies, and materials they have taken without asking and are surprised by other children's anger. They fail to respect personal space and physically crowd, jostle, or bump others who resent the intrusion. Consequently, they are involved in more verbal and physical altercations with other students.

It is true that the original Individuals with Disabilities Act (1997) provided extensive procedure protection for students with disabilities with regard to school discipline. For example, if a student's actions were found to be the result of their disabilities, they could receive "lighter sentences" than nondisabled students would. Objections to these protections were so strong, however, that when the bill was amended in 2004, the number of available modifications were reduced. This change was particularly true for behavior that fell into the "zero tolerance" category for students without disabilities. In the revised bill, students with disabilities may be removed to on interim alternative educational setting for up to forty-five school days not only for weapon- or drug-related violations but also if they have inflicted serious bodily injury upon another person at school or at a school function (IDEA, 2004). The revised bill also eliminates the right of students with disabilities to remain in their current educational placements while they appeal a disciplinary decision if their violation of the school code would usually result in removal for more than ten days (IDEA, 2004). What is problematic about such provisions is that they undo decades of work to prevent students with disabilities from being excluded from schools. These policies allow school administrators to remove students with disabilities from classrooms, and even schools, for behavior that is a result of their disabling condition—that is, students are removed *because* they are disabled. A recent study revealed that, although administrators said they were aware of their responsibility to protect the rights of students with disabilities, most were more likely to give priority to what they perceived as the safety of the larger school community. They argued that their primary responsibility was to preserve order for the good of the entire school and "most, but not all, viewed their obligation to implement IDEA's disciplinary regulations as a deterrent to that goal" (McCarthy and Soodak, 2007, p. 463). Instead of providing students with disabilities with the needed supports to behave appropriately in the least restricted setting possible, it appears that the "safety" of some schools may be achieved through the sacrifice of those students' civil rights.

Effects of Zero-Tolerance Policies

Despite the highly publicized support for zero-tolerance policies, there is little proof that they actually make schools safer and some evidence that schools with such policies actually have more problems with discipline, a more negative school climate, and lower academic achievement (Billeteri, 2008; Brady, Balmer, and Phenix, 2007). In addition, there is a great deal of evidence that the consequences they mandate have highly negative impacts on young people.

What *has* been studied is the impact on students of consequences mandated by zero-tolerance policies. Despite arguments that applying one-size-fits-all consequences are fair, it is clear that the effects of the policies are not the same for all students. ". . . for some, zero tolerance adds another risk factor to lives that are already overburdened with risk factors. Although some students may have the support and know-how to wrangle and maneuver their way back to success after an expulsion or suspension, other students cannot. Applying the policy consistently does not mean that all students receive the same punishment. For example, there are great differences in expulsions when one student is expelled but can afford tutoring and another is expelled but cannot afford to be tutored" (Casella, 2003b, p. 881).

Researchers demonstrate that out-of-school suspension, the most commonly applied zero-tolerance consequence, is linked to continued academic failure, grade retention, negative school attitudes, less participation in extracurricular activities, higher placement in special education programs, lower grades, poorer attendance, and continued disciplinary problems (Nichols, 2004). Most serious of all, being involved with school disciplinary practices is a strong predictor of dropping out.

These consequences should come as no surprise. When students are suspended, they obviously lose instructional time. They are usually at home and most are provided with no access to their teachers or to the assignments on which their classmates are working. There are very few publicly funded alternatives to schools, and most places in those settings are reserved for students with disabilities. Delays in getting back into school are common even when students have "served their time" or been found "not guilty." In addition, they often feel ostracized and rejected by the adults to whom they had previously looked for help. They often believe—sometimes correctly—that they have been unfairly singled out and lose faith in the integrity of teachers and administrators. Excluded students often become "transients," moving in and out of various educational settings, never feeling quite at home and never being able to establish the kind of relationships with other students that lead to academic success (Brown, 2007).

In fact, the increase in dropouts that is connected to mandatory suspensions and expulsions may not be accidental at all. Students whose behavior is inappropriate are often young people who are struggling with academic tasks. They "act out" their frustration with schools' inability to meet their needs. In an era of high-stakes testing, poor performance on standardized assessments negatively impacts the school's "report card." It is plausible that administrators may use zero-tolerance policies to raise test scores by "pushing out" low performing students. Certainly that remedy is more affordable than providing students with small classes, tutoring, mentoring, and after-school programs that might actually help improve their academic performance and, in turn, decrease their inappropriate behavior.

In addition to increasing the number of students who drop out of school—or perhaps more precisely, as a result of doing so—zero tolerance has also created a "school to prison pipeline." Many schools have increased the deployment of police officers in schools. In New York City, these "school safety officers" often take upon themselves authority that goes beyond violence prevention. "They enforce school rules relating to dress and appearance. They make up their own rules regarding food or other objects that have nothing whatsoever to do with school safety. On occasion they subject educators who question the NYPD's treatment of students to retaliatory arrests" (New York Civil Liberties Union, 2007, p. 4). More than 400,000 arrests are made in schools each year, the vast majority for nonviolent offenses. Misbehaviors that would have been taken care of by school administrators in the past have been criminalized. The "over-policing" of schools interferes with instructional time, subjects students to intrusive searches with sexual overtones, and provides them with evidence of society's disregard for their rights. The schools become "drop-out" factories, where fewer than 30 percent of ninth-graders make it to senior year (New York Civil Liberties Union, 2007).

Changes in the juvenile justice system have been taking place simultaneously. "Since 1992, 45 states have passed laws making it easier to try juveniles as adults, 31 have stiffened sanctions against youths for a variety of offenses and 47 loosened confidentiality provisions for juveniles. Despite a precipitous drop in juvenile crime during the last half of the 1990s, the number of formally processed cases involving juveniles—mostly non-violent—increased, along with the number of youths held in secure facilities for non-violent offenses" (Wald and Losen, 2004, p. 3).

Statistics also provide insight into the connection between school failure and incarceration. "Drop-outs are eight times more likely to be in jail or in prison as are high school graduates" (Bridgeland, DiIulio, and Morrison, 2006). "Approximately 68 percent of state prison inmates in 1997 had not completed high school. 75 percent of youths under age 18 who have been sentenced to adult prisons have not successfully passed tenth grade. An estimated 70 percent of the juvenile justice population suffers from learning disabilities and 33 percent read below the fourth grade level. The "single largest predictor" of later arrest among adolescent females is having been suspended, expelled, or held back during the middle school years" (Wald and Losen, 2004, p. 4).

The school-to-prison pipeline is self-perpetuating. Zero-tolerance policies have a chilling affect on relationships between adults and young people. Those most in need of assistance, including the mentally ill, are discouraged by such policies from seeking it, for fear that their concerns will be misinterpreted or misunderstood and will result in punishment in school or in prisons (Skiba et al., 2006). Consequently, they receive no assistance in changing or dealing with the underlying causes of their behaviors. The acting out continues, harsh school penalties follow, suspension leads to referrals to the criminal justice system or to behavior "on the street" that results in arrest and time in jail. The viciousness of this systemic connection led one scholar to declare it an example of how "America still eats her young" (Ladson-Billings, 2001, p. 84).

Democratic Discipline

Admittedly, it is challenging to create disciplinary policies that exemplify the American ideal—protection of both individual rights and the common good. It is also necessary if young people are to believe that democratic values like fairness and justice are more than mere words.

School disciplinary policies can be crafted to incorporate the best characteristics of the U.S. justice system. For example, schools could act under the assumption that students are presumed innocent until their guilt is proven. Administrators could have the right to consider the facts of each case—including the student's intent, the circumstances surrounding an incident—before applying consequences. School districts could establish disciplinary codes that clearly spell out due process procedures.

In addition, violations of school disciplinary codes could be seen as "teachable moments." Instead of meting out punishments that do little, democratic disciplinary policies could provide students with instruction in acceptable behavior or problem solving (Skiba and Peterson, 2003). Ronnie Casella argues alternatives like "restorative justice"—community service that replaces suspension—do just that. Instead of sitting at home watching TV or in an in-school suspension room doing meaningless busy work, students provide academic tutoring for younger children, work in community agencies, or even improve the school building or campus through physical work. Schools establish peer mediation teams that work to resolve conflicts among students and recommend consequences for inappropriate behaviors. Such teams involve victims of students' aggression in deciding what would constitute appropriate restitution. The offenders also are required to take responsibility for ways to restore order and to remedy any damage their actions have caused (Skiba et al., 2006).

Involving adults in meaningful ways is another important aspect of democratic disciplinary policies. Bringing school officials and parents together first to work out acceptable consequences means that the students are faced with a united front of adults who are working in the students' best interest and that of the community. In such cases, contracts are created that spell out the responsibilities all parties will take on in order to avoid future problems. Students create problem-solving plans that require them to describe what they need in order to change their behaviors, and are provided with mentors—older students or adults—with whom they check-in weekly to report progress or seek advice (Casella, 2003b).

These models not only address problems that have already taken place; they also go a long way in preventing future ones. They also send students the message that public authority in the United States is fair and operates in the best interest of all its citizens. By creating and sustaining such beliefs, disciplinary policies that allow administrators discretion in determining consequences and involve students, families, and communities in implementing them, provide greater assurance than do policies that prescribe one-size-fits-all remedies.

With the evidence mounting that the benefits of zero-tolerance policies are negligible, why do we not to have the political will to demand that they be abandoned? Perhaps because the real purpose of such laws is actually not to help young people change their behaviors but to give adults reassurance that they are still "in charge." It turns out that the benefits of zero-tolerance policies are illusory and merely the stuff of good public relations campaigns.

Society can do better for young people. The original message for zero-tolerance policies—concern for their well-being—can be communicated in more effective ways by creating schools that attend to students' real needs. There are models for doing so. Schools in which disorder, disrespect, and disruption are minimized are small enough to reduce anonymity, alienation, and isolation, and attend to minor infractions quickly and use them as an opportunity to teach students how to manage their behavior more effectively (Bridgeland, DiIulio, and Morrison, 2006). Even at our most idealistic, however, we must acknowledge that some students will need to leave or be removed from an educational setting in which their needs can not be adequately served and in which they can not manage their behavior. However, this should be our last resort, a result agreed upon by caring adults—parents, administrators, teachers, psychologists, and, when necessary, police officers and the courts. "The accumulated evidence points to a clear need for change in how zero-tolerance policies are applied, and toward the need for a set of alternative practices. These alternatives rely upon a more flexible and common-sense application of school discipline, and on a set of prevention practices that have been validated in ten years of school violence research. It is time to make the shifts in policy, practice, and research to implement policies that can keep schools safe *and* preserve the opportunity to learn for all students (Skiba et al., 2006).

For Discussion

1. Opponents of zero tolerance argue that it is particularly harmful to students of color and that by giving administrators more discretion in disciplinary matters, the effects of prejudice could be lessened. However, administrators, like teachers have biases. How can a district's disciplinary procedures protect students of color from racial prejudice without resorting to mandated consequences?
2. Are there some situations where zero tolerance is the correct or the only option? Discuss what they might be and why you think discretion is inappropriate in those cases.
3. Felons are allowed "three strikes" before mandatory life sentences are imposed. Would it be appropriate for schools to allow a similar "three offense" policy before suspension or expulsion were imposed?
4. Interview a school administrator about his/her experiences with disciplining students with disabilities. Ask about the hardest situation he/she has faced. Ask whether the administrator believes making allowances for students with disabilities is appropriate. Discuss your findings in class. Drawing on class discussions and interviews, write an essay arguing for or against IDEA regulations regarding discipline.

References

ACHILLES, G., McLAUGHLIN, M. and CRONINGER, R. (2007). "Sociocultural Correlates of Disciplinary Exclusion Among Students With Emotional, Behavioral, and Learning Disabilities in the SEELS National Dataset." *Journal of Emotional and Behavioral Disorders* 15(1): 33–45.

THE ADVANCEMENT PROJECT AND THE CIVIL RIGHTS PROJECT, HARVARD UNIVERSITY. (2005). "Education on Lockdown." www.advancementproject.org/reports/FINALEOLrep .pdf.

AMERICAN CIVIL LIBERTIES UNION. (2005). "Students' Rights." www.aclu.org/StudentsRights/.

ANYON, J. (1997). *Ghetto Schooling.* New York: Teachers College Press.

AYERS, W., DOHRN, B. AND AYERS, R. *Zero Tolerance.* New York: The New Press.

BEATTY, P., PETTERUTI, A., AND ZIEDENBERG, J. (2007). "The Vortex: The Concentrated Racial Impact of Drug Imprisonment and the Characteristics of Punitive Counties." Washington, DC: The Justice Policy Institute. www.justicepolicy.org/images/upload/07-12_REP_Vortex_AC-DP.pdf.

BILLETERI, T. (2008). "Discipline in Schools." *Congressional Quarterly Researcher* 18(7):145–168.

BRADY, K., BALMER, S. AND PHENIX, D. (2007). "School-Police Partnerships Effectiveness in Urban Schools." *Education and Urban Society* 39(4):455–478.

BRIDGELAND, J., DIIULIO, J., AND MORISON, K. (2006). "The Silent Epidemic: Perspectives of High School Dropouts." Report prepared for the Bill and Melinda Gates Foundation. Washington, DC: Civic Enterprises.

BROWN, T. (2007). "Lost and Turned Out: Academic, Social, and Emotional Experiences of Students Excluded from Schools." *Urban Education* 42(5): 432–455.

Butler v Rio Rancho Public School Board. 2002. 245 F. Supp. 2d 1188 (2002 U.S. Dis. LEXIS 26238).

CASELLA, R. (2003a). "Zero Tolerance Policy in Schools: Rationale, Consequences, and Alternatives." *Teachers College Record* 105(5): 872–892.

———. (2003b). "Security, Schooling, and the Consumer's Choice to Segregate." *The Urban Review* 35(2): 129–148.

COMMON GOOD (2008) "Overruled." http://commongood.org/burdenquestion-2.html.

FENNING, P. AND ROSE, J. (2007). "Overrepresentation of African American Students in Exclusionary Discipline The Role of School Policy." *Urban Education* 42(6): 536–559.

GIROUX, H. (2003). "Racial Injustice And Disposable Youth In The Age Of Zero Tolerance." *Qualitative Studies in Education* 16(4): 553–565.

IYENGAR, R. (2008). "I'd Rather Be Hanged For A Sheep Than A Lamb: The Unintended Consequences Of 'Three-Strikes' Laws." *NBER Working Papers Series, Working Paper 13784.* Cambridge, MA: National Bureau of Economic Research.

JONES, G., CONNELLY, M. AND WAGNER, K. (2001) "Three Strikes Law: Does It Really Work?" Maryland: State Commission on Criminal Sentencing Policy. www.msccp.org/publication/strikes.html.

KOLD News. (2007). "Suspended for Doodling." www.kold.com/Global/story.asp?S=6971974&nav=14RT.

LADSON-BILLINGS, G. (2001). "America Still Eats Her Young" in *Zero Tolerance,* ed. W. Ayers, B. Dohrn and R. Ayers. New York: The New Press.

LEMAGIE, S. (2008). "Students Expelled For Replica Swords," *Minneapolis Star Tribune,* April 25.

LIPS, D. (2008). "School Choice: Policy Developments and National Participation Estimates in 2007–2008." *Backgrounder.* Washington, DC: Heritage Foundation. www.heritage.org/Research/Education/bg2102.cfm.

McCARTHY, M. and SOODAK, L. (2007). "The Politics of Discipline: Balancing School Safety and Rights of Students With Disabilities." *Exceptional Children* 73(4): 456–474.

Mississippi Youth Justice Project. (2008). *Effective Discipline for Student Success.* Montgomery, Alabama: Southern Poverty Law Center.

National School Safety and Security Services. (2008). "Zero Tolerance: School Safety and Discipline Policies." www.schoolsecurity.org/trends/zero_tolerance.html.

New York Civil Liberties Union (2007). *Criminalizing the Classroom.* New York: author. www.nyclu.org/policinginschools.

New York City Department of Education (2008). "Citywide Standards of Discipline and Intervention Measures." www.nycenet.edu/parents/PDFs/DisciplineCode.pdf.

NICHOLS, J. (2004) "An Exploration of Discipline and Suspension Data." *The Journal of Negro Education* 73(4): 408–424.

ORFIELD, G. and LEE, C. (2007). "Historic Reversals, Accelerating Resegregation, and the Need for New Integration Strategies."Los Angeles: The Civil Rights Project. www .civilrightsproject.ucla.edu/research/deseg/reversals_reseg_need.pdf.

SCHULTE, B., (2008). "For Little Children, Grown-Up Labels As Sexual Harassers," *Washington Post,* April 3, 2008.

Seal v Morgan. 2000. 229 F. 3rdd 567 (6th Cir.).

SHEPHERD, JOANNA M. (2002), "Fear of the First Strike: The Full Deterrent Effect of California's Two-and Three-Strikes Legislation." *Journal of Legal Studies* 31: 159–201.

SKIBA, R. (2000) "Zero Tolerance, Zero Evidence: An analysis of School Disciplinary Practice." Bloomington, IN: Indiana Education Policy Center. Policy Research Report #SRS2. www.indiana.edu/~safeschl/ztze.pdf.

SKIBA, R. AND PETERSON, R. (2003) "Teaching the Social Curriculum: School Discipline as Instruction." *Preventing School Failure* 47(2): 66–74.

SKIBA, R., et al. (2006). "Are Zero Tolerance Policies Effective in the Schools? An Evidentiary Review and Recommendations." A Report by the American Psychological Association Zero Tolerance Task Force. Washington, DC: American Psychological Association.

STADER, D. (2004). "Zero Tolerance as Public Policy: The Good, the Bad, and the Ugly." *The Clearing House* 78(2): 62–66.

STEIN, N. (2007). "Bullying, Harassment and Violence Among Students." *Radical Teacher* 80: 30–35.

SULLIVAN, L., (2008). "The Crackdown on New York City Students," *Gotham Gazette,* February 11.

TURNER, S. (2000). RAND Corporation Criminal Justice Program, Justice Research and Statistics Association. "Impact of Truth-in-Sentencing and Three Strikes Legislation on Crime," *Crime and Justice Atlas 2000.* Washington, DC: U.S. Department of Justice.

U.S. DEPARTMENT OF EDUCATION. (2001). No Child Left Behind Act. www.ed.gov/policy/ elsec/leg/esea02/index.html

———. (2007). "Indicators of School Crime and Safety, 2007." National Center for Educational Statistics. http://nces.ed.gov/pubsearch/pubsinfo.asp?pubid=2008021.

U.S. Department of Justice (2008). COPS in Schools. www.cops.usdoj.gov.

WALD, J. AND LOSEN, D. (2004). "Defining and Redirecting A School to Prison Pipeline." Paper presented at the 2004 Midwest Conference on the Dropout Crisis: "Assessing the Problem and Confronting the Challenge." http://www.woodsfund.org/ community/Folder_1036081004377.

WALSH, J., (2008). "Sent Home: The Suspension Gap." *Minneapolis Star Tribune,* May 18.

CHAPTER 16

Teacher Unions and School Leadership: Detrimental or Beneficial

Should teachers and their unions be given a larger role in running public schools?

POSITION 1: TEACHERS AND TEACHER UNIONS SHOULD PLAY A MAJOR ROLE IN SCHOOL LEADERSHIP

It is as much the duty of the union to preserve public education as it is to negotiate a good contract.

—Shanker, AFT, 2008

Forcing Teachers to Unionize

In the early part of the twentieth century, teachers were trained to believe that sacrifice was the essence of their profession. Teachers worked long hours; their classes often numbered fifty or more students; their salaries were low; and schools were at times poorly heated, poorly ventilated, and unsanitary. Women teachers were not allowed to go out unescorted (except to attend church) or frequent places where liquor was served; and in many communities, when women teachers married, they were forced to resign from their jobs. In addition to living truncated social lives, teachers served at the whim of school boards, without any promise of tenure or health or retirement benefits. They were not considered worthy of participating in the book selection process and were excluded from the more substantive deliberations about curriculum. As school systems developed into large bureaucratic organizations, teacher powerlessness became institutionalized. School principals became part of management and separated themselves from the teachers. Once referred to as the "principal teacher" or the "main teacher," the head of a school stopped teaching and became a manager who shared few of the problems of teachers and little of their perspective.

Most of the new school principals were male; most of the classroom teachers were female. Throughout the history of public education, most teachers have been women—especially in the lower grades—and principals and superintendents have been primarily men. As one historian notes, in the mid-1850s, the sanctioned occupations for women were limited to teaching, printmaking, and dressmaking (Kessler-Harris, 2007). Education was traditionally thought of as "women's work." Women were considered more nurturing and better suited to be moral guides for children. In the early days of public schools, with few other work opportunities open to them, women were ready recruits. Educated only slightly better than the students they would eventually teach, women were hired to work for very low wages and expected to serve in schools without tenure or any promise that they could assume positions of leadership.

During the nineteenth century, it was assumed that those who taught school would do so for only a short time. Women typically chose marriage and homemaking after a few years in the classroom. Ambitious men were expected to move from teaching to loftier, better-paying occupations. Classroom teaching was seldom the chosen lifetime work of the more able. Teaching was considered as employment for workers who were "passing through" on their way to more serious pursuits (Holmes Group, 1986). At best, teaching was seen as a good short-term job, but most people disparaged it as a career choice, and those who chose to stay in the classroom for more than a few years often encountered social derision. In 1932, the sociologist Willard Waller observed that teachers were not treated like other workers, and certainly not like professionals. He noted that in small towns, unmarried teachers were expected to live in a teacherage—a special boardinghouse—apart from other single adults who held nonteaching jobs. Waller also noted the popular prejudice against teachers commonly held by wealthier and better-educated members of the community. "Teaching," he wrote, "is quite generally regarded as a failure belt . . . the refuge of unmarriageable women and unsaleable men" (Waller, 1932, p. 61).

Administrators treated teachers as low-skilled temporary workers who needed to be told what to do. The authority to run schools was vested in men in administrative offices, and teachers were not to challenge their authority. Over time, teachers realized what they were being asked to give up in the name of professionalism was not good for them or their students, and through organized and collective action, schools could be improved for everyone.

Teachers have been joining together for well over one hundred years, but their earliest organizations were not really unions. The National Education Association (NEA), for example, was established in 1857, to represent the views of "practical" classroom teachers and administrators. Annual NEA conventions were not union meetings but settings for the exchange of ideas about teaching. Members typically avoided discussing labor issues or how teachers could influence decisions about their work or wages. The NEA was less concerned with the personal welfare of classroom teachers than it was with advancing the profession of education. In its early years, the NEA was a male-dominated organization for teachers that was led by school superintendents, professors of education, and school principals (Wesley, 1957). As one critic of the old NEA notes, the role of classroom teachers, especially women teachers, was "limited to listening" (Eaton, 1975, p. 10).

Teacher unionism dates to the early twentieth century, when Chicago teachers organized to fight for better working conditions. In 1916, the American Federation of Teachers (AFT) was formed as an affiliate of the American Federation of Labor. Initially, the older NEA and the upstart AFT cooperated. The NEA focused on professional and practical sides of teaching; the AFT concentrated on improving economic aspects of teachers' lives (Engel, 1976). Over the years, local affiliates of the NEA and the AFT have become rivals in their efforts to become the teachers' bargaining agents. More than 80 percent of U.S. teachers belong to either the NEA or the AFT, and more than 60 percent work under a formal collective bargaining agreement.

Teachers were never eager to join unions; they were forced to because the culture of administrative managers was at odds with the culture of working teachers (Jessup, 1978; Urban, 1982; Murphy, 1990). Teachers urged their colleagues to use unions and collective bargaining to improve their working conditions and gain a voice in improving education. Today, teacher organizations often bear a greater resemblance to professional associations (for example, the American Bar Association or the American Medical Association) than to labor organizations (the International Ladies Garment Workers Union or the United Automobile Workers). Leaders of the old AFT, however, identified with unionized workers in other industries. They believed problems common to all workers could be solved through cooperation and collective action. They wanted teacher organizations to provide economic benefits for their members, and argued that teacher unions also could assist labor by improving the education offered to working-class children. Despite numerous efforts to organize teachers and revitalize education, including development of a workers' college and special public schools for workers' children, AFT membership declined in the 1920s and remained flat throughout most of the 1930s. Teachers were reluctant to join unions, and most school administrators were openly hostile to organized labor. In the 1920s, fearing worker radicalism and union activity, many school superintendents demanded teachers, as a condition of employment, sign "yellow dog contracts," agreements they would not join a union.

The National Labor Relations Act (NLRA) of 1935 changed the status of unions by recognizing workers in private industry had the right to bargain collectively. Employees are at a disadvantage when they bargain singly with employers, working alone against the power and resources at management's hand. Under collective bargaining agreements, employees, as a group, and their employers negotiate about wages and employment conditions. Collective bargaining laws recognize workers have the right to join together and elect a bargaining agent (a union) to negotiate with management on their behalf. The NLRA required employers and unions to "meet at reasonable times and confer in good faith with respect to wages, hours, and other terms and conditions of employment."

Questions about its constitutionality clouded the NLRA's early history. The Supreme Court eventually decided the issue, judging the act constitutional

(*NLRB v. Jones and Laughlin Steel Company,* 1937). This was a major victory for organized labor, and represented a great change in the thinking of the courts. In earlier cases the courts had ruled unions were illegal and workers who joined unions were guilty of entering into an illegal "conspiracy" to improve their wages. By the mid-nineteenth century, courts no longer held that those who advocated collective bargaining were involved in criminal conspiracies (*Commonwealth v. Hunt,* 1842), but unions and collective negotiations did not earn full legitimacy until the Supreme Court's 1937 decision.

The NLRA affects only workers in the private sector. It does not cover employees of federal, state, or local government, so this law did not guarantee collective bargaining for public school teachers. Teachers could still be fired by school boards simply for joining a union (Kahlenberg, 2007, p. 41). Public schools are considered extensions of the state. School boards are, in a sense, state employers, and thus they are excluded from federal labor legislation. It has been left up to the states to regulate employment relations in public education. Following Congress's lead, the majority of state legislatures have taken action to recognize the rights of workers to organize and negotiate with employers.

The organization of teachers in New York City in 1960 is considered a watershed for public school unions (Lieberman and Moscow, 1966, p. 35). The United Federation of Teachers (UFT), a local affiliate of the AFT, was made up of several New York City teacher organizations. The UFT asked the Board of Education to recognize the teachers' rights to bargain collectively and conduct an election to determine which organization should represent them. The board was unsure how to implement collective bargaining, and it did not move swiftly. The unions accused the board of stalling, and on November 7, 1960, the UFT declared the first strike in the history of New York City education.

It was a brief but effective job action. The teachers were back in the classrooms the next day and the board agreed to hold elections and not to take reprisals against striking teachers. Union estimates put pickets at about 7,500, and it was claimed that another 15,000 teachers stayed home (Eaton, 1975, p. 165). The strike alerted the nation to the power of unions, and teachers began to recognize the advantages of collective negotiation as well as the power potential of the strike. Collective bargaining changed the relationship between classroom teachers and administrators. It promised teachers more pay, better job security, and an audible voice in education. As one labor historian puts it, "It essentially refined and broadened the concept of professionalism by assuring [teachers] more autonomy and less supervisory control" (Murphy, 1990, p. 209).

The New York City strike reverberated nationally. The results encouraged teachers, and sent the two largest unions, the NEA and the AFT, scrambling for members. The NEA represents about 3.2 million teachers, more than twice the number represented by the AFT. These organizations differ on specific issues. (You can examine the views of the AFT at www.aft.org and the NEA's views at www.nea.org.)

The decision to join the labor movement no doubt came hard to many teachers. Teachers tended to be politically conservative, first-generation college graduates who identified with management more than with labor (Rosenthal, 1969; Aronowitz, 1973). They belonged (and still belong) to a special category of white-collar employees called "knowledge workers." Paid for what they know and how they use their knowledge to produce value, these workers, as a group, are highly individualistic, and difficult to unionize and organize into collective action (Kerchner, Koppich, and Weeres, 1997, p. 34). Strikes are anathema to most members of teacher unions (Rauth, 1990). The fact that the union movement has succeeded in recruiting teachers speaks well for unions; teachers believe unions are necessary and useful. Most teachers now belong to some sort of union, despite a decline in union membership in other fields and continued middle-class antipathy toward unions. Today, surveys find teachers supportive of unions, professional organizations they regard as a necessary protective shield in a workplace too eager to ignore them (Galley, 2003).

Protecting Teachers' Rights

Unions have been good for classroom teachers. The research literature indicates unions have had a positive effect on teachers' working conditions. As a result of collective bargaining, teachers' salaries have increased,[1] and teachers have gained protection against unreasonable treatment. Unlike the pre-union days, teachers cannot be dismissed simply because they consume alcohol, change their marital status, or express unpopular political views. The philosopher John Dewey, described as the "intellectual guru" of the AFT, believed a union was necessary to protect teachers' intellectual and academic freedom (Kahlenberg, 2007, p. 35). Unions also have been good for students. They have put the faculty squarely in the front ranks of the battle for better schools and better education for children. Unions have given faculty a collective voice in matters of curriculum and school improvement.

Teacher unions have always attracted some bad press. Some of it is traditional antilabor rhetoric, and some is simply misinformed. No doubt you have heard unions are to blame for declining student performance and that unions have hurt education by protecting weak teachers who deserve to be fired. This is not the case. In fact, it is mystifying when unions are blamed for protecting weak teachers. Before teachers are awarded tenure, they must be graduated from state-approved teacher education programs, convince administrators to hire them, and survive an extended probationary period, typically from three to five years. Unions currently play virtually no part in any of these processes. Weak teachers may make it through this system, but they do so with no help from organized labor. Teacher unions are embarrassed by poor teachers, just as the American Bar Association and the American Medical Association are discomfited by ineffective, corrupt, or lazy members in their ranks. No responsible union wants to protect incompetent workers.

---

[1]In the 2004–05 school year, the average teacher salary was $47,602, up 2.2 percent from the previous year, and the average beginning salary was $31,753. For the most current state-by-state listings, see the "Salary Survey" of the American Federation of Teachers at www.aft.org.

Unions' Stake in Education Reform

By the late twentieth century, a growing number of educational theorists and researchers had come to realize that tapping classroom teachers' intellectual understandings and creative energies would lead to improved education (Barth, 1990; Schlechty, 1990; Smylie, 1994). The traditional top-down, male-dominated leadership model of public schools had outlived its usefulness. Schools faced a wider array of vexing issues than ever before. The problems of education had become far too complex for one or two "leaders" to manage, no matter how skilled and able they might be. In addition, most people recognized that teachers too had changed: Not only were they invested in teaching as a career, they were well educated and possessed curricular expertise and immediate classroom experiences essential to school improvement. School administrators may have been good teachers at one time, but removed from the day-to-day life of instruction, their knowledge of what works and what needs to be done pales in comparison to what teachers know. Above all, experience has shown that for reforms to be successful, the reform agenda must be widely shared by everyone in the school. The best ideas and most worthwhile proposals for change are doomed to failure if viewed as the "principal's plan" rather than a plan shaped and shared by everyone. No single person—no matter how thoughtful and creative that person may be—has a vision that can measure up to the teachers' collective visions of how to help students learn. School leadership is the work of everyone in the schools (Lambert, 2002; Spillane, 2006; Gaffney, 2007).

Most school boards now accept that teachers have the right to bargain over working conditions, but many remain unconvinced of the legitimacy of labor's voice in policy issues and matters of school leadership.[2] Unions have always recognized their role in school reform, and continue to insist teachers have a collective voice in bringing about better schooling. Teachers know what needs to be done to improve schools (Rauth, 1990; Watts and McClure, 1990; Kerchner and Koppich, 1993). Today's unions understand that teacher leadership is central to improving student learning. If you look at countries with high-achieving school systems, you will find that beginning teachers not only have solid academic backgrounds, subject matter expertise, and a reasonable command of education in pedagogy, but they also are inducted into their profession through a clinical, real-world training process that is organized and managed by practicing teachers (AFT, 2003).

Today's teacher unions are as dedicated to school improvement as they are to serving teachers. In fact, they realize the best way to serve teachers is to improve schools. The relationship between schools and unionized teachers is not unlike the new relationship forged between the United Auto Workers (UAW) and the General Motors (GM) Saturn assembly plant.[3] Both GM and

[2]Teacher leadership refers to the use of teacher expertise to organize and improve student learning, on both the classroom and school levels, through involvement in curriculum decision making, personnel matters, and financial and resource allocation (York-Barr and Duke, 2004, p. 261).

[3]The AFT recognizes union-management cooperation through its Saturn-UAW Partnership Award. The award celebrates "exemplary models of union-management collaboration that demonstrate trust, teamwork, shared decision making, training accountability, a focus on quality and the ability to survive conflict and change." For more information, go to www.saturnuaw.com.

the UAW recognized that to compete against foreign and domestic automakers in a fiercely competitive market, both sides needed to develop a new labor-management relationship (Kerchner, Koppich, and Weeres, 1997, p. 113). The old us-versus-them antagonism has given way to a new and cooperative partnership. The goal is to make a better product. For teacher unions, the goal is to build better schools though the development of a high-quality teaching force. As the AFT notes, to develop and sustain good teachers, "union[s] must play a role in developing and/or implementing quality preservice teacher education, effective recruiting and hiring practices, strong induction and mentoring programs, high-quality professional development, meaningful evaluation, and when necessary, fair, timely intervention and dismissal procedures" (AFT, 2003, p. 5).

What Do Teacher Unions Really Want?

Parents, legislators, and unions agree: The ultimate goal of schools is to help every student succeed. Unions want to use their collective strength to improve schools through appropriate policies and practices. Unionized teachers would like to add their collective voice to the debates about accountability and school assessment programs, teacher education and development, school administration, and policy issues such as "No Child Left Behind" legislation, vouchers, merit pay, as well as salaries and working conditions of teachers.

Nowhere is the union voice more necessary than in the support of teachers. What do classroom teachers need and how can unions help? While salaries have always been a major issue for teachers, teachers typically indicate that a "lack of support" is their top concern (NEA, 2005). Teachers need real-world mentors who have mastered the practical skills necessary to help children learn. Teacher unions want a voice in recruiting and sustaining a high-quality teaching force. Unions want to play a significant role in everything to do with teaching, from participation in preservice teacher education to the development of strong induction programs and meaningful evaluation of teachers. The unions know that to improve schools, they have to support everything necessary and central to the preparation, recruitment, and work of good teachers.

Everyone supports good schools. Too many schools are failing, and most are not doing well enough. Unions are supportive of many school reform proposals and suspicious of others. (See the NEA and AFT websites for their positions on specific policy issues, from testing to school discipline, as well as the teaching of specific subject areas and the No Child Left Behind legislation.) Unions are particularly wary of policies and procedures that are imposed on schools without the consultation of teachers and that exclude the teaching staff from the decision-making process. Since it is largely up to the teachers to make schools successful, unions believe that the teachers should have a strong voice in all school decisions. As the AFT notes, by guaranteeing that the teachers play a formal role in school leadership, the school not only benefits from their expertise but also provides teachers with a greater stake in making the program work (AFT, 2006).

POSITION 2: TEACHERS AND TEACHER UNIONS SHOULD NOT PLAY A ROLE IN SCHOOL LEADERSHIP

The simple fact is that the NEA and other belligerent teacher unions are with-out par as school reform barriers. School reform initiatives are almost always doomed when the NEA chooses to oppose them, as they usually do.

—Rod Paige, former U.S. Secretary of Education, 2001–2005
(2006, p. 191)

A History of Self-Serving and Unsupported Union Claims

Teacher union officials say that when public monies are spent to improve working conditions for teachers, children are the ultimate beneficiaries. Their arguments are, no doubt, familiar: Public school students suffer because teachers are underpaid. Hardworking, devoted teachers deserve greater compensation. Unless teachers earn higher salaries, not only will the current crop of teachers become discouraged, but the most able college graduates will not consider a teaching career. Union leaders further argue that teachers need a stronger voice in school affairs. They claim teachers will be more effective if allowed to join administrators in all areas of school leadership, including school improvement and supervision and evaluation of teaching.

The logic in these examples is simple: What is good for teachers is good for children. If the public wants better education for its children, the public should support union efforts to improve education through increased remuneration and greater authority for teachers. Collective bargaining practices, picket lines, work stoppages (strikes), and expansion of union control over schools should be considered beneficial to the community, parents, and students. Convincing? Not really. Making schools better places for teachers does not necessarily serve the public interest. The public's interest is not measured in teachers' job satisfaction but in the quality of learning provided to students. Despite the rhetoric of organized labor, teacher unions do not have a positive effect on student achievement. Researchers find negligible differences in achievement between public school students in union and nonunion schools. While research indicates evidence that collective bargaining improves teachers' salaries, benefits, and working conditions, it is more difficult to find a consistently positive influence of unions on student learning (Goldhaber, 2006; Stone, 2000). Unions cannot claim to make a difference where it counts most: students' academic performance. Despite failures of teacher unions to prove their worth in student achievement, the positive wage effect of unions—that is, their power to improve teachers' pay—clearly ensures unions will remain players in education. Less clear is whether or not unions are good for schools, a hindrance to school reform, or merely irrelevant (Finn, 1985). A review of the available research indicates

> There are many well-reasoned assertions and even some data-based inferences about the effects of teacher leadership on student learning, but little evidence

exists to support these claims . . . What is known about teacher leadership? . . .
The collective literature still is more robust with argument and rationale than
with the evidence of effects of teacher leadership. (York-Barr and Duke, 2004,
pp. 285–287)

Although only about 15 percent of American workers belong to labor
unions, most teachers in America's schools are unionized. Over 80 percent of
teachers belong to an affiliate of the National Education Association (NEA) or
the American Federation of Teachers (AFT), and with millions of dues-paying
members, unions have great resources and great power. Not only can teacher
unions exert influence on the day-to-day workings of schools, their political
activities have given them unrivaled influence in the local, state, and federal
governments. As Terry Moe points out, "The key to the unions' preeminence
in American education is that they are able to combine collective bargaining
and politics into an integrated strategy for promoting union objectives" (Moe,
2001, p. 166). Moe goes on to note that "On education issues, the teacher unions
are the 500-pound gorillas of legislative politics, and especially in legislatures
where the Democrats are in control, they are in a better position than any other
interest group to get what they want from government" (Moe, 2001, p. 175).

Teacher unions work for the benefit of teachers. Please, do not be misled
when unions call for more rigorous training of teachers or stricter licensing standards. While there is little evidence such changes would result in better education or improved student learning, there is abundant evidence to indicate these
policies would make good economic sense for teachers. Stricter standards for
teacher certification, whether academic (requiring all teachers to have master's
degrees) or arbitrary (requiring all teachers to be over 6'5" tall), would result in a
diminished supply of teachers at a time when demand is increasing. Obviously,
unions are hopeful that market forces will result in improved salaries. It is hard
for the public to trust unions. Who can say with certainty that union advocacy
of smaller class size represents a desire to help children or if it is simply a way
to make teachers' work easier and, concurrently, increase the demand for teachers? Consider another union recommendation: mentorship programs through
which experienced classroom teachers help new teachers learn the ropes. When
teachers serve as mentors for other teachers, does it benefit students or is this
simply driving up the cost of education through featherbedding—the addition
of unnecessary workers? (Ballou and Podgursky, 2000)

From Bread and Butter to Policy Issues

While the evidence shows small but significant effects of leadership actions on
student learning across the spectrum of schools, existing research also shows
that demonstrated effects of successful leadership are considerably greater in
schools that are in more difficult circumstances. Indeed, there are virtually no
documented instances of troubled schools being turned around without the
intervention of a powerful leader. (Leithwood et al., 2004, p. 3)

Encouraged by their ability to improve teachers' salaries—the union-wage
effect is in the neighborhood of 5 to 10 percent—unions have extended their

influence beyond bread-and-butter work issues. Past union efforts typically were limited to traditional labor concerns: wages and hours, working conditions, fringe benefits, grievance procedures, organization rights, and such specific work-related issues as extra pay for extra duty (athletic coaching or directing school plays, for example). Over time, teacher unions began to demand a voice in policy issues, including curriculum reform, class size, disciplinary practices, textbook selection procedures, in-service training, teacher transfer policies, and personnel matters—including hiring and awarding tenure (Kerchner, 1986; Kerchner and Koppich, 1993). Today, affiliates of both the NEA and the AFT want teachers to expand their activities and participate in discussions about school improvement, staff development, and student assessment. These demands go well beyond the traditional bargaining issues of salaries and working conditions. Some union contracts give teachers the right to make decisions about how schools spend money, how teachers teach, and how students are to learn. In strongly unionized urban districts, union contracts can be hundreds of pages long (Moe, 2001). Under the familiar argument that collective negotiations will create a better education for children, union leaders now claim that increased teacher participation in all the decision-making and managerial aspects of education also will improve schools. The public has greeted the new union arguments with a healthy skepticism. Unions grew up on industrial principles. They have used organizing and negotiating techniques borrowed from industrial unions in mining and manufacturing—collective bargaining and the threat of strikes—to improve their members' working conditions. There is every reason to be suspicious that unions can use the same tactics to improve the quality of student learning.

Turning schools over to unions would distort the authority structure of public education. No matter how it is packaged, capitulating to demands for teacher empowerment destroys community control of education. The unions were not hired by the community, and they may not represent the most effective classroom teachers. Over the years, teacher unions have become stronger, and teachers have increased their political power. While teachers were winning, parents and the community were losing (Friedman and Friedman, 1979; Moe, 2006; Moo, 1999). If unions are allowed to bargain collectively about school policy and curriculum issues, schools will become less responsive to the community and more an agency of the unions. Responsibility for running schools should be entrusted only to those the voters have chosen. Collective bargaining should not be allowed to erode the community's control over the education of its children.

Apologizing for Bad Teachers

Unions have become apologists for poor teaching and an obstacle to school reform. On the one hand, unions heap praise on the magical effect good teachers have on children's lives. On the other hand, they fail to admit weak teachers may be a cause of many of education's problems. Everyone familiar with public schools knows the quality of classroom instruction varies tremendously. Nestled among the great teachers, the good teachers, and the marginally adequate teach-ers are those who fail to convey enthusiasm for learning and, unfortunately, more than a few who have neither the personal qualities nor the skills and knowledge necessary to teach children. While the good teachers whet students' appetites for academic achievement, bad teachers kill interest, leave students with enormous gaps of information, and tarnish the reputation of the profession.

Unions talk about boosting teacher morale and teacher self-esteem, but they regularly oppose merit pay for good teachers. Some districts have proposed pay-for-performance plans that would reward unusually successful teachers—those who produce above-average learning gains in students—with higher raises, whereas those who evidence less success would earn lower-than-normal raises. Typically, teacher unions reject these plans, claiming the plans are "sub-ject to administrator bias" (Lieberman, 1997; Harshbarger, 2000) or that the con-cept of a "highly qualified teacher" is subjective, "unworkable," or "unfair" to otherwise qualified teachers who might not be able to pass subject matter tests in the areas they are teaching (American Federation of Teachers, 2004). The inability to reward good teachers upsets the public more than the inability to rid the schools of bad teachers (Brimelow, 2003, p. 184). The public believes schools are designed to treat each child individually and to make judgments about those who should be rewarded and those who deserve to be dismissed. It suspects schools would benefit if teachers were subject to similar judgments. Good teachers should reap the fruits of their individual talent; bad teachers should be dismissed. As one advocate of performance pay notes:

> And people wonder why public education is going down the tubes. . . . The Union leadership and the dolts who follow the leader seem to think that teach-ing is the only profession in the world that shouldn't be subject to performance-based pay or goals-based bonus systems. We have teachers who are teaching solely because of the pay, and no matter how good or poor that teacher is, he/she will get the same pay as everyone around him/her. No wonder there's been no true innovation in education in the last 100 years, there's no incentive to do so. When pay is based solely on number of years in the profession, there's no reason to do a good job. It's akin to socialism, and we've seen what that does to economies. (Dwyer, 2001)

The public is generally sympathetic to teachers, but not to teacher unions, and it is not hard to understand why. The sad fact remains that too many schools have teachers who are not able to do the work expected of them. Unfortunately, because of unions and tenure laws, even the poorest teachers will probably stay on the job until retirement. Union opposition to culling ineffective teachers from classrooms has forced school districts to decide whether to spend money on new books and programs or on litigation. In many states, union rules have brought administra-tive actions against ineffective teachers to an absolute halt[4] (VanSciver, 1990). The

---

[4]In New York, it takes well over a year's time and costs the schools almost $195,000 to prosecute a single teacher accused of misconduct. It is not surprising that although the New York City Board of Education employs over 172,000 teachers, it sought to dismiss only three of them over a recent two-year period (Brimelow, 2003, p. 41).

unions cry for greater involvement in managing schools, but their opposition to pay-for-performance plans and refusal to allow dismissal of incompetent teachers cast great doubt on their potential contribution to school improvement. The public would be more supportive of unions if unions were as concerned about the quality of teaching as they are about protecting individual teachers.

Schools Must Be Led by Administrators, Not Unions

[E]ducation leadership has been called the "bridge" that can bring together the many different reform efforts in ways that practically nothing else can. Teachers are on the front lines of learning. But principals at the school level, and superintendents at the district level, are uniquely positioned to provide a climate of high expectations, a clear vision for better teaching and learning, and the means for everyone in the system—adults and children—to realize that vision. (Wallace Foundation, 2007, p. 2)

Public schools are hierarchical by design. They were not structured to be workplace democracies that function to serve teachers or their union representatives. It is not within the role of teachers to shape policy or control schools. Teachers are not entitled to vote on decisions about school procedures, curriculum issues, or the vacation schedule (Owens, 2001). No reasonable school administrator would ignore teachers or deny them a voice in school matters, but to extend leadership authority to teachers would be to distort school authority and the ends for which schools were established.

School "authority" refers to the legally-designated exercise of responsibility over education. In public education, the state has given school administrators the authority to run schools and provide constitutionally mandated instruction. Good management principles demand that, in large organizations, one person or one small group of people can be expected to have the responsibility to direct corporate outcomes and to be accountable. Leading schools is a daunting, full-time set of tasks. One recent report, while highly critical of the education of school administrators, recognizes the complexity of the task assigned to school superintendents and other school administrators. Arthur Levine, the president of Teachers College, Columbia University, writes,

[School administrators] no longer serve as supervisors. They are being called on to lead in redesign of their schools and systems. In an outcome-based and accountability-driven era, administrators have to lead their schools in rethinking goals, priorities, finances, staffing, curriculum, pedagogies, learning resources assessment methods, technology, and the use of time and space. They have to recruit and retain top staff members and educate newcomers and veterans alike to understand and become comfortable with an education system undergoing dramatic and continuing change. (Levine, 2005, p. 13)

Levine, a recognized scholar of higher education, urges broad changes in the preparation of school administrators, but he does not argue that teachers should have expanded roles in school leadership. Administrators need to lead schools. It is part of the culture of American life to view management as accountable for an organization's success or failure. Parents know that this is the pattern in government and industry, and they expect the same rules to apply to education. In schools, authority and responsibility rest with the administration. When parents have questions about school policy or curriculum, they call the administrators. Parents expect school administrators to manage teachers and conduct the educational process for the good of the children.

One of the key roles for any administrator is to transform and inspire the efforts of teachers (Hoy and Hoy, 2006). Good schools could not exist without good teachers, but excellent teachers alone are not sufficient to provide good education. Good teachers have a demonstrated impact on the learning that takes place in their classrooms, but at the school level, the evidence is convincing that student learning is strongly influenced by administrators. As researchers note, "There seems to be little doubt that both district and school leadership provides a critical bridge between most educational reform initiatives, and having those reforms make a genuine difference for all students. Such leadership comes from many sources . . . but those in formal positions of authority in school systems are likely still the most influential" (Leithwood et al., 2004, p. 12.)

The problem with schools is not that principals control them, and it is not likely schools would improve if we handed control over to teachers or the unions. In the final analysis, administrators are responsible for schools, and must exert leadership and accept consequences for educational outcomes. Schools need effective leaders who can encourage learning, support and reward good teaching, and ensure schools serve the community (Smylie and Hart, 1999; Blase and Blase, 2001; Fullan, 2001; Creighton, 2005). The conflicting expectations that the state, community, teachers, and students exert on schools demand a specially trained group of managers. Without intelligent leadership from educational administrators, schools would be unlikely to meet any of their academic and social goals. Without skilled, carefully selected administrators to lead educational reform, positive change becomes less likely. School improvement is a very complex process, and it depends largely on the principal's ability to create and manage the conditions necessary for sustained improvement (Fullan, 2002). Teachers may determine the success or failure of any education reform or change in school policy, but the burden of leadership falls mainly on administrators. "Above all, the principal must communicate a clear vision of instructional excellence and continuous professional development consistent with the goal of improvement of teaching and learning" (Hoy and Hoy, 2006, pp. 2–3). School administrators play a complex, demanding role in learning and instruction. It is a role that requires special skills and talents.

As a matter of practicality, administrators, not the teachers, need to run schools. As one school administrator argues, "Democratic decision making doesn't work! I can't hold a meeting and call a vote every time we need to make a decision; [teachers] haven't got time for that either" (Owens, 2001, p. 287). Most teachers would agree. They neither want to nor have time to be involved in every aspect of school leadership. Most faculty do not want to be involved in decisions not affecting them, such as the technicalities of tasks only remotely related to the classroom or the teacher's welfare (Drake and Roe, 1999, pp. 122–123). Even in schools that have tried to empower teachers and enlist their aid in decision making, most new ideas still come from administrators. The research shows that shared decision making does not improve teacher morale, nor does it necessarily lead to school reform or improved learning (Weiss, 1993; Smylie, 1994). It is still up to administrators to lead schools and school improvement. Practicing teachers gladly give their support to administrators who assume the role of instructional leader (Fullan, 2001). Teachers want to be consulted, but they do not want to abandon teaching to run the schools.

The call for increased teacher leadership is nothing new. For decades, schools have experimented with extending greater leadership authority to teachers, and the results have been disappointing. First of all, research indicates that the current system of school management—one led by highly qualified school superintendents and building principals—does not need to be changed. The current leadership arrangement of schools produces significant positive effects on student learning across a wide spectrum of schools (Leithwood et al., 2004). Furthermore, research fails to document the benefits of teacher leadership for student achievement on a school-wide basis (York-Barr and Duke, 2004). The rhetoric is more glowing than the reality; teacher leadership may sound like a good idea, but there is little evidence of its value. Furthermore, we wonder why, for all the talk of unions reforming schools and improving learning, researchers find that most union officials spend most of their time "attending to the nuts and bolts of conventional unionism: representing teachers in grievance processes, negotiating contracts, training teachers for union leadership posts, and attending to the union organization itself" (Kerchner and Koppich, 2007, p. 354). Where is the evidence that union leadership improves student learning? Where are the union voices demanding that they be held accountable for student achievement? As one scholar notes, so-called reform unionism is "an exercise in wishful thinking" (Moe, 2006, p. 252). Until union behavior matches union rhetoric, it is unwarranted and not in the best interests of students to support union demands for increased teacher leadership in public schools.

For Discussion

1. Fourteen states* and the District of Columbia require candidates for school principal and school superintendent to pass a standardized examination as part of the licensure process. The School Leaders Licensure Assessment "consists of twenty-five constructed response questions ranging from short vignettes requiring brief responses to much longer case study exercises" (Educational Testing Service, 2008). Consider one of the sample exercises and the exam scoring rubric used to evaluate the candidate's response:

   Read this vignette and briefly and specifically answer the question that follows:
   > It is early December and the students in an elementary school are practicing for the annual holiday concert. A parent phones the school to insist that her child not be required to sing any of the Christmas songs. The principal excuses the child from participation in music practice.

---

*The states include Arkansas, California, Connecticut, Indiana, Kentucky, Maine, Maryland, Mississippi, Missouri, North Carolina, Pennsylvania, South Carolina, Tennessee, and Virginia.

Do you agree with the principal's action? Give a rationale, citing factors that are relevant to a principal's decisions in such situations.

Scoring Guide

> **Score 2:** Response specifically cites the civil and/or religious rights of the parent/student, and includes at least one of these:

- meeting with the parent and student to discuss the objections
- suggesting some alternative activity for the student
- examining the content of the concert to determine its appropriateness for all students

> **Score 1:** Response specifically cites one of these:

- the civil and/or religious rights of the parent/student
- meeting with the parent and student to discuss the objections
- suggesting some alternative activity for the student
- examining the content of the concert to determine its appropriateness for all students

> **Score 0:** Response is vague or omits reference to any of the essential factors.

What do you think principals should know and be expected to do? Can the knowledge and skills necessary to be a good administrator be measured by standardized exams? Does the sample exercise tap the abilities you consider important for a school leader? If teachers themselves want to be involved in school leadership, should they be required to take and pass exams required of school principals and other administrators?

2. The next generation of teachers is likely to hold views about their work differently from the views of the teachers they will replace. Susan Moore Johnson (2004) argues that the new generation is "less accepting of top-down hierarchy and fixed channels of communication, less respectful of conventional organizations, and generally more entrepreneurial than their predecessors." Johnson also notes that the new teachers—whether they are first-career or mid-career entrants—do not seek uniform treatment, do not expect to or want to work alone, and do not want to be isolated in the classroom without feedback about their performance. They also expect their salaries to reflect their success as teachers (p. 252).

   Do these values of the next generation of teachers match your own? Do you enjoy teamwork over the autonomy of a single-teacher classroom? Do you enjoy risk-taking entrepreneurial opportunities that could affect your salary?

   Looking at Johnson's findings, another researcher argues that the values of previous generations of teachers—job security and single-teacher classes with little competition among teachers—are a better fit for collective bargaining and teacher unions than are the values of the new teachers (Koppich, 2005, p. 108). Do you agree? Can teacher unions be attractive to a new generation of teachers?

3. Unions typically support a uniform salary structure, a pay scale based on years of service and additional increments for post-baccalaureate college work. Since the mid-nineteenth century, school officials have proposed various payment-for-results plans, whereby teachers would be rewarded for the performance of their students. Today, pay-for-performance plans and similar merit pay plans are typically tied to how well or how poorly students perform on standardized tests. One opponent of these plans, Alfie Kohn, writes, "The premise of merit pay, and indeed of all rewards is that people, *could* be doing a better job but for some reason have decided to wait until it's bribed out of them. This is as insulting as it is inaccurate" (Kohn, 2003, p. 1). Do you agree with Kohn's argument? Do you favor a uniform salary structure for teachers based on experience and education or would you prefer a performance-based salary system based on criteria that could change year by year based on student performance?

References

AMERICAN FEDERATION OF TEACHERS. (2003). The Union Role in Assuring Teacher Quality. www.aft.org/teacher-quality.

———. (2004). NCLB: "Its Problems and Promise." AFT Teachers Policy Brief Number 18/July 2004. www.aft.org/policybrief/18.

———. (2006). Redesigning Schools to Raise Achievement: Key Components. www.aft.org/topics/school-improvement/components.

———. (2008). Albert Shanker quoted. www.aft.org.

BALLOU D., AND PODGURSKY, M. (2000). "Gaining Control of Professional Licensing and Advancement." In T. Loveless, ed., *Conflicting Missions?* Washington, DC: Brookings Institution.

BARTH, R. (1990). *Improving Schools from Within: Teachers, Parents, and Principals Can Make the Difference.* San Francisco: Jossey-Bass.

BLASE, J. AND BLASE, J. (2001). *Empowering Teachers.* 2nd Ed. Thousand Oaks, CA: Corwin.

BRIMELOW, P. (2003). *The Worm in the Apple: How the Teacher Unions are Destroying American Education.* New York: HarperCollins.

Commonwealth v. Hunt. (1842). 445 Mass (4 met.) 111, 38 Am. Dec 346.

CREIGHTON, T. (2005). *Leading Below the Suface; A Non-Traditional Approach to School Leadership.* Thousand Oaks: Corwin.

DRAKE, T.L. AND ROE, W. H. (1999). *The Principalship.* 5th Ed. Upper Saddle River, NJ: Prenctice Hall.

DWYER, G. (2001). NEA Today Debate Question. http://nea.org/neatoday. Oct. 15.

EATON, W. E. (1975). *The American Federation of Teachers, 1916–1961: A History of the Movement.* Carbondale: Southern Illinois University Press.

EDUCATIONAL TESTING SERVICE. (2008). *School Leadership Series: School Licensure Assessment* [and] *School Superintendent Assessment.* Princeton: Author.

ENGEL, R. A. (1976). "Teacher Negotiation: History and Comment." In E. M. Cresswell and M. J. Murphy, eds., *Education and Collective Bargaining.* Berkeley, CA: McCutchan.

FINN, C. E. (1985). "Teacher Unions and School Quality: Potential Allies or Inevitable Foes?" *Phi Delta Kappan* 66, 331–338.

FRIEDMAN, M., AND FRIEDMAN, R. (1979). *Free to Choose.* New York: Harcourt Brace Jovanovich.

FULLAN, M. (2001). *Leading in a Culture of Change.* San Francisco: Jossey-Bass.

———. (2002). "The Change Leader." *Educational Leadership* 59, 16–20.

GAFFNEY, D. (2007). *Teachers United; The Rise of the New York State United Teachers.* Albany, NY: SUNY Press.

GALLEY, M. (2003). "Survey Finds Teachers Supportive of Unions." *Education Week.* June 4, pp. 1–3. www.edweek.org/ew/articles/2003/06/04.

GOLDHABER, D. (2006). "Are Teachers Unions Good for Students?" in *Collective Bargaining in Education*, ed. J. Hannaway and A. J. Rotherman. Cambridge, MA: Harvard University Press.

HANNAWAY, J. AND ROTHERMAN, A. J. eds., (2006). *Collective Bargaining In Education: Negotiating Change in Today's Schools.* Cambridge, MA: Harvard.

HARSHBARGER, B. (2000). "NEA Today Debate Question." Feb. 23. www.nea.org/neatoday.

———. (2001). "NEA Today Debate Question," Sept. 30. www.nea.org/neatoday.

HOLMES GROUP. (1986). "Tomorrow's Teachers: A Report on the Holmes Group." East Lansing, MI: Author.

HOY, A. W. AND HOY, W. K. (2006). *Instructional Leadership: A Research-Based Guide to Learning in School.* 2nd Ed. Boston: Allyn and Bacon.

JESSUP, D. K. (1978). "Teacher Unionization: A Reassessment of Rank and File Education." *Sociology of Education* 51, 44–55.

JOHNSON, S. M. et al. (2004). *Finders and Keepers; Helping New Teachers Survive and Thrive in Our Schools.* San Francisco: Jossey-Bass.

KAHLENBERG, R. (2007). *Tough Liberal; Albert Shanker and the Battles Over Schools, Unions, Race, and Democracy.* NY: Columbia University.

KERCHNER, C. T. (1986). "Union-Made Teaching: Effects of Labor Relations." In E. Z. Rothkopf, ed., *Review of Research in Education,* Vol. 13. Washington, DC: American Educational Research Association.

KERCHNER, C. T., AND KOPPICH, J. E. (1993). *A Union of Professionals: Labor Relations and Educational Reform.* New York: Teachers College Press.

———. (2000). "Organizing around Quality: The Frontiers of Teacher Unionism." In T. Loveless, ed., *Conflicting Missions?* Washington, DC: Brookings Institution.

———. 2007. "Negotiating What Matters: Collective Bargaining and Student Achievement." *American Journal of Education* 113: 349–365.

KERCHNER, C. T., KOPPICH, J. E., AND WEERES, J. G. (1997). *United Mind Workers: Unions and Teaching in the Knowledge Society.* San Francisco: Jossey-Bass.

KESSLER-HARRIS, A. (2007). *Gendering Labor History.* Urbana and Chicago: University of Illinois Press.

KOHN. A. (2003). "The Folly of Merit Pay. How Should We Reward Teachers? We Shouldn't." September 17. www.edweek.org/ew/articles/2003/09/17/03.

KOPPICH, J. (2005). Addressing Teacher Quality Through Induction, Professional Compensation and Evaluation: The Effects of Labor Management Relations." *Educational Policy* 19: 90–111.

LARUE, A. H. (1996). "The Changing Face of Tenure." www.aft.org/research/reports/tenure/laruep.htm.

LEITHWOOD, K. et al. (2004). *How Leadership Influences Student Learning.* www.wallacefoundation.org.

LEVINE, A. (2005). Educating School Leaders. www.edschools.org.

LIEBERMAN, M. (1997). *The Teachers Unions: How the NEA and the AFT Sabotage Reform and Hold Students, Parents, Teachers, and Taxpayers Hostage to Bureaucracy.* New York: Free Press.

LIEBERMAN, M., AND MOSCOW, M. H. (1966). *Collective Negotiations for Teachers: An Approach to School Administration.* Chicago: Rand McNally.

LOVELESS, T. ed. (2004). *Conflicting Missions? Teachers Unions and Educational Reform.* Washington, DC: Brookings Institution.

MOE, T. M. (2001). "Teachers Unions." In T. M. Moe, ed., *A Primer on America's Schools.* Stanford: Hoover Institution.

———. (2006). "Union Power and the Education of Children." in *Collective Bargaining in Education,* ed. J. Hannaway and A. J. Rotherman. Cambridge, MA: Harvard Press.

MOO, G. G. (1999). *Power Grab: How the National Education Association is Betraying Our Children.* Washington, DC: Regnery.

MURPHY, M. (1990). *Blackboard Unions: the AFT and the NEA, 1900–1980.* Ithaca, NY: Cornell University Press.

NEA. (2005). "NEA Committed to Improving Teacher Quality." www.nea-org/teacher-quality.

NLRB v. *Jones and Laughlin Steel Company.* (1937). 301 U.S. 1, 57 S.Ct.615.

OWENS, R. G. (2001), *Organizational Behavior in Education: Instructional Leadership and School Reform.* 7th Ed. Boston: Allyn and Bacon.

PAIGE, R. (2006). *The War Against Hope; How Teacher Unions Hurt Children, Hinder Teachers and Endanger Public Education,* Nashville, TN: Thomas Nelson.

RAUTH, M. (1990). "Exploring Heresy in Collective Bargaining and School Restructuring." *Phi Delta Kappan* 71, 781–784.

ROSENTHAL, A. (1969). *Pedagogues and Power: Teacher Groups in School Politics.* Syracuse, NY: Syracuse University Press.

SCHLECHTY, P. S. (1990). *Schools for the 21st Century: Leadership Imperatives for Educational Reform.* San Francisco: Jossey-Bass.

SMYLIE, M. A. (1994). "Redesigning Teachers' Work: Connections to the Classroom." In L. Darling-Hammond, ed., *Review of Research in Education.* Washington, DC: American Educational Research Association.

———. and HART, A. W. (1999). "Redesigning Teachers' Work: Connections to the Classroom." In L. Darling Hammond, ed., *Review of Research in Education.* Washington, DC: American Educational Research Association.

SPILLANE, J. (2006). *Distributed Leadership.* San Francisco: Jossey-Bass.

STONE, J. A. (2000). "Collective Bargaining and Public Schools." In T. Loveless, ed., *Conflicting Missions?* Washington, DC: Brookings Institution.

URBAN, W. J. (1982). *Why Teachers Organized.* Detroit: Wayne State University Press.

VANSCIVER, J. H. (1990). "Teacher Dismissals." *Phi Delta Kappan* 72, 318–319.

WALLACE FOUNDATION. (2007). "Education Leadership, A Bridge to School Reform." www.wallacefoundation.org.

WALLER, W. (1932). *The Sociology of Teaching.* New York: John Wiley & Sons.

WATTS, G. D., AND McCLURE, R. (1990). "Expanding the Contract to Revolutionize School Reform." *Phi Delta Kappan* 71, 765–774.

WEISS, C. H. (1993), "Shared Decisions About What? A Comparison of Schools With and Without Teacher Participation." *Teachers College Record* 95, 69–92.

WESLEY, E. B. (1957). *NEA: The First Hundred Years.* New York: Harper and Brothers.

YORK-BARR, J. AND DUKE, K. (2004). "What Do We Know About Teacher Leadership? Findings From Two Decades of Scholarship." *Review of Educational Research* 74, 255–316.

CHAPTER 17

Academic Freedom: Teacher Rights or Responsibilities

How should the proper balance between teacher freedom and responsibility be determined?

POSITION 1: FOR INCREASED ACADEMIC FREEDOM

In short, discussing controversy in the classroom is an imperative in a democracy.
—Misco and Patterson, 2007

Intellectual freedom is the belief in the fundamental dignity of individual inquiry and the right to exercise it.

—LaRue, 2007

Sex, Politics, and Religion: A Few Cases

A parent in Olathe, Kansas, demanded that John Steinbeck's *Of Mice and Men* be banned from the school curriculum and classroom because the book is "worthless" and "profanity-filled." Two school board members actually voted to have the classic banned, but the majority rejected the effort.

In Oakley, California, some parents wanted the same Steinbeck book banned for racial epithets.

School use of the popular Philip Pullman book, *The Golden Compass*, was protested by a group of parents and Christian leaders in Winchester, Kentucky, because Pullman was called "an atheist" and the book "anti-Christian."

A tenured teacher in Colorado was dismissed for showing the publicly available Bertold Bertolucci film, *1900*, as part of a class discussion about fascism. The teacher appealed, the teachers' association provided an attorney for a hearing, and the teacher was reinstated.

Some years earlier, a well-respected high school history teacher in the Denver Public Schools was dismissed because the city newspaper published his and other candidates' views as they ran for a Congressional seat; the district thought his views were too controversial. He appealed and won reinstatement, but the district limited him to teaching basic English and forbade his teaching history.

A high school student paper in Bakersfield, California, was prohibited from publishing a story with interviews about gender identity; but a county judge ruled that students have the right to exercise freedom of speech and press without prior restraint.

In Metuchen, New Jersey, the high school principal threatened a student-financed and -edited paper that included some material from national news magazines (like *Time* and *Newsweek*), with the magazines' permission, because he considered it too controversial. The Board refused to back the principal.

Words about puberty and homosexuality were cut by school administrators at the last minute from a New York high school production of *A Chorus Line*; one student danced a part in silence.

Field trips at a Pennsylvania high school to see *MacBeth* and *Schindler's List* were cancelled after some citizen complaints.

Efforts to restrict or ban books, films, speakers, topics of study, magazines, speech, press, dress, art, drama, field trips, and other student and teacher activities have permeated and undercut school life for generations. Most of these efforts involve controversies surrounding sex, politics, or religion, though other issues, like race and economics, sometimes arise.

Over the past two decades, the most frequently banned books include: *Harry Potter, Diary of Anne Frank, Catch-22, Farewell to Arms, Deliverance, The Great Gatsby, Adventures of Huckleberry Finn, To Kill a Mockingbird, The Chocolate War,* and *Slaughterhouse Five.*

Among the most censored authors are Judy Blume, Mark Twain, Maya Angelou, John Steinbeck, J. D. Salinger, Toni Morrison, R. L. Stine, Maurice Sendak, William Golding, and Robert Cormier.

(Sources: *Newsletter on Intellectual Freedom*, 1996–2009; Sherrow, 1996; author; Foerstel, 2002)

A Climate of Fear

This is a small sample of incidents of censorship and politically-based restrictions of ideas in schools. Many more incidents are recorded each year across the United States, and many do not get recorded. Restrictions on inquiry, knowledge, and education, unfortunately, are commonplace. They are also responsible for a climate of fear in schools that causes cautious teachers to self-censor or severely limit controversial topics in order to avoid similar situations. School administrators often fear parental or citizen complaints, and take preemptive action to try to limit teachers and students by cumbersome, and sometimes illegal, school policies and practices that encroach on the rights of teacher and student.

Teachers may think they have academic freedom, but they sometimes engage in self-censorship to avoid threats or uncomfortable situations. Administrators may impose questionable restrictions but encounter no protest by teachers who fear problems. Parents may threaten teachers and cause them to limit inquiry. In good school districts, however, the legitimate rights of teachers and students, as well as the rights of parents and the public to raise questions about what is taught and how, are protected by well-prepared policies and practices on academic freedom.

Although some censorship and political restriction stories show a positive result, where teacher and student academic freedom is protected, many incidents do not end so well. Teachers lose jobs, students are suspended, students and teachers avoid controversy, education suffers. Furthermore, the long and continuing history of efforts to control, censor, and restrict teachers and students shows that the idea of academic freedom is not so well established in society that it is no longer an issue. There is a need for constant vigilance to retain the intellectual freedom that education in a democracy requires. That freedom, academic and intellectual, is the central purpose for education.

A Necessity, Not a Frill

A society cannot be free when its schools are not. The need to provide strong support to academic freedom for teachers and their students should seem obvious to anyone who supports a free society. Ideas are the primary ingredients of democracy and education, and the realm of ideas is protected by academic freedom. This simple, elegant concept is not well enough understood by some of the public, and even by some teachers. Academic freedom requires diligent effort, exercise, and expansion in schools. It is under constant threat (American Association of University Professors, 1986; American Library Association, 1996; Newsletter on Intellectual Freedom, 1986–current; Nelson, 1990, 2003; McNeil, 2002; Stone, 2004; Lindorff, 2005; LaRue, 2007; Wilson, 2008).

The continuing development of American democracy requires that academic freedom be further expanded in schools for both students and teachers. Noddings (1999) points out that democratic education requires debate and discourse—only with teacher freedom can this happen. The basic principles are clear—enlightened self-governance is basic to democracy and academic freedom is basic to enlightened self-governance. Freedom to teach and learn is basic to good education.

Historic arguments against academic freedom for teachers were based on a mix of traditional ideas such as: teachers were not "scholars," they have a captive audience, they can influence impressionable minds, and they are public employees subject to the will of boards and administrators. These arguments falter against the more important necessity for teacher freedom to educate in a democracy. Teachers are now required to have scholarly qualities; students are expected to inquire and challenge rather than be captive receptacles; teachers' professional ethics do not countenance brainwashing; and to fulfill their professional and contractual responsibilities to educate, teachers must have the freedom to examine and present topics.

We are well beyond the period when teachers were prohibited from marrying, dancing, or participating in politics. In contemporary schools, teachers are expected to do more than force-feed students memorized material; we have come to expect education and critical thinking. Yet there remain strong efforts to censor and restrain educators in performance of their profession.

Pat Scales (2001), a school librarian honored by the American Library Association's (ALA) Intellectual Freedom Award, writes:

> The problem is obvious. Censors want to control the minds of the young. They are fearful of the educational system, because students who read learn to think. . . . As educators, we cannot for the sake of the students, allow ourselves to be bullied into diluting the curriculum into superficial facts. We must talk about the principles of intellectual freedom. We must challenge students to think about the intent of our forefathers when they wrote the Bill of Rights. (p. 2)

Unfortunately, some people and groups with strong moralistic or other narrow agendas have increased their efforts to restrict schools and impose censorship on students and teachers (Newsletter on Intellectual Freedom; Nakaya, 2005; Seesholtz, 2005). They hope to advance their own political, religious, or economic views and to deny the views of others. They see education as a way to indoctrinate the young to become noncritical believers or as a way to inoculate and insulate students from controversial ideas. They see evil or controversy in anything that differs from their own beliefs.

Zealots on different sides of political, economic, and religious fences have tried to use schools as agents to impose their views and values on the young. They don't want schools to present opposing views or conflicting evidence and are against real critical thinking. That zealotry has increased the vulnerability of teachers who realize good education requires dealing with controversial issues (Thelin, 1997; Pipkin and Lent, 2002).

Now we are seeing efforts to change the argument against teacher freedom by changing the definition of academic freedom to suit a political agenda. The "Academic Bill of Rights" (Students for Academic Freedom, 2003; Dogan, 2006) is touted as a protection for academic freedom, demanding neutrality for institutions and requiring a "diverse" faculty along political lines. this proposed Bill of Rights is for colleges, but has obvious implications for precollegiate schools. It claims support of academic freedom, but some think it is a cover to require the hiring of more conservative faculty members and to impose new restrictions on teachers in schools and colleges (American Association of University Professors, 2003; Wilson, 2006). While the neutrality of schools and the impartiality of teachers are good educational concepts, the proposed Academic Bill of Rights implies political litmus tests for teachers and contains the seeds of censorship and self-censorship to avoid controversial subjects.

The good teacher, willing to examine controversial topics, runs risks far beyond those who are fearful, docile, and self-censoring. Teachers who fulfill the basic educational responsibility to provide intellectual freedom may encounter threats, ostracism, or ridicule. Ominous overt threats and subtle pressure from administrators, school boards, parents, special interest groups, and even peer teachers can cool a teacher's ardor for freedom of ideas. Teacher self-censorship—where fearful teachers screen ideas from classroom use in order to avoid controversy—is a common but hidden threat to academic freedom.

Teachers hear about others being fired or threatened and often try to avoid any topic that could have similar repercussions for them. It is true that a few teachers have been fired for doing what our society should expect all good teachers to do. It is also true that many times these firings are reversed when the teacher is given due process and facts become known. Still, such events produce a chilling effect on other teachers, restricting academic freedom for themselves and their students. It takes courage to remain professional in the pursuit of education, but it is necessary. When the censors win, education and democracy lose (McNeil, 2002; Stone, 2004; Fuentes, 2005).

The Essential Relationship of Academic Freedom to Democracy

One inescapable premise in a democracy is that the people are capable of governing themselves. That premise assumes people can make knowledgeable decisions and select intelligently from among alternative proposals. Education and free exchange of ideas are fundamental to the premise. To think otherwise is to insult the essential condition of democracy.

Academic freedom is the freedom of teachers to teach, of schools to determine educational policies and practices unfettered by political restraints or censorship, and the freedom of students to engage in study of ideas. It is essential to democracy. A society that professes freedom should demand no less freedom for its schools (Rorty, 1994; Wilson, 2008).

The U.S. Supreme Court demonstrated its commitment to the principle of academic freedom in a 1967 decision, finding that a state law that demanded teachers take a loyalty oath was unconstitutional. The Court noted that academic freedom is a "transcendent value":

> Our nation is deeply committed to safeguarding academic freedom, which is of transcendent value to all of us and not merely to the teachers concerned. That freedom is, therefore, a special concern of the First Amendment, which does not tolerate laws that cast a pall of orthodoxy over the classroom. . . . The classroom is peculiarly the "marketplace of ideas." (*Keyishian v. Board of Regents,* 1967)

Propaganda and public deceit are practiced in all countries, including democracies, but citizens of a democracy are expected to have the right and the ability to question and examine propaganda and expose those deceits. Dictatorial regimes do not need, and do not desire, the masses to have an education enabling them to question information the government presents. Totalitarian states maintain their existence by using raw power and threats, utilizing censorship and restriction, and keeping the public ignorant. Governments in democracies can attempt the same maneuvers, but they run the risk of exposure and replacement. The more totalitarian the government, the more it uses threats, censorship, and denial of freedom in education. The more democratic the society, the less it employs threats, censorship, and restriction of education. This litmus test of a democracy is also a significant measure of the level of academic freedom.

The Evolution and Expansion of Academic Freedom

Academic freedom has evolved and expanded from early American education when a narrow definition limited it to a few scholars in colleges, and even there it was not well practiced. It has since become a fundamental educational concept embracing both the general framework of schooling and work of teachers at all levels. We are closer now to the historic dual German intellectual freedoms—*lehrfreiheit* and *lernfreiheit*—the freedom of teachers to teach and of learners to learn without institutional restriction (Hofstadter and Metzger, 1968). The American concept of academic freedom evolved from this dual and mutually supportive freedom for teachers and students (Daly, Schall, and Skeele, 2001). It still has not evolved sufficiently to assure educators and the public that schools are places of real and critical education, but it is significantly more embedded in the culture of schools and educated society than it was.

Socrates, charged with impiety and corruption of youth, defended himself by claiming that he and his students had the freedom to pursue truth. All wickedness, he argued, was due to ignorance; freedom to teach and learn would uncover knowledge, eliminate ignorance, and improve society. The judges did not agree and Socrates was sentenced to death. Academic freedom, over time, has fared better. Though it is regularly battered, it has survived and expanded.

Unfortunately, differences in state laws and confusing court opinions have produced a mixed view of what specific actions are legally protected under the idea of academic freedom in the United States (O'Neil, 1981; *Newsletter on Intellectual Freedom*, 2000–2009). The broad concept of academic freedom is generally understood, but practical application of that freedom in classrooms and schools often is contested and local and state court decisions often are murky. While some courts have supported school board discretion over curricular and student newspaper matters, in general, courts have exhibited an expanding awareness of the need for academic freedom in schools and have provided protection for teachers. If this good trend continues, and educators remain vigilant, this foretells a proper expansion of the concept to cover the work of competent teachers across the nation.

Courts often have been highly supportive of academic freedom for public school teachers. Justices Frankfurter and Douglas (*Wieman v. Updegraff*, 1952) argued that all teachers from primary grades to the university share a special role in developing good citizens, and all teachers should have the academic freedom necessary to be exemplars of open-mindedness and free inquiry. In *Cary v. Board of Education* (quoted in Rubin and Greenhouse, 1983), the decision included:

> To restrict the opportunity for involvement in an open forum for the free exchange of ideas to higher education would not only foster an unacceptable elitism, it would fail to complete the development of those not going to college, contrary to our constitutional commitment to equal opportunity. Effective citizenship in a participatory democracy must not be dependent upon advancement toward college degrees. Consequently, it would be inappropriate to conclude that academic freedom is required only in colleges and universities. (p. 116)

At the global level, a statement adopted by the International Federation of Library Associations and Institutions (IFLAI) holds that: "Human beings have a fundamental right to access to expressions of knowledge, creative thought, and intellectual activity, and to express their views publicly" (IFLAI Statement, 1999). Academic freedom for all teachers is consistent with this position. It needs continual nurturing, expansion, and vigilance in support of global democratization.

Educational Grounds for Academic Freedom

Where, if not in schools, will new generations be able to explore and test divergent ideas, new concepts, and challenges to propaganda? Students should be able to pursue intriguing possibilities under the guidance of free and knowledgeable teachers (First Amendment Schools, 2008). Students can test ideas in schools with less serious risks of social condemnation or ostracism. In a setting where critical thinking is prized and nurtured, students and teachers can engage more fully in intellectual development. This is in society's best interests for two fundamental reasons: (1) new ideas from new generations are the basis of social progress, and (2) students who are not permitted to explore divergent ideas in school can be blinded to society's defects and imperfections and will be ill-equipped to participate as citizens in improving democracy (Puddington, et al., 2008).

Although teaching can be conducted easily as simple indoctrination, with teachers presenting material and students memorizing it without thought or criticism, that leads to an incomplete and defective education. Teaching also can be chaotic, with no sense of organization or purpose—this, too, is incomplete and defective education. Neither of these approaches to teaching offers education. Education consists of ideas and challenges, increasingly sophisticated and complex. Indoctrination stunts the educational process, shrinking knowledge and constricting critical thinking. Chaotic schools confuse the educational process, mix important and trivial ideas, and muddle critical thinking. A sound education provides solid grounding in current knowledge and teaches students to challenge ideas as a part of the process of critical thinking.

The defining quality of academic freedom is freedom in the search for knowledge. This freedom extends to all students and teachers engaged in the quest for knowledge. The search for knowledge is not limited to experts, but is the primary purpose of schooling. Learning best occurs as people test new ideas against their own experiences and knowledge—that testing requires academic freedom. This active learning does more than just help clear up student confusion. It offers intellectual involvement and ownership. In addition, it is often students who recognize flaws in existing knowledge or who find new ways to understand. When only experts control knowledge or when censors limit ideas, we risk conformity without challenges or conflicting opinions. We may not like challenges to ideas we find comfortable, but those challenges are the stuff of progress. Limiting the search for knowledge to a cadre of established experts is not in the interest of student learning, human progress, or social development.

Most young people encounter radical ideas in conversations with friends or in films, TV, and other media. In an educational setting, students can more fully consider controversial ideas, and they have the opportunity to criticize each view. The real threat to society is that students will not examine controversial material in schools, and that students will come to distrust education and society as places for free exchange of ideas (Evans, 2007). Daly and Roach (1990) call for a renewed commitment to academic freedom to pursue these social and educational ends.

The Center of the Profession

Academic freedom is at the heart of the teaching profession (Nelson, 1990, 2003). Professions are identified by the complex, purposeful nature of the work, educational requirements for admission, and commonly held ethics and values. Medical professionals, for example, work to protect and improve health, have a specialized education in medical practice, and share a commitment to life. Attorneys work in the realm of law, have specialized training in the practice of law, and are dedicated to the value of justice. Teachers work to educate children, have subject knowledge and specialized education in teaching practice, and share a devotion to enlightenment.

The nature of teachers' work and their shared devotion to enlightenment require a special freedom to explore new ideas in the quest for knowledge. This freedom deserves protection beyond that provided to all citizens under the constitutional guarantee of free speech. Unlike other citizens, teachers have a professional obligation to search for truth and assist students in their search for truth (Zirkel, 1993; Nelson, 2003). The National Science Teachers Association (NSTA) states: "As professionals, teachers must be free to examine controversial issues openly in the classroom" (www.nsta.org). The National Council for Social Studies (2007) policy supports freedoms of teachers to teach and of students to learn. Similar statements advocating academic freedom for classroom teachers appear in the major documents of most national teacher associations. The Foundation for Individual Rights in Education (FIRE) maintains a website that archives such academic freedom statements from all over the world (www.thefire.org). Teachers' jobs must not be at risk because they explore controversial material or consider ideas outside the mainstream.

A general misunderstanding of the central role schools play in a free society causes teachers and students to live a peripheral existence in the United States. Teaching has been viewed as less than professional; oftentimes teachers are considered low-level employees, hired to do what managers ask. Excessive restrictions are sometimes imposed on what teachers can teach and methods of instruction they can use. School boards and administrators try to censor teachers and teaching materials. And students are virtually ignored, are treated as nonpersons, or are expected to exhibit blind obedience. There may have been some historic reason to treat teachers as mere functionaries; some came as indentured servants and others had inadequate academic preparation. Now all states require undergraduate degrees and a majority of teachers have graduate degrees. Increasingly rigorous teacher credential regulations and improved professional study and practice offer no grounds for demeaning restrictions on a teacher's work. Academic freedom, the essence of the teaching profession, has been insufficiently developed as a necessary idea in our society and in teacher education. A dual educational effort would increase public awareness of the need for academic freedom and inform and inspire the people who go into teaching.

Academic Freedom and Teacher Competency: The Tenure Process

Provision of academic freedom for teachers is not, however, without limits or conditions. Not all persons certified to teach nor every action they take deserve the protection of academic freedom. The basic condition for academic freedom is teacher competence. Incompetent teachers do not deserve and should not receive that extra protection; they should be dismissed if a fair and evidential evaluation finds them incompetent. A license to teach is not a license to practice incompetence (Bernard, 2008).

Teacher competence is a mix of knowledge, skill, and judgment. It includes knowledge of the material and of the students in class, professional skill in teaching, and considered professional judgment. Competence depends on more than just accumulation of college credits; it includes a practical demonstration that teachers can teach with knowledge, skill, and judgment. As in other professions, competence is measured by peers and supervisors, and continues to be refined as teachers gain experience. In teaching, initial competence is expected as the new teacher completes the teaching credential program. That program of four or more years includes subject field and professional study and practice teaching under supervision. Then, according to the laws of various states, teachers serve full-time for several years under school supervision and are granted tenure only if they are successful. This long test of actual teaching should be sufficient to establish competence. Incompetent teachers should not get tenure.

The main legal protection for academic freedom in schools is state tenure law. Under tenure laws, teachers cannot be fired without due process and legitimate cause. The tenured teacher who is threatened with firing has a right to know specific allegations, a fair hearing, and an evidentially based decision. This protects tenured teachers from improper dismissal as a result of personality conflicts or local politics. Grounds for dismissal, identified in state law, usually include moral turpitude, professional misconduct, and incompetence. The allegation must be clearly demonstrated and documented for the dismissal to be upheld. There should be a high standard for becoming a teacher and for obtaining tenure; there also should be a high standard for dismissing a teacher. Teachers should not be dismissed on the basis of personal or political disagreements with administrators or others.

Nontenured probationary teachers also deserve the general protection of academic freedom because they, too, are expected to engage in enlightening education. However, they do not have the same legal claims as tenured teachers (Standler, 2000). Tenured teachers serve on "indefinite" contracts that schools need not renew formally each year. Dismissal or nonrenewal of the probationary teacher's one-year contract can occur at the end of any given school term, often without specifying cause for dismissal. Dismissal for dealing with controversial topics in a competent manner should, however, be prohibited by school policy as a condition for all teachers. Many excellent school districts honor this concept. Tenured faculty, protected from improper interference, need to assure that nontenured teachers are not subjected to dismissal for performing their proper teaching function. It is a professional responsibility.

Obstacles to Academic Freedom

Notwithstanding the compelling reasons that support academic freedom, there are historical, political, and economic pressures that can be overwhelming (Wilson, 2008). Sadly, censorship, political restraint, anti-intellectualism, and illegitimate restrictions on teacher and student freedom have a long and sordid history in the United States. Early schools, under religious domination, imposed moralistic requirements on teachers, firing them for impiety, for not attending religious services, or for not exhibiting sufficient religious zeal. In the nineteenth century, many contracts required teachers to remain single, avoid drinking and smoking, attend church each Sunday, substitute for the minister on occasion, not associate with "bad elements," and avoid controversy. Communities required strict conformity to social norms, and teachers could be dismissed for dating, visiting pool halls, or simply disagreeing with local officials. Teachers whose political views differed from those with power in the community were summarily fired. No recourse was available to stop vigilante school boards or administrators.

In the first half of the twentieth century, political restraint and censorship replaced religious and moralistic restrictions on teachers (Pierce, 1933; Beale, 1936; Gellerman, 1938). College teachers often fared no better, and many suffered great indignities at the hands of college officials (Veblen, 1918/1957; Sinclair, 1922; Hofstadter and Metzger, 1955). Academic freedom was an ideal, not a common practice. John Dewey and a few other widely known scholars founded the American Association of University Professors in 1915 for the primary purpose of organizing to protect the academic freedom of college teachers. Dewey recognized even then that all teachers, not just those in colleges, needed academic freedom.

In the twenty-first century, teachers clearly have gained much in professional preparation and stature, but they are not yet free. Significant threats to academic freedom continue to limit education and place blinders on students. Censorship attempts have been launched in virtually every state. Some states have numerous censorship attempts each year, and thousands of teachers and students are restricted by actions of vigilante groups, school boards, and school administrators.

Figure 17.1 shows institutions receiving the most complaints and challenges to materials being available between 1990 and 2000; schools are the leading institutions for efforts to censor.

Textbook publishers shy away from controversial content to avoid censors. Texas censors forced a major American history textbook by highly respected historians to be stricken from Texas high schools because of two paragraphs (out of 1,000 pages) suggesting prostitution was rampant in the West in the late nineteenth century (Stille, 2002).

FIGURE 17.1 Which Institutions are Targets of Censorship?

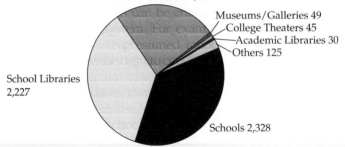

Public Libraries 1,561

Museums/Galleries 49
College Theaters 45
Academic Libraries 30
Others 125

School Libraries
2,227

Schools 2,328

Source: Office of Intellectual Freedom, American Library Association. In Foerstel,
H. N. (2002). *Banned in the USA*. Westport, CT: Greenwood Press. Data from
1990–2000.

The Internet is the most recent focus of censors, with scare tactics used to block access to many legitimate Internet sites (O'Neil, 2008). A 1999 report of the Censorware Project shows that Utah blocks access for all public schools and some libraries to such material as: The Declaration of Independence, The U.S. Constitution, the Bible, the Koran, all of Shakespeare's plays, and Sherlock Holmes ("Censored Internet Access in Utah Schools and Libraries," 1999). Websites that protest such censor intrusion into libraries include the Electronic Frontier Foundation (www.eff.org), the Foundation for Individual Rights in Education (www.thefire.org), and Peacefire (www.peacefire.org).

Topics that arouse the censors vary over time and across locations, and span both ends of the political spectrum. Socialism and communism were visible targets in the 1920s and again in the 1960s, surfacing again in the Reagan administration. Sexual topics and profanity are constant targets of school censors. A more recent issue is the charge that schools teach secular humanism—teachers and materials are anti-God, immoral, antifamily, and anti-American. Among other current topics stimulating people who want to stifle academic freedom are drugs, evolution, values clarification, economics, environmental issues, social activism, and the use of African American, feminist, or other minority literature (Jenkinson, 1990; Waldron, 1993; Japenga, 1994; Sipe, 1999; Horowitz, 2005; Seesholtz, 2005; Lindorff, 2005.)

Publicized censorship and restraint activities have a chilling effect on school boards, administrators, and even many teachers (Whitson, 1993; Ross, 2004). The possibility of complaints on a controversial topic leads to fear. Daly (1991) found that few school districts had policies to protect teacher and student rights to academic freedom. As a result, teacher self-censorship denies students and society the full exploration of ideas. Many teachers avoid significant topics, or they neutralize and sterilize them to the point of student boredom. Table 17.1 indicates that parents are the people most likely to initiate censorship efforts in schools and libraries.

A statement by the American Association of University Professors (AAUP, 1986) in support of academic freedom for precollege-level teachers identified a

Rank	Initiator	Number of Challenges over Ten Years
	Table 17.1 Who Initiates Challenges to School and Library Materials?	
1	Parents	3,891
2	Patrons	936
3	Administrator	596
4	Board Member	232
5	Teacher	176
6	Pressure Group	175
7	Other Group	162
8	Religious Organization	108
9	Clergy	92
10	Government	53

Source: Office of Intellectual Freedom, American Library Association. In Foerstel, H. N. (2002). *Banned in the USA.* Westport, CT: Greenwood Press. Data from 1990–2000.

variety of political restraints imposed on such teachers. The American Civil Liberties Union (www.aclu.org) has a long tradition of support for academic freedom for teachers and students, and assists in court proceedings to redress censorship and political restriction. Since 1970, the frequency of reported censorship incidents has tripled. Moreover, estimates suggest that for each incident formally reported, about fifty other censoring activities go unreported (Jenkinson, 1985). The National Coalition Against Censorship (www.ncas.org), affiliated with dozens of professional and scholarly associations, formed because of this increase in censorship.

A Free Society Requires Academic Freedom

Despite the often weak protection of academic freedom and often powerful political pressures brought to bear to stifle it, attaining freedom for teachers and students is worth the strenuous effort it demands. There are compelling democratic, educational, and professional grounds for expanding the protection of academic freedom to competent teachers and all students. And there are important social reasons why the public should support academic freedom in public education. Academic freedom is more than a set of platitudes, state regulations, and court decisions. It should be a fundamental expectation of schools in a free society. Academic freedom is a central truth for the profession of teaching.

POSITION 2: FOR TEACHER RESPONSIBILITY

Freedom of speech does not imply a right to an audience. . . . Unfortunately, many of those who talk the loudest and longest about "freedom of speech" and "academic freedom" are in fact trying to justify the imposition of propaganda on a captive audience in our schools and colleges.

—Sowell, 2005, p. 1

> . . . *the K–12 public school establishment has adopted a quasi-official pedagogy that encourages the classroom teacher to shape students' beliefs on contemporary issues like race, gender, sexual preference, and American foreign policy.*
>
> —Stern, 2006

Freedom from Indoctrination

Academic freedom involves more than unbridled indoctrination to one view. Yet, some college professors and the K–12 teachers' unions have asserted a right to academic freedom of that type. Stern (2006a) notes that "leftist political indoctrination in the classroom is now even more pernicious in K–12 education than it is on the university campus" (p. 1). Kline (2008) reports on a survey showing that about 40 percent of Americans said professors often use their classroom for political platforms. This is not academic freedom and teachers at any level who engage in it should not be protected.

Academic freedom consists of the presentation of balanced views, with the teacher as a neutral to be sure there is fairness. This can't be done if schools continue to hire teachers who think indoctrination is their right, and if teacher education programs continue to emphasize political goals like "teaching for social justice" or progressivism. We need a professional code of ethics for teachers that emphasizes the teaching of basic skills to help students do schoolwork, not to turn them into activists. "If educators won't do this voluntarily, then let the legislators do it for them" (Stern, 2006a, p. 1). Freedom for teachers is directly linked to their responsibilities; a suitable code of ethics makes that clear.

Power and Responsibility in Teaching

All rights and freedoms are connected to responsibilities. Teachers' freedoms must be tied to their responsibilities, and their rights and freedoms are conditioned on their acceptance of those responsibilities. Teachers' freedoms are supported and limited by their responsibilities to parents, society, the child, and to the profession.

Society gives teachers authority to develop sound knowledge and values in children; school is compulsory for that purpose. The child, weaned from parental influence, looks to teachers for guidance. This is a particularly important responsibility. Teachers bear duties to parents, society, and the child to provide a suitable education. They also have ethical duties to the profession of teaching. These multiple responsibilities require accountability from teachers and schools.

Teaching is among the most influential positions in society. Teaching is next to parenting in its power to carry values and ideas from generation to generation. In some respects, teachers exert more influence on children's views and values than do parents. Parents have great control over what their children see, hear, and do during the earliest years, but after the child starts school, parents relinquish increasing amounts of that influence to teachers. That should be a good thing, with children becoming more mature and independent while studying under responsible, committed teachers. Parents retain strong interests in what their children see, hear, and do long after primary school, and good schools and teachers give them nothing to fear. The influence of teachers goes well beyond the classroom doors, school grounds, and school term; teachers exert influence that can last for years, even lifetimes. This capacity to influence the young carries heavy responsibilities.

Parental Rights

Parents have general, moral, and legal rights and obligations to and for their children, rights and obligations that teachers and schools must not undermine. Parents are expected to provide for the child's safety and welfare—physical, emotional, spiritual, and moral. Provision of food, clothing, and shelter is a parental obligation given up only when parents are incapable. Parents have moral obligations and rights, including instructing their children in determining right from wrong, good from bad. Parents instruct their children in ethical conduct by providing them with a set of socially acceptable behaviors, including integrity, honesty, courtesy, and respect. Under the law, parents can be held accountable for lack of adequate and appropriate care of their children; they can even be held legally responsible for their children's acts.

Because parents are presumed to have the child's interests at heart, they are given great latitude in providing care and upbringing. Parents are even permitted to exercise appropriate corporal punishment, more than any other person would be permitted to inflict upon a child, under the legal idea that the parent has broad responsibilities and rights. At the root of laws regarding parents' rights and obligations is the idea that they are responsible for their children's upbringing, morality, and behaviors. Teachers, however, act as surrogate parents only in certain situations, with a number of limitations, and should not deviate from the norms of the good parent in the good society.

Children are not put in schools as punishment, or as a way to make up for family irresponsibility. Schools, therefore, must continue the cultural heritage by inculcating positive and supportive social and family values in the young.

The comparative youthfulness of students, influential role of teachers, and authoritative nature of instruction make schools and teachers even more responsible to social and parental values and interests. Especially in public schools, where attendance is mandatory, schools and teachers need a greater sensitivity to the role of positive parental surrogate. Thus, public school teachers are even more accountable than private ones to the community and to parents for what they teach and how.

Teacher Responsibilities to Parents

Schools, then, have a special obligation to be responsive to parents' concerns for their children. This reasoning lies behind the legal concept that teachers act in loco parentis, or in place of the parent. That concept, with deep social and legal roots, protects teachers in handling student discipline and evaluation. It also requires teachers to remain sensitive to parental interests.

Teachers, standing in place of the parents, take on similar responsibilities for children's development and protection. Teachers have responsibilities for providing a safe, healthy classroom environment, and they assume protective moral, ethical, and legal duties. In addition, they have educational responsibilities: They must teach children necessary knowledge and skills. Discharging these responsibilities demands responsiveness to parental concerns about the kinds of knowledge and values taught.

Teachers cannot have license to do anything to students, physically or mentally. No one today would argue that teachers should be permitted to abuse children physically. Teachers can require students to be attentive to lessons, be orderly, and be civil, but they are prohibited from abusive activities, such as striking students. Malevolent teacher behavior is outside the standards of professional conduct.

Mental abuse of students is equally abhorrent, but is less easy to detect. Mental abuse is no less harmful, however, to students, parents, or society. It can consist of vicious verbal personal attacks, indoctrination in antisocial values or behaviors, or manipulation of children's minds against parents or morality (Sowell, 2005; Stern, 2006b). Parents have a right to insist teachers not subject their children to these tactics, but often are unaware of them until after the damage has been done.

Parents have a right to monitor what schools are teaching their children, hold the school accountable for it, and limit potential for damage to their children. Beyond necessary limits on teachers, schools also must be subject to limits that conform to social mores. For example, book, video, and film purchases for school libraries should be continuously and vigilantly screened so only proper material is made available to our children. A parent review committee can be used to determine which books are suitable, with opportunity for any parent to complain about library materials and have that complaint acted on effectively.

We need not only worry about what teaching materials are used in classrooms, we also must be vigilant about other areas of schools where underage students have access. In school media centers, there is an increasing problem with Internet access. The Internet can be a valuable resource for children. There are many excellent websites for adding educational quality in such areas as science, history, the arts, literature, math, and other subjects. The opportunity to observe geographic locations, ancient art and culture, current news, scientific experiments and achievements, and to engage in available educational work via the Internet is exceptional and otherwise not available. However, there exists a serious problem in Internet usage when websites containing inhumane, anti-American, racist, antiauthority, sexual, antireligious, or other inappropriate material are available in schools. Parents can exert control in their children's computer use at home to screen out undesirable sites; schools have a greater responsibility in screening out any such sites from their computers since schools serve a broad cross section of children.

Teacher Responsibilities to Children

The paramount responsibility of teachers is to their students. Because students are immature and unformed, teachers must carefully exercise their influence and temper freedom with responsibility. Teachers hold great potential power over children's lives, and teacher authority needs to be weighed heavily in teacher decisions as to what to teach and how. Teachers derive power from maturity, physical size, and position. Children are vulnerable.

In forming and testing ideas, attitudes, and behaviors, children look to teachers for direction. Children naturally are curious and positive, but cannot yet fully discern between good and bad, proper and improper. Teachers have a responsibility to continue the moral and ethical education that parents have begun.

Teacher Responsibilities to Society

Society, as well as parents, has a significant interest in children's education. Schools were established to pass on the cultural heritage; to provide the skills, attitudes, and knowledge needed to produce good citizens; and to prepare children to meet their responsibilities in family, work, and social roles. Schools are social institutions, financed and regulated to fulfill social purposes. Society has values, standards of behavior, and attitudes that schools must convey to children. These standards have evolved over a long period, and they represent our common culture. Society charges schools and teachers to ensure that social standards, and ideals these standards represent, are taught by example and by word.

Schools do not exist as entities separate from society, able to chart their own courses as though they had no social responsibilities. They were not intended to instruct students in antisocial, anti-American, or immoral ideas or behaviors, nor will society allow them to continue to do so. Society trusts teachers to develop the young into positive, productive citizens. Those few teachers who use their position to attempt to destroy social values or create social dissension are violating that trust. Those who sow the seeds of negativism, nihilism, or cynicism also are violating that trust. Society has the right to restrict, condemn, or exclude from teaching those who harm its interests.

Teacher Responsibilities to Their Profession

The teaching profession has an extensive and illustrious history. It is based on the idea of service to children and society. The teachers' code of ethics recognizes teacher responsibilities as singularly important. Teachers want to convey the cultural heritage to their students, along with a strong sense of social responsibility. Teachers can ask no less of themselves.

A basic responsibility of the teaching profession is to prepare young people for life in society. That includes teaching students social values and knowledge, and teachers' personal conduct should exemplify society's ideals. The teaching profession recognizes both children's needs and society's needs. Teachers have an obligation not to go beyond professional bounds, and to reject those who would tarnish the profession's reputation.

Teachers are the key to good education. They are also the key to poor education. When teachers are excellent, a school is excellent. But, as is widely known, many schools are not excellent, and many teachers are weak and ineffective. In fact, much of the great problem in U.S. education is due to teachers who should not be in classrooms. These teachers should be weeded out, but tenure laws and teacher unions protect the weakest and ensure poor educations for many of our children. These protections not only burden students, parents, and citizens, they pose a more serious threat to decency, patriotism, and social values (Limbaugh, 2005; Sowell, 2005).

Zealotry and Teacher Irresponsibility

Pied Piper teachers are not weak in their beliefs and sales techniques, but often are weak in their intellectual capabilities and acceptance of fundamental responsibility to society and its values. These teachers fail to recognize the proper role of a teacher. Not only does tenure cover up poor teaching, it also protects socially dangerous teachers. They use the hollow claim of academic freedom to camouflage their attempts to distort the minds of the young. Weak teachers who actually believe they have a special freedom to do as they wish in the classroom are a major threat to our culture.

Teachers can be captured by radical ideas, and have a captive audience of immature minds. Oftentimes the academically weak teacher misunderstands the threats of anarchism, atheism, satanism, socialism, communism, and other extreme positions. They often have a simplistic utopian view and want their students to adopt the same, so impose their radical views on vulnerable young people. They may advocate extreme views of politics, economics, religion, family relations, drug use, sexual preferences, and other controversial topics. Students are expected to recognize the teacher's authority and may not be in a position to challenge the teacher's opinions. This denies the concept of education and threatens society. Nevertheless, state laws and unions protect teachers, no matter how radical and socially detrimental their concepts are. This protection, under tenure laws and the false cloak of academic freedom, allows miseducation in schools. Tenure laws make it almost impossible to rid schools of poor teachers or those who are zealots.

The false claim that academic freedom gives teachers the right to do what they wish does not take into account the real history of academic freedom. The historic idea of academic freedom protects scientists and university scholars in pursuing and publishing their research. Even in this restricted setting, there are some limits for researchers; they cannot do any research they might want, certainly none that knowingly harms people. Academic freedom in its original conception has little to do with schoolteachers and their work. Nor does the historic sense of academic freedom reflect social responsibilities attendant on teaching in public elementary and high schools. Because young, impressionable children must attend school by law, we demand greater accountability from public school teachers than we do from teachers in colleges, where students may be old enough to resist brainwashing. Students are a captive audience of relatively unsophisticated children; they are the ones who need protection. The historic definition of academic freedom applies solely to the protection of university scholars as they research their specialties. It was not intended to cover schoolteachers and their students.

Where current applications of academic freedom involve schoolteachers and their students is in assuring that no indoctrination or politicization takes place in classrooms of our schools (Stern, 2006a, b). The National Academic Freedom Conference provided significant evidence of the problems created when teachers attempt to impose their views without challenge (Dogan, 2006). Students subjected to teacher rants against the president or in support of foreign governments or ideologies make sad stories in the report.

Academic Freedom as License

A license to teach is not a license to impose one's views on others. Corruption of the young is at the least a moral crime; it is ethically reprehensible. The majority of teachers accept this and discharge their duties with integrity and care. For them, teaching is a calling to instruct the young in society's knowledge and values. This represents the best in the profession and is a great support to the well-being of the community and nation. Unfortunately, some teachers do not subscribe to the values of their profession.

There are teachers who are caught in drug raids, who have cheated on their income tax returns, and who have committed robbery—but these are exceptions (O'Connor, 2005). Most teachers are not criminals. When teachers do engage in criminal conduct, they are subject to criminal penalties and possible loss of employment. They do not receive special treatment. However, there is another form of crime, intellectual crime, that teachers may engage in under the guise of academic freedom.

Intellectual crimes include ridiculing student or family values, advocating antisocial attitudes, indoctrinating children in secular humanism, and influencing students to think or act in opposition to parent and community norms. These crimes may have an even greater, more devastating, effect on children and society than legal transgressions because they tear at the nation's moral fiber. Perpetrators should not have special protection. There is nothing academic about confusing and confounding children about their families and society; teachers who commit such crimes deserve no consideration under the rubric of academic freedom. Distorting the minds of the young is misteaching and should be penalized.

A child brought up to revere the family, believe in traditional marriage, support the United States, and respect people in authority may find it traumatic when a teacher expresses approval of such activities as participating in homosexual acts, supporting abortion rights, espousing anti-Americanism, engaging in civil disobedience, or sexually using children. Teachers should not have the right to damage children in this manner. Stretching the idea of academic freedom to protect such teachers is an affront to the true meaning of academic freedom.

Some schoolteachers and their unions want to open a large umbrella of academic freedom to cover anything a teacher does or says. Their claims to protection are not justified, but make school administrators wary. Administrators do not want the American Civil Liberties Union or other local vigilante groups interfering in school affairs. Thus, radical teachers often get away with their preaching and mind-bending for years because the administration is afraid to reprimand them. Instead, the problem is hidden. Parents who protest are allowed to have their children transferred to other classes, but unsuspecting parents fall prey to these unprofessional classroom Fagins. It takes a courageous, persistent parent to thwart such a teacher. Often, public disclosure of the teacher's actions will arouse the community and force school officials to take action.

Radical teachers also have misused state tenure laws, which typically place excessive impediments to obstruct efforts to dismiss a teacher. As a result, very few school districts find it worthwhile to try to fire even the most incompetent teachers, and radical teachers recognize this. Tenured teacher firings are very rare; the radical teacher merely has to sit tight until tenure, and then anything is permissible. Tenure laws create burdensome requirements that save teachers' jobs even when those teachers have demonstrated a lack of respect for parents, students, and community values. We need to make it easier to dismiss teachers who behave irresponsibly.

Teachers may have views that differ from community norms, but the classroom is not the place in which to express them. Teachers should not have the freedom to preach radical ideas in schools. Schools are not meant to be forums for teachers whose viewpoints differ sharply from those of the community. Instead, schools are intended to express and affirm community values. Malleable students are a captive audience; teachers must not have the right to impose contrary views on the young (Sowell, 2005).

Academic Freedom and Teacher Freedom

We must bear two important considerations in mind in any discussion of academic and teacher freedom in the schools. First, academic freedom provides limited protection to university-level scholars who are experts in their specialized fields, and the concept is more limited when applied to teachers below the college level. Second, other freedom for teachers below the college level is not unlimited or unrestrained; it is necessarily related to traditional teacher responsibilities.

There is no doubt that, within the limits of responsibility, teachers deserve respect and some freedom to determine how to teach. That is, teacher freedom can be separated from academic freedom, which is intended to protect the rights of experts to present their research results. This separation does not denigrate teachers any more than it denigrates lawyers, doctors, and ministers as respected people with no claim to special freedom in their work. Teacher freedom is protected by community traditions and the constitutional protection of free speech. Teachers do not need additional protections.

The U.S. Constitution's protections of free speech for all citizens are more than sufficient for teachers. Under the Constitution, any of us can say what we wish to say about the government, our employers, or the state of the world, provided it is not slanderous, imminently dangerous, or obscene. Obviously, we cannot say false things about someone without risking a libel suit, and we cannot yell "Fire!" in a crowded theater or "Bomb!" in an airport without risking arrest. Though we have the freedom to say them, we also must accept the consequences for our statements (Standler, 2000).

Public expression of controversial views, as in letters to a newspaper editor, is a right of all people in the United States. Teachers, of course, have the same right. But that does not mean that teachers are any different from other citizens or more deserving of job security no matter how inane or anti-American their public statements. Teachers' jobs are not safe regardless, any more than are jobs of those employed by private firms who make controversial public statements. Anyone who wishes to make public statements must recognize the risks involved. Teachers, more than most citizens, should be aware of the responsibilities surrounding public discourse. A teacher's inflammatory comments can lead to public outrage. For public school teachers, the public is the employer.

Schoolteachers should not expect job guarantees when they make negative comments about schools, the community, or the nation, or when they teach children by using propaganda or inaccurate or provocative material. Classroom statements by teachers are actually public statements, subject to the same conditions as letters to the editor or public speaking. There is no special privilege granted to teachers merely because they close the classroom door.

Private schools can expect their teachers to uphold school and parent values because private school administrators and boards have more latitude in dismissing teachers they consider unsatisfactory in teaching or in judgment. State tenure laws do not apply to them. Public school boards and administrators are under some constraints because of those tenure laws and active teacher unions, but they should be more aggressive in weeding out poor teachers and those who engage in controversial acts. Each board of education has a responsibility to provide children with information, skills, a set of social values, and a moral code that strengthen society. Teachers cannot abrogate that responsibility.

Academic Freedom as a Function of Academic Position

Academic freedom protects scholars who recognize the academic responsibilities inherent in it. Scholars who have developed expert knowledge in a subject field may conduct research challenging accepted views—this is how we continue to refine knowledge. Academic freedom allows such scholars to publish or present their research without fear of losing their positions, but only in those areas in which they have demonstrated expert knowledge. They have no greater freedom than any other citizen in areas outside their own expertise.

The Constitution protects everyone's speech, but does not and should not protect a faculty job. There is a difference between academic freedom and license, and no academic freedom should exist for those who indoctrinate others. Kirk (1955), Hook (1953), and Buckley (1951) provide philosophic grounds for limiting teacher freedom to expert scholars engaged in publication of their research. They would deny scholars or any other educators the right to proselytize or indoctrinate students under special protection of academic freedom (Limbaugh, 2005).

Unfortunately for teachers and scholars, the idea of academic freedom has been abused in current times. Teacher unions and lawyers, attempting to save the jobs of teachers who are incompetent or who espouse antisocial propaganda, have clouded the positive idea of academic freedom. Academic freedom should not become a shield for incompetent, antisocial, or un-American teaching. Rather, academic freedom should offer protection for expert scholars in the search for truth, and provide a rationale for teachers to subscribe to a code of ethics that assures a balanced presentation of views in precollegiate classrooms. Linking teacher responsibility and accountability to teacher freedom is a much sounder approach to the protection of teachers and integrity of society.

Goldstein (1976) argues that academic freedom is unsuited to elementary and secondary schools because of the age and immaturity of the students, the teacher's position of authority, the necessarily more highly structured curriculum, and the dominant role of schools in imparting social values. These factors cannot be easily dismissed. Elementary and secondary school teachers are different from university scholars in their training, functions, employment status, and responsibilities. Elementary and secondary schools have broad responsibilities to parents, community, and state that do not permit license. Schools and teachers serve in capacities that require support for and advocacy of social and family values. Rhetoric about academic freedom does not diminish that significant responsibility.

Teachers deserve respect and appreciation for their contributions to society, decent salaries, and comfortable working conditions. They deserve the protection the Bill of Rights gives to all U.S. citizens: freedom of speech, association, and assembly. For all of us, including teachers, these freedoms entail responsibilities. Teacher responsibilities to students, parents, school officials, the teaching profession, and to society make classroom teachers one of our most treasured resources. Teachers do not, however, merit special treatment in regard to their freedom. Tenure should not protect them from losing their jobs for subverting students, advocating radical ideas, insubordination, or proselytizing.

For Discussion

1. Dialectic exercise: The idea that academic freedom is limited to university researchers in their field of study only can be considered a thesis. What would be an antithesis? What evidence exists on each side? What philosophic grounds and logic support each position? What would be a suitable synthesis? How would your synthesis affect the current situation for K–12 teachers in regard to the exercise of academic freedom?

2. If you were asked by a local school board to be on a committee to prepare school district policies related to:
   Teacher freedom,
   Student freedom,
   Dealing with controversial material,
   and handling parental or citizen complaints about teaching material, methods, or school curriculum,
   What policies would you recommend? Draft an example set of policies to govern how a school district should handle such matters.
3. Dialogue ideas: Should there be any restrictions on what a teacher can discuss in class? What set of principles should govern establishment of those limits? Should students have the same freedoms and limits? Is student age or teacher experience a significant factor in this determination? How should schools handle questions that arise about how a teacher handles controversy?
4. Which, if any, of these topics should be banned from schoolbooks or class discussion?

Explicit sexual material	Violence
Sexism	Anti-American views
Racism	Antireligious ideas
Fascism	Socialism
Inhuman treatment of people	Animal, child, or spouse abuse

   What are the grounds for justifying censorship of any of these? Who should decide? What are some good examples of thesis and antithesis statements about censorship? How would you construct a dialect on this topic?
5. What role should teachers play in learning about and responding to efforts at censorship? Should censors be censored? How should a teacher be prepared to deal with censors and political restraint?

References

AMERICAN ASSOCIATION OF UNIVERSITY PROFESSORS (AAUP). (1986). *Liberty and Learning in the Schools.* Washington, DC: Author.
————. (2003). "Academic Bill of Rights." Statement from Committee A. December. www.aaup.org.
AMERICAN LIBRARY ASSOCIATION. (1996). *Intellectual Freedom Manual.* 5th Ed. Chicago: ALA.
Attacks on the Freedom to Learn. (1985–1994). Washington, DC: People for the American Way.
BEALE, H. (1936). *Are American Teachers Free?* New York: Scribner's.
BERNARD, S. (2008). "Should There Be Limits on Teachers' Freedom of Speech?" *Edutopia.* www.edutopia.org. March.
BUCKLEY, W. F. (1951). *God and Man at Yale.* Chicago: Regnery.
"CENSORED INTERNET ACCESS IN UTAH SCHOOLS AND LIBRARIES." (1999). Report, Censorware Project. March 23. www.censorware.org.
COHEN-ALMAGOR, R. (2008). "Hate in the Classroom." *American Journal of Education* 114(2), 215–241. Feb.
DAHL, T. (2008). "Surveys in American's Classrooms: How Much do Parents Really Know?" *Journal of Law and Education.* 37(2), 143–192. April.
DALY, J. K. (1991). "The Influence of Administrators on the Teaching of Social Studies." *Theory and Research in Social Education* 19:267–283.

DALY, J. K., AND ROACH, P. B. (1990). "Reaffirming a Commitment to Academic Freedom." *Social Education* 54:342–345.

DALY, J. K., SCHALL, P., AND SKEELE, R. (2001). *Protecting the Right to Teach and Learn.* New York: Teachers College Press.

DEWEY, J. (1936). "The Social Significance of Academic Freedom." *The Social Frontier* 2:136.

DOGAN, S. (2006). "A Rousing Success." Report on the First National Academic Freedom Conference. April 11. www.frontpagemag.com.

EVANS, R. W. (2007). *This Happened in America: Harold Rugg and the Censure of Social Studies.* Charlotte, NC: Information Age Publishing.

FIRST AMENDMENT SCHOOLS. (2008). First Amendment Center News. www @firstamendmentschools.org.

FOERSTEL, H. N. (1994). *Banned in the USA.* Westport, CT: Greenwood Press.

————. (2002). *Banned in the USA.* Westport, CT: Greenwood Press.

FOUNDATION FOR INDIVIDUAL RIGHTS IN EDUCATION. (2005). www.thefire.org.

FUENTES, C. (2005). *This I Believe.* New York: Random House.

GELLERMAN, W. (1938). *The American Legion as Educator.* New York: Teachers College Press.

GOLDSTEIN, S. (1976). "The Asserted Right of Teachers to Determine What They Teach." *University of Pennsylvania Law Review* 124:1, 293.

HENTOFF, N. (1991). "Saving Kids from Satan's Books." *The Progressive* 55:14–16.

HOFSTADTER, R., AND METZGER, W. (1955, 1968). *The Development of Academic Freedom in the United States.* New York: Columbia University Press.

HOOK, S. (1953). *Heresy, Yes—Conspiracy, No.* New York: J. Day Co.

HOROWITZ, D. (2005). "Academic Freedom: David Horowitz vs. Russell Jacoby. *Front Page.* July 29. www.frontpagemag.com.

IFLAI STATEMENT. (1999). "Libraries and Intellectual Freedom." International Federation of Library Associations and Institutions, The Hague, Netherlands. March 25.

JAPENGA, A. (1994). "A Teacher at War." *Mother Jones* 19:17.

JENKINSON, E. B. (1985). "Protecting Holden Caulfield and His Friends from the Censors." *English Journal* 74:26–33.

————. (1990). "Child Abuse in the Hate Factory," in *Academic Freedom to Teach and to Learn,* ed. A. Ochoa. Washington, DC: National Education Association.

JONES, B. M. (1999). *Libraries, Access, and Intellectual Freedom.* Chicago: American Library Association.

Keyishian v. Board of Regents. (1967). 385 U.S. 589.

KIRK, R. (1955). *Academic Freedom.* Chicago: Regnery.

KLINE, M. A. (2008). "Cold War on Campus." Campus Report 23(4), 1,5. www.academic .org. Accuracy in Academia.

LA RUE, J. (2007). *The New Inquisition.* Westport CT: Libraries Unlimited.

LIMBAUGH, D. (2005). "False Promises of Academic Freedom." Town Hall. www.townhall .com/columnists.

LINDORFF, D. (2005). "Academic Freedom? What Academic Freedom?" *Common Dreams.* February 10. www.commondreams.org.

MAWDSLEY, R. D., AND MAWDSLEY, A. L. (1988). *Free Expression and Censorship: Public Policy and the Law.* Topeka, KS: National Organization on Legal Problems of Education.

McNEIL K. (2002). "The War on Academic Freedom." *The Nation.* November 25. www. thenation.com.

MELNICK, N., AND LILLARD, S. D. (1989). "Academic Freedom: A Delicate Balance." *Clearing House* 62:275–277.

MENAND, L., ed. (1996). *The Future of Academic Freedom.* Chicago: University of Chicago Press.

MISCO T. AND PATTERSON, N. C. (2007). "A Study of Pre-Service Teachers' Conceptualizations of Academic Freedom and Controversial Issues," *Theory and Research in Social Education.* 35(4), 520–550.

NATIONAL COUNCIL FOR THE SOCIAL STUDIES (NCSS). (1974). "The Freedom to Teach and the Freedom to Learn." Washington, DC: Author.

NATIONAL COUNCIL FOR THE SOCIAL STUDIES. (2007). *Academic Freedom and the Social Studies Teacher.* www.ncss.org.

NAYAKA, A. C., ed. (2005). Censorship: Opposing Viewpoints. New York: Thomson Gale.

NELSON, J. (1990). "The Significance of and Rationale for Academic Freedom," in *Academic Freedom to Teach and to Learn,* ed. A. Ochoa. Washington, DC: National Education Association.

————. (2003). "Academic Freedom, Academic Integrity, and Teacher Education." *Teacher Education Quarterly* 30(1):65–72.

NEWSLETTER ON INTELLECTUAL FREEDOM. (Bimonthly). Chicago: American Library Association.

NOBLE, W. (1990). *Bookbanning in America.* Middlebury, VT: Paul Ericksson.

NODDINGS, N. (1999). "Renewing Democracy in Schools." *Kappan* 80(8):579–583.

O'CONNOR, E. (2005). "Academic Freedom Does Time." *Critical Mass.* www.ericoconnor.org.

O'NEIL, R. M. (1981). *Classrooms in the Crossfire.* Bloomington: Indiana University Press.

O'NEIL, R. M. (2008). *Academic Freedom in the Wired World.* Cambridge MA: Harvard University Press.

PICO, S. (1990). "An Introduction to Censorship." *School Media Quarterly* 18:84–87.

PIERCE, B. (1933). *Citizens' Organizations and the Civic Training of Youth.* New York: Scribner's.

PIPKIN, G. AND LENT, R. C. (2002). *The Schoolhouse Gate:Lessons in Intellectual Freedom.* Portsmouth, NH: Heinemann.

PUDDINGTON, A. MELIA, R. O. AND KELLY, J. (2008). *Today's Americans: How Free?* Lanham MD: Roman and Littlefield.

REICHMAN, H. (1993). *Censorship and Selection: Issues and Answers for Schools.* Chicago: American Library Association and American Association of School Administrators.

The Rights of Students. 3rd Ed. (1988). Washington, DC: American Civil Liberties Union.

RORTY, R. (1994). "Does Academic Freedom Have Philosophical Presuppositions?" *Academe* 80:52–63.

ROSS, S. J., "21st Century Book-Burning," *Los Angeles Times,* October. 14, 2004. www.commondreams.org.

RUBIN, D., AND GREENHOUSE, S. (1983). *The Rights of Teachers: The Basic ACLU Guide to a Teacher's Constitutional Rights.* Rev. Ed. New York: Bantam.

SACKEN, D. M. (1989). "Rethinking Academic Freedom in the Public Schools." *Teachers College Record* 91:235–255.

SCALES, P. (2001). *Teaching Banned Books.* Chicago: American Library Association.

SEESHOLTZ, M. (2005). "Diversity, Academic Freedom and Conservative T-Shirts." *Counterbias.* July 11. www.counterbias.org.

SHERROW, V. (1996). *Censorship in Schools.* Springfield, NJ: Enslow Publishers.

SIMMONS, J. (1991). "Censorship in the Schools: No End in Sight." *ALAN Review* 18:6–8.

————, ed. (1994). *Censorship: A Threat to Reading, Learning, Thinking.* Newark, DE: International Reading Association.

SINCLAIR, U. (1922). *The Goose-Step.* Pasadena, CA: Sinclair.

————. (1923). *The Goslings.* Pasadena, CA: Sinclair.

SIPE, R. B. (1999). "Don't Confront Censors, Prepare for Them." *Education Digest* 64(6):42–46.

SOWELL, T. (2005). "Academic Freedom?" Feb. 15. www.townhall.com/columnists.

STANDLER, R. B. (2000). "Academic Freedom in the USA." www.rbs2.com/academicfreedom.

STERN, S. (2006a). "Social Justice and other High School Indoctrinations." April 13. www.frontpagemag.com.

————. (2006b). "Pinko Teachers, Inc." *New York Post.* March 12. www.nypost.com.

————. (2006c). "High School Indoctrination." www.frontpagemagazine.com Mar. 8.

STILLE, A., "Textbook Publishers Learn to Avoid Messing with Texas," *New York Times,* June 29, 2002. www.nytimes.com.

STONE, G. R. (2004). *Perilous Times: Free Speech in Wartime.* New York: W.W. Norton.

STUDENTS FOR ACADEMIC FREEDOM. (2003). *Academic Bill of Rights.* www.studentsforacademicfreedom.org.

THELIN, J. (1997). "Zealotry and Academic Freedom." *History of Education Quarterly* 37(3):338–420.

THOMAS, C. (1983). *Book Burning.* Manchester, IL: Crossway Books.

TURNER-EGNER, J. (1989). "Teachers' Discretion in Selecting Instructional Materials and Methods." *West's Education Law Reporter* 53:365–379.

VEBLEN, T. (1918/1957). *The Higher Learning in America: Memorandum on the Conduct of Universities by Businessmen.* New York: Sagamore.

WEINER, I., ed. (1973). *Dictionary of the History of Ideas.* New York: Scribner's.

WHITSON, J. A. (1993). "After Hazelwood: The Role of School Officials in Conflicts over the Curriculum." *ALAN Review* 20:2–6.

Wieman v. Updegraff. (1952). 244 U.S. 183.

WILSON, J. K. (2006). "Interview with David Horowitz." March. www.collegefreedom.org.

WILSON, J. K. (2008). *Patriotic Correctness: Academic Freedom and its Enemies.* Boulder, CO: Paradigm Press.

ZIRKEL, P. (1993). "Academic Freedom: Professional or Legal Right?" *Educational Leadership* 50:42–43.

CHAPTER 18

Inclusion and Mainstreaming: Common or Special Education

When and why should selected children be provided inclusive or special treatment in schools?

POSITION 1: FOR FULL INCLUSION

Implementing inclusion effectively requires schools to make adjustments in order to fully accommodate students with disabilities. Unfortunately, many schools failed to make these changes.

—Ferri and Connor, *Teachers College Record,* 2005, p. 467

. . . the sad irony has been that minorities have been disproportionately perceived as needing to be served in separate programs that have increased their isolation from the educational mainstream and limited their access to the kind of education valued by that mainstream.

—Harry et al., 2008

Full inclusion of all children into school life is a fundamental principle in a free, democratic society. Full inclusion means that students classified "special" or "exceptional" because of individual physical or mental characteristics would not be isolated into separate schools, separate classes, or pull-out sessions. They would be full citizens and members of the school community, not only in regular classes but also as legitimate participants in schools' multiple activities. Inclusion is consistent with fundamental principles of our society and with the law (Vargas, 1999; Kluth et al., 2002; Ferri and Connor, 2005; Oakes, 2005). The United States should do no less than provide full inclusion (Grossman, 1998; Koenig and Bachman, 2004; Wolbrecht and Hero, 2005; Cameron, 2008).

As a matter of human concern and fairness, we should not separate those who differ from the rest. Inclusive schools recognize the richness in human diversity. Cushner, McClelland, and Safford (2000) offer a philosophic and historic case for the inclusion of exceptional children:

> From its inception, a fundamental characteristic of American schooling has been its intended inclusiveness, across social boundaries, of gender, class, and—belatedly—race. Today, the term inclusion refers to the practice of including another group of students in regular classrooms, those with problems of health and/or physical, developmental, and emotional problems. . . . Like societal inclusion, inclusive education implies fully shared participation of diverse individuals in common experiences. (pp. 161, 163)

Not only is inclusion a matter of fundamental principles and law, it is better educationally—for students and teachers.

Exclusion and Segregation: Racism and Ableism

The long and strong effort to exclude some special needs students from regular school classes and activities has remarkable parallels with the racial segregation efforts of times past, as Ferri and Connor (2005) suggest:

> As in the case of school desegregation, the movement from segregated placements toward more inclusive ones for students with disabilities has involved a long and often difficult struggle. . . . Yet even when school systems have shifted to more inclusive practices because of legal requirements, the results were often characterized as cosmetic or shallow. . . .

There are many parallels between how our society has treated minority children and how it has treated disabled children in schools. One is a function of forms of racism, the other a function of forms of ableism. Where they coincide is corrosive of our democracy and social values. One of the striking things about school-based classification of children into special education classes, programs, or schools is that students placed in the special category come disproportionately from minority ethnic and social class groups of society (Educational Testing Service, 1980; Heller, Holtzman, and Messick, 1982; Anderson and Anderson, 1983; Brantlinger and Guskin, 1987; Ferri and Connor, 2005; Artiles and Bal, 2008). Obviously, this combination of class, race, and classification as disabled becomes a recipe for discrimination. This parallel discrimination should be addressed as a civil rights issue on principle and a political issue in practice. Class and ethnicity have been used politically to limit the full participation of groups without wealth and power. Children with special needs have been subject to a similar political agenda restricting access, opportunity, and fulfillment of the democratic ideal (Barton, 1988; Harry et al., 2008).

Meier (2005), studying school board actions and educational politics, argues:

> At the extremes this [grouping and sorting children] includes sorting students into a variety of special education classifications or into various honors or college prep options. . . . Studies consistently find that minorities are assigned in disproportionate numbers to special education, lower ability groups, and vocational tracks and at the same time are less likely to gain access to

advanced classes, advanced placement classes, gifted programs, and college prep tracks. (p. 239)

Oakes (2005), following up on her famous study of inequality in schools, notes, "Thus, through tracking, schools continue to replicate existing inequality along lines of race and social class and contribute to the intergenerational transmission of social and economic inequality" (p. xi).

Exceptionality among individuals is a constant in human history. This condition of "abnormality" has historically been the basis for a variety of destructive actions by those in power, from infanticide to institutionalization. Winzer's (1993) comprehensive history of special education is based on a pertinent principle: "A society's treatment of those who are weak and dependent is one critical indicator of its social progress. Social attitudes concerning the education and care of exceptional individuals reflect general cultural attitudes concerning the obligations of a society to its individual citizens" (p. 3). This, in the United States and in the civilized world, is a civil rights issue based on the most fundamental documents and foundational moral principles.

Inclusion Is More Than Mere Addition

Full inclusion expects far more of good education than merely adding classified students to general classes or mandating all students to run, climb, read, write, draw, or compute in only one way and at the same speed. Full inclusion assumes schools will provide high-quality, individualized instruction, with well-prepared teachers, suitable and varied teaching materials, and appropriate schedules to support the idea that all students are capable of success. The principle of full inclusion merely extends the democratic principle of quality education for all to include children with special needs (Skiba et al., 2008).

Kluth and colleagues (2001) note that the 1994 policy guidelines established by the U.S. Department of Education specify schools may not use lack of resources or personnel as an excuse for not providing free and appropriate education—in the least restrictive environments—to students with disabilities (p. 24). But school districts have been very slow to follow the law and the policies. During the twelve-year period, 1977 to 1990, there was an actual decline of only 1.2 percent in the number of students with disabilities who were moved from separate to regular classrooms. A National Council on Disability study reported in 2000 that "every state was out of compliance with the requirements of the Individuals with Disabilities Education Act and that U.S. officials were not enforcing compliance" (reported in Kluth et al., 2001). The common excuses of schools simply do not meet the standards set by the law: "we don't provide inclusion"; "this child is too disabled to be in a regular classroom"; "we give them special programs." The law, and supporting court decisions, requires inclusion unless the severity of the disability precludes satisfactory education in regular classes. This high standard does not allow schools to ignore or dismiss the requirement to provide inclusion for the vast majority of students with disabilities (Kluth et al., 2001; Cigman, 2007).

The concept of inclusion involves a set of school practices that Stainback, Stainback, and Jackson (1992) describe:

1. All children are to be included in the educational and social lives of their schools and classrooms.
2. The basic goal is to not leave anyone out of school and classroom communities (thus, integration can be abandoned since no one has to go back to the mainstream).
3. The focus is on the support needs of all students and personnel.

Full inclusion does not mean schools should bring in students with special needs only to insist on blind conformity to a single standard for all students; nor does it mean nonconforming students should be ignored or mistreated in "regular" schools. Rather, the concept of inclusion assumes that the individual needs of every student, whether classified "special" or not, seriously must be considered to provide a quality education. This assumption undergirds the idea of full inclusion for students who are "special" or "exceptional."

The Legal Basis for Full Inclusion

Over the past quarter-century, the U.S. Congress clearly has shown its intent that all children with disabilities be provided a free and appropriate education in public schools. A series of modifications in supportive legislation, from 1975 to the present, have improved the educational rights of children with disabilities and their families. Full inclusion is the next logical step. Turnbull and Turnbull (1998) defined this evolving policy as "Zero Reject" and noted an important effect was "to redefine the doctrine of equal educational opportunity as it applies to children with disabilities and to establish different meanings of equality as it applies to people with and without disabilities" (p. 92). Earlier laws relied on a concept of equality that meant equal access to different resources; children attended separate special education classes and schools. The newer laws assume equal access means full access to regular resources—regular classes and schools, but with special support, to help students "more like than different from people without disabilities" (Turnbull and Turnbull, 1998, p. 93).

The principle of inclusion goes well beyond the mainstreaming that has developed since the 1975 landmark federal legislation, the Education of All Handicapped Children Act (Public Law 94–142). At the time Congress was considering this law, 1 million out of 8 million disabled children under age 21 were completely excluded from the U.S. public school system. They were "outcast children" (Dickman, 1985, p. 181). Mainstreaming grew out of an important clause of the law, offering the concept of the "least restrictive environment"—meaning students with special needs who "demonstrate appropriate behavior and skills" should be in general classrooms rather than segregated programs. The law gave some children with special needs the educational, emotional, and social advantages offered to other students. It also gave parents the right to be advocates in fashioning an appropriate education for their differently abled children.

Amendments and modifications to the 1975 law have included changes in the language—for example, replacing handicapped with disabled and renaming the law, calling it the 1990 Individuals with Disabilities Education Act (IDEA). Other important changes in the law have increased the expectations for mainstreaming and led toward full inclusion. The 1990 IDEA law, and its 2004 renewal, requires schools to offer a set of placement options to meet the needs of students with disabilities, and that to the maximum extent appropriate, children with disabilities are to be educated with other children. Further, the law expects schools to provide supplementary aids and services for disabled children when needed; and it requires that any separate schooling or other removal of children with disabilities from the regular environment occur only when the child cannot learn in regular classes even with supplementary aids and services. This sets a high standard for schools to meet in order to exclude disabled students from regular classes.

Laws and court decisions are becoming more expansive in their recognition of individual and social benefits of inclusion. *Mills v. Board of Education of the District of Columbia* (1972) produced a judgment in class-action litigation based on the foundational arguments of equal opportunity and due process. The judge in the *Mills* case decreed that children with physical or mental disabilities had a right to a suitable and free public education, and lack of funds was not a defense for exclusion. Mainstreaming offered an interim process toward inclusion. Parents have pursued full inclusion and drawn increasing support from the courts (*Oberti v. Board of Education of the Borough of Clementon School District*, 1993).

Democratic Purposes for Inclusion

At the center of education in a democracy are the concepts of equal opportunity and justice. Democracy, by its very nature, requires all citizens to have the opportunity to be fully educated. Equal opportunity and fairness underscore the idea of inclusion. There are many other important reasons for inclusion of special students in regular school classes and activities, but the fundamental premise of democracy expects no less (Burrello et al., 2001).

Education is the primary means for realizing the goals of the Declaration of Independence and the Constitution. Isolating special education students not only labels and stigmatizes them, it limits their full interaction with others during their most formative years. This is detrimental to these students, and also is detrimental to the perceptions of nonexceptional students about life in the full society.

In addition to the obvious educational value of allowing all students to participate fully in the schools, inclusion is also a civil rights issue. Discrimination against persons with disabilities has been legally outlawed in the United States. The 1990 Americans with Disabilities Act (ADA) barred such discrimination, just as other laws barred discrimination based on race, gender, or age.

Some institutions meet the access requirements of ADA on purely physical grounds, providing ramps and elevators as well as stairs and modifying doors and bathrooms. This minimal approach would be the equivalent of simply removing "White Only" signs after racial discrimination was ruled illegal and doing nothing more; it still would not deal with underlying, more pervasive instances of institutional discrimination restricting access and opportunity. In a larger context, education is a primary means of access to all of society's opportunities. Separate-but-equal education for African Americans was actually separate but not equal; similarly, separate special education is also separate but not equal.

Social Policy Considerations

Beyond the obvious democratic and civil rights concerns raised by separating special needs children from their peers in schools, there are other defects in this policy. As a matter of social policy, separation is inconsistent with the larger-scale interests of the United States (Sailor, Gerry, and Wilson, 1991).

Broad social policy goals underlie the tenets of inclusion for special needs youth in all society's activities and institutions. Full participation in the society requires full inclusion in the schools. Denying those rights to the disabled denies society the skills, the economic productivity, and the social and political values inherent in full participation of individuals with disabilities.

In the period before 1910, the United States had a pattern of institutionalizing children with disabilities in isolation from society. Families of these children hid them, provided private care, or sent them to institutions where they would live out their lives away from public view or participation. Changing public attitudes regarding our social responsibility for persons with disabilities, as well as a recognition of the general economic value in providing training for disadvantaged people, led to a variety of alterations in social policies and educational practices. This occurred at the same time as public schooling expanded in the early twentieth century. For the disabled, this meant segregation in separate schools and/or separate classes, teachers, and programs. The intent may have been benign, but segregation is inadequate as a social policy.

Social and Psychological Arguments for Inclusion

In addition to persuasive arguments based on fundamental democratic principles and on fair social policy in favor of full inclusion, social and personal psychology offer other important arguments. Separation of exceptional children from the mainstream of children in schools has been recognized as traumatic for those separated, whether by race, gender, or abilities. In the landmark Supreme Court decision that declared racially segregated schools and the concept of "separate but equal" unconstitutional (*Brown v. Board of Education*, 1954), Chief Justice Earl Warren argued that separation in schools can cause children to "generate a feeling of inferiority as to . . . status in the community that may affect their hearts and minds in a way unlikely ever to be undone" (p. 493). Senator Lowell Weicker stated: "As a society, we have treated people with disabilities as inferiors and made them unwelcome in many activities and opportunities available to other Americans" (quoted in Stainback and Stainback, 1990, p. 7).

Obviously, perceptions of special needs children are strongly influenced by their separation. It goes beyond individual feelings of insecurity to the concept that society values them less and prefers them out of sight.

Research confirms children with special needs do better in both academic work and social adjustment in mainstreamed schools and in regular classes. Semmel, Gottlieb, and Robinson (1979) report results from several studies showed regular class placement was a factor in superior academic achievement among special students, and special needs students did at least as well in academic work in regular classes as they had in special classes. In addition, Carlberg and Kavale (1980) found social adjustment of special needs youth was improved by mainstreaming into the school's life. If social interaction improves for these students, while academic achievement improves or remains at least as high, then inclusion is a positive school practice. Wang, Reynolds, and Walberg (1990) report multiple studies supporting inclusion.

Avoiding Foreseeable Failures in Inclusive Practices

Positive inclusion in schools depends on collaborative efforts by regular and special education teachers, parents, and administrators. Ill-prepared, poorly organized past efforts at mainstreaming must be avoided in inclusion. Teacher preparation and in-service programs should integrate the most useful knowledge from special education research and practice and should emphasize special methods for dealing with a wide range of students and for individualizing lessons (Cooley, 2008).

Not only are there serious detrimental consequences for the individual exceptional children who are placed in isolated or separated situations, but "average" children are likewise deprived of realistic social interaction and a more compassionate understanding of others' lives. Additionally, the community as a whole suffers from the suspicion, distrust, and misunderstanding created by separation (Risko and Bromley, 2001).

The "Exceptional" and the "Average"

Identification and measurement of exceptionality is a tradition in modern society, though it varies to some extent by nation and time period (Taylor, 2003). Currently, in the United States, exceptionality usually refers to observable or measurable differences in physical, mental, emotional, or other abilities. In school terms, exceptional children differ from nonexceptional ones based on school achievement, for example, in reading, writing, listening, sitting attentively, seeing and hearing, and so on. Exceptionality in the United States has included both extremes of mental ability—the severely mentally or learning impaired and the gifted and talented. Both get special treatment and school support. The category of exceptional children also includes those with a variety of measured physical differences from "average" children, including differences in sight, hearing, and use of limbs, but does not include those with extraordinary physical abilities. Similarly, only one end of the potential spectrum of emotional abilities is included in the exceptional category; only those labeled emotionally impaired. There are some problems, then, with consistency in the way we apply the definition of "exceptional."

Causes of exceptionality include genetics, at-birth disabilities, improper medical practice, disease, parental irresponsibility, accidents, and inadequate health care. These exceptionalities are not self-inflicted; they are often chance happenings, as in afflictions caused by accidents, birth defects, or childhood disease. Although exceptionality, in these terms, is relatively rare, it should not create a wall of separation from the rest of society; human variety is extraordinarily complex and incredibly wide ranging. We have improved our measures, but the extent of human variability remains unknown. Further, the classifications themselves reflect cultural norms and prejudices.

The category of "disabled," "exceptional," or "handicapped" depends on the society, time period, and societal norms. *Disability*, according to Dickman (1985), is a deficit that occurs at birth or through disease or some other event, while handicaps are the secondary problems that occur because of discrimination, mistreatment, or help that is denied or delayed. The term *handicapped*, by this definition, represents a social problem of bias and discrimination, while disability is an individual problem. For another example, the category of "learning disabled," used widely in U.S. schools, varies significantly in the measures used to define it. The term is not used in developing nations, where certain forms of technological literacy are not as important, nor is it used much in the corporate world to define categories of people (Cushner, McClelland, and Safford, 2000; Cameron, 2008).

Much of the history of prejudice and discrimination against exceptional children has been based on a false sense of the meaning of "average," and on people's insecurities about their own abilities and talents. Those who differ often are labeled negatively to maintain the status of the favored. Although we often refer to an average, there may be no actual "average" person, in genetic traits, social characteristics, or preferred individual behavior. Who among us come from a family of 2.3 children, are exactly average in height, weight, IQ, and shoe size, earn average grades or average test scores, and desire an average marriage when over 50 percent end in divorce? Each of us does many things far better or far worse than the average. Average also suggests dullness and conformity; richness comes from diversity. Average is suitable as a broad guide for making tentative comparative judgments about many conditions such as income tax deductions or sleep time needed each day, but should not be mindlessly used as a criterion to rank human qualities against. Exceptional children are exceptional when compared with certain measures of average, but every child differs from average in some respect.

Meeting Potential Problems in Full Inclusion

Full inclusion of all children into the lives of schools is not an easy task. As is clear from the history of special education, many problems are associated with implementing full inclusion. Schools must address the fears of some parents, teachers, administrators, and community members by developing strong programs of information, discussion, preparation, and positive interaction. Special education teachers may fear losing their expert status and, perhaps, their jobs; regular teachers are concerned about their lack of preparation and about no longer being able to send annoying students to special education classes. Thousand and Villa (1995) identify frequently cited causes of school intractability as: "(1) inadequate teacher preparation; (2) inappropriate organizational structures, policies, and procedures; (3) lack of attention to the cultural aspects of schooling; and (4) poor leadership" (p. 53).

These factors have a detrimental impact on efforts to develop full inclusion programs in schools. We need improved teacher education to better prepare teachers for educating diverse students and meeting individual student needs. Regular education teachers also need assistance in changing their teaching practices and working with special education teachers and parents on well-designed and well-implemented plans for individual students. We need to shake the lockstep curriculum, tracking, and teacher isolation common in the current school structure. We must seek involvement and support, provide high-quality assistance and incentives for improvement, and enlist school faculty and administrators in the process of full inclusion to implement the best forms.

We can learn from some of the mistakes made in trying to implement mainstreaming without thorough preparation. Mainstreaming has been a success in many schools and in the lives of many individual students who had previously been shunted to separate schools or classes. It also has been especially successful in alleviating the separation and isolation of special education students and in bringing their situation to light. The needs of these students, and previous inadequacies of schools in meeting their needs, now are part of the public discourse.

Mainstreaming failures in some schools usually occurred where students with special needs were dumped into existing classes without adequate support, without preparing school staff or community or considering students' individual needs. Some special needs students were unable to demonstrate "appropriate behavior and skills" under school guidelines, and these schools made little effort to change programs or personnel to ensure students' success (Lombardi and Ludlow, 1996; Low, 2007). Mainstreaming became popular in the 1980s, but many schools and teachers were unprepared to handle special needs and faltered, or were unnecessarily limited in their vision and operation. The most severely disabled students still are mainstreamed in only a few classes each day, usually classes such as art and physical education.

The Individualized Education Plan (IEP) increases participation of general education teachers in planning for special needs students through membership on IEP teams and the development of a student's IEP. In addition, schools must consider how the student's disability affects involvement and performance in the school's general curriculum.

Inclusion, beyond mainstreaming, offers children with special needs the opportunity to be educated to "the maximum extent appropriate" (Public Law 94–142) in "the school or classroom he or she would otherwise have attended if he or she did not have a disability" (Rogers, 1993). Inclusion offers a broad educational program even more consistent with a society based on democracy and ethics.

Global Needs for Inclusive Education

Full inclusion is not a topic limited to the United States. Moderate to severe disabilities affect about 5.2 percent of the world population. This figure includes

7.7 percent of populations of developed countries and 4.5 percent of populations of less developed regions. The total number of disabled persons is estimated to reach over 300 million in the early twenty-first century. Disparity between proportions of disabled persons in developed and less developed areas of the world reflects differences in the definitions of disabled, in health practices, and in governmental policies on reporting disabilities in different nations. Improvements in health practices throughout the world are expected to cause an increased proportion of disabled persons, since children who previously might have died at birth or in infancy will survive, but may have serious impairments (Mittler, Brouillette, and Harris, 1993; UNESCO, 2008).

In many nations, integration of children with special needs into regular schools is a contemporary movement. For example, Italy has developed national policies for integration, the United Kingdom has established legislative policies encouraging local schools to integrate, and Austria provides model experimental projects to demonstrate the value of integration (Wedell, 1993; Sefa Dei et al., 2000). The United Nations has a history of concern for children, including children with disabilities; the 1959 Declaration of the Rights of the Child recognized the right of every child to develop to his or her full capacity. The United Nations Convention on the Rights of the Child (1989) affirmed the right to an education and, for disabled children, services that "shall be designed to ensure that the disabled child has effective access to and receives education, training, health care services, rehabilitation services, preparation for employment, and recreational opportunities in a manner conducive to the child's achieving the fullest possible social integration and individual development . . ." (article 23, 3). The United Nations Convention on the Rights of Persons with Disabilities (2007) is a current international document recognizing global dimensions of disability issues. UNESCO (2008) sponsors a major program, Education for All, having a focus on quality inclusive education. The United States has, over the past several decades, met or surpassed the legislative expectations of international human rights documents regarding disabled children.

A sense of justice in society requires that all citizens have equal opportunity to build fulfilling lives in the society and the economy. We don't need, as individuals or as a society, forced separation and the stigmatizing that results. It is ethically and practically inconsistent to continue separating children with special needs from other children in our schools.

POSITION 2: SPECIAL PROGRAMS HELP SPECIAL STUDENTS

I have heard stories from high school friends of mine who used to go to regular schools about what it was like to be "mainstreamed." They didn't get all the attention they needed, which is why they made a change and came to my school."

—Charlotte Farber, in Buchman, 2006, p. 194

General-education teachers are the primary caregivers in these full-inclusion classrooms, but their load and the classroom responsibilities have already increased with the additional number of classified special education students, not to mention the additional crowding in already crowded regular-education classrooms!

—Callard-Szulgit, 2005, p. xii

A central point of the Individuals with Disabilities Education Act (IDEA) is that "to the maximum extent appropriate," disabled children will be educated with those who are not. Claims that this requires schools to place all disabled children in regular classrooms are faulty. Full inclusion advocates ignore the significance of the term *maximum extent appropriate* in the law.

For many disabled children, placement into regular classrooms is a physical, mental, and emotional challenge that should not be mandated, and is not "appropriate." Inclusion as an idea can mislead regular teachers into inappropriate treatment of special students in their classes. Special needs of individual students come in many varieties and regular teachers are often unprepared for all of them. Teacher actions may be well-intentioned but inappropriate. School conditions may also be inappropriate.

Academic requirements of the No Child Left Behind Act, overcrowding, district curricular or testing requirements, and financing problems cause schools and teachers to standardize classroom work and limit individualization (Kabzems, 2003; Taylor, 2003; Koenig and Bachman, 2004). That is detrimental to students with special needs. Inclusion may not be the best choice for all (Cromwell, 2004). But full inclusion advocates seem to ignore significant distinctions among children and the pressures on teachers and schools. With misdiagnosis and inappropriate treatment, inadequate preparation of regular teachers, and the increasing standardization in regular classes, full inclusion means that special children are not treated specially (Kauffman, 2002; Buchman, 2006).

Disabled youngsters have a particularly difficult situation, one that requires special treatment by special people. There was a time when disabled children were considered less than human, and were sacrificed, shunned, ignored, and institutionalized. Thankfully, that bleak period passed long ago. In the United States, recognition of the special educational and emotional needs of disabled children is one of our finest traditions over the last half-century. These children need more than what we provide in regular classrooms; they deserve special care. That special care does not include poor-quality education, improperly prepared teachers, misdiagnosis of disabilities, prejudiced classmates and school staff, unsuitable curriculums, or dumping in regular classrooms to satisfy the unthoughtful do-gooders. We need only read the papers and reports to recognize regular schools leave much to be desired in the education of regular students; how can they be expected to educate special students?

Humane and thinking people would not require a truly disabled child to undergo even more traumatic experiences to satisfy a stark, inflexible, and ill-informed interpretation of a law. But that is the apparent position of those who press for full inclusion of children into standard classroom settings. Certainly, for some mildly disabled children, placement in regular classes, along with specially trained teachers, special programs, and appropriate instruction and standards, will help and should be provided. Inflexible interpretation of laws adds further to potential damages to children and to schools.

For Careful Inclusion of Individuals

Full inclusion is not necessary in schools. Thoughtfully involving certain children with special needs in regular school classes and activities, on an individual basis and in suitable situations, offers benefits to schools and to children. Careful inclusion of many students, offered by a well-prepared school district to parents of children whose academic work is likely to be enhanced and whose behavior is not likely to disrupt the education of others, is a positive step. But careful inclusion is not full inclusion. Some describe the difference as "hard versus soft" inclusion, the radical universalists versus the moderates (Low, 2007).

Obviously, we already have careful inclusion in many good schools. Expert diagnosis, classification, parental involvement, individually developed special education programs, close evaluation of progress, and, for some, graduated access to regular classes have provided inclusion for individual students in many schools. These schools provide disabled children and their families with excellent resources, fine-tuned to the child's specific needs and carefully crafted to support the child's development. A focus on the child's highly individual needs and development is fundamental to this process.

Fads and schools go hand in hand. The best place to find the newest fads in young people's language, music, dress, and manners is in schools. Not only are fads in popular culture highly noticeable, but schools are the birthplace of many other types of fads, often as a response to calls for school or social reform. Unfortunately, many of these educational fads are poorly thought out and counterproductive.

Full inclusion appears to be one of the latest examples of education's susceptibility to fads and slogans. The damage that full inclusion policies and practices may create for the very children they claim to help can be significant. Full inclusion carries negative implications for schools, teachers, parents, children, and the community. Worse, the "pro-inclusionists" hide the inherent defects of inclusion behind noble-sounding slogans; they label opponents who speak against full inclusion as insensitive, inhumane, or undemocratic (Petch-Hogan and Haggard, 1999; Cromwell, 2004).

The mainstreaming movement, which thrust many disabled children into regular classrooms without adequate preparation for them and their new teachers, and with excessive expectations, elicited the same type of defensive rhetoric. Reasonable people who argued against large-scale mainstreaming have been chastised, pilloried, or ignored. Full inclusion has become another politically correct view, even though it would damage effective special assistance programs our schools have spent years to develop and improve. As many experts (Kauffman and Hallahan, 1995; Kauffman, 2002) suggest, full inclusion is an illusion because general classrooms and schools will never be capable of meeting the needs of all special or exceptional students. These children require separate assistance and facilities to meet their needs. Children with special needs suffer most from full inclusion. Kennedy and Fisher (2001) point out that "After almost 20 years of specific federal support through the Individuals with Disabilities Education Act (IDEA) of 1990, Public Law 101–476, [and other legislation], fewer than half of the students who receive special education services graduate with a diploma."

Regular classrooms and schools are designed to have nearly all students complete a diploma; they are not appropriate places to have the necessary interest, capabilities, and support for the special needs child. It will not be long before the early blush of full inclusion wears off for those teachers, students, and school staff—leaving the special needs child and family without proper attention and education. This is the fallout from the uncritical rush toward full inclusion.

Typical special education programs provide specially trained teachers and paraprofessionals, smaller class sizes, adjusted curricula, and fairer competition. Such programs allow parents and teachers to jointly fashion an individualized program that maximizes the child's strengths and remediates areas of need. They are also able to access experts outside the school to assist children with special needs in preparing for the transition from school to work life.

Full Inclusion and Common Classroom Limits

Full inclusion limits regular classroom teachers by requiring them to allot extra time, materials, and energy to children who need extra support, as well as requiring them to prepare and monitor individual education plans for each of these children. Full inclusion also limits nondisabled children by diverting time and energy from teachers to meet the special needs of a few students and by sometimes disrupting their schoolwork when the behaviors of a child with special needs are inappropriate in a general classroom. Finally, full inclusion limits the school's ability to make educational decisions in the best interests of individual students. Full inclusion is a form of social engineering that cannot fulfill what it promises without serious repercussions for children and schools. Disruption and discipline problems can occur when some disabled students are mainstreamed or fully included in regular classes.

A study by the General Accounting Office ("Student Discipline: Individuals with Disabilities Act," 2001), noted that 81 percent of public middle and high schools surveyed responded that they had one or more incidents of "serious misconduct" during 1999–2000. Further, when the study accounted for the relatively small numbers of specially classified students in schools, the rate of serious misconduct for special education students in regular schooling was over three times as high as for regular students (15 per 1,000 regular students, and 50 per 1,000 of special students). Misconduct, of course, can be by regular or special students, but a situation of taunting or disrespect against the special student in regular classes offers good reason for a special student's misbehavior. Such situations are not always controllable by teachers and school staff, and clearly do not provide the proper setting and special treatment special young-sters deserve.

In addition, one in five principals reported that protective disciplinary procedures required for special students under the IDEA regulations are "bur-densome and time-consuming." Many students with behavioral problems are mistakenly classified as special for a number of reasons, including the addi-tional school income from state and federal sources. As Navarrette (2002) indi-cates, "Thus the mischievous and the misdiagnosed are mixed with those who really need special education, those with mental retardation and other disabili-ties." Full inclusion needs full examination before implementation.

Full Inclusion and School Reality

Theoretically, inclusion could provide all the good things special education now provides—special teachers, individualization, more self-esteem, but with the added benefit of allowing exceptional children to participate fully in the school program. Long-term experience with school reforms suggests that any imme-diate, positive effects of inclusion are likely to be overcome by long-standing conformist standardization, bureaucracy, and funding requirements that make most schools dull and ineffective even for many regular students. The special needs child will be overlooked in these schools.

The focus will shift from giving special attention to individual children's strengths and disabilities toward conforming to group standards imposed by federal or state officials, meeting community expectations in test scores, or fac-ing other accountability measures of group success. Large class size will make it difficult for regular teachers to provide special assistance to exceptional chil-dren. Schools will not be able to fully control other students' disparaging or hurtful comments, and exceptional children again will suffer. School funds will decrease to a common standard, without special funds for special children. Exceptional students require exceptional effort, but schools will be stretched and unable to provide it (Noonan, 2008).

In addition, advocates of full inclusion are wrong when they argue that interaction with regular students in a regular program will benefit those who are disabled. A sorry history of taunting, labeling, ridicule, and exclusion by regular students is not likely to disappear because of some legislated program of interaction. There is no evidence that nondisabled children will suddenly develop appropriate classroom behavior when full inclusion takes place. Lec-tures and admonitions by school officials, no matter how well-intentioned, are not likely to make a dent in the problem. Even if the majority of children are well behaved and nonprejudiced, it takes only a few to spoil the school setting for children with disabilities who already have been subjected to frequent stares and slights. School is tough enough for many regular students who happen to be different from the group. Life in many schools is not pleasant for children from poor families, children who stutter, are noticeably shorter or taller or more plump, are slower in speed or intellect, are from certain cultural backgrounds, or are not as gregarious or athletic or pretty as others. School subcultures create cauldrons of despair for many students who are not accepted because of minor differences (Palonsky, 1975); consider the problem those with significant disabilities would face in regular schools. Buchman (2007) describes the benefits of a special education for her daughter; her daughter agrees and wishes all children with learning disabilities could have that special treatment (Farber, 2007).

Laudable But Unrealistic Goals

The goal of inclusion may be laudable under some conditions and for some individuals. However, full inclusion for all students represents an ideal that does not mesh with day-to-day reality for large numbers of students. Many children now are participating successfully in effective special education classes and schools. Zigler and Hall (1986) noted a problem regarding excesses in the 1980s mainstreaming movement. This movement was based on the "normalization" principle, an idea that we should provide more "normal" school settings to socialize disabled children:

> Ironically, the very law that was designed to safeguard the options of handicapped children and their parents (the 1975 Education for all Handicapped Children Act) may, in the end, act to constrict their choices and result in disservice to the very children the legislators sought to help, by forcing schools to place them in programs that are not equipped to meet their needs. The normalization principle and the practice of mainstreaming may have deleterious effects on some children by denying them their right to be different. . . . Underlying the very idea of normalization is a push toward homogeneity, which is unfair to those children whose special needs may come to be viewed as unacceptable. (p. 2)

Full inclusion goes well beyond mainstreaming (Ryndak and Alper, 2003). As a result, it runs even greater risks of homogenizing our educational approach and causing a decline in special care and attention for children with exceptional needs. The political support for special programs and funds, support that took years to develop, will atrophy. Special education budgets will diminish. School administrators, with declining special education budgets, will be unlikely to champion the needs of this small and expensive proportion of their student populations. Regular class teachers, already overworked in large classes, will be unable to extend themselves even further for children who need more individualized help. Parents of nondisabled children may be sympathetic, but are unlikely to support the diversion of general education funds, resources, and teacher time from the education of their own children.

McKleskey and Waldron (2000) may advocate inclusive education, but they point out that studies have shown regular school staff continue to hold several unfortunate assumptions that undermine inclusion practices in schools. These include the significant assumption that "inclusion" students should still be perceived as "irregular" even when they are in regular classes, and the assumption that inclusion students require specialized material and support that "could not be provided by the classroom teacher," depending instead on a special educator (p. 70). These assumptions are understandable, but they portend major problems in large-scale inclusion practices in school districts.

We want as many disabled children as possible to be self-reliant, equipped for successful and productive lives, participate constructively in the larger society, and develop feelings of personal worth. We want no less for any child, but the child who is disabled needs special attention and support to reach these goals. One of the primary purposes of special education programs is to provide the setting and individualized attention these children need to develop self-reliance, success, productivity, and feelings of personal worth. These programs are jeopardized by the steamroller tactics of the full inclusionists.

Well-Deserved Special Treatment

It is easy to fling out high-sounding phrases about full inclusion and democracy, but more difficult to critically examine potential consequences of a major change in the way we treat exceptional children in our schools. Inclusion of special needs children into regular schools and classes is an educational policy needing critical assessment. Waving the flag of democracy may stir the faddists in education, but will not hide the serious problems inherent in full inclusion.

Over history, children with disabilities have suffered; they have been reviled, ostracized, ridiculed, ignored, and destroyed. Some became members of circuses; some were hidden by their families; others were placed in ill-funded and ill-supervised institutions with no chance for improvement. The families of disabled children also suffered social maligning. And society lost the contributions it could have had from the many talents of people with disabilities.

Fortunately, society has made dramatic changes in the way it views the disabled. We now recognize that the special needs of these children require special treatment. Exceptional children can find success and develop on their own terms in school and life. Special programs offer a ray of hope to children who were ostracized and ignored in the past. Many special education schools and programs have been successful in preparing students to contribute to society.

Extra funding for special education provides more individualistic education, better-prepared teachers, more appropriate teaching materials, superior facilities, and a setting better organized to help these children. Full inclusion could be used to control school budgets by decreasing current special funding for special education and gifted and talented programs. Of course, it is cheaper to educate children with special needs in regular classes, an unwise and, in the long run, economically foolish move. The actual proportion of exceptional children is very small, in the range of 5 percent nationally. That small number deserves special financing, special treatment, special teachers, and special programs to ensure they will become productive members of society, with the necessary self-respect.

Special education and exceptional programs offer important benefits to the child: a low student-teacher ratio for increased individualized instruction and attention; teachers especially trained to educate and develop the skills of exceptional students; experts organized into study teams to provide diagnosis, treatment, and evaluation of student development; homogeneous grouping to permit the teacher to concentrate on common needs and characteristics; more opportunity for student success among peers and more realistic competition in academics and/or athletics; funds for facilities, special equipment, and specially designed student learning materials; and increased student self-esteem from individual attention and by limiting negative interaction with nondisabled students. In addition, special education programs offer opportunity for remedial education that could return mildly disabled children to the regular program. These benefits continue to accrue to special education programs; they will be reduced with the advent of inclusion. Regular schools are unprepared to offer them in addition to their usual efforts, and initial extra funding will dry up or be absorbed into the ongoing operation of the schools.

Treating Other Exceptional Children: The Gifted

Presumably, full inclusion would require schools to eliminate separate, special programs, forcing all exceptional students into regular classes in regular schools. Deviation from this would occur when parents and school agree that a child cannot be educated in a regular class. But special school programs for exceptional children come in many varieties. Among them are programs for gifted and talented children, honors programs, and tracking.

Gifted and talented programs, for example, often are separately organized, taught, and evaluated. As Clark (1996) notes in a comprehensive analysis of such programs: "Gifted and talented students have more complex needs than average and below average learners . . . if these needs are not met we now know that ability cannot be maintained; indeed, brain research tells us that ability will be lost. . . . When no programs are available to this group of learners a disservice is done, not only to these students but to all of society, as our finest minds not only lack nurture, they are wasted" (p. 60). This is special education also; should these students be fully included in regular classes and activities to meet the law as seen by inclusionists?

Political realities surround efforts to end special programs for gifted, honors, or high-achieving students. These programs usually include children from the more powerful families in a community, demonstrate how special treatment makes a difference in student achievement, and enhance the school's academic reputation. Under full inclusion, gifted and talented children would be moved back into regular classes. Similarly, honors and remedial classes and tracking would be doomed. One-size-fits-all schooling, as full inclusion ideology proposes, is a prescription for mediocrity.

Classification and Myths

Many myths exist about the classification of children into separate special education programs. One myth is that classified students are unhappy or ill served by programs and they drop out. In fact, the national dropout rate for all students over age 14 is about 50 percent, but for students with disabilities the rate is only about 4 percent (Carlson and Parshall, 1996; Heckman and LaFontaine, 2008). Another myth is that classification into special education is a one-way street, that those selected for special education never return to the regular program. In fact, the declassification rate of special education students is higher than their dropout rate, running from about 4 to 9 percent annually (Carlson and Parshall, 1996). A third, and most deleterious myth, is that classified children who are placed into separate special education programs are not challenged and are never able to make the school, social, and behavioral adjustments needed to fit into regular school or society. A significant study by Carlson and Parshall (1996) analyzed data about the approximately 7 percent of special education students who were declassified annually and placed into regular classes in Michigan over a five-year period. This study revealed two important arguments against a one-size-fits-all full inclusion program:

1. Special education programs work, and students can achieve successful declassification; the vast majority of declassified children were well adjusted in academic, social, and behavioral categories.
2. There is a continuing need for special attention for a minority of declassified children; about 11 percent of the declassified students needed extra care, and about 4 percent returned to special education classes.

On the one hand, it is remarkable that a sizable proportion of students in special education programs are able to join regular classes and be successful in terms of school, social, and behavioral criteria. On the other hand, the very small proportion of those who still need special care suggests we should keep separate programs available for those who, for whatever reasons, are better served in classified programs or are unable to make necessary adjustments to the regular school. Carlson and Parshall's study noted the poorest results from declassification efforts occurred for students with emotional impairments. For those whose declassification was successful, Carlson and Parshall state: "Presumably, without special education services, these students would not have done as well in school as they did" (p. 98).

Slogans and Myths: Equal Education

There are many slogans in our society: save the whales, do your duty, and keep a stiff upper lip. Each of these ideas is significantly more complicated than putting a bumper sticker on a car, boycotting, or voting. Unfortunately, the simplicity and moral righteousness of such slogans can be deceptive. Life's problems are complex; slogans ignore the complexity and offer a tantalizingly singular answer. Simplistic answers may make problems worse. Making education a cornerstone of democracy is an excellent idea, but to make it work requires more than unsubstantiated claims and moral posturing (Meier, 2005).

Free and open education, equally available to all with no differences in treatment or result, is an interesting utopian idea so far from reality it is painful. Yet this basic concept underlies the current interest in inclusion. We don't yet have free and equal education, equal treatment, or equal results for the wide variety of students who attend "regular" public schools. It is unrealistic to believe students shifted to meet inclusion goals actually will obtain equal access, treatment, or results. The "regular" classroom is a figment of ideological imagination; schools do not offer equality now.

Currently, even outside of separate special education classes, access to education differs along several dimensions. Tracking or ability-grouping students based on how they score on tests and how teachers evaluate them separates students for most of their school careers (Oakes, 1985, 2005; Urban and Waggoner, 1996; Spring, 1998; Meier, 2005). Schools in different communities offer differing advantages to their students as a result of funding differences citizens vote on (Kozol, 1991). High school athletes are more costly to a school district than humanities students, and only the best athletes are selected for team membership. Good readers are placed in one group and poor readers in another in elementary school classes. Not all students are admitted to college preparatory or honors classes. Advanced woodshop is limited to select students, as are advanced Latin and chemistry. Students who misbehave and disrupt others are separated in schools, and may be denied access by suspension or expulsion. Special education costs are about 2.3 times the cost of regular classrooms, most of which is covered outside of district funds. This funding, even with recent sizable increases in numbers of students classified as special, remains a relatively small proportion of school expenditures (Moe, 2002).

Where students live is related to how well they will do in school and in gaining access to further education; higher-income communities have schools where students obtain higher standardized test scores and higher rates of college admission. Female students have less access to higher-level math and science classes than males. Generally, minority students have less access to highly ranked colleges than majority students. When viewed on the basis of equality, these circumstances may not be ideal or even always supportable, but are the reality of schooling. Democracy does not require exact equality of condition. The economic ideas behind capitalism, which have made this nation so successful, are inconsistent with mandated egalitarianism; capitalism requires we reward competition and entrepreneurship.

On the Fairness of Life

Life, as we know, is unfair. We see unfairness in human relations of all kinds, including those in schools. We can't fix all unfairness, but need to limit inappropriate discrimination and prejudice. Discrimination is inappropriate if based on criteria that are illogical, unethical, or lack a scientific basis. Discrimination is appropriate if it means separating existing individual differences to treat, protect, or nurture them. We discriminate among people by granting academic awards, among people with certain illnesses by treating them and protecting the society, and among animals by determining which are endangered and therefore deserving special treatment. Prejudice means that we "prejudge" without knowledge; but making a judgment based on an understanding of available information is not prejudice. It is prejudice to claim, before ever tasting it, that broccoli tastes bad—but not to make the statement after tasting. Throughout life, we make judgments. Some may turn out to be wrong, but we can only try to use the best, most complete available information and reasoning to inform a judgment.

Fairness sometimes may mean providing different strokes for different folks if the criteria are sensible and consistent with social goals and individual interests. Putting all students into advanced Latin or into woodshop does not make sense; keeping disruptive or violent children in regular classes regardless of their behavior does not make sense; admitting all students to any college they desire does not make sense. We use criteria to limit those who can drive cars, handle food, practice medicine, cut and style hair, be convicted of a crime, or run for president. These limits are unfair only if they are abused, prejudicially applied, or not sensible.

One of the interesting ironies of the effort to establish full inclusion of exceptional children into regular schools is that many of its strongest advocates come from the special education network, and they do not want, themselves, to be integrated into "regular" departments or schools of teacher education. Surveys of leaders of schools of education across the United States in 1989 and 1994 found that almost three-fourths believed special education is best served by separating teacher education into general education and special education departments (Heller, 1996). One of the most frequent reasons given for the desirability of separation is the need to "identify with persons of equal interest, expertise, and common purpose" (p. 258). Another major reason was the increased status of or attention paid to special educators as a result of separation. Special education specialists do not want to be fully included in higher education for good reasons. Separate special education programs in the schools, when constructed properly, offer the same advantages to children with different needs.

Affirmative action programs, when they use quota systems and remove merit considerations, have engendered strong criticism from all parts of the political spectrum. They are defended now mainly by a hard core of disciples. The main purpose of affirmative action, to assure equal opportunity under the Constitution, has been subverted by legislative zealotry and bureaucratic manipulation. Reasonable people from all sides decry prejudice, bias, hate crimes, and discrimination based on stereotypes—but they do not want government to mandate actions on matters best left to individual choice. That is a difficult line to draw, but it is important to do so in a democracy.

Legislation, Courts, and Problems Caused by Full Inclusion

Full inclusion of children with disabilities into regular classes runs some of the same risks of arousing overzealous legislation and activist court interpretation. Legislated mainstreaming has created significant problems—for schools, teachers, communities, and for both disabled and nondisabled children. Court interpretations of laws threaten to leave mainstreaming in another social engineering predicament akin to those of affirmative action. Extending mainstreaming to full inclusion promises to cause even more complicated problems and more bureaucratic, bungling answers. A court case, *Oberti v. Board of Education of Clementon (NJ) School District* (1993), illustrates problems associated with mainstreaming, the laws governing it, and court interpretations.

The case involves an eight-year-old Down's syndrome child with impaired intellectual functioning and ability to communicate. The school district, after testing and review by specialists, determined his educational interests would best be served by placing him in a developmental kindergarten class in the morning to observe and socialize with peer children, but his academic work would be done in a separate special class in the afternoon. During the morning class, the child exhibited serious behavioral problems, including repeated toilet accidents, temper tantrums, crawling and hiding under furniture, and hitting and spitting on other children. Also, the child repeatedly hit the teacher and teacher's aide.

Obviously, he was disruptive and the frustrated teacher sought help from the district Child Study Team. The Individual Education Plan required under the IDEA law and used for the original placement did not cover ways to handle his behavioral problems. Interestingly, the child did not exhibit disruptive behavior in the separate afternoon special education class. After study, the district wanted to place the child in a completely separate program, but the parents refused. After a hearing, there was an agreement that he would be placed in a separate program for one year. In that year, his behavior improved and he made academic progress. When the parents found, however, that the district did not plan to place him back into "regular" classes the following year, they objected and another hearing occurred before an administrative law judge. The judge agreed with the district that the separate special education class was the "least restrictive environment" under the IDEA law, the child's misbehavior in the developmental kindergarten class was extensive, and there was no meaningful educational benefit from that class. Unsatisfied, the parents went to court, getting an expert witness professor from Wisconsin who claimed the child could be in regular classes, provided there were supplementary aids and special support, such as:

1. Modifying the existing regular curriculum for this student;
2. Modifying this child's program to provide for meeting a different set of criteria for performance;
3. Using "parallel" instruction—the child would be in the classroom, but would have separate activities; and
4. Removing the child for instruction in certain special areas.

The district's expert witness claimed the child could not benefit from placement in a regular class, his behavior could not be managed, the teacher could not communicate with him because of his communication problems, and the curriculum could not be modified enough to meet this child's needs without compromising its integrity. Other witnesses, including people who had worked with the child in other public school and Catholic school settings, testified that he had very disruptive behavior, including hitting, throwing things, and running away.

This judge, citing the IDEA law, held that the district had the burden of proof and they had failed to meet the law's requirement for mainstreaming (*Oberti v. Board of Education*, 1993).

This case suggests a series of problems for schools, parents, communities, and children under full inclusion. The court directed that a disruptive and misbehaving child is to attend regular classes, where his actions are likely to be detrimental to other students' academic work and to the teacher's ongoing work. The disabled child's schoolwork, apparently satisfactory in separate special education classes, suffered significantly in the regular placement, even on a part-time basis; yet under the court's order, he now would be in regular classes full time. The child's parents may feel better that their child is in regular classes, but how will he progress? Parents of the nondisabled children do not have the same right to refuse placement, require formal hearings on details they don't like, or protest in court when their children are subjected to a significantly modified curriculum or class disruption. School rules established for all children to provide order and safety are placed in jeopardy by a court order that makes the school ultrasensitive to the parents of a single student.

A number of classroom issues are raised by the suggestion of the expert witness from Wisconsin to mainstream with supplementary activities and support. Teachers work hard on a school curriculum and finding ways to teach it; how are they to modify that curriculum adequately for one severely disabled student without compromising the integrity of the curriculum as a whole? Is it equal and fair treatment if the teacher gives very special treatment to one disabled child, designing different activities and individual levels of performance, but does not do so for each of the other children? If the special needs child has "parallel" instruction provided in class and is removed from the class for certain special instruction, how does that differ in substance from a separate special education program? Although the child is in a regular class, he is to be separated for much of his work, and he may even become more of a target for other children because of his differential treatment.

Excessive mainstreaming caught schools unprepared, frustrated good teachers, diminished special services provided to individual children, and created confusion in schools. Well-prepared schools, specially trained teachers, clear guidelines for diagnosis and education, smaller classes, special materials to enhance learning, and a setting conducive to the best education now exist in many places: special education and gifted and talented programs offer these advantages. Full inclusion would overturn these in favor of a mandate for standardization and chaos beyond what occurred in excessive mainstreaming programs.

Schools vary significantly: It is impossible to define a "regular" school or classroom. Is a one-room school in rural Nevada "regular"? What about an urban school in Manhattan, or a suburban school in Beverly Hills? Schools have some common patterns, but much schooling occurs with separate groups of students. The Bronx High School of Science, vocational-technical high schools, tracking programs, honors programs, remedial courses, basic and advanced courses, reading groups, and selection for music and athletic programs illustrate the common practice of educating certain students separately for particular reasons. Full inclusion threatens these efforts to provide the best individual education for different students.

For Discussion

1. Dialectic exercise: Identify the best arguments for and against full inclusion. Do they provide a thesis and antithesis? Analyze the evidence presented for each. What kinds of research would be needed to provide that evidence? Where would you go to find that kind of research? What research is currently available on these matters? What is your current view and what would be the most convincing evidence for you to change your mind on full inclusion? Is there a synthesis for this argument that serves social policy, educational interests, and individual students and parents?

2. Discussion: How should the movement toward full inclusion influence teacher education programs? What would you propose for teacher preparation in this area? What should teachers know about and be able to do for special students included in general classrooms?

3. Data from the U.S. Department of Education show the annual growth rate in children ages 3 to 21 who receive special education (over 3 percent) continues to exceed the annual growth rate in the general population between ages 3 and 21 (about 1 percent). The proportion of children evaluated as gifted and talented is about 3 percent of the student population. What reasons would explain an increase in proportion of children needing special education? What difference should this annual increase mean for school decisions on full inclusion? To critically examine this topic, what evidence would you need, and where would you expect to find that evidence?

4. How should gifted and talented programs be treated in terms of full inclusion policies? Should they be abolished, separated, enhanced, diminshed, or . . . ? On what grounds do you argue? Who should decide and on what criteria? Are separate programs appropriate in public schools in a democracy? How is this issue similar to and different from treatment of special education students under IDEA law?

References

ANDERSON, G. R., AND ANDERSON, S. K. (1983). "The Exceptional Native American," in *The Politics of Special Education,* ed. L. Barton. London: Falmer Press.

ARTILES, A. J., AND BAL, A. (2008). "The Next Generation of Disproportionality Research," *Journal of Special Education.* 42(1), 4–14 May.

BARTON, L. (1988). *The Politics of Special Education Needs.* London: Falmer Press.

BATES, P., ET AL. (1984). "The Effect of Functional vs. Nonfunctional Activities on Attitude/ Expectations of Non-handicapped College Students: What They See Is What We Get." *The Journal of the Association for Persons with Severe Handicaps* 9:73–78.

BRANTLINGER, E. A., AND GUSKIN, S. L. (1987). "Ethnocultural and Social Psychological Effects on Learning Characteristics of Handicapped Children," in *Handbook of Special Education,* Vol. 1, ed. M. C. Wang et al. Oxford: Pergamon.

Brown v. Board of Education of Topeka, Kansas. (1954). 347 U.S. 483.

BUCHMAN, D. (2006). *A Special Education.* Cambridge, MA: DeCapo Press.

BURRELLO, L. C., ET AL. (2001). *Educating All Students Together.* Thousand Oaks, CA: Corwin Press.

CALLARD-SZULGIT, R. (2005). Teaching the Gifted in an Inclusive Classroom. Lanham, MD: Scarecrow Press.

CAMERON, L. (2008). "The Maine Effect or How I Finally Embraced the Social Model of Disability," *Intellectual and Developmental Disabilities* 46(1) 54–57. Feb.

CARLBERG, C., AND KAVALE, K. (1980). "The Efficacy of Special Versus Regular Class Placement for Exceptional Children: A Meta-Analysis." *Journal of Special Education* 14:295–309.

CARLSON, E., AND PARSHALL, L. (1996). "Academic, Social, and Behavioral Adjustment for Students Declassified from Special Education." *Exceptional Education* 63(1):89–100.

CIGMAN, R. ed., (2007). *Included or Excluded?* New York: Routledge.

CLARK, B. (1996). "The Need for a Range of Program Options for Gifted and Talented Students," in *Controversial Issues Confronting Special Education,* 2nd Ed, ed. W. and S. Stainback. Boston: Allyn and Bacon.

COOLEY, S. M., ET AL., (2008). "A Field at Risk: The Teacher Shortage in Special Education." *Kappan* 89(8), 597–600. April.

CROMWELL, S. (2004). "Inclusion: Has It Gone Too Far?" *Education World. www.education-world.com.*

CUSHNER, K., MCCLELLAND, A., AND SAFFORD, P. (2000). *Human Diversity in Education.* 3rd Ed. New York: McGraw-Hill.

DICKMAN, I. (1985). *One Miracle at a Time.* New York: Simon and Schuster.

EDUCATION WEEK ON THE WEB. (1998). "Inclusion." Washington, DC: Editorial Projects in Education. www.edweek.org.

EDUCATIONAL TESTING SERVICE. (1980). "New Vistas in Special Education." *Focus* 8:1–20.

EIDE, B. AND EIDE, F. (2006). The Mislabeled Child. New York: Hyperion.

FARBER, C. (2006). "Afterword." In Buchman, D. (2006). *A Special Education.* Cambridge, MA:DeCapo Press.

FERRI, B. J., AND CONNOR, D. J. (2005). "Tools of Exclusion: Race, Disability, and (Re)segregated Education." *Teachers College Record* 107(3):453–474.

GORE, M. C. (2004). *Successful Inclusion Strategies for Secondary and Middle School Teachers.* Thousand Oaks, CA: Corwin.

GROSSMAN, H. (1998). *Ending Discrimination in Special Education.* Springfield, IL: Charles C Thomas.

HARRY, B. AND KLINGNER, J. (2006). *Why Are so Many Minority Students in Special Education?* New York: Teachers College Press.

————, ET AL., (2008). "Schooling and the Construction of Identity Among Minority Students in Spain and the United States," *Journal of Special Education* 42(1) 15–25. May.

HECKMAN, J. J. AND LAFONTAINE, P. A. (2008). "The Declining American High School Graduation Rate," *National Bureau of Economic Research Report.* www.nber.org.

HELLER, H. W. (1996). "A Rationale for Departmentalization of Special Education," in *Controversial Issues Confronting Special Education,* 2nd Ed, ed. W. and S. Stainback. Boston: Allyn and Bacon.

HELLER, K. A., HOLTZMAN, W. H., AND MESSICK, S., eds. (1982). *Placing Children in Special Education: A Strategy for Equity.* Washington, DC: National Academy of Sciences Press.

HUXLEY, T. (1897). *Evolution and Ethics, and Other Essays.* New York: D. Appleton.

Inclusive Education. (2008). www.inclusive-international.org. June.

KABZEMS, V. (2003). "Labeling in the Name of Equality." Chapter in Devliger, P., et al., *Rethinking Disability.* Philadelphia: Garant.

KAUFFMAN, J., AND HALLAHAN, D., eds. (1995). *The Illusion of Full Inclusion.* Austin, TX: Pro-Ed.

KAUFFMAN, J., ET AL., (2002). "Separate and Better." Exceptionality 10(3) 149–170.

KENNEDY, C. H., AND FISHER, D. (2001). *Inclusive Middle Schools.* Baltimore: Paul H. Brookes.

KLEINFIELD, S. (1979). *The Hidden Minority: America's Handicapped.* Boston: Little, Brown.

KLUTH, P., et al. (2001). "'Our School Doesn't Offer Inclusion' and Other Legal Blunders." *Educational Leadership* 50(4):24–27.

KOENIG, J. A., AND BACHMAN, L. F., eds. (2004). *Keeping Score for All.* Washington, DC: National Academies Press.

KOZOL, J. (1991). *Savage Inequalities.* New York: Crown Publishers.

LIPSKY, D. K., AND GARTNER, A. (1996). "Inclusion, School Restructuring, and the Remaking of American Society." *Harvard Education Review* 66(4):762–796.

LOMBARDI, T. P. (1994). *Responsible Inclusion of Students with Disabilities: Fastback 373.* Bloomington, IN: Phi Delta Kappa Educational Foundation.

LOMBARDI, T. P., AND LUDLOW, B. L. (1996). *Trends Shaping the Future of Special Education.* Bloomington, IN: Phi Delta Kappa Educational Foundation.

LOW, C. (2007). "A Defense of Moderate Inclusion and the End of Ideology," in Cigman, R. ed., (2007). *Included or Excluded?* New York: Routledge.

MCKLESKEY, J., AND WALDRON, N. (2000). *Inclusive Schools in Action.* Alexandria, VA: ASCD.

MEIER, K. J. (2005) "School Boards and the Politics of Education Policy." Chapter in Wolbrecht, C., and Hero, R. E., *Politics of Democratic Inclusion.* Philadelphia. PA: Temple University Press.

MEISEL, C. J., ed. (1986). *Mainstreaming Handicapped Children.* Hillsdale, NJ: Lawrence Erlbaum.

MERRITT, S. (2001). "Clearing the Hurdles of Inclusion." *Educational Leadership* 59(3):67–70.

Mills v. Board of Education of the District of Columbia. (1972). 348 F. Supp. 866.

MITTLER, P., BROUILLETTE, R., AND HARRIS D., eds. (1993). *Special Needs Education: World Yearbook of Education.* London: Kogan Page.

MOE, T. M. (2002). *A Primer on America's Schools.* Stanford, CA: Hoover Institution Press.

NAVARRETTE, R. "The Special Ed Dumping Ground," *San Diego Union-Tribune,* April 17, 2002.

NOONAN, M. A. (2008). "When Special Education as We Know it Ends—What, if Anything Will Replace It?" *Educational Horizons* 86(3) 139–141. Spring.

OAKES, J. (1985). *Keeping Track: How Schools Structure Inequality.* New Haven, CT: Yale University Press.

———. (2005). *Keeping Track: How Schools Structure Inequality.* 2nd Ed. New Haven, CT: Yale University Press.

Oberti v. Board of Education of the Borough of Clementon (NJ) School District. (1993). 995 f.2d 1204 (3rd Cir. 1993).

PALONSKY, S. (1975). "Hempies and Squeaks, Truckers and Cruisers: A Participant-Observer Investigation in a City High School." *Educational Administration Quarterly* 2:86–103.

PETCH-HOGAN, B., AND HAGGARD, D. (1999). "The Inclusion Debate Continues." *Educational Forum* 35(3):128–140.

RICHEY, D., AND WHEELER, J. (2000). *Inclusive Early Childhood Education.* Albany, NY: Delmar.

RISKO, V., AND BROMLEY, K. (2001). *Collaboration for Diverse Learners.* Newark, DE: International Reading Association.

ROGERS, J. (1993). "The Inclusion Revolution." *Phi Delta Kappa Research Bulletin* 11:1–6.

RYNDAK, D. L., AND ALPER, S., eds. (2003). *Curriculum and Instruction for Students with Significant Disabilities in Inclusive Settings.* 2nd Ed., Boston: Allyn and Bacon.

SAILOR, W., GERRY. M., AND WILSON, W. C. (1991). "Policy Implications of Emergent Full Inclusion Models," in *Handbook of Special Education: Research and Practice,* Vol. 4., ed. M. C. Wang et al. Oxford: Pergamon.

SEFA DEI, G., ET AL. (2000). *Removing the Margins.* Toronto: Canadian Scholars' Press.

SEMMEL, M. I., GOTTLIEB, J., AND ROBINSON, N. M. (1979). "Mainstreaming." *Review of Research in Education* 7:223–279.

SKRTIC, T. M. (1995). *Disability and Democracy.* New York: Teachers College Press.

"THE SPECIAL EDUCATION FIASCO." (2001). *Wilson Quarterly,* Autumn. Review of W. F. Horn, and D. Tynan, "Revamping Special Education," in *The Public Interest,* Summer 2001.

SKIBA, R. J., ET AL., (2008). "Achieving Equity in Special Education." *Exceptional Children* 74(3) 264–288.

SPRING, J. (1998). *American Education.* 8th Ed. New York: McGraw-Hill.

STAINBACK, W., AND STAINBACK S. (1990). *Support Networks for Inclusive Schooling.* Baltimore, MD: Paul H. Brookes.

STAINBACK, S., STAINBACK, W., AND JACKSON, H. J. (1992). "Toward Inclusive Classrooms," in *Curriculum Considerations in Inclusive Classrooms,* ed. S. and W. Stainback. Baltimore, MD: Paul H. Brookes.

"STUDENT DISCIPLINE: INDIVIDUALS WITH DISABILITIES ACT." (2001). *Report to Committees on Appropriations: House and Senate.* Washington, DC: General Accounting Office.

TAYLOR, R. E. (2003). *Assessment of Exceptional Students.* 6th Ed. Boston: Allyn and Bacon.

THOUSAND, J. S., AND VILLA, R. A. (1995). "Managing Complex Change Toward Inclusive Schooling," in *Creating an Inclusive School,* ed. R. A. Villa and J. S. Thousand. Alexandria, VA: Association for Supervision and Curriculum Development.

TURNBULL, H. R., AND TURNBULL, A. P. (1998). *Free Appropriate Public Education: The Law and Children with Disabilities.* 5th Ed. Denver: Love Publishing.

UNESCO. (2008). "Inclusive Quality Education," Education for All. www.portal.unesco .org. Apr.

UNITED NATIONS CONVENTION ON THE RIGHTS OF THE CHILD. (1989). New York: United Nations.

URBAN, W., AND WAGGONER, J. (1996). *American Education: A History.* New York: McGraw-Hill.

VARGAS, S. R. L. (1999). "Democracy and Inclusion." *Maryland Law Review* 58(1):150–179.

WANG, M. C. (1990). "Learning Characteristics of Students with Special Needs," in *Special Education: Research and Practice,* ed. M. C. Wang et al. Oxford: Pergamon.

WANG, M. C., REYNOLDS, M. C., AND WALBERG, H., eds. (1990). *Special Education: Research and Practice.* Oxford: Pergamon.

———. (1991). *Handbook of Special Education: Research and Practice.* Oxford: Pergamon.

WEDELL, K. (1993). "Varieties of School Integration," in *Special Needs Education: World Yearbook of Education,* ed. P. Mittler et al. London: Kogan Page.

WINZER, M. A. (1993). *The History of Special Education: From Isolation to Integration.* Washington, DC: Gallaudet University Press.

WOLBRECHT, C., AND HERO, R. E. (2005). *The Politics of Democratic Inclusion.* Philadelphia: Temple University Press.

ZIGLER, E., AND HALL, N. (1986). "Mainstreaming and the Philosophy of Normalization," in *Mainstreaming Handicapped Children,* ed. C. J. Meisel. Hillsdale, NJ: Lawrence Erlbaum.

CHAPTER 19

Violence in Schools: School Treatable or Beyond School Control

Can schools deal effectively with violent or potentially violent students?

POSITION 1: SCHOOLS CAN AND SHOULD CURB VIOLENCE

I believe that school is primarily a social institution. Education being a social process, the school is simply that form of community life in which all of those agencies are concentrated that will be most effective in bringing the child to share in the inherited resources of the race, and to use his own powers for social ends. . . . I believe that education, therefore, is a process of living and not a preparation for future living.

—Dewey, 1897, "My Pedagogic Creed," Reprinted in Dworkin, 1959, p. 22

John Dewey helped define the relationship between Americans and their public schools. Schools are extensions of the community in this country, he argued. Schools share in the burden of caring for the community's children and for equipping them with skills and habits necessary to survive and succeed. Schools take the community's highest ideals and translate them into academic and social programs for all children. Everyone is responsible for the education of the community's children. As Dewey wrote, "What the best and wisest parent wants for his own child, that must the community want for all its children" (Dworkin, 1959, p. 54).

Dewey recognized social conditions constantly change and schools always have to adjust to new demands placed on communities. When social problems overwhelm community resources, schools are expected to lend strength and assistance. In a speech delivered in 1899, he said, "It is useless to bemoan the departure of the good old days of children's modesty, reverence, and implicit obedience, if we expect merely by bemoaning and by exhortation to bring them back. It is radical conditions which have changed, and only an equally radical change in education suffices" (Dworkin, 1959, p. 37).

In the late nineteenth century, the Industrial Revolution had upset the community's traditional structure and nature of work. Parents were working long hours, away from home, separated from their children. Many children also worked, at hard and often dangerous jobs. As a result, families had changed, and were not able to carry out the full range of their former functions. Schools were pressed to expand their role, to go beyond providing instruction in reading and arithmetic and help children adjust to the "radical conditions" of the day. Helping children adjust to the problems of a new industrial economy imposed a great burden on public education. Helping children understand and overcome the radical conditions of the twenty-first century may require even greater effort, but it is not a problem schools can shirk. The community's problems are always the school's problems. We are concerned with violence here, a social problem with a long history and many causes.

The Violent Community

Violence is among the most "radical conditions" now confronting the nation and its school-age children. Violence increasingly affects the daily lives of children, and violence-prevention and aggression-management programs have become part of the common curriculum in schools. Society has changed in the past decades, and students' lives are filled with problems never before the concern of schools.

In some ways school violence is a new American problem; in other ways, it is as old as the nation. American society is violent, and has been so for a long time. You may recall that Andrew Jackson shot and killed a man who made insulting comments about his wife, and Aaron Burr killed political rival Alexander Hamilton in a New Jersey gun duel. The United States was born of revolution. It has made heroes of gunfighters and warriors. Americans have witnessed assassinations of national figures, racial lynchings, and riots by organized labor, farmers, and students. Violence is said to be as American as apple pie (Alvarez and Bachman, 2008). Until the 1930s it was not possible to quantify the rate of violence, but since that time, the FBI's *Uniform Crime Reports* document a dramatic increase in violent crime, including murder, forcible rape, robbery, and aggravated assault over time. The U.S. murder rate is the highest in the industrialized world, and we remain a leader in school violence.

Violence and the Media

Violence currently presents unprecedented dangers to school-age children. U.S. films, music videos, and television are the most violent in the world. Messages about aggressive behavior enter the world of children no matter how hard families work to screen them out. These messages flow not only from children's direct experiences, but also from news reports, film, music, and advertising. War toys line store shelves; cartoon heroes destroy villains on television and in films; music videos play darkly on themes of anger and destruction; and computer games encourage interactive simulations of murder and mayhem. Many children suffer nightmares stemming from the violence in their lives (Jordan, 2002).

Television brings a steady volume of vicarious violence into living rooms. Over 97 percent of U.S. households have at least one television set, and young children watch about four hours of television daily. They likely watch passively—typically without adults present—acts of violence at unprecedented levels. The typical child in the United States views an estimated 8,000 murders and 100,000 acts of televised violence before the end of elementary school (Galezewski, 2005) and another 100,000 hours before the end of high school. Among other things, researchers have found that viewing portrayals of violence leads to aggressive behavior, and media violence is a significant correlate of real-world violence (Kunkel and Zwarun, 2006). Some researchers note the absence of a causal relationship between children viewing media violence and subsequent violent behavior (Trend, 2007; Grimes, Anderson, and Bergen, 2008). However, other researchers find that viewing media violence can desensitize viewers to real violence, as well as make them excessively fearful of the potential for violence in their own lives (Galezewski, 2005).

Violence is an increasingly familiar aspect of students' lives (see Figure 19.1), and bullying[1] has become an all too common experience for school-age children. In the most recent report of school crime and safety, 78 percent of schools report one or more incidents of violent crime during the previous school year, and 28 percent of students between the ages of twelve and eighteen report that they had been victims of bullying during the previous six months (U.S. Department of Justice, 2007). Students report incidents of bullying beginning as early as pre-school. Almost half of all middle and high school students avoid school bathrooms for fear of being assaulted or harassed (Smith-Heavenrich, 2005). It may be naïve for us to think we are not vulnerable to violence. Although violence is more prevalent in urban areas and among poor and minorities, no one in any neighborhood is immune. School violence affects the suburbs and rural areas as well as cities. In fact, the number of students reporting the presence of gangs, one indicator of school violence, increased more for rural and suburban students than in it did for urban students (U.S. Department of Justice, 2007).

Recent reports of school crime contain both bad and good news. The bad news is that in 2005, students between the ages and twelve and eighteen were victims of 1.5 million crimes in school. Ten percent of the male students and 6 percent of the female students were threatened or injured with a weapon. The

---

[1] Bullying has no standard definition (Zins, Elias, and Maher, 2007). According to the National Conference of State Legislatures, bullying is pattern of behavior over time designed to cause injury or discomfort. Bullying includes "harassment, intimidation to varying degrees, taunting and ridicule. Sometimes bullies are motivated by hate and bias, sometimes by cultural norms, peer pressure or the desire to retaliate . . . Sometimes there is no readily identifiable reason for bullying; when kids are asked who school bullies target, their answers can be disturbing precisely because they are not extraordinary: bullies pick on kids who are 'weaker,' 'smaller,' 'funny looking,' or 'dumb'" (National Council of State Legislatures, 2008). (www.ncsl.org/programs/educ/schbullying .html). Bullying and violence are not limited to acts that cause bodily harm; they include actions that deny others the ability to be effective actors in their world. Bullies trade in threats and intimidations as often as they deliver physical blows. The victims of bullying suffer more embarrassment, rejection, and anxiety than cuts and bruises, but their pain is real and lasting (MacNeil, 2002).

FIGURE 19.1 Percentage of Public Schools Experiencing and Reporting Incidents of Crime That Occurred at School, By Various Type of Crime

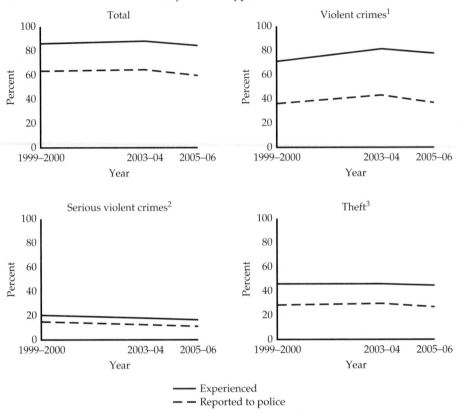

[1] Violent crimes include rape, attempted rape, sexual battery, physical attack, and threat of physical attack or fight with or without a weapon, threat of physical attack and robbery with or without a weapon.
[2] Serious violent crimes include rape or attempted rape, sexual battery, physical attack or fight with a weapon, and robbery with or without a weapon.
[3] Theft includes incidents of takings worth over $10 without physical confrontation.

Source: U.S. Department of Education, National Center of Education Statistics, Indicators of School Crime and Safety, December 2007. http://nces.ed.gov/programs/crimeindicators2007.

good news is that the percentage of schools reporting crimes in 2005–2006 was lower than the previous year and similar to the percentage of schools experiencing crime in 1999–2000 (U.S. Department of Education, 2007). The bad news may not be getting worse, but it is disturbing nonetheless. From the standpoint of any victim of school violence or the parents whose children have been victimized, there are no levels of acceptable violent behavior in schools.

Violence-Prevention Curricula

The bad news is easy to tabulate. The statistics are alarming: Violence is common in schools; too many children feel unsafe in schools; many schools have to invest in metal detectors and guards instead of books and field trips. The good news is harder to quantify, but it should be reassuring: School programs can make a difference in preventing childhood aggressive behavior and future adult violence (*Recess from Violence,* 1993; Astor et al., 2002; Bowen et al., 2002; Zins, Elias, and Maher, 2007). While schools alone cannot overcome the problem of violence, they are central in the struggle to protect children from violence and teach them physical aggression is never the preferred solution to problems. The problem of violence is complex, and there are no simple solutions. It is not the sort of problem, however, likely to be solved by applying zero-tolerance policies and simple punitive measures. To solve the problem of school violence, children must learn how to understand and control their anger and practice using non-violent problem-solving techniques. Schools can help students manage their aggression by teaching alternatives to violence through violence-prevention curricula.

Consider a few violence-prevention strategies. We present them as illustrative examples rather than prescriptive remedies. Many schools now are using schooltime conflict-resolution approaches, teaching children to handle their own disputes and assume responsibility for helping other children find peaceful resolutions to their disagreements. These programs are disarmingly simple and effective. First, children are taught conflicts are inevitable, and in most disputes, both sides are apt to believe they and they alone are in the right. Conflict resolution approaches encourage students to listen to each other and take responsibility for ensuring they resolve conflicts by conversation and negotiation rather than by physical means. The process is similar for younger children and students in secondary schools. What varies is the nature and complexity of the problems. Consider this example for resolving a classroom conflict in elementary school: The teacher begins the activity by distributing an "activity card" to the class with a conflict that might be familiar to them.

> Mariah is riding the bus to school. Kateesha, another girl on the bus, is having a bad day, and she calls Mariah a bad name. Mariah is very upset and mad at Kateesha. When they get off the bus, they start yelling at each other and shoving each other until a teacher breaks up the fight. Both children are taken to the office for fighting, and both children are still mad at each other. What is the solution to their problem? (Osier and Fox, 2001, p. 10)

The teacher reads the card to the class and asks students to identify the problem. When the class agrees about the nature of the problem, the teacher asks students to recommend actions they could take to solve it. Younger children may draw a picture of the solution; older children write one. The teacher then asks the class to share their solutions and identifies those supported by students in the class. Students are asked to save the favored solutions and apply them when a new conflict arises in or outside of class.

Secondary school students are encouraged to use similar role-playing strategies to examine critical incidents in their lives. The goal is to have students see how simple, commonplace events can escalate into violence. In this example, taken from a videotape transcript written by eighth-grade students, one young woman taunts another:

> "I heard that she was at the movies with your boyfriend last night. All over him."
> "I wouldn't take it," adds another girl.
> "She doesn't need your boyfriend. What was she doing with him anyhow?"

The young women simulate pushing and shoving. They break off from the simulation with self-conscious laughter, recognizing, perhaps, that in real life the angry words they scripted all too often escalate into real acts of violence. On the videotape, the classroom teacher applauds the students' effort, and the class examines what has taken place. A rumor was spread; it led to an exchange of words; verbal accusations threatened to become physical. In real life, it could easily have resulted in injury. The teacher asks, how could this have been avoided? What did others do to make the situation worse? What could they have done to help (*Violence in the Schools,* 1993)?

Many schools have adopted schoolwide prevention programs that teach students a series of consistent, reasonable approaches to contend with conflict. Students learn to view conflict situations as constructive rather than destructive experiences (Smith and Daunic, 2005). In these schools, when a playground dispute occurs, an older child, trained by the teachers, asks both parties to tell their sides of the story. Certain ground rules are agreed to beforehand: no yelling, no cursing, no interrupting, no put-downs of the other person. The older student, acting as a conflict manager, seeks to guide the disputants to solutions of their problems. If they cannot, the conflict manager tries to help. A teacher or administrator always is available. The goal is to provide a caring community in which all children feel safe, where they can resolve their problems, and where everyone is responsible for others' well-being. Caring communities teach children to handle problems without resorting to violence, and violence prevention is promoted by student vigilance and an increased sense of shared responsibility (Davies, 2004).

School programs can help students find alternatives to violence. Nonviolence can be an important curriculum strand running through social studies, language arts, and other subject areas. Violence is a learned response, and because it is learned, it can be unlearned (Noguera, 1995). Schools, working with social service agencies and psychologists, can replace antisocial behaviors with prosocial behaviors and provide positive role models for children. Violence-prevention curricula are new and their successes have not been carefully evaluated or scientifically assessed (Devine and Lawson, 2003). The evidence collected thus far, however, supports the effectiveness of conflict resolution programs and other violence-prevention interventions (such as anger management and anger-coping programs and antibullying strategies) in teaching students to manage conflicts through nonviolent means (Bowen et al., 2002; Devine and Cohen, 2007). Even more convincing is the observable difference these curricula bring to schools. As one school administrator notes, "It makes a difference in my school, and I have a reduction of 10 percent in some problems. These materials are OK by me, and I don't need researchers to say it works" (Lawton, 1994, p. 10).

College and university students can help through mentorship programs. The absence of appropriate parental supervision is a strong predictor of trouble complying with school discipline. Once thought of as a problem confined to the poor, lack of supervision and absence of positive role models now are recognized as much broader problems. Students from all social classes need sources of support other than the family. Many undergraduate programs now match volunteer mentors with at-risk students. The mentors act as role models, older brothers or sisters, and surrogate parents. They help with homework and teach study skills. They are models of problem solvers who do not resort to violence and examples of succesful adults who have not succumbed to the temptations of crime. Above all, they offer at-risk children a caring, thoughtful person in their lives. Their presence cannot be underestimated. Children at risk for violence have had too few positive role models in their lives. Schools and teachers can help. Research indicates that "the involvement of just one caring adult can make all the difference in the life of an at-risk youth" (Sautter, 1995, p. K8).

Viewed simply, violence is irrational destruction, an explosion of spontaneous rage. But violence doesn't just happen. It is not an act without cause or one that defies understanding. To prevent violence, schools and society should examine how history, economics, and culture find an outlet in violent behavior. Violent acts cannot be prevented unless schools and communities attend to social and political forces producing them. Violent behavior is one of the most frequently studied social phenomena of our day. The social and behavioral sciences have learned a lot about violence, and we have every reason to assume schools can successfully stem the tide of violent behavior and protect children and society from the violent among us. We are ultimately very optimistic about schools and the ability of school personnel to make schools more just and more satisfying places for all students. Teachers and principals can extend the power of schooling into students' daily lives. Schools can help to reduce social conflicts and individual violence. The process likely will be slow and expensive, but if not begun in schools, future social and personal costs will be more costly. Potentially violent children and their problems will not go away by themselves. To paraphrase John Dewey, what the best and wisest parents in the community want for their children should be made available to all children through the agency of the schools.

POSITION 2: THE PROBLEM OF SCHOOL VIOLENCE IS BEYOND SCHOOL CONTROL

Social scientists and educators have developed school-based antibullying programs in an effort to combat the perceived problem of school violence. These programs are unnecessary because, contrary to public belief, school violence is decreasing rather than increasing. They are also ineffective because they do not impart useful tools for responding to bullying but simply teach children how to identify and express their feelings. Several rigorous studies have failed to prove such programs actually reduce bullying. Antibullying

> *programs may do more harm than good by leaving children even less*
> *prepared for the interpersonal conflicts that have always been a normal, albeit*
> *unpleasant, part of school life.*
>
> —Labash, 2005, p. 13

U.S. schools began with modest academic goals: teach children to read and write. Over the years, schools enhanced their curricula to include academic instruction in content as well as skills, subject matter from art to social studies. The argument in this section is simple, direct, and straightforward: Schools should teach academic content in the most compelling and academically legitimate ways possible. This is the job schools are entrusted with, and is what teachers are trained to do. Without academic skills, students are at a disadvantage, will be unable to compete for places in the best colleges, earn scholarships, land good jobs, or launch satisfying careers. Schooling is primarily about teaching and learning academic subject matter and mastery of skills necessary for success in life. When society asks schools to engage in social engineering programs—such as preventing violence or solving the problems of crime and delinquency—it blurs the focus on cognitive learning, and spreads their efforts across too many areas (Finn, 1993). Schools must teach about our history and literature and instill in students a sense of civic responsibility, if we are to survive as a nation. School must equip students with intellectual skills necessary to understand science, math, the arts, and humanities, if they are to succeed individually. School focus should not be on social reform, but academic achievement. A school's success is measured by the rigor and quality of teaching, not by the extent to which it confronts social problems (Ravitch, 2001).

We will further argue that (1) violence in schools is an overstated problem; (2) violence-prevention curricula are of questionable value; and (3) schools should not try to do the job of welfare agencies, police, or social psychologists.

Decline of Family Values

To spend much energy arguing that these are not normal times is to belabor the obvious. Everyone knows that the family is in disarray, and family values are all but lost to many Americans. Thirty percent of all children are born to single mothers, and the problem is even greater in some minority populations. Too many youngsters have no one to teach them basic skills, socially appropriate behavior, and other family values. Too many children show up at the doors of the nation's schools with only a vague sense of right and wrong, no self-discipline, and a limited ability to get along with other children. Increasing numbers of today's youth claim that the counterculture or gang life offers the sense of belonging, worth, and purpose they fail to find within their families. Too many students refuse to accept responsibility for their actions, and teachers commonly report hearing excuses such as, "It's not my fault; other kids were doing it," and, "I wasn't late; the bell just rang before I got there" (Conrath, 2001, p. 586).

Children do not show up for the first day of kindergarten as blank slates: The experiences of their early lives have etched upon them many complex impressions, both good and bad. Most children are ready to begin school; their parents have invested tremendous amounts of time and energy in them. These children are self-controlled. They demonstrate mastery over their emotions, enthusiasm for learning, and respect for the teacher's authority. Others are not ready for school. Victims of poor parenting or no parenting at all, they come to school with insufficient preparation for the academic side of school and inadequate control over their own behavior to get along with classmates. Teachers spot these students quickly. They are overly impulsive, physically aggressive, and uncooperative. Psychologists have developed profiles of school bullies and other potentially violent youth. Among other things, they tend to be loners who lack empathy for others; frequently are victims of violence at home; have a great deal of pent-up anger, a low frustration tolerance, a record of involvement in substance abuse and other risky behavior, and a lack of moral conscience (MacNeil, 2002). These troubled youth likely have average or above-average intelligence, but are not likely to do well in school, and threaten the educational quality and physical well-being of other children and themselves.

Only a small fraction of students, however, exhibit aggressive behaviors or other traits that predict violence. In fact, school violence is an overstated problem. Potentially violent students represent only 1 percent of children who enter school, and the rate of violence in school has not increased in twenty years. In 2008, the National Center for Education Statistics website (http://nces. ed.gov) reported data indicating a general decline in the victimization rate for violent crime between 1992 and 2005. The declining pattern holds true for the total crime rate reported by students ages twelve to eighteen. In 2005, the crime victimization rate for this population of students was 57 crimes per 1,000 students while at school, and 47 crimes per 1,000 students while away from school (see Figure 19.2).

Despite widespread publicity depicting schools as dangerous places, rife with crime and violence, the conclusion drawn from student reports of violence seems to say school violence may be more of a media creation than a serious school problem. For the moment, at least, it seems fair to argue that schools are probably less dangerous for students than they have been in the past two decades. Every year since 1969, Phi Delta Kappa and the Gallup Organization conduct a poll of the public's attitude toward the public schools. For the first sixteen years of the poll, when asked to identify the biggest problem the schools in their communities faced, most of those polled put "discipline" at the top of the list. "The use of drugs" replaced discipline in the top spot until 1991, when it was tied with "lack of financial support." Since 2000, "lack of financial support" has been unchallenged in the public's view as the major problem facing public schools. In 2007, "lack of discipline" was in second place among perceived school problems, identified by only 10 percent of the public as the major problem faced by the schools in their communities (Rose and Gallup, 2007, p. 44).

Teaching is among the nation's safest professions. According to statistics compiled by the Department of Education, and similar to the data for crimes against students, reported crimes against teachers continue to decline in both private and public schools. Compared with a decade earlier, 7 percent fewer

FIGURE 19.2 Rate of Student-Reported Nonfatal Crimes Against Students Ages 12–18 per 1,000 Students, By Type of Crime and Location: 1992–2005.

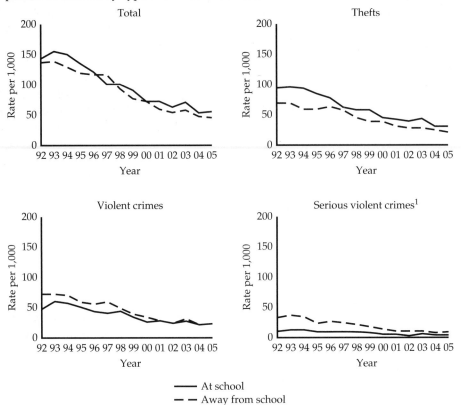

[1]Serious violent crimes also include violent crimes.

Note: Serious violent crimes include rape, sexual assault, robbery, and aggravated assault. Violent crimes include serious violent crimes and simple assault. Total crimes include violent crimes and theft.

Source: U.S. Department of Education, National Center of Education Statistics, Indicators of School Crime and Safety, December 2007. http://nces.ed.gov/programs/crimeindicators2007.

teachers report being physically threatened by students. Male teachers are more likely than female teachers to be the victims of violent crimes. Secondary school teachers are at greater risk than elementary teachers, and urban teachers experience more violent crimes committed against them than reported by their rural and suburban colleagues, but the rate of crime committed against all categories of teachers is on the decline (U.S. Department of Education, 2007).

Schools are generally safe places, but disruptive students do exist. What responsibilities do schools have to teach the distracting handful of children who are unable to control their aggression? This is a difficult question. None of us wants to appear callous or indifferent to children, but schools are not social welfare agencies. Teachers are not social workers or psychiatrists. Educators are trained to teach children reading, math, social studies, and other important content and skills. We cannot reasonably expect schools and teachers to function as anger-management therapists or violence-control specialists. Violence-prevention curricula sound noble and high-minded, but they are a diversion from the schools' academic mission and are of doubtful benefit. After reviewing 70 federally funded programs with a total of $2.4 billion in funds aimed at reducing school violence and substance abuse, the General Accounting Office concluded these programs had not demonstrated their worth (U.S. General Accounting Office, 1997).

Similarly, a survey of nearly 400 schools in Ontario, Canada, indicated that "schools are investing significant resources into antibullying programs, despite scant evidence of program effectiveness . . . Few schools evaluated their antibullying programs and the rigour of these evaluations was generally low." (Smith, Ryan, and Cousins, 2007, p. 120)

In other words, a great deal of money is being spent on a small minority of children with little to show for the expenditure. Today a small group of problem students is attracting a disproportionate share of curriculum attention as well as federal and state dollars. The education of the majority of cooperative students is being held ransom by an unruly minority.

Who Are the Potentially Violent?

We know who is likely to commit crimes, the early experiences that lead to violent behavior, and the personal and family traits that tend to protect children from becoming violent adults. We know behaviors that alert teachers and administrators to the potentially troublesome. (See Table 19.1.) Unfortunately, beyond identifying troubled students, research has not yet developed a strong knowledge base about the causes of violent behavior or the ways it can be prevented. No one knows how to prevent potentially violent children from becoming violent adults. Schools now embracing one violence-management curriculum or another are doing so without adequate evidence of its effectiveness. Many causes of violence are not within the schools' control (Weishew and Peng, 1993). Violent children become violent adults, and if children have not learned to control their aggression by the time they come to school, it may not be possible for them to disentangle the patterns of violence that took shape in their early years.

In a perfect world, all children would come to school with no violent inclinations. All children would be raised in loving, drug-free, nurturing homes. They would all bond with an adult who dispenses love freely and teaches them they belong to someone and someone belongs to them. Children's earliest experiences would have shown them that disagreements are part of life, but discord can be settled through calm discussions rather than rancor or violence. We would like all children to have high IQs, to have parents who are literate adults, free from alcohol and drug addiction, who study books about child rearing, read stories to their children, and place limits on television viewing. We would like all these things and more, but social policies cannot create them. Too many children are born to single mothers unprepared for the task or unable to give

---

Table 19.1 Characteristics of Troubled Students*

1. Has a history of tantrums and uncontrollable angry outbursts.
2. Characteristically resorts to name calling, cursing, or abusive language.
3. Habitually makes violent threats when angry.
4. Has previously brought a weapon to school.
5. Has a background of serious disciplinary problems at school and in the community.
6. Has a background of drug, alcohol, or substance abuse or dependency.
7. Is on the fringe of his or her peer group with few or no close friends.
8. Is preoccupied with weapons, explosives, or other incendiary devices.
9. Has previously been truant, suspended, or expelled from school.
10. Displays cruelty to animals.
11. Has little or no supervision and support from parents or a caring adult.
12. Has witnessed or been a victim of abuse or neglect in the home.
13. Has been bullied and/or bullies or intimidates peers or younger children.
14. Tends to blame others for difficulties and problems she/he causes her/himself.
15. Consistently prefers TV shows, movies, or music expressing violent themes or acts.
16. Prefers reading material dealing with violent themes, rituals, and abuse.
17. Reflects anger, frustration, and the dark side of life in school essays or writing projects.
18. Is involved with a gang or an antisocial group on the fringe of peer acceptance.
19. Is often depressed and/or has significant mood swings.
20. Has threatened or attempted suicide.

---

* The National School Safety Center tracks school-associated violent deaths in the United States and has developed a checklist of behaviors to alert teachers and administrators to troubled students.

Source: www.nssc1.org/reporter/checklist.htm.

---

them what they need to be successful in life. Drug addiction, crime, and poverty are beyond school control. Schools cannot redistribute wealth or solve social problems. For better or worse, schools reflect society; they are not now nor have they ever been agents of social change. They have a mission to educate students and have little power and no authority to do anything else.

Although public schools must work with all students, they do not have to mix the disruptive and the potentially violent with the well behaved; nor do they have to encourage violent students to stay in school until graduation. Students who arrive at school ready to learn should be introduced to a rigorous, sound academic education. The academic side of school will matter to them in life. Children come to school to improve their academic skills and increase their store of intellectual capital—the knowledge needed for success in life. As Hirsch notes, "Sociologists have shown that intellectual capital (i.e., school knowledge) operates in almost every sphere of modern society to determine social class, success or failure in school, and even psychological and physical health" (1996, p. 19). Students are disadvantaged by too small a share of intellectual capital, and need to start early and move quickly in securing as much of it as they can. The vast majority of students do not need special curriculum treatments to teach them how to get along with others, settle disputes without violence, or manage aggression. They need academic content to succeed in life, and that's what schools should deliver.

Conflict-resolution curricula distract students from academic pursuits and send students an undesirable, if unintended, message: "We expect school to be violent, so let's talk about it" (Devine, 1996, p. 165). Violence is not a way of life for most children. Directing conflict-management programs to all students, rather than at the violent minority, sends a negative message that violence is a normal part of life and everyone must learn to manage it or otherwise cope with it.

Schools and Violence

Let's look at what we know about potentially violent children and what schools can reasonably do about them: Overly aggressive children should be identified in kindergarten and trained to work on anger management. Although a school cannot replace the family, it can provide some supports found in homes of self-controlled, high-achieving students. For example, school discipline policies should incorporate the reward-and-punishment systems successfully used by middle-class parents. Students should learn that appropriate behavior earns teacher praise and special privileges, while inappropriate behavior results in loss of praise and privilege. This would be reasonable, inexpensive, and not too intrusive on the privacy rights of students or their parents. Working individually with counselors—and not consuming instructional time—violent and potentially violent students should be the focus of appropriate intervention and prevention strategies (Bemak and Keys, 2000).

Schools alone cannot solve problems of violence (Casella, 2001; Bowen et al., 2002). Influences of early family experiences and the greater society are pervasive. Research provides little encouragement that school interventions successfully prevent violence, and the research may simply be confirming public knowledge. Of course, schools should try to help all students, but not impede the progress of the well behaved. Schools should try every measure to help young children adapt to school and school discipline. But some children never will adjust to academic demands and self-discipline required for success. According to one analysis of U.S. Justice Department statistics, about 6 percent of adolescents are responsible for two-thirds of violent crimes committed by juveniles (Bodine and Crawford, 1998, p. 6). This tiny percentage of students should not be a major focus of school attention and a constant drain on school budgets. If these students have not learned to control themselves by early adolescence, schools should waste no more time or money on them.

Alternative Schools

When Cesar was in the ninth grade, his career ambition was to become an assassin. His credentials were impressive, urban gang member, hardened street fighter, handgun aficionado. . . Three years later [as a student in a public alternative high school] he was a captivating poet with a scholarship to a private college. (Leiding, 2008, p. 29)

Educators have long recognized that alternatives in public education are sometimes necessary to serve special populations of students—teenage mothers, for example, or the physically disabled. The one-size-fits-all model of the comprehensive public high school does not serve everyone equally well, and some students rebel against the competition, perceived conformity, and order of traditional education. Many educators now recognize the academic demands and social structure of traditional high schools may contribute to school violence. Students unaccustomed to impersonal rules governing school behavior and emphasis schools place on quiet compliance may lash out at teachers and other students (Epp and Watkinson, 1997; Brown and Beckett, 2007). By the time they reach middle school, students learn the focus of schooling is on academic achievement, and unfortunately students who do not achieve well often develop indifferent or hostile attitudes. As one supporter of alternative schools notes, "Their behavior is not irrational. Just as it is rational to embrace the repetition of successful experiences, it is equally rational to avoid repetitions of unsuccessful experiences" (Conrath, 2001, p. 587).

Alternative schools can siphon off the troubled, disaffected, potentially violent, and others for whom traditional schooling is not a good fit. Alternative schools often are better able to serve nonacademic students while allowing traditional schools to focus on the majority's academic needs. Sometimes housed within the regular school building, and sometimes in separate facilities of their own, alternative schools are designed for students who, because of any number of problems—academic but more often behavioral or social—are not able to learn well in a traditional school environment. Today, 40 percent of all public school districts have some form of alternative school program, sometimes as part of the school, other times as separate buildings with their own faculty and administrators. Alternative schools and programs serve students who are at risk of dropping out of school for any number of reasons. About 6 percent of elementary and secondary schools are alternative schools (U.S. Department of Education, 2007).

Alternative schools are likely to be less formal than traditional schools, and typically offer a lower student-to-teacher ratio. The record indicates these schools can go a long way toward ameliorating the anonymity and isolation some students experience in traditional schools (Dunbar, 2001; Brown and Beckett, 2007). Many formerly disruptive students behave better when they work in a small, supportive setting. They are able to find a niche that eluded them in traditional schools and teachers willing to focus on personal and social problems they bring with them to school (Conchas and Rodriguez, 2008).

Alternative schools can be very effective and should be viewed as appropriate educational options for disruptive students who have not responded to special curricular treatment and counseling in regular schools and classes. Unfortunately, although alternative schools try to accommodate students with a wide range of problems, they do not work for everyone. In fact, they may not work well for many of the most disruptive students. The same students that caused problems in traditional schools often continue to present problems when they transfer to alternative schools. For these students, more dramatic action is likely to be in order.

Schools should embrace all students equally when they first begin school. Special curriculum interventions—the so-called conflict- and dispute-resolution curricula—should be reserved exclusively for students who demonstrate behaviors associated with violence in adults (for example, physical aggression and lack of self-control). Schools should use every technique at their disposal to curb disruptive behavior and bring the unruly child back into the fold. However, by middle school, students who impede the learning process of their classmates or threaten the welfare of other children should be considered as candidates for alternative schools. Students who are not likely to succeed in one kind of school should be given another chance in a different kind of school. These alternative schools have amassed a sound, though not perfect, record for educating the disaffected. For the small handful of very disruptive students who are unable to cooperate in an alternative school, expulsion is a harsh but sensible last resort.

Will expelling problem students from the public school system be likely to increase their inclination toward further violence and criminality? Will these students inevitably wind up in the criminal justice system? It is hard to know. Research indicates future dropouts have high levels of criminal behavior while in school, but some evidence indicates that after these students drop out of school, they may have less trouble with the law (Herrnstein and Murray, 1994). Schools often add to the problems of young people. Many students who do not succeed academically feel frustrated. Others feel confined by alienating school rules and the abrasiveness of school crowding (Noguera, 1995; Neumann, 2003; Leiding, 2008). Some students may learn better in another environment, and schools should find places for such students. Schools are ultimately academic institutions designed to teach cognitive skills. Students who cannot learn to play by the rules of civilized behavior—to exercise self-discipline, order, and respect for others—ultimately have no place in school.

For Discussion

1. Teenage boys are the most frequent perpetrators as well as the most common victims of school violence. One researcher argues that young males suffer from the Boy Code: "Violence committed by and acted upon boys seems to be, more often than not, from what we teach (or do not teach) boys about the behavior we expect from them. It comes from society's set of rules about masculinity, the Boy Code that says, 'To become a man, you must hold your own if challenged by another male. You can show your rage, but you must not show any other emotions. You must protect your honor and fight off shame at all costs'" (Pollack, 2005, p. 64).

   Is violence in boys an inevitable consequence of what our society expects of males and male behavior? Can schools discourage or modify the Boy Code without running afoul of established, social expectations?

2. Researchers find that students and other youth express bullying in different ways according to gender. Boys tend to be physically aggressive, while girls are "relationally aggressive," that is, harming others through gossip, spreading rumors, and excluding them from social contact (Leff et al., 2007). Does this finding reflect your experiences with bullying and violence in elementary and secondary school? In your experience, did the schools handle bullying appropriately for both victim and bully?

Did the schools respond differently to incidents involving the physical violence of boys and the relational violence of girls? Should they?

3. In Scandinavian countries, corporal punishment is prohibited by law in schools and in homes. Minnesota is the only state in the United States to prohibit corporal punishment of any sort, even by parents (Smith, 2003). The 2006 Program Accreditation Criteria of the National Association for the Education of Young Children include the following statement about the interactions among teachers and children in preschools, kindergarten, and childcare centers: "Teachers [should] abstain from corporal punishment or humiliating or frightening discipline techniques."

Is this a reasonable standard? Should parents have the right to determine whether or not corporal punishment can be used as a form of discipline on their own children at home or in the public schools they attend?

References

ASTOR, R. A., ET AL. (2002). "Public Concern and Focus on School Violence, in *Handbook of Violence*, ed. L. A. Rapp-Paglicci et al. New York: John Wiley and Sons.

BARBOUR, S. (2005). *How Can School Violence be Prevented?* Detroit, MI: Greenhaven.

BEMAK, F., AND KEYS, S. (2000). *Violent and Aggressive Youth: Intervention and Prevention Strategies for Changing Times.* Thousand Oaks, CA: Corwin Press.

BODINE, R. J., AND CRAWFORD, D. K. (1998). *The Handbook of Conflict Resolution Education: A Guide to Building Quality Programs in Schools.* San Francisco: Jossey-Bass.

BOWEN, G. L., ET AL. (2002). "Reducing School Violence: A Social Capacity Framework," in *Handbook of Violence*, ed. L. A. Rapp-Paglicci et al. New York: John Wiley and Sons.

BROWN, L. H. AND BECKETT, K. S. (2007). *Building Community in an Alternative School.* New York: Peter Lang.

CONCHAS, G. Q. AND RODRIGUEZ, F. F. (2008). *Small Schools and Urban Youth.* Thousand Oaks, CA: Sage.

CONRATH, J. (2001). "Changing the Odds for Young People: Next Steps for Alternative Education." *Kappan* 82:585–587.

DAVIES, L. (2004). *Education and Conflict; Complexity and Chaos.* New York: Routledge Falmer.

DEVINE, J. (1996). *Maximum Security.* Chicago: University of Chicago Press.

DEVINE, J., AND Lawson, H. A. (2003). "The Complexity of School Violence; Commentary from US, in *"Violence in Schools; the Response in Europe,* ed. P. K. Smith. New York: Routlege Falmer.

DEVINE, J., AND COHEN, J. (2007). *Making Your School Safe; Strategies to Protect Children and Promote Learning.* New York: Teachers College Press.

DOWD, N. E., SINGER, D. G., AND WILSON, R. F., eds. (2006) *Handbook of Children, Culture, and Violence.* Thousand Oaks, CA: Sage.

DWORKIN, M. S. (1959). *Dewey On Education.* New York: Teachers College Press.

EPP, J. R., AND WATKINSON, A. M. (1997). *Systemic Violence in Education: Broken Promise.* Albany: State University of New York.

FINN, C. E., JR. (1993). "Whither Education Reform?" in *Making Schools Work*, ed. C. L. Fagnano and K. N. Hughes. Boulder, CO: Westview Press.

GALEZEWSKI, J. (2005). "Bullying and Aggression Among Youth," in *Violence in Schools; Issues, Consequences, and Expressions*, ed. K. Sexton-Radek. Westport, CT: Praeger.

GRIMES, T., ANDERSON, J. A. AND BERGEN, L. (2008). *Media Violence and Aggression: Science and Ideology.* Los Angeles, CA: Sage.

HERRNSTEIN, R. J., AND MURRAY, C. (1994). *The Bell Curve: Intelligence and Class Structure in American Life*. New York: Free Press.

HIRSCH, E. D., JR. (1996). *The Schools We Need and Why We Don't Have Them*. New York: Doubleday.

JORDAN, K. (2002). "School Violence Among Culturally Diverse Populations," in *Handbook of Violence*, ed. L. A. Rapp-Paglicci et al. New York: John Wiley and Sons.

KUNKEL, D. AND ZWARUN, L. (2006). "How Real is the Problem of TV Violence?" In *Handbook of Children, Culture, Culture, and Violence*, eds. N. E. Dowd and R. F. Wilson. Thousand Oaks, CA: Sage.

LABASH, M. (2005). "Antibullying Programs are Ineffective and Unnecessary," in *How Can School Violence be Prevented*? ed. S. Barbour. Detroit, MI: Greenhaven.

LAWTON, M. (1994). "Violence-Prevention Curricula: What Works Best?" *Education Week*, Nov. 9, pp. 1, 10–11.

LEFF, S. S. ET AL. (2007). "Using a Participatory Action Research Model to Create a School-Based Intervention Program for Relationally Aggressive Girls—The Friend to Friend Program. *"In Bullying, Victimization, and Peer Harrassment*, eds. J. E. Zins, M. J. Elias, and C. A. Maher. New York: Hayworth.

LEIDING, D. (2008). *The Hows and Whys of Alternative Education*. Lanham, MD: Rowman and Littlefield.

MacNEIL, G. (2002). "School Bullying: An Overview," in *Handbook of Violence*, ed. L. A. Rapp-Paglicci et al. New York: John Wiley and Sons.

NATIONAL ASSOCIATION FOR THE EDUCATION OF YOUNG CHILDREN. (2005). "Early Childhood Program Standards and Accreditation Criteria." (www.naeyc.org/accreditation/criteria98.asp).

NEUMANN, R. (2003). *Sixties Legacy; A History of the Public Alternative Schools Movement, 1967–2001*. New York: Peter Lang.

NOGUERA, P. A. (1995). "Preventing and Producing Violence: A Critical Analysis of Responses to School Violence." *Harvard Educational Review* 65:189–212.

OSIER, J., AND FOX, H. (2001). *Settle Conflicts Right Now! A Step-by-Step Guide for K–6 Classrooms*. Thousand Oaks, CA: Corwin Press.

POLLACK, W. S. (2005). "Changing Society's Expectations of Boys Can Prevent School Violence," in *How Can School Violence be Prevented*? ed. S. Barbour. Detroit, MI: Greenhaven.

RAVITCH, D. (2001). "Education and Democracy," in *Making Good Citizens: Education and Civil Society*, ed. D. Ravitch and J. P. Viteritti. New Haven, CT: Yale University Press.

Recess from Violence: Making Our Schools Safe. (1993). Hearings Before the Subcommittee on Education, Arts, and Humanities of the Committee on Labor and Human Resources. U.S. Senate, One Hundred Third Congress, First Session on S.1125 (Sept. 23). Washington, DC: U.S. Government Printing Office.

ROSE, L. C. AND GALLUP, A. M. (2007). The 39th Annual Phi Delta Kappa/Gallup Poll of the Public's Attitudes Toward the Public Schools." *Kappan* 89:33–45.

SAUTTER, C. R. (1995). "Standing Up to Violence." *Kappan* 76:K1–K12.

SMITH, J. D., RYAN, W., AND COUSINS, J. B. (2007). "Antibullying Programs. A Survey of Evaluation Activities in Public Schools." *Studies in Educational Evaluation* 33:120–134.

SMITH, P. K., ed. (2003). *Violence in Schools: The Response in Europe*. New York: Routledge Falmer.

SMITH, S. W., AND DAUNIC, A. P. (2005). "Conflict Resolution and Peer Mediation." In K. Burns, ed., *School Violence*. Detroit, MI: Greenhaven.

TREND, D. (2007). *The Myth of Media Violence; A Critical Introduction*. Malden, MA: Oxford.

U.S. DEPARTMENT OF EDUCATION. (2007). *Number and Types of Public Elementary and Secondary Schools from the Common Core of Data: School Year 2005–06.* www.nces.ed.gov .pubsearch/pubid2007354.

U.S. DEPARTMENT OF JUSTICE. *Indictors of School Crime and Safety,* 2007. http://nces.ed.gov/ programs/crimeindicators2007.

U.S. GENERAL ACCOUNTING OFFICE. (1997). "Substance Abuse and Violence Prevention." Testimony before the Subcommittee on Oversight and Investigations, Committee on Education and the Workforce House of Representatives. Washington, DC: Author.

VAN ACKER, R. (2007). "Antisocial, Aggressive, and Violent Behavior in Children and Adolescents Within Alternative Education Settings: Prevention and Intervention." *Preventing School Failures* 51:5–12.

Violence in the Schools. (1993). National Education Association Video, Teacher TV Episode #15. West Haven, CT: National Education Association.

WEISHEW, N. L., AND PENG, S. S. (1993). "Variables Predicting Students' Problem Behaviors." *Journal of Educational Research* 87:5–17.

ZINS, J. E., ELIAS, M. J., AND MAHER, C. A. (2007). *Bullying, Victimization, and Peer Harassment; A Handbook of Prevention and Intervention.* New York: Haworth.

Index